Schriftenreihe des
ZENTRUMS FÜR EUROPÄISCHE RECHTSPOLITIK
der Universität Bremen (ZERP)

Band 78

Christiane Gerstetter

Substance and Style

WTO judicial decision-making in 'trade and ...' cases

Nomos

Gedruckt mit Unterstützung des Förderungsfonds Wissenschaft der VG WORT.

The Deutsche Nationalbibliothek lists this publication in the Deutsche Nationalbibliografie; detailed bibliographic data are available on the internet at http://dnb.d-nb.de

a.t: Bremen, Univ., Diss., 2017

ISBN 978-3-8487-5768-8 (Print)
978-3-8452-9942-6 (ePDF)

British Library Cataloguing-in-Publication Data
A catalogue record for this book is available from the British Library.

ISBN 978-3-8487-5768-8 (Print)
978-3-8452-9942-6 (ePDF)

Library of Congress Cataloging-in-Publication Data
Christiane Gerstetter
Substance and Style
WTO judicial decision-making in 'trade and ...' cases
Gerstetter, Christiane
634 pp.
Includes bibliographic references.

ISBN 978-3-8487-5768-8 (Print)
978-3-8452-9942-6 (ePDF)

Onlineversion
Nomos eLibrary

1st Edition 2021

An unlikely dedication in a book such as this, but still:

*To those that continue to believe
that it is unnecessary to conquer the world,
because it is sufficient to build it anew.*

(Remember: Pessimism of the intellect, optimism of the will)

Preface

Writing this book has taken a very long time (so long, in fact, that I am hesitant to disclose when it all started). With lapses and life happening in between, researching and writing it has been (mostly) a pleasure. If I had finished this work earlier, it would almost certainly have looked different, both in content and in language (and probably length). I am grateful for having had all this time to think about it, develop it, polish it, and to learn so much in the process. At the same time, it is immensely satisfying to see it finished. And it is a relief to know that there will no longer be a reason for this constant nagging feeling that there is still this writing project to be completed.

Given that I have taken such a long time to finish, this work has travelled with me through life, but also through the world. It has been researched and written in a number of different places. Among the ones that I can remember are rooms, offices, cafés, libraries, hostels, hotels, balconies, rooftops and even a camping site and an artist's atelier in Bremen, Berlin, Schwäbisch Hall, Heidelberg, Geneva, Beirut, Florence, the small Palestinian village of Yanoun in the West Bank, Istanbul, pre-war Damascus, Vienna, Belgrade, Sana'a (Yemen), Zagreb and, of course, "my" beloved Jerusalem. And an endless number of trains, fast and slow, old and new that took me from one place to another.

More important than places are, however, the people that in manners direct or indirect have contributed.

From the academic world, I owe the greatest debt of gratitude to Josef Falke, who was my primary supervisor. Josef Falke has been extremely supportive and patient over the years and has generously shared his immense knowledge of the details of EU and WTO law as well as the latest research. Without his offer to publish this book as part of the publication series of the Centre of European Law and Politics (ZERP), I am not sure the work would actually have turned into a book. Christian Joerges, my other supervisor, has also provided important intellectual guidance, in particular from private law and theoretical perspectives.

Both of them co-directed the research project on "Trade liberalisation and social regulation in transnational structures“ at the University of Bremen, where I started the research that ultimately has led to this book. We were a mixed team of lawyers and political scientists in a larger Collaborative Research Centre on "Transformations of the State", dominated by political scientists. This is were I first understood the beauty, but also the challenges of interdisciplinary work. I have learnt a lot from the other members of our small research team – Christine Godt, Leonhard Matthias Maier and Ulrike Ehling deserve being mentioned in particular. More generally, I have also benefitted from the intellectual environment and the exchange with so many young and more established researchers working in the mentioned research centre. Funding by the German Research Foundation (DFG) (and thus ultimately taxpayers in Germany) made it all possible.

From the University of Bremen, I would also like to thank Gerd Winter who not only taught me a thing or three about environmental law in my undergraduate studies, but also was willing to be a part of the committee for the oral "defense" of my PhD – and his dedication to environmental law, to teaching it and to interdisciplinary work were inspiring.

This work has benefited hugely from substantial comments by Ralph Bodle, Hanna Goeters and Maike Schmidt-Grabia, who each reviewed a (long) part of an earlier draft version. I also acknowledge with gratitude the proof-reading carried out by Anne Baumann, Olaf Heinrich, Damaris Mühe, Dagmar Seybold and Jürgen Weber.

At the very end, Pete Langman accepted the challenge of editing a PhD in a discipline that is not his own – and has not so much polished as thoroughly and brilliantly scrubbed chapters 2-4. If the text sounds English-English rather than German-English now, that is his work (and I like to believe that I have learned something from his edits above and beyond this specific text).

All errors remain mine, of course.

The "Förderungsfonds Wissenschaft der VG Wort" has provided generous financial support for the printing costs.

There have been more people, however. People who may not have directly contributed to this work, but without whom I would not be who I am, nor think or write the way I do.

I wish to thank my parents, Beate Scherrmann – Gerstetter and Albert Gerstetter, who have supported me in many ways over the years. They raised me to be interested in the world and trust my intellectual abilities; both were, to my mind, essential ingredients for successfully completing my legal studies and ultimately a PhD.

I am also indebted to the people at the Ecologic Institute, an environmental think tank where I have worked for a longer time than I had ever imagined working in one place. I have had the privilege to cooperate with and learn from many brilliant colleagues and partners, coming from many disciplines (and places). In particular, I would like to thank the co-founder and (now former) director of this institute, R. Andreas Kraemer, as well as its present director, Camilla Bausch, for their constant encouragement, for giving me space to pursue my interests and grow and for altogether making the institute such a unique place (including one where it is fully acceptable that people may want to do different things in life and therefore work part-time).

I am also thinking – with no little gratitude and joy – of friends, flatmates, and the intense emotional and intellectual companionship of joint political activism. I have learnt from you and you have kept me going. I trust you know who you are and hope you know what you mean to me.

Thank you all, lovely people!
Christiane Gerstetter

Table of Contents

Tables

Abbreviations

AB	Appellate Body
AD	Anti-dumping
ADA	Anti-Dumping Agreement
AIDCP	Agreement on the International Dolphin Conservation Programme
BISD	Basic instruments and selected documents (GATT/WTO)
CBD	Convention on Biological Diversity
CITES	Convention on International Trade in Endangered Species of Wild Fauna and Flora
CTE	Committee on Trade and Environment
CLS	Critical Legal Studies
DS	Dispute settlement
DSB	Dispute Settlement Body
DSU	Dispute Settlement Understanding
EC	European Community
ECJ	European Court of Justice
ECtHR	European Court of Human Rights
EU	European Union
EPA	(US) Environmental Protection Agency
FTA	Free trade agreement
GATS	General Agreement on Trade in Services
GATT	General Agreement on Tariffs and Trade
GMOs	Genetically modified organisms
GSP	General system of preferences
IAC	Inter-American Convention for the Protection and Conservation of Sea Turtles
IACHR	Inter-American Commission on Human Rights
ICC	International Criminal Court
ICJ	International Court of Justice
ICTY	International Criminal Tribunal for the Former Yugoslavia
IEC	International Electrotechnical Commission
ILC	International Law Commission
IMF	International Monetary Fund
ISO	International Organization for Standardization
ITLOS	International Tribunal for the Law of the Seas
MEA	Multilateral environmental agreement
NAFTA	North American Free Trade Agreement
NGO	Non-governmental organisation
PCIJ	Permanent Court of International Justice
SCM	Agreement on Subsidies and Countervailing Measures

SPS	Agreement on Sanitary and Phytosanitary Measures
TBT	Agreement on Technical Barriers to Trade
TFEU	Treaty on the Functioning of the European Union
TRIMS	Agreement on Trade-Related Investment Measures
TRIPS	Agreement on Trade-Related Aspects of Intellectual Property Rights
TTIP	Transatlantic Trade and Investment Partnership
UNCLOS	United Nations Convention on the Law of the Sea
US	United States
USTR	Office of the United States Trade Representative
VCLT	Vienna Convention on the Law of Treaties
WIPO	World Intellectual Property Organization
WTO	World Trade Organization
WTOA	Agreement Establishing the World Trade Organization

List of WTO/GATT cases cited

1982	*United States — Prohibition of Imports of Tuna and Tuna Products from Canada BISD 29S/91.*
1987	*Canada — Measures affecting exports of unprocessed herring and salmon, BISD 35S/98.*
1989	*United States — Section 337 of the Tariff Act of 1930, L/6439 - 36S/345.*
1990	*Thailand — Restrictions on importation of and internal taxes on cigarettes, DS10/R.*
1994	*United States — Restrictions on import of tuna, DS29/R (unadopted).*
1994	*United States — Taxes on Automobile (unadopted).*
1996	*United States — Standards for Reformulated and Conventional Gasoline, WT/DS2/R.*
1996	*United States — Standards for Reformulated and Conventional Gasoline, WT/DS2/AB/R.*
1996	*Japan — Taxes on Alcoholic Beverages, WT/DS8/AB/R, WT/DS10/AB/R, WT/DS11/AB/R.*
1997	*United States — Measures Affecting Imports of Woven Wool Shirts and Blouses from India, WT/DS33/AB/R.*
1997	*European Communities — Measures Concerning Meat and Meat Products, WT/DS26/R.*
1998	*European Communities — Measures Concerning Meat and Meat Products, WT/DS26/AB/R, WT/DS48/AB/R.*
1998	*Argentina — Measures Affecting Imports of Footwear, Textiles, Apparel and other Items, WT/DS56/AB/R.*
1998	*United States — Import Prohibition of Certain Shrimp and Shrimp Products, WT/DS58/R.*
1998	*Australia — Measures Affecting Importation of Salmon, WT/DS18/R.*
1998	*European Communities — Measures Affecting the Importation of Certain Poultry Products, WT/DS69/AB/R.*
1998	*Korea — Alcoholic Beverages, WT/DS75/R, WT/DS84/R.*

1998 *United States — Import Prohibition of Certain Shrimp and Shrimp Products, WT/DS58/AB/R.*

1998 *Australia — Measures Affecting Importation of Salmon, WT/DS18/AB/R.*

1998 *Japan — Measures Affecting Agricultural Products, WT/DS76/R.*

1999 *Korea — Alcoholic Beverages, WT/DS75AB/R, WT/DS84/AB/R.*

1999 *Japan — Measures Affecting Agricultural Products, WT/DS76/AB/R.*

1999 *India — Quantitative Restrictions on Imports of Agricultural, Textile and Industrial Products, WT/DS90/AB/R.*

1999 *Argentina — Safeguard Measures on Imports of Footwear, WT/DS121/AB/R.*

1999 *United States — Sections 301-310 of the trade act of 1974, WT/DS152/R.*

2000 *Australia — Measures Affecting Importation of Salmon, WT/DS18/RW.*

2000 *Canada — Patent Protection of Pharmaceutical Products, WT/DS114/R.*

2000 *Korea – Measures Affecting Government Procurement, WT/DS163/R.*

2000 *Korea — Measures Affecting Imports of Fresh, Chilled and Frozen Beef, WT/DS161/R, WT/DS169/R.*

2000 *European Communities — Measures Affecting Asbestos and Products Containing Asbestos, WT/DS135/R.*

2000 *Korea — Measures Affecting Imports of Fresh, Chilled and Frozen Beef, WT/DS161/AB/R, WT/DS169/AB/R.*

2000 *Argentina — Measures Affecting the Export of Bovine Hides and the Import of Finished Leather, WT/DS155/R.*

2001 *European Communities — Measures Affecting Asbestos and Products Containing Asbestos, WT/DS135/AB/R.*

2001 *United States — Import Prohibition of Certain Shrimp and Shrimp Products, WT/DS58/RW.*

2001 *United States — Import Prohibition of Certain Shrimp and Shrimp Products, WT/DS58/AB/RW.*

2002 *European Communities — Trade Description of Sardines, WT/DS231/R.*

2002 *European Communities — Trade Description of Sardines, WT/DS231/AB/R.*

2003 *Japan — Measures Affecting the Importation of Apples, WT/DS245/R.*

2003 *Japan — Measures Affecting the Importation of Apples, WT/DS245/AB/R.*

2003 *European Communities — Conditions for the Granting of Tariff Preferences to Developing Countries, WT/DS246/R.*

2004 *Canada — Measures Relating to Exports of Wheat and Treatment of Imported Grain, WT/DS276/R.*

2004 *European Communities — Conditions for the Granting of Tariff Preferences to Developing Countries, WT/DS246/AB/R.*

2004 *Canada — Measures Relating to Exports of Wheat and Treatment of Imported Grain, WT/DS276/AB/R.*

2004 *United States — Measures Affecting the Cross-Border Supply of Gambling and Betting Services, WT/DS285/R.*

2004 *Dominican Republic — Measures Affecting the Importation and Internal Sale of Cigarettes, WT/DS302/R.*

2005 *United States — Measures Affecting the Cross-Border Supply of Gambling and Betting Services, WT/DS285/AB/R.*

2005 *Dominican Republic — Measures Affecting the Importation and Internal Sale of Cigarettes, WT/DS302/AB/R.*

2005 *European Communities — Customs Classification of Frozen Boneless Chicken Cuts, WT/DS269, 286/AB/R.*

2005 *Mexico — Tax Measures on Soft Drinks and Other Beverages, WT/DS308/R.*

2006 *Mexico — Tax Measures on Soft Drinks and Other Beverages, WT/DS308/AB/R.*

2006 *European Communities — Measures Affecting the Approval and Marketing of Biotech Products, WT/DS291/R, WT/DS292/R, WT/DS293/R.*

2007 *Brazil — Measures Affecting Imports of Retreaded Tyres, WT/DS332/R.*

2007 *Brazil — Measures Affecting Imports of Retreaded Tyres, WT/DS332/AB/R.*

2008 *United States — Continued Suspension of Obligations in the EC – Hormones Dispute, WT/DS320/R.*

2008 *United States — Final Anti-Dumping Measures on Stainless Steel from Mexico, WT/DS344/AB/R.*

2008 *United States — Measures Relating to Shrimp from Thailand, WT/DS343/AB/R.*

2008 *United States — Continued Suspension of Obligations in the EC – Hormones Dispute, WT/DS320/AB/R.*

2008 *European Communities — Regime for the importation, sale and distribution of bananas, second recourse to Article 21.5 of the DSU by Ecuador, WT/DS27/AB/RW2/ECU.*

2008 *China — Measures Affecting Imports of Automobile Parts, WT/DS339/AB/R, WT/DS340/AB/R, WT/DS342/AB/R.*

2009 *Colombia — Indicative Prices and Restrictions on Ports of Entry, WT/DS366/R.*

2009 *China — Measures Affecting Trading Rights and Distribution Services for Certain Publications and Audiovisual Entertainment Products, WT/DS363/R.*

2009 *China — Measures Affecting Trading Rights and Distribution Services for Certain Publications and Audiovisual Entertainment Products, WT/DS363/AB/R.*

2010 *Australia — Measures Affecting the Importation of Apples from New Zealand, WT/DS367/R.*

2010 *United States — Certain Measures Affecting Imports of Poultry from China, WT/DS392/R.*

2010 *Australia — Measures Affecting the Importation of Apples from New Zealand, WT/DS367/AB/R.*

2011 *European Communities and Certain Member States — Large Civil Aircraft, WT/DS316/AB/R.*

2011 *United States — Measures Affecting the Production and Sale of Clove Cigarettes, WT/DS406/R.*

2011 *United States — Measures Concerning the Importation, Marketing and Sale of Tuna and Tuna Products, WT/DS381/R.*

2012 *China — Measures Related to the Exportation of Various Raw Materials, WT/DS394/AB/R, WT/DS395/AB/R, WT/DS398/AB/R.*

2012 *United States — Measures Affecting the Production and Sale of Clove Cigarettes, WT/DS406/AB/R.*

2012 *United States — Measures Concerning the Importation, Marketing and Sale of Tuna and Tuna Products, WT/DS381/AB/R.*

2012 *United States — Certain Country of Origin Labelling (COOL) Requirements, WT/DS384/AB/R, WT/DS/386/AB/R.*

2012 *China — Measures Related to the Exportation of Various Raw Materials, WT/DS394/R, WT/DS395/R, WT/DS398/R.*

2012 *Canada — Certain Measures Affecting the Renewable Energy Generation Sector, WT/DS412/R and Canada — Measures Relating to the Feed-in Tariff Program, WT/DS426/R.*

2013 *Canada — Certain Measures Affecting the Renewable Energy Generation Sector, WT/DS412/AB/R and Canada — Measures Relating to the Feed-in Tariff Program, WT/DS426/AB/R.*

2013 *European Communities — Measures Prohibiting the Importation and Marketing of Seal Products, WT/DS400/R, WT/DS401/R.*

2014 *European Communities — Measures Prohibiting the Importation and Marketing of Seal Products, WT/DS400/AB/R, WT/DS401/AB/R.*

2014 *China — Measures Related to the Exportation of Rare Earths, Tungsten, and Molybdenum, WT/DS431/AB/R, WT/DS432/AB/R, WT/DS433/AB/R.*

2016 *India — Certain Measures Relating to Solar Cells and Solar Modules, WT/DS456/AB/R.*

Introduction

"Oracular decisionmaking, the authority of which rests on the status of the decisor, rather than the quality of the reasoning, is antithetical to the judicial function."[1]

Several years ago, when I started working on this study, there was much concern about the impact of the World Trade Organization (WTO) on non-trade regulatory objectives and national policy-making. The concern was voiced at the academic level and in newspaper editorials, but also in the streets of Geneva, Seattle, Genoa and other places around the globe. Many – I among them – feared and continue to be concerned that the WTO serves to enforce trade liberalization at the global level at the expense of non-trade concerns, such as poverty reduction, environmental protection, public health, human rights or labour standards, making it more difficult for democratically elected national governments to make choices in favour of such objectives.

Today, the clamour – both academic and activist – around the WTO has become much quieter[2], with good reasons: Negotiations at the WTO about a number of topics have seen little progress over the years. There is also an ever-growing network of regional or bilateral investment and free trade agreements (FTAs) in place. These days, heated public debates about the relationship of international trade and investment rules and environmental issues are mostly triggered by negotiations about FTAs such as the EU - US Transatlantic Trade and Investment Partnership (TTIP)[3] or the

1 Weiler 2009, 137.

2 A piece of anecdotal evidence supporting this observation is that in the 1990ies and in the beginning of the 2000 decade almost every book or article carrying the terms "trade and environment" would in some way have a focus on WTO law or politics. By contrast, of the roughly two dozen chapters of a 2009 "Handbook on Trade and Environment" only three dealt directly with the WTO, see Gallagher 2009. Another indicator is the relative absence of protests during more recent high-level meetings of the WTO.

3 See for example on public opinion on TTIP in Germany Chan and Crawford 2017.

EU-Mercosur Trade Agreement[4] rather than by anything happening at the WTO.

However, the WTO has by no means become irrelevant to the trade and environment debate. WTO Members continue to discuss issues of trade and sustainability.[5] Moreover, WTO law is a reference point for other treaties: numerous bilateral or regional trade agreements take up or refer to formulations used in WTO law.[6] As a result, interpretations of WTO law have also become relevant for the interpretation of other trade and investment treaties.[7] Yet the influence of the WTO dispute settlement bodies' interpretation of WTO law is not *prima facie* limited to international economic law. The WTO dispute settlement system is the most active international judicial mechanism in existence. Thus, how it interprets the WTO treaties may also have an impact on the interpretation of international law more broadly.[8] Moreover, with the WTO dispute settlement system being the most prolific judicial mechanism at the international level it can also provide useful insights on judicial decision-making at the international level – itself an important topic given what some have described as the judicialization of international law. Hence, WTO dispute settlement still deserves attention.

Criticism of the WTO is predominantly linked to the way that non-trade concerns may be affected by WTO law and politics.[9] WTO law extends much beyond the non-discrimination approach and goods-only focus of the era when only the GATT existed. It includes substantive harmonization requirements in such agreements as the Agreement on Sanitary and

---

4 See for example Gruni 2020.

5 See for example WTO, New initiatives launched to intensify WTO work on trade and the environment, 17 November 2020, https://www.wto.org/english/news_e/news20_e/envir_17nov20_e.htm.

6 For an empirical analysis, see Allee, Elsig, and Lugg 2017.

7 Charlotin 2017, 294f finds an overall limited number of citations of WTO case law in non-WTO judicial decisions, but does not include an analysis of judicial decisions from inter-state dispute settlement under FTAs into his analysis. Marceau, Izaguerri, and Lanovoy 2013 identify 150 references to WTO rules and case law in judicial decisions taken by non-WTO international dispute settlement institutions. Peel 2012, 432 mentions one case where several ICJ judges in a dissenting opinion referred to a certain aspect of WTO dispute settlement practice, the reliance on scientific experts, as "best practice".

8 For example Livermore 2006, 789ff suggests that WTO judicial oversight could help improve and legitimize decision-making in the Codex Alimentarius Commission.

9 See for example Kelly 2006.

Phytosanitary Measures (SPS) and Technical Barriers to Trade (TBT) Agreements, the Agreement on Trade-Related Aspects of Intellectual Property Rights (TRIPS) or provisions on liberalization in the service sector in the General Agreement on Services (GATS). Much of the concern stems from the fact that the WTO has one primary aim, which is, according to the preamble of the WTO Agreement, to "develop an integrated, more viable and durable multilateral trading system".[10] This distinguishes WTO law, and hence also the judicial bodies faced with the task of interpreting it, from other parts of the international legal system that protect broader objectives, such as safeguarding core human rights.

Concerns over the negative impact of WTO law and FTAs on non-trade interests are intertwined with a second dimension: the way that the WTO legal framework may restrict the scope for democratic, legitimate decision-making at the national level, in particular through its strong dispute settlement mechanism. This mechanism deprives, as some have argued, WTO Members of an option they otherwise have in practice when it comes to norms of international law – non-compliance at relatively low political and economic cost.[11] Indeed, establishing an international judicial[12] body means delegating certain choices about the institutions that ultimately decide on certain matters to that body. In the case of the WTO, the WTO dispute settlement bodies will have to decide, for example, whether a national measure may remain in place (meaning that national level authorities decide), whether they hold the measure to be inconsistent with WTO law (meaning that the WTO decides), or whether they defer to provisions of non-WTO international law or strengthen international standards (meaning deference to the decisions of those who created these international

10 Obviously, the preamble of the WTO Agreement also mentions other objectives, namely raising standards of living, ensuring full employment and a large and steadily growing volume of real income and effective demand, expanding the production of and trade in goods and services, and securing a share for developing countries in international trade growth. However, those are, according to the WTO approach, dependent on the attainment of the primary objective, i.e. an enhanced international trade system.

11 On this point and its significance for the problem of democratic legitimacy of WTO norms see Bogdandy 2003, 106–109; Howse 2003a, 93. The reputational and political costs of non-compliance are probably not different in the WTO legal universe than concerning other international legal agreements.

12 For the use of the word "judicial" when referring to the WTO dispute settlement, see chapter 1, section 4.1.1.

norms).[13] These questions carry all the greater urgency given that the international (legal) system is in general under the suspicion of suffering from a democratic deficit.[14]

An assessment of judicial decision-making by an international dispute settlement mechanism can obviously follow different approaches; indeed, scholars have researched the WTO dispute settlement system from various methodological and disciplinary angels and sought answers to a number of different questions.[15] This study looks at two dimensions of WTO judicial decision-making, both with a particular focus on the Appellate Body: the substantive outcome produced by and the judicial style of the WTO dispute settlement bodies.

Concerning the substantive outcome, the research question is how the WTO dispute settlement bodies have in practice decided the cases where non-trade issues were at stake. These "trade and ..." or non-trade cases are the ones that tend to receive most public, critical attention and raise the most serious legitimacy issues with regard to the WTO's role in resolving them. In these "trade and ..." cases, is there a pattern that the WTO adjudicators favour trade and economic concerns over other regulatory objectives to an extent not required by the wording of the law? In other words, can it be argued that the WTO dispute settlement system exhibits a pro-trade bias? When seeking to answer these questions, the present study goes beyond individual case notes or the analysis of specific legal issues of WTO case law. While it does contain summaries of specific aspects of WTO case law, notably the interpretation of certain articles, as well as a technical-legal discussion and critique of the way that the dispute settlement bodies have dealt with these issues, it does not stop there. Concerning the analysis of the substantive outcome in "trade and ..." cases, the discussion of the case law only forms the basis for a systematic cross-case assessment of whether the interpretations chosen by the WTO adjudicators are more restrictive of the regulatory freedom of WTO Members than required. For assessing whether WTO law "requires" a certain interpretation, existing legal scholarship is used as a yardstick; for identifying defensible alternative interpretations, I will rely primarily on existing comments by legal observers, but also on differences between Panel and Appellate Body reports. This ap-

13 The fact that judicial decision-making at the WTO involves institutional choices has been most clearly pointed out by Shaffer 2009.

14 See from the voluminous literature on the legitimacy of international law only Stein 2001; Weiler and Motoc 2003.

15 See chapter 1, section 5.1.

proach is based on the assumption that if there are alternative interpretations that a number of renowned legal scholars or practitioners agree on, this is an indication that the WTO adjudicators could also have defensibly interpreted the law in a different way. By implication, their actual interpretation must be considered a deliberate choice, rather than the only possible interpretation of WTO law.

The statement that adjudicators have a choice presupposes that the law actually provides them with such choices, i.e. that the law is indeterminate. However, if the law does not pre-determine outcomes, how is a given substantive interpretation justified by judicial decision-makers? This leads to the second topic of this work, the WTO's judicial style. The research question concerning the judicial style of the WTO dispute settlement bodies is how they justify their decisions. What methods of interpretation are used? What type of arguments and mode of reasoning can be found in the reports? How can the observed style be explained?

Altogether, this work is concerned primarily with the legal reality as it unfolds in the WTO universe. My aim is not to make a contribution to the debate on how WTO law *should* be interpreted – even though there are some dispersed comments on that as well – but to analyse how it *has* been interpreted, what effects the chosen interpretations have, and what could be reasons why they were chosen. The new insights I hope to add to the vast body of existing legal scholarship are both substantive and methodological: In substance, I purport to systematically assess the degree to which the interpretations contained in WTO case law in "trade and ..." cases is restrictive or permissive vis-à-vis WTO Members' regulatory freedom via a reading of the judicial decisions. This is combined with an analysis of the rhetoric, the judicial style, used for justifying these decisions. These aspects have only infrequently been brought together in the existing literature on an equal footing and connected to a defined theoretical framework. Yet bringing them together is important: The legitimacy[16] of judicial decisions depends on both the substantive outcomes of cases, i.e.

16 A brief explanation is in place on the use of the terms legitimate and legitimacy. A distinction is frequently made between two meanings of this term, namely legitimacy in a normative sense and in an empirical or social sense. Legitimacy in an empirical sense means acceptance of a norm, decision, or policy by relevant constituencies as justified, legitimacy in a normative sense means that "a claim of authority is well founded" or "worthiness of acceptance", see Bodansky 1999, 601; Krajewski 2001, 168. The term will be used in both senses in the following, but I will try to make clear in which sense it is used in each instance where not evident from the context.

who wins and loses and what interpretations are adopted, and the way a judicial decision is justified. A judicial outcome that is perceived as unjust or inappropriate or not in line with the law is likely not to gain the acceptance of relevant constituencies, i.e. the parties to a case, the actors using an international dispute settlement mechanism, legal communities, or the larger public. At the same time, a judicial decision that is poorly reasoned, refers to arguments that by conventional wisdom should not be relevant for a judicial decision, or is inconsistent is not likely to be accepted, either. Thus, both the substance and style of judicial decisions matter – and this applies to WTO dispute settlement as well.

Concerning methodology, this study has a stronger interdisciplinary character than most WTO-related works coming from the legal discipline. The conceptual framework described further in chapter 1 is not taken primarily from the discipline of law; rather, it is informed by theoretical writings on the indeterminacy of law as well as insights on the real-world functioning of courts, taken mainly from political science studies. Chapters 2 and 3, constituting the empirical part of the study, follow partially a standard legal methodology; they describe and criticize how WTO law has been interpreted and discuss potential alternative ways how it could have been interpreted. However, they also go beyond a standard legal methodology in inquiring about the substantive and discursive effects of the case law. This work uses theoretical approaches, developed mainly by political scientists, on courts as strategic actors, as a conceptual framework while undertaking an in-depth empirical analysis of relevant case law with the methods of lawyers. It also bears noting that the overall approach of this work – having a theoretical framework which is brought to bear upon empirical material – is an approach not normally found in the discipline of law, but prevalent in social sciences. This work would not have been possible at a stage where there was little discussion about WTO law; the study can hence also be read as an attempt to reap the fruits of the lively discourse on WTO law of the past 25 years.

The study is structured as follows: The underlying theoretical assumptions are explained in chapter 1. The chapter first justifies and explains the assumptions on judicial decision-making at a general level, drawing on relevant works from legal theory and comparative studies of courts' reasoning. One assumption is that law in general and WTO law in particular are indeterminate, at least to a degree. This means that judges regularly need to decide cases on other than strictly legal grounds. Furthermore, I assume that judges are generally interested in maintaining and enhancing the reputation, credibility, legitimacy and mandate of the court they work for.

They will therefore seek to make their judgements acceptable to relevant constituencies. For doing so, the judge/s must observe certain standards of what is considered an acceptable legal argument. Having justified these assumptions about judicial decision-making in general terms, I discuss to which extent the resulting insights are also valid within the WTO context and what hypotheses concerning the outcome and style of the WTO dispute settlement can be formulated on their basis. For this purpose, the main point of reference is prior research by political scientists conceiving of courts in general and the WTO dispute settlement bodies in particular as strategic actors. Finally, chapter 1 also explains in more detail the methodology underlying the work.

Chapter 2 focuses on the substantive outcome produced by the WTO dispute settlement bodies. It reviews the relevant "trade and ..." cases of the WTO with a view to how certain core norms of WTO law are interpreted in substance. The aim of this chapter is to ascertain the balance between trade and non-trade objectives, between international legal norms and national regulatory space that the WTO dispute settlement bodies strike through their interpretations. The review will focus on those norms which, by their rather indeterminate wording, offer judicial decision-makers considerable leeway, and are at the same time most relevant in cases where environmental protection, public health or other non-trade concerns are at stake. These are selected norms from GATT, the SPS and TBT Agreements and the GATS. Chapter 2 contains sections on each of these agreements.

Each of the sections is structured alike: I will first present the relevant case law on each of the agreements and will then analyse the respective case law from a legal-technical point of view in a part entitled "discussion". The rationale behind this approach is that, as discussed above, the type and quality of arguments that judges use matter for the legitimacy of a ruling. For example, when a certain interpretation is widely perceived as not covered by the everyday meaning of the term it seeks to interpret or there are inconsistencies between different parts of a ruling, this will undermine the perceived quality and thus acceptance of the respective judicial finding. In a part entitled "assessment", I will then assess the case law from a more normative-political point of view. I will inquire what alternative interpretations could have been chosen and whether the interpretations actually chosen are more or less restrictive of WTO Members' regulatory freedom than the potential alternatives. The chapter ends with an overall assessment of the case law in "trade and ..." cases. This assessment summarizes the insights on whether an interpretive pattern is discernible that the WTO adjudicators favour trade and economic concerns over other regulatory objectives to an extent not required by the wording of the law.

Chapter 3 is dedicated to the judicial style of the WTO dispute settlement bodies. Attention is paid, among others, to the methods of interpretation used (including the role of non-WTO international law), the standard of review, the role of principles and balancing in the jurisprudence, and the use of precedents and techniques to avoid deciding certain issues. In addition certain other aspects of the case law are discussed that are more rhetorical in character. For each of these issues, I will first explain in the respective section why the topic is important. I will then briefly summarize the most important insights and, where pertinent, discuss them from a legal-technical point of view, drawing also on relevant scholarship. For all of the aspects of the WTO judicial style, I will assess the discursive effects of the approach chosen by the adjudicators, what the approach means in terms of legitimizing the decisions and how it can be explained. The discussion and assessment sections feed into a description and assessment of the specific judicial style of the WTO in the last section of chapter 3.

Chapter 4 offers conclusions drawing on the insights on substance and style. It starts by offering evidence for the often-heard claim that the WTO dispute settlement system is a success by investigating the relative absence of counter-measures of WTO Members against it so far. I will then bring together the key results from chapters 2 and 3 concerning the substance and style of judicial decision-making at the WTO respectively in an attempt to explain the perceived success of the WTO dispute settlement system.

Chapter 1: Judicial decision-making at the WTO (and elsewhere) – a conceptual outline

"Courts and judges always lie. Lying is the nature of the judicial activity."[17]

In a simplifying and generalising statement one could say that 20th century theories on judicial decision-making largely agree that law is – sometimes/often/usually – indeterminate and that hence judicial decision-makers have a – limited/certain/large – degree of discretion or autonomous space when deciding a case brought before them. While the basic insight that law is indeterminate seems to be widely shared, the slashes in the previous sentence indicate that disagreement persists on various related questions: To which degree is the law indeterminate? What do judges do when faced with the indeterminacy of the law? And what ought they do? Obviously, judges and courts are different from each other. Yet the real-world differences between judicial systems and processes do not seem to fully explain why scholars have developed such diverse portrayals of the judicial decision-making process.

This chapter discusses insights into judicial decision-making and the applicability of these insights to the dispute settlement system of the WTO. In this context, judicial decision-making refers both to the way that judges "really" come to a decision and the way they justify their decision in the text of their judgement, which is often published.[18]

The study draws on existing theoretical accounts of judicial decision-making as well as on empirical studies on specific courts. Yet, given the longevity of judicial decision-making as a research topic and the resulting breadth of the literature, it is impossible to take into account all relevant theoretical or empirical literature.[19] For this reason the focus is on courts

---

17 Shapiro 1994, 159.

18 The assumption that both dimensions are different, i.e. that the factors motivating a judicial decision and the reasons given for justifying it are not necessarily identical, will be explained in this chapter.

19 Lindquist and Cross 2009, 2 observe that in the US context discussions about activist judges date back until the time of the framing of the US constitution; Hig-

at the international (rather than regional or national) level,[20] given that the WTO Appellate Body is itself such a "court"[21]. In addition, literature on the European Court of Justice (ECJ)[22] is taken into account. Similar to the WTO dispute settlement bodies, the ECJ frequently has to decide cases where trade, or, in the language of the EU[23], internal market concerns and non-trade concerns (e. g. environmental policy objectives) are pitched against each other.[24] Given that WTO law shares at least some features and functions with constitutional law, some studies on constitutional courts are also taken into account.[25] On the basis of the literature review, I proceed to formulate cautious hypotheses on what may be expected from the Appellate Body in terms of style and substance in "trade and ..." cases.

This chapter is structured as follows: Section 1 briefly summarizes the debate on the indeterminacy of the law, explaining the assumption that law is inherently indeterminate and describing different accounts of how

---

gins 1968, 63 observes that the distinction between "legal" and "political" questions was first made in 1758.

20 More concretely, there are, besides the WTO dispute settlement system, currently three permanent international courts: the International Court of Justice (ICJ), the International Criminal Court (ICC) and the International Tribunal for the Law of the Sea (ITLOS). The ICC is considerably different from the others in that its mandate is to judge the behaviour of individuals rather than that of states.

21 For a discussion of the court-likeness of the Appellate Body, see below section 4.1.1.

22 With the Lisbon Treaty, the name of the Court has changed to "Court of Justice of the European Union" which is usually abbreviated CJEU. In this work, I still use the old and more widely known terminology, given that the events and cases I refer to are mostly from the pre-Lisbon era.

23 I use the term European Union (EU) to refer to the entity called this way since the Lisbon Treaty, even when a matter in the pre-Lisbon era is concerned. However, some of the earlier dispute settlement cases involved the predecessor "European Communities". In the context of such cases (and only there), I still use "EC" or "European Communities".

24 These similarities have given rise to a body of literature that compares EU and WTO legal rules and dispute settlement decisions, see Cheyne 2006; Neumayer 2001; Hohmann 2000; Holmes 1999; Joerges and Godt 2005; Ortino 2004; Notaro 2003; Scott 2004b; Slotboom 2003; Weiler 2000; for a discussion of differences and similarities between the WTO and the EU, see Búrca and Scott 2001.

25 Eeckhout 2010, 8. Another "court" that could arguably be taken into account is the dispute settlement procedures of NAFTA. Indeed, in some of the discussions of WTO dispute settlement, NAFTA is also taken into account, see for example Flett 2010, 310ff. However, NAFTA is a trilateral, rather than a multilateral agreement, and its dispute settlement system does not include an appellate review. Thus, similarities with the WTO are likely to be limited.

judges decide cases in the face of such indeterminacy. Section 2 presents different factors that influence the substantive outcome of judicial cases. Section 3 deals with what I call "judicial style" in this work; I discuss in this section what kind of arguments judges may and do use for justifying decisions that are based on indeterminate legal norms. In other words, section 1 sets the scene, section 2 relates to the "context of discovery", i.e. the non-textual factors determining the outcome of a case[26] and section 3 deals with the "context of justification", i.e. the reasoning used in judicial decisions to justify them. In section 4, I discuss to which extent general insights into factors influencing judicial decisions and judicial apply to the WTO context. This leads to several hypotheses on factors influencing the substantive outcome of cases brought before the Appellate Body and its judicial style. Section 5 serves as methodological double-check and presents details on the aspects of the WTO's judicial decision-making process that will be investigated in the remainder of this work.

1. *Judicial decision-making in the face of the indeterminacy of the law: a debate revisited*

The insight that the law is pervasively and inherently ambiguous and indeterminate and more than one interpretation can often be justified by established methodological standards was called a *"Gemeinplatz"*, a truism, years ago.[27] When the actions of judges are discussed is when the indeterminacy of the law becomes particularly relevant: it is the judges' task to decide what the law mandates in a specific case. Parties come to them to obtain an answer of "yes" or "no" or at least a "yes, but" or "partially no". Thus, the debate on judicial decision-making is as old as the one on the indeterminacy of the law, leading the author of one book published in 1999 to begin his work by stating that yet another book on adjudication required justification.[28] What follows cannot, therefore, be more than a rough sketch.

Before presenting the thoughts of some of the leading figures in the debate on the indeterminacy of the law and judicial decision-making, it is useful to take a closer look at the word indeterminacy, itself not a determi-

26 For the terms "context of discovery" and "context of justification", see, for example, Beck 2012, 46f; Martineau 2007, 994.

27 Enderlein 1992, 83.

28 Lucy 1999, 1.

nate term. What does it mean? One possible definition is that the law is indeterminate whenever it is not evident to a legal professional, immediately or after some reflection, what the law mandates in a certain factual constellation. A second possible definition is that the law is indeterminate whenever two legally trained readers, acting in good faith, arrive at divergent conclusions on a legal issue after careful reflection. A third possible definition is that the law is indeterminate when a court's decision in a given case situation cannot be predicted.[29]

Indeterminacy is a matter of degree. Take, for example, a provision that stipulates a prohibition to park a "car" in a certain designated area and provides for a fine as a consequence of any breech of that prohibition. It would be difficult for the police to make the case for fining someone for having his dog wait in this area while shopping. It may be disputable whether the same provision warrants fining a woman for parking her motorcycle in this area. Yet a truck driver, leaving her truck in the area, will undoubtedly have to pay a fine. Conversely, the limits that terms like "appropriate" impose on what a defensible judicial interpretation is are much less clear. Of course, there is no precise threshold for when precisely a law is "indeterminate" and when it is not. Moreover, a norm may appear determinate at first sight, but in the process of interpretation it may become clear that it is not.[30]

In the following, I will lay the foundations for the later analysis by briefly revisiting the main positions on the indeterminacy of the law and its implications for what judges do. The following broad overview is not nearly comprehensive or detailed enough to do justice to each piece of empirical research or all theoretical works on judicial decision-making.[31] My ambition here is more limited: I seek to establish that analysing WTO judicial decisions as involving at least a degree of discretion of the people taking them is a meaningful approach, in light of existing research on judicial decision-making. For this purpose, I draw on two well-known strands in legal theory on the indeterminacy of the law and judicial decision-making: formalist and realist approaches.[32]

---

29 See Kennedy 1997, 60; some theorists arguing that the law is not determinate have replaced the term "predictability" of judicial decisions by the term "reckonability", meaning that outcomes may be predicted in most, but not in all cases, see Beck 2012, 3.

30 An example from German civil law is given by Rafi 2004, 41f.

31 For a more detailed account see Lucy 1999.

32 For a brief description see for example Beck 2012, 17ff who calls them "scientific vs heuristic" legal reasoning. Lucy 1999, 2 also identifies the two approaches, call-

Legal formalism can be both an empirical and prescriptive approach. The central basic assumption in legal formalism is (or maybe: was[33]) that positive legal norms are a more or less closed and comprehensive system adopted on the basis of, for example, political, economic and moral considerations by the responsible legislative bodies.[34] The judges' role is to apply and interpret these norms. When doing so, they lay bare what is already there, without letting themselves be guided by their own non-legal personal preferences and without considering the economic, political and social reality outside of the courtroom. Judge are constrained by legal norms, interpret these norms, use the established methods of legal interpretation, but do so in isolation of factors outside the textual universe of the law. Thus, it does not matter who the judge is. Whoever decides the case will arrive at the same conclusion, assuming that no (professional) mistake is made. There is one right solution, a legal truth that a judge can and must find.

What I describe here is, however, a rather strong version of formalism, which may not exist in this pure form;[35] indeed it may be more correct to say that according to formalist accounts of judicial decision-making adjudicators are "*relatively* constrained by standards *relatively* determinate of the dispute before them"[36]. Some scholars argue that while the law is *prima facie* indeterminate, at a deeper level it is not, or at least not in most cases. Dworkin may be the most prominent example,[37] but is certainly not the only proponent of this idea.[38] According to these scholars, the indetermi-

---

ing them orthodox and heretical. Guthrie, Rachlinski, and Wistrich 2007, 2f also describe the two different strands, but hold themselves that neither formalist nor realist assumptions are entirely correct and posit that "judges generally make intuitive decisions but sometimes override their intuition with deliberation", at 3.

33 Or maybe not even that. Tamanaha 2009, 4 claims that "the age of 'legal formalism' never really existed as such" and was basically an invention of its critics. However, as I hope to show in this work, e.g. below in section 5.1., influential portrayals of WTO adjudication exist that can only be described as formalist.

34 For a good overview see Schauer 1988.

35 For example Beck 2012, 19 states that to his knowledge no pure example exists of what he labels a "scientific legal theory'" but what would be a formalist understanding in this work.

36 Lucy 1999, 2.

37 Dworkin developed his theory in a series of books with considerable change in detail over time, especially as far as terminology is concerned, see Watkins-Bienz 2004, 75–76. As all that is needed for the present context is a rough sketch, this need, however, not concern us here.

38 A more doctrinally-minded author that uses the Dworkinian model is Hector 1992, especially at 178; another example is Emmerich-Fritsche 2000.

nacy thesis is correct with regards the surface of the law, consisting of a set of written legal norms. These norms may indeed confront the judge with "hard cases", in which it is not clear at first or second sight what the law stipulates.[39] Yet Dworkin and others do not think that in such cases a "right answer" is simply not available, i.e. one interpretation of the law that captures what the law "really" says does not exist. They hold that a legal system will provide unequivocal answers, if judges do what they ought to do. To them, the law sets forth clearly what rights individuals have. Dworkin demonstrates this by inventing judge Hercules, a judge endowed with super-human capacities in all relevant judicial disciplines.[40] When faced with a hard case, judge Hercules will initiate a process of theoretical reconstruction of the existing legal system. In this process, judge Hercules will consider the principles underlying the existing legal rules, institutions as well as prior case law. Judge Hercules' reconstruction will allow identifying the interpretation that fits best into the existing legal system as a whole, among the different legal interpretations that are defensible from a linguistic point of view. Dworkin insists that a judge does – and should[41] – not make new law according to his or her own preferences, but is able and bound to detect a solution already present in the existing law.[42] Dworkin still accepts, however, the idea that identity of a judicial decision-maker in a given case may be of relevance.[43] His thesis is softer than it seems to be at first sight. Dworkin acknowledges that the "judgement" of the individual judge who endeavours to "detect" the right solution within the existing legal system is needed for deciding the case. He does not deny, though, that two judges may come to different conclusions in a given case.[44]

Alexy draws a similar conclusion; he shares Dworkin's idea that a legal system does not consist only of rules, but also of principles.[45] Concurring with Dworkin, Alexy holds that what distinguishes rules and principles is how they function in a collision case: Rules have a clear "if … then" struc-

---

39 The "hard case" terminology is the one of Dworkin 1981, 81–130.

40 See ibid., 101–125 for the following.

41 There is some ambiguity as to whether Dworkin's model is a normative ideal or an empirical description, see Soper 1983, 13–14.

42 Dworkin 1981, 117–118, 127.

43 Ibid., 123–129.

44 Another possible way of reconciling the idea that law is ultimately determinate with the idea that it does matter who is the judge, would be to argue that principles do not narrow, but enlarge the space for judicial decisions. This is what Raz 1983, 76 seeks to demonstrate.

45 Alexy 1995, 177–212.

ture. Consequently, when two rules mandate different consequences in a certain factual situation, one of those rules must be invalid or inapplicable.[46] By way of contrast, principles define certain points or interest that must necessarily be taken into account when a legal decision is taken. When two principles contradict each other, judicial decisions-makers have to decide which principle is more important and take the decision accordingly; this does not mean, however, that the underlying principle is invalid, just that it is less "weighty" in the specific case.[47] Rules are specified in advance of the conduct that they apply to, while principles are not.[48] Reacting to criticism, Alexy states that the principles model of legal systems does not mean that there is always one solution to a case. The reason is that it is impossible for law-makers to pre-establish a hierarchy between all principles applicable to all cases ever.[49] Rather, principles help to considerably reduce the *prima facie* indeterminacy of the law.[50]

Historically, the strand of legal theory competing with legal formalism was (legal) realism,[51] on which later strands like Critical Legal Studies have built. A core assumption of legal realism is that the written law allows, and in many cases even requires, judges to consider what is a morally just or politically appropriate solution in light of the wider economic, political and social context of the case at hand. Furthermore, judges are not primarily or exclusively judges, but human beings.[52] They bring a human factor to their judgements, in the form of individual convictions, preferences, attitudes and even stereotypes. Some authors, who do not belong to the

---

46 Of course, the difference between rules and principles is sometimes also described in different terms, see for example Lydgate 2012, 624ff.

47 Alexy 1995, 216–219; Dworkin 1981, 24–28.

48 Trachtman 2003, 140; Trachtman speaks of standards rather than principles, but appears to mean the same.

49 Alexy 1995, 224–255; this is also the point that Dworkin seems to have in mind when he calls his model judge "Hercules" and emphasizes that he must be superhuman.

50 Many authors build on the distinction between rules and principles by Dworkin and Alexy, also in the context of WTO law. See for example Andenas and Zleptnig 2007, 376f.

51 On US-American legal realism see Bechtler 1978, 5-48, and for the realist concept of the legal process especially 23-30. It should be noted that US American legal realists focused mainly on common law, much less on statutory interpretation.

52 This formulation is borrowed from a 2010 lecture by Frederick Schauer "Do lawyers think and if so how?", video online at http://www.youtube.com/watch?feature=player_embedded&v=_l7FcYzvl7k#!.

school of (US) legal realism, share these basic ideas about the indeterminacy of the law and their implications for judicial decision-making.[53]

There are several obvious objections as well as potential qualifications to the assumption that the law is indeterminate, which may require its restatement in a less far-reaching manner.[54] An obvious objection to the indeterminacy thesis is the following: Are there not accepted tools of legal interpretation, recognized methods of legal interpretation – textual interpretation of the norm, interpretation of a norm in its context, historical interpretation and teleological interpretation (to name the important ones) – and the typical forms of legal arguments like inferences *e contrario, ad absurdum* as well as analogies that judges may use to find out what the law says? Can indeterminacy not be eliminated by using them? Does a judicial decision reached in line with established rules of legal interpretation not have to be considered acceptable? In this sense, methods of interpretation help judges (and other lawyers) cope with the indeterminacy of the law. However, how judges use them and which rule of interpretation they prefer, is largely left to them. Canons of legal interpretation are themselves general rules and give rise to ambiguities of their own, which can only be resolved through interpretation.[55] There is usually no pre-established hierarchy among the methods of interpretation in domestic law, once textual interpretation does not deliver.[56] Much the same has been observed for the rules of interpretation in public international law.[57] Hence, the canons of legal interpretation do not fully eliminate the indeterminacy of the law.[58]

---

53 For example, Kelsen appears to have shared this idea as well, see Zarbiyev 2012, 5.

54 See for a criticism of the indeterminacy thesis and different responses to it also Habermas 1992, 246ff.

55 See Enderlein 1992, 329f; Hart 1994, 126; Pauwelyn and Elsig 2012, 448 specifically with regards to the rules of interpretation for international treaties contained in the VCLT; Habermas 1992, 276 also notes the circularity of an argument that relies on the established methods of legal interpretation to reduce the indeterminacy of the law.

56 See Rafi 2004, 19–24.

57 Alvarez 2008, 620ff; Cartland, Depayre, and Woznowski 2012, 987; Foltea 2012, 92; Mavroidis 2006, 352; Steinberg 2004, 258; van den Bossche 2006, 308.

58 Beck 2012, 6, 134f therefore differentiates between "primary uncertainty", i.e. indeterminacy of legal rules, and "secondary uncertainty", i.e. indeterminacy of rules of interpretation. He also discusses some of the reasons for secondary uncertainty.

Even when using them, judges can still arrive at a number of divergent interpretations on the same matter.[59]

Model solutions to the case at hand are a second tool that judges may use to reduce indeterminacy; these model solutions exist in the form of precedents[60] and, less importantly, scholarly writing. Precedents can obviously help reduce legal indeterminacy from the perspective of a judge. In common law systems precedents perform the very function of legal rules.[61] However, as long as there is no formal rule requiring judges to take into account a decision by a different court, they are free to do or not do so.[62] Even judges are legally bound by certain precedents, they need to decide whether both cases are similar enough for a precedent to apply. It has been observed that "a multitude of legal positions can be wriggled out of precedents if only one is willing to argue accordingly"[63], irrespective of whether there are formal rules on precedents in a given legal system. Similarly, when resorting to the opinions of legal scholars, judges must take a decision on whether these opinions are relevant to the case at hand. To complicate matters, the legal discourse rarely offers monolithic conclusions about how specific legal norms ought to be interpreted.[64] Thus, judges still have to decide which suggested interpretation is sounder. Altogether, the indeterminacy dilemma is not resolved through either legal-interpretive tools or precedents,[65] although both may help mitigate it.

The idea that the law is indeterminate and that where determinacy ends the judge decides a case on non-legal grounds[66] can be found in stronger and weaker versions. The strong version, which has most prominently

59 With regard to WTO dispute settlement Ruiz Fabri 2006, 132; Cartland, Depayre, and Woznowski 2012, 987.

60 Precedents are, of course, only an *additional* potential tool for reducing the initial indeterminacy of legal norms, where there are such legal norms. Where there is no such legal norm in first place, precedents fulfill the very role of legal norms.

61 But even with regard to codified systems, it has been observed that sometimes a legal norm is nothing but the codification of established case law Hector 1992, 195.

62 See Rafi 2004, 56.

63 Jacob 2012, 49.

64 An illustrative example is provided by German legal textbooks. There is a series of books in the fields of civil and penal law whose exclusive content is to point out to long-standing doctrinal controversies, enumerating the arguments that are put forward in support of each of the differing interpretative views. See for example Hillenkamp 2006.

65 Bourdieu 1987, 826.

66 See below section 2 for a discussion of these non-legal grounds.

been propounded by legal realism and subsequent strands like Critical Legal Studies (CLS),[67] assumes that indeterminacy is the normal case. Hence, judges routinely do not interpret, but rather make law when deciding a case. Others propose a weaker version of the thesis. To H. L. A. Hart, a prominent representative of this line of thinking, the cases, in which judges make law, are only the tip of a legal iceberg. To a larger part, the iceberg is made of clear legal rules, open to application by the judge. The indeterminate cases are only a minor part;[68] there are shades of indeterminacy.[69]

In conclusion, major thinkers in contemporary legal theory, representing different theoretical strands, concur that judges will be faced, at least sometimes, with legal norms that do not mandate a specific outcome and thus have a space of their own for influencing the outcome of the cases they decide. It is a widely accepted assumption that some norms are – as one author has put it – "clear, self-executing, fully specified in advance and not in need of interpretation"[70] and others are not.[71] Disagreement seems to be mainly about how deeply indeterminacy is entrenched in the law and whether it can be remedied by resorting to the more fundamental principles of a legal order.

---

67 See for a recent CLS contribution holding such conception of adjudication Kennedy 1997; Bourdieu 1987, 827 probably also comes in this category when referring to the "extraordinary elasticity of texts, which can go as far as complete indeterminacy or ambiguity".

68 See Hart 1994, 35–136, 152–154. Moreover, Hart stresses that formalism, i.e., an attitude that considers it desirable that judicial choice be reduced to a minimum by making rules as clear and precise as possible, is not necessarily normatively desirably, 128-136; on the differences between US American legal realism and Hart see Bechtler 1978, 46–47.

69 For a WTO scholar subscribing to this account of legal indeterminacy, see Trachtman 1999, 351.

70 Ibid., 338 who draws on the distinction between rules and standards developed in the law and economics literature.

71 This basic starting point is shared by some of the eminent authorities in current legal theory, even though they put it differently. Hart 1994, 124–135 describes at some length the "open texture" of law; Dworkin 1981, 83 speaks of "hard cases", in which "no settled rule dictates a decision either way"; Habermas 1992, 266 writes that all legal norms with the exception of few highly specified ones, are originally (von Haus aus) indeterminate. This insight, which initially belonged to the disciplines of law in general and legal theory in particular, has through the recent debate on legalization also gained some prominence in international relations theory. One of the criteria used for measuring how legalized a certain regime is, is the precision of its norms, see Abbott et al. 2000, 401.

There are different reasons why legal provisions are indeterminate.[72] The first reason, which I am tempted to call an ontological one, is that the law *qua lege* is and must be abstract and general.[73] The law provides for categories of future factual situations that are to be treated in a certain way. When the legal categories are applied, it is frequently unclear whether a specific factual situation belongs to one legal category or the other. In other words, indeterminacy is built into the relation between the abstract and the concrete. The second reason for the law's indeterminacy is that law is always a text, i.e. language. Language is no precision tool and misunderstandings and ambiguities occur frequently. The indeterminacy of the law, as language, reflects the indeterminacy of language itself.[74] The third reason for the indeterminacy of the law is more empirical. Law is written by human beings and they may either be unwilling to or incapable of making the law more precise.[75] Non-intended indeterminacy occurs, for example, when law-writers fail to see conflicts between a draft law and existing legal norms or when a formulation in a legal provision is accidentally more ambiguous than necessary (in the light of the indeterminacy of language as such). For example, the Uruguay Round negotiators may not have had much legal expertise, contributing to WTO law being indeterminate.[76] Indeterminate legal norms may also be attributable to a lack of imagination on part of the law-writers, who simply do not envisage certain future factual constellations and therefore do not cater for them.[77] By way of contrast, intended indeterminacy reflects a lack of political will to make the law more precise, in the absence of a political consensus.[78] In international law, countries sometimes deliberately agree on indeterminate legal norms, since this enables them to conclude an agreement despite prevailing politi-

72 For a brief discussion of these reasons with regard to WTO law, see Picciotto 2005, 4ff.

73 Hart 1994, 1; 20–21.

74 Some, for example ibid., 26, do not distinguish between the two reasons, but instead hold that it is only language that causes the problems when the more concrete situation is matched with the abstract rule. This implies that concepts do not "exist" beyond language.

75 See for example Feteris 1999, 7.

76 Bartels 2004, 871.

77 This point is emphasized by Hart 1994, 128–135.

78 For international law see Alter 2003, 793.

cal controversies.[79] Finally, indeterminacy also serves to delegate decision-making to a lower governance level or a judicial body.[80]

Indeterminacy takes different forms in written law. A brief typology of the sources of legal indeterminacy[81] a judge may be faced with in the course of judicial proceedings has to include at least the following ones:[82]

One source of indeterminacy is the language used to formulate the law. Scholars have described this phenomenon in different ways: sometimes the wording of the law is considered to be a mere *topos,* one aspect to be taken into account among others when interpreting legal text.[83] Others describe the wording of legal provisions as the outer, sometimes blurred borderline of what is still a valid interpretation.[84] Obviously, this also depends on the specific terms used in legal provisions. For example, a term like "a person" is less ambiguous and open to interpretation than words like "reasonable" or "good faith".[85]

A situation sometimes distinguished from the indeterminacy of a legal provision is when no legal provision is *prima facie* applicable to a concrete situation, i.e. a *lacuna* or gap in the law exists.[86] Again, a distinction can be made between questions left open deliberately and questions left open un-

---

79 See Pauwelyn 2003a, 93; Daku and Pelc 2017, 235, 237.

80 This has been observed both for domestic law and international law. For national law see Hubmann 1977, 51; for international law see Trachtman 1999, 336, 351; for the ICC see Wessel 2006, 386.

81 Obviously, apart from legal indeterminacy (or uncertainty), factual uncertainty, i.e. the question what actually happened and which part of that can be proven by the admissible procedural means, is also of great practical relevance in court proceedings, but is not discussed here.

82 The model of a legal order underlying this typology is one of codified law, i.e. a civil law system or statutory law in common law systems. A similar model developed with respect to common law would have to include the rules of precedential effect while some of the other types on indeterminacy presented here might be less important. International law, which WTO law is a part of, is a system of codified law and does not follow a common law model. This justifies basing this typology on the former type of legal system.

83 Rafi 2004, 41; Trachtman 1999, 337f.

84 See Barak 2005, xiii: "Semantic meaning sets the limits of interpretation.".

85 Alexy 1995, 24 describes the kind of indeterminacy inherent to the last kind of expressions as „evaluative openness“ and distinguishes it from semantic vagueness.

86 Steinberg 2004, 251 noting also that the distinction between indeterminacy and a "real“ lacuna is ultimately fragile.

intentionally by law-makers.[87] Yet it may be difficult to distinguish between the non-applicability of legal provisions and their non-existence, i.e. whether a provision covers a certain factual situation, but does not support a specific claim, or whether no provision applies to the type of factual situation in dispute and hence a *lacuna* exists.[88]

The opposite of a situation where too little law exists, i.e. a *lacuna*, is a conflict or collision of several provisions[89] applicable to the same factual situation. This is a situation of too much law and represents a third type of legal indeterminacy. Conflicts or collisions occur in different forms.[90] A conflict may stem from the fact that legal rules governing a certain matter exist at different governance levels, e.g. at EU and Member State level.[91] In such cases, there are typically rules on the hierarchy between legal provisions at different governance levels. Examples are the supremacy of Euro-

87 See for international law Hector 1992, 183–185; whether a question was left open deliberately or unintentionally is important from a legal point of view, because judges may legitimately "fill" a gap left open by the law-makers unintentionally, for example by creating analogies, while the same is not true for a deliberate lacuna.

88 On this and other "lacuna problems" in international law, see Fastenrath 1991, 213–251.

89 When precisely one should speak of a conflict of norms, i.e. a collision is not entirely clear. In a narrow understanding a conflict exists where one norm mandates what a second norm forbids. But sometimes one norm only permits what a second norm forbids – which would effectively render the first norm meaningless and could thus also be described as a collision. For an in-depth discussion of the notion of conflict see Vranes 2009, 10ff who subscribes himself to a broad notion of conflict. Pauwelyn 2003a, 164ff also discusses the notion of conflict in international law extensively and suggests a broad understanding of conflict: "Essentially, two norms are [...] in a relationship of conflict if one constitutes, has led to, or may lead to, a breach of the other.", at 175f; the ILC report on the matter subscribes to a broad notion of conflict according to which a conflict is "a situation where two rules or principles suggest different ways of dealing with a problem", see Study Group of the International Law Commission 2006, para. 25. For different notions of conflict in WTO law see also Neumann 2002, 60–63 on the one hand; Marceau and Trachtman 2002, 868 on the other. Marceau 2006, 345 and Pauwelyn 2003a, 188ff provide different accounts of how conflict is defined in WTO case law.

90 The ILC report on the fragmentation of international law distinguishes the following relationships that underlie legal conflicts: between special and general law, between prior and subsequent law, between law at different hierarchical levels and relations of law to its "normative environment" more generally, see Study Group of the International Law Commission 2006, para. 18.

91 For an example of a case involving a clash between Art. 103 UN Charta and European rule of law principles in ECJ and ECtHR jurisprudence, see Nickel 2010, 3.

pean law over national law or the supremacy of constitutional norms over "simple" legal rules within national legal systems. In addition, conflicts between two legal norms or sets of legal norms belonging to the same legal system also occur, for example between different international treaties or between two laws at the national level. The more complex a legal system is, the greater is the likelihood of frictions and tensions between laws protecting different values, rights and interests.[92] Conflicts within a legal system can be solved through specific collision norms, e.g. one treaty sets forth that it is not applicable where a second one is) or general collisions norms, most notably the *lex specialis* and *lex posterior* rules.

More than one of these types of indeterminacy may be present in a given situation. For example, the conclusion that there is a *lacuna* sometimes depends on prior interpretations of the law – for which linguistic indeterminacy plays a role. Another example is when two colliding provisions are each vaguely phrased. The latter example also shows that the presence of more than one type of indeterminacy does not necessarily increase indeterminacy overall. If two conflicting norms both use indeterminate language, a judge may arrive at the finding that the *prima facie* conflict can (and some would argue: must) be solved through an interpretation which brings both norms into accord, i.e. harmonious interpretation.[93]

All this is, of course, a very rough sketch. Indeterminacy can undoubtedly also be described by a different kind of typology; the categories above are different aspects of the same phenomenon rather than radically separate.[94]

While the above discussion has probably revealed my own preference for a non-formalist understanding of the law, the nuances of the debate do not matter for purposes of the present work. Here, the key insight of the literature review above is that law is indeterminate and it matters who the judges are, at least in some or many situations. By implication judicial law-making is an integral part of adjudicatory decision-making; judges do more than merely applying the law. There will nonetheless also be cases in which it is absolutely clear what the law mandates (e.g. the above parking example); the written law does have a constraining function upon those in-

92 See Leisner 1997, 12.

93 See Pauwelyn 2003a, 247 who also points to the existence of a presumption against conflict in international law, at 240ff; Study Group of the International Law Commission 2006, para. 412.

94 For other "checklists" of situations of indeterminacy in the law and the steps of judicial decision-making see Beck 2012, chaps 2–4; Fastenrath 1991, 213–235; Rafi 2004, 18; Hubmann 1977, 55; Trachtman 1999, 337.

terpreting it at least to a certain extent. As will be discussed at greater length below,[95] indeterminacy is also inherent in WTO law and the WTO judicial decision-makers will have to come to terms with it.

2. *Factors determining the outcome of cases in the face of the indeterminacy of the law*

If the law is indeed indeterminate, then it cannot be its wording alone that determines the outcome of a court case. Researchers from a number of disciplines, including sociology, psychology and political science have investigated, which factors, besides the wording of the law, play a role for the outcome of cases. In this section, some of this research is presented, focusing on international, and to a lesser degree, national courts. However, it should be noted upfront that studies on judicial decision-making at the international level are much fewer in number than those focusing on the national level.[96]

Researchers have identified several types of factors: First, some hold the view that courts are strategic actors and their judgements are a reaction to external pressures and events, for example the threat of a reversal of judicial decisions by political bodies or public opinion on a certain matter (section 2.1). Others consider judgements to be deliberately or unconsciously influenced by given preferences and attitudes of judges (section 2.2). Moreover, the institutional set-up of a court and its rules of procedures are also mentioned as factors influencing the outcome of judicial cases (section 2.3). While some contributions only focus on some of the factors, others look at all three of them, maintaining that only all of the factors together can sufficiently explain what courts do.[97]

As a *caveat*, it should be stated that the following discussion of non-legal factors motivating judicial decisions does not mean that the wording of the law does not matter at all. Indeed, some of the works on judicial decision-making summarized further below in this section have been criticized for underestimating the normative power of the law and the particularities

95 See section 4.1.2.

96 Ginsburg 2006, 2; Maton and Maton 2007, 322; Zarbiyev 2012, 4 observes that the concept of judicial activism has not received much attention in international law; Wessel 2006, 380.

97 An example is Wessel 2006.

of judicial institutions.[98] Other studies hold that non-legal factors partially explain certain judicial outcome, but also take account of the degree of (in)determinacy of the law as another factor.[99] Thus, the existence of non-legal factors that influence judicial decisions does not mean that the wording of the law never matters. Rather, the perspective underlying my work is that the wording of the law does matter in the world of professional judges, and the more determinate the law is the more it matters. At the same time, the law is unlikely to be the only factor influencing the outcome of a judicial case. This starting point is shared by many other researchers.[100]

2.1. Courts as strategic actors

One important factor influencing the acceptance of a certain judgement is the substantive outcome of individual cases and the aggregated outcome of the decision-making of a court over a period of time.[101] A judge may give very good legal reasons for her decision and support it by excellent legal arguments – when the decision is perceived as unjust or biased or as not resulting from the law, it is unlikely to be accepted as legitimate by the parties to the dispute, the general public, and political actors.[102] If a court produces such decisions regularly, this is likely to fundamentally undermine its legitimacy. Equally, if an international court departs too often from what states thought they had agreed on, this may undermine the legitimacy of the respective court.[103]

---

98 Beach 2001.

99 Garrett and McCall Smith 2002, 7; Kelemen 2001; McCall Smith 2003, 67.

100 See Wessel 2006, 384f with further references.

101 See for example Glennon and Strother 2019, 243 with various references. By contrast, Benvenisti and Downs 2012, 101 maintain that the "most important determinant of political legitimacy [...] is [...] the extent to which a given court is perceived to be sufficiently independent of the powerful actors that dominate the political sphere to take less powerful and minority interests into consideration". I would maintain that this aspect is a subdimension both of what I call here style, i.e. how a decision is justified, and substance, i.e. the actual, material outcome of cases.

102 Indeed, it has even been observed that the criticism of a certain judicial style may become silent once observers are re-assured that it leads to outcomes that are at opposing ends of the political spectrum, i.e. the result is sometimes politically "liberal", sometimes "conservative", see Aleinikoff 1987, 944.

103 Du 2011, 646.

Anticipated reactions from relevant actors could, in turn, influence the judges when taking a decision. Indeed, in existing research, mainly by political scientists, courts are perceived as rational and strategic actors that work to maintain and enhance their own legitimacy, authority and power.[104] A court, it is argued, should not be expected to take decisions that would lead to a legislative backlash, i.e. a legislative overturn of certain decisions or a permanent clipping of the court's wings by changing its mandate or cutting its funding.[105] In other cases, a court might be motivated by fear that the parties might not comply with a ruling. This is the case for international courts, in particular.[106] Frequent non-compliance would also weaken a court.

Indeed, some international judges have "admitted" (if that is something requiring a confession) that strategic, political considerations are not absent from their deliberations when deciding a case.[107] Similar considerations are also likely to motivate the decisions of lower-level courts that seek to prevent their decisions from being amended or nullified by higher level courts.[108] Political or public preferences that judges respond to will not necessarily and probably not normally take the form of direct pressure being put on judges outside of the court-room – at least this has been observed to be rarely the case by former judges at international courts.[109] Instead, the question is what reactions and countermeasures judges *expect* when taking a certain decision.

In political science, there are two ways[110] of describing the relationship between international courts and the states that can resort to the respective

---

104 Busch and Pelc 2019, 464; Cooter and Ginsburg 1996; Daku and Pelc 2017, 240; Dunoff and Pollack 2017; Glennon and Strother 2019, 243; Stone Sweet 2004, 20; Zarbiyev 2012, 9f, 17ff.

105 As Wessel 2006, 382 puts it: "[...] states influence international adjudication through their consent, financial backing, and ability to limit the effects of decisions through changes in the law and through non-compliance".

106 Sweet and Brunell 2013, 67.

107 Terris, Romano, and Swigart 2007, 157.

108 Zarbiyev 2012, 9.

109 Terris, Romano, and Swigart 2007, 156. However, some examples have even made it into the news; for an example from the ICTY, see "Hague court was pressured in recent verdicts, judge says", International Herald Tribune, 15/16 June 2013, 1.

110 It is not entirely clear whether these are simply ways of placing different courts on a continuum or conflicting theories about the same courts. The first position seems to be held by Sweet and Brunell 2013, 62.

court.[111] One strand in the literature describes the relationship as one between principals and agents. The states are the principals that delegate certain decision-making power to courts as their agents, providing them with a certain degree of discretion and autonomy. As a result, the court-agents are independent from their principals, but only to a degree; the principals still have ways to influence a court's decisions after its establishment.[112] Others view courts not as "agents", but as "trustees".[113] They maintain that courts, once established, are largely beyond the influence of the states they work for; their judicial behaviour is seen as being guided "primarily by rhetorical and legitimacy politics"[114]. Hence both theories differ with regards the degree of autonomy the court is considered to have.

One court that has been studied rather intensively is the ECJ, in particular with regard to its far-reaching early judgements on the supremacy and direct effect of EU law.[115] Scholars have come up with different theories why the political sphere, i.e. the Member States and/or the EU's political bodies, let the ECJ get away with it. Some have argued that the ECJ in some cases decided the way it did, because the Member States did not pay enough attention to the ECJ's decisions or were unlikely to agree on a coordinated reaction against the ECJ or its specific decisions.[116] Another explanation is that many ECJ decisions were in line with what the majority of the EU Member States or important Member States favoured, at least in cases where no clear rules or precedents existed that would have made such

111 See for the following Elsig and Pollack 2012, 2ff.

112 Such a model is supported, for example, by Wessel 2006, 383.

113 See for example Sweet and Brunell 2013.

114 This is a description by Elsig and Pollack 2012, 2; however these authors themselves favour the principal-agent approach.

115 See for example Alter 1998, 129ff.

116 Ibid., 136ff observes that policy-makers act on a different rationale than courts. They are concerned with the immediate material impact of court decisions. As the ECJ in its landmark decisions established long-term legal principles, but did not bring them to immediate application, policy-makers were not concerned regarding the ECJ judgments. Later, according to her argument, Member States' governments were unable to reverse a legal development they had not wanted. Moreover, she holds that the ECJ managed to turn national courts into its allies; Weiler 1991, 2428 holds that being a supreme court, the ECJ had an inherent legitimacy that was difficult to politically contest; Burley and Mattli 1993, 72f argue that it was the non-political veneer of judicial decisions that made them hard for politicians to contest. They acknowledge that this veneer is more myth than reality, but the judicial use of nominally neutral legal principles "masks" the politics of judicial decisions, gives judges legitimacy, and "shields" judges from political criticism.

a judicial decision difficult.[117] Others consider a weakly developed EU legislature[118] to be one of the reasons behind the ECJ's early bold judicial decisions.[119] On the other hand, instances have been observed where the ECJ "back-pedalled" in reaction to "strong political signals that it had gone too far"[120]. It does not matter for the present purpose which of the different accounts of the ECJ's decision-making is correct; however, the fact is important that a court, in this case the ECJ, is found to behave as a political and strategic actor and its actions are influenced by the anticipated reaction of other actors. The other European court, the European Court of Human Rights (ECtHR), has also been described as taking into account the "degree of consensus or harmony among the national laws of signatory states"[121], when deciding how much deference – or in the language of the ECtHR how large a margin of appreciation – to afford the defendant state in the case at hand.

Similar insights were produced for courts at the national level. For example, a 1996 comparative study on judicial discretion in several countries concludes that courts are "more daring" in countries where the legislative bodies are unlikely to enact new legislation.[122] Several other studies have shown similar effects for US constitutional review.[123] Stone Sweet concludes that the strategic "zone of discretion" enjoyed by any court is determined by a combination of the power delegated to the court and the possibility of a non-judicial authority to shape or annul outcomes. He argues that constitutional courts operate in an unusually permissive strategic environment, because changing the constitution is difficult in most countries.[124]

Apart from the studies on the ECJ, there are few ones on factors influencing judicial decisions at the international level. One such study is the one by Wessel on the ICC. Concerning external pressure factors relevant for the ICC, he investigates the threat of states to withdraw from the ICC

117 Garrett, Kelemen, and Schulz 1998; for a criticism of this theory, see Stone Sweet 2004, 253ff.

118 This obviously relates to the early years of the European Union, which was then called the European Community.

119 Poiares Maduro 1998, 11 with reference to the absence of a strong parliamentary body; Pollicino 2004, 284.

120 Slaughter and Helfer 1997, 315.

121 Ibid., 316f.

122 Cooter and Ginsburg 1996.

123 Whittington 2003.

124 Stone Sweet 2004.

regime ("exit"), the need to attract new signatories ("entry"), far-reaching revisions of the relevant legal texts, lack of financial support, and lack of support from states in providing evidence and enforcement.[125] Zarbiyev also points to mechanisms of political control as one factor influencing whether an international court is activist or restrained.[126] Ginsburg identifies three possible reactions of states that do not like the jurisprudence of a certain court: exit (i.e. leaving a certain organization and by implication the jurisdiction of the respective court), willy-nilly compliance, and compliance combined with efforts to modify relevant rules (including budgetary cuts for the respective court).[127] It has also been pointed out that international courts have more independent decision-making space when they serve several powerful states that have diverging positions on certain matters than when there is a more limited number of dominant actors.[128]

Yet it is not only the preferences of political actors that matter, but also public opinion.[129] At the national level, evidence has been found on judges being influenced by public opinion. For example, German criminal judges are significantly influenced by media reports on the cases they have to decide.[130] In the US context, a change in courts' attitude towards the legal effect of international treaties in the US legal order was prompted by a (failed) constitutional amendment proposal dealing with this issue.[131] At the international level, public pressure is generally likely to play a somewhat lesser role given that not each and every case actually receives a lot of media and public attention. Indeed, some opine that international courts get rather too little public attention.[132] Still, there are exceptions. For example, Wessel describes the area of international humanitarian law as one where the respective courts are faced with quite intensive advocacy efforts by NGOs.[133]

There are other factors that may influence how a court acts. Gaining acceptance for judgements may be of more importance to courts at some stages of their existence than at others. For example, international courts

---

125 Wessel 2006, 423ff.
126 Zarbiyev 2012, 7ff.
127 Ginsburg 2006, 33ff.
128 See Pauwelyn and Elsig 2012, 463.
129 Beck 2012, 35f.
130 See Kepplinger and Zerback 2009. Their finding resulted from a survey among judges and prosecutors.
131 Hathaway, McElroy, and Solow 2011, 69.
132 Terris, Romano, and Swigart 2007, 170.
133 Wessel 2006, 390.

have been described as particularly vulnerable to external pressure when the treaty they supervise is under re-negotiation.[134] The openness of courts to political pressure or public opinion may vary over time. A court that is controversial at the time of its creation and hence has a weak institutional legitimacy is likely to tread more carefully. Whether a court is controversial may depend, among other factors, on the authority of the legal source that a tribunal has to interpret.[135] Moreover, permanent courts have been described as less "politicized" than *ad hoc* tribunals.[136]

Altogether, there is substantial evidence that courts are not left untouched by their surroundings.

2.2. Fostering judges' legal or non-legal preferences and attitudes

Judges act strategically in the sense of taking into account political or other preferences of actors outside the court. Yet it is, of course, also conceivable that a judge or a group of judges are guided by their *own* political or moral preferences and attitudes, possibly even unconsciously. Such preferences can be of a legal or non-legal nature, they can relate to what a judge considers a desirable outcome of a case, but also to what a judge sees an appropriate role for a court or as acceptable professional behaviour.[137]

Many studies demonstrate the impact judges' preferences on judicial decisions taken at the national level; research has focused on countries such as the US or Israel that have a relatively heterogeneous population. Moreover, such research also seems to be more prevalent in common law jurisdictions, probably due to the more central role that judicial decisions play in these legal systems.[138] Several studies have investigated the influence of liberal versus conservative policy preferences of US Supreme Court judges on the outcome of cases[139] and there are similar studies for other coun-

134 Kelemen 2001, 625.

135 Slaughter and Helfer 1997, 304; Foltea 2012, 26.

136 See Tumonis 2013, 44f for references; the author only seems to share this view to a certain extent.

137 On the latter see from a sociological perspective Bourdieu 1987, 833; see also the "internal" factors that Wessel 2006, 385f mentions.

138 For a brief overview of the role of precedents in civil, common and international law, see Blackmore 2004, 495ff.

139 See for example Lindquist and Cross 2009 with further references.

tries[140]. For non-constitutional courts, a number of studies on different countries has shown that the ethnic bias of judges has influenced the outcome of court cases.[141] Similarly, there are studies on how the gender, racial or ethnic identity of judges influences the outcome of cases.[142] Also, in a study on how German labour courts handle law suits on dismissals, the authors find that

> "courts are more likely to rule in favor of employees in regions with depressed labor markets even after controlling for a host of individual characteristics of the claimants, defendants and judges involved in a particular case".[143]

So sometimes a sentiment akin to compassion may motivate a judge's decision. In general, one observer has concluded, that "there can be no doubt […] that factors such as age, ethnicity, and gender play a role in how a judge will operate".[144]

At the international level, there seem to be fewer studies by comparison. This may be reflective of the lower overall number of cases decided by international courts as well as the fact that in international court proceedings individual preferences and attitudes relating to factors such as the gender or ethnicity of the individuals involved in a court case are likely to play a smaller role; judges in international cases are mostly not required to decide about an individual's behaviour.[145]

While racist, sexist etc. attitudes of judges are unlikely to matter in international court cases, this limitation does not necessarily apply to political or macro-economic preferences or ideas on what constitutes proper judicial decision-making. Indeed, a few studies have investigated international courts and the influence of individual judges' legal, political or other opinions on outcomes. When several judges are involved in taking a decision, it has been shown that rulings are sometimes the results of negotiations and compromises among judges that go beyond legal-interpretive questions in

140 On the Portuguese Constitutional Court, see Coroado, Garoupa, and Magalhães 2017.

141 See for an example from Israel Gazal-Ayal and Sulitzeanu-Kenan 2010; and for a study on the US Morrison Piehl and Bushway 2001.

142 See for example Peresie 2005; Harris and Sen 2019.

143 Berger and Neugart 2012, 57.

144 Dickson 2007, 8.

145 The ICC is an important exception of course; moreover, human rights tribunals, while not judging an individual's behaviour, deal with claims brought by individuals.

a narrow sense.[146] Thus, it is not necessarily and only individual preferences that matter for the outcome of a case, but it could also be a collectively agreed version of such preferences.

Related to the ICJ, McWhinney[147] maintains that throughout the different phases of the ICJ's existence, the composition of the ICJ bench of judges, with their origin in certain legal traditions and preconceived ideas on the appropriate role of the ICJ, did influence the outcomes of individual cases. Smith[148] finds only weak links between the decisions of ICJ judges and their nationality and finds these links to become even weaker in recent years, as concepts of nationality have changed. The same author also observes that in different international courts and tribunals states more and more often support the nomination of judges from another state.[149] By contrast, Posner et al. conclude on the basis of a statistical analysis that ICJ judges have sided with their home states "about 90 percent of the time"; in cases where their home states were not involved, judges supported states similar to their home states concerning wealth, culture, and political regime.[150] Generally, the influence of an international judge's nationality on his/her decisions is contested.[151] A hypothesis has also been formulated that whether a judge is experienced or new to a tribunal may matter for the way he decides.[152] In a study on the ICJ, Wessel observes that judges are likely to follow their own preferences in situations where the text of the law is indeterminate and not strongly constraining and where there are no credible external constraints (in the form of potential counter-measures by other actors). In the case of the ICC he expects decisions that tend to expand the scope and reach of international humanitarian provisions, given the demonstrated concern of many judges for humanitarian and human rights issues and the absence of judges with a military background on the bench.[153] In conclusion, personal political ideas and attitudes of judges

146 Alvarez-Jiménez 2009a, 295ff investigating the US Supreme Court, the ICJ and GATT Panels.
147 McWhinney 2006.
148 Smith 2004.
149 Ibid., 229ff.
150 Posner and de Figueiredo 2005, 624.
151 See Terris, Romano, and Swigart 2007, 153f for an overview.
152 Busch and Pelc 2010, 269.
153 Wessel 2006, 383, 434ff; he also points to one case where the political preferences of a certain judge allegedly quite clearly influenced the jurisprudence of the ICC, at 391f, as well as a shift in the degree to which the ICTY embraced a

cannot be dismissed as factors influencing an international court's judgements.

Altogether, there is substantial evidence that individual preferences and attitudes of judges matter in deciding cases, even when they should be legally irrelevant.[154] Yet most of the studies are not uncontroversial given that it is difficult to control for all factors that could influence the outcome of cases other than the attitudes and preferences of individual judges.[155] And, again, the influence of individual preferences is likely to be more limited at the international level compared to the national level.

2.3. Mandate and procedural rules

Finally, a third set of factors having an influence on the outcome of judicial decisions are the mandate of a court and the procedural rules it needs to observe. Wessel refers to "creational constraints" in this regard, i.e. constraints created by the state parties to an international treaty when establishing the respective judicial institution.[156]

The mandate given to a court matters for what it can and cannot decide. For example, Art. 22 of the Rome Statute governing the ICC mandates that the definitions of crime contained in the Statute "shall be strictly construed and shall not be extended by analogy". Moreover, "[i]n case of am-

---

more restrictive stance following the appointment of an individual as President of the Tribunal who was critical of the Tribunal's earlier expansionist tendencies, at 395.

154 Who the individual is that decides a case does not only matter in terms of political preferences or stereotypes that judges hold. It may matter in even more mundane terms: A 2011 study took the common mis-portrayal of legal realism as saying that the outcome of court cases is influenced by "what judges ate for breakfast" as starting point for an investigation on how experienced Jewish-Israeli judges on parole boards decided their cases. Based on a statistical analysis of a significant number of cases, the study found that the likelihood of a ruling in favour of the prisoner was greater at the beginning of the work day or after a food break than later in the sequence of cases. While the authors of the study do not claim to be able to fully demonstrate the mental/psychological mechanisms behind this trend, they conclude that their "results do indicate that extraneous variables can influence judicial decisions, which bolsters the growing body of evidence that points to the susceptibility of experienced judges to psychological biases", Danziger, Levav, and Avnaim-Pesso 2011, 4.

155 For a discussion on different studies on the Israeli judicial system see Gazal-Ayal and Sulitzeanu-Kenan 2010, 7ff.

156 Wessel 2006, 384.

biguity, the definition shall be interpreted in favour of the person being investigated, prosecuted or convicted". Given these rather clear instructions, it will arguably be difficult for the ICC to interpret the definitions of crime contained in the Rome Statute in a manner that would bring more types of behaviour within their purview. In addition, the Rome Statute also contains a clear guidance for the judges on the hierarchy of applicable law in Art. 21.[157] Again, it is likely quite difficult for judges to go against this hierarchy. The universe of legally defensive interpretations is limited in these regards.

Another factor mentioned as potentially influencing the outcome of court cases is how judges are appointed. Wessel observes that when many actors are directly or indirectly involved in the selection of judges, courts are more likely to be activist.[158] Actors indirectly involved in a selection process can be NGOs advocating for certain candidates or lawyers' associations. It is argued that when many such actors are involved and judges "owe" their appointment to many actors, the power of the political branch is "diluted" and so is the need for judges to adhere to preferences of the political establishment.[159] Moreover, the ease with which judges can be removed from office may also influence how willing international judges are to honour the actual or assumed preferences of states.[160]

There may be a more indirect link between procedural and institutional features of a certain court and the substance of its decisions. Institutional aspects such as the composition of a court[161] and its procedural rules[162] also influence whether a court is perceived as legitimate actor by relevant constituencies. As argued above, the degree to which a court rests on a firm "legitimacy fundament" may in turn also influence how it acts and what substantive decisions it takes.

---

157 These norms are mentioned by ibid., 400f in his analysis of ICC judicial law-making; Wessel himself argues that they do not put any significant constraints on expansionist judicial law-making by the ICC.

158 Ibid., 417f.

159 Ibid.

160 For the ICC, see ibid., 422.

161 Helfer and Slaughter have developed a list of criteria for the effectiveness of supranational/international courts; effectiveness for them is closely related to legitimacy, see Slaughter and Helfer 1997, 299ff; their list of factors includes the composition of the court.

162 Jetzlsperger 2003, 27.

3. Judicial styles in the face of the indeterminacy of the law

Until here, I have discussed the indeterminacy of the law and theoretical reconstructions of how judicial decision-makers decide a case. I have then discussed what factors are likely to influence the substantial outcome of a case, if not the law alone. What is missing, is an account of what reasons judicial decision-makers may be expected to give for their decisions, which are taken sometimes or regularly in the face of the indeterminacy of the law and at least partially or sometimes for non-legal reasons. This is the question I turn to next. I will first discuss more general insights on judicial modes of reasoning and styles (section 3.1), and then present the comparative analysis Lasser[163] has conducted on the judicial styles of different courts (section 3.2).

I use the term "judicial style" to refer to more or less consistent patterns of reasoning, discernible from the decisions of an individual court or even judge. Sub-aspects of judicial style include the methods of interpretation used, the length and tone of judgements, the intensity of dealing with the arguments of the parties and evidence, and the types of arguments used (e.g. references to considerations of justice or policy objectives, use of precedents).[164] While judicial style can also refer to the general writing style or quality of writing in judicial decisions (e.g. whether sentences are long or short, whether humour is used), this is not an aspect of the WTO's judicial style investigated in this work.

3.1. Judicial styles in the face of the indeterminacy of the law – general insights

If the law is, at least sometimes and to a degree, indeterminate and judges therefore need to choose between competing interpretations, the justifica-

---

163 Lasser 2004; Lasser 2003.

164 Prott 1970, 75 uses the term "style of judgment" to depict "not only those canons of good style which one considers in literature, such as language, sentence structure, tone and so on, but also such things as the method of argument used and the subject matter which it is thought proper to include". Zarbiyev 2012, 12 uses the terms "organizational identity" or "center of narrative gravity". Van Damme 2010, 606 and passim uses the term "hermeneutics" in what I take to be a similar intention. By contrast, Posner 1995, 1422 seems to use a narrower definition when defining style as the "specific written form in which a writer encodes an idea".

tion of such choices becomes important. Indeed, in some jurisdictions there is a statutory obligation to justify and give reasons for judicial decisions.[165] In other jurisdictions there may not be such a legal requirement, but it is clear that a judicial decision will always come with an at least short explanation on what has motivated it. Explaining a judgment is how courts try to convince the addressees of a decision and the wider audience of its correctness and legitimacy as well as the need to follow it.[166] In particular, judges must explain their decision to the losing party.[167] As described above, if judicial decisions are not perceived as legitimate, political opponents of a court may seek to abolish or weaken it through institutional reforms.[168] Judges have been described as using a "strategy of impression management" for this reason[169]. All of this is true, in particular, for judges of international courts, which lack effective enforcement mechanisms.[170]

However, the fact that judges (must) explain their decisions does not mean that they will necessarily give all or the "real" reasons for a decision.[171] For example, many of us would – I hope – be appalled by a judge writing into his or her judgement that, as the accused is a person of colour, he or she is more likely than a white person to commit further crimes if not punished severely. Today, such a statement would also be legally prohibited as racist discrimination in many countries of the world. This does not, however, mean that such stereotypes never influence a judge's decision. As discussed above[172], a significant number of studies do show how such biases influence the outcome of judicial deliberations. Nevertheless, and leaving aside formal prohibitions of racist behaviour for a moment, such (racist) considerations cannot be written explicitly into a judgement, because they would not be considered proper legal reasoning. They are not a relevant, recognized basis for a legal argument. Judicial decisions are con-

---

165 Feteris 1999, 6; von Bogdandy and Venzke 2013, 56 even maintain that justifying a judicial decision is always a legal requirement.

166 See Meagher 2020, 143ff for a summary of why judges routinely provide written and reasoned decisions even in cases where they are not legally compelled to do so.

167 Ibid., 161f.

168 See above, section 2.1.

169 Venzke 2016, 241.

170 Busch and Pelc 2019, 465ff; Henckels 2006, 281; Krüger 2013, 55; Lovric 2010, 60; Meagher 2020, 148; Slaughter and Helfer 1997, 318f observe for the ECJ that the court in its early years successfully established its own legitimacy mainly due to the quality of reasoning of its judgments.

171 Charlotin 2017, 281f; Pauwelyn and Elsig 2012, 449.

172 See above section 2.2.

sidered legitimate if they are supported by the right[173] kind of arguments. Providing these arguments is thus an important strategy for judges to with a view to legitimising their decisions and thus avoiding opposition to their judgements and a lack of acceptance.

Engaging in reasoning that is legal in character means that the speaker (or in most legal practice: the writer) is faced with certain constraints. At the most general level, the "legitimacy of judicial pronouncements depends on their rationality and soundness"[174]. There is a perception that "the more fully a point is argued the more likely it will be successful"[175]. A minimum standard that judicial decisions need to satisfy in order to be accepted as sound legal decisions is that they are coherent[176], i.e. free of internal contradictions. Moreover, they should normally not stray too far from the ordinary meaning of language (unless it can be shown that a term has a specific technical-legal content).[177] The degree to which a judicial decision will be considered persuasive and create the kind of legal normativity it is aimed at also depends on the degree to which it is rational, its methods of interpretation can be reproduced, and its findings generalized.[178] Arguments must not be phrased in terms of purely private interests.[179] Judges may not be seen as succumbing to political pressures or interests[180] or deciding a case in line with their own policy preferences[181]. Or, as another author has put it, "judges cannot decide cases in a legally unrecognizable way and continue […] to claim to be doing law"[182]. Or, to re-iterate the same thought in yet another way:

> "the judge must situate the case and the judgment within the boundaries of the law, lest the decision be illegitimate and even unlawful"[183].

---

173 Obviously, what is considered a "right" argument varies across societies and is subject to changes over time, see below and sections 3.2 and 3.3 of this chapter.
174 Kleinlein 2012, 254.
175 The quote is by Jacob 2012, 60.
176 Henckels 2006, 281; Slaughter and Helfer 1997, 319 observe that most commentators concur that coherence is a central element of good legal reasoning.
177 Beck 2012, 32.
178 Kleinlein 2012, 254.
179 Neyer 2010, 40f.
180 With reference to the Appellate Body, see Krüger 2013, 55; more generally Slaughter and Helfer 1997, 312f.
181 Greenwald 2003, 115.
182 Zarbiyev 2012, 5.
183 Terris, Romano, and Swigart 2007, 102.

The arguments that a judge can give, the way he or she can speak in a judicial decision, are part of what Bourdieu calls a "field". A field is structured by the "internal logic of juridical functioning, which [...] constrains the range of possible actions"[184]. Hence, judicial decisions

> "can be distinguished from naked exercises of power only to the extent that they can be represented as the necessary result of principled interpretation of unanimously accepted texts".[185]
>
> By implication, judges have been said to "always aim to generate a particular rhetorical effect [...]: that of legal necessity of their solutions without regard to ideology"[186]. Bogdandy and Venzke write:
>
> "Judges apply the law, this is the source of their authority, and whenever the impression gains currency that this is not what they are actually doing, they are usually in trouble."[187] [footnote omitted]

Beck also comments:

> "Judges themselves probably go further than anyone else in claiming, though not necessarily believing in, methodological or quasi-scientific certainty for their own judgments."[188]

Other authors have offered similar observations.[189]

There are different views on what a good or acceptable legal argument and justification is, above and beyond the above minimum standards for acceptable judicial reasoning.[190] When comparing the arguments used by functionally comparable courts in different jurisdictions it is possible to empirically identify a common set of arguments used by most of the courts, albeit with different frequency.[191] In other words, while there are competing theories on what a good and acceptable legal argument is, there

184 Bourdieu 1987, 816.

185 Ibid., 818.

186 Kennedy 1997, 2.

187 Bogdandy and Venzke 2012, 10.

188 Beck 2012, 19.

189 See D'Aspremont and Mbengue 2014, 243; Venzke 2016, 240; Zarbiyev 2012, 29.

190 For an overview of different theories, see Feteris 1999.

191 This is the conclusion from a comparative study on the arguments used by the highest courts in nine different countries, see Summers and Taruffo 1991, 462ff.

seems to be, factually, a basic consensus transcending individual jurisdictions.

The observed constraints on the arguments that judges can use are related to the fact that there is, at least in democracies, but potentially also in other political systems, a role that judges are expected and allowed to fulfil. The term "allowed" in the previous sentence refers to both what the respective legal (constitutional) rules set forth and to what is considered to be socially, politically and/or professionally permissible, with a view to not endangering a court's legitimacy and the acceptance of its judgements. Classically, the role of judges is opposed to that of law-makers.[192] Judges must avoid appearing as making the law; courts are not supposed to be political decision-makers.[193] In international law, a principle has also been identified that "judges cannot legislate".[194] A court that oversteps the boundaries of what is considered the judicial realm is vulnerable to being criticized as activist[195] and not exercising enough judicial self-restraint. International courts crossing the line between interpreting law and making law have been observed to "put at risk the future of the court itself, if not the whole edifice of international law"[196].

This risk of decisions or a court being perceived as illegitimate has implications for the judicial style that judges are likely to use in their decisions. The table below illustrates differences in the reasoning or rhetoric of different, but functionally similar courts and clarifies what are, hence, constitutive elements of the judicial style of various courts. It was originally compiled by Summers and Taruffo as the result of an empirical analysis of the

192 See Kulovesi 2011, 181ff.

193 Or, as formulated concisely by Iancu 2009, 1: "Public law, albeit 'political', must not be politics"; see also Ginsburg 2006, 5.

194 Van Damme 2009, 161 with references to several PCIJ and ICJ judgments; conversely von Bogdandy and Venzke 2013, 56 point out that it is "inevitable that statements about what international law requires also, to varying degrees, contribute to its making". While this is true, there is, of course, still a difference between creating a general legal rule (adopted by law-makers) and interpretive decisions on very specific questions (taken by courts).

195 For a discussion of the term judicial activism, see below section 5.3.2. It should be noted that the discussion on judicial activism and judicial law-making is heavily US dominated, both in terms of who contributes and what is researched. However, for the European context it has been observed that charges of "judicial activism" have recently been more frequently voiced in the academic and wider public realm, see Nickel 2010, 4ff.

196 Terris, Romano, and Swigart 2007, 130.

"justificatory style of opinions"[197] of higher courts in nine countries.[198] I have slightly modified it, reducing the eight characteristics contained in the original table to six.[199]

Table 1: Styles of judicial reasoning compared

	Formalist rhetoric or reasoning[200]	Non-formalist/less formalist rhetoric or reasoning
1	Genuine issues of interpretation not openly acknowledged Only one answer possible	Open acknowledgment of alternative readings of statute More than one possible answer
2	High proportion of legalistic, technical and bureaucratic language in the opinion	Lower proportion of legalistic and technical language in opinion
3	Abbreviated and terse opinion	Extended and elaborate opinion
4	Implicit model of rationality is logico-deductive, i.e. syllogistic subsumption Evaluative and creative role (of courts, C. G.) not recognized, decisional process viewed as essentially one of cognitive ascertainment and application of the law that "is"	Implicit model of rationality is not deductive but discursive – open choice Acknowledgment of some evaluative and creative role
5	High proportion of formal rather than substantive reasons	Lower proportion of formal rather than substantive reasons
6	Magisterial and authoritative	Argumentative and dialogic

Most of these categories are self-explanatory. What may require some elaboration are the attributes in rows 5 and 6. With regard to row 5, Summers and Taruffo explain the difference between both types of arguments in the following terms:

> "[...] formal reasons are ones that arise essentially from authoritative sources of law including the statute itself and related statutes, any constitution, any precedent on the meaning of the statute, any precedent

197 Summers and Taruffo 1991, 496.

198 Ibid., 501; some of the characteristics of judicial style that Summers/Taruffo identify are also mentioned by Posner 1995, 1429f as characterising "pure" and "impure" judicial styles respectively. The former, according to Posner, is the technical, formalist style of lawyers, while the latter involves writing a judicial opinion with the aim of "explaining to a hypothetical audience of laypersons why the case is being decided in the way that it is".

199 Summers and Taruffo had kept the aspects contained in line 1 and line 4 respectively as separate categories; however, to my mind they are so closely linked that it is hardly conceivable that a court being classified as "formalist" in one respect, would have to be considered "non-formalist" in the other.

200 Column headings added by me.

on interpretational method, any relevant regulations or official interpretations, any general principles of law, the logic of relevant legal concepts, any authoritative policies in the areas, and official *travaux préparatoires*. Independent substantive reasons [...] are reasons of essentially moral, economic, political and social content the force of which depends more or less on their weight and not on whether they happen to be linked to some authoritative source or sources [...]."[201]

The differences between a "magisterial and authoritative" way of reasoning and an "argumentative and dialogic" one (row 6) are described by Summers and Taruffo in the following way:

"In the magisterial style, the court's opinion is presented as an impersonal, authoritative, unsigned, imperial 'Staatsakt' whereas in the argumentative style the opinion is more personalized, is duly signed by the authors, and bears at least some recognizable stylistic traits of the author. Further, in the magisterial style, the courts proceeds as if there is only one possible answer – the court's answer – to the issue of interpretation, whereas in the argumentative style the court assumes that more than one answer might be possible, rehearses the arguments for and against, and seeks to show by argument why the answer given is the most justified one. Additionally, in the argumentative style, the court enters into what might be construed as a dialogue with its various addressees. That is, some or all of the opinion can often be construed as a dialogic response to arguments of losing counsel, or to arguments of a lower court judge, or to arguments of a concurring or dissenting judge of the same court."[202]

The style of judicial reasoning characterized by the attributes in the first column of the table, here labelled "formalist", is closely associated with the classical image of the judge as an interpreter, as the "mouth"[203], rather than the maker of the law. A judge uses that manner of reasoning when he or she appears to be guided by the "letter of the law", in a formal, deductive syllogistic exercise, when he or she turns into an interpretation au-

201 Summers and Taruffo 1991, 499f.

202 Ibid., 500.

203 See Bogdandy and Venzke 2012, 9; they call this style of reasoning the "cognitive paradigm of adjudication."

tomat[204] that merely follows a predefined script and is not visible as an individual person behind the judgement. A formalist judicial decision is a techno-linguistic exercise, performed with the help of a dictionary to find out a word's meaning or by resorting to scholarly writing or precedents without looking at the respective weight and importance of the interests involved; the judge's personal attitudes, policy preferences and interests are not openly acknowledged to influence the outcome. As observed above, this is how judges tend to portray their decision-making process in public.[205]

At the same time, as shown by the analysis of Summers and Taruffo, a formalist way of reasoning is not the only way how a court can frame its findings nor is literal interpretation the only established[206] method of interpreting the law. Other established methods are teleological interpretation, systematic/contextual interpretation and historic interpretation. These different methods involve different degrees of discretion of a court. Notably, teleological interpretation is frequently seen as a method that allows judges to exercise more discretion than when resorting to literal interpretation.[207] This is due to the fact that while legislators, in particular at the international level, state the objectives of a law or an international treaty in the preamble to a treaty (or elsewhere), they do not normally do the same for individual paragraphs or articles. Moreover, both national law and international treaties are frequently a result of compromises and pursue different, not necessarily consistent objectives.[208] This leaves judicial decision-makers considerable space for dwelling on their own views of the objectives of a certain paragraph and for determining priorities among different objectives. At the same time, teleological interpretation is still in line with a classical role description of a judge and not necessarily considered judicial activism.

---

204 Miguel Poiares Maduro, *We, The Court* (Oxford: Hart, 1998) at 20 talks about an ideal "robot-court" associated with syllogistic reasoning in the application and interpretation of law.

205 See above note 186 et seq.

206 "Established" does not equal "written" or "codified". For international treaties, Art. 31 VCLT sets forth which methods of interpretation are to be used primarily, and Art. 32 VCLT sets forth "supplementary means of interpretation". However, in other legal orders (e.g. the German one) methods of interpretation and a hierarchy between them are not set forth anywhere in the law explicitly, but are instilled in the minds of future lawyers through textbooks and academic education.

207 See Arup 2003, 913.

208 Beck 2012, chap. 3.

Even beyond teleological interpretation, using a more normatively oriented way of reasoning or a more personal tone is not always considered inappropriate for judges. Generally, the more indeterminate the law is, the more leeway judges have with regard to how they justify a decision. Judicial discretion increases with the indeterminacy of the law.[209] Abbott et al. write: "precision narrows the scope for reasonable interpretation"[210]. Notably, legal provisions may contain words such as "appropriate", "good faith", "fair" or "reasonable". When faced with such terms, a judge can obviously not present any purely linguistic or semantic conclusion on what a certain term means, because these words themselves have a normative connotation to them. Here, the law itself calls for judges to talk about policy objectives, interests, principles, values, expectations, maybe even justice, and weigh them against each other, stating that one is more important than the other; judges will need to engage in what is usually referred to as balancing.[211] Balancing is a normative exercise, which is likely to involve the exercise of some measure of discretion or subjective judgement by judges; in the case of balancing, "judges are most clearly exposed as policy-makers"[212]. Balancing is likely to be the more easily accepted as a form of judicial argument, the larger the *prima facie* indeterminacy of the law is.[213] Thus, terms such as the ones above have a specific function in law – they enable judges to go beyond mere syllogistic deduction, while at the same time allowing them to be formally faithful to their role of judges and to comply with the letter of the law.

Balancing is even a legal requirement in some cases, not only allowing, but mandating judges to weigh different interests at stake. One very prominent example for a legal requirement to balance, taken from the realm of public law both at the national and international level, is the proportional-

209 Zarbiyev 2012, 9; Beck 2012, 9.

210 Abbott et al. 2000, 412.

211 Or in the words of Aleinikoff 1987, 945: "By a balancing opinion, I mean a judicial opinion that analyses a constitutional question by identifying interests implicated by the case and reaches a decision [...] by explicitly or implicitly assigning values to the identified interest".

212 Stone Sweet 2004, 10.

213 See for example Ossenbühl and Erbguth 1996, 25; Arup 2003, 899; Kelemen 2001, 625 puts this phenomenon in slightly different words when saying: "The constraints imposed by the need to maintain legal consistency will be greatest where treaty requirements, established case law, and general legal norms point clearly in one direction. By contrast, where treaties or legal norms are vague or where precedents are absent or contradictory, the desire to maintain legal consistency imposes less of a constraint."

ity principle. The basic rationale of the proportionality principle is to guarantee that in situations where different interests of *prima facie* equal weight are at stake the more important interest will prevail, while the others are encroached upon to the least degree possible.[214] Proportionality is considered a fundamental, constitutional principle of many legal orders.[215] In international law, proportionality has not (yet) achieved the status of a general principle,[216] but is viewed as an "essential concept"[217] and is relevant in several areas of international law[218].

A test whether a government action has been taken in line with the proportionality principle usually involves several steps.[219] Proportionality tests vary between legal orders.[220] The German and the European legal order are particularly similar in this regard; they both have a fully articulated and

---

214 However, it should be noted that there is always one "fundamental" value or right in comparison to which the measures reviewed need to be proportional. For example, a measure affecting a human right recognized in the German *Grundgesetz* must be a proportional restriction of this right; it is not the human right that needs to be proportional in light of the restriction. Thus, there is an implicit bias in favour of the fundamental value or right protected. While this may seem an obvious and more than justified choice in the case of human rights, this structure is not necessarily equally defensible in other cases. For example, in EU law national environmental measures restricting fundamental freedoms must be justified in light of these freedoms, and not the other way round – one may indeed question whether such a structural bias in favour of economic freedoms is politically and economically appropriate.

215 See Emmerich-Fritsche 2000, 140 – 188 for an overview of the legal orders of the EU Member States. In EU law, the case usually cited as being the one in which the ECJ first recognized the proportionality principle is the case C-11/70, Judgment of the Court of 17 December 1970, Internationale Handelsgesellschaft. In this case, the ECJ, after a thorough review of possible alternatives, found that the regulation in dispute was both "necessary and appropriate" for the end pursued (para. 12). Today, the principle of proportionality is enshrined in Art. 5 TFEU.

216 Krugmann 2004, 12. Still, the proportionality principle is relevant in an increasing number of areas of public international law.

217 Andenas and Zleptnig 2007, 401.

218 The most important areas seem to be the legal rules governing self-defense and reprisals, humanitarian law and human rights law, and maritime boundary law, see Andenas and Zleptnig 2007, 396ff; Bleckmann 1981; Cottier et al. 2017; Delbrück 1997, 1141–1143; Krugmann 2004, 15–40.

219 For an overview of the characters and elements of the principle in different legal orders, see Desmedt 2001, 444ff.

220 For a brief comparative overview see Kulick 2012, 173ff.

frequently used proportionality principle[221] that often serves as a point of reference in more general discussions on proportionality. In the EU and German versions of the proportionality principle, a measure is reviewed in a first step[222] as to whether it is suitable for pursuing the intended goal, i.e. whether it contributes to the realization of the intended goal at all. It is unusual for a measure not to pass this hurdle. The next step consists of an examination of whether the measure is necessary, i.e. whether among a set of equally suitable and feasible measures the measure in question least afflicts competing interests. This test is somewhat harder to pass. For example, the German Federal Constitutional Court *(Bundesverfassungsgericht)* has applied this test rather strictly sometimes.[223] The criteria of suitability and necessity pertain to factual or empirical questions that can, in theory, be answered with the help of science.[224] By way of contrast, the last step of the proportionality test is much more normative in character than the steps preceding it.[225] It is referred to as test of proportionality in the narrow sense ("*sensu stricto*") or "weighing" (*Abwägung* in German). The final step of the proportionality test comprises a process of weighing and balancing[226] different interests, rights, policy objectives or values, which includes determining whether all relevant interests have been taken into account, what legal importance each of the competing interests has and what consequences it would have for each of them, if the measure at issue was upheld or struck down. On that basis, judges decide whether the measure is proportional and should therefore be allowed to stand. The last prong of the proportionality test does not contain any substantive guidance on what value is to take precedence. However, it does comprise a procedural requirement that whoever takes the decisions (authority, parliament or

221 Several authors stress the influence that German public law has had in this respect on European law, see Hilf and Puth 2002, 202; Jacobs 1999, 2; Neumann and Tuerk 2003, footnote 17.

222 See for the following Andenas and Zleptnig 2007, 387ff; Desmedt 2001, 446; Jans 2000, 240–241; Neumann and Tuerk 2003, 199–233. It should be noted, however, that the terminology used varies; Notaro 2003, 66, for example, discusses "causal links" under the label "necessity" and the availability of less restrictive measures as "proportionality".

223 See for example the so called "Brokdorf" decision of the *Bundesverfassungsgericht* (Federal Constitutional Court), Case No 1 BvR 233/81 of 14 May 1985.

224 Emmerich-Fritsche 2000, 60 with further references.

225 See for example Ruozzi 2009, 475.

226 With regard to proportionality in the narrow sense as an obligation to balance divergent interests, see ECJ, C-169/91, Jugdement of 16 December 1992, Stoke on Trent, para. 15.

court) must take into account all legally recognized interests and values and use them to rationally justify the decision taken.[227]

Altogether, the proportionality principle combines, in a structured framework, an element of seemingly formal syllogistic deduction with the possibility of judges engaging in balancing and a more normative manner of reasoning. Although judicial balancing is a legal requirement at least in certain cases and widely recognised as acceptable at least in some settings,[228] it is far from immune to criticism. Some regard it as inappropriate judicial activism at the cost of the legislative branch.[229] Others have criticized balancing for its alleged irrationality.[230] While these views do not seem to be widely shared within the legal community, and in particular not among the judiciary, a normative style of reasoning is generally not deemed appropriate where the law is relatively determinate. In these cases, it is difficult for judges to base their decision explicitly on an analysis of the underlying interests, values and considerations of justice. This does not mean that indeterminacy is not a pre-requisite for a more deductive kind of interpretation as well – if the meaning of the law is plain and clear at first sight, there is simply nothing that must be interpreted. Yet a higher degree of textual indeterminacy is required when the stated reason for a certain judicial decision is derived from a balancing of interests.[231] Even when judges interpret indeterminate terms and balancing is mandated by the law, there are lines that judges are well-advised not to cross. For exam-

---

227 Andenas and Zleptnig 2007, 379.

228 For example, Aleinikoff 1987, 944 wrote already in 1987 that in the US the debate about balancing in constitutional jurisprudence had "all but disappeared". However, Aleinikoff himself is critical of the view that balancing is inevitable, arguing that many (constitutional) decisions can be made by resorting to principles that are not themselves subject to balancing, see, 997f.

229 Ladeur 2004, 33, 44, 69. Criticism relates, *inter alia*, to the fact that judges do not have any objective criterion to guide them in valuing and comparing the interests at stake and courts' failures to take account of all relevant interests, see Aleinikoff 1987, 972ff; also see Iancu 2009, 8ff for further points of criticism.

230 For an overview of this debate see Schauer 2009.

231 Dworkin 1981, 34 makes a distinction between discretion in a strong sense and in a weak sense. Discretion in a weak sense exists where for some reason the standards an official must apply cannot be applied mechanically but demand the use of judgment. Discretion in a strong sense exists where an official is simply not bound by any specific standards set by the authority who usually sets such standards, although she might be bound by more general standards of fairness or impartiality. In terms of these definitions, balancing would require a kind of discretion which is much closer to discretion in the strong sense than in the weak sense.

ple, judges may not state that they find a certain legal rule politically unwise and will therefore not apply it. They would overstep their competences, and their decision would likely not be regarded as legitimate and be vulnerable to criticism.[232]

At the same time, a formalist manner of reasoning is not considered favourably by everyone, either.[233] For example, in one recent contribution, the author observes that it is not a "pleasant qualification in a legal context" for a court to be called "formalistic".[234] Some observers consider using a very formalist style of reasoning to be an act of hiding or disguising what is really going on. For example, Maduro writes that the ECJ "hides" behind formal legal reasoning and indicates that the ECJ's formal style of reasoning serves to insulate the ECJ against criticism. According to Maduro, the self-referential nature of legal formalism makes it difficult to enter into a critical legal discourse on ECJ jurisprudence.[235] Similarly, Picciotto writes that since formalist reasoning "is closed and coded, intelligible only to insiders, it may [...] provide a cloak for activist decision-making"[236]. Nonetheless, using a formalist approach in a given situation is not necessarily an act of bad faith. It could also reflect the fact that judges only unconsciously let their personal preferences influence the outcome of a case.[237] A formal way of reasoning might also be "compensated" by the opinions and explanations of other actors that are part of a given legal system.[238] Others have stated that for the perceived legitimacy of a court's decision

> "the precise nature of reasoning involved, whether deductive, syllogistic, analogical, or some combination [...] is less important than that judicial decisions be reasoned in the first place [...]"[239].

232 See Burley and Mattli 1993, 73; Busch and Pelc 2019, 469 also observe that when "judges use their discretion to rely on strong sentiment [...] they do so at the risk of being seen as overly politicized".

233 See Slaughter and Helfer 1997, 320 for a short overview of different views on how courts should reason.

234 Loth 2009, 3.

235 Poiares Maduro 1998, 20–22; another observer who criticizes the ECJ's style of reasoning as "too succinct and leav[ing] too little room for arguments and persuasion" is Schmid 2010, 296.

236 Picciotto 2005, 5.

237 Poiares Maduro 1998, 23.

238 See Lasser's description of the *French Cour de Cassation*, below section 3.2.

239 Slaughter and Helfer 1997, 320.

In sum, courts are clearly expected to fulfil a role that is different from that of parliaments, and judges are expected to behave differently from lawmakers. For this reason it is a plausible assumption that formalism is the choice of the moment, whenever it is particularly important for a court to insulate its judgements against criticism.[240] Yet, if and when precisely a court is regarded as inappropriately "activist"[241] for using a non-formalist way of reasoning also depends on the wording of the law, the individual observer, and the mandate of the court. Empirically, courts use different ways of reasoning. Choosing an appropriate judicial style matters for whether a court's decisions are perceived as legitimate.

3.2. Lasser's work on judicial styles as part of a judicial system

In the preceding section, the types of arguments that courts can legitimately use were described, in relation to the determinacy of the legal norms under interpretation, among others. Yet the legal system of which the court is part and the political and legal discourse of the time also play an important role with regard to which judicial style a court can adopt.[242] In this context some of the factors that have been mentioned above as potentially influencing the outcome of judicial decisions are relevant to their style as well.[243]

---

240 For example Pair 2001, 211 observes that the ICJ "in the early phase of interpretation of the United Nations Charter and a time when legal positivism was a preferred form of interpretation [...] had not yet established enough strength to rule on the basis of purpose and intent alone, not only because of its own weakness and inexperience, but also because of the credibility of the organization and its purpose". Similarly, Poiares Maduro 1998, 25 states that the ECJ, which in its early years adopted several decisions of sweeping legal significance for the European legal order, was only able to do so, because it portrayed the decisions as an inevitable consequence of the wording of the EC Treaty; see also more generally Picciotto 2005, 5.

241 For a discussion on what is meant by judicial activism, see below section 5.3.2.

242 This aspect is emphasized by Zarbiyev 2012, 5f who states the following: "In every legally organized community, there is a range of courses of action that are considered to be appropriately judicial: there is a rough consensus about what judges are permitted to do as well as the limit that the judiciary cannot legitimately transgress".

243 See in particular Pauwelyn and Elsig 2012.

I will now proceed to provide an overview of the influential[244] and in-depth analysis by Mitchel Lasser on different courts. He investigates what I call judicial style and what he calls "models of judicial control, debate and legitimacy"[245], analysing the US Supreme Court, the French *Cour de Cassation* and the ECJ. Although all of the courts that Lasser compares have a functionally equivalent position within the respective legal system, their judgements differ fundamentally in style, as do the sources of authority they draw on.

One extreme of judicial style, according to Lasser, is the one of the French *Cour de Cassation*.[246] Its published judgements are extremely short and impersonal in tone and entirely formalist in approach; they present the findings as the only and inevitable conclusion from the wording of the law. This does not mean, according to Lasser, that considerations of equity or the larger social needs and personal perspectives of individual judges do not influence the judgements of the French *Cour de Cassation*. Discussions of more political or normative aspects are, however, confined to the interaction of the different judicial players in the courtroom and do not appear in the judgements. Explaining the doctrinal as well as social and political implications of judgements is left to academic observers, whose case notes are often published together with the judgements. Thus, a split, or, in Lasser's words, a "bifurcation", occurs: a formalist legal discourse is what the *Cour de Cassation* engages in publicly, while discussions of the more normative arguments supporting a judicial decision are relegated to the non-public or less-public realm or – as far as they are made public – unveiled mainly by academics.

The US Supreme Court, as the other extreme, produces long decisions and strives to make the reasons for taking them transparent to the utmost degree.[247] The US judicial style incorporates two kinds of discourse: a formal legal discourse and a more socially-responsive, equity-oriented one.

244 For example, the contributions in Huls, Adams, and Bomhoff 2009 all build on or discuss Lasser's analysis.

245 Lasser 2004; Lasser 2003.

246 The *Cour de Cassation* is the highest court in France and unique in that it is the only such court in France, with responsibility for civil, criminal or other cases, see "The Role of the Court of Cassation" at the court's website, http://www.courdecassation.fr/about_the_court_9256.html.

247 Kennedy 1997, 73ff discusses at length the origins of the US style of judicial decision-making. His description is rather similar to Lasser's: "In American judicial opinions and in doctrinal writing, the most common mode is neither deduction nor policy but an intermediate mode, deductive argument supplement-

Both, in Lasser's view, tend to "control" each other. Neither a plainly formalist style of judicial reasoning nor an open reference to, for example, the term "policy" as a justification for a judicial decision seem to be acceptable.

An intermediate position is occupied by the ECJ. Originating in and like in the French tradition the court's judgements are comparatively short and rather formalist, textualist in style.[248] One particular feature of the ECJ's jurisprudence is that, the Court by and large adopts a teleological approach, frequently justifying decisions with reference to the overall objectives of the European legal and political order. The centrality of the overall objectives of the EU legal order in the ECJ's reasoning is, in part, indebted to the fact that the ECJ has a public counterpart, the Advocate General. The Advocate General's reasoning is much more subjective and policy-oriented in tone than that of the ECJ and also takes scholarly doctrines into account. Thus, the existence and content of the opinions of the Advocate General draw attention to the fact that the final decision of the ECJ represents a choice, which the Court needs to justify – and it does so by resorting to *telos.* Like in the French system, there is a bifurcation of the discourse. Different from the French system, however both parts of the legal discourse are made public – the more formalist ECJ reasoning and the more subjective, policy-oriented ones of the Advocates General.

As Lasser shows, all three courts (and the wider legal systems of which they are part) need to defend their judgements in legal terms, and ensure their responsiveness to political and social needs at the same time. The three courts have developed different models for doing so.

The decisive point about Lasser's comparison for the present purpose is that he relates the different judicial styles he describes to certain features of the overall political-legal order, of which the respective court is a part, and to the function that individual cases have within this system.[249] Basically,

ed or "guided" by policy arguments" (at 104); Lasser 2001 in turn criticizes Kennedy's distinction between the US approach and the European judicial discourse, which Kennedy describes as not policy-oriented and deductionist-formalist, as overly simplistic. Lasser argues that policy is also used as an argument in European judicial decisions.

248 On judges' views on how the use of French as the ECJ's working language leads to a use of notions and a style of argumentation belonging to the French tradition, see Terris, Romano, and Swigart 2007, 78.

249 Lasser 2003 seems to be somewhat ambiguous concerning whether to describe the relationship between the more general features of the respective judicial sys-

these courts have different models of authority on which they draw for legitimizing their decisions.

The French judiciary is composed of a small number of lawyers that have undergone a long, strict and highly selective training in public academic and judicial institutions. They are regarded as national, republican elite. As such, they are considered trustworthy enough not to have to make the more socially responsive, equity-oriented reasons for their decisions public. At the same time, the fact that judicial deliberations take place in a judicial black box and are eliminated from the published decisions, makes the French decisions appear as mere application of the law rather than law-making. Individual cases have a less central role in the French judicial system than in other legal systems. Notably, it is considered perfectly legitimate for judges to change their interpretations as needed in line of the specific circumstances of a given case. They can do so, because judicial decisions are not seen as an instance of making and re-writing the law, but a mere application of the law in a given, confined case. This, in turn, lowers the burden of justification resting on the shoulders of judges. The French *Cour* draws mainly on institutional sources of authority, including notably the persons making the judgements and the mechanisms to select them.[250]

By way of contrast, US judges have not gone through a comparably monolithic process of public education and selection. There is also no US "republican spirit" comparable to the French one. Thus, it is the US Supreme Court's judgements themselves that carry the entire burden of justification. For lack of another source of authority, the US Supreme Courts relies on judicial discourse and explanation – the court makes its reasoning transparent and understandable, aiming at its decisions being understood and accepted. The US Supreme Court is not entirely free of the constraints of textualism; rather, it needs to integrate a more normative, policy-oriented discourse and the traditional judicial formalist-textualist discourse. Judges must make all reasons for their decisions transparent – the more formal legal and the more socially and politically motivated or equity-oriented ones. In Lasser's observation this has led to the emergence of "multi-part" or "multi-prong" judicial tests in US jurisprudence (e.g. a proportionality test), which fuse a more textualist and more normative

tem and the judicial style in terms of causation. In some instances, he explicitly assumes that the phenomenon can only be understood as a "chicken-and-egg-type" of problem (see at 33), elsewhere he seems to assume that there is, after all, some sort of causality involved, see for example at 56.

250 Lasser 2004, 179ff; for a good summary of Lasser's argument, see Loth 2009, 4.

mode of reasoning. Another corollary of the need to reconcile textualism and policy discourse is, according to Lasser, that there is an "expectation of individual judicial responsibility for the judicial opinion and for its reasoning"[251]. The US judicial style correlates with the centrality of the judgements within the overall judicial system: judges are more or less officially entrusted with the task of law-making through precedent and a "judicial decision serves as the absolute center of attention"[252]. The relation between the centrality of judgements and the style of reasoning they exhibited is, according to Lasser, a circular one: because the judgements are so well-reasoned they are so central, and because they are so central they must be so well-reasoned.

The ECJ's teleological style, in turn, needs to be understood against the backdrop of both its historical roots in the French tradition and the peculiar features of the European scene, according to Lasser. Like US American judges – and even more so – ECJ judges lack a unified educational background and have not passed a process of strict professional selection. They even come from different legal systems. Moreover, there is no unitary European *demos*, different from the French setting.[253] The ECJ's deductionist, formalist and concise style is in need of being complemented by references to the overall, accepted objectives of the European legal order. In this context, Loth, building on Lasser's work, argues that the ECJ also relies on a discursive model of authority, but in a different manner from the US Supreme Court.[254] The ECJ ties its findings to the overall objectives of the EU and their legitimacy, basically "borrowing" their authority. Moreover, the ECJ has a counterpart, the Advocate General, whose published opinions feature a less formalist style of legal reasoning and rely more strongly on personal views, precedents and doctrinal writing as well as equity-related and policy arguments. Even though some of the justification of the ECJ decisions is "outsourced" to the Advocate General in the ECJ system, Lass-

251 Lasser 2003, 31.

252 Ibid., 32.

253 On a critical note, one may question the view that there is ever something like a unitary "demos", because this notion disguises conflicts of class, race and gender that permeate every society. Positing the existence of a unitary "demos" is also a first step towards constructing an ethnically, religious or "racially" homogenous entity from which whoever does not fit into dominant categories is excluded, which then can easily become the basis for different types of discrimination. This, however, is not the topic of this work and can thus not be developed further here.

254 Loth 2009, 7f.

er observes that the normative power and weight of ECJ decisions are close to that of the US ones.

Other authors have used an approach similar to Lasser's for analysing other courts, for example the ECtHR and the *Dutch Hoge Raad.*[255] These courts have all been described as being located between the French *Cour de Cassation* on the one extreme and the US Supreme Court on the other with regard to their style, but also concerning the sources of authority – institutional and discursive ones – they rely on. Moreover, Lasser's description of judicial styles has also been confirmed by authors.[256]

In conclusion, the style of a court is determined by a number of factors; this is the main point to be learned from Lasser's analysis for purposes of the present work. These factors include the overall judicial system of which the court is part, the way the court operates in conjunction with other actors within the judicial system, the role of individual judgements in the overall legal system, as well as the extent to which the authority of a court stems from other sources than the judgements themselves, for example, the educational background of the judges and institutional mechanisms for their selection. Other authors have offered similar explanations, arguing for example that the ECJ's preference for teleological interpretation can be explained by the broader nature of the EU's constitutive legal texts (as compared to WTO law), the different institutional balance, and different expectations on part of Members, among others.[257]

To put things into perspective, it must also be noted that even if observable judicial styles are more or less consistent over longer periods of time, this does not necessarily mean that a court cannot be bolder in some cases than in others[258] or will refrain from modifying its judicial style in a long-term perspective.

---

255 See ibid., 8ff with references to other authors.

256 Summers and Taruffo 1991, 502ff describe the French judicial discourse (not restricted to the Court de Cassation) and that of the US Supreme Court as the extremes observed in terms of formalist (French) and non-formalist (US) orientation. This is based on case studies, see Troper, Grzegorczyk, and Jean-Louis Gardies 1991 and Summers 1991.

257 Lennard 2002, 86.

258 For example, Bogdandy and Venzke 2012, 8, observe that the "lawmaking impetus" of the ICJ differed considerably in its Kosovo and Wall opinions. See also references in n. 240 above.

3.3. Additional factors influencing judicial styles

Besides the literature on the strategic behaviour of courts quoted above[259] and Lasser, a number of other studies have discussed additional factors influencing judicial styles; there is a rich debate in the US context in particular.[260] The following overview is focussed on studies that are of more immediate relevance to the WTO context.

One point that several authors have stressed is that the judicial style of a court may vary across times. Sometimes, it may become acceptable or necessary for a court to modify its style in light of broader legal, political and social developments.[261] The line between the "judicial" and the "political" may change its position over time.[262] A court may also modify its style once its legitimacy has been established and the risk of backlash has become less acute.[263]

Moreover, it has also been claimed that the style of dispute settlement decisions varies, depending on how politically sensitive a case is. According to Busch and Pelc, the Appellate Body uses more "affect", i.e. emotionally charged language in cases that are politically sensitive and where the defending governments may have to win the support of domestic constituencies for the needed policy changes.[264] Other courts have also been observed to vary their style by types of cases.[265]

It has also been argued that judges care about being perceived positively by relevant audiences[266] and this, in turn, leads them to adapt their style to

259 Section 2.1.
260 See for example Aleinikoff 1987; Posner 1995.
261 Thus, for example Aleinikoff 1987, 949ff observes that the US Supreme Court moved towards a style that heavily involved balancing only in the second half of the 20th century, from what Aleinikoff calls a "non-balancing past". The factors behind this move were, according to his analysis, a mounting criticism of the Supreme Court jurisprudence as being out of touch with political and social realities which individual judges on the Court's benches subscribed to and broader intellectual currents, such as pragmatism and realism in legal theory. These intellectual currents rejected formalism, both in jurisprudence and in other disciplines.
262 Ehlermann and Lockhart 2004, 493.
263 For example, several authors have observed that the Appellate Body's reliance on textual interpretation has become less pronounced over the years, see van Damme 2010, 641ff; Lang 2016, 1101; more generally Pauwelyn and Elsig 2012, 467.
264 Busch and Pelc 2019, 464.
265 See references in Pauwelyn and Elsig 2012, 450.
266 Baum 2006, 3.

their audience.[267] At a less personal level, courts may also consider which style is expedient for reaching difference audiences and/or avoiding to antagonize others. For example, it has been observed that courts that "talk to" national courts (e.g. national courts of appeal, but also – in some cases – the ECJ) may have a different, more formalist style than those seeking to reach policy-makers.[268] Courts "talking" to political decision-makers have even been described as deliberately avoiding clarity in their writing and using "legalese" in some cases for avoiding political backlash.[269]

Generally, international courts have been observed to be in a particularly precarious position: while international law tends to be less determinate than national law, states are at the same time wary of delegating decision-making to courts – and the fact that international treaties once agreed are difficult to change further compounds the situation.[270]

The function of courts has also been identified as a factor influencing their judicial style. For example, *ad hoc* tribunals tasked with settling a specific dispute (for the past) can be expected to act differently from more permanent bodies (e.g. concerning their approach to precedents).[271] Moreover, which actors besides states and the courts are involved in judicial proceedings (e.g. civil society) may also matter.[272]

At an international court the legal background of the judges (e.g. coming from common or civil law systems) and how they deal with the diversity may also matter.[273] Lastly, preferences of individual judges may also have an impact on judicial style, even though they are likely to be less important in settings where several judges decide jointly.[274]

267 Venzke 2016, 252ff.
268 Busch and Pelc 2019, 466.
269 See the references in ibid., which mainly relate to the US context.
270 Pauwelyn and Elsig 2012, 447.
271 Ibid., 462; see also Charlotin 2017, 296f.
272 Pauwelyn and Elsig 2012, 465f.
273 Ibid., 467f.
274 Meagher 2020 points out that common and civil law systems tend to favour different styles of judicial reasoning, but overall holds the view that the judicial style used by a court is mainly a result of the preferences of individual adjudicators (see at 164).

4. Hypotheses on judicial decision-making within the WTO

With these different aspects in mind, I now turn to a discussion of what may be expected of the WTO dispute settlement bodies, when the existing insights on factors influencing the judicial style and substance of judicial decisions are applied to the WTO context. As argued above, it is necessary to look at both the substantive outcome of judicial cases as well as the judicial style deployed to justify them: neither of them alone will suffice to ensure that a court and its judgements are perceived as legitimate.

Generally, applying insights from one political and legal system to another is a complex exercise. In particular, it has been cautioned that analogies between domestic and international courts are misplaced and differences rather than similarities between them should be emphasized.[275] Yet, other scholars have applied the insights gained from the analysis of various courts to the world of WTO dispute settlement[276] and more generally insights on the decision-making of national courts to the international level.[277] When I discuss in the following sections what the insights on judicial decision-making presented in the previous sections may mean for the substance and style of WTO dispute settlement decisions, this is not to imply that insights on other courts are all automatically applicable to the WTO dispute settlement system. Rather, this section develops hypotheses on how the Appellate Body's judicial decision-making is likely to look like, considering the existing more general research on judicial decision-making. In the subsequent chapters of this work, I will then discuss whether relevant aspects of the WTO dispute settlement decisions match these expectations. In the final chapter of this work I will link my results to the hypotheses presented here[278] and clarify, which of them seems to apply in a WTO context. I will also discuss the reasons for the observed results, considering the general insights on judicial decision-making presented in this chapter.

It is necessary, however, to initially clarify two points: First, the above insights on judicial decision-making can only be applied to the WTO dis-

275 Tumonis 2013, 49; however, some of the reasons he gives for this caveat are not applicable to WTO dispute settlement, e.g. an absence of a sanctioning mechanism.

276 Garrett and McCall Smith 2002; Alvarez-Jiménez 2009a; Flett 2010, 319, also states that the WTO exhibits a unique set of characteristics, but is closer to the ECJ model than to any other judicial model at the international level.

277 Ginsburg 2006.

278 See chapter 4, section 2.

pute settlement bodies if they are courts or something akin to a court. Second, it is important to understand to what degree WTO law is indeterminate. These questions will be discussed in section 4.1. Section 4.2 features a brief overview of how (former) Appellate Body Members have portrayed the decision-making process of the Appellate Body.

For developing several hypotheses on the likely substantive outcomes of WTO judicial decision-making and its style I will proceed as follows: Features of the WTO dispute settlement system that are likely to influence both the style and outcome of WTO judicial decision-making are discussed in section 4.3. Additional factors that could be relevant for the substantive outcomes of appellate proceedings are presented in section 4.4 and additional factors of importance for the WTO judicial style in section 4.5. Section 4.6 presents the conclusions in the form of hypotheses.

A further *caveat* is in place with regards hypotheses on what behaviour can be expected from the Appellate Body need to be understood. Steinberg notes that

> "[p]olitical science lacks cognitive models that are robust enough, and the complete information necessary, to make perfect predictions about the political consequences of WTO judicial decisions. These deficiencies suggest that the precise boundary of the strongest political constraint on judicial lawmaking is uncertain ex ante."[279]

These limitations apply to this work as well. Thus, the hypotheses I formulate below in section 4.6 are no predictions, but at most informed suggestions or assumptions. They are based on prior research on judicial decision-making presented in sections 2 and 3 and the characteristics of the WTO dispute settlement system and WTO law discussed in section 4. The hypotheses may in the end be confirmed or refuted through the in-depth reading of relevant aspects of the WTO dispute settlement decisions in chapters 2 and 3 of this work.

4.1. The WTO dispute settlement system and its law

In this section, I will first present insights on whether the WTO dispute settlement system, and in particular the Appellate Body, can be classified as "judicial" or "court" (section 4.1.1). Moreover, the character of WTO

279 Steinberg 2004, 267.

law is discussed, in particular with regard to its degree of indeterminacy (section 4.1.2).

4.1.1. The dispute settlement system: a judicial mechanism?

The WTO's dispute settlement system has often been described in the literature;[280] thus, only a brief summary is needed here: When a WTO Member wishes to obtain a judicial decision and consultations between the parties concerned have failed, the first institution to decide a case is a Panel. Panels are composed of three individuals nominated *ad hoc* from a roster of experts maintained by the WTO for this purpose.[281] If a party to a case is dissatisfied with a Panel decision, it can bring the case before the Appellate Body who re-decides issues of law, but not of fact.[282] Both Panel and Appellate Body reports need to be adopted by the DSB, composed of all WTO Members, to become binding.[283]

The selection of Appellate Body Members is governed by Art. 17.2 DSU. Accordingly, the DSB appoints persons to serve on the Appellate Body for a term of four years, which is once renewable. Prior to the decision by the DSB, WTO Members nominate candidates, who are then subject to a screening process at the WTO.[284] The DSB decides by consensus on the appointment of candidates, in line with the usual decision-making practice of the WTO.[285]

There is today consensus that the Appellate Body can be described as a court[286] or at least a "quasi-juridical"[287] or "quasi-judicial"[288] entity. It has even been called a trade "supercourt"[289]. One scholar has described the WTO dispute settlement system as the "most powerful dispute settlement system at the international level that we have today or perhaps ever in the

280 See for example Kulovesi 2011, 130ff.
281 See Art. 8 DSU for the procedures.
282 See Art. 17.6 DSU.
283 See Art. 16.4 DSU for Panel reports, Art. 17.14 DSU for Appellate Body reports.
284 Krüger 2013, 13.
285 See Art. IX.1 WTOA.
286 See for example Gourgourinis 2016, 11f.
287 Conti 2011, 60.
288 The "quasi" is due to the fact that there are some "political" elements in the WTO dispute settlement process, including notably mandatory consultations between the parties, the adoption of dispute settlement reports by the DSB and the instruction to Panels to help settle disputes, see Davey 2000, 293ff.
289 Shell 1995, 831.

history of the world"[290]. Others have compared the Appellate Body to other international tribunals and found a high degree of similarity.[291] One practitioner engaged in WTO dispute proceedings even has commented that the Appellate Body "is easily the most judicial instance before which I have litigated"[292]. A certain semblance of the WTO dispute settlement system to a domestic court has sometimes been noted.[293]

Some features make the Appellate Body particularly similar to an international and in some regards even domestic court and help justify the assumption that "the Appellate Body is a court in all but name"[294]. These include the quasi-automatic adoption of dispute settlement decisions[295], the move away from full confidentiality of proceedings[296], the Appellate Body's compulsory jurisdiction[297], and procedural rules that include strict deadlines. The most important point is probably the "quasi-enforceability" of dispute settlement decisions.[298] The most important feature that the Appellate Body lacks as compared to a regular court is the immediate binding effect of its decisions on the parties. For that, a decision by the Dispute Settlement Body (DSB) is required. Given that the DSB adopts the dispute settlement reports almost automatically, this is not a major minus concerning the court-likeness of the Appellate Body, though.[299]

290 Statement by Jackson during a panel discussion, see Taniguchi et al. 2008, 388.
291 Sacerdoti 2006, 42ff.
292 Flett 2011, 4.
293 Costa 2011, 21.
294 Weiler 2001, 201.
295 According to Art. 17.14 DSU the DSB must adopt, and the parties must unconditionally accept, an Appellate Body report unless the DSB decides by consensus not to adopt the report. As the winning party is unlikely to agree to the non-adoption, such a case has so far not occurred and is unlikely to occur in the future.
296 As Weiler 2001, 196 observes it was in the GATT era even difficult to obtain the Panel reports. However, important parts of the dispute settlement proceedings are still non-public – to an extent not normally found at the national level, or the EU level, see Conti 2011; Stein 2001 observes that the fact that dispute settlement proceedings are closed is „in sharp conflict with the concept of a modern judiciary".
297 Watson 2013, 89.
298 See for example Costa 2011, 8; Reusch 2007, 119ff.
299 See Sacerdoti 2006, 49.

The Appellate Body is not only a court by its procedures, but also by the people who decide[300] cases. Indeed, Members of the Appellate Body occasionally have used the term "judges" to describe themselves.[301] At least as important as the self-conception of the Members of the Appellate Body is their professional background. Among Panelists, there is a substantial proportion of individuals without a background in law.[302] Conversely, there are few Appellate Body members without a legal background.[303] Thus, the advent of the WTO has not only been accompanied by the introduction of a court-like appellate stage, but also by the establishment of a body of professional lawyers performing the appellate review.[304] By their professional education, lawyers are more likely than e.g. diplomats of other professions to understand the specific judicial role of interpreting the law, to feel committed to its ethos of, and to have the capacity to fulfil it. More specifically, the lawyers appointed to the Appellate Body initially were "distinguished jurists, not eminent experts in GATT/WTO law"[305].

Appellate Body Members serve for a once renewable term of four years. This is shorter than the term of office of judges of other international courts (such as the ECJ and ICJ);[306] at the same time it is much closer to a permanent position and hence judicial independence than the position of the Panelists who are selected *ad hoc* for each case. Given that the Appellate Body is composed of lawyers that enjoy a certain permanence of pos-

300 In the remainder of this work, terms like "decide" or "rule" will be used to describe the activities of Panels and the Appellate Body; however, strictly speaking a certain dispute settlement report only becomes legally effective once adopted by the DSB.

301 See for example Bacchus 2002, 1024.

302 Costa 2011, 14 puts the figure of Panelists with no legal background at 45 % for the period 1995 - 2015; Johannesson and Mavroidis 2015, 5f indicate that "40% of all Panels have had Panelists with a legal background". Costa also notes, however, that the number of Panelists without legal background has been declining over the years, i.e. the Panels are becoming more legalized in terms of the professional background of their members.

303 Costa 2011, 14 mentions a share of 10 % for the period 1995 - 2010.

304 On the wider implications of the move towards a legal culture within the WTO, see Weiler 2001, 197ff.

305 Howse 2016b, 27; Meagher 2020, 157ff also points out that the WTO judicial decision-makers come from both civil and common law systems. While he does not discard the possibility that this may have an influence on the WTO's judicial style, he concludes that questions of personality may ultimately be more important than the common/civil law background of a WTO judicial decision-maker.

306 Matsushita 2005a, 1390.

ition, it is *prima facie* a reasonable assumption that the above insights on judicial decision-making are of relevance in the context of WTO dispute settlement, too.[307]

This statement on "courtness" is applicable to a lesser extent to Panels: they operate on an *ad hoc* basis and are generally described as still being permeated by a more or less diplomatic spirit[308]; they may still be characterized, at least to a degree, as what Weiler has called "diplomacy through other means"[309] with reference to Panels under the GATT. However, given that the Panels operate in the shadow of the Appellate Body, this seems to be of secondary relevance when discussing the overall characteristics of the dispute settlement system.

In the description of the functioning of the WTO dispute settlement system given until here one actor is missing: the WTO Secretariat. According to Art. 27.1 DSU, the role of the Secretariat is to "assist panels, especially on the legal, historical and procedural aspects of the matters dealt with". Generally, the Secretariat's role has not been much researched.[310] Nonetheless, from the few descriptions available, it is known that the division assisting the Panels has quite a substantial role in the proceedings and in drafting the reports.[311] One account of how this works in practice is the following:

> "The Secretariat is always there. It provides panelists with the summaries and analysis of the cases and list of questions. Panelists tend to gain experience as they sit on more panels. Often they are much quieter the first time they serve. Experienced panelists will sometimes develop their own questions [...]. After the last round of meetings, the panelists will tell the Secretariat what they want and what they do not want in the final reports. The Secretariat will then draft the outlines of the final report. The scope for its initiative will depend on how detailed the panelists' instructions are. The Secretariat will then go through the outline with the panelists and make the necessary

---

307 This conclusion is also drawn by Colares 2009, 386; and from a legitimacy perspective by Howse 2001, 41.

308 See for example Conti 2011, 79ff.

309 Weiler 2001, 194.

310 The only study focusing on the role of civil servants within GATT/the WTO seems to be Xu Yi-chong and Weller 2004; however, they concentrate on the Uruguay Round negotiations and say little about the WTO reality.

311 See for example Krüger 2013, 13; Flett 2011, 23 who in addition criticizes the unduly heavy involvement of the Secretariat in the process of selecting Panelists, see at 21f.

changes. If panelists are less experienced state delegates, the Secretariat can have significant influence in the process as well as the final report. When panelists are state delegates, according to some staff at the Legal Division, the panelists would handle the politics of the dispute and the Secretariat would do the law. If panelists are academic, that is less the case. When panelists are current state delegates or formal trade officials, time constraints may allow the Secretariat to play a major role in the process."[312]

Obviously, this account relates to Panels rather than the Appellate Body. The Appellate Body has its own secretariat. One observer actively involved in WTO dispute settlement describes the Appellate Body Secretariat as "tightly separated from the rest of the organization" and "more influenced by the objective rules of interpretation than the rest of the Secretariat". He also indicates that it has played an "important ancillary role" in developing WTO jurisprudence.[313] In the remainder of this work the role of the Secretariat in WTO dispute settlement will, however, be neglected for two reasons: First, assessing this role in detail would be methodologically very difficult. Second, it is the Appellate Body Members that sign the dispute settlement decisions by names – signalling that they ultimately are personally responsible for the content of the decisions.

To conclude, it is appropriate to use existing insights on judicial-decision making when performing research on the WTO dispute settlement system, given the "court-likeness" of the Appellate Body.

4.1.2. The degree of indeterminacy of WTO law

WTO law is clearly a part of international law; international law generally is considered to be more indeterminate than domestic law. In international it is frequently not only unclear what the law says, but also what constitutes a legal principle or rule in the first place.[314] In any case, the indeterminacy of law is always a matter of degree; a likeness of WTO law to national constitutional law has been observed when it comes to the degree of indeterminacy and the functions of WTO law.[315] This characterization is

312 Xu Yi-chong and Weller 2004, 223.

313 Flett 2011, 23.

314 This is a re-phrasing of a sentence by Sir Gerald Fitzmaurice, as quoted by Zarbiyev 2012, 13.

315 Cass 2001, 42; Eeckhout 2010, 8.

mostly based on the fact that WTO law is more densely structured than international law normally is;[316] it has been characterized as having a higher degree of precision than other norms of international law.[317] Thus, it is probably fair to say that some parts[318] of WTO law exhibit a higher degree of determinacy than can be found in some other areas of international law.[319]

Even if at least some parts of WTO law are more determinate than some other international legal agreements, the WTO legal order is still less densely structured than national legal orders. Bartels, for example, holds the view that

> "[i]ndeterminacy is, of course, a feature common to all legal systems—and probably inherent in them as well—but it is particularly marked in the WTO, where the substantive agreements are especially characterized by gaps, overlaps, and conflicts."[320]

Others have also highlighted the indeterminacy of WTO law,[321] which has been characterized as "replete with contradictions, gaps and ambiguities"[322]; WTO rules have been described as "pitched at such a level of generality [...] that they invite competing interpretations"[323]. The Appellate Body itself has sometimes critically commented on the lack of clarity of WTO law, saying for example that Art. 3.3 SPS was "not a model of clarity in drafting and communication".[324] In the terminology of political scientists, WTO law is a case of an "incomplete contract", into which adjudication is a built as a mechanism for making the law more "complete".[325]

---

316 Cass 2001, 50.

317 Abbott et al. 2000, 406.

318 Ibid. give the TRIPS Agreement as an example.

319 This is not to say that there is no other international law as determinate and precise as WTO law. For example, some of the norms currently under negotiation in the UNFCCC framework are extremely detailed and technical; the same is true for some of the WIPO agreements.

320 Bartels 2004, 871.

321 Goh and Morgan 2007, 483; Picciotto 2005, 12f; Du 2011, 652ff discusses some of the reasons behind it.

322 Barfield 2001, 7.

323 Arup 2003, 910.

324 *European Communities – Measures Concerning Meat and Meat Products, WT/DS26/AB/R, WT/DS48/AB/R* 1998, para. 175.

325 Sweet and Brunell 2013, 68f; Trachtman 1999, 346ff.

Indeed, the various types of indeterminacy discussed above[326] are also present in WTO law. Several authors have pointed out that some of the most central terms of WTO law are fuzzy and highly in need of judicial interpretation.[327] Some of these norms are very relevant for "trade and ..." cases. Notable examples are the "appropriate level of protection" in Art. 5 SPS or the term "necessary" contained e.g. in Art. 2.2 SPS, XX GATT, XIV GATS and 2.2 TBT. There are also issues with regard to where in the legal text certain terms are used and where they are not. For example, Weiler makes the point that some form of a necessity test would seem to be warranted for all justification measures within the remit of Art. XX GATT, but the word "necessity" is distributed "almost haphazardly" in that article.[328] With regard to gaps, WTO law is like other treaty law almost necessarily not complete[329].

With regard to conflicts, potential collisions exist within WTO law as well as between WTO law and other international law.[330] The most prominent type of (potential) external collision of WTO law is probably with multilateral environmental treaties (MEAs), but conflicts could also occur, for example, in relation to other free trade agreements.[331] An example of a (potential) internal collision is the somewhat unclear relation between the SPS Agreement and the GATT.[332]

Interestingly, WTO law itself recognizes that there sometimes may be more than one defensible interpretation; Art. 17.6 (ii) of the Anti-Dumping Agreement states:

> Where the panel finds that a relevant provision of the Agreement admits of more than one permissible interpretation, the panel shall find the authorities' measure to be in conformity with the Agreement if it rests upon one of those permissible interpretations.

This implies the possibility of various defensible interpretations of WTO law, which are, in turn, only possible when the law is indeterminate.

326 See above section 1.

327 Arup 2003, 911; for a discussion of various instances of "ambiguity" in WTO law from a practitioner's perspective, see Flett 2011, 11ff.

328 Weiler 2009, 137.

329 Van Damme 2009, 110.

330 The most comprehensive study of these conflicts is probably Neumann 2002.

331 For an overview, see Matsushita 2004.

332 See for differing views on this relationship on the one hand Winter 2003, 123; and on the other hand Quick and Blüthner 1999, 627.

The observed indeterminacy of WTO law is, *inter alia,* attributed to a deliberate decision of the negotiators to leave the agreements as they were in order to attain consensus[333] and present domestic constituencies with a success story.[334] Flett, an EU Commission official involved in WTO dispute settlement proceedings, relates the following telling episode:

> "I recall that, having spent a number of years working in this area, I participated in the preparation of legal document [sic] containing guidance for negotiators. The gist of the document was to recall some of the past WTO cases in which the judicial construction of ambiguity had gone against the EU, and to suggest means of avoiding such outcomes by negotiating different treaty language in the future. The reception of this document among negotiators was somewhat muted, to put it mildly. The general sense of the reaction was that it must have been written by people who had never actually participated in WTO negotiations. It was then that the improbable realisation dawned on me. A significant amount of the time the negotiators were not actually trying to avoid such outcomes. Or at least they were taking interpretative risks, sometimes very considerable risks, because the other side was doing exactly the same thing, and there was no other means to conclude the agreement."[335]

According to Flett, WTO law is "not ambiguous by accident, but by design and of necessity"[336]. In a similar vein, Maier observes that countries could not agree on certain issues when negotiating the SPS Agreement and therefore left certain questions open and deliberately kept some provisions of the agreement vague.[337] Other reasons for the indeterminacy of WTO law are the "complexity and scope of the agreements and uncertainty about future circumstances".[338]

The combination of leaving legal norms indeterminate and establishing a judicial mechanism is sometimes considered to constitute a conscious choice of delegating decision-making power to the WTO's judicial branch.[339] While this explanation is theoretically appealing, there are some doubts about whether WTO negotiators really intended to delegate consid-

333 Conti 2011, 60.
334 Holmes 1999, 65; see also Picciotto 2005, 12.
335 Flett 2011, 11.
336 Flett 2010, 319.
337 Maier 2017, 235.
338 Shany and Shlomo-Agon 2014, 195.
339 Trachtman 1999, 344ff.

erable decision-making powers to the Appellate Body. Accounts of the DSU negotiations during the Uruguay Round indicate that negotiators did not expect the Appellate Body to play quite the central role it plays today.[340] Moreover, the DSU was negotiated relatively late, when advanced drafts of several agreements had already been negotiated, without the fact being known that something like an Appellate Body would be created.[341] Negotiators dealing with the various agreements may therefore not have been fully aware of the consequences of leaving certain norms indeterminate.[342] Nonetheless, in practice, leaving the law indeterminate and at the same time creating a binding adjudication mechanism has the effect of delegating decisions to adjudication.

In sum, WTO law is indeterminate – probably more so than the bulk of domestic law, and less so than many other international legal rules.

4.2. The Appellate Body as described by its (former) Members

In a few instances (former) Members of the Appellate Body have published their views on the actual or desirable functioning of the WTO dispute settlement system. These publications convey what these judicial decision-makers consider to be an adequate description of their work to a larger audience. They provide important insights into what judicial style can expected from the Appellate Body and how restrained or activist it is likely to be. At the same time, these statements illustrate how the individuals populating the Appellate Body seek to generate legitimacy by portraying what the Appellate Body did or does in a certain manner. The images of the Appellate Body they convey are remarkably similar.[343] In this section, I will summarize what is public knowledge about the Appellate Body's understanding of its own roles and tasks, as evident from extra-curial sources.

Generally, the Appellate Body is portrayed as deferring to the decisions of the WTO Members, i.e. the political branch of the WTO. For example, James Bacchus, a former Member of the Appellate Body from the US,

340 Steinberg 2004, 250f.

341 Maier 2017, 226f.

342 This account of the negotiations is given by Cartland, Depayre, and Woznowski 2012, 986.

343 They were also confirmed in interviews with other WTO officials, see the quotes in Shlomo-Agon 2015, 553.

states on the Appellate Body's decision to allow private counsels to represent WTO Members in dispute settlement proceedings:

> "Basically, we concluded that it was not for us to second-guess a member of the WTO on who that member wanted to include in its delegation in an Appellate Body proceeding. So we let in the lawyer." [344]

In a similar vein, James Bacchus also stresses that

> "Members of the Appellate Body leave the politics and the policy entirely to the Members of the WTO. That is not their job."[345]

In another instance he writes:

> "Some have suggested that the Appellate Body should interpret the text of the WTO treaty in a way that makes economic sense. But there are no such instructions from the Members of the WTO to the Appellate Body in the DSU. The Members of the Appellate Body are instructed by the Members of the WTO to assist them in their efforts to uphold the existing rules on which the Members of the WTO have agreed. The Members of the WTO – and not the Members of the Appellate Body – must decide whether those rules make economic sense. Some have suggested that the Appellate Body should embrace expediency by making pragmatic, 'political' decisions. […] It necessarily follows […] that the Appellate Body must never make political decisions, and I have never once heard even one national or other political consideration uttered by anyone in deliberations of the Appellate Body."[346]

Bacchus here projects an image of the Appellate Body as being, in all cases, loyal to the will of the WTO Members and being a faithful executioner of what the Members of the WTO wrote into the agreements, thus fulfilling the classical function of a judge as interpreting the law rather than making it. This is also evident from another quote:

> "Do the words used by the Appellate Body evidence a bias by the Appellate Body toward trade liberalization? Not at all. […] In their work for the Members of the WTO, the Members of the Appellate Body favor trade liberalization only to the extent that the words the Members of the WTO have chosen to put into the WTO treaty require trade lib-

344 Bacchus 2001, 957.
345 Bacchus 2004b, 19.
346 Bacchus 2005, 506.

> eralization. Here, too, the 'Appellators ' are true to the words of the treaty."[347]

Similarly, Mitsuo Matsuhita from Japan, writes that

> "Panels and the Appellate Body should not make their findings on the 'political' basis of whether it is a political view of a national constituency or an international community. They owe their allegiance only to WTO agreements which they are charged to interpret and apply."[348]

On the other hand, Bacchus also makes the following statement:

> "Is there, inevitably, an element of personal judgment that enters into the making of such decisions? Of course there is. This is so of the decision making of any deliberative body anywhere in the world, whether 'quasi-judicial' or otherwise. And the Members of the WTO certainly know and assume this. This is why they have required in the DSU that '[t]he Appellate Body shall comprise persons of recognized authority, with demonstrated expertise in law, international trade and the subject matter of the covered agreements generally'. The Members of the WTO have chosen the Members of the Appellate Body in part for their judgment, in the hope that, within the bounds of the DSU, they will use it."[349] [footnote omitted]

George Abi-Saab, a former Appellate Body Member of Egyptian descent who is also a former judge at the ICJ and the ICTY, describes the Appellate Body as having a "judicial policy" towards interpretation which is

> "strict constructionism, insisting heavily that we must remain very close to the text, even the words, of the agreements, and not add to or diminish from the rights and obligations of the contracting parties, or fill any gaps, et cetera [...]".

He voices a measure of dissatisfaction with this approach, when going on to say:

> "Moreover, because of this judicial policy, there is not much room for legal reasoning and theorizing. [...] There is usually one, sometimes two, international lawyers on the Appellate Body. But there is no general conviction that we should open up to general international law or

347 Ibid., 517.

348 Matsushita 2003, 203.

349 Bacchus 2005, 518.

> inject a Third World sensibility into our interpretation. […] If you act as a judge, you cannot tamper with rules. You have to interpret them within the permissible margin for interpretation. But as the Appellate Body has this restrictive judicial policy, it reduces even further that margin."[350]

The image of the Appellate Body as being faithfully devoted to executing the Members' will is closely linked to the portrayal of the Appellate Body as being governed by particularly high professional standards, in the words of Bacchus:

> "I have heard renowned, experienced advocates who have also appeared before many of the other notable international and other tribunals of the world say that no other tribunal in the world is as demanding, as exhausting, as inquisitive, or as downright persistent as the Appellate Body of the WTO in the pursuit of legal truth."[351]

The formulation "in the pursuit of legal truth" is remarkable, as it implies that there is indeed one legal truth that a court could – and the Appellate Body will – find. This implies a rejection of the ideas presented above, that there is often more than one way a legal question can be answered and that judges inevitably have a degree of freedom in deciding their cases. A statement such as the one of Bacchus can thus be interpreted as an attempt to lend the Appellate Body additional legitimacy by presenting it as a body that finds a "truth" that is already "in the law", rather than as an entity constructing one defensible "truth" among others. At the same time, others involved in the workings of the WTO appellate system have indicated that they do not consider WTO law to be a model of clarity and determinate language, which nonetheless the Appellate Body has to interpret.[352]

Bacchus also relates the following anecdote:

> "I recall in one of our early appeals in our very first year, Japan–Alcohol, someone saying around the table soon after the notice of appeal was filed, 'This is a chance for the Appellate Body to write the definitive treatise on the meaning of national treatment.' And I recall my close friend and colleague Julio Lacarte-Muro, the wise man that he is,

---

350 As cited by Terris, Romano, and Swigart 2007, 139f.

351 Bacchus 2004b, 16.

352 See the quotes by Julio Lacarte-Muró, a former Member of the Appellate Body, and Debra Steger, a former Director of the Appellate Body Secretariat, in Alvarez-Jiménez 2009a, 300f.

> saying very quickly in reply, 'No, this is our chance to address the legal issues raised in this one dispute.' This has always been the approach of the 'Appellators' to fulfilling their task, and this, I submit, is the very opposite of 'overreaching'."[353]

Again, here is the portrayal of a judicial entity that does what it has been mandated to do and resists the temptation of doing anything above and beyond it. However, not everyone is as careful. An anonymous Member of the Appellate Body is quoted as saying:

> "You cannot really fulfillf even the settlement of dispute function without having some leeway. There is, of course, a kind of an incremental development, but it is being kept to a minimum in order not to shock."[354]

While the quotes above present the WTO judicial decision-makers as having little (or no) choice of their own, this latter quote conveys that they do have a choice, a fact of which they are not only aware, but which they also use strategically.

Members of the Appellate Body have stressed that they are mindful of the difficult position of the WTO dispute settlement system within the wider WTO system. For example German Claus-Dieter Ehlermann writes that the

> "judge's job becomes much more delicate, if the political decision-making process is slow or – as in the case of the WTO – practically blocked."[355]

Furthermore he states:

> "The WTO is characterized by an imbalance between the strong (quasi-) judicial structure set up by the DSU and the weak political decision-making process which is all too often blocked, between major trade rounds, by the traditional consensus rule. [...] In view of the weakness of the political decision-making process, the responsibility of the AB is enormous. It must proceed with extraordinary circumspection and care. It is therefore advisable to pursue the cautious, case-spe-

353 Bacchus 2005, 508.
354 Terris, Romano, and Swigart 2007, 128.
355 Ehlermann 2002, 632.

> cific approach that the AB has adopted in motivating its findings and conclusions."[356]

Ehlermann also writes that Members of the Appellate Body wanted to contribute to the strength and authority of the new institution and were aware that they had to build the reputation and acceptability of the new institution and ensure its legitimacy from the scratch. He also states that Members of the Appellate Body had a common understanding of contributing to "building an independent (quasi)judicial institution".[357] Some Members of the Appellate Body have also expressed their regret about fact that the likelihood of political correction of WTO judicial decisions is so low, given that the Appellate Body Members are "human beings and [we] can always make mistakes."[358]

Moreover, it has also been observed that the Appellate Body has adopted – or at least been advised to adopt – a restrained approach to judicial decision-making. Steinberg indicates that senior officials of the WTO Secretariat have

> "met with and advised members of the Appellate Body to show restraint, when those officials perceived that the Appellate Body was leaning toward an activist stance".[359]

Bacchus writes that the Members of the Appellate Body

> "exercise a considerable measure of what I would describe – and what I believe almost any objective observer would also describe – as 'quasi-judicial' restraint".[360]

Overall, the image of the Appellate Body that emerges from these and other[361] (self)descriptions is that of a body which has adopted a philosophy of self-restraint as well as of faithful dedication to the wording of the law and the intentions of WTO Members. Conversely, there are also statements that convey a certain sense of hesitancy concerning this picture. For example, Abi-Saab observes that the

> "ambiguities in the language and the institutional procedures, as well as the common reference to the Appellate Body as a 'quasi-judicial' or-

356 Ibid., 606.
357 Ehlermann 2003a, 695ff.
358 As quoted by Terris, Romano, and Swigart 2007, 128.
359 Steinberg 2004, 266.
360 Bacchus 2003, 439.
361 Also see the quotes in Meagher 2020, 151ff.

gan, combine to maintain, be it subconsciously, the question about its legal nature, and have cast it from the outset into the [...] role of an organ in search of identity."[362]

In any case, as discussed in the preceding sections, what judges say they do is not necessarily congruent with what they actually do, whether consciously or unconsciously. Thus, the statements above do not need to be taken at face value; a reading of the dispute settlement decisions is still warranted. These statements are nonetheless important, since they corroborate the insight that judges are strategic actors that seek to decide cases in a way that is perceived as legitimate.

4.3. Characteristics of the WTO dispute settlement system relevant for style and outcome

This section discussed two characteristics of the WTO legal and political order that are likely to be relevant for both the style of the Appellate Body and the substance of decisions: first, the fact that the WTO dispute settlement system is, for a variety of reasons, a rather contested entity (4.3.1), and second, the mandate and some of the procedural rules applicable in WTO dispute settlement (4.3.2).

4.3.1. The dispute settlement system: a (relatively) new and contested mechanism

Courts care about the perceived legitimacy and acceptance of their decisions by relevant constituencies[363]; the Appellate Body is no exception, as revealed by the statements of former Appellate Body Members quoted in the last section. The adjudicators' desire that their decisions be perceived as legitimate and be accepted can be expected to influence both the judicial

362 Abi-Saab 2006, 454.

363 In the WTO context, relevant constituencies include in particular WTO Members, with their variety of institutions, NGOs, business communities, academics working on WTO-related matters, other international institutions and trade law practitioners. However, perceptions among, e.g. the wider public, are also relevant; see also Shany and Shlomo-Agon 2014, 193.

style of the WTO dispute settlement bodies and the substantive outcome of cases.[364]

As noted above, a court that has a tenuous and controversial position is likely to tread carefully in style and/or in substance. Moreover, as also discussed briefly above, the legitimacy of outcomes is also based, to a degree at least, on whether the law that a court decides on is perceived as legitimate.[365] Both insights are relevant for the WTO context: Right after its establishment, the WTO dispute settlement system had, at best, a tenuous legitimacy. Many observers were (and are) strongly critical of the idea of trade liberalization. They therefore took no particular liking to the WTO (an organization whose *raison d'être* is achieving this very goal) and consequently not to its dispute settlement system, either.[366] Others were less concerned about free trade than about the democratic legitimacy of the new organization.[367] Social movements and NGOs have tended to portray the WTO as a powerful actor, whose decisions have a strong impact on the lives of millions of people worldwide; this was true at least in the 1990ies, when the WTO was founded.[368] While it may be true that trade liberalization achieved through WTO rules has indeed a strong impact on the lives of people worldwide, the fact that it is not "the WTO" that produces these effects, but rather its Members, sovereign states, has sometimes got lost in a discursive fog. Observers close to the WTO have correctly pointed out that the WTO, i.e. the entity with a seat in Geneva, is not a powerful actor at all.[369] The WTO Members decide what happens at the WTO.[370] The WTO budget and staff number are minimal compared to those of the administration of any large developed country, amounting to about CHF 197

364 McCall Smith 2003, 75; Shlomo-Agon 2015, 541ff.

365 For the WTO, see specifically Broude 2004, 67.

366 See Esty 2002 for a description of different aspects of what he calls the WTO's "legitimacy crisis"; Shlomo-Agon 2015, 548ff.

367 See for example Beviglia Zampetti 2003; Magnuson 2010, 123f also observes that while all courts face problems when deciding cases that some consider to belong into the political realm, the Appellate Body's situation is particularly difficult as it has an "even more attenuated democratic pedigree" than national courts.

368 See for example Laura Carlson, A knife to the heart - the WTO kills farmers, 12 September 2003, https://www.counterpunch.org/2003/09/12/wto-kills-farmers/.

369 Bacchus 2004a, 668.

370 See for example for the WTO Committee on Trade and Environment (CTE), Shaffer 2001, 81f.

million and ca. 620 employees respectively in 2019.[371] They are also smaller than those of other international institutions dealing with trade and economic matters.[372]

The statement that the WTO has only limited powers of its own applies with only one major exception: the WTO dispute settlement system. Dispute settlement is, according to Art. III:3 WTOA[373], truly and originally a function of the WTO, although WTO Members, by selecting the disputes they bring before the WTO, decide to which extent it is used. The considerable powers of the WTO dispute settlement system are not counterbalanced by a comparably strong political branch[374] nor by similar international judicial heavyweights in other policy fields, e.g. environmental politics. This is the setting which gave raise to concerns about the decision-making and potential lack of restraint of the WTO dispute settlement bodies.[375] Indeed, Stein observes that the discourse on the democratic legitimacy deficit of the WTO "originated in the use of adjudicatory power of the organization".[376]

While several observers have commented on the initially (politically) precarious position of the Appellate Body,[377] Weiler has pointed out an additional, less obvious dimension of the fragile legitimacy of the WTO dispute settlement system. He argues that the Appellate Body also had (and maybe has) to come to terms with the expectations and views of trade officials in Geneva who were used to the former, more diplomatic *modus operandi*. While the dispute settlement bodies could not stray too far from the path of a proper court for their "external" observers, they could not be

371 See WTO, Annual Report 2020, https://www.wto.org/english/res_e/booksp_e/anrep_e/anrep20_e.pdf, 179ff.

372 Eeckhout 2010, 19.

373 See for a reading of this norm in particular Bogdandy 2001, 615.

374 See below section 4.4.1.

375 Barfield 2002, 8.

376 Stein 2001, 530; Broude 2004, 66 also acknowledges that the perception that the WTO dispute settlement system is powerful has been central to the debate about the legitimacy of the WTO. However, he maintains himself that the "possibility that the problems of legitimacy in the WTO stem from the substance and design of WTO law itself, and [...] from the malfunctioning political processes of the WTO [...] has not been sufficiently explored to date". An in-depth discussion of how the term legitimacy can be understood in the WTO context is provided by Kulovesi 2011, 28–53.

377 Garrett and McCall Smith 2002, 11; Howse 2016b, 24; McCall Smith 2003, 66.

too audacious and too far from the previous model for constituencies inside the WTO, either.[378]

While many question the legitimacy of the WTO and its dispute settlement system, others see the WTO, its law and its judicial function as "device that can alleviate democratic deficits in the post-national constellation"[379]. Their idea is that WTO law is an instrument that forces states to take into account the interests of those outside their borders that do not normally play a pivotal role in domestic decision-making processes. However, these voices do not seem to have gained the upper hand in the debate – those questioning the legitimacy of the WTO still seem to prevail.

In any event, legitimacy was and continues to be a major issue for the WTO dispute settlement system. This is true for other international courts, in particular newly established ones as well, but probably applicable to a larger extent for the WTO dispute settlement mechanism than for other international courts. In any event, the need for legitimacy is likely to influence WTO dispute settlement.

4.3.2. Mandate and procedural rules

The mandate and procedural rules governing the functioning of the WTO dispute settlement bodies are other factors that potentially influence the outcome and judicial style of WTO dispute settlement. Some aspects of how the mandate of a court and procedural rules that it must observe can influence outcomes have been summarized above:[380] For example, a rule stating that a court can only interpret certain provisions in a non-expansive manner is likely to lead to a different outcome than if no such rule existed. Such a rule at the same time influences certain aspects of the style of reasoning of a court, for example the methods of interpretation it uses.

One very important norm for WTO judicial decision-making is Art. 3.2 DSU. It defines the role of the WTO dispute settlement system and reads:

---

378 Weiler 2001. He also argues that the decision not to call the dispute settlement mechanism a court was taken to assuage fears of a powerful court among some actors within the WTO and some of its Members; however, not being called a court in turn weakens the broader, external legitimacy of the dispute settlement.

379 Bogdandy and Venzke 2012, 7; for a similar position see Joerges 2009, 75; Scott 2004a.

380 See above, section 2.3.

> The dispute settlement system of the WTO is a central element in providing security and predictability to the multilateral trading system. The Members recognize that it serves to preserve the rights and obligations of Members under the covered agreements, and to clarify the existing provisions of those agreements in accordance with customary rules of interpretation of public international law. Recommendations and rulings of the DSB cannot add to or diminish the rights and obligations provided in the covered agreements.

Art. 3.2 DSU states twice (!) that dispute settlement decisions are not to alter the substantive balance of rights and obligations enshrined in WTO law; this is mentioned again in a similar fashion in Art. 3.4 and 3.5 DSU and is repeated *verbatim* in Art. 19.2 DSU. The extraordinary emphasis put on this point through the various, rather unusual repetitions strongly indicates that the dispute settlement bodies are interpreters of the law, not law-makers, according to the concept underlying the DSU. One observer supposes that Art. 3.2 DSU was worded against the background of ECJ jurisprudence, constituting an attempt to prevent EU-style jurisprudential developments at the WTO level.[381] Goldberg and Steinberg indeed indicate that those involved in the negotiations of the DSU expected that Art. 3.2 and 19.2 DSU would prevent any law-making of the Appellate Body.[382]

As argued above, more often than not a court that wishes to avoid any appearance of judicial law-making is well advised to adopt a textualist, formalist approach towards interpretation. Thus, Art. 3.2 DSU could be read as requiring such an approach and judicial restraint.[383] In a similar vein, it could also be argued that providing "security and predictability" to the multilateral trading system can best be achieved by the method of interpreting the law that is closest to the text of the law. As the text of the law is written, parties to a dispute and the WTO membership at large can predict the outcome of a case more easily when the latter is based closely on the

381 Bogdandy 2001, 617.

382 Goldstein and Steinberg 2007, 19 quoting interviews with A. Jane Bradley, former chief US dispute settlement negotiator and Assistant USTR for Enforcement (March 2007) and with Kenneth Freiberg, USTR Deputy Gen. Counsel (March 2007) to this end.

383 This is indeed suggested by Guan 2014, 242f.

text as compared to relying on some unwritten points that the dispute settlement bodies deem to be relevant.[384]

Yet these are not necessarily very strong arguments justifying the expectation that the dispute settlement bodies would adopt a formalist style. In most cases brought before the dispute settlement bodies, it will be unclear what precisely the text of the law says; otherwise parties would be unlikely to bring a case and would rather amicably settle a case they might well lose. Thus, while the mandate given to the WTO dispute settlement bodies seems to make a textualist approach to interpretation the choice of the day, it is improbable that mere textualism will always produce conclusive results. Indeed, Art. 3.2 DSU also stipulates that WTO dispute settlement is to clarify the meaning of the agreements "in accordance with customary rules of interpretation of public international law". According to the ICJ, the customary rules of interpretation of international law are enshrined in Art. 31 VCLT.[385] Art. 31.1 VCLT, in turn, stipulates that a "treaty shall be interpreted in good faith in accordance with the ordinary meaning to be given to the terms of the treaty in their context and in the light of its object and purpose". Art. 32 VLCT furthermore allows, under certain conditions, the use of supplementary methods of interpretation, such as reliance on the preparatory work of a treaty.

For the WTO dispute settlement bodies, the reference to the customary rules of interpretation of public international law in Art. 3.2 DSU means that they can legitimately use at least these three methods of interpretation as well as the supplementary methods mentioned in the VLCT. Altogether, while Art. 3.2 DSU can be read to favour a textualist approach to interpretation, it does by no means mandate it.[386] It has been observed that WTO adjudicators enjoy a "significant zone of interpretive discretion"[387].

384 By contrast Weiss 2003 seems to argue that to provide security and predictability the WTO dispute settlement bodies need to apply methods of interpretation consistently, but it does not matter very much which methods are used.

385 ICJ, Territorial Dispute (Libyan Arab Jamahiriya v. Chad), Judgment of 3 February 1994, para. 41.

386 This view is also held by Steinberg 2004, 258; Mitchell 2007, 809; by contrast Kneubuehler 2001, 51 argues that the rules of the DSU prevent the WTO dispute settlement bodies from acting in a way similar to the ECJ and boldly advancing WTO 'integration', as they are bound to deploy a textualist approach.

387 Shell 1995, 904.

A second important provision, mainly for the judicial style of the dispute settlement bodies, is Art. 11 DSU. It reads:

> The function of panels is to assist the DSB in discharging its responsibilities under this Understanding and the covered agreements. Accordingly, a panel should make an objective assessment of the matter before it, including an objective assessment of the facts of the case and the applicability of and conformity with the relevant covered agreements, and make such other findings as will assist the DSB in making the recommendations or in giving the rulings provided for in the covered agreements. Panels should consult regularly with the parties to the dispute and give them adequate opportunity to develop a mutually satisfactory solution.

By its wording this provision only applies to Panels, since they are the only ones to produce an "assessment of the facts of the case"; the Appellate Body is limited to discussing matters of law. Art. 11 DSU sets forth, according to the Appellate Body[388], the standard of review, i.e. a yardstick for how intensively Panels are to review measures taken by WTO Members. The standard of review used in WTO dispute settlement has a significant bearing on what decision-making authority and power the WTO adjudicators have or assume as compared to WTO Members. For the style of the dispute settlement bodies, the most relevant part of this clause is that Panels are required to

> "make an objective assessment of the matter before it, including an objective assessment of the facts of the case and the applicability of and conformity with the relevant covered agreements".

The term "objective assessment" appears twice in this sentence. It is neither clear, however, what constitutes an "objective assessment" nor to what extent a requirement to engage in such an assessment imposes actual restriction on the WTO adjudicators. The opposite of an "objective" assessment of matters of fact and law would be a "subjective" one. Yet as argued above, making "subjective" assessments is very clearly not in line with the classical role description of judges. Against this background, Art. 11 DSU could be read to merely state the obvious; at most, it could be read as an attempt to prevent a too "activist" stance of the WTO adjudicators or judicial law-making. In other words, similar to Art. 3.2 DSU, Art. 11 DSU could be construed to be somewhat more compatible with a formalist ori-

388 See chapter 3, section 2.1.

entation of the WTO adjudicators than with a more normative, policy-oriented style. Still, a wide range of types of judicial reasoning seems ultimately compatible with the term "objective assessment". Art. 11 DSU does not present a real constraint on Panels and none on the Appellate Body (to which it does not apply).

In conclusion, Art. 3.2 and 11 DSU do not impose very strong constraints on the dispute settlement bodies, if any at all. While they do not mandate a restrained or formalist approach, they certainly allow the adjudicators to hold back and show sensitivity to concerns of WTO Members[389] and allow the use of different judicial styles[390].

A third point that is likely to be relevant mostly for the substantive outcome of cases is that the dispute settlement system is a two-stage system. It is a plausible assumption that Panels, like other lower instance courts, will seek to prevents their decisions from being modified or nullified by the Appellate Body, i.e. their decision will at least partially motivated by certain expectations on what the Appellate Body's position on a certain matter will be. The Appellate Body, in turn, has no remand authority; it cannot send a case back to a Panel. As a consequence the Appellate Body has to decide on claims brought before it to the extent necessary to resolve the dispute, provided there is a sufficient factual basis to do so.[391] Moreover, the Appellate Body is likely to ensure that Panels take into account its case law, by giving it some kind of precedential value.

A fourth point to note is that the WTO dispute settlement bodies do not pick their own cases: they must decide on the cases brought before them. According to Art. 3.7 DSU a WTO Member "shall exercise its judgement" as to whether bringing a dispute would be "fruitful". But there is no similar provision for the dispute settlement bodies; it is therefore at least questionable whether a Panel could decline hearing a case on the basis of this

389 Goh and Morgan 2007, 483.

390 Meagher 2020, 148f.

391 There is, however, a procedure, according to Art. 21.5 DSU, whereby WTO Members can ask the WTO dispute settlement bodies to review whether a measure adopted by another WTO Member in order to bring its measures into conformity with the recommendations of WTO dispute settlement body is in fact compliant with WTO law. The Art. 21.5 DSU proceedings in some cases fulfil a similar function to another round of revision by the initial Panel, allowing another full review of a measure on the basis of the Appellate Body's legal position. In at least one case, the Appellate Body actually recommended the DSB to request the parties of the initial dispute to make use of the Art. 21.5 course of action, see *United States – Continued Suspension of Obligations in the EC – Hormones Dispute, WT/DS320/AB/R* 2008, para. 737.

provision.[392] Moreover, Panels and the Appellate Body have no authority to suspend proceedings of their own motion, e.g. in order to wait for a decision by the political branch of the WTO.[393] WTO dispute settlement bodies are not to exercise their judgement on whether or not to decide a case, e.g. because it might be too political.[394] Moreover, the adjudicators cannot refuse to address the legal issues that need to be decided upon to settle the case, either[395] – even though they do not necessarily need to decide on all the issues the parties raise.[396]

Once the DSB establishes a Panel and unless the parties notify a mutually agreed solution during the judicial procedures, a Panel has few choices but rendering a report. The situation is similar for the Appellate Body. In sum, the WTO dispute settlement system has an "effectively compulsory jurisdiction"[397] under the DSU rules: the defending Member does not need to agree to dispute settlement proceedings being initiated, a demonstration of legal interest is no pre-condition for bringing a case, and there is no rule on the exhaustion of local remedies, either.[398] Consequently, the WTO judicial decision-makers cannot "dodge" sensitive issues, or at least not all of them.[399] Instead, they will have to find ways to come to terms with sensitive issues, in terms of substance and in terms of legitimizing their decisions.[400] The fact a WTO complaint goes forward quasi-automatically is rather unique among international legal institutions; many other international tribunals have a built-in mechanism for resolving jurisdic-

---

392 Bartels 2004, 886 seems to hold the view that based on the text of the provision, a Panel might have the power to reject hearing a case; however, he also notes that the Appellate Body rejected this option in one of its decisions.

393 Ibid., 891ff.

394 Ehlermann 2002, 632; McCall Smith 2003, 77; Reusch 2007, 264–267.

395 Bacchus 2005, 507.

396 For national higher courts see Summers and Taruffo 1991, 489ff; for the ECJ Poiares Maduro 1998, 19.

397 Lovric 2010, 36.

398 Ibid., 36ff.

399 This does not mean that issues of standing and justiciability have never been at issue in the WTO judicial setting; indeed there have been a few cases, in which the adjudicators needed to decide on such matters. An example was the *EC – Bananas* case where one issue was whether the US, not producing any bananas on its territory, could actually bring a claim relating to trade in bananas, see for an overview of this and later cases Bhala 1999b, 61. However, these cases have been infrequent. In the Bananas case, the Appellate Body indeed decided that WTO Members had a significant degree of discretion on which cases to bring.

400 McCall Smith 2003, 79.

tional issues before the main proceedings.[401] Similarly, higher courts at the national level often have some type of discretion concerning the selection of cases they want to decide on merits

Finally, the Appellate Body is a standing body, with its Members serving for periods of several years. This gives it the opportunity to develop a proper "jurisprudence", a body of law that is consistent across cases.[402] At the same time, the fact that candidates for the Appellate Body need to be nominated by their home state and then be accepted by all Members means that, once elected, they have a high degree of accountability to all WTO Members.[403]

4.4. Additional factors relevant for the substantive outcome of WTO cases

Two factors that could influence the outcome of cases have been discussed above – first, the situation of the dispute settlement system as a new and controversial entity and, second, its mandate and some important procedural rules. In this section, I will turn to additional factors that have been identified as potentially influencing the substantive content of judicial decisions and discuss whether they are present in the context of the WTO. Two main approaches were identified above: one that focuses on the strategic agency of courts (section 4.4.1) and a second one that focuses on how individual judges' preferences, attitudes and ideas unconsciously or deliberately influence the outcome of a case (section 4.4.2).

4.4.1. Maintaining and expanding judicial power

One factor that has been shown to influence the content of judicial decisions is a court's desire to maintain or expand its power. Courts have been demonstrated to act in a manner that avoids negative consequences when policy-makers dislike too many of their decisions; such consequences could consist in a court's decision being reverted through a legislative one as well as a court's wings being clipped permanently through changes in its mandate or procedural rules or the withholding of funding. It has been

401 Howse and Essermann 2006, 63, referring to ITLOS, the ICJ and investor-state arbitration under ICSID and UNCITRAL rules.

402 Ibid., 64.

403 Dunoff and Pollack 2017, 11.

argued that the WTO dispute settlement decisions can also be understood in these terms.[404]

There are various authors who have looked at if and how the dispute settlement bodies position themselves vis-à-vis anticipated preferences of WTO Members.[405] Kelemen has undertaken a study in which he relates the outcome of certain trade and environment cases decided by the ECJ and the WTO dispute settlement bodies to both the degree of legal indeterminacy and public opinion in these cases. He finds that where legal indeterminacy is relatively pronounced, and the political threat posed by the potential defiance of a state or a group of states towards a certain outcome is great, the judicial bodies are likely to yield to the political pressure.[406] In other words, political and legal constraints correlate with the substantive decisions of the WTO dispute settlement bodies and the ECJ in trade-environment disputes. However, the analysis is based on a limited number of cases. Similarly, Garrett and McCall Smith hypothesize that the WTO dispute settlement bodies would not want to take decisions not supported by the US, Japan or the EU. They argue that there is evidence, again based on the analysis of a limited number of cases, that at least partially supports the hypothesis that when the defendant in a certain case is a powerful state, the dispute settlement bodies are more likely to rule in favour of the defendant than in other cases.[407] Steinberg also argues that the interests of powerful WTO Members, notably the US and the EU, are likely to influence the outcome of judicial decisions, but does not test this assumption empirically.[408] Stone Sweet and Brunell find that the Appellate Body follows a strategy of "majoritarian activism". By this, they mean a

> "disposition of judges to produce rulings that reflect outcomes that states might adopt under majoritarian, but not unanimity, decision rule".[409]

---

404 However, this not the only approach to explaining the outcomes of WTO dispute settlement procedures with reference to example factors. For example Maton and Maton 2007, 333 observe that the only factor that influences the outcome of a judicial decision in favour of the complaint is the respective complainants' expertise in WTO dispute settlement, as evident from prior cases.

405 For an overview of the corresponding research on the outcome of GATT Panel decisions, see Busch and Reinhardt 2002, 475f.

406 Kelemen 2001.

407 Garrett and McCall Smith 2002, 44f.

408 Steinberg 2004.

409 Sweet and Brunell 2013, 63f.

They find that the Appellate Body seeks to identify consensus among WTO Members on the legal issues at hand (e.g. by looking at relevant state practice outside the WTO) and then orients its decision along these lines. At the same time, the authors also conclude that the Appellate Body engages in such a strategy less often than other courts such as the ECJ and the ECtHR; they relate this to the different mandate of the WTO.[410] A similar account is provided by Knox, who argues that the Appellate Body has devised strategies to find out where areas of consensus between WTO Members may lie and has maximized political support for its decisions through this strategy.[411] He argues that the Appellate Body's "incorporation of moderate environmental proposals" into its jurisprudence stems from a desire to win support for its decisions from the WTO Membership.[412] Another scholar, Krüger, states the following:

> "For a litigant to be successful, a certain degree of convergence between its own preferences and those of the Appellate Body is thus helpful, if not needed: in its efforts to strengthen its own position and that of the WTO in general, while similarly avoiding political opposition and noncompliance, the Appellate Body will leave its generally conservative stance towards interpretation and activism only in the wake of a certain degree of member state support."[413]

Krüger considers the adjudicators to be aware of constraints posed by possible counter-measures from WTO Members.[414] Moreover, he observes that the Appellate Body usually shows its creativity in procedural matters and is responsive to political pressures in highly sensitive cases, in particular where compromises between trade and non-trade objectives are involved. He furthermore concludes that the Appellate Body

> "departs from its textual approach only in certain cases, more readily on procedural issues and more easily if it sees a backing for its approach by one or more member states."[415]

Other authors share the basic assumption that the adjudicators behave strategically, but have not investigated the matter empirically or in-depth.

---

410 Ibid., 85.
411 Knox 2004, 2, 47ff; he does not make any comparative statement on other courts, though.
412 Ibid., 3, 47ff.
413 Krüger 2013, 57.
414 Ibid., 56.
415 Ibid., 101.

The WTO dispute settlement bodies, and in particular the Appellate Body, are conceived of as strategic actors concerned with preserving their legitimacy, influence and reputation.[416] They are described as seeking to maintain and expand their role in resolving international trade disputes as well as to ensure that WTO Members, including those losing a case[417], respect and comply with their decisions.[418] In this context, the Appellate Body has been described as "an agent of the membership, not a principal".[419] Moreover, WTO dispute settlement has also been discussed in the context of legitimizing the WTO regime more broadly.[420]

In existing research three main "dangers" for the WTO dispute settlement system have been identified that the adjudicators may seek to preempt.[421] First, a risk of modification of either WTO substantive rules or the rules of the DSU, second a risk of non-compliance with decisions that parties do not like (in the worst case with approval or support from other WTO Members) and, third, a risk of boycott, i.e. non-use of the dispute settlement system.[422] The last category includes the risk of a permanent withdrawal of Members from the jurisdiction of the WTO. In addition, it has also been suggested that the (re)-appointment of Appellate Body Members by the DSB and the selection of Panelists by the WTO Secretariat and the Parties to a dispute are mechanisms for controlling the adjudicators' behaviour.[423] Conversely, some of the external pressure factors that have been found to play a role for other courts are not relevant for the WTO dispute settlement bodies. For example, the WTO dispute settlement bodies do no need to seek to ensure the continued support of states in enforcement or collecting evidence, different from the ICC.[424]

I will first take first a look at the risk of political overturn of either substantive WTO rules or the DSU in response to dissatisfaction among WTO Members, in particular powerful ones, with the Appellate Body's decision-making in general or in a concrete case. The risk of WTO judicial decisions being overturned or the dispute settlement bodies' powers being permanently curtailed by WTO Members through a change in the DSU appears

416 See for example Shaffer 2009, 33.

417 Schmid 2001, 19.

418 Ginsburg 2006; Pauwelyn and Elsig 2012.

419 Hoekman 2016, 1085.

420 Foltea 2012, 26ff; Shany and Shlomo-Agon 2014, 193.

421 For an overview see Krüger 2013, 13ff.

422 Garrett and McCall Smith 2002, 3; McCall Smith 2003, 75; Steinberg 2004, 249.

423 Elsig and Pollack 2012; Steinberg 2004, 249.

424 See above section 2.1 for Wessel's study on the ICC.

to be weak. Changing specific rules in any of the WTO agreements, either the substantive agreements or the DSU, in response to a specific judicial decision is not impossible, but faced with high political hurdles.[425] Art. IX.1 WTOA states that "[t]he WTO shall continue the practice of decision-making by consensus followed under GATT 1947"; only "where a decision cannot be arrived at by consensus, the matter at issue shall be decided by voting", unless otherwise provided. Decision-making by consensus is the practice that the WTO has mostly followed.[426] Formally, Art. X WTOA contains a scale of finely tuned majorities required for changing specific rules in WTO agreements. Changes to the more fundamental norms require acceptance by all Members, or at least the consent of those Members for whom the amendment is to take effect. Others can be changed with the support a two-third majority, with effect for all WTO Members. While the Ministerial Conference and the General Council can, according to Art. IX.2 WTOA, adopt authoritative interpretations of the WTO agreements by a three-quarters majority, notwithstanding any interpretations given by a Panel or the Appellate Body, such an authoritative interpretation has never been agreed on and doing so has been described as practically impossible[427]. Finally, WTO Members also have the possibility to express disagreement with a dispute settlement decision during sessions of the DSB according to Art. 16.2 DSU (Panel reports) and 17.14 DSU (Appellate Body reports); such comments go on record in the minutes of the respective DSB session according to Art. 16.3 DSU. This is a different situation than exists for other international courts where states are "legally or ethically restrained" from criticizing rulings.[428] Nonetheless, the mere possibility of expressing a view on a judicial decision is not a very powerful tool. The WTO adjudicators are not forced to take such views into account; views are also like to differ among WTO Members. Altogether, the WTO is characterized by an imbalance between a strong judicial branch and a weak political one,[429] if not on paper, then at least in practice.[430]

Briefly, it should also be noted that there is no serious risk of WTO Members withdrawing funding for the WTO dispute settlement system,

425 For a detailed discussion of the different rules see Ehlermann and Ehring 2005.
426 See Bartels 2004, 865 for a few exceptions from the consensus practice.
427 Du 2011, 649.
428 Broude 2004, 197.
429 Conti 2011; Bogdandy 2001; Ehlermann 2002, 606.
430 The point that the strength of the WTO's judicial mechanism is rather a matter of how things work in practice than of rules on paper is stressed in particular by Broude 2004, 277ff.

thus undermining its functioning through imposing financial constraints. The funding for the dispute settlement system is part of the general WTO budget. That budget is, in turn, fuelled by contributions that all WTO Members need to make according to Art. VII WTOA. Contributions are based on a country's share in world trade or a set minimum contribution if the trade share is minimal.[431] Altogether the WTO dispute settlement bodies are less vulnerable than other judicial entities in this regard.[432]

Second, there is the risk of non-compliance of WTO Members with dispute settlement decisions that they do not like. Frequent non-compliance would likely undermine the authority and credibility of the WTO dispute settlement system and ultimately weaken it. There are several theories on why states comply with international generally, and with WTO law more specifically. The first is that states comply, because they are coerced to do so, the second is that they comply if and when compliance is in their interest, and the third is that states comply out of a sense of obligations with norms they consider legitimate.[433]

When considering the relative importance of these factors in the WTO context, an important point to note is that WTO Members are legally bound by dispute settlement decisions adopted by the DSB, according to a wide-spread view also held by the Appellate Body.[434] According to Art. 17.14 DSU, the non-adoption of a dispute settlement report by the

---

431 Member's contributions are listed in the WTO's Annual Reports, see for example WTO Annual Report 2020, https://www.wto.org/english/res_e/booksp_e/anrep_e/anrep20_e.pdf, p. 180 for the 2019 contributions.

432 Ginsburg 2006, 53f compares the judicial discretion that the ECJ, the ICJ, NAFTA dispute settlement bodies, ad hoc tribunals and the WTO dispute settlement bodies have. Based on an analysis of the possibility of certain counter-measures by members, he concludes that only the ECJ and the WTO dispute settlement bodies have very high discretion. Benvenisti and Downs 2012, 113f also conclude that the ICJ is not quite as independent at least as far as the five permanent members of the Security Council are concerned, and would be hesitant to go against the joint interests of all five of them, even though not being as reluctant when going against only of them; see also Garrett and McCall Smith 2002, 10. By contrast Bogdandy and Venzke 2012, 22 seem to hold the view that the risk of legislative overturn is small in equal measure for any international court.

433 For an overview of the different theories, see Broude 2004, 67ff; Shany and Shlomo-Agon 2014, 205 stress the role of legitimacy in inducing compliance.

434 For an overview of the discussion on whether WTO judicial decisions are legally binding, see Shany and Shlomo-Agon 2014, 209f. Two authors holding that the judicial decisions are legally binding are Reusch 2007, 122; McBride 2001, 652.

DSB requires consensus[435], including the agreement of the winning party, and is hence unlikely.[436]

Generally, the existence of an international legal obligation does not necessarily equal state compliance with that legal obligation. Yet, different from other judicial or quasi-judicial mechanisms at the international level, the WTO dispute settlement system includes an option that, while not amounting to a full-fledged enforcement mechanism, fosters compliance. The DSU contains procedures for determining a time frame for compliance of the losing Member with the dispute settlement decision (Art. 21.3 and 21.4 DSU) as well as procedures for monitoring and reviewing compliance (Art. 21.5 and 21.6 DSU). More importantly, the DSB can authorize the winning party to suspend the application of concessions or other obligations vis-à-vis the losing party (Art. 22 DSU). Under these circumstances, coercion is likely to have a comparatively larger role in inducing Members' compliance with judicial decisions than in other judicial settings. Still, it cannot be ruled out that the other two factors – the interest of countries involved and a sense of obligation to comply with a legitimate judicial decision – play a role as well. All in all, it seems that the threat of non-compliance is not as powerful a threat in the WTO judicial setting as in the case of other international tribunals.[437] Nonetheless, the adjudicators may want to enhance the chances for compliance by deciding in a way they anticipate the parties to find appropriate.

Third, there is the risk of the WTO dispute settlement system being boycotted, or in a more benign version, being used less.[438] This is an important factor for international judicial bodies in general – and there is no rea-

---

435 Flett 2011, 36 indicates that a way for a defendant Member to prevent the adoption from happening would be to block the adoption of the agenda of the meeting where the respective judicial decision is to be adopted. Adopting the meeting agenda also requires consensus. Flett indicates that this has once happened, at least temporarily, but considers this practice illegal himself.

436 One author that does not seem to consider the possibility of a non-adoption of a dispute settlement report entirely unrealistic is Broude 2004, 192f.

437 Howse 2016b, 30 concludes, however, that "non-compliance with its purported binding rulings poses a greater risk on balance to the Appellate Body's legitimacy than perceptions that it is overly deferential".

438 There are obviously different reasons for why a court might get used less. Apart from the factors discussed here, a very basic factor is whether there are real-world conflicts a court needs to solve. If there are no or fewer such conflicts resulting in fewer judicial cases, judges might consider this a favourable development, because it could mean that a certain legal system functions well and smoothly. So if a court is used less at a certain stage of its existence, this is not

son why the WTO judicial system should be an exception. Still, the degree to which WTO Members are satisfied with the Appellate Body's performance is unlikely to be the only factor determining a WTO Member's decision to bring a claim – and it can be assumed that the judicial decision-makers are aware of this situation. Research on the circumstances under which countries are likely or unlikely to initiate WTO disputes has identified the following factors inhibiting the initiation of a specific trade dispute: inadequate capacity for trade retaliation, inability to cover the legal costs associated with WTO proceedings, the reliance on bilateral assistance from the opponent country, and the existence of preferential trade agreements with the respondent country.[439] The lack of capacity to launch effective legal cases is also a factor that prevents developing countries, in particular, from using the WTO dispute settlement system more often.[440] Further factors identified as influencing the decision to pursue a WTO dispute settlement claim are the legal merits of a case, economic stakes, the effectiveness of enforcement, political credit to be gained from domestic constituencies by initiating proceedings, and who is the opponent.[441] An observer with an inside perspective of the functioning of the WTO dispute settlement system maintains that whether a dispute proceeds to the stage of appellate review is frequently mainly linked to domestic political constraints:

> "[...] often cases do not come to litigation because both parties are convinced of the correctness of their positions, but rather because an internal domestic rigidity demands adjudication before ceding"[442].

Altogether, the extent to which WTO Members are likely to use the system in the future, as a result of WTO judicial decisions, can be assumed to be a relevant factor to WTO adjudicators. At the same time, whether or not a case enters the WTO dispute settlement system does not only, and proba-

always a development that the individuals populating it may seek to avoid. However, in the case of the WTO, with a still increasing number of Members, globalization and statistically increasing levels of international trade (see chapter 4, note 2645), the scenario that there will be less trade-related conflicts in the near or longer- term future appears unlikely.

439 Bown 2005, 308.

440 Guzman and Simmons 2005.

441 Busch and Reinhardt 2002, 475ff.

442 Flett 2010, 319. Flett is a staff member of the European Commission Legal Service, WTO Team, and indicates that he frequently represents the European Union in WTO dispute settlement cases.

bly not even predominantly, depend on the satisfaction of WTO Members with the system.

In this context, it should be noted that it would be very difficult and costly for WTO Members to permanently "escape" the authority of the WTO dispute settlement mechanism. The only way for a WTO Member to do so would be to exit the WTO, given that the DSU is an integral part of the WTO. While some states have withdrawn their consent to compulsory jurisdiction of the ICJ as a result of decisions they disliked,[443] a WTO Member leaving the WTO is so unlikely an event to appear almost as a fictive scenario. Huge economic and political costs would be involved in such a WTO withdrawal. These high costs of "exit" also enhance the independence of the WTO's judicial bodies.[444]

Finally, the appointment of Members of the Appellate Body is another avenue through which WTO Members can try to influence the decision-making of the Appellate Body.[445] According to 17.2 DSU Members of the Appellate Body are appointed by the DSB; according to Art. 2.4 DSU the DSB decides by consensus. This gives individual WTO Members considerable influence over the appointment of specific candidates, but also the appointment process in general, i.e. the possibility of rejecting any kind of re-appointment. The latter can effectively stop the Appellate Body from functioning, once the term of office of existing Members runs out. Candidates, at least in more recent years, undergo quite intensive scrutiny before being nominated by Members;[446] after their nomination, there is another round of screening within the various WTO committees.[447] The candidate's approach to judicial decision-making apparently plays a role in countries' decisions to support him or her.[448] Candidates have been questioned by WTO Members about their attitude to issues of gap-filling, the role of international law in WTO interpretation, dissenting opinions, judicial activism, and DSU reform, among other topics.[449] There are usually more candidates than places available.

Once a Member of the Appellate Body has been appointed, the influence of WTO Members over that person is quite limited. While parties to a dispute must agree to a specific Panelist deciding their dispute, they have

443 See Posner and de Figueiredo 2005, 604.
444 See Benvenisti and Downs 2012, 120.
445 See for example Broude 2004, 166.
446 See Elsig and Pollack 2012.
447 Krüger 2013, 12.
448 Steinberg 2004, 249.
449 See Elsig and Pollack 2012, 15ff.

no influence on the selection of the Members of the Appellate Body. Thus, the latter are closer to an ideal of judicial independence than Panelists.[450] The only tool that WTO Members have to "discipline" an individual Appellate Body Member is a refusal to re-appoint him or her for a second four-year term of office. Whether the threat of not being re-appointed is indeed powerful enough to prompt individual Members of the Appellate Body to decide in line with powerful WTO Members' expectations or whether an ethos of judicial independence is stronger, is not clear. Until present, only one case has been identified in the literature, in which an Appellate Body Member is said to have acted in line with the expectations of the WTO Members nominating her.[451] Generally, given that Appellate Body Members are appointed by consensus, even powerful states can only exercise, through appointment politics, a modest degree of influence over the Appellate Body's individual decisions or general direction.[452] Moreover, there is also evidence that the nominees themselves act strategically in providing evidence to the WTO Members on the preferences that the latter inquire about.[453] This is another reason why the influence of WTO Members over Members of the Appellate Body is ultimately limited. Finally, neither the DSU nor the Appellate Body's self-given procedural rules contain provisions for the removal of an Appellate Body Member during his or her term of office.[454] It is unclear, whether and by which procedures WTO Members could remove a serving Member of the Appellate Body against his/her will.[455]

All in all, it seems that the risk of various forms of political backlash from WTO Members is relatively limited in the case of the WTO dispute settlement mechanism. One exception is, however, the appointment process for Appellate Body Members, since individual WTO Members have the power to block appointments. Commentators have stated that the Appellate Body has a high degree of autonomy vis-à-vis the preferences of

---

450 See Ehlermann 2003b, 1507.

451 See Elsig and Pollack 2012, 19.

452 Ibid., 9.

453 Ibid., 20.

454 By contrast, the "Working Procedures for Appellate Review" cover the voluntary resignation or incapacity of an Appellate Body Member, see rules no. 12–15.

455 Broude 2004, 167 identifies the following possibilities: There could be simply no possibility to legally remove an Appellate Body Member, or the DSB, or the WTO General Council could remove him/her.

WTO Members[456] and formulated an expectation that the WTO dispute settlement bodies, and the Appellate Body in particular, will be considerably less constrained in their decision-making than the contemporary ECJ is[457]. They have, however, also pointed to some constraints[458]. However, it is not *ex ante* clear what this means.[459] As discussed in greater detail below in section 4.6, it could either lead the WTO adjudicators to adopt a posture of restraint or to seek to actively "form" WTO law.

4.4.2. Judges' legal or non-legal preferences

Existing research also identifies judges' legal or non-legal preferences[460] as a factor influencing the outcome of judicial cases. For the WTO, it has been observed that judicial actors come

> "with professional concerns, with shared and sometimes contested meanings about the law, and both practical and normative ideas about the operations and role of the WTO in world affairs"[461].

This section therefore briefly discusses if and how theories on how judges' individual preferences, stereotypes, or opinions influence the outcome of a case apply in the WTO context as well.

As explained above[462], individual factors generally tend to be more important in a national context, where judges have to decide about the rights, obligations and behaviour of individuals, rather than on states' rights and obligations. The views of judges on whether the free trade rules of the WTO should be given the broadest possible or narrowest scope of application, or anything in between, could, however, matter in the WTO context.

Another aspect that has been shown to be of some relevance in the international judicial context is the inclination of judges to rule in favour of the

456 Krüger 2013, 12.

457 Garrett and McCall Smith 2002, 4.

458 Shany and Shlomo-Agon 2014, 205.

459 For a similar statement applying to international courts more broadly, see Bogdandy and Venzke 2012, 24.

460 Obviously, in this section preferences other than the wish to extend and maintain judicial power, which was the topic of the previous section, are discussed.

461 Conti 2011, 14; see also Colares 2009, 422. Costa 2011 compares the background of Panelists and Appellate Body Members to those of ICSID arbitrators, based on the idea that who a judge is may influence what he decides.

462 See above, section 2.2.

interests of the states whose nationality they have. In the WTO realm, this factor cannot play a role in the case of Panels; according to Art. 8.3 DSU Panelists are barred from deciding a dispute involving a country whose nationality they have. Yet no similar prohibition exists for Members of the Appellate Body; they have indeed frequently decided on cases involving their home country.[463] While no comprehensive statistical analysis on the matter seems to exist, anecdotal evidence suggests that the nationality of an Appellate Body Member is unlikely to play a major role for outcomes. For example, the EU lost the *Hormones I* case, a major case surrounded by an intensive public debate; the division of the Appellate Body deciding the case was comprised of Florentino Feliciano (Philippines), Claus-Dieter Ehlermann (Germany) and Mitsuo Matsuhita (Japan). None of the judges deciding the case had the nationality of the (successful) complaining parties while one had the "quasi-nationality" of the EU, the defendant and losing party. It has also been observed that in the first ten years of WTO dispute settlement, no defeated party ever accused an Appellate Body Member of a national bias.[464] Cottier, who served as a Panelist in WTO cases, also relates his personal experience that none of his co-Panelists "defended interests apparently and closely related to their constituencies"[465]. Other statements in the literature also corroborate that the WTO adjudicators are not guided by national bias.[466]

Yet the nationality of the judges may matter in a different respect. Pauwelyn observes that certain features of WTO dispute settlement are to some extent a result of US influence; he speculates that one way how this influence materializes is through the predominance of US-educated lawyers working in the Secretariat of the WTO and pleading in WTO dispute settlement proceedings.[467] However, this is of less relevance for the

463 McCall Smith 2003, 82 calculates that one Member of the division making the decision had the nationality of the defendant state in 54 % of all cases decided by the Appellate Body in the time period from 1995 until July 2002.

464 Howse and Essermann 2006, 62; for a similar observation see Krüger 2013; Hughes 2009, 281. Lacarte-Muró, a former Member of the Appellate Body, even claims that that "there was never any doubt in anybody's mind that there was anything but complete impartiality on the part of the member of the Appellate Body" when deciding a case where their home country was involved, even in high profile cases - see the statement in Taniguchi et al. 2008, 392.

465 Cottier 1998, 348.

466 See Shany and Shlomo-Agon 2014, 203 with further references.

467 Pauwelyn 2003d, 121; Bhala 1999b, 9 makes a similar observation for the use of precedents in WTO dispute settlement.

present context as it is unlikely to influence the substantive outcome of cases.

Finally, general preferences of the Appellate Body Members on judicial decision-making may matter. Indeed, this seems to be a factor of certain importance for some WTO Members when Appellate Body Members are appointed: Steinberg relates that the Office of the US Trade Representative (USTR)

> "carefully vet[s] each candidate, reading his or her past work and judicial decisions (if any), and interviewing each in Washington or Geneva, prior to deciding whether to endorse the candidacy. In recent years, these interviews have focused on the candidate's qualifications and approach to judicial decision making, without raising any legal issues that are concurrently or prospectively at any stage of the dispute settlement process". [468]

Only a few Appellate Body Members held any judicial offices prior to their WTO appointment, however.[469] Others also maintain that it matters whether the Members of the Appellate Body are "WTO-insiders", who were involved e.g. in the Uruguay Round negotiations, or lawyers specialized in other areas of law (e.g. international law more broadly).[470] Generally, the Appellate Body Members' ideas on judicial decision-making are not public knowledge and may ultimately be more important for the style of judicial decision-making than its substance. Consequently it is, in the context of the present work, not possible, but maybe also unnecessary, to formulate any *ex ante* expectations in this regard.

The fact that WTO dispute settlement decisions are always taken jointly by a group of judges[471] reduces the risk of the preferences of an individual judge influencing the outcome. What is even more, Rule 3.2 of the Working Procedures sets forth that the

---

468 Steinberg 2004, 264.

469 See the short bios of Appellate Body Members at http://www.wto.org/english/tratop_e/dispu_e/ab_members_bio_e.htm.

470 Krüger 2013, 97; more generally Meagher 2020, 142.

471 Panels have three members; the Appellate Body has seven permanent Members of whom three decide any given dispute. These three Members, however, exchange views with the other Members of the Appellate Body before making a decision, see Appellate Body Members, http://www.wto.org/english/tratop_e/dispu_e/ab_members_descrp_e.htm. For a more in-depth description of the internal decision-making processes of the Appellate Body see Alvarez-Jiménez 2009a, and Matsushita 2005a, who is a former Member of the Appellate Body.

> "Appellate Body and its divisions shall make every effort to take their decisions by consensus. Where, nevertheless, a decision cannot be arrived at by consensus, the matter at issue shall be decided by a majority vote."

The Working Procedures, including this consensus rule, were adopted by the Appellate Body itself and modified various times.[472] Thus, WTO Members cannot directly influence the Working Procedures.

In conclusion, it can be expected that non-legal preferences of individual judicial decision-makers at the WTO play, at most, a limited role for the substantive outcome of cases. In any case, in what direction such preferences are likely to influence decisions cannot be stated with any reasonable degree of certainty *ex ante*.

4.5. Additional factors relevant for the style of the Appellate Body

Above, I have discussed several factors likely to influence the judicial style of the WTO dispute settlement bodies – the mandate given to them, the degree to which the adjudicators anticipate that a certain decision would be perceived as legitimate, the degree of indeterminacy of WTO law, and procedural rules. Adding to this, I will now go back to the additional characteristics of judicial entities that Lasser has shown to influence the style of the respective entity[473] as well as factors discussed by other authors[474].

The main factors identified by Lasser were the degree to which other actors within the legal system (e.g. the Advocate General in the EU) take over certain functions in explaining the reasons behind judges' decisions, the role that individual decisions have within the wider legal system, and the degree to which judges are a relatively homogenous, professional and rigorously selected elite.

First, the WTO dispute settlement system has no strong institutional control mechanisms to ensure that judges are a hand-picked elite with a unified educational and professional background – one of the mechanisms that Lasser considers to be behind the formalist style of the French *Court de Cassation*. Quite to the contrary, Appellate Body Members all come from different countries, in line with the requirement of Art. 17.3 DSU

---

472 For an overview of the changes see Appellate Procedures, http://www.wto.org/english/tratop_e/dispu_e/ab_procedures_e.htm.

473 See above section 3.2.

474 See above section 3.3.

that the "Appellate Body membership shall be broadly representative of membership in the WTO".[475] The WTO judicial decision-makers do not come from the same legal tradition and have not gone through the same (prestigious) legal education. WTO judicial decision-makers cannot rely on any pre-existing authority they have *qua* their position and professional status in the eyes of observers, but need to give good reasons for their decisions in the dispute settlement reports.

Second, the burden of giving reasons for a judgement and legitimizing it cannot be outsourced to other actors in the judicial realm in the WTO context. Neither is there a figure comparable to the Advocate General in the ECJ setting, nor does some of the justification and explanation of judgements come in the form of more or less authoritative comments on the judgements such as in the French tradition; at least there was no such tradition for the Appellate Body to build on right after its establishment. Altogether institutional sources of authority appear weak in the case of the WTO. Thus, the dispute settlement reports themselves need to justify and legitimize any specific decision.

Despite the weight that individual WTO judgements carry in terms of justification, there is no formal *stare decisis* rule in the WTO context.[476] There is an inherent logic to this: If a judicial body is explicitly not to "make law" according to is mandate and the WTO dispute settlement bodies must not change the rights and obligations of WTO Members, individual judgements cannot have the same weight as in a precedent-based system where judgements basically are the law.

Most of the other factors potentially influencing judicial styles that I have discussed above appear not be relevant in the WTO context or not within the framework of research of this work. For example, it is quite possible that the WTO's judicial style will vary over time or depend on the type of case under judicial review. However, the methodology of this work[477] does not allow analysing such changes.

One of the above factors that could be relevant is that (national) policy-makers are an important audience for the WTO dispute settlement bodies; this tends to make a judicial style more likely that can also be understand by policy-makers without a background in law more likely. Moreover, the fact that the WTO dispute settlement system is a permanent one, with the express task of creating predictability for WTO Members, could also influ-

---

475 On the background of Appellate Body Members see Meagher 2020, 156ff.

476 See chapter 3, section 3.1.

477 See below section 3.2.

ence the WTO's judicial style in at least some respects. For example, as a permanent judicial body, the Appellate Body is likely to seek to avoid (manifestly) contradicting itself and thus give its own prior decision some kind of precedential value, even without a formal *stare decisis* rule.

4.6. Conclusion: hypotheses

What do these observations mean in terms of the judicial style of the WTO dispute settlement bodies and the likely outcome of judicial cases?

First of all and most fundamentally, it is reasonable to assume that the WTO dispute settlement bodies will – like other courts – behave strategically, in an attempt to gain legitimacy. There is no reason why the WTO dispute settlement bodies should be different from other courts in this regard. In fact, given the indeterminacy of WTO law and the fact that they have almost no way of not accepting a case that a WTO Member brings, they have no choice but to make choices. This also means that the dispute settlement bodies have to give reasons for the choices they make, reasons that will convince relevant constituencies of the legitimacy of the WTO dispute settlement system and its decisions.

Nonetheless, the WTO adjudicators have – like other courts – a certain leeway concerning the style of reasoning they adopt. Neither the mandate nor the procedural rules of the WTO dispute settlement bodies prescribe a certain approach.

The absence of a homogenous, hand-picked judicial elite and figures such as the Advocate General mean that the WTO dispute settlement reports carry the entire burden of justification. Combine this with the controversial legitimacy of the WTO dispute settlement system – and pure and short textualism like in the French model appears not to be a viable option for the WTO dispute settlement system.

At the same time, a predominantly formalist-textualist approach seems a safe and likely choice in cases where a court cannot take for granted that its decisions will be perceived as legitimate – and this is the situation of the Appellate Body. Equally, the mandate of the WTO dispute settlement bodies tends to support a formalist style of reasoning, without prescribing it. A predominantly formalist in approach is also the most likely expectation based on the statements of former Appellate Body Members quoted above.

For ensuring that dispute settlement decisions are accepted by the (losing) parties, other WTO Members, the "peer group" of legal commentators and the wider public, this approach would, however, likely need to be complemented by non-formalist elements of reasoning and the decisions would have to be explained well. Consequently, it is to be expected that the WTO dispute settlement decisions – while predominantly formalist in style – will not look like those of the French *Court de Cassation* and will be considerably longer and supported by more arguments. It can also be expected that the Appellate Body will be very careful to present any of its findings as being rooted in WTO law and being justified by the use of established method of interpretation. It is also likely that the Appellate Body will seek to be or at least appear to be consistent in its decision-making by attributing its own case law some kind of precedential value. It is also like that the adjudicators will avoid any appearance of being guided by their own political or economic preferences.

Hypotheses are even harder to formulate on substantive outcomes. The indeterminacy of WTO law gives the WTO dispute settlement bodies "considerable creative room for manoeuvre"[478]; the judges have relatively more leeway to decide cases in line with their own preferences than if WTO law was more determinate. Moreover, the possibilities and likelihood of serious potential backlash by WTO Members are rather limited. Altogether, as observed above, the adjudicators have significant discretion.

In what way can they be expected to use that space? Generally, there is a widely shared assumption in the literature that "greater amounts of judicial discretion create the *potential* for greater amounts of judicial policy-making"[479].

One possible scenario is that in the absence of political constraints the WTO dispute settlement bodies make "bold" decisions. This scenario could build, in particular, on findings that some of the bold and far-reaching judgements of the ECJ were possible, because Member States were not interested in or not in a position to take counter-measures. In the words of Bartels:

> "Political stalemate and an active dispute settlement system is truly a recipe for judicial activism."[480]

Assuming for a moment that the Appellate Body would indeed choose the route of judicial activism, i.e. rather leaning towards far-reaching, creative decisions, this does not answer the question whether these decisions would be rather "pro-trade" or crafted in a way to uphold WTO Members' discre-

---

478 Scott 2004b, 311; see also Choi 2003, 6ff.
479 Wessel 2006, 384; emphasis in the original.
480 Bartels 2004, 866.

tion to regulate in favour of non-trade goals to the greatest extent possible. One observer stated in 1995 that there were

> "reasons to believe that the Appellate Body decisions will drift toward reliance on economic free trade theory and doctrine of comparative advantage to ground their legal analysis"[481].

Yet WTO Members often hold divergent views on how a certain norm should be interpreted. In the larger public there are probably even more concerns in relation to a possible pro-trade agenda of WTO judges and a broader range of views on what the WTO dispute settlement bodies should do. In their statements quoted above, Appellate Body Members portray themselves as being very aware of the sensitivities involved in WTO appellate review and being very careful and mindful of WTO Members' intentions as enshrined in the WTO agreements. If one takes this seriously, it is quite plausible that the WTO dispute settlement bodies would adopt a restrained stance and issue balanced judgements that allow WTO Members a certain, but not excessive leeway to implement policies they want to adopt. In other words, it is reasonable to assume that the adjudicators will not consistently side with any specific political agenda or maximalist views on how certain norms should be read.[482] Moreover, to the extent that Appellate Body Members are not primarily specialized in international trade law, but are international lawyers more broadly, this is also likely to reduce any one-sided pro-trade decision-making.

Yet the above assumption that the Appellate Body would choose the route of judicial activism in the absence of a strong political branch is not the only one that can reasonably be made. An eminent commentator has suggested that the adjudicators can be expected to rather avoid "broad pronouncements of law", precisely because there are relatively weak checks on judicial power in the WTO universe.[483] It has also been observed that

> "for most international courts, jurisprudential coherence and minimal policy-making are the best ways to maintain states' confidence"[484].

Considering all these insights, the Appellate Body cannot be expected to exploit its discretion to the maximum and only in a pro-trade way. In light

---

481 Shell 1995, 905.

482 For WTO dispute settlement see McCall Smith 2003, 75; Alvarez 2008, 628; for a similar conclusion on the ICJ Shahabuddeen 1996, 230.

483 Alvarez in Abi-Saab 2008, 713f.

484 Wessel 2006, 426.

of divergent preferences among WTO Members on how WTO law should be interpreted and in view of the self-description of WTO adjudicators as being very mindful of WTO Members' intentions as enshrined in the WTO agreements, the most plausible scenario is that there will be a mixed picture in terms of substantive outcome, or the Appellate Body will find other ways of avoiding outcomes that would lead to significant opposition from WTO Members.

5. *Methodology*

It is now time for a more precise outlook over the remainder of this work. The section is structured as follows: In 5.1, I will discuss different methods that have been or could be applied for analysing WTO dispute settlement decisions. I will justify the method chosen in this work, i.e. an in-depth reading, re-construction and assessment of selected aspects of the WTO dispute settlement decisions. With the basic approach established I proceed to explain the selection of cases and legal provisions (5.2) as well as the aspects of the WTO judicial style (5.3) that I will analyse. Section 5.4 contains a table with an overview of the research approach to chapters 2 and 3.

5.1. Methods for analysing court decisions – and their limits

I have indicated in the introduction to this work that I intend to engage in an in-depth reading of some aspects of the "trade and ..." cases decided by the WTO dispute settlement bodies. The aim is to find out how the WTO adjudicators, in particular the Appellate Body, have decided these cases and how they justify their decisions. Thus, what I will do is at least partially good old lawyering: looking at what the law says, at what judges have decided, looking at what other lawyers write, and discussing what alternative decisions judges could have taken. At the same time, I go beyond traditional legal methods by systematically assessing the case law with regards to how restrictive the decisions are on WTO Members' regulatory freedom. Moreover, I look at the judicial style used to justify the decisions taken.

Other research methods have also been used for analysing certain aspects of WTO dispute settlement. These include statistical analysis[485], more

485 Bown 2005; Colares 2009; Colares 2011; Davey 2005; Elsig and Pollack 2012; Guzman and Simmons 2005; Maton and Maton 2007.

qualitative work carried out mostly by political scientists that relates external factors to the outcome of judicial decisions[486] or investigates WTO Members' use of the dispute settlement system[487], purely legal-doctrinal exegesis of individual cases or the analysis of overarching questions based on a formalist understanding of the judicial process carried out by lawyers[488], socio-legal research based on interviews[489], more or less empirical descriptions of the decision-making processes within the WTO dispute settlement system[490], a "Habermasian" discourse analysis[491], economic analysis[492], quantified computer-based textual analysis of judicial decisions[493], citation analysis[494], and different combinations of these methods.[495] What, then, justifies the proposed method, in particular in the light of the volumes that have already been written on the WTO dispute settlement system in general and individual cases? And what can and cannot be found out through that approach?[496]

In my view, reading the dispute settlement decisions is the approach that works best for what I intend to do, which is finding out how much leeway the WTO dispute settlement bodies afford WTO Members in the "trade and ..." cases, while at the same time giving due importance to the professional restrictions under which the adjudicators operate when justifying their decisions, in an attempt to find acceptance among the relevant constituencies. It is the legal details of the dispute settlement reports, the interpretations offered in these reports that set forth what WTO law mandates. The reports help define what WTO Members can and cannot do legally in the future. Or to put it differently, if the WTO agreements are a map at a scale of 1:500 000, the dispute settlement reports are, taken together, a map at a scale of 1:200 000. There are cases, in which the WTO Member that lost a dispute actually welcomed the outcome, while the win-

486 Daku and Pelc 2017; Garrett and McCall Smith 2002; McCall Smith 2003; Steinberg 2004.

487 Krüger 2013; Zangl et al. 2012, 375ff.

488 See the footnotes in the next chapters for examples.

489 Conti 2011; Costa 2011.

490 Alvarez-Jiménez 2009a; some of the contributions by former Appellate Body Members quoted above in section 4.1 also fall in this category.

491 Ceva and Fracasso 2010.

492 Rigod 2015.

493 Busch and Pelc 2019.

494 Charlotin 2017.

495 For a more comprehensive overview of political science studies on WTO dispute settlement see Krüger 2013, 33ff.

496 For a similar methodological issue and possible responses, see Bhala 1999b, 9ff.

ning WTO Member was dissatisfied with the outcome in light of the way that certain provisions had been interpreted and what that meant for the future.[497] There are also cases in which the WTO Member that won appealed certain findings of a Panel.[498] Only when reading judicial decisions can we find out what a court has decided as compared to what could have been decided. And only when looking at the nuances of the reasoning of a court can we understand its way of justifying these decisions and ideally come closer to understanding why decisions are justified in a certain way.

Other methods are unlikely to work equally well for this purpose. For example, interviews with the judicial decision-makers would probably not: If the point made above is taken seriously that there are some arguments that judges can legitimately use to support their decisions, and others, for example purely political or individual preferences, they cannot, then it is unlikely that research interviews would be able to pierce the protective wall of this professional code of conduct. Why should a judge "confess" to be doing or have been doing what he/she should not be doing, for example taking a politically motivated decision?[499] This would undermine his/her legitimacy as judge or the legitimacy of the institution he/she works for.[500]

---

497 For example, Winham 2003, 140 notes that in the *Hormones I* case the EU, which actually lost the case, expressed support for the results, while the US, which had prevailed with its claims, criticized the Appellate Body's decision; Gaines 2001, 749 states that India and Thailand whose complaint against the US in *Shrimp – Turtles* was successful, expressed the view that in reality the US won the dispute, because the Appellate Body interpreted WTO law in a way favored by the US.

498 See Busch and Pelc 2019, 466 for examples.

499 For a comparable statement on the limits of interviews when studying WTO dispute settlement decisions, see Bhala 1999b. There is indeed some empirical evidence to support this assumption. Glennon and Strother 2019, 246 in an analysis of TV interviews given by US Supreme Court judges conclude that the judges "justices spend a very large share of their time in interviews reinforcing the Court's institutional legitimacy. They do so in three primary ways: they discuss the importance of a neutral arbiter of law to uphold the rule of law and the centrality of such an institution to the American style of democracy, often expressly rejecting claims that the Court is 'political'; they describe the fundamentally legal nature of their decision-making practices; and they discuss their jurisprudential philosophies and distinguish those from partisan or political influence.".

500 This is not to deny, of course, that interviews are a meaningful method for investigating certain aspects of the functioning of the WTO, and even its dispute settlement, see for example Conti 2011; Alvarez-Jiménez 2009a; Shlomo-Agon 2015.

Assuming that people do what they say (rather than lying about it) is nonetheless reasonable. In the words of Aleinikoff: "The best evidence that we have are the words used by the judges."[501] If some kind of evidence is to be found why the WTO judges take certain decisions and what outcome they favour, that evidence is as likely to be in the WTO dispute settlement reports as in the mouth of any of the professional dispute settlers of the WTO. Indeed, when Members of the Appellate Body have engaged in public self-reflection and disclosed some aspects of the internal functioning of the judicial body to which they belong(ed), they have stuck to an image of the Appellate Body as a dutiful executioner of the WTO Members' will and as abstaining from any type of judicial policy-making.[502] Moreover, individual preferences may also find their way into judgements without the respective judicial decision-maker being aware of it or having any intention to this end.[503] Conversely, the style of reasoning used judicial decisions in can be revealing. Altogether, interviews would be unlikely, for purposes of this work, to have significant added value as compared to analysing the judicial decisions themselves and reading extra-curial statements that the WTO judicial decision-makers have published.

The statistical analysis of dispute settlement decisions also has significant limitations in terms of assessing how judges behave, at least in the case of the WTO. The number of cases decided is one limiting factor for a statistical analysis of overall outcomes. Moreover, statistics on how many cases are won and lost, and by whom, do not say a great deal on the way that WTO law is interpreted[504] and is likely to be applied in the future.[505] Statistical analysis can hardly capture the precise interpretation of a norm contained in a judgement, and whether it is e.g. broad or narrow.[506] Yet this is precisely what matters from a legal point of view. In legal terms it is not primarily of interest whether a certain party lost or won a case; it is of

---

501 Aleinikoff 1987, 952.

502 See the contributions cited above, section 4.2.

503 Kennedy writes that judges pursue "conscious, half-conscious or unconscious ideological projects", Kennedy 1997, 14. At the semantic level, the notion of someone "pursuing" a project unconsciously is somewhat problematic though.

504 As noted by Conti 2011, 65 the notion of "winning" a case is problematic: consider cases where a claimant "wins", because a WTO dispute settlement body supports one minor claim, but not all others or when a court supports the legal views of a claimant, but the claimant still "loses" because the facts are not seen as supporting his/her claim.

505 Garrett and McCall Smith 2002, 9.

506 Steinberg 2004, 255.

interest on what (factual, legal, procedural) grounds a measure was upheld or struck down. Only this allows an assessment of whether a judgement was e.g. "pro-environment" or "pro-trade". Also, whether a certain judgement is considered acceptable and legitimate does, as I have argued above, not depend only on the outcome, but equally on the judicial reasoning employed – a point that statistical analysis misses completely. Conversely, a statistical analysis of the WTO judicial style would be a meaningful exercise, in principle; the dispute settlement reports could be coded for certain stylistic traits and then analysed statistically. Results could be compared with the reasoning of other courts. Yet such an approach also has serious limitations as it cannot properly take account of the legal constraints under which judges operate when embracing a certain judicial style. For example, if one judicial body relies mainly on textual interpretation, whereas another judicial institution embraces a more teleological orientation, this difference is only significant if there is no formal legal rule requiring that the courts primarily use either of these methods of interpretation. In conclusion, while statistical analysis of judicial decisions may be a useful method for some purposes, it would not be the appropriate method for answering the research questions underlying this work.

Yet the method chosen here is not without limitations, either. The insight that judges' real reasons for deciding a case in a certain way are not necessarily the reasons they give for their decisions is important. As one author has recently put it:

> "[...] even though international courts justify their decisions only by reference to legal rules, it does not necessarily mean that they actually decide cases that way. Thus, they are not necessarily better at disregarding political considerations, but they are better at pretending to do so."[507]

This implies that the method used in the present work, i.e. reading and critically assessing the WTO case law, will not allow any empirically grounded, robust conclusions with regard to the "real" motives for why the WTO adjudicators have taken a certain decision and whether there was a conscious choice of making it, e.g. as "pro-trade" as possible or the opposite. As McCall Smith writes:

> "The Appellate Body's rationale in these rulings, of course, is not directly observable or verifiable. The rulings themselves provide some

507 Tumonis 2013, 45.

> guidance, but they are necessarily incomplete as a record of the decision-making process. As with other judicial institutions, complete documentation of internal Appellate Body deliberations is unlikely to be disclosed in writing or in interviews. Even if such information were available, unstated reasons could lie behind certain decisions. As a result, the reliability of any causal inferences ultimately depends on close analysis of how the Appellate Body behaves."[508]

This work undertakes such a close analysis of WTO case law, but I do not purport to achieve more than offering observations on WTO judicial decision-making that are more well-founded than could have been achieved without such exercise. This work will not provide any beyond-the-doubt conclusions on why a certain case has been decided in a certain way or why the Appellate Body has a certain style.[509]

There is a further limitation: while it is true that the WTO dispute settlement system is among the most active international judicial institutions, the case law on individual norms is often still limited. So whatever analysis can be carried out now is but a snapshot taken at a certain point in time.[510] The method chosen here also neither allows any statements about variations in WTO judicial decision-making over time nor does it allow any inferences to be drawn on the basis of comparisons with what other courts do.

5.2. Substance: cases and norms to be considered

A wide range of substantive issues in WTO law could obviously be analysed. As explained in the introduction, the focus of this work is on "trade and ..." cases, i.e. cases in which measures taken for non-trade reasons were at stake. This focus is chosen as these cases are sensitive from a

---

508 McCall Smith 2003, 74.

509 A similarly cautious statement is made by Beck 2012, 11 in his analysis of the reasoning of the ECJ. He writes: "It is not realistically possible [...] to provide conclusive evidence in relation to the claims advanced in this study as regards the broad heuristic patterns of legal reasoning [...] any evidence cited cannot be conclusive but only illustrative. The 'enlightened' reader [...] must decide whether the views advanced in the study cohere with his ordered experience and whether they enrich it. If they do, much of what can be done, has been done". Apart from the assumption that a reader is always a "he", Beck's statement also applies to this work.

510 For a similar caveat see Bacchus 2005, 520f.

political point of view[511], tend to receive public, critical attention, and raise the most serious legitimacy issues with regard to the WTO's role in resolving them.

Yet even in these cases there are so many legal issues that the scope of the work needs to be narrowed further to be manageable. Based on the argument that judges are more likely to exercise discretion where the law is relatively indeterminate, a focus on norms that exhibit this characteristic is warranted. Unfortunately, given the observation that many WTO provisions are indeterminate,[512] this criterion does not narrow down the scope of analysis enough, either. Thus, concerning the analysis of the substance of WTO judicial decision-making the specific focus of this work is on the way that the WTO adjudicators interpret the justification norms[513] of WTO law. "Justification norms" is used to denote those provisions of WTO law that are of specific relevance for assessing the WTO legality of measures taken for non-economic purposes. Any interpretation of such provisions inevitably entails a position that is either "pro-trade" or the opposite. Thus, analysing the interpretation of justification norms in WTO law is ideal for assessing the outcome of WTO dispute settlement in terms of the degree to which it is "pro-trade".

In GATT and GATS, the core justification norms are Art. XX GATT and XIV GATS respectively. They determine under which conditions WTO Members can deviate from the trade disciplines of these agreements for non-trade-related purposes, including environmental and health protection, among others. The necessity test contained in the various sub-paragraphs of these two articles has been characterized as the primary tool to distinguish between (illegitimate) protectionist measures and (legitimate) regulatory measures.[514] Other provisions in these agreements, e.g. Art. III or XI GATT, often play a role in non-trade cases, but also in cases that have no relation with non-economic objectives. For this reason I will only discuss Art. XX GATT and XIV GATS.

The SPS Agreement is different from GATT and GATS in that the entire SPS Agreement contains disciplines on WTO measures pursuing certain health-related objectives. It goes beyond the non-discrimination ambition of GATT.[515] The SPS Agreement contains clauses imposing substantive

511 Busch and Pelc 2019, 466; Shlomo-Agon 2015, 541; Sweet and Brunell 2013, 63.
512 See above, section 4.1.2.
513 The term "justification norms" is used for example by Zleptnig 2010.
514 Kapterian 2010, 90.
515 Van Calster 2008, 130; Hudec 2003, 187f; Kelly 2006, 91.

limits as well as procedural requirements to be observed when adopting SPS measures. Differently from GATT and GATS, the focus when looking at the case law can hence not be on exception norms: the SPS Agreement only contains positive obligations, no exception provisions.[516] Of the 14 articles of the SPS Agreement only Art. 2 - 6 SPS impose substantive obligations on WTO Members. It is these substantive obligations and their interpretation that are most relevant for this work. The balance struck by the adjudicators between trade and non-trade objectives hinges upon the interpretation of substantive rather than procedural provisions; both a measure favouring health protection at the expense of trade and one favouring trade at the expense of health protection could be violating (procedural) requirements relating to e.g. the publication or notification of measures or due process. Among the substantive norms of the SPS Agreement, only Art. 2, 3 and 5 have played an important role in WTO dispute settlement and will be analysed in this work.

The structure of the TBT Agreement is similar to that of the SPS Agreement; it contains rules for a certain type of measures, namely those that satisfy the definition of "technical regulation" or "technical standard" in the TBT Agreement. Similar to the SPS Agreement and different from the basic approach of GATT and GATS, the TBT Agreement does not only prohibit certain actions by WTO Members, but defines substantive and procedural criteria that each technical regulation or standard must fulfil. It goes beyond the requirement of non-discrimination. As a consequence, the analysis in the case of the TBT Agreement should be, like in the case of the SPS Agreement, on the substantive disciplines; they are mainly contained in one article of the agreement, Art. 2 TBT.

The interpretation of other WTO agreements is not covered in this work, because they seem to be less relevant. The TRIPS Agreement arguably does not contain a general justification norm,[517] while it does provide for the possibility of exceptions to intellectual property rights that WTO Members have to grant and protect. For patents, which are probably the most controversial type of intellectual property right regulated in the

516 Kapterian 2010, 96.

517 Art. 8 TRIPS states that "Members may [...] adopt measures necessary to protect public health and nutrition, and to promote the public interest in sectors of vital importance to their socio-economic and technological development", but also stipulates that such measures need to be TRIPS consistent. Thus, there is no real justification norm under TRIPS.

TRIPS agreement[518], the relevant norm is Art. 30 TRIPS. That norm has indeed become relevant in one case, *Canada – Pharmaceutical Patents*[519]. Nonetheless, the TRIPS Agreement has not been included in the present analysis. Its character is quite different from that of other WTO agreements since it contains what could be called "positive" regulation, i.e. prescriptions on what regulation WTO Members must adopt, rather than negative regulation, i.e. rules on what measures WTO Members are prohibited from taking (such as in GATT) or what standards they need to observe when they adopt certain measures (such as in the SPS and TBT Agreements). Other WTO agreements such as the SCM or AD Agreements do not seem *prima facie* relevant in the context of this work, since measures in dispute under these agreements are not usually taken for non-economic regulatory goals. More recently, there have been some environment-related cases, in which some of these other agreements were at stake. One example is *Canada – Renewable Energy*[520], involving a Canadian province's scheme for fostering the generation of renewable energy. In this case, the TRIMS and SCM Agreements were decisive. The measures in dispute in that case were not taken exclusively for environmental purposes, but also with the objective of supporting domestic industries, e.g. through local content requirements. Given this fact and, in addition, the need to limit the scope of this work, the case law interpreting these agreements is not discussed in this text.

Cases where one of the above norms was in dispute were identified from the chronological list of disputes and the short description of the disputes on the WTO website[521] as well as through the WTO Analytical Index[522] and literature[523]. The cut-off date for taking into account cases and literature was September 2014; a few updates have been made concerning quan-

518 See from various perspectives for example Haugen 2007; Carvalho 2002; Dutfield 2003; El-Said and El-Said 2005; Sun 2003.

519 *Canada – Patent Protection of Pharmaceutical Products, WT/DS114/R* 2000.

520 *Canada – Certain Measures Affecting the Renewable Energy Generation Sector, WT/DS412/AB/R and Canada – Measures Relating to the Feed-in Tariff Program, WT/DS426/AB/R* 2013.

521 Chronological list of disputes cases, http://www.wto.org/english/tratop_e/dispu_e/dispu_status_e.htm.

522 The Analytical Index offers an overview of case law by agreement and article, see http://www.wto.org/english/res_e/booksp_e/analytic_index_e/analytic_index_e.htm.

523 It is, at this stage of the discussion, very difficult to take into account all academic contributions ever published on the WTO in general or even only its dispute

titative figures and for taking account of more recent political developments as well as literature published after this date. All links have been revisited in spring 2020.

As I am interested in the present study in the implicit or explicit choices that the WTO adjudicators make when deciding cases, I will look at how each of the norms identified above has been interpreted in the case law. The purpose is not to make suggestions on how these norms *should* be interpreted, but to understand how they *have been* interpreted. The underlying assumption is that the WTO adjudicators often have a choice between various defensible interpretations; in other words, the interpretation they choose is only one in a universe of other at least plausible judicial interpretations. Thus, when assessing the interpretation of the relevant norms in the dispute settlement reports, the focus will be on finding out if the interpretation chosen by the WTO judicial decision-makers is mandated by the wording of the law, or whether other interpretations would also have been legally defensible. If the latter is the case, I will also discuss if the interpretation chosen in WTO dispute settlement is rather "pro trade" or "pro non-trade" regulatory goals – or, in other words, whether the WTO dispute settlement decision limits the discretionary space of national policy makers more than alternative, equally defensive interpretations would have.[524] By focusing on the substantive impact of the judicial decisions I seek to avoid criticism sometimes levelled against a purely legalist-doctrinal analysis of case law – that it misses and even masks what the adjudicators actually do.[525]

---

settlement system. The task becomes virtually unmanageable when, like in this study, reference is made to works in different languages and from different disciplines. In this work, I have put the focus on central contributions by WTO scholars engaged in research on the WTO over long periods of times, on works by (ex)practitioners close to the WTO dispute settlement system, on literature analyzing WTO case law and the dispute settlement system in a theoretically informed or overarching manner (rather than e.g. individual case notes), and more recent contributions. Chapter 1 contains, in particular, references to more theoretical works on judicial decision-making in general and within the WTO, rooted mostly in legal theory and political science. Chapters 2 and 3 build mainly on legal scholarship covering certain overarching features of the WTO case law, but also some individual case notes. Chapter 4 links the insights from this work to selected strands of WTO scholarship from various disciplines in an attempt to make clear what is new and points to instances where existing research is either confirmed by or inconsistent with what I find.

524 Other authors have assessed the case law from a similar perspective, see for example Osiro 2002, 124; Kapterian 2010.

525 See criticism by Shaffer 2009, 8.

Obviously, this approach has some difficulties: whether there is a defensible alternative interpretation to the one that the Appellate Body adopts is often open to debate. Nonetheless, other scholars have adopted a similar approach. For example, Davey[526] analyses WTO cases by focusing on whether the outcome was unexpected (i.e. was in line with relevant precedents and the wording of the law) and whether the result significantly constrains governments in reaching desired policy goals. Pair[527] and Yung[528] both maintain that judicial activism can be identified by measuring either the behaviour of judges against objective criteria, or the results achieved against other possible results. In a similar vein and given the difficulties of finding more objective criteria, I will use published opinions of other lawyers as an at least somewhat objective yardstick. Analyses by legal scholars, *amicus curiae* briefs, and differences between the decisions of Panels and the Appellate Body all provide useful insights for this purpose, because they delineate the universe of acceptable legal interpretations of a certain norm.

In cases decided by the Appellate Body the focus of the analysis will be on the appellate reports; this is the case for the majority of cases discussed here. From a legal point of view only the Appellate Body reports matter in cases where they exist, as the DSB only adopts the Appellate Body report (and not the Panel reports) when there is such a report (Art. 16.4, 17 DSU). While the focus is on the Appellate Body reports, there will be occasional references to what Panels have decided as well. In some cases there is no appeal and hence not Appellate Body decision. Moreover, as already stated, the differences between Panel and Appellate Body reports are often illustrative of different possible interpretations of WTO provisions. Finally, Panel reports are sometimes needed for understanding the facts of the case and the Appellate Body's legal analysis.

5.3. Judicial style: issues to be considered

This work is based on the assumption that the reasoning employed in judicial decisions merits close analysis. Such reasoning is crucial for legitimizing judicial decisions and there are different styles that courts deploy to this end. What style they use can, in turn, be explained at least partially by

526 Davey 2003.
527 Pair 2001, 184.
528 Yung 2011, 19.

certain external factors, such as the institutional set-up of a court or its interactions with other actors in the system. To be manageable and replicable, an analysis of the judicial style of a particular judicial entity needs to look at specific issues, however. In other words, the concept of "judicial style" needs to be operationalized. For doing so, I will draw on two sources: the analysis by Summers/Taruffo, already quoted above, and works on judicial activism.

Summers/Taruffo are primarily concerned with describing and categorizing different styles, rather than explaining them.[529] By contrast, Lasser, provides a thorough analysis of potential factors behind the observed differences in courts' judicial styles, but does not offer a classification of arguments that is as systematic as the one by Summers/Taruffo. He mainly classifies the judicial discourses he investigates on two "sliding scales" covering the spectrum from "more formal" to "more open-ended" and "less disclosure" to "more disclosure"[530]. For this reason the analysis by Summers and Taruffo is a more useful starting point for *describing* the style of argumentation that the WTO dispute settlement bodies use; by contrast, Lasser's analysis is likely to be more helpful in trying to *explain* the style observed. Here, I will therefore first discuss what can be learnt from Summers/Taruffo for the analysis of the judicial style of WTO dispute settlement (section 5.3.1).

A second source I will draw on for identifying relevant aspects of the WTO judicial style is the debate on how to identify and measure judicial activism/judicial-law-making (section 5.3.2). That debate is relevant to the present context, because both judicial "activism" and "law-making" are normally used to denote a behaviour of a court viewed as negative and undesirable.[531] A court keen to establish a reputation of "good" judicial decision-making and to be perceived as an authoritative and legitimate voice of the law is therefore likely to try to avoid behaviour considered to constitute judicial activism. As discussed above, the WTO dispute settlement bodies were, at the time they were established, very much in a position where they needed to work on their legitimacy credentials; in conse-

529 However, they offer some hypotheses on reasons behind the observed differences. The main reasons they refer to are different political traditions on the role of courts, concepts of democracy, institutional set-ups, and legal cultures, see Summers and Taruffo 1991, 502ff.

530 Lasser 2004, chap. 8.

531 See for example de Visser 2013, 188.

quence, they can plausibly be expected to try and avoid any appearance of being "activist".

In a concluding section (5.3.3), I will link the insights from the previous sections and specify those aspects of the WTO judicial style to be analysed in the work – and those left out of the analysis.

5.3.1. Issues from the analysis by Summers/Taruffo

Summers/Taruffo show that there is a wide array of empirically identifiable ways of how courts reason and justify their decisions – courts all use a different rhetoric and style. To recap, the dimensions along which Summers/Taruffo find various courts' reasoning to diverge are the degree to which issues of interpretation and the existence of more than one possible interpretation are openly acknowledged, the respective proportions of legalistic and technical language in a judicial decision, whether the opinion is short and terse or extended and elaborate, the implicit model of rationality (logico-deductive or discursive), the proportion of formal rather than substantive reasons, the recognition of the evaluative and creative role of the courts, and whether the decision is framed in a "magisterial and authoritative" or an "argumentative and dialogic" way.[532]

Summers/Taruffo classify judicial decisions on the basis of descriptions of the styles of various courts provided by experts familiar with the respective legal order. These country case studies are based on a list of guiding questions, which is, however, too long and detailed to be reproduced here.[533] The questions relate, among others, to gap-filling, the types of arguments recognized as acceptable and their respective importance, the types of material used in interpretation and their respective importance, the structure of opinions, the role of the courts in the overall legal system, positive legal and constitutional rules on interpretation, the role of general principles in justifying decisions, and the impact of the character and mandate of the courts as well as legal culture on interpretation. Other studies discussing the judicial style of courts have used similar elements.[534]

532 See above, section 3.1 and Table 1 in particular.

533 It is contained in the Appendix of MacCormick and Summers 1991, 545ff.

534 For example Pauwelyn and Elsig 2012 look at methods of interpretation, the use of original vs. evoluationary interpretation, gap filling, use of precedents, and linkages to other treaties and tribunals.

I have already discussed some of these issues for the WTO context, e.g. the role of the "court" in the WTO legal system as well as existing rules on interpretation. Other questions are somewhat difficult to use in the WTO system. An example is the influence of "legal culture" on interpretation. Immediately after the establishment of the WTO, a pronounced WTO legal culture did not exist; it is doubtful whether it will ever exist in international legal practice to the same extent as in a national legal system. In the international legal system, and any of its sub-areas, practitioners and scholars come from a variety of legal traditions; this makes the notion of a unique and uniform "culture" of international law generally or WTO law more specifically difficult. By contrast, several others of the dimensions of judicial reasoning in the analysis by Summers/Taruffo are useful and applicable in the WTO context as well. These are the approach toward gap-filling, types of material used in interpretation and their respective importance, and the role of general principles in justifying decisions. A particularly important issue is which types of arguments are recognized as acceptable as well as their respective importance and prevalence in the dispute settlement reports. This includes both the methods of interpretation used and the extent to which the WTO judicial decision-makers use a more normative, policy-oriented style of reasoning. The latter is particularly apparent from the way the judicial decision-makers engage in balancing. Balancing is, as explained above, a normatively oriented way of reasoning that takes into account different interests, rights and values at issue in a given case. As described more in-depth below[535], balancing is related to the use of (substantive) principles in general and the use of the proportionality principle or elements of it in particular. The proportionality principle is a test established by courts to be able to "fuse" more formal legal arguments with a more normatively oriented style of reasoning.[536]

Finally, two other issues are the length and elaborateness of the judicial decisions and the degree to which different possible interpretations are openly acknowledged and discussed; these issues are not captured directly by the guiding questions underlying the Summers/Taruffo analysis, but appear in their overall assessment of courts' reasoning as being formalist.

535 See chapter 3, section 4.
536 See above, section 3.1.

5.3.2. Lessons from discussions on judicial activism

Debates on "judicial activism" yield some important insights for the purpose of identifying aspects of judicial styles that are relevant to this work.[537] The purpose of this work is not to find out whether the Appellate Body is "activist" or not – the added value of sticking such a rather vague label on anyone or anything seems limited.[538] At the same time, my endeavour is somewhat similar to that of those who are chasing judicial activism. Like them, I am trying to find out what a judicial entity "really" does, on the basis of the assumption that something else may be going on below a surface of the interpretation of the law as communicated in the judicial decisions.

Few contributions deal explicitly with how to "measure" or operationalize judicial activism. Frequently, "judicial activism" seems to be primarily used to denigrate a decision that people do not like – for whatever reason.[539] Authors often use the term without giving precise indications on how to identify it. Such "I know it when I see it (and don't like it)" approaches are rightly criticized as not satisfactory from a methodological, academic point of view.[540] The frequent lack of proper definitions of judicial activism may be related to the fact that judicial activism is indeed not

537 Bogdandy and Venzke 2012, 24f discuss the terms judicial activism and judicial law-making as contending concepts and find the first term more suitable. I use judicial activism, because it denotes, to my mind, more clearly that the approach of judges it refers to is seen as undesirable and inappropriate.

538 Moreover, there is also a degree of cultural bias inherent in how the term gets used. Judicial activism seems to be more of a concern in the United States than, in for example, Europe, see Ruiz Fabri 2006, 126.

539 A former Appellate Body Member writes with certain acumen and probably based on experience: "A lawyer who has convinced his country to spend several years, and who has convinced his client to spend several million dollars, in a losing case, is unlikely when he loses, to admit that his was, from the beginning, a losing case. That lawyer is more likely to blame those who have judged the case for supposedly 'overreaching'." Bacchus 2005, 502; for a similar view see also for the WTO Bartels 2004, 984; and more generally Lindquist and Cross 2009, 29f. Kmiec 2004, 1475 also quotes a US Supreme Court decision where one of the judges bases a dissenting opinion on the observation that the majority opinion would amount to judicial activism.

540 Rasmussen 1986, 6; de Visser 2013, 188.

easy to detect; there is "rarely smoking gun evidence".[541] What are the options?[542]

Lindquist/Cross who have recently dedicated an entire book to the question of how to measure judicial activism define "judicial activism" on a continuum of "more" or "less".[543] They list four dimensions of "judicial activism" commonly identified in research on national courts:[544]

(1) a lack of deference to decisions of the legislative or administrative branches of government,

(2) a willingness to not follow precedents or a lack of fidelity to the text, intent or history of the law,

(3) the expansion of judicial authority to hear cases and controversies, and

(4) result-oriented judging, i.e. judging that fosters judges' individual preferences.

Lindquist/Cross analyse each of these dimensions in the jurisprudence of the US Supreme Court through a statistical analysis of the outcome of cases as well as the known policy preferences of judges.

Yung presents a list of signs of judicial activism as identified in the existing literature on national courts:

> "overruling actions by other federal branches or state governments, failing to follow textual meaning, departing from history or tradition, issuing maximalist and not minimalist holdings, using broad remedial powers, basing decisions upon partisan preferences, failing to follow an originalist view of the Constitution, issuing an opinion inconsistent with prior precedent, exercising power beyond a court's jurisdiction, creating new rights or theories, altering prior doctrines or interpretations, establishing substantive policy, and failing to use an accepted interpretative methodology".[545]

He also suggests that a useful way of measuring activism would be to identify what a formalist court would have decided in a given case and view any deviation from this as activism.[546]

---

541 Kmiec 2004, 1476.

542 Zarbiyev 2012, 4ff also gives an overview of some definitions of judicial activism in the literature.

543 Lindquist and Cross 2009, 31.

544 Ibid., 32ff.

545 Yung 2011, 10.

546 Ibid., 19.

Pair states that judges can be considered "judicially active" when they refuse to take an attitude of deference to legislative or executive power or judgement, relax requirements of justiciability, break precedent, or construe constitutions, statutes or binding precedent loosely.[547] Kmiec argues that there are five "core meanings" of judicial activism, namely invalidation of arguably constitutional actions of other branches of government, failure to adhere to precedent, judicial legislation, departures from accepted interpretive methodology, and result-oriented judging.[548] De Visser observes that a court is most at risk of being charged with judicial activism when appearing to strike down legislation, i.e. to define policy outcomes, or to extend its own jurisdiction.[549]

At the EU level, a piece of research that explicitly discusses how to measure judicial activism is Rasmussen's study on the ECJ. He measures judicial activism by ascertaining the reaction of "countervailing powers" to individual judgements or a group of judgements; in the case of the ECJ these are the other EU institutions and EU Member States.[550] Muir et al. do not give a definition of judicial activism in relation to the ECJ, but observe that accusations of judicial activism are increasingly not directed at the substantive outcome of ECJ proceedings, but the reasoning the court employs.[551] This highlights that perceptions of judicial activism can be related both to the substance and the style of judicial decision-making. Kaupa, also in a work on the ECJ, describes judicial activism to mean that

> "judges follow an ideological agenda instead of ruling what the law, or society at large, would demand. It essentially means that judges rule in bad faith".[552]

In his study on judicial activism in international law, Zarbiyev, while acknowledging difficulties of defining the concept, indicates that judicial activism can be understood in the following terms:

> "In every legally organized community there is a range of courses of action that are considered to be appropriately judicial: there is a rough consensus about what judges are permitted to do as well as the limits that the judiciary cannot legitimately transgress. In this light judicial

547 Pair 2001, 184.
548 Kmiec 2004, 1444.
549 De Visser 2013, 199.
550 Rasmussen 1986, 7.
551 Muir, Dawson, and Witte 2013, 3.
552 Kaupa 2013, 56.

> activism would be a term of art to characterize a course of action that goes beyond the boundaries of what is deemed appropriate for the judiciary in a given context."[553]

For one specific international court, the International Criminal Court (ICC), Wessel describes "judicial policy-making" as consisting of two elements: gap filling and judicial activism. The latter is described to exist if a court's decisions are against the intent of the states that are parties to the underlying legal framework.[554] More in detail, Wessel maintains that the following two elements are useful to detect judicial activism by the ICC: first, the recognition of new legal obligations by the Court that govern behaviour previously unregulated; second, a narrow interpretation of the complementarity clause that defines the division of labour between the ICC and the signatory states, leading to an expansion of the power of the ICC and a lack of deference to national institutions.[555]

With regard to the WTO, the Appellate Body has been described as an "activist tribunal" based on the number of Panel reports it has reversed.[556] Steinberg observes a general tendency to measure judicial activism in terms of the rates at which (constitutional) courts strike down laws[557], but suggests himself that judicial activism should be measured by the proportion of dispute settlement reports in which ambiguity is clarified or gaps are filled.[558] McCall Smith argues in his study on WTO dispute settlement that judges cannot appear to ignore unambiguous treaty rules or previous decisions for the sake of accommodating political preferences without doing harm to their reputation for independent, impartial judgement.[559] Howse maintains that judicial activism in international law consists of imposing on states legal constraints not justified "by the strict rule of international law"[560]. He bases this understanding of judicial activism on the basic principle of international law that sovereign states may do what they wish, unless there is a specific rule binding them. Goldstein and Steinberg use the "rate and scope of judicial gap filling and ambiguity clarification, fac-

553 Zarbiyev 2012, 5f.
554 Wessel 2006, 387.
555 Ibid., 387ff.
556 Davey 2005, 22; similarly Cartland, Depayre, and Woznowski 2012, 989 use the title "judicial activism" for an analysis of how frequently the Appellate Body has modified Panels' findings.
557 Steinberg 2004, 254.
558 Ibid., 255; see also Goldstein and Steinberg 2007, 19.
559 McCall Smith 2003, 67.
560 Howse 2003c, 35.

tored by the volume of dispositive dispute settlement reports" for measuring the "expansiveness of judicial law-making"[561], which seems to be a concept similar to judicial activism. Guan seems to hold the view that the Appellate Body is "activist", because its interpretative approach (allegedly) departs from "general international practice" and established jurisprudence.[562]

Not all of these approaches are helpful in the present context. Obviously, those approaches that do not involve a reading of the actual text of a judicial decision and instead rely e.g. on statistical analysis of the outcome of cases are not useful for my purpose, for the reasons described above (5.1). Some other approaches are conceptually interesting, but they only seem to shift the problem from identifying judicial activism with any degree of objectivity to identifying with any degree of objectivity result-oriented judging (Lindquist/Cross and Kmiec), partisan preferences (Yung), the intent of state parties (Wessel), or the creation of new legal constraints as opposed to such already contained in the law (Howse). Others have also observed that using some of the suggested "indicators" for judicial activism is difficult, requiring qualitative judgements from the analyst.[563]

For the purpose of the present work, the following parameters for measuring judicial activism are both relevant and can be used in a feasible way: the degree of deference to decisions by WTO Members, the use of precedents, the methods of interpretation used, in particular the degree to which the text of WTO provisions plays an important role, and the attitude towards gap-filling. How broadly or narrowly the WTO adjudicators construe justiciability and admissibility is also, in principle, relevant, but has not played a very important role in existing WTO case law. The reason is probably that there are no separate requirements of admissibility in WTO law or provisions that would allow the adjudicators to easily restrict the justiciability of certain matters. Given that these issues are relatively unimportant in the WTO legal universe, the analysis will focus instead on other ways how the WTO adjudicators can avoid taking a decision on certain matters: the use of so-called avoidance techniques, notably judicial economy and reasoning *arguendo*.

561 Goldstein and Steinberg 2007, 24.

562 Guan 2014, 240ff.

563 Goldstein and Steinberg 2007, 24.

5.3.3. Conclusions on judicial style

Certain aspects of the judicial style and reasoning of a court are mentioned in both of the preceding sections, while others appear in only one of them. In sum, I will discuss the following aspects of the WTO's judicial style in chapter 3 of this work:

First, the methods of interpretation used obviously matter. As discussed extensively above in section 1, courts rely on different methods of interpretation, reflecting, among others, the accepted modes of judicial reason-giving in a certain legal system and a court's interaction with other actors within the judicial system. Different methods offer judicial decision-makers different degrees of freedom in deciding a case and are also linked to different images of judicial decision-making: using teleological interpretation more easily allows and perhaps even more strongly calls for the exercise of individual, subjective judgement and normative judgements than textual interpretation.[564] Teleological interpretation also has an easy, almost natural link with basing a judgement on the discussion of policy objectives and their respective weight, given that teleological interpretation is about the objectives that a law pursues. One of the indicators of judicial activism proposed by Yung and Pair is therefore a loose attitude towards the wording of the law; equally, a failure to follow established methods of interpretation is seen as an indicator of judicial activism by Yung.[565] In the Summers/Taruffo scheme, methods of interpretation are also relevant. The model of rationality that a decision conveys depends on the prevalence of different methods of interpretation and as well as on the proportion of formal and substantive reasons used respectively. If textual interpretation prevails, the model of rationality projected is a logical-deductive one, in which facts are related to the legal text through a syllogistic argument. When teleological interpretation is used more frequently, substantive policy arguments are likely to be more frequent than in textual or contextual interpretation. Hence, methods of interpretation are an important aspect to discuss with regard to the WTO's judicial style. The extent to which non-WTO international law is used in WTO dispute settlement closely related to methods of interpretation. It is also relevant since non-WTO international legal

564 James Bacchus, a former Member of the Appellate Body advises parties not to request the Appellate Body to apply a teleological approach, because such an approach "would enable the members to impose their purely personal views on the meaning of the 'covered agreements'", Bacchus 2004b, 21.

565 See above n. 545 and 546.

rules and principles often serve other objectives than liberalizing international trade. The extent to and the manner in which they are used may not only influence outcomes, but also contribute to (de)legitimizing WTO judicial decisions.

Another aspect of judicial decisions that scholars take to be indicative of judicial activism is the standard of review a court uses and the degree of deference it affords to decisions by political entities. As explained above (2.3), Art. 11 DSU requires a Panel to conduct an "objective assessment of the matter before it". However, what precisely constitutes an "objective" assessment is not very clear: Art. 11 DSU does not seem to express much more than what is generally expected of judges. The standard of review the adjudicators apply and related questions of how they deal with expressions of the political will of WTO Members (e.g. gap-filling) constitute, therefore, a second dimension of the WTO's judicial style that I will look at.

A third issue are precedents. Failure to adhere to precedents is identified as an indicator of judicial activism by the aforementioned Yung[566] and Kmiec[567]. In the Summers/Taruffo scheme, precedents are important, because the existence of a precedent is a formal (rather than substantive) argument; moreover, if a court presents decisions as inevitable resulting from prior case law it also assumes an implicit model of logico-deductive rationality. Continuity and consistency and the application of the same rules to the same factual issues, regardless of the parties involved, are an important source of legitimacy for any adjudicator.[568]

Along with looking at precedents, I will also consider avoidance techniques. In the WTO context, the concept has been used by Davey. He defines as "issue avoidance techniques" certain techniques that courts have developed to "dispose of cases or issues within cases where a decision seems unnecessary, inappropriate or perhaps simply too controversial"[569]. By adopting a case-specific approach and by not deciding on certain issues a judicial body preserves scope for future decisions that may be particularly suitable to the concrete case, or for responding to political pressure in a future case, thereby avoiding criticism of its jurisprudence.[570] At the same

566 See above n. 545.
567 See above n. 548.
568 Charlotin 2017, 282 observes that the use of precedents by international courts can be attributed to the fact that "tribunals cite authorities to emphasize the soundness of their reasoning or, at the very least, to prevent themselves from an accusation of arbitrariness"; see also Palmeter and Mavroidis 1998, 402.
569 Davey 2003, 58.
570 This point is made in particular by McCall Smith 2003.

time, a court that produces more legal findings than necessary to resolve the case at hand is more likely to be considered activist and law-making.[571] While this issue cannot be easily located in the Summers/Taruffo scheme for assessing the degree to which a judicial body has a formalist style of reasoning, it does appear in discussions on judicial activism. For example, Yung identifies maximalist rather than minimalist findings as one indicator of judicial activism[572]; a decision that avoids certain issues can be characterized as minimalist.

A fourth question in the analysis of judicial style is the use of principles, in particular the principle of proportionality, and balancing language. To recap[573], balancing is a normatively coloured type of judicial reasoning, in which the rights and interests of different actors as well as policy objectives are taken int account. In some legal orders, the proportionality principle explicitly requires balancing. More generally, some authors conceive of balancing and principles as being intimately connected. Different from rules that have an "if … then" structure, principles require taking into account certain interests to different degrees, but do not require an "either/or" decision. Against this background, it is clear that balancing and the use of principles involve the use of substantive rather than formal arguments. Moreover, balancing clearly makes the creative role of a court visible and also tends to highlight the possibility of a different balance of interests being struck, and hence of an overall different outcome of a case. Balancing and the use of principles are hence relevant to several dimensions of the Summers/Taruffo scheme. Moreover, balancing and the use of principles also increase the likelihood for a judicial decision to be considered "activist". For example, a failure to follow textual meaning or result-oriented judging are considered to be indicators for judicial activism by some of the authors quoted above. In practice, balancing is not necessarily result-oriented judging in the sense of fostering the preferences of judges; judges can engage in balancing by resorting to what they think is an objective order of values enshrined in a given legal order. However, judicial reasoning that involves resorting to the relative importance of various interests is likely to make it easier to foster individual preferences. It is also likely to more easily convey an impression of such individual preferences having determined the outcome than a more textualist, formalist style of reasoning.

571 See Zarbiyev 2012, 8.
572 Yung 2011, 10.
573 For a more extended version of this argument see above section 3.1.

Finally, I will analyse some other aspects of the WTO's judicial style that are mainly derived from the modified Summers/Taruffo scheme. Two of them are the length and tone of reports and the use of what I call "appeasement techniques". I use this term to describe instances, in which the adjudicators verbally re-assure the parties (and the larger public) that their concerns and arguments have been considered and their interests been properly taken account of, without these statements necessarily having any legal value of their own. Both aspects relate primarily to the dimension of whether a decision is framed in a "magisterial and authoritative" or "argumentative and dialogic" way. In a distinct section, I will also address the degree to which different interpretations are presented in the WTO judicial decisions as potentially defensible, elaborating on the respective dimension of the Summers/Taruffo scheme.

The analysis of the WTO's judicial style is not aimed at investigating WTO judicial procedures as such. This also why some procedural aspects of WTO law are not investigated (e.g. the burden of proof): they are not closely related to the judicial style prevailing in WTO dispute settlement, because they do not generate a certain legitimizing rhetoric effect or have a significantly constraining effect on what reasons the WTO judges may give for their decisions. For example, the rules on burden of proof have been described as hardly constraining for the WTO judges.[574]

The above aspects of the WTO's judicial style will be analysed as evident from the reports in the "trade and ..." cases, with a focus on the Appellate Body reports. However, given that the WTO dispute settlement bodies are likely to develop a consistent style in both "trade and ..." and other cases, it will be necessary to take account of the larger body of case law as well. As it is impossible to read as part for this work all the hundreds of thousands of pages of WTO case law that exist today, the analysis of the judicial style of the WTO will partially draw on existing research on the respective matters.

5.4. Overview: research approach to chapters 2 and 3

The following table shows the research approach to chapters 2 and 3 in an overview.

574 Flett 2011, 29; Cho 2009a, 691.

Table 2: Overview of research approach for chapters 2 and 3

	Chapter 2: Substance	Chapter 3: Style
Overarching research question	How have the WTO dispute settlement bodies interpreted the justification provisions of WTO law in substance?	How can the WTO's judicial style be described?
Guiding questions for legal-technical analysis of case law	Are there any shortcomings of the case law from a legal-technical point of view (logic, internal consistency, compatibility with wording of law etc.) and if so which ones?	Are there any shortcomings of the case law from a legal-technical point of view (logic, consistency etc.) and if so which ones?
Guiding questions for normative-political assessment of case law	What is the outcome in "trade and ..." cases in terms of whether it is more restrictive of WTO Members' freedom to take measures for non-trade purposes than required by the wording of WTO law?	What is the (rhetoric) effect of the adjudicators' way of reasoning? How can the observable features of the WTO's judicial style be explained in terms of the fact that the WTO dispute settlement system and its individual decisions need to win acceptance from WTO Members as legitimate?
Use of case law	In-depth analysis of Appellate Body reports of all "trade and ..." cases decided under GATT, GATS, SPS and TBT Agreement as well selected Panel reports (decided between establishment of WTO and September 2014)	In-depth analysis of Appellate Body reports of all "trade and ..." cases decided under GATT, GATS, SPS and TBT Agreement as well selected Panel reports (decided between establishment of WTO and September 2014) Analysis of selected other Appellate Body reports mentioned as relevant in literature for respective aspect of judicial style
Use of literature	Literature serves – to inform the legal-technical analysis – as a benchmark for assessing the degree to which the substantive outcome is more restrictive of WTO Members' freedom to take measures for non-trade purposes than required by wording of the law	Literature serves – to add to the analysis of characteristics of WTO judicial style – to inform the legal-technical analysis – to contribute to potential explanations of observed the characteristics

Chapter 2: Substance: The case law on justification norms

> *"It is not rare for the law, as a docile, adaptable, supple instrument, to be obliged to the ex post facto rationalization of decisions in which it had no part."*[575]

This chapter discusses the outcome of WTO cases, notably the substantive interpretations that the dispute settlement bodies have come up with so far. The focus in this chapter is on justification norms – those norms of WTO law that contain rules that are of particular relevance when WTO Members take measures aimed at non-trade policy objectives, notably environmental or health protection. In other words, I do not look at the interpretation of *all* norms contained in WTO law and interpreted in "trade and ..." cases so far, but at a more limited selection of core norms that are likely to be relevant in many "trade and ..." cases, but not in other cases. The norms identified as relevant above are Art. XX GATT, Art. XIV GATS, Art. 2 TBT and Art. 2, 3, 5 SPS. The selection of cases to be discussed as well as the approach to the analysis have been explained in greater detail above.[576]

As explained in the first chapter of this work, the outcome of cases is one of the factors influencing the degree to which judicial decisions are acceptable to relevant constituencies. The substantive choices that judges make matter. For this reason, my analysis of each of the agreements will go beyond mere summaries of existing case law. For each of the agreements I will also engage in a "discussion" and "assessment" of the related case law. The "discussion" is an analysis of the case law from a legal-technical point of view. Such an analysis is necessary because both the type and quality of arguments that judges use in a ruling have an effect on its legitimacy. For example, if in the view of relevant constituencies a certain finding is manifestly not covered by the meaning of the term it seeks to interpret, or there are inconsistencies within a ruling, this will undermine the perceived quality and potentially the acceptance of judicial findings. The "assessment"

575 Bourdieu 1987, 827.
576 See chapter 1, section 5.2.

looks at the case law from a more normative-political angle. I will inquire after potential alternative interpretations that could have been chosen, and consider whether the interpretations actually chosen are more or less restrictive of WTO Members' regulatory freedom than the potential alternatives.[577] In order to identify defensible alternative interpretations, I will rely primarily on existing comments by legal observers, but also on differences between Panel and Appellate Body reports. This approach is based on the assumption that if a number of renowned legal scholars or practitioners agree on alternative interpretations, this is an indication that the WTO adjudicators could also have interpreted the law in a different way. By implication, their actual interpretation must be considered to constitute a deliberate choice and cannot be considered to be the only possible interpretation of WTO law.

The chapter is hence structured as follows: Section 1 presents the case law on Art. XX GATT and Art. XIV GATS; these two norms are similar in wording and cases discussing them often contain cross-references to the interpretation of the respective other norm. Section 2 is dedicated to the case law on the SPS Agreement, section 3 to the TBT Agreement. Each of the sections contains an overview of the relevant case law and then discusses the case law from a "lawyerish" perspective, i.e. with a view to overarching trends, eventual inconsistencies etc. Each of the sections concludes with an assessment of the interpretation offered in the case law with regard to how restrictive it is to WTO Members' non-trade measures, as compared to defensible alternative interpretations. Section 4 contains the overall conclusions, bringing together the insights on the different agreements.

1. *Art. XX GATT and XIV GATT*

Art. XX may well be the single norm of GATT that has received most overall scholarly attention.[578] This is due to the fact that Art. XX GATT is one of the critical points at which compromises between trade and other concerns are made. Moreover, it contains indeterminate terms such as "neces-

---

577 For a similar approach by political scientists, see Sweet and Brunell 2013.

578 To cite just some publications that refer to Art. XX GATT in the title: Bartels 2002; Bentley 2000; Epiney 2000; Feddersen 2002; Fontanelli 2012; Manzini 1999; Thiedemann 2005; Bowen 2000; Briggs 2001; Charnovitz 1991; Chi 2014; Doyle 2011; Espa 2012; Gaines 2001; Gu 2012; Klabbers 1992; Leyton 2001; Mattoo and Mavroidis 1997; McRae 2000; Regan 2007; Hippler Bello and Shenk 1996; Urakami 2001; Venzke 2012; Waart 1998.

sary" or "discrimination" that provide courts with significant interpretive discretion, as evident also in other areas of international law.[579]

Art. XX GATT consists of the chapeau and several sub-paragraphs, of which only (a), (b), (d) and (g) have played a major role in dispute settlement so far. Paragraphs (b) and (g) are, based on their wording, obviously relevant for environmental and health measures. Paragraph (a) has also been invoked to justify non-trade measures in several cases. Paragraph (d) does not deal explicitly with such measures. In practice, it has been invoked most often for defending measures and regulation put in place to enforce intellectual property, tax or competition law, an exception being the *Brazil – Tyres* case which involved environmental issues.[580] Still, paragraph (d) cannot be left out of the present analysis: it uses similar wording as paragraphs (a) and (b) and it also constitutes a part of their context that would have to be taken into account in contextual interpretation. In addition, all of the paragraphs are united under the same chapeau; the interpretation of the chapeau in an Art. XX (d) case may be relevant to its interpretation in a later paragraph (b) or (g) case. Thus, Art. XX (d) GATT will also be included in the analysis. Concerning the order of reviewing the chapeau and the individual sub-paragraphs the Appellate Body has decided that adjudicators must review first the sub-paragraphs and only after this the chapeau.[581] This order is followed in this section.

Art. XIV GATS is similar to Art. XX GATT in character as it contains clauses on "General Exceptions" that allow WTO Members to take measures otherwise prohibited under the GATS. Like Art. XX GATT it contains several subparagraphs pertaining to particular regulatory objectives and partially identical in wording with the sub-paragraphs of

579 For example, see on the use and interpretation of "necessity" in international investment law Parish 2010.

580 In this case, Art. XX (d) was only an issue before the Panel, not at the appellate stage. However, the Panel did not discuss the provision in detail, as it had already found that the controversial measure could not be justified under Art. XX (b) GATT and the chapeau of Art. XX GATT, see *Brazil – Measures Affecting Imports of Retreaded Tyres, WT/DS332/R* 2007, para. 7.381ff.

581 The Appellate Body used this order of investigation for the first time in *United States – Standards for Reformulated and Conventional Gasoline, WT/DS2/AB/R* 1996, sec. III, at 13ff albeit in a casual manner. In *United States – Import Prohibition of Certain Shrimp and Shrimp Products, WT/DS58/AB/R* 1998, para. 115–121, the Appellate Body was more explicit, chiding a Panel that had not applied this order of investigation; later Panels have applied this order of investigation, see for example *European Communities –Measures Affecting Asbestos and Products Containing Asbestos, WT/DS135/R* 2000, para. 8.167.

Art. XX GATT. In addition, Art. XIV GATS contains like Art. XX GATT a chapeau stipulating that measures taken under any of the sub-paragraphs

> "are not applied in a manner which would constitute a means of arbitrary or unjustifiable discrimination between countries where like conditions prevail, or a disguised restriction on trade".

The section is structured as follows: First, some overarching issues concerning the scope and applicability of Art. XX GATT are presented (section 1.1). In line with the order of investigation that the WTO dispute settlement bodies follow when discussing the above paragraphs in the case law, the case law on the different sub-paragraphs of Art. XX GATT (section 1.2) and GATS (section 1.3) is then presented. This is followed by an investigation of the case law on the chapeau clauses of both norms (section 1.4). At the end, the findings are discussed from a legal-technical point of view (section 1.5) and assessed from a more normative-political perspective (section 1.6).

1.1. Overarching issues

Certain aspects relating to the interpretation of Art. XX GATT concern more than one sub-paragraph. One is whether relevant sub-paragraphs of Art. XX GATT can also be invoked for the protection of extra-territorial resources. A second issue is whether Art. XX GATT can be used to justify deviations from the norms of agreements other than the GATT. Both issues are investigated in the following sections.

1.1.1. Protection of extraterritorial resources

Whether Art. XX GATT (and a similar issue could arise under Art. XIV GATS) can only be taken to cover measures taken for protecting interests, goods, or resources within the territory of the state taking the measure, or whether it can also justify measures that seek to protect resources or influence the politics in another state is a much debated issue in the literature.[582] An example would be the placing of import restrictions on goods that have been produced in contravention of fundamental labour standards in the importing country.

582 See for example Diebold 2008, 70ff; Zleptnig 2010, 297ff; Conrad 2011, 283ff.

The issue came up for the first time in WTO history in the *Shrimp – Turtles* case; in this case, the US had taken measures to protect sea turtles outside its territory. The Appellate Body in this case stated that, *if* a territorial nexus between the state taking the measure and the resource protected was required by Art. XX (g) GATT, it was present in the case at hand given the migratory behaviour of sea turtles; the Appellate Body did not elaborate further on whether a territorial nexus was indeed required.[583] In the Art. 21.5 DSU proceedings in the same case, the Appellate Body accepted the US measure as conforming to GATT rules.[584] Implicit in this is a rejection of the view that a state's protective measures have to be limited to the inside of that state's boundaries and also a rejection of the view, propounded at one point by Malaysia, that such a restrictive interpretation of Art. XX GATT was mandated in order to avoid violating the sovereignty of the importing country.[585] In *EC – Seal Products,* the Appellate Body referred to this finding because the EU measures that were controversial in this case were also aimed at addressing methods of seal hunting used outside of EU territory. However, given that the parties to the dispute had not presented any claims on an implicit territorial limitation of Art. XX GATT, the Appellate Body did not decide the question in this case, either, merely recognizing "the systemic importance of the question"[586]. The question as to whether the Appellate Body's application of Art. XX (a) GATT to a WTO Member's measure that was aimed at a method of production taking place outside of that Member's territory (in this case, hunting), implies a statement that there is no territorial limit to the application of Art. XX GATT is a valid one: any answer, however, would necessarily be speculative.

To conclude, it is not clear at present whether measures aimed at the protection of interests and resources outside a WTO Member's borders can only aim at "migratory" or "shared" resources, or whether trade-restrictions for the sake of, for example, animals or plants ("resources") or the

583 *United States – Import Prohibition of Certain Shrimp and Shrimp Products, WT/DS58/AB/R* 1998, para. 133.

584 *United States – Import Prohibition of Certain Shrimp and Shrimp Products, WT/DS58/AB/RW* 2001.

585 For Malaysia's argument see *United States – Import Prohibition of Certain Shrimp and Shrimp Products, WT/DS58/R* 1998, para. 7.24.

586 *European Communities – Measures Prohibiting the Importation and Marketing of Seal Products, WT/DS400/AB/R, WT/DS401/AB/R* 2014, para. 5.173.

rights of workers living only in the exporting state are amenable to justification.[587]

1.1.2. Applicability of Art. XX GATT under other WTO agreements

Whether Art. XX GATT can be invoked in defence of violations of agreements other than the GATT has so far only been discussed by the Appellate Body in three dispute settlement cases, with one additional case considered by a Panel. Only the Panel dealt with the applicability of Art. XX GATT under a WTO agreement other than the GATT, while the appellate cases related to whether Art. XX GATT could be invoked as a defence of a violation of China's WTO Accession Protocol.

The case, in which the Panel discussed whether a defendant could rely on Art. XX (b) GATT to justify a breach of the SPS Agreement, was *United States – Imports of Poultry from China.* The Panel first observed that there was no explicit textual reference to the SPS Agreement in Art. XX (b) GATT, because the GATT pre-dates the SPS Agreement; yet it noted that there was a reference to measures "necessary to protect human, animal or plant life or health".[588] Next, the Panel described that the SPS Agreement contained several references to Art. XX (b) GATT and featured terms identical to those in Art. XX GATT. It also concluded that the SPS Agreement "explained in detail" how to apply Art. XX (b) GATT.[589] On the basis of this latter observation, it concluded that it had

> "difficulty in accepting that an SPS measure which is found inconsistent with provisions of the SPS Agreement such as Articles 2 and 5, which are explanations of the disciplines of Article XX(b), could be justified under that same provision of the GATT 1994. Additionally, we recall that Article 2.1 of the SPS Agreement provides that Members have a right to take SPS measures necessary for the protection of human, animal, or plant life or health, provided that such measures are

---

587 In practice, numerous measures conditioning the importation of certain natural resources upon the fulfilment of certain conditions within the country of origin have been adopted by WTO Members, see for example EU Regulation 995/2010 of 20 October 2010 laying down the obligations of operators who place timber and timber products on the EU market or the US Lacey Act.

588 *United States – Certain Measures Affecting Imports of Poultry from China, WT/DS392/R* 2010, para. 7.468.

589 Ibid., para. 7.469–7.477.

> not inconsistent with the provisions of the SPS Agreement. Therefore, the Panel is of the view that an SPS measure which has been found inconsistent with Articles 2 and 5 of the SPS Agreement, cannot be justified under Article XX(b) of the GATT 1994."[590] [footnotes omitted]

The argument seems to be that the SPS Agreement is a *lex specialis* in relation to Art. XX (b) GATT so that there can be no case in which the conditions of Art. 2 and 5 SPS are not fulfilled, but the conditions of Art. XX (b) GATT would be.

In *China – Publications and Audiovisual Products*, China had invoked Art. XX (a) GATT to defend measures which had been found to be in violation of a certain norm in China's WTO Accession Protocol and China's Accession Working Party Report. The Panel in that case had not taken a decision on the applicability of Art. XX GATT, but had first investigated whether the substantive conditions contained in Art. XX (a) GATT were met; as it found this not to be the case, it did not investigate the applicability of the article.[591]

The Appellate Body did tackle the question, however, concluding that China could, in principle, invoke Art. XX GATT in order to justify deviations from the legal documents governing its WTO accession. This decision was based, however, on a specific clause contained in Art. 5.1 of China's Accession Protocol. The article reads:

> "Without prejudice to China's right to regulate trade in a manner consistent with the WTO Agreement, China shall progressively liberalize the availability and scope of the right to trade, so that, within three years after accession, all enterprises in China shall have the right to trade in all goods throughout the customs territory of China, except for those goods listed in Annex 2A which continue to be subject to state trading in accordance with this Protocol. Such right to trade shall be the right to import and export goods."

The Appellate Body concluded that the reference to China's "right to regulate trade in a manner consistent with the WTO Agreement" was a refer-

---

590 Ibid., para. 7.481.

591 *China – Measures Affecting Trading Rights and Distribution Services for Certain Publications and Audiovisual Entertainment Products, WT/DS363/R* 2009, para. 8.2(a)(ii).

ence to "the WTO Agreement as a whole, including its Annexes".[592] One of the Annexes of the WTO Agreement is the GATT 1994, which according to its Art. 1 "consists of" the GATT 1947, among others. Hence, the Appellate Body held that the phrase above was to be interpreted as encompassing

> "both China's power to take regulatory action provided that its measures satisfy prescribed WTO disciplines and meet specified conditions [...] and China's power to take regulatory action that derogates from WTO obligations that would otherwise constrain China's exercise of such power—that is, to relevant exceptions".[593]

In consequence, China could invoke Art. XX GATT in defence of a certain measure if "the measure has a clearly discernible, objective link to the regulation of trade in the goods at issue"[594]. In the case, the Appellate Body found – based on the factual conclusions drawn earlier by the Panel – that the provisions in dispute did possess a clearly discernible, objective link to China's regulation of trade in goods; hence, China could invoke Art. XX GATT to justify these measures.

In *China – Raw Materials* the question was decided again by the Appellate Body; this time with regard to Art. 11.3 of China's Accession Protocol. This norm reads:

> "China shall eliminate all taxes and charges applied to exports unless specifically provided for in Annex 6 of this Protocol or applied in conformity with the provisions of Article VIII of the GATT 1994."

Unlike its decision in *China – Publication and Audiovisual Products*, the Appellate Body decided in that case that Art. XX GATT could not be invoked to justify a breach of that norm. The Appellate Body seemed to rely mainly on two arguments:[595] First, the above article and the Annex to which it refers already provide for specific exceptions of the type that China sought to justify; second, Art. VIII GATT, to which the article also refers, excludes from its scope precisely the type of (export) measure that China sought to justify. By way of contrast, the Appellate Body neither took up its earlier

592 *China – Measures Affecting Trading Rights and Distribution Services for Certain Publications and Audiovisual Entertainment Products, WT/DS363/AB/R* 2009, para. 222.

593 Ibid., para. 228.

594 Ibid., para. 230.

595 See *China – Measures Related to the Exportation of Various Raw Materials, WT/DS394/AB/R, WT/DS395/AB/R, WT/DS398/AB/R* 2012, para. 284ff.

decision in *China – Publications and Audiovisual Products* on trade in goods, nor did it systematically investigate the context of Art. 11.3 of China's Accession Protocol.

The Panel and the Appellate Body returned to the question of whether a breach of Art. 11.3 of China's Accession Protocol could be justified by resorting to Art. XX GATT in *China – Rare Earths*. China had argued that there were new arguments not previously presented and discussed by the adjudicators that justified departing from the finding of the earlier case.[596] The Panel discussed China's arguments, but ultimately concluded that China had not presented any "cogent reason" for departing from the decision in the earlier case. However, one Panelist had a dissenting opinion, arguing that China should be allowed to rely on Art. XX GATT for justifying a breach of Art. 11.3 of its Accession Protocol.[597] China's appeal on the matter was limited, extending only to a rejection of one of its "new" arguments for the applicability of Art. XX GATT to Art. 11.3 of its Accession Protocol. In response, the Appellate Body did not explicitly deal with the availability of "cogent reasons" for departing from its earlier finding, but did approve the way that the Panel had dealt with China's arguments. In other words, the Appellate Body upheld both the Panel's findings in the current case and the earlier precedent.[598] When discussing the arguments it made very clear that whether Art. XX was an available defence with regard to violations of China's Accession Protocol required a case-by-case decision for each provision in question, on the basis of a thorough analysis of

> "the relevant provisions, starting with the text of the relevant provision in China's Accession Protocol and taking into account its context, including that provided by the Protocol itself, and by relevant provisions of the Accession Working Party Report, and by the agreements within the WTO legal framework. The analysis must also take into account the overall architecture of the WTO system as a single package of rights and obligations and any other relevant interpretative elements, and must be applied to the circumstances of each dispute, including the measure at issue and the nature of the alleged violation".[599]

596 China's arguments are summarized in *China – Measures Related to the Exportation of Rare Earths, Tungsten, and Molybdenum, WT/DS431/AB/R, WT/DS432/AB/R, WT/DS433/AB/R* 2014, para. 5.4ff.

597 Finding of the Panel as summarized in ibid., para. 1.13, 5.7.

598 Ibid., para. 5.8–5.74.

599 Ibid., para. 5.51; for the detailed arguments of the Appellate Body, see para. 5.52ff.

Overall, there is no unified approach in the WTO case law to the applicability of Art. XX GATT to violations of non-GATT provisions.

1.2. Sub-paragraphs of Art. XX GATT

1.2.1. Art. XX (a) GATT

Art. XX (a) GATT allows countries to take measures "necessary to protect public morals". As with the other subparagraphs of Art. XX GATT, there are two requirements. One is that a measure serves a certain non-trade policy objective, and the second concerns the relationship between the measure and the objective, qualified in Art. XX (a) GATT by the word "necessary".

The Appellate Body has discussed Art. XX (a) GATT in two cases so far, *China – Publications and Audiovisual Products* and *EC – Seal Products*. The Chinese case was the first one. China sought to defend measures that were ultimately aimed, to put it bluntly, at censorship. These measures had been found to be in violation of a certain norm in China's WTO Accession Protocol, and the Appellate Body decided that Art. XX GATT could in principle be invoked to defend these measures. In *EC – Seal Products*, the EU invoked Art. XX (a) GATT in defence of measures aimed at public moral concerns over the killing of seals.[600] This shows that Members may use the public morals exception to defend measures taken for a wide variety of policy objectives lying behind public moral issues.

Protection of public morals

What is understood by the term "public morals" and how the adjudicators ascertain whether a certain measure protects them is an interesting point in the context of the WTO. The WTO membership is so broad and diverse that ideas of public morals are unlikely to be consistent throughout it: compare, for example, those expected in countries like Sweden, Jordan, In-

600 See *European Communities – Measures Prohibiting the Importation and Marketing of Seal Products, WT/DS400/R, WT/DS401/R* 2013, para. 7.625ff.

dia or Burkina Faso.[601] *China – Publications and Audiovisual Products* is a case in point; the censorship measures that China sought to defend might be viewed by other societies as contrary to their democratic political-ethical standards and public morals. How do the adjudicators deal with this sensitive issue?

In *China – Publications and Audiovisual Products*, the Panel drew on the prior findings of the Panel on Art. XIV (a) in *United States – Gambling* on the definition of public morals and public order, which the Appellate Body had approved. Accordingly,

> "the content of these concepts for Members can vary in time and space, depending upon a range of factors, including prevailing social, cultural, ethical and religious values."

and Members

> "should be given some scope to define and apply for themselves the concepts of 'public morals' [...] in their respective territories, according to their own systems and scales of values."[602]

When applying these standards to the measures at issue, the Panel observed that China claimed that these measures protected public morals, a claim the other party to the dispute did not contest, and proceeded on the basis of this assumption to investigate the remainder of Art. XX (a) GATT.[603] The Appellate Body did not investigate the matter.

In *EC – Seal Products* the controversial measure was a ban on the import of products containing seals, which contained certain exceptions. Seal products could only be imported into the EU market if the seals had been hunted by Inuit or other indigenous communities, for purposes of marine resource management, or if the seal products were brought by travellers in-

601 However, questions of morals are also contested within societies or regions. For an overview of morals-related cases of the US Supreme Court, the ECtHR and the ECJ, see Delimatsis 2011, 266ff.

602 These quotes are originally from *United States – Measures Affecting the Cross-Border Supply of Gambling and Betting Services, WT/DS285/R* 2004, para. 6.465, 6.461 respectively; they are quoted by the Panel in *China – Measures Affecting Trading Rights and Distribution Services for Certain Publications and Audiovisual Entertainment Products, WT/DS363/R* 2009, para. 7.759.

603 *China – Measures Affecting Trading Rights and Distribution Services for Certain Publications and Audiovisual Entertainment Products, WT/DS363/R* 2009, para. 7.763.

to the EU in limited circumstances.[604] To find out whether the measure was aimed at protecting public morals, the Panel looked at the text, structure, design and legislative history of the measure as well as considering other evidence. It found that there were indeed public concerns over seal welfare in the EU and that the main objective of the measure was to address these concerns, even though it also accommodated other interests through its exception clauses. Consequently, the Panel addressed whether public concern over seal welfare was an issue of "public morals" in the EU. On the basis of various pieces of evidence, the Panel concluded that seal welfare was a moral or ethical issue in the EU and the measures were therefore aimed at addressing it.[605] Before the Appellate Body considered the issue there was no question over whether the EU's regime addressed public concerns over seal welfare, but the complainants made the point that these were not "moral" concerns; moreover, they pointed out that the measure also addressed certain other objectives through its exceptions. Generally, the Appellate Body held that Panels

> "should take into account the Member's articulation of the objective or the objectives it pursues through its measure, but it is not bound by that Member's characterizations of such objective(s). Indeed, the panel must take account of all evidence put before it in this regard, including 'the texts of statutes, legislative history, and other evidence regarding the structure and operation' of the measure at issue. A panel's identification of the 'objective' of a measure is a matter of legal characterization subject to appellate review under Article 17.6 of the DSU."[606] [footnotes omitted]

The Appellate Body then relied on the Panel's factual findings and confirmed its analysis that the EU measure addressed issues of public morals.[607] Unlike the approach taken in *EC – Asbestos* to the interpretation of the term "protection" in Art. XX (b), the Appellate Body did not hold

---

604 See the description of the measure in *European Communities – Measures Prohibiting the Importation and Marketing of Seal Products, WT/DS400/AB/R, WT/DS401/AB/R* 2014, para. 1.4.

605 See the summary of the Panel's reasoning in ibid., para. 5.135ff. The Panel had actually discussed the measure's objective under Art. 2.2 TBT, but then drawn on its analysis also under Art. XX (a) GATT. The Appellate Body followed this approach and reviewed in its analysis for Art. XX (a) GATT the Panel's statements on the objective of the measure under Art. 2.2 TBT, see para. 5.133.

606 Ibid., para. 5.144.

607 Ibid., para. 5.167.

that the term "to protect" in Art. XX (a) GATT implied that a risk to public morals had to be demonstrated. It argued explicitly that protecting public morals was different from protecting public health in this regard; risks to public morals could not be ascertained in the same manner as risks to public health.[608] The Appellate Body also stressed that the right of WTO Members to choose a level of protection appropriate to themselves also involved a right to "set different levels of protection even when responding to similar interests of moral concern".[609]

Necessary

A measure that aims at protecting public morals also needs to be necessary to this end under Art. XX (a) GATT.

When investigating the criterion of "necessity" under Art. XX (a) GATT, the Panel in *China – Publications and Audiovisual Products* found that China had not demonstrated that the measures at issue were necessary to protect public morals, because a less trade-restrictive measure was available. The Appellate Body referred to its own approach in *Korea – Various Measures on Beef* (in the context of Art. XX (d) GATT), *United States – Gambling* (in the context of Art. XIV (a) GATS), and *Brazil – Tyres* (in the context of Art. XX (b) GATT); it observed that in these cases the act of interpreting the term "necessary" had always been taken to involve "weighing and balancing" a number of factors relating both to the measure to be justified and to possible alternative measures reasonably available.[610] The Appellate Body also expressed the view that in all of these cases it had taken the same approach towards interpreting the necessity criterion.[611]

Accordingly, the Appellate Body re-iterated findings from earlier case law that

> "the term 'necessary', in the abstract, refers to a range of degrees of necessity. The Appellate Body explained that determining whether a measure is 'necessary' involves a process of weighing and balancing a series of factors that prominently include the contribution made by

608 Ibid., para. 5.197f.
609 Ibid., para. 5.200.
610 *China – Measures Affecting Trading Rights and Distribution Services for Certain Publications and Audiovisual Entertainment Products,* *WT/DS363/AB/R* 2009, para. 239.
611 Ibid., para. 242.

> the measure to secure compliance with the law or regulation at issue, the importance of the common interests or values protected by that law or regulation, and the accompanying impact of the law or regulation on imports or exports. The greater the contribution a measure makes to the objective pursued, the more likely it is to be characterized as 'necessary'."[612] [footnotes omitted]

It also stated that

> "[...] if a Member chooses to adopt a very restrictive measure, it will have to ensure that the measure is carefully designed so that the other elements to be taken into account in weighing and balancing the factors relevant to an assessment of the 'necessity' of the measure will 'outweigh' such restrictive effect."[613]

Moreover, WTO adjudicators

> "need to identify relevant factors and undertake a weighing and balancing process including, where relevant, with respect to proposed alternative measures that may be less trade restrictive while making an equivalent contribution to the relevant objective".[614]

According to the adjudicators, the question of the availability of a less trade-restrictive measure is also a matter of balancing. The Appellate Body also indicated that there may be more than one way to carry out the test in a concrete case, stating that the way the Panel had applied the necessity test in the case at hand was not the only way that the Panel could have approached its task, but neither did the Panel's approach amount to an error in law.[615]

The Appellate Body also re-confirmed a finding from an earlier case that for demonstrating that a measure was necessary a party should induce "data or evidence".[616] At the same time, and again drawing on an earlier decision, the Appellate Body stressed that the threshold for demonstrating "necessity" was not too high as it could be difficult to isolate the contribution of a specific measure to the realization of a defined objective. Thus, in the eyes of the Appellate Body, a Panel can also conclude that a measure that is apt for contributing to a certain objective is also necessary to that end.

---

612 Ibid., para. 251.
613 Ibid., para. 310.
614 Ibid., para. 242.
615 Ibid., para. 249.
616 Ibid., para. 252.

Such a conclusion needs to be based on quantitative projections or qualitative hypotheses.[617] In the concrete case the Appellate Body found that the Panel's decision was not based on such evidence.[618]

In terms of balancing the objectives at stake, none of the parties appealed the Panel's finding that the protection of public morals was a highly important governmental interest and that China had adopted a high level of protection of public morals within its territory,[619] and hence the Appellate Body did not pass judgement upon it.

The Appellate Body did review the Panel's finding on whether the measures at hand *de facto* made a contribution to the objective pursued, the protection of public morals, however. After stating that this was not the case, the Appellate Body analysed the Panel's findings on the trade-restrictive effects of the measure. In that context, the Appellate Body investigated whether only the restrictive effects of a measure on *actual* imports or also the effects on *potential* importers had to be investigated; the latter had been the approach of the Panel. The Appellate Body concluded in this regard that the analysis had to be conducted in light of the specific norm whose breach a party sought to justify, in this case Art. III:4 GATT. According to the Appellate Body, Art. III:4 GATT protects the equality of competitive opportunities for imported products as compared to like domestic products. Moreover, the measures in dispute contained rules on who could import publications and audiovisual products into China; in other words, the Appellate Body found no fault with the Panel's approach which investigated the trade-restrictive impacts of the measure also with regard to potential importers. Indeed, it even found such approach to be pertinent, as it allowed the Panel to distinguish between different measures by the degree to which they restricted trade. This, in turn, had an impact on how likely

617 Ibid., para. 253.

618 Ibid., para. 294. In the case at hand, there had been a rule that publication import entities could only be approved and hence import publications to China if they were in conformity with the State plan for the number, structure, and geographical coverage of publication import entities. However, according to China that "State plan" did not exist in writing, see para. 281ff.

619 See *China – Measures Affecting Trading Rights and Distribution Services for Certain Publications and Audiovisual Entertainment Products, WT/DS363/R* 2009, para. 7.836.

they were to be considered as necessary, with the more trade-restrictive measures being harder to justify.[620]

In terms of potential alternative, less trade-restrictive measures, the US, the claimant, made a suggestion which the Panel investigated and found to be both available to China and less trade-restrictive than the measures in dispute. The Appellate Body, when reviewing this finding, repeated the *dictum* of earlier appellate reports that an

> "alternative measure may be found not to be 'reasonably available' where it is merely theoretical in nature, for instance, where the responding party is not capable of taking it, or where the measure imposes an undue burden on that Member, such as 'prohibitive costs or substantial technical difficulties'. Moreover, a 'reasonably available' alternative measure must be a measure that would preserve the responding party's right to achieve its desired level of protection with respect to the objective pursued under Article XX of the GATT 1994."[621] [footnotes omitted]

Moreover, it also clarified that a party invoking Art. XX (a) does not have to demonstrate that there were no alternative measures that it could have taken. Yet if the complainant suggests a concrete measure, the defendant must show that such measure is no proper alternative or not "reasonably available".[622] This can be the case either because the proposed alternative measure would not lead to the desired level of protection, or because it could only be adopted at undue financial or economic cost. In any case, the defendant party must base its claims on the alternative measures on sufficient evidence.[623] In the case at hand, the Appellate Body found that the Panel had proceeded correctly when deciding that a certain alternative measure proposed by China's opponent was reasonably available to China, even though it might require the allocation of additional human and financial resources to authorities implementing the measures.

In *EC – Seal Products*, the Panel concluded that the EU measure was necessary for protecting public morals within the EU on the basis of the *Korea – Beef* formula. It found that the goal of protecting public morals was an

---

620 *China – Measures Affecting Trading Rights and Distribution Services for Certain Publications and Audiovisual Entertainment Products, WT/DS363/AB/R* 2009, para. 305ff.

621 Ibid., para. 318.

622 Ibid., para. 319.

623 Ibid., para. 327.

important value or interest, that the measure contributed to a "certain extent" to its objective of addressing the EU public moral concerns on seal welfare, and that the trade-restrictive effects of the measures were described casually as "severe".[624] The Panel also found that an alternative measure proposed by the complainants was not reasonably available to the EU.[625] The Panel drew on its prior analysis under Art. 2.2 TBT to this end.

The finding that the measure was necessary was challenged on appeal. The Appellate Body first re-iterated that making a decision on the necessity of a measure involved a process of "weighing and balancing" a "series of factors, including the importance of the objective, the contribution of the measure to that objective, and the trade-restrictiveness of the measure". It also stated that "in most cases", a comparison between the measure in dispute and potential alternatives should then be carried out.[626] Subsequently, it rejected the Panel's reliance on the appellate report in *Brazil – Tyres* to the end that a highly trade restrictive measure needed to be apt to make a "material" contribution to the end pursued to be necessary. The Appellate Body stressed that its finding in the Brazilian case was a result of the specific circumstances of the case, rather than a generally applicable yardstick.[627] It emphasized that the balancing exercise required as part of the necessity analysis was a holistic and flexible exercise. In other words, only one of the relevant factors, the contribution for the measure to the end pursued, could not on its own be determinative of a measure's necessity and no specific threshold that a measure needed to meet in this regard could be set *ex ante*.[628] At the same time, the Appellate Body also stressed that a Panel has certain latitude in ascertaining the contribution of a measure to the end pursued, and its approach may be qualitative or quantitative.[629] In the case at hand, as some of the aspects of the disputed measure had only been fully operational for a short time, the measure's effects could not yet be fully appreciated; indeed, there was a shortage of data on the effects of the measure. Hence, the Panel had conducted a predominantly qualitative analysis

---

624 *European Communities – Measures Prohibiting the Importation and Marketing of Seal Products, WT/DS400/R, WT/DS401/R* 2013, para. 7.630ff.

625 Ibid., para. 7.639.

626 *European Communities – Measures Prohibiting the Importation and Marketing of Seal Products, WT/DS400/AB/R, WT/DS401/AB/R* 2014, para. 5.169.

627 Ibid., para. 5.213.

628 Ibid., para. 5.215.

629 Ibid., para. 5.221.

on the extent to which the measure contributed to protecting public morals. The Appellate Body approved of this approach.[630]

Due to the limited character of the appeal, the Appellate Body did not fully review the Panel's balancing exercise, but it did discuss its analysis of the availability of alternative, less trade-restrictive measures. Here, the Appellate Body first recalled earlier findings that an alternative measure may be found not to be reasonably available where it is merely theoretical in nature, for example, because the defending WTO Member is not capable of taking it, or where taking it would impose an undue burden. The Appellate Body also clarified that in some cases it might not only be the costs to the country itself that mattered, but also the cost or difficulties created through alternative measures for the affected domestic industry.[631] Moreover, the alternative measure must also preserve the desired level of protection of the defendant.[632] In this case, the proposed alternative to the EU's trade ban (with exceptions) was market access for seal products complying with animal welfare standards, and fulfilling certification and labelling requirements in this regard.[633] The Panel found the alternative measure to be less trade-restrictive than the regime in place, but held the alternative measure was not reasonably available as it did not attain the EU's desired level of protection.[634] This was appealed by the complainants who argued that the Panel had based its comparison between the proposed alternative measure and the measure in place on the assumption that the measure in place fully attained the EU's objective of protecting public morals, rather than on the actual extent to which it did so.[635] However, the Appellate Body rejected the complainants' reading of the Panel's findings.[636] All in all, the Appellate Body upheld the Panel's finding that the EU seal regime was justified under Art. XX (a) GATT.

630 Ibid., para. 5.221f.
631 Ibid., para. 5.277.
632 Ibid., para. 5.261.
633 Ibid., para. 5.262.
634 A similar conclusion had also been drawn in the literature before the Panel report was published, see Fitzgerald 2011, 94.
635 *European Communities – Measures Prohibiting the Importation and Marketing of Seal Products, WT/DS400/AB/R, WT/DS401/AB/R* 2014, para. 5.262.
636 Ibid., para. 5.269ff.

1.2.2. Art. XX (b) GATT

Art. XX (b) GATT is the second relevant sub-paragraph of Art. XX GATT in the context of this work. Textually, the norm contains two requirements, namely that in order to be justified under this norm, a measure must be taken to protect human, animal or plant life or health and that it be necessary to this end. Given that the norm relates not only to human but also to animal or plant life or health, it may also be used to justify measures that serve an environmental objective as e.g. in the *Brazil – Tyres* case.[637] It could also have been invoked (but was not) in the *EU – Seal Products* case, where animal welfare concerns were among the issues at stake.[638]

It should be noted that the Spanish and French versions of the text are formulated slightly differently from the English version;[639] in the English version, the paragraph refers to measures "necessary for the protection of human, animal and plant life or health", whereas the Spanish and French versions relate to measures

> "necesarias para proteger la salud y la vida de las personas y de los animales o para preserver los vegetales", and
> "nécessaires à la protection de la santé et de la vie des personnes et des animaux ou à la préservation des végétaux" respectively.

These versions mean in English "necessary to protect the health and life of person or animals or to conserve plants" and "necessary for the protection of the health and life of person or animals or to conserve plants" respectively.

---

637 The Appellate Body in this case agreed with the Panel that the measures at issue served environmental objectives next to health objectives and both were important; see *Brazil – Measures Affecting Imports of Retreaded Tyres, WT/DS332/AB/R* 2007, para. 179; however, it is doubtful whether the Appellate Body made a statement to the end that Art. XX (b) GATT can generally be invoked to justify measures protecting the environment, as e.g. Kaufmann and Weber 2011, 513 seem to contend.

638 Several commentators see the possibility of justifying the EU measure under Art. XX (b) GATT in this case, see Howse and Langille 2011, 419ff; Pitschas and Schloemann 2012, 23; by contrast, Fitzgerald 2011, 124f is less optimistic in this regard. It is not clear why the EU did not invoke Art. XX (b) GATT in this case.

639 I owe this insight to Condon 2010, 209f.

Protection of human, animal or plant life or health

The first requirement has, until today, not caused any major controversies or required sophisticated interpretations. In most cases it was plain whether the requirement was met and the adjudicators simply stated so[640]; in other cases what was difficult to clarify were the facts rather than the law.[641]

One aspect that dispute settlement bodies have begun to clarify what constitutes an appropriate approach to ascertaining the protective character of the measure at issue: In *EC – Asbestos*, the Panel in its discussion of Art. XX (b) GATT investigated the existence of a health risk, because Art. XX (b) GATT deals with measures "to protect" human, animal and plant health – and this presupposes a risk that measures need to protect against.[642] Unlike the SPS Agreement the GATT does not contain any specific requirements concerning the kind of evidence that must be offered to demonstrate the existence of a risk. Nonetheless, the Panel's assessment of the evidence in *EC – Asbestos* strongly resembles the way that other Panels had dealt with the evidential material in the SPS cases.[643] It stated that in assessing the evidence it had to keep in mind that the measure under review related to public health.[644] It found that the evidence tended to prove the existence of a health risk rather than the opposite and that therefore a decision-maker in the field of health policy could reasonably conclude that a health risk existed.[645] When the complainant in this case challenged the Panel's findings on the existence of a risk, the Appellate Body stated that the "Panel enjoyed a margin of discretion in assessing the value of the evi-

---

640 *United States – Standards for Reformulated and Conventional Gasoline, WT/DS2/R* 1996, para. 6.21.

641 *Brazil – Measures Affecting Imports of Retreaded Tyres, WT/DS332/R* 2007, para. 7.56ff.

642 See the summary of the Panel's reasoning in *European Communities – Measures Affecting Asbestos and Products Containing Asbestos, WT/DS135/AB/R* 2001, para. 157. The Panel in this case had consulted experts and relied on various studies quoted by the parties to the dispute to ascertain the existence of a risk, see para. 8.174–8.175, 8.184–8.195 of the Panel report.

643 See below section 2.1.

644 *European Communities – Measures Affecting Asbestos and Products Containing Asbestos, WT/DS135/R* 2000, para. 8.184.

645 Ibid., para. 8.193; the Appellate Body in the same case approved the Panel's approach, see *European Communities – Measures Affecting Asbestos and Products Containing Asbestos, WT/DS135/AB/R* 2001, para. 159–163.

dence, and the weight to be ascribed to that evidence",[646] relying on earlier findings to this end in non-health related cases. Consequently, it did not find that the Panel erred in its assessment of the evidentiary material.[647]

The Panel in *Brazil – Tyres* adopted a more light-handed approach when stating that the policy objective

> "as declared by the Member taking the measure falls within the scope of policies to protect human, animal or plant life or health".[648]

This approach is different from the approach taken by the Appellate Body in other situations where the objective of a measure needed to be verified, e.g. in the context of Art. III GATT. Here, the Appellate Body had decided that the objectives of a Member's measure should be determined objectively by the adjudicators, using such factors as, for example, the text of the measure and legislative history.[649]

Necessary

The difficult part of Art. XX (b) GATT is, of course, the interpretation of the necessity requirement. The approach used by the world trade adjudicators until today was begun under the GATT, by the Panel in the GATT *Thailand – Cigarettes* case. The Panel in that case recycled – in light of the identical wording and objectives of both provisions – the interpretation of Art. XX (d) GATT that a previous Panel had developed in the *United States – Section 337* case.[650] Accordingly, a WTO Member

> "cannot justify a measure inconsistent with another GATT provision as 'necessary' in terms of Article XX(d) if an alternative measure which it could reasonably be expected to employ and which is not inconsistent with other GATT provisions is available to it. By the same token, in cases where a measure consistent with other GATT provisions is not

646 *European Communities – Measures Affecting Asbestos and Products Containing Asbestos, WT/DS135/AB/R* 2001, para. 161.

647 *European Communities – Measures Prohibiting the Importation and Marketing of Seal Products, WT/DS400/R, WT/DS401/R* 2013, para. 7.636.

648 *Brazil – Measures Affecting Imports of Retreaded Tyres, WT/DS332/R* 2007, para. 7.101.

649 For references from the case law see McGrady 2009, 156.

650 *Thailand – Restrictions on importation of and internal taxes on cigarettes, DS10/R* 1990, 75.

> reasonably available, a contracting party is bound to use, among the measures reasonably available to it, that which entails the least degree of inconsistency with other GATT provisions."[651]

The first WTO case in which Art. XX (b) GATT played a role was *United States – Gasoline*. In this case only the Panel decided on Art. XX (b) GATT as the findings on Art. XX (b) GATT were not appealed and the Appellate Body consequently only dealt with the interpretation of Art. XX (g) GATT. The Panel opened the necessity analysis by saying that it was not its task to investigate whether the environmental objectives pursued were necessary.[652] It then resorted to the *United States – Section 337* formula and proceeded to investigate the existence of reasonably available, less GATT-inconsistent alternative measures.[653] After a relatively short analysis it discarded US statements that certain alternative measures that the Panel itself had identified were either not of comparable effectiveness as those in place or not feasible; the Panel ultimately concluded that the controversial US measures were not necessary.

The Appellate Body also used the earlier GATT formula when first dealing with Art. XX (b) GATT in the *EC –Asbestos* case, but in a far less deductive manner than had earlier GATT Panels. It posited a relationship between the magnitude of the risk at stake and the strictness with which the necessity test would be applied: the smaller the hazard, the less vigorous measures can be.[654] The Appellate Body relied for its interpretation of Art. XX (b) GATT on its report in the *Korea – Beef* case, a report that was issued after the Panel had taken its decision in the *EC – Asbestos* case and where Art. XX (d) GATT was at stake. The Appellate Body in *EC – Asbestos* said that

> "one aspect of the 'weighing and balancing process [...] comprehended in the determination of whether a WTO-consistent alternative measure' is reasonably available is the extent to which the alternative measure 'contributes to the realization of the end pursued.' In addition, we observed in that case, that '[t]he more vital or important [the] common interests or values' pursued, the easier it would be to accept as

651 *United States – Section 337 of the Tariff Act of 1930, L/6439 - 36S/345* 1989, para. 5.26.

652 *United States – Standards for Reformulated and Conventional Gasoline, WT/DS2/R* 1996, para. 6.22.

653 Ibid., para. 6.25ff.

654 *European Communities – Measures Affecting Asbestos and Products Containing Asbestos, WT/DS135/AB/R* 2001, para. 171f.

> 'necessary' measure designed to achieve those ends."[655] [footnotes omitted]

This reading of Art. XX (b) GATT establishes a close relationship between the two elements of Art. XX (b) GATT. If the way to qualify a measure as protecting human, animal or plant health is to verify the existence of a health risk and the magnitude of the risk is decisive for determining what counts as a necessary measure, the elements are no longer entirely separate. In *EC – Asbestos*, the Appellate Body also observed, drawing on earlier findings under the SPS Agreement, that

> "'responsible and representative governments may act in good faith on the basis of what, at a given time, may be a *divergent* opinion coming from qualified and respected sources.' [emphasis added]. In justifying a measure under Article XX(b) of the GATT 1994, a Member may also rely, in good faith, on scientific sources which, at that time, may represent a divergent, but qualified and respected, opinion. A Member is not obliged, in setting health policy, automatically to follow what, at a given time, may constitute a majority scientific opinion. Therefore, a panel need not, necessarily, reach a decision under Article XX(b) of the GATT 1994 on the basis of the 'preponderant' weight of the evidence."[656]

The Appellate Body, implicitly, appears to concur with the Panel's view that the term "reasonably available" ought not to be interpreted too loosely nor too strictly when pointing out that a measure can neither be ruled out as not being reasonably available because it is difficult to implement nor can it only be ruled out if it is impossible to implement.[657] Ultimately, the Appellate Body deferred to the Panel's (factual) finding that it was doubtful whether alternative measures would have been effective in reaching the level of protection France had opted for.[658] While it did not fully

655 Ibid., para. 172.

656 Ibid., para. 178; Howse 2009, 229 makes the point that deference here is only afforded to democratic, representative governments. However, it is not clear whether this is not an over-interpretation of the Appellate Body's findings. Treating WTO Members differently because of their internal political structure would certainly not meet with the consent of many WTO Members, has clearly no textual basis and may lead to charges against the adjudicators of being biased against certain countries.

657 *European Communities – Measures Affecting Asbestos and Products Containing Asbestos, WT/DS135/AB/R* 2001, para. 169.

658 Ibid., para. 173f.

conduct the balancing test with all of its elements, this is perhaps because it considered that the alternative measures proposed by the claimant would not reach the desired level of protection and thus, by implication, the measure in place was indispensable.[659]

The next case in which Art. XX (b) GATT became relevant concerned the EU's system of trade preferences for certain developing countries: *EC – GSP*. Only the Panel decided on Art. XX (b) GATT in this case, as its findings on Art. XX (b) GATT were not appealed. In this case, the EU had argued that granting certain trade preferences to countries with a major role in drug production and trafficking was justified under Art. XX (b) GATT. It argued that drugs posed a risk to human life and health in the EU and that tariff preferences contributed to the protection of human life and health by supporting measures against drug production and trafficking, thereby reducing their supply to the EU.[660] The EU here made a complex factual argument, based on a rather long, if plausible, causal chain between the EU measure, increased income in developing countries, political decisions in those countries on how to invest that income in certain measures, the effects of those measures, and the desired health effect in the EU. The Panel, when interpreting Art. XX (b) GATT stated explicitly that it considered the approach followed by the Appellate Body in *Korea – Beef* regarding Art. XX (d) GATT also appropriate for the analysis of a measure under Art. XX (b) GATT, albeit without giving any specific reason for this finding.[661] Yet the Panel then only relied on the *Korea – Beef* approach in relation to identifying the proper order of analysis. In its later analysis of necessity, it did not mention the various elements identified by the Appellate Body in *Korea – Beef* as relevant for the necessity analysis, but just discussed the extent to which the EU measure contributed to the stated health objective. Its analysis was rather curt: it observed that the product coverage of the EU scheme had been narrowed and tariff cuts had been reduced in the preceding years. On this basis, the Panel concluded that the contribution of the EU scheme to the realization of the claimed health objective was "insecure for the future".[662] Another reason for Panel's rejection of the EU claim that its measure was necessary for health purposes was that the EU had no system in place for monitoring whether the measure actually con-

659 See Ruozzi 2009, 479.

660 *European Communities – Conditions for the Granting of Tariff Preferences to Developing Countries, WT/DS246/R* 2003, para. 7.180.

661 Ibid., para. 7.196.

662 Ibid., para. 7.213.

tributed to the envisioned health objective. The Panel therefore concluded that it could not assess whether the measure actually contributed to the objective pursued.[663] In addition, the Panel observed that the EU measure also granted tariff preferences and provided for the suspension of such preferences for a number of reasons unrelated to drug trafficking and the seriousness of the drug problem in a certain country. In the view of the Panels, this cast further doubt on the measure's effectiveness in pursuing the declared health objective.[664] Finally, the Panel also looked at alternative measures, concluding, again in a rather brief manner, that the provision of technical and financial assistance to countries concerned and the multilateral negotiation of tariff reductions constituted a less trade-restrictive alternative.[665] In sum, the Panel concluded that the EU measure was not necessary in the sense of Art. XX (b) GATT.

The next appellate case involving Art. XX (b) GATT, *Brazil – Tyres,* is very interesting with regards the interpretation of Art. XX (b) GATT for two reasons: First, the interpretation of Art. XX (b) GATT was the only subject matter of the appeal; second, the appellant, the EU, explicitly claimed that the Panel had not carried out a proper weighing and balancing of the relevant factors.[666] When reviewing this claim, the Appellate Body first referred to the *Korea – Beef* decision stating that

> "a 'necessary' measure is [...] located significantly closer to the pole of 'indispensable' than to the opposite pole of simply 'making a contribution to'".[667]

It also re-iterated the *Korea – Beef* formula that determining whether as measure is necessary

> "involves in every case a process of weighing and balancing a series of factors which prominently include the contribution made by the compliance measure to the enforcement of the law or regulation at issue, the importance of the common interests or values protected by that law or regulation, and the accompanying impact of the law or regulation on imports or exports".[668] [footnote omitted]

663 Ibid., para. 7.214.
664 Ibid., para. 7.215–7.218.
665 Ibid., para. 7.222.
666 *Brazil – Measures Affecting Imports of Retreaded Tyres, WT/DS332/AB/R* 2007, para. 133.
667 Ibid., para. 141.
668 Ibid., para. 142.

It then went on to state that

> "If this analysis yields a preliminary conclusion that the measure is necessary, this result must be confirmed by comparing the measure with its possible alternatives, which may be less trade restrictive while providing an equivalent contribution to the achievement of the objective pursued."[669]

The Appellate Body here seemed to posit a two-step analysis; a preliminary analysis followed by one that is more in-depth. It then went on to re-iterate some of the findings from earlier reports such as *United States – Gambling*, including the finding that if a complaining Member has put forward an alternative measure, the responding Member may try to demonstrate that that measure is not reasonably available, e.g. because it is merely theoretical in nature or because the measure would impose an undue burden on the defending Member.[670]

When applying the *Korea – Beef* formula, the Appellate Body first described the Panel's finding on the objective pursued through the measure and its importance, without investigating it at any length.[671] The Appellate Body then went on to review the methodology used by the Panel in analysing the contribution of the challenged measure to the achievement of its objective, re-iterating that such a contribution existed "when there is a genuine relationship of ends and means between the objective pursued and the measure at issue"[672]. In this regard, it observed that Panels had certain latitude in designing a proper methodology for carrying out the analysis, depending on the facts of the case and the evidence available. Consequently, the Appellate Body accepted the Panel's choice of a qualitative approach which the EU had appealed.[673] It also noted that in some cases the contribution of one specific measure to a public health or environmental objective among several measures in place could be difficult to establish. Moreover, it observed that sometimes the contribution of measures to such objectives as mitigating climate change could only be evaluated in the long-term, which would not keep such measures from being justifiable under Art. XX (b) GATT.[674] All in all, the Appellate Body accepted that the

669 Ibid.
670 Ibid.
671 Ibid., para. 144.
672 Ibid., para. 145.
673 Ibid., para. 147.
674 Ibid., para. 151.

"Panel's analysis supports its conclusion that the [measure at issue] is capable of making a contribution" to the end pursued.[675]

After accepting the Panel's finding that the measure at issue was capable of contributing to the stated objectives, the Appellate Body went on to investigate whether the measure was "apt for" making a "material contribution" to the objective. Considering the connotations of suitability concomitant with "apt for", this is a somewhat curious choice of word, given that the Appellate Body had already stated that the measure was capable of contributing to the objective pursued. A measure that is capable of contributing to a certain objective is certainly at the same time also suitable to this end. Looking at "apt" in addition to "capable" would make sense, if "apt" had a meaning going beyond that of "capable". Yet it is not clear from the Appellate Body report if "apt" is used as a synonym for appropriate. In the Spanish version of the report, the word "apropriada"[676], which is the equivalent of "appropriate", is used for describing the quality of the measure; by contrast according to the French version, the Appellate Body investigates

> "si […] l'interdiction d'importer est à même d'apporter une contribution importante à la réalisation de l'objectif"[677],

which translates as

> "whether the import ban is capable of making an important contribution to the attainment of the objective".

A different division of the Appellate Body in a later case shed some light at the approach of the Appellate Body in *Brazil – Tyres.* It observed that the Appellate Body in the Brazilian case was faced with a situation in which there was a bundle of measures in place; this made a determination of the actual contribution of any specific measures to the objective pursued difficult. This is why the Appellate Body investigated the "aptness" of the measure to contribute – in theory and in the future – to the objective pursued, rather than its actual impact.[678] In sum, the Appellate Body concluded that the measure at issue, an import ban, was "likely to bring a material contri-

675 Ibid., para. 150.

676 See para. 152 of the Spanish version of *Brazil – Measures Affecting Imports of Retreaded Tyres, WT/DS332/AB/R* 2007.

677 See para. 152 of the French version of ibid.

678 *European Communities – Measures Prohibiting the Importation and Marketing of Seal Products, WT/DS400/AB/R, WT/DS401/AB/R* 2014, para. 5.213.

bution to the achievements of its objective" and approved of the Panel's analysis.[679]

Given that the preliminary analysis of the relevant factors,

> "particularly the extent of the contribution to the achievement of a measure's objective and its trade restrictiveness, in the light of the importance of the interests or values at stake",

led to the preliminary conclusion that the measure was necessary,[680] the Appellate Body went on to investigate possible alternative measures. One of the reasons why the Panel had concluded that some of the measures proposed by the EU, the complainant in this case, were not reasonably available was that they were already in place as part of a comprehensive approach. The Appellate Body accepted this finding. The Appellate Body also reviewed some of the Panel's factual findings on whether the proposed alternative measures reached the level of protection that Brazil aimed at and approved of the Panel's finding that they did not.[681] It is interesting that the Appellate Body made a distinction between "remedial" and "preventive" measures, arguing that all of these would be needed, rather than being interchangeable for one another.[682]

Finally, the Appellate Body examined the Panel's "weighing and balancing" which the EC had criticized as improper. The Appellate Body, having reviewed the individual factors to be balanced by the Panel, came to the conclusion that the Panel had carried out this process properly. Interestingly, the Appellate Body did not refer to any "discretion" or space of judgement that the Panel had when weighing the different factors.

Another case where Art. XX (b) was at stake was *China – Raw Materials*. In this case, only the Panel had to deal with Art. XX (b), as its interpretation of Art. XX (b) was not appealed. The Panel invoked the formula of *Brazil – Tyres* and hence found it had to

> "consider the relevant factors, particularly the importance of the interests or values at stake, the extent of the contribution to the achieve-

679 *Brazil – Measures Affecting Imports of Retreaded Tyres, WT/DS332/AB/R* 2007, para. 155.
680 Ibid., para. 156.
681 Ibid., para. 174f.
682 Ibid., para. 211.

> ment of the measure's objective, and its trade restrictiveness".[683] [footnote omitted]

China had argued that its export restrictions on certain metals reduced the production of these metals through curbing demand for them outside China, leading to a reduction of the pollution associated with their production and thus protecting the health of the Chinese population. China had also argued that certain export duties concerning scrap metals served environmental protection objectives, as these duties were necessary to ensure a steady supply of scrap within China and to facilitate a shift from primary to secondary production of the metals.[684] The Panel first investigated the objectives of the measures as evident from the measures themselves and whether they contributed or were at least apt to contribute to health protection at the time of the Panel's decision and in the future. The Panel concluded that neither was the case. It then proceeded to investigate the trade-restrictive impacts of the Chinese measures. One factor it considered important in this regard was that China was a major exporter of the raw materials to which the export restrictions related; hence the overall restrictive effect of such measures was more severe than it would have been if China were not such a major exporter.[685] The Panel then observed that, according to the Appellate Body's decision in *Brazil – Tyres*, it was only to investigate the availability of alternative measures if a preliminary conclusion could be drawn that the measures at issue were necessary. Even though the Panel had not drawn such a conclusion, it proceeded to discuss *arguendo* a number of alternative measures suggested by the complainants.[686] A particularity of the case was that China had already adopted all of the measures suggested by the complainants: it argued that the controversial measures it proposed were needed in addition to these existing measures. The Panel concluded rather the opposite: It argued that the fact that China had already adopted certain measures indicated that they were available, that China had the necessary expertise, and could just intensify, expand, tighten or simply apply the other existing measures so that it might reach its desired objectives.[687] This is a different outcome from the one in *Brazil – Tyres* where the fact that a bundle of measures was in place was taken as an

683 *China – Measures Related to the Exportation of Various Raw Materials, WT/DS394/R, WT/DS395/R, WT/DS398/R* 2012, para. 7.483.

684 Ibid., para. 7.494.

685 Ibid., para. 7.555ff.

686 Ibid., para. 7.564f.

687 Ibid., para. 7.565ff.

indication that the measures were all needed and the measures at issue were therefore necessary.

1.2.3. Art. XX (d) GATT

The next subparagraph of Art. XX GATT that has played a role so far in the jurisprudence of the WTO is Art. XX (d) GATT. Like the other sub-paragraphs, Art. XX (d) GATT comprises two elements. A measure can be justified under this norm, if it secures compliance with laws and regulations that are themselves consistent with GATT, and is necessary to this end.[688]

Compliance with law and regulations

With regard to the first requirement, compliance with laws and regulations themselves consistent with GATT, the most interesting point in the present context is an issue discussed in *Mexico – Softdrinks*: does a non-WTO international legal norm constitute a law and regulation in the sense of Art. XX (d) GATT? In *Mexico – Softdrinks*, Mexico sought to invoke a clause contained in the North American Free Trade Agreement (NAFTA) in defence of its measure, arguing that the measure in question was needed for it to comply with a NAFTA provision. The Appellate Body noted that up until that point the terms "laws and regulation" had always referred to domestic rules in earlier dispute settlement cases.[689] In further support of this position, the Appellate Body pointed to the examples given in Art. XX (d) of laws and regulation,[690] and also noted that a contextual interpretation would further corroborate the position, as terms like "international law" or "international obligations" are used in other clauses when referring to non-WTO international law.[691] The Appellate Body thus rejected the idea that international legal provisions could be "laws and regulations" in the sense of Art. XX (d) GATT.

---

688 *Korea – Measures Affecting Imports of Fresh, Chilled and Frozen Beef, WT/DS161/AB/R, WT/DS169/AB/R* 2000, para. 157.

689 *Mexico – Tax Measures on Soft Drinks and Other Beverages, WT/DS308/AB/R* 2006, para. 69.

690 Ibid., para. 70.

691 Ibid., para. 71.

Necessary

Concerning the "necessary" requirement, Art. XX (d) GATT is related to subparagraphs (a) and (b) in that the term "necessary" contained in these paragraphs is interpreted by the Appellate Body in an identical way. Still, in the context of the *problématique* underlying this work, sub-paragraph (d) is different from (a), (b) and also (g) in an important respect: It does not explicitly relate to policies designed to promote non-trade interests. In most cases decided so far, it has been invoked in defence of laws and regulations enforcing economic interests in a broad sense, such as rules on taxation, intellectual property, and subsidies for domestic publishers.

The first case to discuss the necessity requirement under Art. XX (d) GATT was *Korea – Beef*. In this case, the Panel drew on the (adopted) GATT *United States – Section 337* decision.[692] The GATT Panel, with a casualness one supposes it might not have displayed had it been aware that it would initiate an entire line of interpretation, had stated that it seemed "clear" that a provision could not be justified as necessary if an alternative measure was available which a party could reasonably be expected to employ and which was not inconsistent with other GATT provisions. Equally, it seemed "clear" to the Panel that, when the only measures available were inconsistent with the GATT, a country had to use the measure that was least inconsistent.[693]

Besides this GATT decision the Panel in *Korea – Beef* also quoted the *United States – Gasoline* case in support of its position that a measure was not necessary if alternative measures were available. *In casu*, the Panel stated that no measures like the incriminated ones were in place in sectors of the Korean economy other than the one concerned by the dispute. From this, the Panel inferred that Korea should have demonstrated that what was sufficient in other sectors was insufficient in the beef sector. This approach transforms the necessity test essentially into a cross-cutting test for internal regulatory consistency. Yet such a test would normally take place under a non-discrimination clause, like Art. 5.5 SPS,[694] a point that Korea

692 *Korea – Measures Affecting Imports of Fresh, Chilled and Frozen Beef, WT/DS161/R, WT/DS169/R* 2000, para. 653 citing the Panel report in *United States - Section 337*, para. 5.26.

693 *United States –Section 337 of the Tariff Act of 1930, L/6439 - 36S/345* 1989, para. 5.26.

694 See below chapter 2, section 2.3.1.

made in its appellate submission.[695] In addition, the Panel in *Korea – Beef* dedicated some attention to alternative measures suggested by the complainants. The fact that such measures were applied in other sectors of the Korean economy led the Panel to conclude that these measures were "reasonably available".[696] Moreover, it stated that Members could not reject taking measures simply because they involved extra costs. Such costs would, given that the WTO system involved "bargains", have to be borne by Members.[697] Finally, in a surprising move, the Panel stated that for these reasons the Korean measure was "disproportionate".[698] This was a surprise as, until that moment, the Panel had not referred to the proportionality of a measure as being a requirement of the "necessity" criterion. It is therefore quite hard to understand what this reference to proportionality is supposed to mean. The Panel did not in the case consider other factors such as the trade-restrictiveness of the measures or the importance of the regulatory goals pursued.

In the same case, the Appellate Body first pointed out that "necessary", as a matter of natural language, held several meanings, ranging from "indispensable for" to "making a contribution to". The Appellate Body held the view that in the context of Art. XX (d) GATT the meaning of "necessary" was closer to the former connotation.[699] It tried to make the term more manageable by introducing various other elements that had to be considered when analysing whether the measures at issue were necessary. As the statements of the Appellate Body in *Korea – Beef* have been quoted in numerous later cases, it is worth reproducing them *verbatim* here at some length. The Appellate Body stated:

> "It seems to us that a treaty interpreter assessing a measure claimed to be necessary to secure compliance of a WTO-consistent law or regulation may, in appropriate cases, take into account the relative importance of the common interests or values that the law or regulation to be enforced is intended to protect. The more vital or important those

---

695 *Korea – Measures Affecting Imports of Fresh, Chilled and Frozen Beef, WT/DS161/AB/R, WT/DS169/AB/R* 2000, para. 22.

696 *Korea – Measures Affecting Imports of Fresh, Chilled and Frozen Beef, WT/DS161/R, WT/DS169/R* 2000, para. 671–672.

697 Ibid., para. 673.

698 Ibid., para. 674–675.

699 *Korea – Measures Affecting Imports of Fresh, Chilled and Frozen Beef, WT/DS161/AB/R, WT/DS169/AB/R* 2000, para. 160f.

> common interests or values are, the easier it would be to accept as 'necessary' a measure designed as an enforcement instrument.
> There are other aspects of the enforcement measure to be considered in evaluating that measure as 'necessary'. One is the extent to which the measure contributes to the realization of the end pursued, the securing of compliance with the law or regulation at issue. The greater the contribution, the more easily a measure might be considered to be 'necessary'. Another aspect is the extent to which the compliance measure produces restrictive effects on international commerce, that is, in respect of a measure inconsistent with Article III:4, restrictive effects *on imported goods*. A measure with a relatively slight impact upon imported products might more easily be considered as 'necessary' than a measure with intense or broader restrictive effects.
> In sum, determination of whether a measure, which is not 'indispensable', may nevertheless be 'necessary' within the contemplation of Article XX(d), involves in every case a process of weighing and balancing a series of factors which prominently include the contribution made by the compliance measure to the enforcement of the law or regulation at issue, the importance of the common interests or values protected by that law or regulation, and the accompanying impact of the law or regulation on imports or exports."[700] [footnotes omitted]

Interestingly, what the Appellate Body presented here is a more or less unreasoned *dictum*. The Appellate Body did not explain how it arrived at the insight that the factors it named were the ones that should be considered in an analysis of whether a measure was necessary; the Appellate Body did not base its opinion on any particular method of interpretation or draw on any non-WTO sources of law that interpreted "necessary" in a similar way. The only way that the Appellate Body tried to justify its approach was by presenting it as being nothing more than an explicit formulation of what had already been built into the "old" *Section 337* formula, which the Appellate Body said "encapsulates the general considerations [...] above".[701] The Appellate Body's reference to this formula would seem to have one important implication: as in *Section 337* the Panel had referred to the existence of available alternative measures as the only criterion for whether a measure was necessary or not, the Appellate Body's *Korea – Beef* formula would logically also have to be understood as an interpretation on that

700 Ibid., para. 162–164.
701 Ibid., para. 166.

point, i.e. a means to understand when an alternative measure is available. Maybe this is the reason why, despite the fact that the Panel in the case had not weighed or balanced any factors and had focused on the availability of alternative measures, the Appellate Body still did not see any need to modify the Panel's conclusions on the necessity of the Korean measures. One passage of the appellate report is particularly illustrative for the Appellate Body's approach to investigating whether alternative measures are reasonably available. The Appellate Body declared it was

> "not persuaded that Korea could not achieve its desired level of enforcement [...] by using conventional WTO-consistent enforcement measures, if Korea would devote more resources to its enforcement efforts on the beef sector. It might also be added that Korea's argument about the lack of resources to police thousands of shops on a round-the-clock basis is, in the end, not sufficiently persuasive. Violations of laws and regulations [...] can be expected to be routinely investigated and detected through selective, but well-targeted, controls of potential wrongdoers. The control of records will assist in selecting the shops to which the police could pay particular attention."[702]

The Appellate Body here made quite far-reaching proposals on what the defending WTO Member should do; it does not seem to intensively deal with the arguments made by Korea to explain why the proposed alternative measures were not feasible in its local context. The Appellate Body also stated in a rather short manner that it did not agree with the way Korea characterized its level of enforcement and that indeed the Korean measures were aimed at a lower level of protection.[703]

The Panel in the next case in which Art. XX (d) GATT was at stake, *Canada – Wheat,* cited the weighing and balancing formula of the Appellate Body in *Korea – Beef* and the factors that the Appellate Body had considered in this case while applying the formula: the importance of the value or interest pursued by the laws with which the challenged measure sought to secure compliance; whether the objective pursued by the challenged measure contributed to the end to be realized, and whether a reasonably available alternative measure existed.[704] This citation is not entirely faithful to the *Korea – Beef* report, however. As described, the Appellate

702 Ibid., para. 180.
703 Ibid., para. 178.
704 *Canada – Measures Relating to Exports of Wheat and Treatment of Imported Grain, WT/DS276/AB/R* 2004, para. 6.223.

Body's *Korea – Beef* formula is most plausibly understood as an instruction on how to ascertain if there is an alternative measure reasonably available. Thus, the availability of alternatives is not one of the factors to be balanced against other factors. Instead, a decision on whether an alternative measure is reasonably available is what should result from the weighing and balancing process.

In effect, the Panel in the *Canada – Wheat* case ran into some problems, due to what is most likely a misquotation of the *Korea – Beef* formula. First, it discussed the importance of the interests and objectives protected through the Canadian measures. Notably, it stated that while the measures' underlying commercial objectives were important, they were not as important as health protection.[705] Next, it stated that the measures also contributed somewhat to the stated objectives of the Canadian government.[706] Then the Panel apparently realized that it had still to determine whether a reasonably available alternative measure existed and quoted, once more, some factors that it intended to rely on in its analysis of reasonable availability, resorting once more to the very same paragraph of the *Korea – Beef* report that it had quoted before, adding the degree of difficulty of implementation to the factors already enumerated.[707] In the following, it did, however, not discuss either of those factors in depth; instead, it suggested, in a rather off-hand manner, some alternative measures to Canada and arrived at the conclusion that they were realizable, less trade-restrictive than the measures in place, and would secure the attainment of Canada's stated objectives.[708] Despite its efforts, the Panel only partially succeeded in performing the expected weighing and balancing in accordance with the Appellate Body's guidelines. As there was no appeal in that case, no appellate correction could take place.

In *Dominican Republic – Cigarettes,* the Panel also followed the weighing and balancing approach, but again, it was not entirely faithful to the Appellate Body's formula in *Korea – Beef.* In its first step, the Panel discussed the trade-restrictive impact of the Dominican measure, which it found to be quite low.[709] The Appellate Body's formula, if taken seriously, posits this as being part of the application of the necessity criterion, a criterion

705 Ibid., para. 6.224.
706 Ibid., para. 6.225.
707 Ibid., para. 6.226.
708 Ibid., para. 6.226 6.228–6.247 and 6.302–6.310.
709 *Dominican Republic – Measures Affecting the Importation and Internal Sale of Cigarettes, WT/DS302/R* 2004, para. 7.214.

the Panel proceeded to discuss after this step. The Dominican Republic had, among others, quoted WHO studies confirming the kind of measures taken by the Dominican Republic as useful, in principle, for controlling trade in tobacco.[710] Although this led the Panel to conclude that such measures could be "useful" for enforcement purposes, it insisted that the concrete way in which the Dominican Republic had implemented these measures still had to be justified as necessary.[711] In the end, the Dominican Republic did not succeed in doing so. It could not demonstrate convincingly that the alternative measure suggested by the complainant would not allow it to reach the level of enforcement already in place.[712] The Panel, at this point, did not base its analysis on the level of enforcement that the defending Member claimed it was seeking to attain, but rather on what the Panel considered to be the lower actual level of enforcement, proceeding in a way similar to the Appellate Body in *Korea – Beef*. Apparently, the Panel assumed that as the measures actually in place did not secure the level of enforcement claimed by the party invoking Art. XX (d) GATT as justification, the Member could not be taken to be all *that* serious about the stated level of enforcement. It followed, therefore, that it had to be acceptable for this Member to take other less trade-restrictive measures that did not reach the stated level of protection. While this reasoning is, to some degree, reasonable, it should not go unnoticed that the adjudicators did not simply accept the Member's statement about its purported level of protection. Instead, they assumed the competence to cross-check and conclude that the actual level of protection diverged from the way that the respective WTO Member had characterized its level of protection.

What did the Appellate Body in the same case make of these findings? The report is remarkable as the Appellate Body faced a claim that the Panel had failed to balance the different factors at stake appropriately.[713] According to the Dominican Republic, the Panel either did not take into account the trade impact of the measure, the importance of the interests protected by the measure (in this case: health), the contribution of the measure to the end pursued, and the existence of alternative measures that the Member could reasonably be expected to employ, or did not do so fully. The

710 Ibid., para. 7. 216.

711 Ibid., para. 7.218.

712 Ibid., para. 7.221–7.229.

713 See the statement by the Dominican Republic in *Dominican Republic – Measures Affecting the Importation and Internal Sale of Cigarettes*, *WT/DS302/AB/R* 2005, para. 10.

mention of the last aspect reflects a degree of confusion that the new *Korea – Beef* formula and its application provoked. The formula is, as discussed above, most easily understood as describing a way of finding out if an alternative measure is reasonably available. As such, it was "comprehended" or "encapsulated"[714] in the test previously used, the "alternative less GATT inconsistent measure available" test. The way the Dominican Republic cited the Appellate Body *Korea – Beef* report, enumerating several factors with the "alternative measure available" issue as one of them, was thus not entirely faithful to the *Korea – Beef* approach. Given that the *Dominican Republic – Cigarettes* Panel report was not, either, this is not too surprising.

How did the Appellate Body respond to the claims of error regarding the Panel's balancing exercise? The Appellate Body confirmed and further corroborated its prior line of reading that interpreting the necessity requirement involved a balancing process. In support, it not only cited *Korea – Beef*, but also *EC – Asbestos*, in which this formula had been used under Art. XX (b) GATT and a case under GATS, *United States – Gambling*.[715] Subsequently, the Appellate Body subscribed to the Panel's and the Dominican Republic's reading of the *Korea – Beef* appellate report, which is not entirely in line with what seems to be the most plausible reading of that report. As pointed out, the *Korea – Beef* "weighing and balancing" approach originally served to make the "no alternative measure available" formula more concrete; the availability of alternative measures was not one of the factors to be balanced in the necessity analysis.

The Appellate Body also re-iterated the *United States – Gambling* conclusion that alternative measures could be found to be not reasonably available when they were merely theoretical in nature, for instance when the responding Member was not capable of taking them, or when they imposed an undue burden on that Member, such as prohibitive cost or substantial technical difficulties.[716] With regard to the application of the test by the Panel, the Appellate Body observed that the Panel had stated that the measure at hand was "useful" for the regulatory objective pursued, but had limited effects in contributing to it, that the objective pursued was important and that the trade impact of the measure was limited, too. The Ap-

714 Both expressions are used by the Appellate Body in *Korea – Beef*, see ibid., para. 166.

715 *Korea – Measures Affecting Imports of Fresh, Chilled and Frozen Beef*, *WT/DS161/AB/R*, *WT/DS169/AB/R* 2000, para. 66–69.

716 *Dominican Republic – Measures Affecting the Importation and Internal Sale of Cigarettes*, *WT/DS302/AB/R* 2005, para. 70.

pellate Body approved this approach of the Panel.[717] The Panel then decided that alternative measures were reasonably available; it concluded that given the measures in place were also of limited effectiveness in reaching the desired regulatory goal, they were not necessary. This finding was also without fault, in the eyes of the Appellate Body, and in line with the precedents set in *United States – Section 337, EC – Asbestos*, and *United States – Gambling*.[718]

In *Mexico – Softdrinks*, the Appellate Body again confirmed the *Dominican Republic – Cigarettes* approach. While in this case it did not have to go into the details of the necessity analysis under Art. XX (d) GATT, it stated incidentally that the degree to which a measure contributed to the realization of the end pursued was an important and indispensable factor in the "necessity" analysis under it.[719]

In *China – Measures Affecting Imports of Automobile Parts*, only the Panel dealt with Art. XX (d) GATT. Having concluded that the controversial Chinese measure did not satisfy the first part of the requirements contained in Art. XX (d) GATT, namely that measures needed to be designed to ensure compliance with certain laws or regulations, it still went on to investigate whether the measure was "necessary" to this end. For this purpose it used the Appellate Body's *Korea – Beef* formula.[720] The interest China claimed it pursued in this case was a fiscal one, the collection of tariff payments in accordance with the schedule of commitments negotiated at the WTO. The Panel stated that collecting WTO-consistent tariff duties imposed on imported goods was an "important interest for WTO Members".[721] At the same time, it also observed that China had not shown that there was any real problem existing for the measure at issue to address, and that the measure was also unnecessarily trade-restrictive. Finally, it also found that an alternative measure was available. In light of all the factors, the Panel held that the Chinese measure was not necessary.[722]

---

717 Ibid., para. 71.

718 Ibid., para. 72. It is remarkable that the Appellate Body considers the Panel to be in line with all three of these reports, given that the *United States – Gambling* appellate report had not yet been published at the time of the decision of the Panel in the *Dominican Republic – Cigarettes* case.

719 *Mexico – Tax Measures on Soft Drinks and Other Beverages, WT/DS308/AB/R* 2006, para. 74.

720 *China – Measures Affecting Imports of Automobile Parts, WT/DS339/AB/R, WT/DS340/AB/R, WT/DS342/AB/R* 2008, para. 7.348.

721 Ibid., para. 7.360.

722 Ibid., para. 7.361–7.364.

In *Colombia – Ports of Entry* the Panel quoted the *Korea – Beef* weighing and balancing formula.[723] It then proceeded to investigate the three factors named by the Appellate Body in *Korea – Beef*, namely the importance of the values or interests protected, the extent to which the measures contributed to the end pursued, and the restrictive impact of the measure. The Colombian interest in this case was combating smuggling and customs fraud, which in turn were related to money laundering and drug trafficking. The Panel concluded that combating these phenomena was a "relatively more important reality for Colombia than for many other countries", indicating that the importance of an interest or value may depend on the respective context.[724] Concerning the extent to which the measure at issue contributed to the end pursued, the Panel considered – predominantly quantitative – evidence presented by Columbia, but was ultimately unconvinced that the measures contributed to the objectives Columbia claimed it pursued.[725] Concerning the third factor, the restrictive impact of the measure, the Panel considered several pieces of quantitative evidence, but ultimately found itself "unable to conclude whether the imposition of the measure has had a suppressing effect on trade volumes, in terms of value or volume".[726] On this basis, the Panel then stated it had to "weigh and balance" different factors in order to arrive at a finding on whether the defending party had established provisionally that the measure was necessary. Instead of doing so on the basis of the three factors it had considered up until that point, the Panel turned to the question of whether alternative measures were reasonably available. Given that the complaining party in this case had not suggested any specific alternative measure,[727] the Panel found that it could only rely on the above three factors to decide whether the measure was necessary and ultimately concluded that Colombia had failed to show that the measure was indeed necessary.[728] As the Panel report was not appealed, the Appellate Body did not decide whether the Panel's findings were correct.

Finally, in a further case involving US anti-dumping measures, the Panel found that the controversial US measures were not necessary, as the US had failed to demonstrate that the measures were reasonably correlated to

---

723 *Colombia – Indicative Prices and Restrictions on Ports of Entry, WT/DS366/R* 2009, para. 7.547f.
724 Ibid., para. 7.563.
725 Ibid., para. 7.588.
726 Ibid., para. 7.608.
727 Ibid., para. 7.611.
728 Ibid., para. 7.610ff.

the objectives it officially pursued. The Panel applied the three factors identified previously by the Appellate Body as relevant for the "necessity" analysis, namely the relative importance of the values or objectives the law or regulation is intended to protect, the extent to which the measure contributes to the realization of the end pursued, and the restrictive impact of the measure at issue.[729] The Appellate Body approved of this analysis, and like the Panel, apparently saw no need for a discussion of whether alternative measures were reasonably available, given that the measure did not reach its intended objective in first place.[730]

1.2.4. Art. XX (g) GATT

Subparagraph (g) of Art. XX GATT is, besides sub-paragraph (b), the norm under which certain environmental measures violating GATT norms can be justified. For a measure to be justified according to this paragraph, it must "be related to the protection of exhaustible natural resources" and "be made effective in conjunction with restriction on domestic production or consumption".

Relating to the protection of exhaustible natural resources

What, precisely, are exhaustible natural resources? Even in the GATT era, the Panels adopted, mostly in agreement with the parties to the dispute,[731] a broad interpretation. Accordingly, the term "exhaustible natural resources" does not only comprise minerals[732], but also living resources like

729 *United States – Measures Relating to Shrimp from Thailand, WT/DS343/AB/R* 2008, para. 316.

730 Ibid., para. 316f.

731 In two cases, the complaining party did not agree with this interpretation. The first one was a GATT case, *United States – Restrictions on import of tuna, DS29/R (unadopted)* 1994, para. 5.14; here, the EC objected to this interpretation. The second one was *Shrimp –Turtles* case, see *United States – Import Prohibition of Certain Shrimp and Shrimp Products, WT/DS58/R* 1998, para. 3.247-3.240; see also the comments of the Appellate Body in *United States – Import Prohibition of Certain Shrimp and Shrimp Products, WT/DS58/AB/RW* 2001, para. 133.

732 See *China – Measures Related to the Exportation of Various Raw Materials, WT/DS394/R, WT/DS395/R, WT/DS398/R* 2012, para. 7.363.

dolphins[733], fish[734], and turtles[735]. Petroleum[736] and clean air[737] have also been treated as exhaustible natural resources. That Art. XX (g) does not only cover non-living resources, but also living species that are capable of extinction, can be considered as established jurisprudence. All in all, the interpretation of this term has not posed any major problems.

Concerning the interpretation of the term "relating to", the first WTO Panel to be confronted with the issue in *United States– Gasoline* decided that this term meant "primarily aimed at"[738], a formula that previous GATT Panels had developed and used in two (unadopted) reports.[739] The parties to the *United States– Gasoline* appellate dispute did not contend this interpretation and the Appellate Body consequently did not further examine or revise it.[740] It just remarked casually that the:

> "phrase 'primarily aimed at' is not itself treaty language and was not designed as a simple litmus test for inclusion or exclusion from Article XX(g)".[741]

Despite its verbal concurrence with the previous Panels' interpretation, the Appellate Body in the *United States – Gasoline* case seemed to apply the formula in a manner that makes it a low hurdle to pass. The measure at issue was upheld under the "relating to" standard on the ground that the aim it pursued might not have been reached without it – bringing the formula into the vicinity of a suitability criterion. The Appellate Body went on to state that the US rules at issue could not be regarded as merely incidentally or inadvertently aimed at conservation purposes. The standard here, hence, was one of plausibility rather than of intense scrutiny.

---

733 *United States – Prohibition of Imports of Tuna and Tuna Products from Canada (BISD 29S/91)* 1982, para. 4.10; *United States – Restrictions on import of tuna, DS29/R (unadopted)* 1994, para. 5.14.

734 *Canada – Measures affecting exports of unprocessed herring and salmon, BISD 35S/98* 1987, para. 4.4.

735 *United States – Import Prohibition of Certain Shrimp and Shrimp Products, WT/DS58/AB/R* 1998, para. 130–131.

736 *United States – Taxes on Automobile (unadopted)* 1994, para. 5.57.

737 *United States – Standards for Reformulated and Conventional Gasoline, WT/DS2/R* 1996, para. 6.37.

738 Ibid., para. 6.39f.

739 *United States – Restrictions on import of tuna, DS29/R (unadopted)* 1994, para. 5.23; *United States – Taxes on Automobile (unadopted)* 1994, para. 5.59.

740 *United States – Standards for Reformulated and Conventional Gasoline, WT/DS2/AB/R* 1996, sec. III B, at 18.

741 Ibid., sec. III B, at 18f.

In *Shrimp – Turtles,* the Appellate Body seemed to embark on a slightly different course, even though it cited its previous finding in *United States – Gasoline*. In *Shrimp – Turtles*, the Appellate Body stated that Art. XX (g) GATT required "a close and genuine relationship between ends and means".[742] This standard was brought to bear to the facts of the case by the Appellate Body in the following way:

> "In its general design and structure, therefore, Section 609 is not a simple, blanket prohibition of the importation of shrimp imposed without regard to the consequences (or lack thereof) of the mode of harvesting employed upon the incidental capture and mortality of sea turtles. Focusing on the design of the measure here at stake, it appears to us that Section 609, cum implementing guidelines, is not disproportionately wide in its scope and reach in relation to the policy objective of protection and conservation of sea turtle species. The means are, in principle, reasonably related to the ends. The means and ends relationship between Section 609 and the legitimate policy of conserving an exhaustible, and, in fact, endangered species, is observably a close and real one, a relationship that is every bit as substantial as that which we found in United States – Gasoline between the EPA baseline establishment rules and the conservation of clean air in the United States."[743] [footnote omitted]

What is new about this approach – as compared to the Appellate Body's *United States – Gasoline* report – is that the Appellate Body here seemed to delve deeper into the facts and their evaluation. It did not simply pass by and state that the measure was more than casually related to the protective end; instead, it looked at the relationship between both more closely and also assumed the role of evaluating and commenting on this relationship using terms like "reasonable", "genuine" and "disproportionate", all terms with a normative flavour.

In *China – Raw Materials*, the Appellate Body re-iterated its finding that Art. XX (g) GATT required "a close and genuine relationship between ends and means".[744] Upon appeal by China, the Appellate Body explicitly rejected the understanding of the Panel that the conservation measures in dis-

742 *United States – Import Prohibition of Certain Shrimp and Shrimp Products, WT/DS58/AB/R* 1998, para. 136.

743 Ibid., para. 141.

744 *China – Measures Related to the Exportation of Various Raw Materials, WT/DS394/AB/R, WT/DS395/AB/R, WT/DS398/AB/R* 2012, para. 355.

pute had to be "primarily aimed at" restrictions on domestic production or consumption.[745] Curiously, the Appellate Body presented this finding as if it had already been contained in its earlier decision on *United States – Gasoline* case. It stated that in that its *Gasoline* report,

> "the Appellate Body did not consider that, in order to be justified under Article XX(g), measures 'relating to the conservation of exhaustible natural resources' must be primarily aimed at rendering effective restrictions on domestic production or consumption. Instead, the Appellate Body read the terms 'in conjunction with', 'quite plainly', as 'together with' or 'jointly with', and found no additional requirement that the conservation measure be primarily aimed at making effective certain restrictions on domestic production or consumption."[746] [footnotes omitted]

This is, at best, an ambitious reading of the earlier Appellate Body decision; as described above, in *United States – Gasoline*, the Appellate Body did not revise the Panel's finding that measures needed to be "primarily aimed at" conservation, as the parties had not appealed the finding. Instead, the Appellate Body in the earlier case had just made a casual statement that the

> "phrase 'primarily aimed at' is not itself treaty language and was not designed as a simple litmus test for inclusion or exclusion from Article XX(g)".[747]

Indeed, the Panel in the *China – Raw Materials* case had taken the Appellate Body in *United States – Gasoline* to have ruled

> "that a measure was 'relate[d] to' conservation if there was a substantial relationship between the export measures and conservation, and 'that a measure must be 'primarily aimed at' the conservation of exhaustible natural resources in order to fall within the scope of Article XX(g)'[748]."[749]

---

745 Ibid., para. 356.

746 Ibid., para. 358.

747 *United States – Standards for Reformulated and Conventional Gasoline, WT/DS2/AB/R* 1996, sec. III B, at 18f.

748 The original footnote in the Panel report is: "Appellate Body Report, *US – Gasoline*, p. 18, DSR 1996:I, 3, at p. 17 (emphasis added)".

749 *China – Measures Related to the Exportation of Various Raw Materials, WT/DS394/R, WT/DS395/R, WT/DS398/R* 2012, para. 7.370. However, the Panel in turn omitted from its quote the part where the Appellate Body said that the phrase "primarily aimed at" was not itself treaty language.

Because the parties' appeal concerning the interpretation of Art. XX (g) GATT in *China – Raw Materials* was limited, the Appellate Body did not have to review the Panel's application of the standard in any depth.[750] The Panel had investigated whether there was "a close and genuine relationship" between the measure in dispute – export duties on certain raw materials – and the conservation objective by examining "the text of the measure itself, its design and architecture, and its context".[751] The Panel observed that the Chinese legislation did not mention the conservation objective explicitly. It also found that restrictions on extraction would be more in line with conservation goals than export restrictions and that extraction of the resources in question had actually increased.[752] Finally, it also noticed that China could not, at the request of the Panel, explain how the export measures actually fostered conservation. In consequence, it concluded that China had not discharged its burden of proof under the first part of Art. XX (g) GATT.

The most recent case so far to discuss Art. XX (g) GATT is *China – Rare Earths*, which featured a measure similar to that at stake in *China – Raw Materials*, i.e. Chinese export restrictions on certain raw materials inconsistent with Art. XI GATT and certain provisions of China's Accession Protocol. China appealed the Panel's finding on the first requirement of Art. XX (g) GATT, i.e. that the Chinese measures were not related to the conservation of exhaustible natural resources. The Panel accepted that rare earths and other minerals were exhaustible natural resources in the sense of Art. XX (g) GATT.[753] Yet it was not convinced that the Chinese export quota actually contributed to the protection of these resources. The Panel accepted China's argument that the export restrictions could signal to foreign consumers of the minerals in question that they needed to look for other sources of supply, which could contribute to conserving China's re-

750 In essence, China, the defendant had not appealed the basic finding of the Panel that the controversial Chinese measures were not justified under Art. XX (g), but had only appealed one specific point of law, see *China – Measures Related to the Exportation of Various Raw Materials, WT/DS394/AB/R, WT/DS395/AB/R, WT/DS398/AB/R* 2012, para. 275.

751 *China – Measures Related to the Exportation of Various Raw Materials, WT/DS394/R, WT/DS395/R, WT/DS398/R* 2012, para. 7.416.

752 See ibid., para. 7.418ff for the Panel's findings.

753 See the summary of the Panel's finding in *China – Measures Related to the Exportation of Rare Earths, Tungsten, and Molybdenum, WT/DS431/AB/R, WT/DS432/AB/R, WT/DS433/AB/R* 2014, para. 5.78.

sources.[754] However, it also saw a risk that export restrictions would lead to lower domestic prices, more domestic consumption of the resources in question, and the relocation of companies to within China to circumvent the export restrictions. In the Panel's view, the decisive flaw of the Chinese measure was the absence of a mechanism to counteract the perverse signals its export quota sent to domestic consumers.[755] While China's appeal was limited to a particular set of the Panel's findings,[756] the Appellate Body nevertheless took the opportunity to re-iterate its approach to the interpretation of Art. XX (g) GATT more broadly. It stated that

> "the generic term 'natural resources' in Article XX(g) is not 'static' in its content or reference, but is rather, 'by definition, evolutionary'. The word 'conservation', in turn, means 'the preservation of the environment, especially of natural resources'. It seems to us that, for the purposes of Article XX(g), the precise contours of the word 'conservation' can only be fully understood in the context of the exhaustible natural resource at issue in a given dispute"[757]. [footnotes omitted]

It also repeated findings of earlier cases that

> "there must be 'a close and genuine relationship of ends and means' between that measure and the conservation objective of the Member maintaining the measure. Hence, a GATT-inconsistent measure that is merely incidentally or inadvertently aimed at a conservation objective would not satisfy the 'relating to' requirement of Article XX(g). Furthermore, the absence of a domestic restriction, or the way in which a challenged measure applies to domestic production or consumption, may be relevant to an assessment of whether the challenged measure 'relates to' conservation."[758] [footnotes omitted]

Moreover, the Appellate Body reiterated the findings from *United States – Gasoline* that an empirical test of the effects of measures on the protection of natural resources was not necessary, while the predictable effects could be of relevance in certain situations for the overall assessment of a matter.[759] However, these findings had been made in *United States – Gasoline* in relation to the second requirement of Art. XX (g) GATT while the Ap-

754 See the summary of the Panel's findings in ibid., para. 5.155.
755 For a summary of the Panel's arguments, see ibid., para. 5.149ff.
756 For a summary of China's appeal, see ibid., para. 5.81ff.
757 Ibid., para. 5.89.
758 Ibid., para. 5.90.
759 Ibid., para. 5.98ff, 5.112f.

pellate Body now transferred it – without giving further reasons– to the interpretation of the first requirement.

Made effective in conjunction with restrictions on domestic production or consumption

With regard to the second part of Art. XX (g) GATT, the Appellate Body in the *United States – Gasoline* case rejected the interpretation by earlier GATT Panels. These had taken the phrase to require that the measures in dispute do not only impose restrictions on imported products, but also on ones of domestic origin. Instead, the Appellate Body stipulated that "even-handedness" in the treatment of both imported and domestic products was needed.[760] According to the Appellate Body, "even-handedness" lies somewhere between identical treatment of imported and domestic products (which is not required) and no restrictions at all on domestic production and consumption (which is not sufficient). When applying the standard, the Appellate Body simply noted that *in casu* there were restrictions not only on importers, but also on domestic producers, which it considered to be sufficient for the "even-handedness" criterion to be satisfied. The Appellate Body also clarified that adjudicators did not need to conduct an "empirical effects test". The Appellate Body related this to the practical difficulties in ascertaining the real-world effect of measures, given that in the area of protection of natural resources the effects of a measure might only become visible in the long term. At the same time, the Appellate indicated that the expected impacts of a measure could be relevant in some situations.[761]

In *Shrimp – Turtles* the adjudicators followed the *United States – Gasoline* approach, using the even-handedness formula and applying it by noting the existence of measures directed at domestic producers.[762] In *China – Raw Materials* the Appellate Body also quoted the *United States – Gasoline* approach,[763] but did not have to apply it to the facts of the case as the appeal of the parties was limited. The Panel in this case concluded that the measures that China quoted as restricting the domestic production and

760 *United States – Standards for Reformulated and Conventional Gasoline, WT/DS2/AB/R* 1996, sec. III C, at 21.

761 Ibid., sec. III C, at 21f.

762 *United States – Import Prohibition of Certain Shrimp and Shrimp Products, WT/DS58/AB/R* 1998, para. 143f.

763 *China – Measures Related to the Exportation of Various Raw Materials, WT/DS394/AB/R, WT/DS395/AB/R, WT/DS398/AB/R* 2012, para. 357.

consumption of the resources in question did not, at the time of the Panel's decision, contain any actual restrictions. Nonetheless, it subsequently proceeded to investigate the even-handedness criterion.[764] It found that as China could not show that there were restrictions on domestic use and consumption, the export-related measures could not be considered to be even-handed.[765]

An interesting side issue was brought up in *United States – Gasoline* by Venezuela, which argued that for its proposed measure to stand the US had to demonstrate that it was effective, i.e. it actually contributed to the protective aim pursued. The Appellate Body rejected this argument, saying that Art. XX (g) GATT contained no such empirical test. This seems to be at least partially motivated by a precautionary approach: given that the effects of a measure may not become visible until years later, a measure should not be struck down for lack of empirical effectiveness. The Appellate Body, however, proceeded to blur this relatively clear line by adding that situations could be imagined where the absence of a causal relationship between the measure and the aim could lead to a finding of a violation of Art. XX (g) GATT.[766]

In *China – Rare Earths*, the Appellate Body also had to deal with Chinese export restrictions on minerals. The defendant appealed some of the findings of the Panel relating to the second requirement of Art. XX (g), including that the Panel had assumed that the paragraph contained an independent, additional requirement of even-handedness of trade and domestic restrictions.[767] The Appellate Body started its analysis by clarifying that

> "the second clause of Article XX(g) refers to governmental measures that are promulgated or brought into effect, and that operate together with restrictions on domestic production or consumption of exhaustible natural resources. [...] Moreover, in order to comply with the 'made effective' element of the second clause of Article XX(g), it would not be sufficient for domestic production or consumption to be subject to a possible limitation at some undefined point in the future.

---

764 *China – Measures Related to the Exportation of Various Raw Materials, WT/DS394/R, WT/DS395/R, WT/DS398/R* 2012, para. 7.458f.

765 Ibid., para. 7.465.

766 *United States – Standards for Reformulated and Conventional Gasoline, WT/DS2/AB/R* 1996, sec. III C, at 21f.

767 See the summary of China's appeal in *China – Measures Related to the Exportation of Rare Earths, Tungsten, and Molybdenum, WT/DS431/AB/R, WT/DS432/AB/R, WT/DS433/AB/R* 2014, para. 5.119ff.

> Rather, a Member must impose a 'real' restriction on domestic production or consumption that reinforces and complements the restriction on international trade."[768]

It was in this sense, that it wished its earlier finding, namely that "even-handedness" between measures restricting trade and measures restricting domestic consumption was required, to be understood.[769] While the Appellate Body did not make a definitive pronouncement on whether the Panel had actually introduced even-handedness of measures as an additional requirement, it clarified that in any case even-handedness was no such additional requirement.[770] In response to arguments by the defendant, the Appellate Body also clarified that even-handedness did not mean that trade restrictions and domestic measures had to evenly distribute the burden of conservation between foreign and domestic actors.[771] Yet the Appellate Body then weakened this statement by saying that

> "it would be difficult to conceive of a measure that would impose a significantly more onerous burden on foreign consumers or producers and that could still be shown to satisfy all of the requirements of Article XX(g)".[772]

For satisfying the second requirement of Art. XX (g)

> "a Member must impose 'real' restrictions on domestic production or consumption that reinforce and complement the restriction on international trade, and particularly so in circumstances where domestic consumption accounts for a major part of the exhaustible natural resource to be conserved".[773] [footnote omitted]

768 Ibid., para. 5.92.
769 Ibid., para. 5.93.
770 Ibid., para. 5.127.
771 More precisely, the Appellate Body stated that such an interpretation would "raise concerns", see ibid., para. 5.131.
772 Ibid., para. 5.134.
773 Ibid., para. 5.132.

1.3. Art. XIV (a) GATS

There is little case law so far on Art. XIV GATS; in fact it has only played a role in one case so far, *United States – Gambling*.[774] In that case, Art. XIV (a) and (c) GATS were discussed by the Panel and only Art. XIV (a) GATS by the Appellate Body. In the following, I will therefore focus on the interpretation of the latter norm. This dispute has gained additional significance from the fact that the Appellate Body drew on prior case law relating to Art. XX GATT in its analysis of Art. XIV GATS. The Appellate Body justified this approach by saying that both norms were similar in character and structure as exceptions and had partially identical wording, such as the term necessary.[775] Conversely, in later cases Panels and the Appellate Body have drawn on the interpretation of "necessary" under Art. XIV GATS for the interpretation of the same term in Art. XX GATT[776] as well as on the interpretation of the term "public morals"[777].

Art. XIV (a) GATS allows measures "necessary to protect public morals or to maintain public order". A footnote *ad* Art. XIV GATS specifies that "[t]he public order exception may be invoked only where a genuine and sufficiently serious threat is posed to one of the fundamental interests of society". Both the Panel and the Appellate Body investigated the clause in *United States – Gambling*, as parties disputed whether US measures restricting the remote supply of gambling and betting services were indeed to protect public morals or order within the US. The Panel against this background needed to interpret the term, which it did making the following statements:

> "We are well aware that there may be sensitivities associated with the interpretation of the terms 'public morals' and 'public order' in the context of Article XIV. In the Panel's view, the content of these concepts for Members can vary in time and space, depending upon a range of factors, including prevailing social, cultural, ethical and religious values. [...] Members should be given some scope to define and apply for themselves the concepts of 'public morals' and 'public order'

774 *United States – Measures Affecting the Cross-Border Supply of Gambling and Betting Services, WT/DS285/AB/R* 2005.

775 Ibid., para. 291.

776 See for example *China – Measures Related to the Exportation of Various Raw Materials, WT/DS394/R, WT/DS395/R, WT/DS398/R* 2012, para. 7.489.

777 See above section 1.2.1.

in their respective territories, according to their own systems and scales of values."[778]

The Panel linked this finding also to earlier case law on Art. XX GATT, according to which Members could choose their appropriate level of protection.[779]

The Panel then proceeded to investigate dictionary definitions of the terms "public", "morals" and "order". It concluded that "public morals" denoted "standards of right and wrong conduct maintained by or on behalf of a community or nation"[780], whereas "public order" referred to the "preservation of the fundamental interests of a society, as reflected in public policy and law"[781]. The Panel also noted that while these two concepts were separate, they had similarities and could overlap some cases.[782] In order to ascertain whether the US measures protected public morals, the Panel then looked at the practice in other jurisdictions (including historic ones) with regard to the practices in dispute; it also referred to international legal documents going back as far as the League of Nations. It found that prohibiting the practices interdicted by the US measures had also been considered an issue of morals and hence concluded that the US measures fell within the ambit of Art. XX (a) GATT.[783] The Appellate Body upheld the Panel's findings.[784]

The Panel further concluded that the measures in dispute were not necessary in the sense of Art. XIV (a) GATS. The Appellate Body summarized the Panel's findings as follows: the interests and values protected by the controversial measures served societal interests that could be characterized as "vital and important in the highest degree"; the relevant acts did "contribute, at least to some extent" to addressing the United States' concerns "pertaining to money laundering, organized crime, fraud, underage gambling and pathological gambling"; the measures in question "have a significant restrictive trade impact", and

---

778 *United States – Measures Affecting the Cross-Border Supply of Gambling and Betting Services, WT/DS285/R* 2004, para. 6.461.

779 Ibid.

780 Ibid., para. 6.465.

781 Ibid., para. 6.467.

782 Ibid., para. 6.468.

783 Ibid., para. 6.471ff.

784 *United States – Measures Affecting the Cross-Border Supply of Gambling and Betting Services, WT/DS285/AB/R* 2005, para. 296ff.

> "[i]n rejecting Antigua's invitation to engage in bilateral or multilateral consultations and/or negotiations, the United States failed to pursue in good faith a course of action that could have been used by it to explore the possibility of finding a reasonably available WTO-consistent alternative."[785]

Both parties had appealed certain aspects of these findings, relating predominantly to the Panel's analysis of the availability of alternative measures in its interpretation of "necessary".

When discussing the term "necessary", the Appellate Body quoted the *Korea – Beef* approach. It explained that first the importance of the protected interest had to be evaluated, and then other factors had to be weighed and balanced, of which the Appellate Body had previously identified two, namely the contribution of the measure to the realization of the end pursued, and the restrictive impact of the measure on international commerce.[786] After this, according to *Korea – Beef*, a

> "comparison between the challenged measure and possible alternatives should then be undertaken, and the results of such comparison should be considered in the light of the importance of the interests at issue".[787]

The Appellate Body also re-iterated earlier findings that a measure that was only theoretical in nature or did not enable a WTO Member to reach its desired level of protection did not constitute a possible alternative.[788] The Appellate Body did not agree with the Panel's analysis of the availability of alternative measures. It observed that the Panel seemed to have understood that the US had to explore and exhaust all possible measures, including consultations with Antigua, before adopting its WTO-inconsistent measure.[789] As the US had not consulted with Antigua, the Panel had concluded that the US measures were not necessary.[790] Rejecting the Panel's approach, the Appellate Body observed that consultations were not an "appropriate alternative for the Panel to consider", as negotiations were necessarily open-ended and the US could not have been sure it would reach its desired objective and therefore this measure was "not capable of compari-

785 Ibid., para. 301.
786 Ibid., para. 306.
787 Ibid., para. 307.
788 Ibid., para. 308.
789 Ibid., para. 307.
790 Ibid., para. 315.

son with the measure in place".[791] Having rejected the Panel's findings, the Appellate Body then conducted its own analysis of the necessity of the measure.

1.4. Chapeau of Art. XX GATT and XIV GATS

The text of the chapeau of Art. XX GATT is, as the Appellate Body noticed in *United States – Gasoline,* not "without ambiguity".[792] The adjudicators do, however, only have to perform the difficult task of interpreting and applying the chapeau after finding a measure to be consistent with the requirements of one of the sub-paragraphs. This has considerably reduced the number of cases in which the chapeau has been discussed so far.

The chapeau clause itself consists of several, alternative elements. A measure may not be applied in a way that might constitute either an arbitrary or unjustifiable discrimination between countries where the same conditions prevail or a disguised restriction on trade. In the case law, these different requirements are often not discussed separately.

In one of the first cases after the establishment of the WTO, *United States – Gasoline,* the Appellate Body laid down some of the cornerstones of the interpretation of the chapeau of Art. XX GATT. First, it stated that, in order for the predicates of the chapeau to be fulfilled, there had to be circumstances in addition to those that had led to the conclusion that one of the sub-paragraphs had been breached. The Appellate Body considered this to be a matter of *effet utile.*[793] As a corollary, the Appellate Body noted that it would be more difficult – in terms of burden of proof – to justify a measure under the chapeau than in one of the sub-paragraphs. In addition, it also found that a "disguised restriction on international trade" was not much different from an "arbitrary or unjustifiable discrimination".[794]

A matter that the Appellate Body mentioned, but did not resolve, in *United States – Gasoline* was whether the reference in the chapeau to "countries where the same conditions prevail" was to conditions in exporting as compared to importing countries or to conditions in different exporting countries. The Appellate Body did not decide on the issue as none of the

791 Ibid., para. 317.

792 *United States – Standards for Reformulated and Conventional Gasoline, WT/DS2/AB/R* 1996, sec. IV, at 23.

793 Ibid., sec. IV at 23.

794 Ibid., at 25.

parties had contested the applicability of Art. XX GATT in the case of a violation of Art. III:4 GATT, the national treatment obligation in which both an importing and an exporting country are always involved.[795]

The way the Appellate Body consequently applied the chapeau requirements in *United States – Gasoline* is somewhat peculiar. Essentially, it carried out a necessity analysis. It found that the US could have taken several alternative measures which were feasible and would also have enabled the US to reach its regulatory objective.[796] One of the alternative measures that, in the Appellate Body's view, the US had failed to take, was entering into negotiations with the countries affected by the measures with the aim of reaching a "cooperative arrangement".[797] The other possible alternative, which the US was reproached for not having considered, was to accord foreign producers the same treatment as domestic producers. In this respect the Appellate Body found that, while the US took certain financial interests of its nationals into account, it did not do the same with regard to foreign producers. These omissions, the Appellate Body concluded,

> "go well beyond what was necessary for the Panel to determine that a violation of Article III:4 had occurred in the first place. The resulting discrimination must have been foreseen, and was not merely inadvertent or unavoidable."[798]

It ultimately concluded that the measures were unjustified discrimination and a disguised restriction on international trade. The Appellate Body did not find the measures to be "arbitrary discrimination", however, for reasons not explicitly stated in the report.

The next case, chronologically, was *Shrimp – Turtles.* It heralded important new insights into the interpretation of the chapeau clause. What makes the case very interesting is that there are four reports in total which deal with similar US measures: the Panel report, the Appellate Body report and finally another Panel and Appellate Body report in proceedings that were initiated by the complainants of the original case under Art. 21.5 DSU, i.e. compliance reports. Significant differences exist between the way that the Panels and the Appellate Body interpreted the chapeau.

795 Ibid., sec. IV, at 24.
796 Ibid., sec. IV, at 25f.
797 Ibid., sec. IV, at 26f.
798 Ibid., sec. IV, at 28.

How did the Panel interpret the requirements of the chapeau? Regarding discrimination, the Panel simply stated that some countries had obtained a certificate necessary for importing shrimp to the US, whereas others had not, and that this alone constituted discrimination.[799] In a next step, the Panel investigated whether the discrimination it had found to exist was unjustifiable. Having stated that the term "unjustifiable" was susceptible to both a narrow and a wide interpretation, the Panel proceeded to discuss whether the chapeau covered measures that made market access conditional upon the adoption of certain regulatory policies by the exporting state. Given that it found the text of Art. XX GATT to be ambiguous, the Panel resorted to contextual and teleological interpretation. The Panel induced two main arguments as to why a political conditionality would make any corresponding measure "unjustifiable". First, looking at the preamble of the WTO Agreement, it found that the fundamental purpose of the agreement was the promotion of economic development through trade.[800] Secondly, the Panel held that measures of WTO Members had to be assessed against the multilateral approach underlying the WTO agreements. If a measure under review *in casu* or similar measures by other Members endangered the multilateral approach underlying the WTO system, the respective measures would have to be considered inconsistent with the chapeau of Art. XX GATT. The Panel took the view that measures that made market access dependent upon the adoption of a specific regulatory measure by the exporting Member posed a threat to the multilateral trading system: Other Members might be provoked to adopt similar measures, which, altogether could lead to a situation where a country wishing to export certain goods would face conflicting requirements. This, the Panel concluded, would endanger the multilateral trading system as it would cause a loss in security and predictability.[801] For these reasons the Panel considered the measure to be unjustifiable.

What is also interesting about the Panel's report is the way the Panel dealt with the US argument that multilateral environmental agreements existed at the international level that permitted precisely the kind of measures that the US had actually taken. In reaction to this argument, the Panel pointed out that there was no concrete rule, either of treaty or customary international law, which permitted the precise measure the US had tak-

799 *United States – Import Prohibition of Certain Shrimp and Shrimp Products, WT/DS58/R* 1998, para. 7.33.

800 Ibid., para. 7.42.

801 Ibid., para. 7.45f.

en in favour of marine turtles.[802] Yet it did *not* state that the arguments induced by the US were not pertinent. The Panel also supported its reading of the chapeau as requiring a multilateral approach with a reference to the Rio Declaration and other international agreements that stress the need for a multilateral approach towards environmental problems.[803]

This latter approach of according importance to rules contained in public international law beyond the WTO legal framework is one of the few similarities that exist between the Panel and the (first) Appellate Body report in the *Shrimp – Turtles* case. Otherwise, the Appellate Body report differs considerably from the Panel report. The first point of divergence is that the Appellate Body did not hold the Panel's view that requiring an exporting Member to adopt certain policies made the measure through which this was done insusceptible to justification under the chapeau of Art. XX GATT *per se*.[804] The Appellate Body stated that it "appeared" that conditioning access to a Member's domestic market on the adoption of certain policies was, to a certain extent, a common feature of all the subparagraphs of Art. XX GATT. In the view of the Appellate Body the reading proposed by the Panel

> "renders most, if not all, of the specific exceptions of Article XX inutile, a result abhorrent to the principles of interpretation we are bound to apply".[805]

Other differences concerning the interpretation of the chapeau also emerged. Although both Appellate Body and Panel emphasized the importance of the preamble of the WTO Agreement, the Appellate embraced a much broader reading of the underlying purpose of the multilateral trading system. The Appellate Body stressed that the preamble referred to the sustainable use of the world's natural resources as one of the objectives of WTO system. The Appellate Body underlined the importance of the *intention* of the negotiators to promote this goal, which, accordingly, had to inform the interpretation of the agreements annexed to the WTOA.[806] Moreover, it also noted developments that had occurred at the political level since the entry into force of the WTO agreements, such as the establish-

802 Ibid., para. 7.49, 7.50, 7.58, 7.59.
803 Ibid., para. 7.52.
804 *United States – Import Prohibition of Certain Shrimp and Shrimp Products, WT/DS58/AB/R* 1998, para. 121.
805 Ibid.
806 Ibid., para. 152, 153.

ment of the Committee on Trade and Environment (CTE). Noting the absence of any specific decision or recommendation of that body that would alter any of the agreements relevant to the case, the Appellate Body stated that it had to

> "fulfil [our] responsibility in this specific case, which is to interpret the existing language of the chapeau of Art. XX by examining its ordinary meaning".[807]

How did the Appellate Body do so? The chapeau, in the eyes of the Appellate Body, is a central element in the balance between the rights and obligations of WTO Members as struck by the negotiators of the agreement.[808] Consequently, the task of the adjudicators is to find the equilibrium appropriate to the concrete case before them. Having made these more general remarks about the nature of the chapeau and the way it was to be interpreted, the Appellate Body proceeded to investigate whether the US measures constituted either unjustifiable or arbitrary discrimination.

The Appellate Body did not elaborate much on the meaning of either of these terms. Rather, it went on to describe why it considered the US measure to be discrimination, both unjustifiable and arbitrary in nature. With regard to unjustifiable discrimination, it found the US measure to be inconsistent with the chapeau of Art. XX GATT on two accounts. Firstly, the measure required a foreign government to adopt "essentially the same" regulatory policies as the US.[809] The point was not the coercive effect of the measures as such, because the Appellate Body had earlier in its report stated that making market access conditional upon the adoption of certain policies by the exporting Member was, to a certain extent, a common aspect of all of the sub-paragraphs of Art. XX GATT.[810] Provisions allowing this kind of conditionality would also permit an (at least mildly) coercive effect. The decisive point about the US measure was that it required all countries to do the same thing, even though conditions in those countries might be different.[811] This is reminiscent of the interpretation of equal treatment or non-discrimination clauses in other jurisdictions. These claus-

---

807 Ibid., para. 154, 155.

808 Ibid., para. 156, 157.

809 Ibid., para. 163.

810 This reading of the appellate report is confirmed by the compliance Panel in the same case, see *United States – Import Prohibition of Certain Shrimp and Shrimp Products, WT/DS58/RW* 2001, para. 5.103.

811 This becomes clear in *United States – Import Prohibition of Certain Shrimp and Shrimp Products, WT/DS58/AB/R* 1998, para. 164, 165.

es do not only frequently forbid the unequal treatment of the equal, but also the equal treatment of the unequal.[812] The US measure, which contained in the eyes of the Appellate Body a rigid and unbending standard, pertains to the second category. Consequently it would seem that the inflexibility of the clause resulted in "discrimination", rather than "unjustified discrimination", but unfortunately the Appellate Body was not very clear on the matter. The second reason that the Appellate Body considered to be decisive for categorizing the US measure as "unjustifiable discrimination" was the failure of the US government to initiate negotiations with the exporting countries aimed at reaching agreement on regulatory policies for the conservation of sea turtles. This statement of the Appellate Body must not, however, be read in isolation from its context. The Appellate Body pointed out quite clearly that the failure to initiate negotiations was fatal in the *Shrimp – Turtles* constellation, because the problem itself – extinction of sea turtles – required a multilateral approach, a fact recognized in other international agreements. Moreover, such an approach had been taken by the US vis-à-vis states other than the complainants with good success, leading to the conclusion of an agreement, the Inter-American Convention for the Protection and Conservation of Sea Turtles (IAC).[813] The Appellate Body, having pointed out these two aspects which, in its view, necessitated the US measure as being considered unjustifiable discrimination, stated that the existence of the IAC showed that an alternative course of action had been open to the US, which the US had not taken.[814]

The Appellate Body report lacked in clarity on why exactly the failure of the US to start negotiations with any of the complaining parties would constitute unjustifiable discrimination. Was it because the US behaved differently towards two countries or groups of countries or because there was an alternative measure potentially available? The Appellate Body report in *Shrimp – Turtles* was ambiguous on the matter; the later reports from the compliance review stage were more helpful in this respect, however.

With regard to "arbitrary discrimination", the Appellate Body several aspects of the case which led them to judge the measure to amount to arbi-

812 For an example from EU law, see Holoubek, in Schwarze et al. 2012 Art. 18 AEUV, para. 5; for German constitutional law, see Boysen, in Münch and Kunig 2012 Art. 3, para. 64ff.

813 *United States – Import Prohibition of Certain Shrimp and Shrimp Products, WT/DS58/AB/R* 1998, para. 166–169.

814 Ibid., para. 171.

trary discrimination. The first was the measure's inflexibility.[815] The second was the absence of provisions in the US regulatory scheme that ensured predictability from the perspective of the exporters regarding fulfilment of pre-conditions for importing into the US, and a formal opportunity for an exporting country to be heard in the administrative decision-making process.[816] The latter finding was also based on (the otherwise infrequently used) Art. X:3 GATT. The Appellate Body observed in this regard:

> "Inasmuch as there are due process requirements generally for measures that are otherwise imposed in compliance with WTO obligations, it is only reasonable that rigorous compliance with the fundamental requirements of due process should be required in the application and administration of a measure which purports to be an exception to the treaty obligations of the Member imposing the measure and which effectively results in a suspension *pro hac vice* of the treaty rights of other Members."[817]

In the period between the initial proceedings and the compliance proceedings under Art. 21.5 DSU in *Shrimp – Turtles*, two other Panels, *EC – Asbestos* and *Argentina – Bovine Hides*, interpreted the chapeau clause. It is of note that the Panel report in *EC – Asbestos* does not suffer from the shortcoming displayed by both the Panel and the Appellate Body reports in *Shrimp – Turtles*. The *Asbestos* Panel distinguished clearly between the inquiry into whether the application of the measure under review was discriminatory – which the Panel conceived of as being an essentially factual question – and the investigation whether the discrimination identified was unjustifiable or arbitrary.[818]

Concerning the interpretation of discrimination, the Panel reiterated the Appellate Body's finding from *United States – Gasoline* that discrimination could occur both on the basis of a comparison between products from different exporting countries and in a comparison between domestic and foreign products.[819] It also cited the Appellate Body as saying that "discrimination" under the chapeau of Art. XX GATT had to have a different

815 Ibid., para. 177.

816 Ibid., para. 183.

817 Ibid., para. 182.

818 *European Communities – Measures Affecting Asbestos and Products Containing Asbestos, WT/DS135/R* 2000, para. 8.226.

819 Ibid., para. 8.227; this finding is also repeated by the Panel in *Argentina – Measures Affecting the Export of Bovine Hides and the Import of Finished Leather, WT/DS155/R* 2000, para. 11.134.

meaning than under Art. III:4 GATT.[820] Given that the measure at issue in the case was neutral in design and there was no claim that it had been applied differently to domestic and foreign products, the Panel concluded that there was no arbitrary or unjustifiable discrimination.[821] If the Panel had wanted to be even more faithful to its approach of distinguishing clearly between the existence of discrimination and its arbitrary or unjustifiable character, it should rather have stated that the decisive point was the absence of discrimination, which would have implied *a fortiori* the absence of unjustifiable or arbitrary discrimination.

As it could find no discrimination in the application of the measure under review, the Panel proceeded to discuss the hitherto seldom discussed issue of what constitutes a disguised restriction on international trade. The meagre precedents available, especially those set by the Appellate Body in *United States – Gasoline*, suggested to the Panel that just because a measure was concealed or not publicly announced did not make it a "disguised" restriction on trade.[822] After adding its own interpretive efforts, it concluded, having followed a literal approach, that a restriction formally meeting the requirements of Art. XX GATT would have to be considered a disguise if formal compliance with the terms of Art. XX GATT was in fact only a way to conceal the pursuit of trade-restrictive objectives.[823] In order to find out whether such concealment tactics had been used by the US, the Panel looked at the design, architecture and structure of the measure under review, in line with the approach taken by the Appellate Body in *Japan – Alcoholic Beverages* for the interpretation of Art. III:2, second sentence GATT. This analysis did not in the eyes of the Panel allow the conclusion that there was a disguised restriction on international trade.

In *Argentina – Bovine Hides*, the Panel started with an investigation of whether there was unjustifiable discrimination. With regard to the existence of discrimination, the Panel only referred to its prior finding under Art. III:2, first sentence, that there was discrimination.[824] This is contrary to the convincing line of reasoning of the Appellate Body in *United States – Gasoline* that for a measure to constitute discrimination under the chapeau of Art. XX GATT there must be circumstances in addition to those that led

---

820 *European Communities – Measures Affecting Asbestos and Products Containing Asbestos, WT/DS135/R* 2000, para. 8.227.

821 Ibid., para. 8.229.

822 Ibid., para. 8.234.

823 Ibid., para. 8.236.

824 *Argentina – Measures Affecting the Export of Bovine Hides and the Import of Finished Leather, WT/DS155/R* 2000, para. 11.315.

the measure to be inconsistent with one of the sub-paragraphs of Art. XX GATT. By contrast, the *Argentina – Bovine Hides* Panel only took into account the different standard of discrimination in Art. XX chapeau GATT and other paragraphs of the agreement when it turned to the investigation of whether the discrimination was "unjustifiable".[825] Essentially, the Panel turned this investigation into a test of whether the measure was necessary to reach the end pursued.[826] This, however, is clearly a matter for discussion in the context of the relevant sub-paragraph, in this case Art. XX (d) GATT. The Panel ultimately found the Argentinean arguments for the necessity of its measures unconvincing, probably rightly so.

What, then, did the reports resulting from the *Shrimp – Turtles* proceedings under Art. 21.5 DSU add to these interpretations? It is noteworthy that both the Panel and the Appellate Body reports gave short shrift to the two intermediate Panel reports. The compliance Panel turned first to the aspects that the Appellate Body had understood to be decisive in considering that the US measure constituted unjustifiable discrimination. The first aspect was the lack of flexibility of the measure which did not take the conditions prevailing in different countries into account.[827] The second aspect was the absence of US negotiations with the countries wishing to import shrimp to the US. The Panel understood the Appellate Body to have stated that the absence of negotiations with the complaining parties was not only problematic, because negotiations had been conducted with other countries, but because the environmental problem at stake could only be solved by joint action, given the migratory nature of sea turtles. The Panel, moreover, took the Appellate Body as saying that the absence of negotiations was unacceptable because several international legal instruments and declarations of the WTO CTE existed that favoured multilateral cooperation for solving environmental problems such as the extinction of sea turtles.[828] The Panel also attributed the Appellate Body's rejection of the measure as non-compliant with the chapeau in part to the fact that the measure under review was an import ban, which is the most trade-restrictive measure conceivable.[829] These were all considered by the Panel as factors to be taken into account in marking out the appropriate equilibrium between the

825 Ibid.

826 Ibid., para. 11.324–11.330.

827 *United States – Import Prohibition of Certain Shrimp and Shrimp Products, WT/DS58/RW* 2001, para. 5.43.

828 Ibid., para. 5.46–5.56.

829 Ibid., para. 5.51.

rights and obligations of the parties under the chapeau. The Appellate Body, in the eyes of the compliance Panel, had found that the scale was tilted in favour of a multi- or bilateral solution in the constellation underlying the *Shrimp – Turtles* case.[830]

The Panel then proceeded to elaborate on each of these aspects. It first discussed the AB's finding that the US ought to have initiated negotiations, and how that finding was to be understood. The compliance Panel went one step further than the Appellate Body and took the principle of good faith, as expressed in the chapeau, to mandate a "continuity of efforts" and, hence, multilateral negotiations with the aim of improving the protection of sea turtles.[831] The Appellate Body, in contrast, had only stated in a much more abstract manner that the principle of good faith prohibited a party from exercising its rights under Art. XX GATT in a manner that would unduly encroach upon the rights of the other Members. Altogether, the Panel took the Appellate Body as saying that in order to avoid unjustifiable discrimination, the US had to initiate, or at the very least make serious efforts to initiate, negotiations with all interested parties, but that there was no obligation to successfully conclude them.[832] It admitted that any test designed to ascertain whether such serious efforts had been undertaken might prove difficult to apply, but found that in the case under review, with the example of the IAC existing and given the considerable diplomatic and financial resources of the US, "rather more than less" could be expected from the US.[833] This would seem to imply, for example, that rather less could be expected from less-developed country in such a situation. Even though the compliance Panel did not explicitly refer to a necessity test, referring to the IAC as a "benchmark"[834] of what behaviour could have been expected from the US also vis-à-vis other countries, these statements plainly moved it to the vicinity of a necessity test. The existence

830 Ibid., para. 5.58, 5.59.

831 Ibid., para. 5.60.

832 Ibid., para. 5.62–5.66; this understanding is confirmed by the Appellate Body in *United States – Import Prohibition of Certain Shrimp and Shrimp Products, WT/DS58/AB/RW* 2001, para. 123.

833 *United States – Import Prohibition of Certain Shrimp and Shrimp Products, WT/DS58/RW* 2001, para. 5.76.

834 Ibid., para. 5.71–5.75; the Appellate Body later on mildly chides the Panel for the use of this term and suggests "example" instead, while approving the Panel's overall approach, see *United States – Import Prohibition of Certain Shrimp and Shrimp Products, WT/DS58/AB/RW* 2001, para. 130.

of the IAC is taken to demonstrate that an alternative, feasible course of action was open to the US.

Applying these criteria, the Panel found that in the interim period between the original and the review proceedings, the US had made sufficient efforts with regard to initiating negotiations.[835] At the end of its discussion of the duty to initiate negotiations, the Panel added an important clarification. It stated that there were two cases in which a unilateral measure could be justified under the chapeau of Art. XX GATT. The first is where serious and 'good faith' efforts had been undertaken by the party imposing the measure to negotiate with the country or countries affected. The second is when the measure taken was allowed under another international agreement.[836] In the first case, the measure is only justified provisionally and would have to be reconsidered at some later point.[837] Continuing its discussion concerning whether the "new" US measure lived up to the guidelines set out in the Appellate Body report, the Panel turned next to the flexibility of this measure and its responsiveness to the conditions prevailing in the respective countries. This absence of such flexibility was one of the decisive reasons behind the Appellate Body finding against the initial US measure. The Panel, having simply reiterated the Appellate Body's interpretation, found that the new measures did not suffer from the same flaw as the initial one: it did not require exporting countries anymore to adopt "essentially the same" regulatory policy, but rather a comparably effective one.[838] Moreover, the Panel found that the new guidelines for applying the US measure allowed for an inquiry into the appropriateness of the US regulatory program for the conditions of countries where different conditions prevailed.[839] Thus, there was no "equal treatment of the unequal" anymore, like before. It is not quite clear why this was discussed with a view to the *unjustifiable* nature of the discrimination, because there are good reasons to assume that treating the unequal in an identical way is *eo ipso* discrimination, and not only unjustifiable discrimination. The Panel found no GATT violation with regard to arbitrary discrimination, ei-

835 *United States – Import Prohibition of Certain Shrimp and Shrimp Products, WT/DS58/RW* 2001, para. 5.87.

836 The Panel here did not elaborate any further on *why* the existence of another international legal agreement permitting the measures in question was relevant, e.g. because of *lex posterior* or *lex specialis* collision rules.

837 *United States – Import Prohibition of Certain Shrimp and Shrimp Products, WT/DS58/RW* 2001, para. 5.88.

838 Ibid., para. 5.94.

839 Ibid., para. 5.102.

ther.[840] As the revised US measure did not require the exporting countries to adopt precisely the same regulatory instrument as the US, the Panel considered it to be more flexible than the old one. Moreover it also posed fewer problems with regards due process as the countries potentially affected by an import ban according to the revised US guidelines would be heard as part of its implementation.

The compliance Panel then went on to discuss whether the US measure constituted a disguised restriction on international trade, given that it did not amount to either unjustifiable or arbitrary discrimination.[841] To this end, the Panel relied on the criteria developed by the Appellate Body in *United States – Gasoline* and *Japan – Alcoholic Beverages*, namely that any potentially protective application of a measure may can be assessed by scrutinizing its design, architecture and structure. The Panel did not, however, look in detail at any of these aspects. Rather, it found that US shrimp fishers had to fulfil similar requirements as the foreign fishers and would not profit from the revision of the measure. Moreover, it also pointed out that third countries could devise their own regulatory scheme for sea turtle protection and were offered technical assistance for this purpose. It is not entirely clear from these findings why the latter two aspects would lead to the finding that there was no disguised restriction on international trade.

Finally, the Appellate Body also issued a report under Art. 21.5 DSU. The Appellate Body approved of several of the Panel's findings, such as the formula that when all that was required was for the exporting state to have a comparably effective regulatory policy, the respective measure could be justified under the chapeau.[842] It also agreed with the Panel's treatment of the question of whether the revised guidelines were flexible enough not to be discriminatory.[843]

On the other hand, the Appellate Body disagreed with the Panel in several respects. In contrast to both its own previous approach and that taken by both Panels, the Appellate Body did not deal with the two qualifications of discrimination separately. First, the Appellate Body turned to the duty to negotiate. Its findings point in a slightly different direction from those of the Panel compliance report. While the Panel had considered a duty to initiate negotiations under Art. XX GATT as inherent to the princi-

840 Ibid., para. 5.121–5.137.

841 Ibid., para. 5.142–5.143.

842 *United States – Import Prohibition of Certain Shrimp and Shrimp Products, WT/DS58/AB/RW* 2001, para. 141–144.

843 Ibid., para, 146–148.

ple of good faith, the Appellate Body emphasized that its prior finding supporting the existence of such a duty was a result of the varied attitudes that the US had taken towards its different trading partners.[844] There was, therefore, not *per se* a duty to negotiate, but rather an obligation to undertake comparable efforts in comparable situations. There is a second point where the Appellate Body's report differs slightly from that of the Panel but does not formally reject it: the Appellate Body does not only refer to the IAC as a background against which the US behaviour towards the complaining Asian states had to be assessed, but also as an indicator that an alternative course of action was available to the US.[845] As discussed above with regard to the initial Appellate Body report, it is not very clear where the Appellate Body is heading with this emphasis on the availability of an alternative course of action, as this is normally a matter of necessity.

The next case to deal with the chapeau was *EC – GSP*. In this case only the Panel decided on the chapeau, as the parties did not appeal its finding on this aspect. As described above,[846] the controversial measure in this case was an EU scheme granting tariff preferences to certain countries where drugs that were later exported to the EU were produced. The Panel investigated whether the conditions set out in Art. XX GATT chapeau were fulfilled, even though it had already concluded that the measure was not necessary in the sense of Art. XX (b) GATT. It found the EU measure to be discriminatory as the measure did not grant trade preferences to all countries that are important drug producers. The Panel could not identify "objective" and "specific" criteria for the selection of those countries included in the preferential trade arrangement.[847]

The chapeau was also at issue in *Brazil – Tyres*. In this case the Brazilian legal framework prohibited the import of retreaded tyres to Brazil, but contained an exception for tyres from Mercosur countries. The respective exemption had been included in the legal framework after a Mercosur tribunal had decided that the Brazilian import ban on retreaded tyres was prohibited under Mercosur rules.[848] In addition, there were exemptions to the import ban for some Brazilian importers resulting from injunctions by Brazilian courts; these importers could e.g. import tyre components from

844 Ibid., para. 119–122.

845 Ibid., para. 126–128.

846 See above section 1.2.2.

847 *European Communities – Conditions for the Granting of Tariff Preferences to Developing Countries, WT/DS246/R* 2003, 7.233f.

848 The Mercosur judgment is summarized by Morosini 2010.

the EU, while EU exporters could not export these to Brazil. The fact that tyres from Mercosur countries were treated differently from identical tyres from other countries constituted discrimination in the eyes of the Panel.[849] In discussing whether the discrimination was also arbitrary or unjustifiable, the Panel referred to the dictionary definitions of the two terms; these

> "suggested the need to be able to 'defend' or convincingly explain the rationale for any discrimination in the application of the measure".[850]

The fact that the exception resulted from a judicial decision taken under a non-WTO international trade agreement led the measure, in the view of the Panel, not to be "capricious" or "random" and hence not "arbitrary", either.[851] In a quite surprising and largely unexplained move, the Panel then stated that if the exemptions from the import ban on re-treaded tyres led to imports taking place in such quantities as to undermine the objective of the measure at issue, the measure including the exemptions would constitute an unjustifiable discrimination.[852] As the Panel observed that court injunctions led to significant imports of tyres, it concluded that the Brazilian measure constituted unjustifiable discrimination.[853] It adopted what has been labelled an "effects-based approach"[854] to the interpretation of the term. Ironically, the Panel thus assumed a partial import ban (i.e. a trade measure less trade-restrictive than a total ban) to constitute unjustifiable discrimination, precisely because it was not a full import ban. The Panel also investigated whether the discrimination occurred between "countries where the same conditions prevail", concluding in the affirmative after observing that there was no origin-based difference between the products in question from a waste-management point of view.[855] With regard to the term "disguised restriction on international trade", the Panel observed that a concealment of a measure was not required for a restriction to be considered as disguised; rather, a number of factors needed to be

---

849 *Brazil – Measures Affecting Imports of Retreaded Tyres, WT/DS332/R* 2007, para. 7.243.
850 Ibid., para. 7.260.
851 Ibid., para. 7.281.
852 Ibid., para. 7.287.
853 Ibid., para. 7.306.
854 Davies 2009, 512.
855 *Brazil – Measures Affecting Imports of Retreaded Tyres, WT/DS332/R* 2007, para. 7.309.

taken into account and a flexible approach to applying the term in a given case was warranted.[856]

The Appellate Body began its analysis by repeating some of its findings from both earlier GATT case law and from *United States – Gambling*, a case relating to GATS. Included amongst these findings was that the chapeau served to ensure that Members' right to use the exceptions contained in Art. XX GATT was exercised in good faith and not to circumvent WTO obligations.[857] It also reiterated the statement that the chapeau contained a balance of rights and obligations constructed by WTO Members, with the "line of equilibrium" moving according to the circumstances of the case.[858]

The Appellate Body observed that any analysis of whether discrimination was arbitrary or unjustifiable was dependent on assessing the cause or rationale of discrimination.[859] The Appellate Body therefore found that it had to examine whether the cause indicated by Brazil for the differentiation between re-treaded tyres from Mercosur and non-Mercosur countries, the ruling by the Mercosur tribunal, was "acceptable as a justification for the discrimination".[860] The Appellate Body stated that the requirements of the chapeau were not met when the reasons given for a discrimination

> "bear no rational connection to the objective falling within the purview of a paragraph of Article XX GATT, or would go against that objective",

relying on an earlier argument by one of the parties in *Shrimp – Turtles*.[861] Quite obviously, there was no such "rational connection" between the exemptions resulting from court decisions and the environmental objectives of the import ban for tyres from other origins; to the contrary, they undermined the objective. The Appellate Body therefore concluded that the Mercosur exemption resulted in the import ban being applied in a manner constituting arbitrary or unjustifiable discrimination.[862] The same reasoning also applied with regard to court injunctions allowing the importing of used tyres in some other cases.[863] In other words, the Appellate Body

---

856 Ibid., para. 7.322.
857 *Brazil – Measures Affecting Imports of Retreaded Tyres, WT/DS332/AB/R* 2007, para. 215.
858 Ibid., para. 224.
859 Ibid., para. 225.
860 Ibid., para. 227.
861 Ibid.
862 Ibid., para. 228.
863 Ibid., para. 246.

did not distinguish between the two terms arbitrary or unjustifiable. It also failed to discuss independently whether the discrimination was between "countries where the same conditions prevail". The Appellate Body explicitly rejected the finding of the Panel which implied that whether discrimination was "unjustifiable" could depend on the factual, quantitative impact of a measure,[864] noting somewhat cryptically that

> "in certain cases the effects of the discrimination may be a relevant factor, among others, for determining whether the cause of discrimination is acceptable or defensible".[865]

In *EU – Seal Products*, the Panel found that an EU measure provisionally justified under Art. XX (a) GATT violated the terms of the chapeau.[866] The complainants appealed certain parts of the Panel's findings, notably that the Panel used the same test under Art. 2.1 TBT and the chapeau, but not its overall conclusion. The defendant did not appeal the Panel's finding. In response to the appeal, the Appellate Body reiterated findings from earlier cases that the chapeau was to preserve the balance of rights and obligations of Members and must be interpreted and applied accordingly.[867] It also recalled that the provisions of the chapeau could not be read to establish the same legal standards as the sub-paragraphs; yet, this does not mean, according to the Appellate Body that the

> "circumstances that bring about the discrimination that is to be examined under the chapeau cannot be the same as those that led to the finding of a violation of a substantive provision of the GATT 1994".[868]

The Appellate Body then provided a summary of the existing case law on the interpretation of the chapeau, but also looked in greater detail than it had done in previous cases at the phrase "same conditions". It noted that while the term conditions could refer to a range of circumstances a country faces, only those conditions

> "'relevant' for the purpose of establishing arbitrary or unjustifiable discrimination in the light of the specific character of the measure at issue

864 Ibid., para. 229.
865 Ibid., para. 230.
866 *European Communities – Measures Prohibiting the Importation and Marketing of Seal Products, WT/DS400/R, WT/DS401/R* 2013, para. 7.644.
867 *European Communities – Measures Prohibiting the Importation and Marketing of Seal Products, WT/DS400/AB/R, WT/DS401/AB/R* 2014, para. 5.297.
868 Ibid., para. 5.298.

and the circumstances of a particular case should be considered under the chapeau".[869]

In the view of the Appellate Body, the regulatory purpose of the measure as considered under the sub-paragraphs of Art. XX GATT and the GATT provisions violated by the controversial measure provided important guidance as to which "conditions" were relevant.[870] With regard to the term discrimination it quoted an earlier finding from *Shrimp – Turtles*, which stated that discrimination exists when countries in which the same conditions prevail are treated differently. When examining whether the discrimination is arbitrary or unjustifiable the rationale provided for the discrimination and its link with the objective pursued by the measure are important, but not the only relevant factors.[871]

When responding to the appellants' argument that Art. 2.1 TBT and Art. XX chapeau required different tests, the Appellate Body first observed that there were indeed important parallels between the two norms. Notably, they both contained the concepts of "arbitrary or unjustifiable discrimination between countries where the same conditions prevail" and of a "disguised restriction on trade". Yet the Appellate Body also found important differences between the two norms: Notably, under Art. 2.1 TBT, a non-discrimination provision, only the regulatory distinction disadvantaging imported products needs to be examined for its legitimacy. By contrast, the chapeau clause requires a wider balancing of the rights and obligations of WTO Members; the grounds on which a violation of the prohibition of arbitrary and unjustifiable discrimination under the chapeau is found are not necessarily the same as those on which a violation of a non-discrimination provision of the GATT is identified. On this basis, the Appellate Body concluded that different tests needed to be conducted for the two norms and reversed the Panel's findings.[872]

Given that Panel had applied a flawed test, the Appellate Body then proceeded to complete the chapeau analysis. The problem at hand was that the EU's trade ban on seal products contained an exception for products from seal hunted by indigenous communities. Seal products imported to the EU from Greenland stemmed mostly from seal hunted by such communities, whereas products from seals hunted in Canada and Norway, the two complainant countries, mostly were from commercial hunts and did

869 Ibid., para. 5.299.
870 Ibid., para. 5.300f.
871 Ibid., para. 5.303, 5.321.
872 Ibid., para. 5.310ff.

not qualify for the exceptional admission to the EU market.[873] When comparing the "conditions" in these countries, the Appellate Body found them to be identical in relation to the objective of the measure pursued – the same concerns over the welfare of seal existed everywhere.[874] As a corollary, the EU measure was discriminatory. The Appellate Body then went on to examine whether

> "the discrimination can be reconciled with, or is rationally related to, the policy objective with respect to which the measure has been provisionally justified".[875]

It relied in this regard on its earlier decision in *Brazil – Retreaded Tyres*, but only said that whether the discrimination was rationally related to the policy objective recognized under Art. XX GATT was "one of the most important factors" (rather than the only factor) in the assessment of arbitrary or unjustifiable discrimination.[876]

In this context it observed that the parties were not disputing whether the exception clause was related to the objective of protecting public morals: they both agreed that it was not. Rather, according to the EU, it was to mitigate adverse effects of the trade ban on indigenous peoples.[877] The Appellate Body therefore concluded that the EU had failed to demonstrate how the way in which seal hunts by indigenous communities were treated could be "reconciled with, or [...] related to" the objective of protecting public morals.[878]

It then went on to examine other factors that could be of relevance in the overall assessment of whether there was a rationale for the observed discrimination. The Appellate Body identified certain ambiguities in the exception clause benefitting indigenous communities, giving the bodies applying them significant discretion. In addition, there were no mechanisms in place for ensuring that the exception provision was not circumvented or only applied to the proper products. The Appellate Body concluded that some products could enter the EU market that were made from seal that had been hunted by indigenous communities in a manner that was similarly harmful to seal welfare as products from commercial

---

873 See also Pitschas and Schloemann 2012, 6.

874 *European Communities – Measures Prohibiting the Importation and Marketing of Seal Products, WT/DS400/AB/R, WT/DS401/AB/R* 2014, para. 5.137.

875 Ibid., para. 5.318.

876 Ibid., para. 5.306.

877 Ibid., para. 5.319.

878 Ibid., para. 5.320.

hunt. The products from indigenous communities were allowed to enter the EU market, the ones from commercial hunt were not. This, in the eyes of the Appellate Body, constituted a means of arbitrary or unjustifiable discrimination between countries where the same conditions prevail.[879] The Appellate Body further investigated whether indigenous communities in different countries benefitted from the exception in an equal manner.[880] At the time of the Panel proceedings only Inuit communities from Greenland were able to do so, and the complainants maintained that this was a result of the design of the exception provision rather than a coincidence or lack of effort by indigenous communities from elsewhere. The Appellate Body held that the EU had not been able to show that the *de facto* exclusive operation of the exception to the benefit of Greenland's indigenous communities was attributable to other factors than the measure itself, e.g. choices by private actors. The Appellate Body was not persuaded that the EU had made "comparable efforts" to facilitate the access of the Canadian Inuit under the exception for indigenous communities as it did with respect to the Greenlandic Inuit; it referred to a finding in *Shrimp – Turtles* that a measure may result in arbitrary or unjustifiable discrimination when the application of the measure "does not allow for any inquiry into the appropriateness of the regulatory program" for the conditions prevailing in exporting countries.[881] Consequently, the Appellate Body held that the EU's seal ban was not justified under Art. XX GATT.

1.5. Discussion of case law on GATT and GATS

WTO judicial decision-makers have interpreted Art. XX GATT and its various sub-paragraphs, as well as Art. XIV GATS, in a number of cases. While this has led to more finely grained rules that WTO Members must observe when taking non-trade measures, the body of case law on these norms has several weak points. I will in the following focus on some central aspects and do not purport to criticize each and every aspect of all the relevant cases.

879 Ibid., para. 5.324ff.
880 Ibid., para. 5.329ff.
881 Ibid., para. 5.337.

1.5.1. Unclear structure and content of the necessity test

Despite the frequent cross-references in the case law and marked attempts at interpreting the term "necessary" in the same way in GATS and GATT cases relating to different subparagraphs of Art. XX GATT, it is not clear how the analysis whether a certain measure qualifies as "necessary" is to be carried out – and this is partially because the way it is conducted seems to vary quite considerably across cases.

What is nominally clear is that the weighing and balancing exercise, as created by the Appellate Body in *Korea – Beef* and mentioned consistently in later cases, involves at least the following three factors: the importance of the interests that a measure is to protect; the effectiveness of the measure in reaching its objective, and the trade-restrictive effect of the measure. Beyond that, much remains open. In particular, it is difficult to find conclusive answers to two questions in the case law. The first concerns the relationship between the balancing of these factors and the requirement that a measure can only be considered necessary if there are no alternative measures reasonably available.[882] The second, concerns whether the balancing formula actually entails a balancing of interests in the sense of the third prong of the EU-style proportionality test, i.e. can a measure that is very trade-restrictive and serves a relatively unimportant regulatory goal be struck down as WTO-inconsistent?

On the first question the following observations can be made:

As described above, the current "weighing and balancing" formula can be traced back to *Korea – Beef*. In that case, it was used in reference to an earlier GATT case that had interpreted the term "necessary" as requiring that no alternative, less trade-restrictive measures were reasonably available. Considering this judicial history underpinning the *Korea – Beef* formula, it is reasonable to read it as a tool for finding out whether an alternative measure is reasonably available.[883]

However, in later cases the relationship between the weighing and balancing exercise and the test whether alternative measures are available

882 That this aspect of WTO case law is rather unclear has been noted by various other commentators as well, see for example Ruozzi 2009, 482ff; van Calster 2008, 135 wrote after the *Brazil – Tyres* decision: "what the current test is under Article XX, its chapeau, and similar provisions in other WTO Agreements, really is anyone's guess." This is still largely true.

883 For a similar understanding of the *Korea – Beef* report see Marceau and Trachtman 2002, 827; Zleptnig 2010, 235.

seems to have been conceived of differently.[884] In some, the "alternative measure" test appears to be an additional one that is initiated only if and once the balancing test has yielded the preliminary result that the measure is necessary (e.g. *Brazil – Tyres* and *Dominican Republic – Cigarettes*).[885] Conceptually, this could create a higher hurdle for national measures that would need to pass two independent tests. In other cases, whether an alternative measure is reasonably available seems to be one more factor to be taken into account for the weighing and balancing procedure (e.g. *China – Audiovisual Products*). While the Appellate Body has presented the *Korea – Beef* formula and subsequent case law building on it as a stringent set of precedents that build upon each other, this is, at close reading, far from the case.[886] This aspect of WTO case law can thus not be considered as settled. This is quite surprising – and even unsatisfactory – given how central the term "necessary" is to WTO law and to the review of the legality of measures taken for non-trade purposes.

Moreover, as Fontanelli and Regan observe, the fact that the Appellate Body refers in *Brazil – Tyres* first to the balancing formula and then to a least-restrictive means test is also puzzling from another point of view: the tests seem to be largely similar.[887] The weighing and balancing formula comprises the following elements: the importance of the interest or value that the controversial measure protects; the degree to which the measure contributes to that end, and its trade-restrictiveness. Yet the least-restrictive means test would also cover the second and third element at least: in order to ascertain whether an alternative measure reaches the objective pursued to the same degree as the measure in place, the effectiveness of this measure at doing so must be assessed. Furthermore, the alternative measure must also be less-trade restrictive than the measure in place, which requires a statement on the degree to which the measure in place restricts trade.

---

884 The fact that this aspect of the Appellate Body's case law is not very clear seems to be missed by some authors, e.g. in the otherwise excellent article by McGrady 2009, 160.

885 Fontanelli 2012, 38f; Ruozzi 2009, 481f.

886 Some commentators offer a slightly more linear narrative of the WTO jurisprudence on necessity. For example, Buchmüller 2013, 257 identifies three stages of the evolution of the test, the old GATT, Korea - Beef and the cases following it and Brazil - Tyres and the cases following it. Given the low number of cases and how little explanation the Appellate Body actually provides on its approach and its transformations, this seems a somewhat too ambitious attempt at systematization for the time being.

887 Fontanelli 2012, 48f; Regan 2007, 354, 357.

The only thing that the weighing and balancing formula adds when compared with the least-restrictive means test is that the adjudicators look at the importance of the interest or value pursued.

WTO Members also seem to perceive a lack of clarity in the balancing test. In *China – Audiovisual Products* the US sought clarification of how to apply the test under Art. XX GATT, arguing that in carrying out the necessity analysis

> "a panel cannot simultaneously assess all relevant factors and undertake the necessary 'weighing and balancing' with respect to the contested measure and proposed alternative measures."[888]

In response, the Appellate Body referred to its own approach in *Korea – Beef* (in the context of Art. XX (d) GATT), *United States – Gambling* (in the context of Art. XIV (a) GATS), and *Brazil – Tyres* (in the context of Art. XX (b) GATT). It observed that in these cases the interpretation of the term "necessary" had always been taken to involve "weighing and balancing" a number of factors relating both to the measure to be justified and to possible alternative measures considered to be reasonably available.[889] The Appellate Body also expressed the view that in all of these cases it had taken the same approach towards interpreting the necessity criterion.[890]

I will now turn to the question of whether the Appellate Body actually engages in a balancing of interests in the sense of the third prong of the EU proportionality test.[891] Opinions are divided on this point in the literature.

Some observers conclude that there is no balancing of trade and non-trade values and interests in the WTO in the sense of proportionality *sensu stricto* either conceptually or in practice.[892] As one observer has put it:

---

888 *China – Measures Affecting Trading Rights and Distribution Services for Certain Publications and Audiovisual Entertainment Products, WT/DS363/AB/R* 2009, para. 238.

889 Ibid., para. 239.

890 Ibid., para. 242.

891 On the following see also Venzke 2012, 208.

892 Andenas and Zleptnig 2007, 374; Bown and Trachtman 2009, 88; Kleinlein 2012, 266; Lovric 2010, 143ff; Neumann and Tuerk 2003, 212f. 227ff; Reid 2010, 893; Regan 2007; Vranes 2009, 274; with regard to the Appellate Body's decision in EC - Asbestos Howse and Tuerk 2001, 323; Van den Bossche 2008, 289; with regard to the TBT and the SPS Agreements see also Ortino 2004, 472; Zleptnig 2010, 244ff.

> "the balancing result is rarely spelled out in clear terms, and virtually never relied upon to decide on the WTO-legality of the measure."[893]

For the most part, these observers give little thought to how they might tread the Appellate Body's reference to the need for assessing the importance of the interest at stake, if it is not supposed to involve balancing. Vranes is a laudable exception. He surmises that the reference to the importance of the interest at stake must be taken to relate to the level of scrutiny that adjudicators will apply, which would be less intensive when the interest is more important.[894] This analysis of what the Appellate Body does is open to question, however: the level of scrutiny applied is, in the normal course of affairs of WTO dispute settlement, often discussed very explicitly and under the heading of standard of review. It would therefore be quite surprising if, in the context of the necessity analysis, the intensity of scrutiny to be applied was addressed in a manner so opaque and indirect as a discussion of the importance of the interest pursued. It has also been surmised that the reference to balancing has been borrowed by the Appellate Body from the German/EU legal tradition, as some of the Appellate Body Members taking the relevant decisions were German/EU-trained lawyers.[895] Yet this still fails to explain what, precisely, the Appellate Body means by referring to balancing in the context discussed here, if no "real" balancing of interests takes place.

By way of contrast to this first group of observers, some consider the Appellate Body's "weighing and balancing" formula under Art. XX GATT, which includes the importance of the regulatory interest at stake as one factor to be taken into account, to involve substantial trade-offs between trade and non-trade regulatory goals.[896] They identify similarities to the third element of the proportionality test in European law.[897] In support, it has been pointed out that the Appellate Body seemed to be less accepting of the defending Member's claim that proposed alternatives would not reach the desired level of protection in two cases involving

893 Fontanelli 2012, 49.

894 Vranes 2009, 274f.

895 Kulick 2012, 182.

896 Marceau and Trachtman 2002, 852ff; Marceau and Trachtman 2014, 406ff; Osiro 2002, 134; van Calster 2008, 135; Weiler 2009, 140; probably also Martineau 2007, 1006ff; see also the authors in the next two footnotes.

897 Buchmüller 2013, 262; probably also of this view Morrison and Nielsen 2013, 217f; Cheyne 2006, 271 even maintains – probably a bit too optimistically – that there is "a clear echo of the principle of EC law that human health takes precedence over economic interests".

Art. XX (d) GATT; in these cases policy goals such as preventing fraud or smuggling than in cases were health issues were at stake.[898] In other words, measures were accepted more easily in the health-related cases in the eyes of these observers.

The divergence in the literature may stem in part from the fact that the contributions were published at different stages of development of the case law, and further from the fact that some of the Appellate Body's findings seem to indicate that it is reluctant to engage in any balancing of substantive interests, while other findings seem to point in an opposite direction.[899] Another source of the confusion may be the fact that while the Appellate Body assumes it has the right to say something on the importance of the interests at stake it has, in practice, almost never explicitly described any interest as un-important[900], even though it has been conspicuously silent on the importance of the interest pursued at least in one case, *Korea – Beef*.[901] More generally, the Appellate Body seems reluctant to fully apply its own test: Bown and Trachtman state that the Appellate Body in *Brazil – Tyres*

> "has shown itself unwilling to evaluate for itself, or to require a Panel to evaluate, in any but the most gross categories, any of [the] four factors"

belonging to the Appellate Body's weighing and balancing formula and has been similarly imprecise in other cases.[902] Another commentator concludes that the weighing and balancing formula has been put to (full) practice in only one Panel report, *Colombia – Entry Ports*.[903] This was a case under Art. XX (d) GATT. The measures at issue were aimed at strengthening customs controls and enforcement, and by implication generating revenue and preventing smuggling and money laundering, also in the context of drug trafficking. The Panel concluded that

---

898 Du 2010a, 1096ff referring to Korea - Beef and Dominican *Republic – Cigarettes* on the one hand, and Asbestos and *Brazil – Retreaded Tyres* on the other; Ruozzi 2009, 482; Morrison and Nielsen 2013, 127f.

899 Probably the most thorough exploration of the textual ambiguity of the Appellate Body's report in Korea - Beef is offered by Regan 2007.

900 See also Lovric 2010, 145. It did make a statement in one case, though, that cost considerations were not sufficient grounds for a discrimination, see Marín Durán 2016, 485.

901 Regan 2007, 360.

902 Bown and Trachtman 2009, 88.

903 Fontanelli 2012, 49; by contrast some other observers maintain that the formula has never been fully applied, e.g. Kleinlein 2012, 266.

> "combating under-invoicing and money laundering associated with drug trafficking is a relatively more important reality for Colombia than for many other countries".[904]

However, it did not say that these interests were of utmost, essential importance for Colombia. This may have made it easier for the Panel to come to the conclusion in the end that the measures were not necessary. Generally, such a comprehensive application of the weighing and balancing formula is rare in the case law.[905]

A reason for the adjudicators' hesitating to fully apply the balancing text in practice may be the fact that the elements the Appellate Body integrates into its balancing formula are not really commensurate. On the one hand, there is an interest and value, while on the other there are factors such as the trade-restrictive effect of the measure and the degree to which the measure contributes to the end pursued. How can one "balance" an interest against such other variables? While the trade-restrictive effect can be "translated" rather easily into an underlying value or interest – unhampered trade – this is not true for the degree to which a measure contributes to the end pursued. The "weighing and balancing" the Appellate Body requires of the adjudicators is, in practice, not at all easy: a WTO dispute settlement body finding an interest pursued by a Member unimportant is likely to be controversial, as is finding a measure too trade-restrictive to be justified. Finally, how to include the remaining factor in a balancing of interests is not clear, given that it cannot be easily translated into an interest to be balanced. However, if there are good reasons for not fully applying the test, then why is it then continually rehashed in Appellate Body case law? Furthermore, that the Appellate Body has hardly ever fully carried out the balancing exercise is not a good argument for being unconcerned over the Appellate Body's balancing ambitions. After all, if the test is there, it can be used in future cases in a way much more intrusive into WTO Members regulatory autonomy than done so far.[906]

Altogether, there is no shortage of critical comments on the current state of the "necessity" analysis and its lack of clarity.[907] The doctrinal state of affairs surrounding the necessity analysis has been called "unfortunate and

---

904 See *Colombia – Indicative Prices and Restrictions on Ports of Entry, WT/DS366/R* 2009, para. 7.566.

905 See also Weiler 2009, 138.

906 Buchmüller 2013, 268f; Venzke 2012, 211.

907 See Du 2010a, 1095; Fontanelli 2012; Foster 2008, 438; Guan 2014, 221; Hoekman, Bernard and Trachtman, Joel 2010, 171; Kapterian 2010, 118; Marwell

dangerous"[908] and doubts about its consistency have been voiced.[909] Yet to put this observation in context, it must be said that the ECJ, which has decided many more cases than the WTO dispute settlement bodies on similar issues, faces similar calls for further clarification of its jurisprudence.[910]

1.5.2. Logical inconsistencies in the case law

In the case law, there are certain inconsistencies between cases. Sometimes, these are of a logical nature – one finding is not logically compatible with another one. Sometimes, the inconsistency stems from the fact that different dispute settlement reports seem to say different things on the matter. The necessity analysis is an example of the latter, but there are more examples.

An important example of inconsistencies between different pronouncements by the adjudicators has to do with the right of Members to choose the level of protection they wish to attain. This right has been wholeheartedly supported by the Appellate Body.

At the same time, it is not clear to which extent WTO Members actually enjoy it. The main argument as to why such an unfettered right may not obtain after all is that the Appellate Body assumes, as part of its weighing and balancing exercise, the right to review the importance of the objective at stake. As discussed in the previous section, it is not entirely clear the extent to which the Appellate Body's formula for how to interpret the "necessity" requirement involves balancing *sensu stricto*, and if it does not, what the reference to the importance of the interest pursued would otherwise mean.

If one takes the Appellate Body's approach seriously it means that a measure is less likely to be accepted as necessary if the goal it pursues is considered less important. However, if only the specific measure in place is capable of reaching the level of protection desired by the WTO Member, the Appellate Body declaring a measure non-necessary also means that the respective WTO Member may in fact not choose its own level of protection.

2006, 827; McGrady 2009, 162; Doyle 2011, 160; Regan 2007; Charnovitz 2007, 697; Weiler 2009, 138.

908 Regan 2007, 350 made this statement several years ago. However, as the case law has not evolved much since, it is still applicable.

909 For example Kleinlein 2012, 267; with regard to the interpretation of Art. XX GATT in the case law more generally, see also Guan 2014, 221.

910 This has been noted by Reid 2010, 878.

Indeed, several observers have noted that there is a contradiction between the Appellate Body's balancing approach and the statement that Members have the right to determine the level of protection they want.[911]

Also, the WTO dispute settlement bodies do not appear particularly consistent in their approach towards ascertaining the actual level of protection of a Member. They decided some cases (e.g. *Korea – Beef*) on the basis of an actual level of protection they found to be lower than the level of protection the defending Member claimed it pursued, but did not do the same in *Brazil – Tyres,* for example.[912]

Another example of inconsistency between decisions is the Appellate Body's finding in *United States – Gambling* and its approach in *Brazil – Tyres.* In the former, it decided that an alternative measure is not reasonably available where it is merely theoretical in nature whereas in the latter, the contribution of the measure actually in place was merely theoretical in nature; the Appellate Body accepted in this case that it was sufficient if a measure was "apt" for making a "material" contribution to the regulatory purpose pursued.[913] Bown and Trachtman make the point that it would be strange to impose a stricter standard on alternative measures than the actual, controversial ones.[914] Taking matters further, the point has been made that the Appellate Body's *Brazil – Tyres* approach to investigating the aptness of the measure in place was not the same as in *China – Audiovisual Products,* either; in the latter case, the Appellate Body investigated the actual contribution of a measure to the aim pursued.[915]

A further (possible) inconsistency has been identified between the Appellate Body's interpretation of the chapeau in *Brazil – Tyres* and *Shrimp – Turtles* respectively.[916] In *Brazil – Tyres*, but also in the later *EC – Seal Products* case, the Appellate Body held that a measure constituted no "arbitrary" or "unjustifiable" discrimination under the chapeau of Art. XX GATT, if a convincing rationale could be offered for treating countries with similar conditions differently. The Appellate Body made clear in these cases that one important factor in considering the WTO legality of the measure was whether the rationale offered by the defendant was connected to furthering the overall regulatory objective of the measure. In the earlier *Shrimp –*

911 Buchmüller 2013, 260; Du 2010a, 1080; Fontanelli 2012, 46; Marceau and Trachtman 2002, 849; Regan 2007, 348; Venzke 2012, 206; Weiler 2009, 141.

912 Bown and Trachtman 2009, 123.

913 Ibid., 127.

914 Ibid.

915 Delimatsis 2011, 263.

916 Buchmüller 2013, 309f; Davies 2009, 519.

Turtles case, however, the Appellate Body had stated that "the policy goal of a measure […] cannot provide its rationale or justification under the standards of the chapeau of Article XX"[917], as the policy goal of a measure was to be investigated under the sub-paragraphs of Art. XX GATT.[918] There are some doubts as to whether the Appellate Body's statement in *Shrimp – Turtles* really should be taken to mean that regulatory goals cannot matter under the chapeau of Art. XX GATT or whether the statement was merely an attempt to delimit the scope of the chapeau and the sub-paragraphs of Art. XX GATT.[919] Yet the above quote from the chapeau is rather clear textually; if the Appellate Body had considered it wrong in hindsight, it could have clarified the matter in a sentence or two in *Brazil – Tyres.*

Altogether, several inconsistencies can be identified in the case law on the justification norms in GATT and GATS. Some of these are logical inconsistencies between two statements, while some are instances where the same issue is dealt with differently in different cases without these differences being made explicit, let alone justified.

1.5.3. Incorrect use of earlier case law

In this section I will look at how the adjudicators use earlier case law. The question here is not, as in the previous section, whether there are (logical) inconsistencies between one finding and another. It is simply whether what the adjudicators claim had been said in an earlier case is indeed a defensible understanding of that earlier case. It appears that there are quite a number of examples in which a more detailed analysis suggests that an earlier case does not actually support the findings in a later case.

It is in *Korea – Beef*, for example, that the balancing formula used in all later cases first appeared related to an interpretation of Art. XX (d). The Appellate Body's point that the importance of the regulatory issue at stake mattered for a finding of necessity was made on the basis of a contextual interpretation and the fact that laws and regulations were mentioned in Art. XX (d) GATT. Such laws and regulations will ultimately protect diverse interests and objectives as defined by the respective WTO Member;

917 *United States – Import Prohibition of Certain Shrimp and Shrimp Products, WT/DS58/AB/R* 1998, para. 149.

918 For a summary and critique of the Appellate Body's reasoning on this point in Shrimp - Turtles, see in particular Gaines 2001, 776ff.

919 Buchmüller 2013, 309.

the interests and objectives may be of varying importance. These textual circumstances do not exist for the term "necessary" under Art. XX (a) and Art. XX (b) where the *Korea – Beef* formula was used subsequently. The text of Art. XX (a) and Art. XX (b) GATT recognizes specific regulatory goals, i.e. there is already a stated consensus among WTO Members that this goal is important. There is hence no strong rationale why the adjudicator should double-check whether these goals are important.

Also, the Appellate Body had initially said in its *Korea – Beef* report that a treaty interpreter "may, in appropriate cases" take the importance of a regulatory goal into account when assessing the necessity of a measure.[920] In the later *Brazil – Tyres* case, the Appellate Body stated that the relevant factors a Panel "must" assess are the contribution of a measure to the achievement of its objective and its trade restrictiveness, in light of the importance of the interests at stake.[921] So from a factor that could be taken into account optionally and where suitable, the importance of regulatory interests at stake was turned into something that the adjudicators are compelled to consider. Similarly, the Appellate Body stated in *Korea – Beef*[922] that the "weighing and balancing" formula was only to apply to measures not "indispensable". This was not taken up again in later cases.[923] Moreover, as described in the previous section, the structure of the necessity analysis has undergone quite some changes in the various cases, but the Appellate Body neither "admits" these changes nor does it discuss their implications openly.[924]

The way that the Appellate Body's findings in *United States – Gasoline* are used in later cases is equally surprising: In *China – Raw Materials*, the Appellate Body observed that in *United States – Gasoline* it had *not* used "to be primarily aimed at" as a translation of "to be related to" in Art. XX (g). This is, at best, an innovative reading of the earlier Appellate Body decision; as described above the Appellate Body in the *United States – Gasoline* case had explicitly not revised the Panel's finding that measures needed to be "primarily aimed at" conservation, as the parties had not appealed the

920 *Korea – Measures Affecting Imports of Fresh, Chilled and Frozen Beef, WT/DS161/AB/R, WT/DS169/AB/R* 2000, para. 162.

921 *Brazil – Measures Affecting Imports of Retreaded Tyres, WT/DS332/AB/R* 2007, para. 156.

922 *Korea – Measures Affecting Imports of Fresh, Chilled and Frozen Beef, WT/DS161/AB/R, WT/DS169/AB/R* 2000, para. 164.

923 Nor has the literature dedicated much attention to this detail, with Regan 2007 being a notable exception.

924 See Ruozzi 2009, 482.

finding. Instead, the Appellate Body had, in the earlier case, just made a casual statement that the phrase was not contained in the treaty itself and not to be taken as a "litmus test" to ascertain whether a measure fell under Art. XX (g) or not.

Another example is the Panel's interpretation of the terms "public morals" and "public order" in *United States – Gambling*. The Panel here referred to the Appellate Body's earlier case law on the right of Members to choose their appropriate level of protection. However, this right had been discussed in the earlier case in the context of the availability of alternative measures as part of the necessity analysis. It had not been used to interpret the regulatory goals in the different sub-paragraph of Art. XX GATT/XIV GATS.[925]

1.5.4. Lack of justification and clarification

A similarly puzzling aspect of the WTO case law on "necessary", on the interpretation of "relating to" in Art. XX (g) GATT, and also on certain aspects of the chapeau is how little justification the judicial decision-makers have offered for their approach. With regard to the necessity analysis, none of these three balancing factors is contained *verbatim* in the text of GATT, nor does GATT make any reference to the availability of alternative measures.

That the WTO adjudicators have developed a jurisprudence that goes beyond the black letter of the law is as such neither surprising nor unusual. As discussed in chapter 1, WTO law often contains vague and indeterminate terms, and "necessary" is one example. The WTO adjudicators have no choice but to try to make the term more manageable by giving it a more nuanced and refined sense. This is in turn virtually impossible without producing some guidelines that are not, *prima facie*, contained in the letters of the law.

The problem with the adjudicators' approach is a different one: one would expect an elaborate and thorough discussion of terms such as "necessary" or "relating to" in support of the interpretation chosen, given how meticulously the adjudicators in other cases often bring to bear various interpretive methods for identifying the meaning of a single term of phrase of WTO law. Yet such a discussion is largely absent from the appellate cases where the present line or lines of interpretation were started, *United*

925 See Diebold 2008, 52f.

States – Gasoline and *Korea – Beef*. In *Korea – Beef*, the Appellate Body did refer to a dictionary definition of necessary and then went on to argue that the importance of the objective pursued was a relevant factor to be balanced, because Art. XX (d) referred to laws and regulations, which typically protect a certain interest.[926] By way of contrast, for the two other aspects to be considered, the extent to which the measure contributes to the realization of the end pursued and the extent to which the measure produced restrictive effects on international commerce, the Appellate Body gave no argument *whatsoever* on how these could be deduced from the text of WTO law.[927] This is all the more surprising given that the Appellate Body's decisions in *Korea – Beef* and *EC – Asbestos* can be seen as departing from earlier GATT case law.[928] The weighing and balancing formula has, from the very beginning, had very little judicial reasoning behind it.[929]

The argumentation supporting the interpretation of the clause "relating to" in Art. XX (g) GATT in *United States – Gasoline* is similarly shaky. As none of the parties to the dispute had directly appealed it, the Appellate Body simply accepted the Panel's interpretation that to fall within the purview of the "relating to" clause in Art. XX (g) GATT, a measure had to "directly aim" at the protection of exhaustible natural resources. Given that the Appellate Body had to decide on and indeed corrected various other flaws in the Panel's analysis of Art. XX GATT, it could reasonably have changed that interpretation, too. Simple consent by parties is a very weak basis for interpreting an important environmental justification norm of WTO law. The Panel's interpretation of the terms "public morals" and "public order" in Art. XIV GATS/XX GATT has been criticized on similar grounds.[930]

A similar lack of argumentative foundation can be stated for the various procedural standards that the Appellate Body found in the chapeau (e.g. the requirement that there should be a possibility for review as well as a transparent, predictable certification process). Two eminent commentators have written that the Appellate Body in *Shrimp – Turtles* articulated them

---

926 *Korea – Measures Affecting Imports of Fresh, Chilled and Frozen Beef, WT/DS161/AB/R, WT/DS169/AB/R* 2000, para. 161, 162.

927 Ibid., para. 163.

928 Bown and Trachtman 2009, 89.

929 This is not the only problem with the Appellate Body's balancing approach; for other aspects see the discussion in chapter 3, section 4.3.

930 Diebold 2008, 51.

"almost from nowhere"[931] and others have also noted a lack of textual foundation for the Appellate Body's requirements.[932]

Another shortcoming of the jurisprudence on Art. XX GATT chapeau is the lack of distinction between the different elements of the chapeau and, more generally, a lack of interpretative clarification of this central clause of WTO law.[933] Generally, there have hardly been any conclusive statements on the term "disguised restriction" so far[934] and the Appellate Body's interpretation of arbitrary discrimination has long been very vague.[935] While in some cases a distinction has been made between the phrases "disguised restriction on trade" and "unjustified or arbitrary discrimination", it is rare for a clear distinction to be made between "unjustified" and "arbitrary" discrimination or between any of these terms and "discrimination".[936] The Appellate Body's chapeau analysis in *Shrimp – Turtles* has been sharply criticized because it offered no convincing discussion on whether there was discrimination between countries where the same conditions prevail.[937]

This does not apply to all of the cases, but to some. For example, the structure of the Appellate Body's investigation of the chapeau in *EC – Seal Products* is an almost textbook approach, in which each element is discussed properly after the other. Also, the Panel in *Brazil – Tyres* is an exception; it decided that a Brazilian measure constituted "unjustifiable", but not arbitrary, discrimination.[938] The Panel's approach was rejected by the Appellate Body. Altogether, there has been a remarkable lack of attention to the wording of the text on the part of a judicial body that has repeatedly stressed that what matters most is the wording of the law.[939]

Moreover, it is also not quite clear what the Appellate Body's means when using the language of balancing for interpreting the chapeau. Some state that the Appellate Body's reference to a balance between the rights

---

931 Búrca and Scott 2001, 22.

932 Goldstein and Steinberg 2007, 21; Kelly 2002, 381; Colares 2009, 433; Knox 2004, 56; by contrast Cho 2009a, 719 supports the Appellate Body's finding as being appropriately procedural in orientation.

933 The point that the Appellate Body has so far failed to give proper significance and content to the different terms of the chapeau is made, in particular, by Bartels 2015, 96ff; Lo 2013, 112ff.

934 Buchmüller 2013, 322.

935 Ibid., 308.

936 See e.g. Búrca and Scott 2001, 18.

937 Gaines 2001, 783f.

938 For a description of the Brazilian measure, see above section 1.2.2.

939 See on the importance of literal interpretation in the workings of the WTO dispute settlement bodies chapter 3, section 1.1.

and obligations of Members involves a balancing of substantive interests – after all the measures in dispute are always about restricting other Members' *trade*-related rights.[940] Yet others find the wording of the Appellate Body reports ambiguous on whether substantive balancing of interests is involved or not.[941] There are also those who that the Appellate Body does not explicitly balance economic and non-economic or any other substantive interests in the chapeau analysis.[942] Again, this seems to be the result of the Appellate Body not always undertaking a step-by-step interpretation of each of the terms of the chapeau, and on its decisions being based on much more vague, case-specific factors.

Finally, as discussed above[943], both structure and content of the necessity test are unclear.

1.5.5. A role for precaution?

A further point I want to look at is the role of precautionary principle under the GATT. There are many different definitions of the precautionary principle or approach, but in the context of this work, I take it to mean something similar to what is stated in Principle 15 of the Rio Declaration on Environment and Development[944]:

> "In order to protect the environment, the precautionary approach shall be widely applied by States according to their capabilities. Where there are threats of serious or irreversible damage, lack of full scientific certainty shall not be used as a reason for postponing cost-effective measures to prevent environmental degradation."

The question is whether WTO law, as interpreted by the dispute settlement bodies, allows WTO Members to follow that approach.[945] In other words, is WTO law interpreted in a precaution-friendly manner?

---

940 Eeckhout 2010, 14.
941 Davies 2009, 524.
942 Zleptnig 2010, 296.
943 See above section 1.5.1.
944 Online at https://www.cbd.int/doc/ref/rio-declaration.shtml.
945 Cheyne 2006, 264 in addition asks whether WTO law mandates WTO Members to take precautionary measures. Given that WTO law serves primarily trade purposes, this seems a rather implausible question to start with.

This is a topic that has been discussed more frequently[946] and arguably more pertinently with regard to the SPS Agreement, where science plays a crucial role. However, the principle in the Rio Declaration relates explicitly to environmental rather than health cases; within the WTO context the former will be adjudicated more frequently under the GATT. Moreover, some health-related measures that do not fulfil the specific definitions of the SPS Agreement may also be adjudicated under the GATT. Thus, the question whether there needs to be scientific evidence in order to allow the inference that a measure serves and contributes to the regulatory objective pursued and what happens if there is no such evidence, is relevant under the GATT, too.

In their interpretation of GATT norms and the application of these interpretations the adjudicators have referred to the term precaution infrequently; scientific evidence has also played a less important role in adjudicating GATT disputes than SPS disputes. Even though no overarching precautionary principle exists in WTO law, there are some reports on GATT from which aspects of precaution are not entirely absent.

One important example is the way in which the Panel assessed the evidence in *EC – Asbestos.* It stated that it had to keep in mind that it was reviewing a public health measure.[947] It found that the evidence tended to prove the existence of a health risk rather than the opposite. Therefore, a decision-maker in the field of health policy might reasonably conclude that a health risk existed and thus take measures which would be eventually justifiable under Art. XX (b) GATT.[948] This can be read as a statement to the end that at least where public health is at stake, decision-makers are entitled to take protective measures in cases of doubt and where evidence indicates, rather than proves, the existence of a health risk. As described above, the Appellate Body approved of and even re-enforced this finding by stating that Members could rely on minority scientific opinions from qualified and respected sources, citing prior case law under the SPS Agreement in support. This goes at least some way towards enabling Members to take precautionary measures; while some scientific evidence is required, the evidence does not have to provide absolute certainty that a risk exists.

Another relevant case is *United States – Gasoline.* In this case, the Appellate Body ruled that in the field of conservation of exhaustible natural re-

946 See below section 2.5.3.

947 *European Communities – Measures Affecting Asbestos and Products Containing Asbestos, WT/DS135/R* 2000, para. 8.184.

948 Ibid., para. 8.193.

sources years might pass before the effects of a measure taken would become visible. This should not, according to the Appellate Body, result in disqualifying such a measure under Art. XX (g).[949] A similar statement can be found in the appellate report for *Brazil – Tyres*. In that case, the Appellate Body noted that sometimes the contribution of measures to such objectives as the mitigation of climate change could only be evaluated in the long-term; this would not keep a measure from being justifiable under Art. XX (b) GATT. According to these findings, a WTO Member is allowed to act if it is plausible that a measure would help it in responding to a certain risk, but the suitability of the measure chosen to that end does not have to be positively and empirically proven.

Another aspect that has been considered as an aspect of precaution in the interpretation of GATT is the Appellate Body's reading of the term "exhaustible natural resources" in *Shrimp – Turtles* as extending to living resources.[950] However, this finding was in no way related to scientific uncertainty. So while it is clear that this interpretation broadens the scope for WTO Members to take measures for environment-related purposes and is hence important, it does not seem to have much to do with the precautionary principle, at least not in the sense contained in Principle 15 of the Rio Declaration on Environment and Development.

In sum, some elements of the case law on GATT can be described as precaution-friendly.

1.6. Assessment

Many of the Appellate Body's findings on Art. XX GATT and XIV GATS are problematic in terms of their weak interpretive, "technical" underpinnings; they are not entirely consistent with each other, or they provide insufficient guidance to adjudicators and parties for future cases. Observers have therefore been rather underwhelmed with the reasoning employed by the Appellate Body when interpreting and applying the justification norms in "trade and ..." cases, even though that does not mean they disagree with the outcome.[951]

---

949 *United States – Standards for Reformulated and Conventional Gasoline, WT/DS2/AB/R* 1996, sec. III C, at 21.

950 Cheyne 2006, 273.

951 See for example Davey and Sapir 2009, 9ff on the interpretation of Art. XX GATT in *Mexico – Softdrinks*.

These observations on the case law from a legal-technical point of view do not, however, say anything about the choices made by the Appellate Body in relation to the range of possibilities open to it, how the choices made affect the regulatory freedom of WTO Members, and whether they have tilted the balance one-sidedly in favour of trade objectives. This is what I turn to next; I will follow the order of analysis in the case law, i.e. move from the issue of applicability of the exceptions, via the interpretation of the definitions of the regulatory objectives in the sub-paragraphs, over the clauses setting forth the required degree of connection between the measure and the objective to the chapeau. Generally, the adjudicators seem to have taken neither the broadest nor the narrowest approach possible when interpreting Art. XX GATT and XIV GATS.

1.6.1. Applicability of Art. XX GATT

While at least one Panel has refused to allow WTO Members to invoke Art. XX (b) GATT as a justification for breaches of the substantive clauses of the SPS Agreement, the Appellate Body has taken a different decision with regard to China's deviation from one of the clauses in its Accession Protocol. The Appellate Body has been taken to say that, in general, Art. XX GATT defences are only available outside of GATT where there is explicit language to this effect.[952] If that reading of the Appellate Body's line of reasoning is correct – which is not clear, given that the relevant appellate cases dealt with a violation of China's Accession Protocol only – this would mean that the Appellate Body has been more restrictive in its application of Art. XX GATT than suggested by some observers.

For example, in an *amicus curiae* brief in *Canada – Renewables*, an NGO coalition argued that Art. XX GATT should be applicable to justify breaches of the SCM, given that the SCM could be read as spelling out the obligations contained in Art. XIV GATT in more detail.[953] It has also been proposed that the Appellate Body might have been more "courageous" and adopted a less limiting interpretation on the applicability of Art. XX GATT in the Chinese cases.[954] Others have pointed out that the Appellate Body's solution to allow China, in principle, to justify export restrictions but not

---

952 Espa 2012, 1407.

953 International Institute for Sustainable Development (IISD), Canadian Environmental Law Association (CELA), and Ecojustice Canada 2012, 6ff.

954 Espa 2012, 1420; Gu 2012; Guan 2014, 225ff.

export duties is unconvincing[955] and that denying a WTO Member the right to rely on Art. XX GATT "tarnishes" the legitimacy of the WTO.[956] By way of contrast, the WTO Members that were third parties in *China – Raw Materials* all concurred with the adjudicators that China should generally not be allowed to rely on Art. XX GATT to defend its measures.[957]

1.6.2. Clause on regulatory objectives

The adjudicators' approach of reviewing the actual objectives of any measure claimed by a Member as within the ambit of one of the sub-paragraphs of Art. XX GATT has been criticized as being at odds with the statement by the WTO dispute settlement bodies that it is not their task to judge the desirability or necessity of the objectives pursued by Members.[958] Yet I do not see an inconsistency here: it is the task of the adjudicators to ensure that the requirements in the legal text are satisfied by a WTO Member's measure. Whether a measure is indeed aimed at a certain objective, as claimed by a defendant, is a factual matter open to review by a Panel.

Generally, the objectives in Art. XX GATT and Art. XIV GATS have been interpreted in a rather expansive manner;[959] showing that a measure falls within the range of policies permitted by one of the sub-paragraphs is relatively easy.[960] For example, it is difficult to imagine any natural resource, whether living or non-living, that does not fall within the term "exhaustible natural resources" in Art. XX (g) as currently interpreted.[961] While the interpretation has mostly been welcomed in legal comments,[962] some have also criticized it as being too broad[963] or even as illicit judicial law-making.[964] In any case, the interpretation of "exhaustible natural resources" is clearly an instance where the Appellate Body has not chosen the

955 Bronckers and Maskus 2014, 399.
956 Ibid., 402.
957 This is pointed out by ibid., 401f.
958 Vranes 2009, 264.
959 Delimatsis 2011, 261 who claims that the dispute settlement bodies' interpretation goes "beyond the ordinary meaning or the negotiators' intent"; supporting the Appellate Body's approach Howse 2016b, 61ff.
960 See for example Doyle 2011, 153.
961 Many observers support that interpretation, see for example Howse 2001, 55ff.
962 See for example Howse 2002b, 500f; Eeckhout 2010, 23.
963 Appleton 1999, 481f; Kelly 2002, 372.
964 Mavroidis 2006, 335; Goldstein and Steinberg 2007, 21.

most "pro-trade" interpretation possible. The adjudicators have also been described as usually showing a high degree of deference when reviewing WTO Members' characterization of the objectives of measures.[965]

Some controversy exists concerning the interpretation of "public morals" in Art. XX (a) GATT and Art. XIV GATS. Some observers agree with the adjudicators' approach,[966] while others criticize it as overly restrictive. One argument employed by critics is that the Appellate Body's approach of relying on practices in different jurisdictions to ascertain whether a certain measure serves the purpose of protecting public morals might be problematic in cases where no society other than the defending Member actually recognizes a certain issue as being a question of public morals.[967] According to this view, whether something is an issue of public morals should only be judged on the basis of evidence submitted by the defending WTO Member to demonstrated the issue's moral significance within its society.[968] Not only would this approach give Members more regulatory freedom than the Appellate Body's current approach,[969] but neither the text of the GATT nor the DSU contains anything preventing such an approach. In this sense, the Appellate Body's approach is more restrictive of WTO Members' freedom than it could be.

On the other hand, the morals clause has been interpreted in broad terms in another respect: According to the understanding of the Appellate Body implicit in *EC – Seal Products*, the clause does not only cover measures aimed at preventing certain immoral behaviour within a given country (e.g. use of pornography, gambling, drug consumption): It also can be used to give "force to intrinsic moral institutions or shared values",[970] which may relate to circumstances beyond the territory of the country invoking the public morals exception. In the seals case, the controversial measure was an EU ban on the import of seal products, motivated by outrage in the EU population over the killing of seals and the often inhumane manner in which it is carried out. The main issue was not that a large proportion of the EU's population was involved in hunting seals; rather, citizens were concerned about what happened elsewhere. In other words, the

965 Fitzgerald 2011, 123.

966 For example, Diebold 2008, 52 notes that the Appellate Body's interpretation of Art. XX (a) GATT has found support among scholars.

967 Kapterian 2010, 111.

968 Marwell 2006, 815ff.

969 Ibid., 824f.

970 Howse and Langille 2011, 412.

EU measure was directed outward, rather than inward.[971] It has been suggested that WTO law should be interpreted to allow only the former category of measures to be justified under Art. XX (a) GATT.[972] Other commentators[973] – and ultimately the Appellate Body – have rejected this view. In this regard, the Appellate Body has consequently not embraced the most "pro-trade" interpretation conceivable.

Another aspect of the case law that has been criticized in the literature is the Appellate Body's decision in *Mexico – Softdrinks* that Art. XX (d) does not extend to compliance with international legal norms, *in casu* NAFTA. The Appellate Body rationale was that if it had decided otherwise it would need to make determinations on WTO Members' compliance with non-WTO international law. Howse has commented that this "seems to get the legal question backward".[974] He observes that if the term "laws and regulations" does, indeed include non-WTO legal provisions, the WTO dispute settlement bodies have jurisdiction to make determinations on these non-WTO provisions. Indeed, the adjudicators have not refrained from looking at non-WTO international law provisions when WTO law contains an explicit reference to such provisions. For example, the adjudicators have scrutinized the decision-making processes under a regional environmental agreement in order to ascertain whether that agreement was an international standard in the sense of the TBT Agreement.[975] Howse also points to an ICJ judgement holding that the fact that another international court had already dealt with certain aspects of the case did not bar the ICJ from deciding on the matter as well.[976] In this light, the Appellate Body seems to have been more cautious concerning the interpretation of Art. XX (d) GATT than is legally required.

---

971 For this distinction, see Wu 2008, 216; the author himself proposes, however, a distinction between three categories of measures: 1) measures safeguarding the morals of inhabitants of the country taking the measures, 2) measures aimed at those producing a product or rendering a service and 3) restrictions aimed at products or services in an exporting state involving actions morally offensive to the importing state, but where these practices are not directly involved in the production of the products or services banned, see 235.

972 Ibid., 243 seems to prefer this narrow interpretation over others.

973 For a discussion of Wu's position, see Howse and Langille 2011, 414f.

974 Howse 2008, 659.

975 See below, section 3.2.

976 Howse 2008, 661. The case he refers to is ICJ Judgment of 26 February 2007, Case Concerning the Application of the Convention on the Prevention and Punishment of the Crime of Genocide (Bosnia and Herzegovina v. Serbia and Montenegro, para. 181.

1.6.3. Clauses on the link between measures and regulatory objectives

Concerning the interpretation of the clauses defining the link between the measure at issue and its objective, "relating to" in Art. XX (g) GATT and "necessary" in the other sub-paragraphs of Art. XX GATT and XIV GATS that have played a role so far, the picture is relatively mixed.

The interpretation of "relating to" in Art. XX (g) GATT as meaning "directly aimed at" amounted to a rather strict standard, which is not required by the wording of WTO law.[977] However, this standard was explicitly given up in *China – Raw Materials.* Certain measures could possibly be justified under either Art. XX (b) GATT or XX (g) GATT. As things stand, Art. XX (g) GATT presents a more lenient standard to achieve as compared to Art. XX (b) GATT.[978]

Concerning the interpretation of "necessary", the balancing approach inscribed into the interpretation of the term by the Appellate Body does not *per se* involve a very restrictive or permissive stance vis-à-vis the regulating state's measures.[979] In practical terms, the balancing formula primarily serves to give the adjudicators a lot of leeway in deciding a concrete case.[980] It involves a somewhat subjective decision on the importance of the regulatory goal at stake and the relationship between the different factors to be balanced.[981] The Appellate Body's balancing formula could actually lead to the threshold for considering a measure "necessary" being lowered in cases where the objective pursued is considered as essential by the adjudicators.[982] There are instances in which the test has been applied rather leniently. For example, the Appellate Body in *Brazil – Tyres* concluded that one of the factors to be considered in the necessity analysis, the contribution of a measure to the end pursued, need not be immediately observable or short-term, and could therefore be described in qualitative terms rather than be quantified. The finding was confirmed in *China – Audiovisual*

977 Bowen 2000, 185.
978 Condon 2004, 12; Appleton 1999, 482.
979 See also Conrad 2011, 337.
980 See Du 2010a, 1101.
981 Pitschas and Schloemann 2012, 19; Martineau 2007, 1003; Doyle 2011, 166.
982 Neumann and Tuerk 2003, 211, 214.

Products.[983] This brings this part of the necessity test in the vicinity of a suitability test,[984] a test usually not difficult to pass.

As part of the necessity test, a standard has been developed for when an alternative measure is reasonably available that is on the surface relatively lenient.[985] It suggests that alternative measures must meet the defending Member's chosen level of protection while not imposing undue burdens on Members, such as prohibitive costs or substantial technical difficulties. Both aspects had not been given much attention by Panels under GATT.[986] It would therefore have been more difficult for the GATT Contracting Parties to justify their measures as necessary than would – theoretically – be the case for WTO Members today.

When these standards have been applied in practice, however, the adjudicators have mostly accepted alternative measures as reasonably available.[987] It has been suggested that, because it would be difficult for the Appellate Body to engage in too "raw" a balancing of the interests at stake, much of the actual balancing work has been moved to the analysis of the link between a measure and its objectives, and this analysis involves quite intensive scrutiny of the measures.[988] Indeed, with regards to some of the alternative measures accepted by the Panel it was not clear if and how they could be implemented. For example, in *China – Rare Earths*, the decisive flaw of the Chinese measure was the absence of a mechanism counteracting the perverse signals sent by its export quota to domestic consumers.[989] Yet, the Panel gave no indication how such a mechanism could look like, or whether indeed it was feasible at all. In other cases, such as *China –*

983 Fontanelli 2012, 52 reads the Appellate Body's decision in *China – Audiovisual* Products as back-pedalling a little from its rather loose interpretation of how the measure must contribute to the end pursued. Personally, I do not think this can be read out of the Appellate Body's statements in that case.

984 Bown and Trachtman 2009, 126.

985 Delimatsis 2011, 262; Neumann and Tuerk 2003, 211 also observe that the interpretation adopted by the WTO dispute settlement bodies gives the regulating Member more leeway than was the case under the old GATT.

986 Kapterian 2010, 101f.

987 Neumann and Tuerk 2003, 208ff.

988 See Lovric 2010, 143ff; Fitzgerald 2011, 119.

989 For a summary of the Panel's arguments, see *China – Measures Related to the Exportation of Rare Earths, Tungsten, and Molybdenum, WT/DS431/AB/R, WT/DS432/AB/R, WT/DS433/AB/R* 2014, para. 5.149ff.

Audiovisual Products, the defendant argued (quite convincingly in my view)[990] that a proposed alternative measure was not reasonably available because it imposed undue financial and administrative burdens; still, the Panel found that the proposed alternative was reasonably available, and the Appellate Body agreed.[991]

Moreover, the "alternative measure" test has been construed by the adjudicators in a way that involves trade-offs between the costs of the trade-restrictive controversial measure (typically and in large part borne by the defendant's trade partners, but potentially also falling to domestic consumers), and the administrative/enforcement costs of either measure (normally financed out of public budgets of the WTO Members taking the measure).[992] WTO case law does not require a WTO Member to take *any* less trade-restrictive alternative measures, but only those that are feasible. While this does not seem to include measures with prohibitive costs, WTO Members will have to bear *some* extra costs for alternative, less-restrictive measures.

The salient normative question behind the application of this test is how costs and benefits of measures are distributed through a dispute settlement decision. This is of particular importance in the relationship between developed and developing countries. Yet the case law so far lacks a clearly articulated test to decide which interests will prevail in which circumstances or even a set of indicators that would allow such inferences to be made. There are some indications that the adjudicators take the differing situations of countries into account while making their necessity analysis; for example, in *Colombia – Ports of Entry* the Panel alluded to Colombia's specific situation as a country where drug-trafficking is a major issue. But it remains unclear whether, for example, the least-developed countries would be expected to bear fewer extra costs for an alternative measure than more

990 Roughly, the issue was that China allowed the importation of certain audiovisual products only to state-controlled enterprises. As an alternative, it was suggested that the import of these products should be allowed to all importers, but the Chinese government could conduct a central review for those products that it considered might be in violation of its provisions. As argued by China, this would have required a massive restructuring of the Chinese system and bureaucratic apparatus; given the size of China and its population, I tend to find this a plausible claim.

991 *China – Measures Affecting Trading Rights and Distribution Services for Certain Publications and Audiovisual Entertainment Products, WT/DS363/AB/R* 2009, para. 312, 322ff.

992 Regan 2007, 349; see also Bown and Trachtman 2009, 126.

developed countries on the grounds that they typically have fewer resources for the enforcement of their regulatory framework. And in any case, in the absence of more detailed guidance over when an alternative measure is reasonably available, it is the adjudicators who decide how the costs and benefits of measures and alternative measures are distributed among the WTO Members involved in the dispute.[993]

There is a clear link to regulatory freedom in this context: If a country is unable to carry even the small extra costs of an alternative measure, but is barred from keeping the original, WTO inconsistent measure, this would obviously restrict a Member's freedom to adopt measures for the benefit of non-trade regulatory goals quite significantly. It is not clear in WTO case law whether this risk currently materializes. If it does, it must be in a relatively small number of cases: there are very few cases in which e. g. least-developed countries that may not be able to relatively swiftly replace a measure by a WTO-consistent alternative one have been defendants in WTO dispute settlement. This lack of practical significance may explain why this issue has received little attention in the literature.

While the least trade-restrictive means test has not been formulated in a very strict manner, it nonetheless bears noting that it is not contained *verbatim* in the GATT or GATS, either. This has led, to complaints from WTO Members over the creation of that test.[994] Moreover, there are several cases in which the adjudicators assumed that certain less trade-restrictive measures were reasonably available and reached the Member's chosen level of protection, without the respective WTO Members sharing this view (e. g. the Panel in *United States – Gasoline* or the Appellate Body in *Korea – Beef*). This has led to criticism that the way the least-restrictive measure test has been applied was used to "tilt the balance in favour of trade liberalization beyond that provided in the treaty",[995] that a Member's chosen level of protection was actually lowered, that the WTO dispute settlement bodies were not consistent in their approach to this matter across cases,[996] or that indeed the term necessary has been interpreted in a strict manner.[997] Given that the text of the law is indeterminate and thus amenable to a variety of interpretations, the first of these criticisms – that a balance has been tilted beyond what is in the text – is not quite convincing. The other

993 Eeckhout 2010, 19.
994 See the quotes in Fontanelli 2012, 41.
995 Kapterian 2010, 104.
996 See for example Delimatsis 2011, 286.
997 Ortino 2004, 385.

points seem be more well-founded: after all, there is an incongruence between the abstract standards that the dispute settlement bodies have formulated on how to assess necessity (not very strict) and the application of that standard (rather strict in some, but not all cases).

A further critical point is the extent to which the judicial decision-makers review the level of protection aimed at by a certain measure. The characterization of the level of protection is of considerable importance for the identification of potential alternative measures. If the level of protection is described in narrow terms, the range of potential alternatives measures that could be used to reach it will be much smaller.[998] The adjudicators have put a strong emphasis on the prerogative of a Member to set and pursue regulatory goals and to characterize the level of protection it seeks to achieve through these measures; yet in practice they have not been shy to come to a different characterization of the level of protection than a WTO Member if they perceived the Member's description to be inadequate. Notably, in *Korea – Beef* and *Dominican Republic – Cigarettes,* the Appellate Body found that there was actually a lower level of protection in place than the Member had claimed it pursued.

Contrary to the opinion of some commentators,[999] reviewing a WTO Member's statements on the level of protection is not as such inappropriate for the WTO's judicial decision-makers nor does it imply a lowering of the level of protection. It is, rather, in line with the mandate of the adjudicators to double-check whether the factual claims of the parties to a dispute are accurate or at least plausible. One particular criticism has been that the Appellate Body re-stated a country's level of protection.[1000] While there are good reasons for assuming that such re-statements must to be undertaken with caution, there is no reason to consider them inadmissible *per se*. If a WTO Member's claim regarding the level of protection it pursues is contradicted by the evidence before the Panel, such a re-statement of the level of protection pursued seems reasonable. Otherwise, WTO Members could make whatever wild claims about their level of protection they wished.

Another aspect of the interpretation of the necessity criterion that has caused observers to worry is that the balancing formula under Art. XX GATT/XIV GATS puts the adjudicators in a position to decide upon the importance of the values or interests at stake. As discussed

998 McGrady 2009, 157.
999 See Vranes 2009, 265.
1000 Du 2010a, 1098 referring to Korea-Beef.

above,[1001] it is not clear whether the test actually involves a "raw" balancing of interests in the sense of proportionality *sensu stricto*. But the Appellate Body uses the language of balancing. A balancing test, where different interests are weighed against each other, is conventionally conceived as being more intrusive upon the decision-making by national regulators than mere means-ends rationality or a least-restrictive means test.[1002] Many feel that regulatory choices on whether an objective is important enough to be pursued by a WTO Member should be an unbridled and sovereign right of that country, rather than a decision made by international adjudicators. I will return to this issue in the chapter on style.[1003]

In sum, while some of the interpretations offered by the Appellate Body on the interpretation of "necessary" are not very restrictive of WTO Members' regulatory freedom, in practice the criterion has become a "significant hurdle"[1004] for WTO Members wishing to defend measures. Justification under the "relating to" standard of Art. XX (g) GATT, however, appears to be easier.

1.6.4. Chapeau

Compared to the "necessity" standard, the interpretation of the chapeau seems to be relatively stricter;[1005] one commentator writes that the Appellate Body's interpretation of the chapeau in *Shrimp – Turtles* has imposed "extra-ordinary preconditions" on WTO Members for resorting to environmental measures and "almost completely closed off the policy space Article XX should leave open".[1006] While the case law has evolved since *Shrimp – Turtles*, restrictive tendencies still prevail in the interpretation of the chapeau.

1001 See above section 1.5.1.

1002 Kapterian 2010, 99f; Cho 2009a, 706 even maintains that "the doctrine strips regulating members of their regulatory autonomy in that the Court, not the regulating country, will weigh in all the details related to a given measure".

1003 See chapter 3, section 4.3.

1004 Doyle 2011, 165; Quick 2013, 971 also states that the necessity requirement in Art. XX (b) "can, at times, be quite difficult to meet".

1005 Appleton 1999, 492 with regard to the *Shrimp – Turtles* case; Alvarez-Jiménez 2008, 475; Delimatsis 2011, 266; McRae 2000, 229ff; Lydgate 2017, 567 with regard to *Brazil – Tyres*.

1006 Gaines 2001, 745, 773.

Earlier GATT jurisprudence understood the term "disguised" in the chapeau of Art. XX GATT to mean that a measure needed to be published (an easy-to-do thing); the current reading is more restrictive on WTO Members[1007] (and more difficult to apply, too). As pointed out above, some observers have been very critical of the Appellate Body's requirement that the US negotiate with certain countries because it had with others, as well as of the other procedural requirements; none of these are easily discernible from the text of the chapeau.[1008] It has also been pointed out that the Panel's approach towards interpreting the chapeau in *Brazil – Tyres* was less strict than the Appellate Body's, giving WTO Members greater regulatory freedom.[1009] The Panel had conducted an effects-based test, implying that a measure differentiating between imported and domestic products could still pass the chapeau test if it had only an insignificant impact on trade; this was clearly rejected by the Appellate Body. Moreover, the Appellate Body in *Brazil – Tyres* did not consider the fact that Brazil had adopted the measure in question as a result of its obligations under the Mercosur agreement, i.e. clearly not in a capricious manner or with a discriminatory intent, sufficient to justify the measure.[1010]

Some of the statements of the Appellate Body also indicate that the Appellate Body considers the clauses in Art. XX GATT to give Members a right that is more limited or weaker than those resulting – as a flip side of the coin – from the "normal" trade-related obligations of WTO Members. For example[1011], the Appellate Body in *Shrimp – Turtles* writes

> "Inasmuch as there are due process requirements generally for measures that are otherwise imposed in compliance with WTO obligations, it is only reasonable that *rigorous compliance* with the fundamental requirements of due process should be required in the application and administration of a measure which purports to be an exception to the treaty obligations of the Member imposing the measure and which effectively results in a suspension *pro hac vice* of the treaty rights of other Members."[1012] [emphasis added]

1007 Snoderly 1996, 293.

1008 See above section 1.5.4.

1009 Davies 2009, 522.

1010 The point is made by Howse 2016b, 74; Lydgate 2017, 568f.

1011 The point is made and the example given by McRae 2000, 231f.

1012 *United States – Import Prohibition of Certain Shrimp and Shrimp Products, WT/DS58/AB/R* 1998, para. 182.

The Appellate Body implies that any measure a WTO Member seeks to justify under Art. XX GATT somehow needs to fulfil more exacting due process requirements; it does not merely have to comply with such requirements, but "rigorously" fulfil them. Similarly, Gaines argues that the equilibrium jurisprudence of the Appellate Body in *Shrimp – Turtles* "gives a trade-favoring bias" to the application of Art. XX GATT.[1013] Such analyses rely on very subtle nuances of the language used in the dispute settlement reports and therefore remain speculative to a certain degree. Moreover, the idea that the exception provisions are a somewhat lesser right than rights deriving from the trade-related obligations cannot be easily squared with the Appellate Body's stance that rights and obligations need to be balanced: balancing would normally presuppose that the interests, rights or values to be balanced are of *ex ante* equal weight.[1014]

The outcomes of the relevant cases are, of course, clearer indicators of how restrictive or lenient the interpretation and application of the chapeau has been. In *Brazil – Tyres* and *EC – Seal Products*, there are two "trade and ..." cases in which a measure satisfied the conditions of one of the sub-paragraphs, but was thereafter held to violate the chapeau of Art. XX GATT by the Appellate Body, because of exception provisions in the respective measures. In both cases, these exceptions attenuated the effect of the original trade-restrictive measure, i.e. they allowed some products to be imported as an exception to a general ban on certain products. In other words, the reasoning of the Appellate Body suggested that if these measures had not contained the exceptions and were hence *more* trade-restrictive, they might have been justified under Art. XX GATT. This is a very curious result, to say the least. In fact, the WTO Members concerned have responded to these decisions with stricter regulation. In other words, in order to achieve the consistency that the Appellate Body demands, they have not removed restrictions, but rather extended them to a larger range of situations.[1015]

In both cases the exceptions in the measures were seen as involving discrimination between countries where similar conditions prevailed; in both cases they were considered not to be justified, because the rationale for these exceptions was not connected to the original regulatory goal as recognized in one of the sub-paragraphs of Art. XX GATT. In terms of real-world policy-making, this is problematic. Often, policies need to accom-

1013 Gaines 2001, 831.
1014 Martineau 2007, 1015ff.
1015 See Lydgate 2017, 562f.

modate different interests; a measure restricting or forbidding a certain behaviour may contain exceptions to alleviate or avoid negative impacts on certain constituencies, for example. This is a very normal outcome of political bargaining processes. Also, institutions at different governance levels, with diverging interests, may be involved in decision-making in federal systems. An approach to interpreting and applying WTO law that considers policies that are the outcome of normal bargaining processes, cater for different constituencies and serve different policy objectives to be illegal, is almost certainly too restrictive.[1016] Indeed, scholars have argued that nothing in Art. XX (a) GATT requires that moral beliefs motivating a measure need to be held to be so important that a measure reflects only these concerns and no other values or interest.[1017] If WTO Members are free to set their level of protection, this would include, of course, the freedom to protect certain moral objectives only to a certain degree. There is also a certain degree of tension between the Appellate Body's verbal acceptance of the fact that WTO Members may pursue several policy objectives through one measure and its decisions in cases where WTO Members actually did so.

Moreover, in *EC – Seal Products*, the exception that ultimately led the EU measures to be struck down was one in favour of indigenous communities.[1018] That these communities need protection is recognized in international law and the EU's measure actually referred to relevant international legal documents.[1019] Protecting indigenous communities could itself be considered a moral endeavour.[1020] In other words, the intent behind the EU's trade-restrictive measure and its exceptions was hardly discriminatory or protectionist.[1021] Several eminent commentators had actually voiced the opinion that the EU's measure was not WTO-inconsistent in analyses published before the Appellate Body report. In their view, even if a violation of GATT was to be found (contrary to what they argued should be the result),

---

1016 For similar views see Conconi and Voon 2016, 223; Lydgate 2017, 575f. Marín Durán 2016, 475 criticizes the rational connection requirement as "excessively rigid and rather senseless when dealing with measures accommodating multiple competing purposes".

1017 Howse and Langille 2011, 418.

1018 Even though the EU's exception was aimed at protecting the interests of indigenous communities, some of these communities challenged the EU seals regime before EU courts, considering it too restrictive, see ibid., 383.

1019 See ibid., 385; Sykes 2014, 497.

1020 Pitschas and Schloemann 2012, 21f.

1021 See Howse and Langille 2011, 404.

the controversial EU measure could be justified under Art. XX GATT.[1022] That experienced WTO lawyers consider the EU measure to be justified under Art. XX GATT is a good indicator that the Appellate Body's approach to interpreting and applying the chapeau of Art. XX GATT is unnecessarily restrictive of WTO Members' regulatory freedom.

1.6.5. Summary

All in all, there seems to be a widespread notion that the Appellate Body has tended to widen the possibilities for justifying measures on non-trade grounds as compared to the GATT case law,[1023] where Panels had set high thresholds for justifying policies under Art. XX GATT.[1024] The Appellate Body's findings are considered to have been rather respectful of WTO Members' regulatory autonomy[1025] and to have made it easier, in some cases, for Members to adopt trade-restrictive measures than the (WTO) Panels' findings[1026].

At the same time, it must be noted that adjudicators have also chosen several interpretations that are more restrictive of Members' discretion to adopt non-trade regulatory measures than mandated by the wording of the law. For example, an interpretation of the term "necessary" that would have been less restrictive of WTO Members' regulatory freedom could certainly have been chosen by the adjudicators: the least-restrictive means test is textually absent from Art. XX GATT and XIV GATS, but is contained in the SPS Agreement and TBT Agreement.[1027] Such textual differences could have been exploited in the WTO case law and could also have been used to justify a departure from earlier GATT case law on the matter. Also, the chapeau analysis has several shortcomings and is a high bar for WTO Members to reach. In light of such decisions, some observers read the WTO case law as being actually quite restrictive on WTO Members' regula-

1022 Ibid., 411ff; Pitschas and Schloemann 2012, 18ff; Sykes 2014, 497f.
1023 Wofford 2000, 563; Bowen 2000, 201; Appleton 1999, 491; Charnovitz 2007, 695f; Venzke 2012, 213.
1024 See Venzke 2012, 185ff.
1025 Osiro 2002, 123.
1026 See for example Doyle 2011, 154.
1027 Kapterian 2010, 105.

tory autonomy[1028] or as having consistently interfered into WTO Members' policies.[1029]

Other decisions, however, have not been taken. For example, the Appellate Body has not yet taken an explicit position on whether GATT law contains any implicit territorial limitations, barring Members from taking measures to protect interests and goods having no nexus with their own territory.

It is probably fair to say that the dispute settlement bodies have chosen neither the interpretation most permissive of WTO Members' measures nor that most restrictive; overall, they are probably closer to the restrictive end of the scale than to the permissive. It is noteworthy that in hardly any of the cases discussed above was the party invoking Art. XX GATT ultimately successful in doing so. The defending parties lost either because their measures were considered to be discriminatory and thus a violation of the chapeau (such as in *United States – Gasoline,* the initial *Shrimp – Turtles, Brazil – Tyres* and *EC – Seal Products*), or because they were not considered necessary given the availability of less trade-restrictive and feasible alternative measures (such as in *Korea – Beef, Dominican Republic – Cigarettes,* and *Mexico – Softdrinks*). The only cases in which Art. XX GATT has been successfully deployed are *EC – Asbestos*, which involved an import ban on asbestos products (arguably a rather clear-cut case because of the high toxicity of asbestos) and *Shrimp – Turtle*, when dealing with the modified US measure.

2. *SPS Agreement*

A further agreement of major relevance for the context of this work is the Agreement on the Application of Sanitary and Phytosanitary Measures (SPS). As described above in chapter 1,[1030] I will analyse the interpretation of the core substantive provisions of this agreement, Art. 2, 3 and 5 SPS.

Art. 2 SPS describes the basic rights and obligations of the parties that are spelt out in greater detail in Art. 3 and 5 SPS. WTO Members have the right to take SPS measures, according to a statement contained in

1028 For example, Du 2011, 651 writes that the Appellate Body has "imposed extraordinary preconditions on Member governments, an approach that results in a very limited role for Article XX"; see also Kapterian 2010, 91.

1029 Fontanelli 2012, 39.

1030 See chapter 1, section 5.2.

Art. 2.1 SPS, but it is made clear that these measures must be consistent with the SPS. Art. 2.2 SPS states, *inter alia*, that measures must be "necessary" to protect the health of living organisms, and may not be maintained without sufficient scientific evidence (except in the case of Art. 5.7 SPS). Art. 2.3 SPS contains a non-discrimination clause.

In its first three paragraphs, Art. 3 SPS regulates the relationship between national SPS measures and international standards with a view to harmonizing Members' SPS measures as far as possible.

Art. 5 SPS contains several more disciplines for SPS measures. The first three paragraphs of this article are, in effect, a specification of the term "necessary" in Art. 2. SPS, as they require an SPS measure to be scientifically justified and spell out what is understood by scientific justification. Art. 5.4 contains a softly worded obligation to take the objective of minimizing negative trade effects into account when choosing the appropriate level of protection. Art. 5.5 SPS contains a consistency or non-discrimination requirement. Art. 5.6 SPS contains a least-restrictive measure requirement, and Art. 5.7 SPS a rule on provisional measures in the absence of sufficient scientific evidence.

In this analysis, I will leave aside some aspects of the interpretation of the SPS Agreement, notably its scope of application. How the provisions on the scope of the SPS are interpreted is quite relevant for the overall regulatory space of WTO Members: the SPS contains stricter requirements for WTO Members than, for example, the GATT and the TBT. In at least one SPS case it was a major issue whether a WTO Member's actions satisfied the definition of an SPS measure.[1031] If the wide interpretation of the definition of SPS measures adopted in that case is used in future cases, then some environmental measures at least may come within the remit of the agreement.[1032] Nonetheless, I will not analyse this issue in depth here, because the norms defining the scope of the SPS contained in its Annex A 1 are relatively determinate and clear, as compared to terms such as "necessary" contained in the other provisions discussed here. Moreover, whether or not a measure constitutes an SPS measure has not often been controversial in the case law.

1031 This case is *European Communities – Measures Affecting the Approval and Marketing of Biotech Products, WT/DS291/R, WT/DS292/R, WT/DS293/R* 2006; for a discussion of the Panel's finding on the applicability of the SPS Agreement in this case see Conrad 2007; Peel 2013, 345ff.

1032 Eeckhout 2010, 10.

The section is structured as follows: Each of the sections is devoted to one of the major substantive disciplines of the SPS Agreement: the science-related clauses Art. 5.1 - 5.3 SPS, 2.2 SPS and 5.7 SPS (section 2.1), Art. 5.6 SPS containing a not more trade-restrictive than necessary test (section 2.2), the non-discrimination clauses Art. 5.5 SPS and 2.3 SPS (section 2.3) and Art. 3 governing the role of international standards under the SPS Agreement (section 2.4). This will be followed by a legal-technical discussion of the case law (section 2.5) and a more normative assessment, discussing what the case law means for the regulatory autonomy of WTO Members and health protection measures (section 2.6).

2.1. Art. 5.1-5.3, 5.7, 2.2 SPS

Art. 5.1 - 5.3 and 2.2 SPS contain the science-related disciplines of the SPS Agreement; Art. 5.7 SPS regulates situations of insufficient scientific evidence. These norms are closely linked; according to the WTO dispute settlement bodies, Art. 5.1 and 2.2 SPS should "constantly be read together".[1033] Art. 5.1 SPS has been described as a "specific application of the basic obligations contained in Article 2.2 SPS"[1034] and as "a particular route leading to the same destination set out in Article 2.2"[1035] SPS. The Appellate Body has also indicated that a violation of Art. 5.1, 5.2 SPS implies a violation of Art. 2.2 SPS;[1036] the opposite, however, is not true – a violation of Art. 2.2 does not automatically entail a violation of the more specific Art. 5.1, 5.2 SPS.[1037] While some aspects of the relationship between Art. 2.2 and 5.1 SPS still await clarification,[1038] it is obvious that these norms are closely related. They are therefore all discussed in this section.

1033 *United States – Continued Suspension of Obligations in the EC – Hormones Dispute, WT/DS320/AB/R* 2008, para. 526.

1034 *Australia – Measures Affecting the Importation of Apples from New Zealand, WT/DS367/AB/R* 2010, para. 209.

1035 *Australia – Measures Affecting Importation of Salmon, WT/DS18/R* 1998, para. 8.52.

1036 *Australia – Measures Affecting Importation of Salmon, WT/DS18/AB/R* 1998, para. 138.

1037 *Australia – Measures Affecting the Importation of Apples from New Zealand, WT/DS367/AB/R* 2010, para. 340.

1038 For an in-depth discussion on the relationship between Art. 2.2 and 5.1 SPS as construed in the case law, see Gruszczynski 2006, 10f.

Art. 5.1 SPS, in particular, has been of significant relevance in WTO dispute settlement so far.[1039]

The section starts with a presentation of the case law on Art. 5.1 – 5.3 SPS (section 2.1.1) and then moves on to the more general Art. 2.2 SPS (section 2.1.2). Finally, Art. 5.7 SPS and its rules for situations of insufficient scientific evidence are discussed (section 2.1.3).

2.1.1. Art. 5.1 - 5.3 SPS

Art. 5.1 SPS contains two requirements, namely that Members' measures must be "based on" a "risk assessment". Art. 5.2 and 5.3 SPS enumerate factors to be considered when performing a risk assessment.

Generally, the WTO dispute settlement bodies do not always clearly distinguish between the two requirements of the existence of a risk assessment and the requirement that a measure be based on it. For example, in *Australia – Apples* the Appellate Body discussed whether the Panel had erred in not accepting certain studies presented by Australia as risk assessment in the sense of Art. 5.1 SPS. When doing so it stated that the Panel should verify the existence of a "rational or objective relationship" between the SPS measures and the risk assessment, on the one hand, and the scientific evidence, on the other.[1040] The relationship between the risk assessment and the measures would seem to belong to the interpretation of "based on", rather than to a discussion of whether the SPS Agreement's definition or risk assessment was fulfilled. Nonetheless, and for the sake of analytical clarity, the two requirements are discussed separately in the following.

Risk assessment

What is understood by a risk assessment in the context of the SPS Agreement is defined in Annex A, para. 4 of the SPS Agreement. Accordingly, a risk assessment is

---

1039 Foster 2008, 438.

1040 *Australia – Measures Affecting the Importation of Apples from New Zealand, WT/DS367/AB/R* 2010, para. 219.

> "[t]he evaluation of the likelihood of entry, establishment or spread of a pest or disease within the territory of an importing Member according to the sanitary or phytosanitary measures which might be applied, and of the associated potential biological and economic consequences; or the evaluation of the potential adverse effects on human or animal health arising from the presence of additives, contaminants, toxins or disease-causing organisms in food, beverages or feedstuffs."

In many of the cases hitherto resolved, a disagreement existed if certain evaluations and scientific studies constituted a valid risk assessment in this sense; this has given the Panels and the Appellate Body ample opportunity to elaborate on the meaning of the term.

Before discussing the case law, it needs to be noted that the interpretation and application of the term risk assessment have a particularly close relationship with the standard of review applied by the WTO dispute settlement bodies; the standard of review in WTO law has to do with how a Panel deals with the facts of a case and how intensively it scrutinizes factual evidence. When interpreting and applying the science-related disciplines of the SPS Agreement, Panelists will often have to assess complex and conflicting factual claims by the parties. Therefore, the substantive requirements set forth in the SPS Agreement and the standard of review applied are both critical for deciding on the ultimate fate of a Member's measure. This close relationship has been noted by the adjudicators themselves. For example, the Panel in *Hormones II* indicated it would not conduct its own risk assessment or impose its own scientific opinions on the EU, but had to make an objective assessment of whether the studies provided by the EU satisfied the definition of risk assessment in the sense of the SPS Agreement.[1041] The standard of review is, however, an issue of procedure and judicial style and is hence discussed in chapter 3.[1042]

It has been clarified in the case law that the two sentences of the definition of risk assessment apply in two different situations. The two types of risk assessment are – in the words of the Appellate Body[1043] – "substantially different", because the first definition in the Annex refers to the evaluation of the *likelihood* of a certain event, whereas the second one refers to a *potential* for adverse effects.

1041 *United States – Continued Suspension of Obligations in the EC – Hormones Dispute, WT/DS320/R* 2008, para. 7.514.

1042 See chapter 3, section 2.1.

1043 *Australia – Measures Affecting Importation of Salmon, WT/DS18/AB/R* 1998, n. 69.

The first definition is relevant when an SPS measure in the sense of para. 1 (a)[1044] and (d)[1045] of Annex A to the SPS Agreement is in dispute. Such measures relate to disease-related or pest-related risks. By way of contrast, a risk assessment in the sense of the second sentence must be carried out when an SPS measure in the sense of para. 1 (b) of the same Annex is at stake.[1046] Such SPS measures relate by the definition in para. 1 (b) Annex A to the SPS Agreement to food-borne risks, i.e. "risks arising from additives, contaminants, toxins or disease-causing organisms in foods, beverages or feedstuffs." A measure in the sense of para. 1 (c) Annex A to the SPS Agreement appears not to have been in dispute so far; given that these measures also serve to prevent disease- or pest-based risks, a risk assessment in the sense of the first alternative is likely required.

A risk assessment in the sense of the first alternative has had to be performed in the majority of cases so far, including the appellate cases *Australia – Salmon, Japan – Agricultural Products, Japan – Apples* and *Australia – Apples.* A risk assessment in the sense of the second alternative had to be performed in *Hormones I* and *Hormones II.* The Panel case *EC – Biotech Products* is special in that the Panel applied both definitions of risk assessment, because it had found that national safeguard measures fulfilled, in certain respects, several of the definitions of SPS measures contained in para. 1 Annex A to the SPS Agreement. Therefore, both definitions for risk assessment were relevant.

In the first of the cases where a risk assessment in the sense of the first alternative was at stake, the *Australia – Salmon* case, the Panel found that this kind of risk assessment had to be conducted in three steps.[1047] The structure was confirmed by the Appellate Body[1048] and used in all relevant later cases.[1049] Accordingly a risk assessment in the sense of the first alternative

---

1044 Ibid., para. 120.

1045 A measure in the sense of Annex A, para. 1 (d) SPS Agreement appears so far only to have been in dispute in the EC - Biotech Products case, see *European Communities – Measures Affecting the Approval and Marketing of Biotech Products, WT/DS291/R, WT/DS292/R, WT/DS293/R* 2006, para. 7.3039.

1046 *European Communities – Measures Concerning Meat and Meat Products, WT/DS26/R* 1997, para. 8.98.

1047 *Australia – Measures Affecting Importation of Salmon, WT/DS18/R* 1998, para. 8.72.

1048 *Australia – Measures Affecting Importation of Salmon, WT/DS18/AB/R* 1998, para. 122.

1049 *Japan – Measures Affecting Agricultural Products, WT/DS76/AB/R* 1999, para. 112; *Japan – Measures Affecting the Importation of Apples, WT/DS245/AB/R* 2003,

(1) has to identify the diseases whose entry, establishment or spread a Member wants to prevent within its territory, as well as the potential biological and economic consequences associated with the entry, establishment or spread of these diseases, and
(2) has to evaluate the likelihood of entry, establishment or spread of these diseases as well as the potential biological and economic consequences and
(3) has to evaluate the likelihood of entry, establishment or spread of these diseases according to the SPS measures which might be applied.

With regard to the interpretation of the term "likelihood", the Appellate Body in *Hormones I* stressed the semantic differences between potential and probability by saying that probability implied a higher degree of potentiality.[1050] Although the Appellate Body has put emphasis on the different meanings of both terms, it is not clear how large the difference is in practice. The Appellate Body has not yet had the opportunity to clarify this issue, as in all cases decided so far national SPS measures were considered inconsistent with WTO law, not because the respective risk was not large or significant enough (in either a quantitative or a qualitative sense), but rather because the underlying risk assessment was not specific or detailed enough, did not offer a proper evaluation or because the scientific evidence did not reveal any risk at all.

The requirement of a risk assessment "according to the sanitary or phytosanitary measures which might be applied" has been understood as granting some case-by-case flexibility to WTO Members when carrying out a risk assessment.[1051] More importantly, it has been read as stipulating that risk-reducing measures alternative to the SPS measure in place must be evaluated as a part of the risk assessment.[1052] The rationale is, in the eyes of the Appellate Body, that a risk assessment is not to justify the measure al-

para. 193; *Australia – Measures Affecting the Importation of Apples from New Zealand, WT/DS367/AB/R* 2010, para. 205.

1050 *European Communities – Measures Concerning Meat and Meat Products, WT/DS26/AB/R, WT/DS48/AB/R* 1998, para. 184; *Australia – Measures Affecting Importation of Salmon, WT/DS18/AB/R* 1998, para. 123.

1051 *Japan – Measures Affecting the Importation of Apples, WT/DS245/R* 2003, para. 8.285.

1052 *Australia – Measures Affecting Importation of Salmon, WT/DS18/AB/R* 1998, para. 132; *Japan – Measures Affecting the Importation of Apples, WT/DS245/AB/R* 2003, para. 208.

ready in place.[1053] The requirement to evaluate alternative measures has some significance for the review of possible alternative measures under Art. 5.6 SPS – a norm that makes it necessary to answer the question whether alternative feasible and less trade-restrictive measures exist.[1054] It is not sufficient to merely describe alternative measures, as there must be an *evaluation* of their possible effects.[1055] At least one Panel stated that the evaluation of alternative measures did not have to be comprehensive, i.e. not all conceivable measures had to be taken into account.[1056]

With regard to risk assessments in the sense of the second alternative, the Panel in *Hormones I* held that the risk assessment should

> "(i) identify the adverse effects on human health (if any) arising from the presence of the hormones at issue when used as growth promoters in meat or meat products, and (ii) if any such adverse effects exist, evaluate the potential or probability of occurrence of these effects."[1057]

The Appellate Body in the same case noted that

> "[a]lthough the utility of a two-step analysis may be debated, it does not appear to us to be substantially wrong."[1058]

The Appellate Body rejected the Panel's use of "probability" in the above definition without offering a definition of its own.

In *Hormones II*, the follow-up case to the initial *Hormones I* case, however, the Panel stated that the second type of risk assessment required the following *three* steps from a Member[1059]:

a) identifying the additives, contaminants, toxins or disease-causing organisms in food, beverages or feedstuffs at issue (if any);
b) identifying any possible adverse effect on human or animal health; and

---

1053 *Japan – Measures Affecting the Importation of Apples, WT/DS245/AB/R* 2003, para. 208.

1054 See below section 2.2 for an analysis of Art. 5.6.

1055 *Australia – Measures Affecting Importation of Salmon, WT/DS18/AB/R* 1998, para. 132–135.

1056 *Australia – Measures Affecting Importation of Salmon, WT/DS18/RW* 2000, para. 7.70.

1057 *European Communities – Measures Concerning Meat and Meat Products, WT/DS26/R* 1997, para. 8.98.

1058 *European Communities – Measures Concerning Meat and Meat Products, WT/DS26/AB/R, WT/DS48/AB/R* 1998, para. 184.

1059 *United States – Continued Suspension of Obligations in the EC – Hormones Dispute, WT/DS320/R* 2008, para. 7.507.

c) evaluating the potential for that adverse effect to arise from the presence of the identified additives, contaminants, toxins or disease-causing organisms in food, beverages or feedstuff.

It made no reference to the Panel report in *Hormones I.* The Appellate Body in *Hormones II*, in a statement that can only be described as confusing, referred to the above quoted paragraph from the Panel report. It stated that the Panel had relied on "Appellate Body's jurisprudence from EC – Hormones and Australia – Salmon."[1060] However, *Australia – Salmon* is a case in which a risk assessment in the sense explained by the first sentence of the definition in the Annex of the SPS Agreement was concerned, whereas in *Hormones II* the second sentence of the definition was relevant. The Appellate Body did not make any further comments or corrections on the definition by the Panel.

Some authors have expressed the view that a risk assessment in the sense of the second alternative is easier to conduct for WTO Members than a risk assessment in the sense of the first alternative.[1061] Yet in practice there appears to be little difference between the two types of risk assessment despite the Appellate Body's seemingly clear-cut distinction. Panels and the Appellate Body frequently refer simply to the "definition of a risk assessment in paragraph 4 of Annex A"[1062] without paying much attention to the fact that the paragraph contains two definitions. Moreover, findings from one case are cited in others, independent of which type of risk assessment is at stake. Therefore, it is most likely that the following interpretations of Art. 5.1 - 5.3 SPS will be applicable, no matter whether an SPS measure in the sense of Annex A (1) (a), (b), (c) or (d) is in dispute.[1063]

The Panel in *Hormones I* characterized a risk assessment, as – generally speaking – a scientific examination of data and factual studies;[1064] the Appellate Body described it as

---

1060 *United States – Continued Suspension of Obligations in the EC – Hormones Dispute, WT/DS320/AB/R* 2008, para. 505.

1061 Iynedjian 2002, 85; Pauwelyn 2001a, 65; Slotboom 2003, 572.

1062 See for example *United States – Continued Suspension of Obligations in the EC – Hormones Dispute, WT/DS320/AB/R* 2008, para. 505.

1063 Iynedjian 2002, 83.

1064 *European Communities – Measures Concerning Meat and Meat Products, WT/DS26/R* 1997, para. 8.94.

> "a process characterized by systematic, disciplined and objective enquiry and analysis, that is, a mode of studying and sorting out facts and opinions"[1065]

and

> "a process in which possible adverse effects are evaluated using scientific methods."[1066]

In *EC – Biotech Products*, the Panel, drawing on risk assessment methodologies by international organizations, stated moreover that a risk assessment

> "should normally address the 'degree of precision', or level of confidence, with which the relevant risks can be, or have been, assessed."[1067]

Risk assessors are not only required to conclude if there is a risk, but rather to evaluate either the likelihood or the potential of damage. The Panel in the Art. 21.5 DSU proceedings in the *Australia – Salmon* case elaborated more in detail on the meaning of "evaluation."[1068] It found that a risk assessment had to be objective to a level that "one can have reasonable confidence in the evaluation made".[1069] This requirement has been taken rather seriously by the dispute settlement bodies; more than one study has been deemed as not constituting a risk assessment due to a lack of evaluation or assessment of the likelihood of certain risks.[1070] To "evaluate" means, in the view of the WTO dispute settlement bodies, more than just stating that

1065 *European Communities – Measures Concerning Meat and Meat Products, WT/DS26/AB/R, WT/DS48/AB/R* 1998, para. 187; *Australia – Measures Affecting the Importation of Apples from New Zealand, WT/DS367/AB/R* 2010, para. 207; *United States – Continued Suspension of Obligations in the EC – Hormones Dispute, WT/DS320/AB/R* 2008, para. 527.

1066 *United States – Continued Suspension of Obligations in the EC – Hormones Dispute, WT/DS320/AB/R* 2008, para. 534.

1067 *European Communities – Measures Affecting the Approval and Marketing of Biotech Products, WT/DS291/R, WT/DS292/R, WT/DS293/R* 2006, para. 7.3240.

1068 *Australia – Measures Affecting Importation of Salmon, WT/DS18/RW* 2000, para. 7.47–7.57.

1069 Ibid., para. 7.51.

1070 *Japan – Measures Affecting the Importation of Apples, WT/DS245/R* 2003, para. 8.275ff; *Australia – Measures Affecting Importation of Salmon, WT/DS18/AB/R* 1998, para. 124ff; *European Communities – Measures Affecting the Approval and Marketing of Biotech Products, WT/DS291/R, WT/DS292/R, WT/DS293/R* 2006, para. 7.3044ff and 7.3079ff.

there is a possibility or probability of a certain damage occurring; vague and general statements are not enough.[1071]

In the eyes of the WTO adjudicators, there is a further and very important requirement that a risk assessment needs to fulfil, namely that it has to be specific enough with regard to the risk in question, including the potential harm concerned and its possible causes.[1072] Depending on what is being debated in a concrete case, a risk assessment may have to be specific to a certain product[1073] or disease. For example, the Appellate Body in *Hormones I* concluded that in the case of hormones administered to cattle, a risk assessment consisting of an evaluation of the carcinogenic potential of entire categories of hormones in humans was not sufficient; rather, the assessment should include an examination of residues of those hormones found in meat from cattle to which the hormones had been administered for growth promotion purposes.[1074] In *Japan – Apples*, the Appellate Body gave in a footnote an illustrative example of its position:

> "[...] an evaluation of risk must connect the possibility of adverse effects with an antecedent or cause. For example, the abstract reference to the 'risk of cancer' has no significance, in and of itself, under the SPS Agreement, but when one refers to the 'risk of cancer from smoking cigarettes', the particular risk is given content."[1075]

In several cases the defendant Member's risk assessment was rejected due to a lack of specificity.[1076] The Appellate Body in *Hormones II* is seen to

1071 *Australia – Measures Affecting Importation of Salmon, WT/DS18/R* 1998, para. 8.83.

1072 *United States – Continued Suspension of Obligations in the EC – Hormones Dispute, WT/DS320/AB/R* 2008, para. 530.

1073 *European Communities – Measures Concerning Meat and Meat Products, WT/DS26/AB/R, WT/DS48/AB/R* 1998, para. 200; *Japan – Measures Affecting the Importation of Apples, WT/DS245/AB/R* 2003, para. 203.

1074 *European Communities – Measures Concerning Meat and Meat Products, WT/DS26/AB/R, WT/DS48/AB/R* 1998, para. 200.

1075 *Japan – Measures Affecting the Importation of Apples, WT/DS245/AB/R* 2003, n. 372.

1076 *European Communities – Measures Concerning Meat and Meat Products, WT/DS26/AB/R, WT/DS48/AB/R* 1998, para. 200; *Japan – Measures Affecting the Importation of Apples, WT/DS245/AB/R* 2003, para. 198–206. The issue was, however, discussed in two different places: in the *Hormones I* case the Appellate Body treated it as part of the „based on“ requirement whereas in the *Japan – Apples* case it formed part of the discussion whether the risk assessment had properly evaluated the risk.

have relaxed the requirement.[1077] While it referred to the requirement of specificity as applied to the risk assessment developed in its earlier case law, it went on to state:

> "This does not mean that the European Communities was required to establish a direct causal relationship between the possibility of adverse health effects and the residues of oestradiol-17βin bovine meat. […] it was sufficient […] to demonstrate that the additional human exposure to residues of oestradiol-17βin meat from treated cattle is one of the factors contributing to the possible adverse health effects. … Where multiple factors may contribute to a particular risk, a risk assessor is not required to differentiate the individual contribution made by each factor."[1078] [footnote omitted]

The evaluation must lead to the conclusion that there is a risk that is ascertainable or identifiable. A hypothetical risk, resulting from the incapability of natural science to supply positive proof is, according to the Appellate Body, not enough.[1079] A *de minimis* threshold – the existence of a risk – must be transgressed. The statement of the Panel in *Australia – Salmon* that a threshold level or a certain degree of risk is not a necessary prerequisite for legitimate SPS measures[1080] is therefore not applicable without qualifications. The Appellate Body in *Hormones II* admitted that there was a certain tension between the statement that no *de minimis* risk was required and the statement that a risk needed to be ascertainable:

> "Although the definition of a risk assessment does not require WTO Members to establish a minimum magnitude of risk, it is nevertheless difficult to understand the concept of risk as being devoid of any indication of potentiality. A risk assessment is intended to identify adverse effects and evaluate the possibility that such adverse effects might arise. This distinguishes an ascertainable risk from theoretical uncertainty.

1077 Du 2010b, 455.

1078 *United States – Continued Suspension of Obligations in the EC – Hormones Dispute, WT/DS320/AB/R* 2008, para. 562.

1079 *European Communities – Measures Concerning Meat and Meat Products, WT/DS26/AB/R, WT/DS48/AB/R* 1998, para. 186; *Australia – Measures Affecting Importation of Salmon, WT/DS18/AB/R* 1998, para. 124; *United States – Continued Suspension of Obligations in the EC – Hormones Dispute, WT/DS320/AB/R* 2008, para. 530, 568.

1080 *Australia – Measures Affecting Importation of Salmon, WT/DS18/R* 1998, para. 8.80.

However, the assessment of risk need not be expressed in numerical terms or as a minimum quantification of the level of risk."[1081]

The Appellate Body went on to explain this still rather unclear formulation in the following way:

> "The terms 'potential occurrence of adverse effects' can be understood as referring to the possibility that the adverse effects might occur, without necessarily requiring that this be expressed in numerical terms. This would be consistent with the definition of 'risk assessment' in paragraph 4 of Annex A of the SPS Agreement [...]. Moreover, it would be consistent with the Appellate Body's view that 'theoretical uncertainty' is not the kind of risk to be assessed under Article 5.1, but rather the risk to be assessed must be an 'ascertainable' risk. In this sense, [...] 'to examine the 'potential' for adverse effects is to ask whether those adverse effects could ever occur'."[1082] [footnotes omitted]

It should further be noted, that although the term risk in the context of Art. 5.1 SPS means "risk other than zero-risk", a government may still choose a measure which is based on the level of protection of zero risk.[1083]

The dispute settlement reports also make it clear that both the parties to the disputes and the adjudicators are well aware of the limits of modern natural science, confirming that scientists are not able to make statements with absolute certainty[1084] and a risk assessment is not required to produce such findings.

For the purposes of a risk assessment in the sense of the SPS Agreement, the Appellate Body acknowledged that a risk could be expressed in quantitative or in qualitative terms.[1085] The difference between the two ways of describing a risk is that the qualitative one is more open to normative

---

1081 *United States – Continued Suspension of Obligations in the EC – Hormones Dispute, WT/DS320/AB/R* 2008, para. 569.

1082 Ibid., para. 572.

1083 *Australia – Measures Affecting Importation of Salmon, WT/DS18/AB/R* 1998, para. 125.

1084 *Australia – Measures Affecting Importation of Salmon, WT/DS18/R* 1998, para. 8.126; *European Communities – Measures Concerning Meat and Meat Products, WT/DS26/R* 1997, para. 8.152; *Japan – Measures Affecting the Importation of Apples, WT/DS245/AB/R* 2003, para. 59.

1085 *Australia – Measures Affecting Importation of Salmon, WT/DS18/AB/R* 1998, para. 124; *United States – Continued Suspension of Obligations in the EC – Hormones Dispute, WT/DS320/AB/R* 2008, para. 530.

judgements. What constitutes a "high" or "serious" risk, for example, is not very clearly defined and depends on what the person performing the risk assessment considers to be a tolerable risk.[1086] With regard to methodology, the Appellate Body further stated that the existence of a risk was not only verifiable by laboratory methods.[1087] Instead, the Appellate Body in a well-known statement held that what needed to be evaluated was the

> "risk in human societies as they actually exist, in other words, the actual potential for adverse effects on human health in the real world where people live and work and die."[1088]

The chosen level of protection can, according to the Appellate Body, also play a role in risk assessments. Notably, the Appellate Body acknowledged in *Hormones II* that a WTO Member that has chosen to set a higher level of protection than contained in an international standard may need to perform certain research different from the risk assessment underlying the relevant international standard as part of its own risk assessment.[1089] At the same time, it still held that the level of protection could not "pre-determine the outcome of the risk assessment".[1090]

Expert judgement can also be part of a risk assessment, but the Appellate Body requires that its use "must be reasoned and explained consistently".[1091] Moreover, the Appellate Body also stated that a risk assessment should be based on objective and coherent reasoning, conducted with scientific and methodological rigor, and come from a respected and qualified source.[1092] The risk assessment does not need to reflect a scientific majority view, but the

---

1086 See the answer given by the experts consulted in *Australia – Measures Affecting Importation of Salmon, WT/DS18/R* 1998, para. 8.79; and *Australia – Measures Affecting Importation of Salmon, WT/DS18/RW* 2000, n. 173.

1087 *European Communities – Measures Concerning Meat and Meat Products, WT/DS26/AB/R, WT/DS48/AB/R* 1998, para. 187.

1088 Ibid.; *United States – Continued Suspension of Obligations in the EC – Hormones Dispute, WT/DS320/AB/R* 2008, para. 527.

1089 *United States – Continued Suspension of Obligations in the EC – Hormones Dispute, WT/DS320/AB/R* 2008, para. 534.

1090 Ibid.

1091 *Australia – Measures Affecting the Importation of Apples from New Zealand, WT/DS367/AB/R* 2010, para. 241.

1092 Ibid., para. 213ff; *European Communities – Measures Affecting the Approval and Marketing of Biotech Products, WT/DS291/R, WT/DS292/R, WT/DS293/R* 2006, para. 7.3240.

> "view must be considered to be legitimate science according to the standards of the relevant scientific community".[1093]

The Appellate Body also wrote that a risk assessment did not have to come to a "monolithic conclusion"[1094].

Another important question with regard to a risk assessment is what kinds of risks can be taken into account. Art. 5.2 and 5.3 SPS name a few possible factors. The list in Art. 5.2 SPS is, according to the Appellate Body, not conclusive.[1095] The Appellate Body, has, in its own words, not yet decided conclusively on the factors that may be considered in a "risk assessment" under the SPS Agreement.[1096]

An interesting question, which the EU brought up in *Hormones I*, is whether entirely non-scientific factors like consumer expectations can also be taken into account in a risk assessment. The Panel answered this question in the negative.[1097] The Appellate Body reversed the Panel's finding, but did not make very clear statements on the matter itself. It stated that

> "there is nothing to indicate that the listing of factors that may be taken into account in a risk assessment of Article 5.2 was intended to be a closed list. It is essential to bear in mind that the risk that is to be evaluated in a risk assessment under Article 5.1 is not only risk ascertainable in a science laboratory operating under strictly controlled conditions, but also risk in human societies as they actually exist, in other words, the actual potential for adverse effects on human health in the real world where people live and work and die."[1098]

Observers agree that, taking the science-oriented language of Art. 5.1 SPS into account, it is unlikely that non-scientific factors alone would suffice to

---

1093 *Australia – Measures Affecting the Importation of Apples from New Zealand, WT/DS367/AB/R* 2010, para. 214.

1094 *United States – Continued Suspension of Obligations in the EC – Hormones Dispute, WT/DS320/AB/R* 2008, para. 529.

1095 *European Communities – Measures Concerning Meat and Meat Products, WT/DS26/AB/R, WT/DS48/AB/R* 1998, para. 187.

1096 *United States – Continued Suspension of Obligations in the EC – Hormones Dispute, WT/DS320/AB/R* 2008, para. 535.

1097 *European Communities – Measures Concerning Meat and Meat Products, WT/DS26/R* 1997, para. 8.105.

1098 *European Communities – Measures Concerning Meat and Meat Products, WT/DS26/AB/R, WT/DS48/AB/R* 1998, para. 187.

justify a measure under this article.[1099] In practice, no WTO Member has tried to defend a measure purely in light of the public perception on a certain matter in an SPS dispute.[1100] Consequently, the judicial bodies have not had to deal with the question explicitly. This is maybe why different observers hold slightly different views on what the position of the Appellate Body concerning the role of public perception or cultural preferences under the science-related disciplines of the SPS Agreement actually is. While some observers take the Appellate Body to say that these aspects cannot be taken into account in a risk assessment,[1101] others consider that the Appellate Body has opened the door to such an exercise, if only slightly.[1102]

The Appellate Body has recognized that risks stemming from an improper use or handling of a certain product and non-compliance with relevant provisions should be taken into account in risk assessments.[1103] Notably, in *Hormones II* the Appellate Body found that the Panel had wrongly interpreted Art. 5.1 SPS because it had failed to consider risks stemming from the mishandling of hormones, even though the EU had referred to, and experts had confirmed, the existence of such risks.[1104]

The Appellate Body accepts that a Member uses available risk assessments for demonstrating that its SPS measure is scientifically warranted.[1105] It does not have to perform its own risk assessment, however, and may draw on already existing data, including, for example, a risk assessment conducted by another WTO Member.[1106] However, reports and opinions of political bodies like the European Parliament are not risk assessments.[1107]

1099 Bohanes 2002, 344; Eggers 2001, 150.

1100 Alemanno 2013, 282.

1101 Foster 2008, 430; Gruszczynski 2006, 16.

1102 Bloche 2002, 836; Neugebauer 2000, 1267; Peel 2012, 433.

1103 *Japan – Measures Affecting the Importation of Apples, WT/DS245/AB/R* 2003, para. 138ff; *United States – Continued Suspension of Obligations in the EC – Hormones Dispute, WT/DS320/AB/R* 2008, para. 545.

1104 *United States – Continued Suspension of Obligations in the EC – Hormones Dispute, WT/DS320/AB/R* 2008, para. 544ff.

1105 *European Communities – Measures Concerning Meat and Meat Products, WT/DS26/AB/R, WT/DS48/AB/R* 1998, para. 190; *Japan – Measures Affecting the Importation of Apples, WT/DS245/R* 2003, 8.247.

1106 *European Communities – Measures Affecting the Approval and Marketing of Biotech Products, WT/DS291/R, WT/DS292/R, WT/DS293/R* 2006, para. 7.3024.

1107 *European Communities – Measures Concerning Meat and Meat Products, WT/DS26/R* 1997, para. 8.109.

Art. 5.1 SPS contains a requirement that relevant techniques developed by the relevant international organizations must be taken into account when conducting a risk assessment. Annex A (3) SPS sets forth what the relevant international organizations are, namely the bodies that adopt the relevant international standards, guidelines and recommendations. This requirement has not been interpreted in very strict or narrow terms. The Panel in *Japan – Apples* found that "taking into account" does not have the same meaning as "conform to".[1108] The Appellate Body in *Australia – Apples* confirmed that "taking into account" was not the same as "to be based on" or "to conform to". On the other hand, using the risk assessment techniques of the relevant international organizations would not, by itself, imply compliance with Art. 5.1 SPS Agreement.[1109] In *Hormones I* the Panel looked at the practices actually used by the Codex Alimentarius Commission as no formal document on risk assessment techniques existed.[1110]

Art. 5.1 SPS further stipulates that measures must be based on a risk assessment "as appropriate to the circumstances". The judicial bodies interpret this clause as granting Members some flexibility when conducting a risk assessment[1111] and warranting a case-by-case approach.[1112] Among the circumstances that have been recognized as being relevant are the source of the risk, the kind of risk (whether it is to human, animal or plant life),[1113] the specific situation of the country of destination (e.g. whether a certain disease has yet to occur there or not)[1114] and the methodological difficulties encountered when assessing a given risk and substance.[1115] In *EC – Biotech Products* the EU had also suggested that the amount of evi-

1108 *Japan – Measures Affecting the Importation of Apples, WT/DS245/R* 2003, para. 8.241.

1109 *Australia – Measures Affecting the Importation of Apples from New Zealand, WT/DS367/AB/R* 2010, para. 269.

1110 *European Communities – Measures Concerning Meat and Meat Products, WT/DS26/R* 1997, para. 8.103.

1111 *Australia – Measures Affecting Importation of Salmon, WT/DS18/R* 1998, para. 8.71; *Japan – Measures Affecting the Importation of Apples, WT/DS245/R* 2003, para. 8.239; *United States – Continued Suspension of Obligations in the EC – Hormones Dispute, WT/DS320/AB/R* 2008, para. 562.

1112 *Australia – Measures Affecting Importation of Salmon, WT/DS18/R* 1998, para. 8.71.

1113 Ibid.

1114 *Japan – Measures Affecting the Importation of Apples, WT/DS245/R* 2003, para. 8.240.

1115 *United States – Continued Suspension of Obligations in the EC – Hormones Dispute, WT/DS320/AB/R* 2008, para. 562.

dence available should be one of the circumstances to be taken into account in the review of the risk assessment. The Panel in response stated that according to the SPS Agreement a risk assessment was required even in cases where scientific evidence was scarce, but conceded that

> "in circumstances where there is little available scientific evidence, the phrase 'as appropriate to the circumstances' may provide a measure of flexibility in terms of how (but not whether) the applicable elements of the Annex A(4) definition, including the likelihood evaluation, are satisfied".[1116]

In *EC – Biotech Products* the Panel added a temporal dimension to the clause; it stipulated that a previously conducted risk assessment could cease to be appropriate to the circumstances if the situation had changed.[1117] The Appellate Body also made clear that the clause does not relieve a risk assessor from performing a proper scientific risk assessment.[1118]

Finally, an important aspect of the case law is how the adjudicators deal with the two stages of risk regulation, risk assessment and risk management. The Appellate Body in *Hormones I* rejected propositions that a narrow interpretation of the term risk assessment in the SPS Agreement could be supported by referring to this common distinction, explaining that the term "risk management" was not contained in the SPS Agreement.[1119] Even though the Appellate Body can be read as having rejected the idea that the risk assessment/management distinction is of any relevance to the interpretation of the SPS Agreement, a very similar distinction was sometimes used in subsequent dispute settlement reports, though without making any explicit reference to risk management. For example, the *EC – Biotech Products* Panel wrote the following:

> "If there are factors which affect scientists' level of confidence in a risk assessment they have carried out, this may be taken into account by a Member in determining the measure to be applied for achieving its appropriate level of protection from risks."[1120]

1116 *European Communities – Measures Affecting the Approval and Marketing of Biotech Products, WT/DS291/R, WT/DS292/R, WT/DS293/R* 2006, para. 7.3053.

1117 Ibid., para. 7.3032ff.

1118 *Australia – Measures Affecting the Importation of Apples from New Zealand, WT/DS367/AB/R* 2010, para. 237, 244.

1119 *European Communities – Measures Concerning Meat and Meat Products, WT/DS26/AB/R, WT/DS48/AB/R* 1998, para. 181.

1120 *European Communities – Measures Affecting the Approval and Marketing of Biotech Products, WT/DS291/R, WT/DS292/R, WT/DS293/R* 2006, para. 7.3240.

In *Hormones II*, the Panel used the Appellate Body's finding in *Hormones I* for what the Appellate Body considered too narrow an understanding of risk assessment.[1121] The Panel had referred to the Appellate Body's finding, reading it to say that because risk management was not mentioned in the SPS Agreement, the SPS Agreement's definition of risk assessment could not be understood to comprise any aspects of risk management. The Appellate Body found it "difficult to reconcile the Panel's understanding of EC – Hormones with what the Appellate Body held in that Report".[1122] Yet it is not entirely clear what, precisely, was wrong with the Panel's reading of the earlier Appellate Body report; the Appellate Body just referred to a too restrictive notion of risk assessment that the Panel had allegedly adopted.[1123]

Based on

What is meant by the phrase" based on" in Art. 5.1 SPS was clarified by the Appellate Body very early in its history.

In *Hormones I,* the Panel had found both a procedural and a substantial aspect to this wording.[1124] The procedural aspect of Art. 5.1 SPS identified by the Panel was that Members were obliged to take a risk assessment into account when enacting or maintaining a sanitary measure.[1125] The Appellate Body did not share the Panel's view of the procedural side of Art. 5.1 SPS. It rejected what it took to be a subjective reading of Art. 5.1 SPS and explained that "based on" was an exclusively objective standard that demanded a rational relationship between the measure in dispute and the risk assessment.[1126] The "objective" reading of "based on" could, besides discarding the procedural requirement proposed by the Panel, also mean that the Appellate Body refuses to assess an SPS measure in the light of the aims the decision-makers might have had in mind. Occasionally, parties aimed to demonstrate that the motive behind a particular

---

1121 *United States – Continued Suspension of Obligations in the EC – Hormones Dispute, WT/DS320/AB/R* 2008, para. 542.

1122 Ibid., para. 541.

1123 Ibid., para. 559.

1124 *European Communities – Measures Concerning Meat and Meat Products, WT/DS26/R* 1997, para. 8.112.

1125 Ibid., para. 8.113.

1126 *European Communities – Measures Concerning Meat and Meat Products, WT/DS26/AB/R, WT/DS48/AB/R* 1998, para. 189.

SPS measure was protectionist.[1127] The Appellate Body neither rejected such arguments outright as having nothing to do with the "based on" standard, nor did it explicitly make use of these arguments. Mostly, the reports have related to a certain relation between the risk assessment and the measure rather than to the objective of a measure.[1128]

The Appellate Body brought several more formulations into play to explain the meaning of "based on", equating it with "sufficiently warranted" and "reasonably supported".[1129] The Panel in *EC – Biotech Products* also referred to an earlier finding of the Appellate Body on Art. 3.1 SPS on the difference between "based on" and "conform to", with the former standard giving WTO Members more leeway.[1130] These formulations have not, however, been taken up by parties or adjudicators in later disputes.[1131]

Despite the Appellate Body's rejection of the procedural notion of "based on", it is not entirely clear whether there are certain limitations on *when* a party could conduct a risk assessment for its measure to remain "based on" it. In *EC – Biotech Products*, the Panel rejected a study cited by the EU in support of its measure, because the study dated from 2004, but the Panel was established in 2003.[1132] However, it seems safe to assume that it is not the evidence available at the time when the measure was enacted that matters, but the one available at the time of the establishment of the Panel (or later).[1133]

The Appellate Body has also introduced one more significant qualification to the "based on" standard. It stated that the required rational rela-

---

1127 See for example *Australia – Measures Affecting Importation of Salmon, WT/DS18/RW* 2000, para. 4.150-4.153.

1128 *Australia – Measures Affecting Importation of Salmon, WT/DS18/R* 1998, para. 8.94ff; *Japan – Measures Affecting Agricultural Products, WT/DS76/R* 1998, para. 8.42 in the context of Art. 2.2 SPS.

1129 *European Communities – Measures Concerning Meat and Meat Products, WT/DS26/AB/R, WT/DS48/AB/R* 1998, para. 193; *United States – Continued Suspension of Obligations in the EC – Hormones Dispute, WT/DS320/AB/R* 2008, para. 528.

1130 *European Communities – Measures Affecting the Approval and Marketing of Biotech Products, WT/DS291/R, WT/DS292/R, WT/DS293/R* 2006, para. 7.3067.

1131 See for example *Australia – Measures Affecting Importation of Salmon, WT/DS18/RW* 2000, para. 4.150-4.153; *European Communities – Measures Affecting the Approval and Marketing of Biotech Products, WT/DS291/R, WT/DS292/R, WT/DS293/R* 2006, para. 7.3030; *Australia – Measures Affecting Importation of Salmon, WT/DS18/R* 1998, para. 8.94.

1132 *European Communities – Measures Affecting the Approval and Marketing of Biotech Products, WT/DS291/R, WT/DS292/R, WT/DS293/R* 2006, para. 7.3075.

1133 See Pauwelyn 1999, 649.

tionship was present even when a measure was not based on majority scientific views. It acknowledged that, while governments often base their measures on the mainstream scientific view,

> "responsible and representative governments may act in good faith on the basis of divergent opinion coming from qualified and respected sources".[1134]

The Appellate Body further detailed its understanding of the "based on" standard by saying that the fact that a certain view was only held by a scientific minority did not signal the absence of a rational relationship,

> "especially where the risk involved is life-threatening [...] and perceived to constitute a clear and imminent threat to public health and safety".[1135]

In *Hormones II,* the Appellate Body gave some indications as to when a minority opinion was a sufficient basis for an SPS measure: it needed to exhibit the necessary degree of scientific and methodological rigor to be considered reputable science and be accepted as legitimate science by the broader scientific community according to its standards.[1136]

In *Hormones I*, the divergent opinion of one single expert was held to be insufficient to counterbalance the cumulative weight of the mainstream. The reason given by the Appellate Body in support of this finding was that the expert in question had not undertaken any research of his own.[1137] Nonetheless, some observers concluded that even a one-person minority might suffice for an SPS measure to pass the "based on" hurdle.[1138] By way of contrast, in later case law the Appellate Body seems to suggest that the relationship between the risk assessment and the measure should be sub-

---

1134 *European Communities – Measures Concerning Meat and Meat Products, WT/DS26/AB/R, WT/DS48/AB/R* 1998, para. 194; *United States – Continued Suspension of Obligations in the EC – Hormones Dispute, WT/DS320/AB/R* 2008, para. 529.

1135 *European Communities – Measures Concerning Meat and Meat Products, WT/DS26/AB/R, WT/DS48/AB/R* 1998, para. 194; *United States – Continued Suspension of Obligations in the EC – Hormones Dispute, WT/DS320/AB/R* 2008, para. 529.

1136 *United States – Continued Suspension of Obligations in the EC – Hormones Dispute, WT/DS320/AB/R* 2008, para. 591.

1137 *European Communities – Measures Concerning Meat and Meat Products, WT/DS26/AB/R, WT/DS48/AB/R* 1998, para. 198.

1138 Iynedjian 2002, 100.

ject to more intensive scrutiny when a WTO Member seeks to rely on a minority view.[1139]

In *EC – Biotech Products*, the Panel stated that a precautionary approach adopted by a WTO Member "could have a bearing" on a Panel's assessment of whether an SPS measure was "based on" a risk assessment and stated that

> "there may conceivably be cases where a Member which follows a precautionary approach, and which confronts a risk assessment that identifies uncertainties or constraints, would be justified in applying (i) an SPS measure even though another Member might not decide to apply any SPS measure on the basis of the same risk assessment, or (ii) an SPS measure which is stricter than the SPS measure applied by another Member to address the same risk".[1140]

Commentators have nonetheless observed that the Panel in *EC – Biotech Products* had a quite narrow understanding of the role of scientific studies that come to different conclusions than the "official" scientific risk assessments.[1141] These studies were rejected because they did not constitute risk assessments.[1142] This means that diverging, minority opinions can only become relevant once they constitute formal risk assessments or are incorporated therein.[1143] However, given that the *EC – Biotech Products* Panel report deviates in its understanding of risk and risk assessments from the later *Hormones II* Appellate Body report, it is unclear whether this line of reasoning will be upheld in future jurisprudence.

The Appellate Body has also explicitly stressed that there is flexibility incorporated into the "based on" standard which depends on the circumstances of each case, the seriousness of the risk involved, the evidence available and the measure at issue.[1144] It is difficult, therefore, to predict how strictly or leniently this standard will be handled in future cases. A strict

---

1139 *Australia – Measures Affecting the Importation of Apples from New Zealand, WT/DS367/AB/R* 2010, para. 221.

1140 *European Communities – Measures Affecting the Approval and Marketing of Biotech Products, WT/DS291/R, WT/DS292/R, WT/DS293/R* 2006, para. 7.3055.

1141 Howse and Horn 2009, 76.

1142 See for example *European Communities – Measures Affecting the Approval and Marketing of Biotech Products, WT/DS291/R, WT/DS292/R, WT/DS293/R* 2006, para. 7.3097ff, 7.3059ff.

1143 Howse and Horn 2009, 76.

1144 *European Communities – Measures Concerning Meat and Meat Products, WT/DS26/AB/R, WT/DS48/AB/R* 1998, para. 194; *Japan – Measures Affecting Agricultural Products, WT/DS76/AB/R* 1999, para. 84.

and narrow interpretation of the "based on" standard means that WTO Members have less leeway in adopting SPS measures that are not identical with international standards.

2.1.2. Art. 2.2 SPS

Art. 2.2 SPS contains three requirements: a measure must be applied only to the extent necessary; it must be based on scientific principles, and it must not be maintained without sufficient scientific evidence. So far, there have been no decisions on the first of these requirements.[1145] One clarification that the dispute settlement bodies have introduced is that the second and third elements of Art. 2.2 SPS, relating to scientific evidence requirements, are violated whenever Art. 5.1 SPS is violated.[1146]

In addition, what has become clear in the case law so far is that Art. 2.2 SPS has a double character as both a substantive and procedural norm due to the scientific evidence requirement. The substantive requirement is that sufficient evidence needs to be brought forward for justifying an SPS measure. In other words, the norm contains an evidence-related and hence procedural requirement as a substantive precondition for adopting a measure. As a consequence, the arguments used by the parties to the dispute are mainly procedural in character;[1147] equally, the findings made are partially procedural in their nature.[1148]

Still, that the Appellate Body understands Art. 2.2 SPS to be a substantive norm became evident in *Japan – Agricultural Products*. The complainant, the US, appealed the decision by the Panel to not decide on a violation of Art. 2.2 SPS for lack of evidence. The US summarized the Panel's suggesting that allegedly the

1145 In at least one case, judicial economy was exercised by the adjudicators, see for example *European Communities – Measures Affecting the Approval and Marketing of Biotech Products, WT/DS291/R, WT/DS292/R, WT/DS293/R* 2006, para. 7.3394.

1146 *Australia – Measures Affecting Importation of Salmon, WT/DS18/AB/R* 1998, para. 137–138; *European Communities – Measures Affecting the Approval and Marketing of Biotech Products, WT/DS291/R, WT/DS292/R, WT/DS293/R* 2006, para. 7.3396.

1147 See the summary of Japan's arguments during the Appellate Body proceedings in *Japan – Measures Affecting the Importation of Apples, WT/DS245/AB/R* 2003, 148f.

1148 See for example ibid., para 152–160.

"Panel found that because there was insufficient evidence of the existence or relevance of varietal differences, it could not find that the evidence was insufficient."[1149]

The US thus did not distinguish between a procedural notion of evidence and scientific evidence in the sense of the SPS Agreement. Such an equation of the two was rejected by the Appellate Body; the Appellate Body stated that under Art. 2.2 SPS the complainant had to comply with the ordinary burden of proof and adduce sufficient evidence to establish a *prima facie* case that the defendant had maintained its measure without sufficient scientific evidence.[1150] The Appellate Body treats Art. 2.2 SPS as a substantive norm for which the normal rules on proof apply.

The fact that Art. 2.2 SPS refers to "scientific" evidence would have given the dispute settlement bodies the opportunity to elaborate on their concept and definition of science. However, the dispute settlement bodies have hardly offered any observations about what science is that are not either circular or more or less self-evident.[1151] The only elaboration on the meaning of the term "scientific" can be found in a footnote of the Appellate Body report in *Hormones I,* which draws on a somewhat unusual source:

> "The ordinary meaning of 'scientific', as provided by dictionary definitions, includes 'of, relating to, or used in science', 'broadly, having or appearing to have an exact, objective, factual, systematic or methodological basis', 'of, relating to, or exhibiting the methods or principles of science' and 'of, pertaining to, using, or based on the methodology of science'. Dictionary definitions of 'science' include 'the observation, identification, description, experimental investigation, and theoretical explanation of natural phenomena', 'any methodological activity, discipline, or study', and 'knowledge attained through study or practice'". (footnotes omitted) United States' Statement of Administrative Action, Uruguay Round Agreements Act, 203d Congress, 2d Session, House Document 103-316, Vol. 1, 27 September 1994, p. 90."[1152]

1149 *Japan – Measures Affecting Agricultural Products, WT/DS76/AB/R* 1999, para. 38.
1150 Ibid., para. 136.
1151 See for example *Japan – Measures Affecting the Importation of Apples, WT/DS245/R* 2003, para. 8.90-8.99, especially 8.93.
1152 *European Communities – Measures Concerning Meat and Meat Products, WT/DS26/AB/R, WT/DS48/AB/R* 1998, n. 172.

With regard to the interpretation of "sufficient", the Appellate Body in *Japan – Agricultural Products* and *Japan – Apples* used the rational relationship standard familiar from Art. 5.1 SPS.[1153] The Panel in *Japan – Agricultural Products* also transported the flexibility of the standard under Art. 5.1 SPS to Art. 2.2 SPS and stated that what was "sufficient" evidence in a case depended on the risk involved and the damage that could result from it.[1154] This is evident from the following quotes:

> "[W]e concluded, on the basis of the elements before us, that there was *not sufficient scientific evidence* to support the view that apples are likely to serve as a pathway for the entry, establishment or spread of fire blight within Japan. Given the negligible risk identified on the basis of the scientific evidence and the nature of the elements composing the phytosanitary measure at issue, the measure on the face of it is disproportionate to that risk."[1155]
>
> "For the reasons mentioned above, we conclude that the phytosanitary measure at issue is clearly disproportionate to the risk identified on the basis of the scientific evidence available."[1156]

The Panel here adopted an interpretation that allows for a great degree of flexibility in the application of the rational relationship standard. This flexibility was also visible from the manner in which the Panel reached a conclusion about whether there was sufficient evidence: the Panel listed the evidence both for and against a scientific justification of the contested SPS measure. Taking the opinions of the experts heard as witnesses into account, the Panel then concluded without further reasoning that there was not sufficient evidence.[1157] The approach was upheld by the Appellate Body in the same case.[1158] The Appellate Body even added flexibility by saying that the approach of the Panel was only one possible approach and others were equally valid, depending on the circumstances of the case.

1153 *Japan – Measures Affecting Agricultural Products, WT/DS76/AB/R* 1999, para. 84; *Japan – Measures Affecting the Importation of Apples, WT/DS245/AB/R* 2003, para. 162.

1154 *Japan – Measures Affecting the Importation of Apples, WT/DS245/R* 2003, para. 8.105 quoting; *European Communities – Measures Concerning Meat and Meat Products, WT/DS26/AB/R, WT/DS48/AB/R* 1998, para. 124.

1155 *Japan – Measures Affecting the Importation of Apples, WT/DS245/R* 2003, para. 8.181.

1156 Ibid., para. 8.198.

1157 Ibid., para. 8.182–8.197.

1158 *Japan – Measures Affecting the Importation of Apples, WT/DS245/AB/R* 2003, para. 164.

2.1.3. Art. 5.7 SPS

Art. 5.7 SPS is closely related to Art. 5.1 and Art. 2.2 SPS, and hence is discussed next. While Art. 5.1 SPS requires WTO Members to base their measures on scientific evidence in the form of a risk assessment presupposing the existence of scientific evidence, Art. 5.7 SPS allows WTO Members to take provisional measures in cases where relevant scientific evidence is insufficient. In practice, no measure has been held to comply with Art. 5.7 SPS in the WTO dispute settlement.[1159]

Art. 5.7 SPS contains four requirements.[1160] According to the first sentence, the precondition for adopting a provisional SPS measure is that it is

(1) imposed in respect of a situation where relevant scientific information is insufficient and
(2) adopted on the basis of available pertinent information.

Furthermore, the Member must, according to the second sentence,

(3) seek to obtain the additional information necessary for a more objective assessment of the risk and
(4) review the measure accordingly within a reasonable period of time.

The Appellate Body holds the view that the first sentence contains requirements pertaining to the adoption of a provisional measure, whereas the second sentence imposes requirements concerned with maintaining such measures.[1161] In *Hormones II*, the Appellate Body held that these requirements needed to be interpreted in the light of the precautionary principle, of which Art. 5.7 SPS was an expression.[1162]

1159 The defendants did not invoke Art. 5.7 in all cases, though. For example, the EU in the Hormones I case held the view that its hormone ban was temporary and hence did not want to rely on Art. 5.7, see *European Communities – Measures Concerning Meat and Meat Products, WT/DS26/R* 1997, para. 4.239, 8.249.

1160 *Japan – Measures Affecting Agricultural Products, WT/DS76/AB/R* 1999, para. 89; *Japan – Measures Affecting the Importation of Apples, WT/DS245/AB/R* 2003, para. 176; *United States – Continued Suspension of Obligations in the EC – Hormones Dispute, WT/DS320/AB/R* 2008, para. 676.

1161 *Japan – Measures Affecting Agricultural Products, WT/DS76/AB/R* 1999, para. 89; *Japan – Measures Affecting the Importation of Apples, WT/DS245/AB/R* 2003, n. 318; also confirmed by the Panel in *European Communities – Measures Affecting the Approval and Marketing of Biotech Products, WT/DS291/R, WT/DS292/R, WT/DS293/R* 2006, para. 7.3248ff.

1162 *United States – Continued Suspension of Obligations in the EC – Hormones Dispute, WT/DS320/AB/R* 2008, para. 680.

Character of the norm and relationship with other articles

Before discussing the case law on each of these requirements, it is important to present the case law on the character Art. 5.7 SPS and its relationship with Art. 5.1 and 2.2 SPS.

The Panel in *EC – Biotech Products* appears to be the first one to have reflected upon this issue extensively. It discussed whether Art. 5.7 SPS was an exception to the rules contained in Art. 2.2 and 5.1 SPS or an autonomous right of WTO Members. While the Appellate Body in *Japan – Agricultural Products* used the term "qualified exemption" when relating to Art. 5.7 SPS, it only did so *passim* and without any substantive discussion of the character of the norm.[1163]

The Panel in *EC – Biotech Products* drew on a distinction between different types of norms made by the Appellate Body in *EC – GSP* and *Hormones I*.[1164] In *EC – GSP* the Appellate Body had concluded the following:

> "In cases where one provision permits, in certain circumstances, behavior that would otherwise be inconsistent with an obligation in another provision, and one of the two provisions refers to the other provision, the Appellate Body has found that the complaining party bears the burden of establishing that a challenged measure is inconsistent with the provision permitting particular behavior only where one of the provisions suggests that the obligation is not applicable to the said measure."[1165]

In other words, only if there is a rule (A) saying that another rule (B) that would otherwise be breached is not applicable, is rule A an autonomous right. In this case, i.e. rule A constitutes an autonomous right, the complainant has the initial burden of proving that the defendant has violated rule A. In other cases, rule A has to be characterized as an exception of rule B and the defending party seeking to rely on it has the initial burden of proof that it fulfils the requirement of rule A.[1166] In *EC – Biotech Products*, the Panel noted textual similarities between Art. 3.1 SPS (in relation to Art. 3.3 SPS) and Art. 2.2 SPS (in relation to Art. 5.7). From these similari-

1163 *Japan – Measures Affecting Agricultural Products, WT/DS76/AB/R* 1999, para. 80.

1164 *European Communities – Measures Affecting the Approval and Marketing of Biotech Products, WT/DS291/R, WT/DS292/R, WT/DS293/R* 2006, para. 7.2963.

1165 *European Communities – Conditions for the Granting of Tariff Preferences to Developing Countries, WT/DS246/AB/R* 2004, para. 88.

1166 Ibid.

ties it inferred that, like Art. 3.3 SPS in *Hormones I*,[1167] Art. 5.7 SPS had to be considered an autonomous right and "qualified exemption" in relation to Art. 2.2 SPS rather than an exception.[1168] The Panel then concluded the same with regard to the relationship between Art. 5.1 and 5.7 SPS, using the quoted criteria of the Appellate Body in *EC – GSP*.[1169] In this understanding, the complaining party bears the burden of proof for showing that Art. 5.7 SPS has been violated by the defending Member.

The Panel in *EC – Biotech Products* decided to investigate the consistency of the controversial measures with Art. 5.7 SPS within the context, and as part, of an examination of the consistency of the same measures with Art. 5.1 SPS. The complaining parties had in that case only claimed a violation of Art. 5.7 SPS and not of Art. 5.1 SPS.[1170] The Panel reasoned that if the complainants were not successful in demonstrating a violation of Art. 5.1 SPS, it would not have to further consider Art. 5.7. By contrast, if Art. 5.1 SPS was considered to be violated, it would need to consider Art. 5.7. If the conditions set forth in Art. 5.7 SPS were fulfilled, Art. 5.1 SPS would become inapplicable.

This leads to a somewhat difficult situation for the complaining party, as it will normally be easier for a complainant to show that Art. 5.1 SPS is violated because its requirements are more burdensome for WTO Members than those contained in Art. 5.7 SPS. As a corollary, the complaining party has an interest in showing that the disputed measure is not "provisional" or that there is sufficient evidence for a full risk assessment. Yet, if it claims a violation of Art. 5.1 SPS only, it may lose the case. Consequently, it will also have to show that the measure at issue does not meet the requirements of Art. 5.7 SPS, either. In other words: to be able to claim a violation of one norm – Art. 5.1 SPS – a complaining party needs to show that the requirements contained in two norms – Art. 5.1 SPS and Art. 5.7 SPS – are violated. Even if the complaining manages to show that Art. 5.1 SPS is violated, it will not automatically win, as Art. 5.7 SPS may still come into the picture. If the requirements of Art. 5.7 SPS are satisfied, Art. 5.1 SPS will be inapplicable. The defending party, on the other hand, has to decide whether there is sufficient scientific evidence for a risk assess-

1167 *European Communities – Measures Concerning Meat and Meat Products, WT/DS26/AB/R, WT/DS48/AB/R* 1998, para. 104.

1168 *European Communities – Measures Affecting the Approval and Marketing of Biotech Products, WT/DS291/R, WT/DS292/R, WT/DS293/R* 2006, para. 7.2967ff.

1169 Ibid., para. 7.2984ff.

1170 Ibid., para. 7.3005.

ment; if that is not the case, the respective WTO Member may choose to take provisional measures in accordance with Art. 5.7 SPS.[1171]

Requirements in Art. 5.7 SPS

After the overall character of Art. 5.7 SPS has been clarified in the preceding section, this section discusses the interpretation of the four requirements of Art. 5.7 SPS in the WTO dispute settlement.

The first of these requirements, i.e. the insufficiency of scientific information, "triggers" the application of Art. 5.7 SPS, as stated by the Appellate Body in *Japan – Apples*.[1172] The issue came up again in *Hormones II*. In this case, the Appellate Body stated that the applicability of Art. 2.2 and 5.1 SPS, on the one hand, and Art. 5.7 SPS on the other, both depended on the sufficiency of the scientific evidence.[1173]

Accordingly, the Panel in *EC – Biotech Products* rejected the EU's position that Art. 5.7 SPS applied whenever a measure was characterized as "provisional" by the WTO Member adopting it. Rather, the Panel clarified by suggesting that Art. 5.7 SPS allowed a measure to be provisionally adopted in such cases.[1174] The provisional character of the measure is thus not a requirement that a Member must fulfil, but defines what a country can do in a given type of situation.

The term "insufficient evidence" in Art. 5.7 SPS is, according to the Appellate Body, to be read in the context of Art. 5.1 SPS. Evidence is therefore insufficient in the sense of Art. 5.7 SPS when a risk assessment in the sense of Art. 5.1 SPS cannot be performed with the scientific evidence available, either because there is not enough evidence in a quantitative sense or because it is not qualitatively satisfactory.[1175] A crucial point here is what constitute legitimate reasons for the insufficiency of scientific evi-

---

1171 *Australia – Measures Affecting the Importation of Apples from New Zealand, WT/DS367/AB/R* 2010, para. 238.

1172 *Japan – Measures Affecting the Importation of Apples, WT/DS245/AB/R* 2003, para. 184.

1173 *United States – Continued Suspension of Obligations in the EC – Hormones Dispute, WT/DS320/AB/R* 2008, para. 674.

1174 *European Communities – Measures Affecting the Approval and Marketing of Biotech Products, WT/DS291/R, WT/DS292/R, WT/DS293/R* 2006, para. 7.2939.

1175 *Australia – Measures Affecting the Importation of Apples from New Zealand, WT/DS367/AB/R* 2010, para. 239; *European Communities – Measures Affecting the Approval and Marketing of Biotech Products, WT/DS291/R, WT/DS292/R,*

dence under Art. 5.7 SPS. Theoretically, at least two possible reasons are conceivable. A first possible reason (1) is simply that no scientist has yet set out to investigate the issue in question. A second (2) is that it is impossible to produce scientific evidence on the matter, either at all or with satisfactory reliability, given the current state of scientific progress; in this second category, there may also be situations of scientific controversy.

Of course, this is an analytical categorization – in practice, it seems both possible reasons will often obtain. This ambiguity is reflected in the Appellate Body's position. In *Japan – Apples*, Japan had contended that Art. 5.7 SPS covered situations of "unresolved uncertainty".[1176] This term was meant to cover an uncertainty that science was not able to resolve, despite accumulated scientific evidence.[1177] It hence relied on reason (2). The Appellate Body rejected this line of argument. Instead it distinguished clearly between a situation of "scientific uncertainty" and one of "insufficiency of relevant scientific evidence", stating further that Art. 5.7 SPS covered only the latter, i.e. reason (1).[1178] This seems clear enough. Yet the Appellate Body then added ambiguity by saying that insufficiency does not necessarily mean the absence of evidence, but it could also mean that available evidence is not reliable.[1179] This is closer to reason (2). In *Hormones II*, the Appellate Body also distinguished a situation of insufficient scientific information under Art. 5.7 SPS from one of scientific controversy on certain aspects; such controversy "in itself is not enough" to conclude that the relevant scientific evidence is insufficient, according to the Appellate Body.[1180] However, it then went on to state that

> "Article 5.7 is concerned with situations where deficiencies in the body of scientific evidence do not allow a WTO Member to arrive at a sufficiently objective conclusion in relation to risk. [...] Where there is, among other opinions, a qualified and respected scientific view that puts into question the relationship between the relevant scientific evidence and the conclusions in relation to risk, thereby not permitting

---

WT/DS293/R 2006, para. 7.3233; *Japan – Measures Affecting the Importation of Apples, WT/DS245/AB/R* 2003, para. 179; *United States – Continued Suspension of Obligations in the EC – Hormones Dispute, WT/DS320/AB/R* 2008, para. 677.

1176 *Japan – Measures Affecting the Importation of Apples, WT/DS245/AB/R* 2003, para. 33f.

1177 This the way the Appellate Body understood the concept in ibid., para. 183.

1178 Ibid., para. 184.

1179 Ibid., para. 185.

1180 *United States – Continued Suspension of Obligations in the EC – Hormones Dispute, WT/DS320/AB/R* 2008, para. 677.

> the performance of a sufficiently objective assessment of risk on the basis of the existing scientific evidence, then a Member may adopt provisional measures under Article 5.7 on the basis of that qualified and respected view."[1181]

Art. 5.7 SPS does, after all, seem to be applicable in situations of scientific controversy as well, i.e. (2) seems to be an acceptable reason behind the insufficiency of scientific evidence. In sum, Art. 5.7 SPS covers, in the words of the Appellate Body, situations

> "where there is some evidentiary basis indicating the possible existence of a risk, but not enough to permit the performance of a risk assessment".[1182]

In other words, at last some situations of scientific uncertainty (and not only insufficiency of evidence) appear to be covered by Art. 5.7 SPS.[1183]

Another point concerning the sufficiency of evidence was raised in *EC – Biotech Products.* In this case, the EU argued that the level of protection sought by the WTO Member whose measure was under scrutiny should be relevant for determining whether the evidence was sufficient – sufficiency should be determined in light of the purpose the WTO Member intended to use the evidence for. The Panel rejected this position, finding nothing to support it in the definition of risk assessment contained within the SPS Agreement.[1184] In *Hormones II*, the EU repeated its position and was supported by the claimants, at least in oral statements at the appellate stage, for a situation in which a WTO Member chooses a higher level of protection than would be achieved by a measure based on the relevant international standard.[1185] The Panel, as in *EC – Biotech Products*, rejected this idea.[1186] In *Hormones II*, however, the Appellate Body held that the level of protection sought could influence the risk assessment: a risk assessment that could justify a higher level of protection may require research to be carried out that is different from the research needed when there is an in-

---

1181 Ibid.

1182 Ibid., para. 678.

1183 See also Gruszczynski 2008, 117.

1184 *European Communities – Measures Affecting the Approval and Marketing of Biotech Products, WT/DS291/R, WT/DS292/R, WT/DS293/R* 2006, para. 7.3234ff, 7.3271.

1185 *United States – Continued Suspension of Obligations in the EC – Hormones Dispute, WT/DS320/AB/R* 2008, para. 682f.

1186 For a summary of the Panel's findings, see ibid., para. 684.

ternational standard that embodies a lower level of protection.[1187] The Appellate Body therefore stated:

> "[...] we disagree with the Panel's finding that 'the determination of whether scientific evidence is sufficient to assess the existence and magnitude of a risk must be disconnected from the intended level of protection.' We emphasize, however, that whatever level of protection a WTO Member chooses does not pre-determine the outcome of its determination of the sufficiency of the relevant scientific evidence. The determination as to whether available scientific evidence is sufficient to perform a risk assessment must remain, in essence, a rigorous and objective process."[1188] [footnotes omitted]

This marks a significant departure from previous case law.[1189]

The Panel in *EC – Biotech Products* also discussed whether the point in time at which the evidence needed to be insufficient was the time of the adoption of the controversial measure or the time the Panel's terms of reference are fixed. Undertaking a contextual reading of Art. 2.2 and 5.7 SPS, it inferred that scientific evidence needed to be insufficient at the time the measure was adopted.[1190]

In the context of the insufficiency of evidence requirement the question arises whether, considering the relationship between Art. 5.7 SPS on the one hand and Art. 2.2/5.1 SPS on the other, scientific evidence is always insufficient in the sense of Art. 5.7 SPS when a measure cannot be justified under Art. 2.2/5.1 SPS. The dispute settlement bodies answered this question in the negative: whether scientific evidence is insufficient needs to be determined under Art. 5.7 SPS independently of the findings under Art. 2.2 SPS.[1191] The explanation given for this is that in the context of Art. 5.7 SPS "sufficiency" refers to the data available for a risk assessment.[1192] This includes data both in support of and militating against the measure in place. The context of Art. 2.2 SPS, however, considers the "supportive" data to be of primary relevance. What must be insufficient is the

---

1187 Ibid., para. 685.

1188 Ibid., para. 686.

1189 Du 2010a, 1083.

1190 *European Communities – Measures Affecting the Approval and Marketing of Biotech Products, WT/DS291/R, WT/DS292/R, WT/DS293/R* 2006, para. 7.3253.

1191 *Japan – Measures Affecting the Importation of Apples, WT/DS245/R* 2003, para. 8.215.

1192 *Japan – Measures Affecting the Importation of Apples, WT/DS245/AB/R* 2003, para. 179.

quantity or quality of the available material in general,[1193] not the evidence relating to a certain sub-aspect.[1194]

An issue that came up in *Hormones II* was whether the existence of an international standard meant that scientific evidence was *eo ipso* also sufficient for a scientific risk assessment, because it could be assumed that international standards were based on risk assessments. The Panel argued that the presumption of WTO consistency in Art. 3.2 SPS for SPS measures conforming to international standards did indeed mean that these standards were also based on a risk assessment that conformed to the requirements of the SPS Agreement. At the same time, it acknowledged that scientific knowledge evolved and as a consequence there could be cases in which a situation changed from one of sufficiency to one of insufficiency of scientific evidence in the sense of Art. 5.7 SPS after the adoption of an international standard.[1195] The Panel, however, posited that there had to be

> "a *critical mass* of new evidence and/or information that calls into question the fundamental precepts of previous knowledge and evidence so as to make relevant, previously sufficient, evidence now insufficient. In the present case where risk assessments have been performed and a large body of quality evidence has been accumulated, this would be possible only if it put into question existing relevant evidence to the point that this evidence is no longer sufficient to support the conclusions of existing risks assessments."[1196]

The Appellate Body rejected outright the Panel's position that the presumption in Art. 3.2 SPS had any significance for the question of sufficiency of information under Art. 5.7 SPS. The Appellate Body pointed to the text of Art. 5.7 SPS, which contains no reference to Art. 3.2 SPS, international standards, or prior risk assessments carried out by entities other than the defending WTO Member. The Appellate Body pointed out that a risk assessment by an international organization could also be considered "available pertinent information" under Art. 5.7 SPS, whereas scientific evidence used in a risk assessment leading to an international standard at a

1193 Ibid., para. 180–182.
1194 Ibid., para. 179.
1195 See the reasoning of the Panel as summarized in *United States – Continued Suspension of Obligations in the EC – Hormones Dispute, WT/DS320/AB/R* 2008, para. 631.
1196 See the reasoning of the Panel as summarized in ibid., para. 632.

certain point in time could be rendered invalid or insufficient by later scientific developments.[1197] Accordingly, while a prior risk assessment by an international organization can be submitted as evidence for the sufficiency of scientific evidence for risk assessment purposes, the defending Member can rebut such evidence.[1198] The Appellate Body then used the discussion of the Panel's "critical mass" standard to make more fundamental observations on the nature of scientific inquiry:

> "[...] the nature of scientific inquiry is such that it is always possible to conduct more research or obtain additional information. The possibility of conducting further research or of analyzing additional information, by itself, should not mean that the relevant scientific evidence is or becomes insufficient. [...] It may be useful to think of the degree of change as a spectrum. On one extreme of this spectrum lies the incremental advance of science. Where these scientific advances are at the margins, they would not support the conclusion that previously sufficient evidence has become insufficient. At the other extreme lie the more radical scientific changes that lead to a paradigm shift. Such radical change is not frequent. Limiting the application of Article 5.7 to situations where scientific advances lead to a paradigm shift would be too inflexible an approach. WTO Members should be permitted to take a provisional measure where new evidence from a qualified and respected source puts into question the relationship between the preexisting body of scientific evidence and the conclusions regarding the risks."[1199]

The Appellate Body then observed that some of the Panel's statements could be read to require such a paradigm shift, which was too exacting a threshold.[1200] In consequence, the Appellate Body reversed the Panel's findings under Art. 5.7 SPS that there was no situation of "insufficient scientific evidence" in the case.[1201]

The second element of Art. 5.7 SPS was discussed by the WTO adjudicators in *Hormones II.* The Appellate Body here clarified that the sources of information that a Member seeking to rely on Art. 5.7 SPS could use infor-

1197 Ibid., para. 694f.
1198 Ibid., para. 696.
1199 Ibid., para. 702, 703.
1200 Ibid., para. 705ff.
1201 Ibid., para. 734.

mation included relevant international organizations or other WTO Members. The Appellate Body also found that there had to be a

> "rational and objective relationship between the information concerning a certain risk and a Member's provisional SPS measure".[1202]

The third and fourth elements of Art. 5.7 SPS were discussed in *Japan – Apples*. In this case, the defending party had not claimed to have actively sought additional information, but the Panel emphasized that it could have done so with relative ease.[1203] The Appellate Body supported this view and said that what constituted a reasonable period of time depended on how easy it was to collect the additional information necessary for a review.[1204] The Appellate Body clarified that the country invoking Art. 5.7 SPS must seek the information it lacks for conducting a proper risk assessment.[1205] In *Hormones II,* the Appellate Body posited that the third element of Art. 5.7 SPS required the "best efforts" of the respective WTO Member to fill the gaps in the available evidence, either through research or by collecting, from a variety of sources, such information as was "germane" to conducting the required risk assessment. The Appellate Body also stated, in a soft formulation, that the Member adopting a provisional SPS measure should be able to identify the insufficiencies in the evidence as well as the steps that it intended to take to fill the needed additional evidence.[1206]

2.2. Art. 5.6 SPS

Art. 5.6 SPS stipulates that SPS measures must not be more trade-restrictive than necessary in order to achieve the appropriate level of protection. According to the Appellate Body, this norm has a close relationship with Art. 2 SPS. The Appellate Body has noted, in particular, the parallels between the requirement in Art. 2.2 SPS that WTO Members apply their SPS measures "only to the extent necessary", and the requirement in

1202 Ibid., para. 678.

1203 *Japan – Measures Affecting Agricultural Products, WT/DS76/R* 1998, para. 8.58.

1204 *Japan – Measures Affecting Agricultural Products, WT/DS76/AB/R* 1999, para. 93.

1205 Ibid., para. 92.

1206 *United States – Continued Suspension of Obligations in the EC – Hormones Dispute, WT/DS320/AB/R* 2008, para. 6.79.

Art. 5.6 SPS that SPS measures be "no more trade-restrictive than required to achieve" the SPS-related objectives.[1207]

The Appellate Body has not yet taken any definite decision on whether that means that whenever Art. 5.6 SPS is violated because an SPS measure is more trade-restrictive than required, Art. 2.2 SPS is also violated, because the measure is not necessary.[1208] Concerning the relationship between Art. 5.1 and 5.6 SPS, the Appellate Body has stated that both are independent obligations.[1209] Art. 5.6 SPS has been stated to be of increasing importance in compliance disputes, as discussions about Art. 5.6 SPS draw attention to measures that a WTO Member found to have violated the SPS Agreement could take to become compliant with WTO law.[1210]

2.2.1. Identification of the appropriate level of protection

Interpreting Art. 5.6 SPS involves a decision on who has to identify the appropriate level of protection and how. The stance taken by the Appellate Body since *Australia – Salmon* is in this respect very clear, at least verbally: WTO Members have to identify the level of protection that they wish to achieve through the SPS measures in dispute.[1211] It is sufficient for a Member to characterize its level of protection as, for example, "high" or "conservative".[1212] Panels or the Appellate Body are only allowed to base their findings on the level of protection as reflected in the measures at stake when a Member either states its desired level of protection imprecisely or

---

1207 *Australia – Measures Affecting the Importation of Apples from New Zealand, WT/DS367/AB/R* 2010, para. 339.

1208 Ibid., para. 340.

1209 Ibid., para. 354.

1210 Foster 2008, 435.

1211 The Appellate Body in *Australia – Measures Affecting Importation of Salmon, WT/DS18/AB/R* 1998, para. 198–206 with this statement explicitly overruled the Panel's decision in; *Australia – Measures Affecting Importation of Salmon, WT/DS18/R* 1998, para. 8.107; see also *Australia – Measures Affecting the Importation of Apples from New Zealand, WT/DS367/AB/R* 2010, para. 343; *United States – Continued Suspension of Obligations in the EC – Hormones Dispute, WT/DS320/AB/R* 2008, para. 523.

1212 This is what Australia did in the case concerning the importation of Salmon, see *Australia – Measures Affecting Importation of Salmon, WT/DS18/R* 1998, para. 8.107.

fails to state it explicitly.[1213] Despite this seemingly unambiguous stance, the Panel in the subsequent report on *Japan – Agricultural Products* did not consider whether it was entitled to infer the level of protection reached by the Japanese measure from the measure itself.[1214] Given that the Appellate Body seems to regard the characterization of an appropriate level as, for example, "conservative" as sufficiently precise, one also wonders what might constitute an imprecise description.

In practice, it is no easy task to determine whether a specific measure reaches a level of protection that is characterized in more or less vague terms. Adjudicators have sometimes pointed to practical difficulties with such a qualitative description of the level of protection. For example, the compliance Panel in *Australia – Salmon* was seemingly puzzled by one of the Appellate Body's findings, and noted, in an unusually critical tone, that:

> "[...] although, according to the Appellate Body, Australia determined its ALOP with sufficient precision to apply Article 5.6, we find it rather difficult to evaluate whether any of the options before us would also meet Australia's somewhat vaguely determined level of 'a high or very conservative level' [...]"

adding further that

> "parenthetically, that a more explicit and in particular a quantitative expression of a Member's ALOP would greatly facilitate the consideration of compliance with not only Article 5.6 but with other provisions of the SPS Agreement as well".[1215]

Nonetheless, the Panel then undertook to investigate the matter based on Australia's qualitative description of its level of protection as it had to.

1213 *Australia – Measures Affecting Importation of Salmon, WT/DS18/AB/R* 1998, para. 207.

1214 *Japan – Measures Affecting Agricultural Products, WT/DS76/R* 1998, para. 8.82. This may, however, be attributable to the fact that both reports were published within one week's interval. The Appellate Body in the *Japan – Agricultural Products* case did not discuss the issue, either.

1215 *Australia – Measures Affecting Importation of Salmon, WT/DS18/RW* 2000, para. 7.129.

2.2.2. Not more trade-restrictive than required

Once the (difficult) hurdle of determining the appropriate level of protection with enough precision has been overcome, the next step is to determine whether the measure is not more trade-restrictive than required to achieve this level. The Appellate Body has emphasized that this is indeed the SPS order of things: the appropriate level of protection determines the SPS measure rather than vice versa.[1216]

The details of Art. 5.6 are contained in a footnote accompanying the article:

> For purposes of paragraph 6 of Article 5, a measure is not more trade-restrictive than required unless there is another measure, reasonably available taking into account technical and economic feasibility, that achieves the appropriate level of sanitary or phytosanitary protection and is significantly less restrictive to trade.

The Panel and the Appellate Body in *Australia – Salmon* developed a three-pronged test[1217] on this basis, suggesting that Art. 5.6 SPS is violated if an alternative SPS measure exists that

> "1) is reasonably available taking into account technical and economic feasibility ; and
> 2) achieves the Member's appropriate level of protection; and
> 3) is significantly less trade-restrictive than the SPS measure contested."

A question logically preceding this test is which alternative SPS measures are to be considered by the adjudicators and who is to suggest them. In *Australia – Salmon* and *Australia – Apples*, the Panels considered alternative measures that had been assessed by the respective defendant party in its risk assessment.[1218] The claimants then invoked these as alternative mea-

---

1216 *United States – Continued Suspension of Obligations in the EC – Hormones Dispute, WT/DS320/AB/R* 2008, para. 523.

1217 *Australia – Measures Affecting Importation of Salmon, WT/DS18/AB/R* 1998, para. 194.

1218 *Australia – Measures Affecting Importation of Salmon, WT/DS18/R* 1998, para. 8.168; *Australia – Measures Affecting the Importation of Apples from New Zealand, WT/DS367/AB/R* 2010, para. 330 describing the approach by the Panel in the same case.

sures under Art. 5.6 SPS.[1219] In other cases, the complainants did not rely on the risk assessment previously undertaken by the defendant. For example, in the compliance dispute in *Australia – Salmon* the complainants suggested alternative measures without relying on a prior risk assessment.[1220] In *Japan – Agricultural Products* the claimant proposed an alternative measure,[1221] but the Panel also examined other alternatives suggested by the experts it had consulted. The parties were given an opportunity to comment on the latter.[1222] The Panel finally found one of the alternatives suggested by the experts to comply with the requirements of Art. 5.6 SPS and that there had therefore been a violation of this norm,[1223] although the US had not – actively – argued for that particular alternative measure and demonstrated it was technically and economically feasible, less trade-restrictive than the measure in place, and attained Japan's desired level of protection.[1224] The Appellate Body did not accept the Panel's approach, stating that the US had failed to establish a *prima facie* case under Art. 5.6 SPS.[1225] In *Australia – Apples*, the complainant suggested some alternative measures that had also been considered by the defendant in its risk assessment.[1226] The Panel did not consider some of the alternatives suggested by the complainant as it did not think that the complainant had demonstrated that the proposed alternatives fulfilled all the requirements of Art. 5.6 SPS.[1227] In practice, this means that the complaining party has to come forward with possible alternatives unless it wants to run the risk of losing for lack of a *prima facie* case. Therefore, the Appellate Body's statement that the complainant is not obliged to suggest alternative measures[1228] appears to be of little practical significance. It does, however, appear to be sufficient for the claimant to rely on alternative measures evalu-

---

1219 *Australia – Measures Affecting Importation of Salmon, WT/DS18/R* 1998, para. 8.169.

1220 See *Australia – Measures Affecting Importation of Salmon, WT/DS18/RW* 2000, para. 7.119.

1221 *Japan – Measures Affecting Agricultural Products, WT/DS76/R* 1998, para. 8.65.

1222 Ibid., para. 8.74ff.

1223 Ibid., para. 8.103, 8.104.

1224 This was acknowledged by the Panel itself in ibid., nn. 328, 332, 333.

1225 *Japan – Measures Affecting Agricultural Products, WT/DS76/AB/R* 1999, para. 126.

1226 See *Australia – Measures Affecting the Importation of Apples from New Zealand, WT/DS367/AB/R* 2010, para. 330.

1227 *Australia – Measures Affecting the Importation of Apples from New Zealand, WT/DS367/R* 2010, para. 7.1119.

1228 *Japan – Measures Affecting the Importation of Apples, WT/DS245/AB/R* 2003, para. 70.

ated in the risk assessment undertaken by its adversary when making such suggestions.

The first[1229] of the three steps in the test did not prove especially controversial.[1230] The *Australia – Salmon* compliance Panel found a measure that was used in a third country to be reasonably available and feasible.[1231] In *Japan – Agricultural Products*, the Panel considered the arguments of the parties and the experts' views, but then decided that it did not have enough evidence to find that a proposed measure was feasible and less-trade restrictive than the measure in place. It did not, therefore, elaborate on the content of this formula nor take any position on the parties' arguments.[1232]

The second criterion, namely that the alternative measure must reach the desired level of protection, concerns the suitability of the measure for this purpose. A first issue here is how to identify the level of protection that alternative measures would reach, which must be compared to that reached by the measure in place. While describing the level of protection at which the measure in place is aimed is the task of the defending WTO Member, identifying the level of protection implicit in alternative measures is the task of the Panels.[1233]

Once the desired level of protection is established, the question is whether alternative measures would reach it. Both the parties and the adjudicators refer to science when discussing this issue.[1234] The Appellate Body stated in one case that it could not

> "conceive of how a complainant could satisfy its burden of demonstrating that its proposed alternative measure would meet the appro-

---

1229 Sometimes, the three elements have been investigated in a different order; for example *Australia – Measures Affecting Importation of Salmon, WT/DS18/RW* 2000, para. 7.127 first investigated whether the alternative measure would reach the desired level of protection.

1230 For example, in *Australia – Apples* the defending party did not contest that the measures suggested by the complainant were feasible, see *Australia – Measures Affecting the Importation of Apples from New Zealand, WT/DS367/AB/R* 2010, para. 331f; see also Schebesta and Sinopoli 2018, 132.

1231 *Australia – Measures Affecting Importation of Salmon, WT/DS18/RW* 2000, para. 7.147.

1232 *Japan – Measures Affecting Agricultural Products, WT/DS76/R* 1998, para. 8.89.

1233 *Australia – Measures Affecting the Importation of Apples from New Zealand, WT/DS367/AB/R* 2010, para. 344.

1234 *European Communities – Measures Concerning Meat and Meat Products, WT/DS26/AB/R, WT/DS48/AB/R* 1998, para 75, 78; *Japan – Measures Affecting Agricultural Products, WT/DS76/R* 1998, para. 8.64, 8.83.

priate level of protection under Article 5.6 without relying on evidence that is scientific in nature."[1235]

Hence, there is a close link between this element of Art. 5.6 SPS and the risk assessment conducted under Art. 5.1 SPS; the risk assessment under Art. 5.1 SPS must, according to the case law, also evaluate possible alternative measures which some of the claimants consequently evoked as possible alternative measures under Art. 5.6 SPS. While the obligations in Art. 5.1 SPS and Art. 5.6 SPS are independent of each other, "factual elements relevant to the analysis under one provision may also be relevant to the analysis under the other provision".[1236] Another way in which the risk assessment that is necessary under Art. 5.1 SPS can be used for the discussion of Art. 5.6 SPS is evident from the *Australia – Salmon* case. In that case, the compliance Panel found that the contested measure was not in its entirety based on a risk assessment and supported by scientific evidence. In its consideration of an alternative measure reaching the desired level of protection, it looked at the contested SPS measure but without the elements for which the defendant had not provided scientific evidence.[1237] In consequence, it could draw on the existing risk assessment when evaluating the alternative measure. The adjudicators consider that they are allowed to decide whether a measure reaches the defendant Member's level of protection,[1238] regardless of an argument put forward by Australia that asserted the opposite.[1239]

A somewhat curious statement on the adjudicators' role in ascertaining whether proposed alternative measures reach the desired level of protection can be found in the Appellate Body report in *Australia – Apples*. The Appellate Body here expressed "certain reservations" about the Panel's approach of asking scientific experts about their views as to whether the proposed alternative measures would reach the defendant's chosen level of protection. As a reason, the Appellate Body indicated that

1235 *Australia – Measures Affecting the Importation of Apples from New Zealand, WT/DS367/AB/R* 2010, para. 356.

1236 Ibid., para. 346f.

1237 *Australia – Measures Affecting Importation of Salmon, WT/DS18/RW* 2000, para. 7.132–7.137.

1238 This can be inferred from the practice of the Panels and the Appellate Body, but also from the text of the reports, see for example *Australia – Measures Affecting Importation of Salmon, WT/DS18/AB/R* 1998, para. 209–212.

1239 *Australia – Measures Affecting Importation of Salmon, WT/DS18/R* 1998, para. 8.172.

> "whether or not an alternative measure's level of risk achieves a Member's appropriate level of protection is a question of legal characterization [...]. Answering this question is not a task that can be delegated to scientific experts."[1240]

This statement is surprising, because whether a measure secures an envisaged level of protection appears to be a factual, not a legal question. This is not only suggested by common sense, but is also the understanding underlying the SPS Agreement: Art. 5.1, 5.2 require a certain type of factual evidence to demonstrate that a measure reaches a desired level of protection; in other words, the link that is required between a measure and risk is clearly a factual one. There is no reason why the situation should be different with regard to alternative measures under Art. 5.6 SPS.

Altogether, the task for the complaining party under Art. 5.6 SPS is more arduous than under Art. 5.1 or Art. 2.2 SPS. Under Art. 2.2 and 5.1 SPS it needs to establish a *prima facie* case that there is not sufficient scientific evidence that the contested SPS measure is suitable for reaching the regulatory objective. Under Art. 5.6 SPS, second element, it needs to demonstrate that an alternative measure is – positively – suitable for reaching the level of protection of the defendant.[1241] In other words, it will be easier for a respondent to defend itself again a claim of violation concerning Art. 5.6 SPS than with regard to Art. 5.1 SPS. There are several cases where the dispute settlement bodies have rejected alternative measures as they did not appear sufficient to reach the level of protection envisaged by the defending WTO Member.[1242] Art. 5.6 SPS seems to be applied in such a manner as to be protective of WTO Members' regulatory space.

With regard to the last element, the significantly less-trade restrictive effect of the alternative measure, much fine-tuning has yet to take place. The issue was either not contentious or an import ban was compared to a situation where imports were allowed under certain conditions, which made it easy to conclude that one measure was significantly more trade-restrictive than the other. There are some indications to be found in the case law regarding how to determine whether an alternative measure is significantly less trade-restrictive than the contested measure, even in less clear-cut cases:

1240 *Australia – Measures Affecting the Importation of Apples from New Zealand, WT/DS367/AB/R* 2010, para. 384.

1241 See *Japan – Measures Affecting Agricultural Products, WT/DS76/R* 1998, para. 8.82.

1242 Du 2010a, 1088 pointing to *Australia – Salmon* and *Japan – Agricultural Products*.

one possibility is showing that there is a demand for a certain product in the country imposing restrictions[1243] – such a demand makes it likely that the removal of the contested measure would lead to an increase in imports.

2.3. Art. 5.5, 2.3 SPS

Art. 2.3 SPS and Art. 5.5 SPS are similar in that they both relate to arbitrary or unjustifiable discrimination.

On the relationship between the two articles, the Appellate Body in *Australia – Salmon* stated that a finding of a violation of Art. 5.5 SPS would "necessarily imply" a violation of either of the first or the second sentence of Art. 2.3 SPS.[1244] In a similar vein, the Panel in *Australia – Apples* stated that the complainant had failed to demonstrate that the impugned measure was inconsistent with Art. 5.5 SPS and "consequently" also failed with regard to Art. 2.3 SPS.[1245] This relationship does not appear to be entirely reciprocal, however, as the Appellate Body in *Australia – Salmon* also found that arbitrary or unjustifiable discrimination in the sense of Art. 2.3 SPS "can be found to exist without any examination under Art. 5.5."[1246]

In other cases, Art. 2.3 SPS has not played a significant role of its own, but rather been used as context for the interpretation of Art. 5.5 SPS.[1247] In the following, I will first discuss Art. 5.5 SPS as the more detailed and practically more relevant norm and then turn to Art. 2.3 SPS.

2.3.1. Art. 5.5 SPS

Art. 5.5 SPS contains a consistency requirement, extending to internal consistency (i.e. the consistency of a measure employed vis-à-vis other states

1243 This is what the Panel accepted as valid reason in *Australia – Measures Affecting Importation of Salmon, WT/DS18/RW* 2000, para. 7.150–7.152.

1244 *Australia – Measures Affecting Importation of Salmon, WT/DS18/AB/R* 1998, para. 252.

1245 Panel's findings as quoted by the Appellate Body in *Australia – Measures Affecting the Importation of Apples from New Zealand, WT/DS367/AB/R* 2010, para. 7.

1246 *Australia – Measures Affecting Importation of Salmon, WT/DS18/AB/R* 1998, para. 252.

1247 *Australia – Measures Affecting Importation of Salmon, WT/DS18/R* 1998, para. 8.109, 8.160.

and one applied to the domestic market) as well as external consistency (i.e. the consistency of measures applied vis-à-vis different other states).[1248] The Appellate Body has made clear that the standard set by Art. 5.5 SPS is not one of absolute or perfect consistency, but rather the avoidance of arbitrary or unjustifiable inconsistencies.[1249]

It has by now been established that for an SPS measure to violate Art. 5.5 SPS three elements must be present.[1250] A Member acts inconsistently with Art. 5.5 SPS if

1) the Member concerned adopts different appropriate levels of sanitary protection in several different situations, and
2) those levels of protection exhibit differences which are arbitrary or unjustifiable, and
3) the measure embodying those differences results in discrimination or a disguised restriction on international trade.[1251]

Different levels of protection in different situations

With regard to the first element, the adoption of different levels of protection in different situations, it is obvious that the situations compared need to be comparable. Situations have been characterized as comparable when they involve a similar disease or similar associated biological and economic consequences (in the case of a risk assessment in the sense of the first alternative)[1252] or the same substance or the same adverse health effect (in the case of a risk assessment in the sense of the second alternative).[1253] That both are relevant criteria is confirmed by "Guidelines to Further the Practi-

---

1248 Pardo Quintillán 1999, 167.

1249 *European Communities – Measures Concerning Meat and Meat Products, WT/DS26/AB/R, WT/DS48/AB/R* 1998, para. 213.

1250 *European Communities – Measures Concerning Meat and Meat Products, WT/DS26/R* 1997, para. 8.175; *Australia – Measures Affecting Importation of Salmon, WT/DS18/R* 1998, para. 8.108.

1251 *European Communities – Measures Concerning Meat and Meat Products, WT/DS26/AB/R, WT/DS48/AB/R* 1998, para. 214.

1252 *Australia – Measures Affecting Importation of Salmon, WT/DS18/AB/R* 1998, para. 146.

1253 *European Communities – Measures Concerning Meat and Meat Products, WT/DS26/AB/R, WT/DS48/AB/R* 1998, para. 216.

cal Implementation of Article 5.5" adopted by the SPS Committee.[1254] The comparison undertaken by the adjudicators between two situations is specific to those situations,[1255] i.e. several comparisons between different situations may be undertaken in one decision.

A passage in the Panel report in *Australia – Salmon* suggests that the comparability of several situations is not necessarily an either/or-issue, but could also be a matter of degree: step 3 of the test, where the existence of a discrimination or disguised restriction on international trade is at issue, would appear to necessitate the consideration of the degree to which the situations are comparable.[1256] It appears that the standard for the comparability of situations under Art. 5.5 SPS is not overly strict, however:[1257] situations have been held as comparable even when it was not entirely clear precisely which diseases could occur in both situations and when the diseases had not actually been detected in both situations.[1258]

Once it has been established that there are comparable situations, differences in the levels of protection applied respectively must be found for a violation of Art. 5.5 SPS. In order to identify the existence of such differences, the level of protection appropriate to each situation must be ascertained. The way in which this might be achieved is also a troubling issue under Art. 5.6 SPS. In one case a party made a respective claim,[1259] which led the Panel to proffer some statements on the issue. It came to the conclusion that the SPS Agreement did not oblige WTO Members to identify or quantify their levels of protection. It therefore felt entitled to rely on the level of protection visible from the SPS measure in its finding,[1260] a level

1254 See WTO Committee on Sanitary and Phytosanitary Measures, Guidelines to Further the Practical Implementation of Article 5.5, 18 July 2000 G/SPS/15, section A 2.

1255 See for example *Australia – Measures Affecting Importation of Salmon, WT/DS18/RW* 2000, para. 7.96-7.99.

1256 *Australia – Measures Affecting Importation of Salmon, WT/DS18/R* 1998, para. 8.119; in this case, the question was whether for two situations to be comparable all of the possible diseases needed to occur in both situations compared or whether it was sufficient that only some of the diseases that might occur in one situation would also occur in the other. The Panel decided for the latter.

1257 See also Pauwelyn 1999, 654.

1258 *Australia – Measures Affecting Importation of Salmon, WT/DS18/AB/R* 1998, para. 150, 230.

1259 See Canada's arguments in *Australia – Measures Affecting Importation of Salmon, WT/DS18/R* 1998, para. 8.105.

1260 Ibid., para. 8.107, 8.123–8.129.

which differed from the characterization offered by the defending WTO Member. In the same case, the Appellate Body failed to touch upon this point – at least not in the context of Art. 5.5 SPS.[1261] In *Hormones I* the Panel simply deduced the level of protection from the measures that were at stake,[1262] and as its approach was not appealed by the parties it was not reconsidered by the Appellate Body.[1263]

In *Australia – Apples*, Art. 5.5 SPS was only discussed by the Panel, as the findings on Art. 5.5 SPS were not subject to appeal. In this case, the Panel observed that Australia had stated very generically that for all comparable situations it aimed at a high level of protection, but not at zero risk.[1264] The Panel then went on to state that the defendant should not be allowed to "hide" behind such a generic statement, as this would "diminish" Art. 5.5 SPS.[1265] It assessed whether there were different levels of protection by looking at both the measures applied and the risks against which such measures were applied.[1266] However, it performed this test under the second step of the test.[1267] It then compared a range of factors for a series of comparable situations in great detail; the measure at issue was a phytosanitary one. The factors included in the analysis, either as proposed by the parties or considered relevant on the basis of the scientific experts' opinions were the following: the facility of transmission of two pests; the potential biological and economic consequences of the pests; the range of host plants, the presence of pests in the exporting areas; the presence of pests in the defendant (importing) state, and the volume of trade.[1268] Ultimately it did not find that different levels of protection existed.

1261 See *Australia – Measures Affecting Importation of Salmon, WT/DS18/AB/R* 1998, para. 143–153.

1262 *European Communities – Measures Concerning Meat and Meat Products, WT/DS26/R* 1997, para. 8.188–8.191, 8.211–8.213.

1263 See *European Communities – Measures Concerning Meat and Meat Products, WT/DS26/AB/R, WT/DS48/AB/R* 1998, para. 218ff.

1264 *Australia – Measures Affecting the Importation of Apples from New Zealand, WT/DS367/R* 2010, para. 7.963.

1265 Ibid., para. 7.970f.

1266 Ibid., para. 7.979.

1267 Ibid., para. 7.987.

1268 Ibid., para. 7.994, 7.1049.

Arbitrary or unjustifiable difference in levels of protection

On the second prong, a review takes place whether the differences in levels of protection are arbitrary or unjustifiable. It is not clear at the present state of the case law if there is any difference in meaning concerning these two terms.[1269]

Generally, a difference in levels of protection is considered arbitrary or unjustifiable when no justification for it can be found.[1270] The way the relation between the first two prongs is construed by the dispute settlement bodies is familiar from other legal norms requiring equal treatment. The existence of differences in levels of protection does not suffice *eo ipso* for a finding that the differences are arbitrary or unjustifiable. In the review stage of *Australia – Salmon*, the Panel found that general statements by the complainant pointing out that different measures applied in different situations did not constitute a *prima facie* case of the violation of the norm, while at the same time both experts and the defendant offered some explanations for these differences.[1271]

With regard to the justification of differences in levels of protection, the Panel in *Hormones I* seemed to be of the view that the larger the differences were, the stronger the justification needed to be.[1272] In the same dispute, the Appellate Body's indication of why it considered certain reasons given by the defendant sufficient justification for the difference in levels of protection was rather short. After repeating the arguments of the EU, the Appellate Body simply expressed its conviction that "on balance" the differences in levels of protection between situations A and B were not arbitrary or unjustifiable.[1273] The Appellate Body then reviewed the Panel's finding that situations A and C were different. Here it concurred with the Panel's

---

1269 Du 2010a, 1085.

1270 *Australia – Measures Affecting Importation of Salmon, WT/DS18/R* 1998, para. 8.133; *European Communities – Measures Concerning Meat and Meat Products, WT/DS26/R* 1997, para. 8.192ff; the Appellate Body also follows this approach in *European Communities – Measures Concerning Meat and Meat Products, WT/DS26/AB/R, WT/DS48/AB/R* 1998, para. 219–235, albeit stating so only casually in para. 221.

1271 *Australia – Measures Affecting Importation of Salmon, WT/DS18/RW* 2000, para. 7.90ff.

1272 *European Communities – Measures Concerning Meat and Meat Products, WT/DS26/R* 1997, para. 8.196; see also Du 2010a, 1085 for a similar reading of this decision.

1273 *European Communities – Measures Concerning Meat and Meat Products, WT/DS26/AB/R, WT/DS48/AB/R* 1998, para. 225.

finding that the differences were unjustifiable, without making clear precisely why. It confined itself to relating the arguments of the parties and findings of the Panel before expressing its agreement with the Panel's conclusions.[1274] This has led one observer to conclude that if a defending party can provide reasonable explanations for the difference, the Appellate Body will accept it and not find the differences to be arbitrary or unjustifiable.[1275] In *Australia – Salmon*, the Appellate Body only discussed the second element of Art. 5.5 SPS very briefly, as the Panel had found that the level of protection applied actually seemed to be lower for situations that presented a higher risk than the one addressed by the controversial Australian measure.[1276]

Discrimination or disguised restriction on international trade

The first question with regard to the third element is whether Art. 5.5 SPS has to be interpreted in the same way as Art. XX GATT chapeau, which also contains the phrase "discrimination between countries where the same conditions prevail, or a disguised restriction on international trade". The Panel in *Hormones I* assumed so and used the existing interpretation of Art. XX under Art. 5.5 SPS as well.[1277] It also referred to the Appellate Body's interpretation of Art. III:2 GATT.[1278] The Appellate Body rejected this attempted interpretative cross-fertilization due to the differences between these norms and Art. 5.5 SPS.[1279]

According to the Appellate Body, the last element of Art. 5.5 SPS warrants a case-by-case approach. Several factors, warning signals or indicators may cumulate in the finding of a violation.[1280] If the first two elements are present, this may be an indicator that also the third element is present.[1281]

1274 Ibid., para. 227–235.
1275 Du 2010a, 1085.
1276 *Australia – Measures Affecting Importation of Salmon, WT/DS18/AB/R* 1998, para. 234f.
1277 *European Communities – Measures Concerning Meat and Meat Products, WT/DS26/R* 1997, para. 8.181, 8.184.
1278 Ibid., para. 8.183.
1279 *European Communities – Measures Concerning Meat and Meat Products, WT/DS26/AB/R, WT/DS48/AB/R* 1998, para. 239.
1280 Ibid., para. 240.
1281 Ibid., para. 215; *Australia – Measures Affecting Importation of Salmon, WT/DS18/AB/R* 1998, para. 161–164.

Yet the Appellate Body has made clear that the fact that there are arbitrary or unjustifiable differences in levels of protection in different situations does not suffice for finding a violation of Art. 5.5 SPS, even where the differences in levels of protection are significant.[1282] It stated that all three elements of Art. 5.5 SPS had to be taken seriously and hence to be examined separately.[1283]

The Appellate Body stated that a lack of scientific justification was a strong indicator that a measure constituted a disguised restriction on international trade,[1284] and has accepted the following factors as also being indicative of a violation of Art. 5.5 SPS:[1285] the arbitrary or unjustifiable character and the magnitude of differences of levels of protection; differences between the draft and the final version of a risk assessment where no scientific justification for such a change could be presented by the defendant, and the absence of internal controls comparable to those applied externally. Given the number of potentially relevant factors, the adjudicators have considerable leeway in deciding whether a discrimination or disguised restriction on international trade is present. What contributes further to the impression that the yardstick used under the third element of Art. 5.5 SPS is rather pliable, is the fact that Panelists do not always seem to attribute the same weight to each of these factors.[1286]

In *Hormones I* the Appellate Body had the opportunity to clarify what factors, on the other hand, might indicate that despite an unjustifiable or arbitrary distinction in levels of protection there was no discrimination or disguised restriction on international trade. It found that both proven consumers' anxieties with regard to hormone-treated beef and the need for the internal harmonization of the common market were convincing rationales for the observed differences in levels of protection. Therefore, the Appellate Body did not share the Panel's conclusion that the EU measures were

---

1282 *Australia – Measures Affecting Importation of Salmon, WT/DS18/AB/R* 1998, para. 164, 177.

1283 *European Communities – Measures Concerning Meat and Meat Products, WT/DS26/AB/R, WT/DS48/AB/R* 1998, para. 215.

1284 *Australia – Measures Affecting Importation of Salmon, WT/DS18/AB/R* 1998, para. 166.

1285 See ibid., para. 161–177; *European Communities – Measures Concerning Meat and Meat Products, WT/DS26/AB/R, WT/DS48/AB/R* 1998, para. 215.

1286 Compare *Australia – Measures Affecting Importation of Salmon, WT/DS18/RW* 2000, para. 7.93, 7.104 on the one hand and; *Australia – Measures Affecting Importation of Salmon, WT/DS18/R* 1998, para. 8.155-8.157. The difference between both becomes even more remarkable when considering that both cases were handled by the same Panelists.

> "not really designed to protect its population from the risk of cancer, but rather to keep out US and Canadian hormone-treated beef and thereby to protect the domestic beef producers in the European Communities".[1287]

The justifications accepted by the Appellate Body are plainly subjective, i.e. the Appellate Body is trying to ascertain the motivation of the legislators at the time the measure was enacted.[1288] At the same time, the Appellate Body also referred to more objective criteria, namely the architecture and structure of the disputed measures.

A final point regarding the last element of Art. 5.5 SPS is the difference between discrimination on the one hand and a disguised restriction on international trade on the other. In the dispute settlement reports, it is rarely stated explicitly which of the terms is actually used for testing the contested measures. This is all the more surprising as in some cases the parties to the dispute based their legal arguments on the distinction between both.[1289] Scholars assume that the difference between a disguised restriction on international trade and discrimination is that the former requires protectionist intent of the government enacting the measure, i.e. a subjective element, whereas discrimination is a purely objective standard.[1290] The WTO judicial bodies have, however, not given any indications in this direction. In *Australia – Salmon* the Appellate Body and the compliance Panel only discussed the existence of a disguised restriction on international trade.[1291]

2.3.2. Art. 2.3 SPS

Art. 2.3 SPS has not played a major role in WTO case law so far.

With regard to Art. 2.3 SPS, the compliance Panel in *Australia – Salmon* found that for a violation three elements had to be present:

1287 *European Communities – Measures Concerning Meat and Meat Products, WT/DS26/AB/R, WT/DS48/AB/R* 1998, para. 245f.

1288 A similar tendency can be found in *Australia – Measures Affecting Importation of Salmon, WT/DS18/RW* 2000, para. 7.106.

1289 See for example ibid., para. 4.19.

1290 Neugebauer 2000, 1265; Iynedjian 2002, 123.

1291 *Australia – Measures Affecting Importation of Salmon, WT/DS18/AB/R* 1998, para. 162, 166, 167; *Australia – Measures Affecting Importation of Salmon, WT/DS18/RW* 2000, para. 7.102–7.107.

"(1) the measure discriminates between the territories of Members other than the Member imposing the measure, or between the territory of the Member imposing the measure and that of another Member
(2) was arbitrary or unjustifiable and
(3) identical or similar conditions prevailed in the territory of the Members compared under the first step."[1292]

With regard to the first element, the Panel stated that the discrimination could be between the Member imposing the measure and another Member, but also between different other Members. Moreover, recalling the statement of the Appellate Body and the original dispute Panel that the finding of discrimination under Art. 5.5 SPS necessarily implied a finding of discrimination under Art. 2.3 SPS, it also found that – as under Art. 5.5 SPS – discrimination could not only be between countries, but also between different products.[1293] Concerning the second element, the Panel found that as there was no violation of the second element of Art. 5.5 SPS, it could not find a violation of the second element of Art. 2.3 SPS, either.[1294] The Panel thus aimed at reading both norms harmoniously. The last element of Art. 2.3 SPS can – by its text – be regarded as the negative of the last element under Art. 5.5 SPS. Certainly, the finding of the compliance Panel in *Australia – Salmon* supports such a reading. In this case – having ascertained that different situations in the sense of Art. 5.5 SPS, first element, existed – the Panel expressed doubts about whether identical or similar conditions in the sense of Art. 2.3 SPS, last element, existed.[1295]

It is not clear from *Australia – Salmon* whether the elements of Art. 2.3 SPS need to be reviewed in the order which the Panel followed in that case and whether – as under Art. 5.5 SPS – the violation of one element implies also a violation of the next one. If this were the case, Art. 2.3 SPS would follow a different logic than Art. 5.5 SPS. Under Art. 2.3, the first step is to decide whether there is discrimination and the third step is to ask whether identical or similar conditions prevail in the territory of the Members compared. Under Art. 5.5 SPS, however, the first step is to decide whether different situations are treated differently.

1292 *Australia – Measures Affecting Importation of Salmon, WT/DS18/RW* 2000, para. 7.111.
1293 Ibid., para. 7.112.
1294 Ibid., para. 7.113.
1295 Ibid.

2.4. Art. 3 SPS

In the words of the Appellate Body, the purpose of Art. 3 SPS is

> "to promote the harmonization of the SPS measures of Members on as wide a basis as possible, while recognizing and safeguarding, at the same time, the right and duty of Members to protect the life and health of their people."[1296]

Art. 3 SPS has not played a major role of its own in the cases that have been brought before the dispute settlement mechanism.[1297] Still, a couple of issues have been controversial in the context of Art. 3 SPS and shall therefore be discussed briefly in the following paragraphs.

In the following, I will first discuss the relationship between the various paragraphs of Art. 3 SPS as construed in the case law (section 2.4.1.) and then summarize the case law on the interpretation of certain norms (section 2.4.2).

2.4.1. Relationship between Art. 3.1, 3.2, 3.3 SPS

This section presents the case law on the relationship between the various paragraphs of Art. 3 SPS. This relationship was outlined by the Appellate Body in *Hormones I*. Accordingly, Art. 3.2 SPS deals with SPS measures conforming to international standards, guidelines or recommendations. Such measures enjoy a rebuttable presumption of consistency with the SPS Agreement and the GATT.[1298]

Art. 3.1 SPS deals with measures that do not conform to, but are based on[1299] international standards, guidelines or recommendations. Such measures do not benefit from a similar presumption as contained in Art. 3.2 SPS, i.e. they must comply with the disciplines of the SPS Agree-

---

1296 *European Communities – Measures Concerning Meat and Meat Products, WT/DS26/AB/R, WT/DS48/AB/R* 1998, para. 177.

1297 It was discussed in *Hormones I* and *Australia – Salmon*. In none of those cases, however, a violation of either of the paragraphs of this article was found in the Appellate Body report.

1298 *European Communities – Measures Concerning Meat and Meat Products, WT/DS26/AB/R, WT/DS48/AB/R* 1998, para. 170.

1299 See the next section for the differences between "based on" and "conform to".

ment.[1300] Still, the Appellate Body has held that Art. 3.1 SPS is a right of WTO Members rather than an exception to Art. 3.2 SPS.[1301] This is relevant for the burden of proof: If Art. 3.1 SPS is a right, the complaining Member must bring a *prima facie* case of its violation, and only then must the defending Member rebut that case. If it is an exception, the onus is on the defending Member.

Finally, the Appellate Body also dealt with Art. 3.3 SPS in *Hormones I*. Art. 3.3 SPS reads:

> "Members may introduce or maintain sanitary or phytosanitary measures which result in a higher level of sanitary or phytosanitary protection than would be achieved by measures based on the relevant international standards, guidelines or recommendations, if there is a scientific justification, or as a consequence of the level of sanitary or phytosanitary protection a Member determines to be appropriate in accordance with the relevant provisions of paragraphs 1 through 8 of Article 5. Notwithstanding the above, all measures which result in a level of sanitary or phytosanitary protection different from that which would be achieved by measures based on international standards, guidelines or recommendations shall not be inconsistent with any other provision of this Agreement."

The footnote ad Art. 3.3 SPS says:

> "For the purposes of paragraph 3 of Article 3, there is a scientific justification if, on the basis of an examination and evaluation of available scientific information in conformity with the relevant provisions of this Agreement, a Member determines that the relevant international standards, guidelines or recommendations are not sufficient to achieve its appropriate level of sanitary or phytosanitary protection."

The Appellate Body stated that, contrary to the Panel's assumption, the norm was not an exception to Art. 3.1 SPS, but rather it offered Members an independent right to enact or maintain SPS measures.[1302] The relationship between Art. 3.1. and 3.3 SPS is relevant for who bears the burden of proof.[1303]

1300 *United States – Continued Suspension of Obligations in the EC – Hormones Dispute, WT/DS320/AB/R* 2008, para. 532.

1301 *European Communities – Measures Concerning Meat and Meat Products, WT/DS26/AB/R, WT/DS48/AB/R* 1998, para. 171.

1302 Ibid., para. 172.

1303 See ibid., para. 104.

Art. 3.3 SPS covers – textually – two constellations. The first sentence refers to measures resulting in a

> "higher level of sanitary or phytosanitary protection than would be achieved by measures based on the relevant international standards, guidelines or recommendations";

the second sentence refers to

> "all measures which result in a level of sanitary or phytosanitary protection different from that which would be achieved by measures based on international standards".

The first sentence, in turn, differentiates between two ways of justifying a higher level of protection than that achieved by international standards; there can be either a "scientific justification" or one in which it is

> "a consequence of the level of [...] protection a Member determines to be appropriate in accordance with the relevant provisions" of Art. 5 SPS.[1304]

Even though the first sentence of Art. 3.3 SPS makes a distinction between two situations, the Appellate Body found that in neither of the two situations were Members relieved of the duty to comply with the requirements of Art. 5 SPS.[1305] It based this conclusion on the second sentence of the norm, which says that "all measures [...] shall not be inconsistent with any other provision of the Agreement"[1306], and the definition of "scientific justification" in the footnote *ad* Art. 3.3 SPS. The Appellate Body noted that this interpretation basically erased the distinction made between various situations in Art. 3.3 SPS, but found that on the basis of the text of the norm it had "no choice" but to adopt this interpretation.[1307]

To summarize: Art. 3.2 and 3.3 SPS cover two distinct situations.[1308] An SPS measure might conform to an international standard and then benefit from the (rebuttable) presumption in Art. 3.2 SPS of being compliant with both the GATT and the SPS Agreement. In this case, the Member's com-

---

1304 Ibid., para. 175.

1305 Ibid., para. 177.

1306 Obviously, this is a very awkward formulation from a grammatical point of view; it would be more correct to say that "no measure shall be inconsistent" with the SPS Agreement. The Appellate Body also quite openly criticized what appears to be a very poor drafting of Art. 3.2, see ibid., para. 175.

1307 Ibid., para. 176.

1308 Iynedjian 2002, para. 70, 77; Slotboom 1999, 483ff.

pliance with Art. 2 and 5 SPS is presumed. In all other cases – an SPS measure is based on an international standard or deviates from it – the measure must conform to all other norms of the SPS Agreement.

2.4.2. Interpretation of certain clauses in Art. 3.1, 3.2 SPS

Having set out the general structure of Art. 3 SPS as conceived of by the adjudicators, I will in the following look at the interpretation of two issues: the terms "based on" and "conform to" and the differences between them and what counts as an international standard for purposes of Art. 3 SPS.

Based on – conform to

A first topic is the interpretation of the terms "based on" and "conform to" which are contained in Art. 3.1, 3.3 and 3.2 SPS respectively. In line with its general interpretative approach, the Appellate Body stressed the differences between both terms. Accordingly, "based on" represents a less strict standard than "conform to". For a measure to be "based on" a standard, only some of the elements of the standard need to be part of the measure in question.[1309] By way of contrast, an SPS measure that "conforms to" a standard would

> "embody the international standard completely and, for practical purposes, converts it into a municipal standard".[1310]

Existence of international standards

A second issue is the existence of a pertinent international standard. What a relevant international standard is can be deduced from Annex A, Art. 3 SPS. So far there is little in clarifying case law.

A point to note is that the Panel in *Hormones I* apparently assumed that it does not matter, for the purposes of WTO law, what happened in the

---

1309 *European Communities – Measures Concerning Meat and Meat Products, WT/DS26/AB/R, WT/DS48/AB/R* 1998, para. 163.

1310 Ibid., para. 170.

course of the adoption of the standards and whether the procedural requirements laid down by the competent international organizations themselves were observed.[1311]

An issue sometimes raised in the literature is whether non-WTO treaties could constitute an international standard. However, this issue has not yet been discussed in WTO case law as the parties to the SPS disputes where the argument might have been brought up have not actually used it.[1312]

2.5. Discussion of case law on the SPS Agreement

In the following, I will discuss some aspects of overarching significance in the interpretation of the SPS Agreement, focusing on legal-doctrinal aspects. As in the summary of the case law above, I deliberately leave aside some issues that have only become relevant in limited circumstances, notably whether the Panel in the *EC – Biotech Products* was right in applying the SPS Agreement.[1313] It should also be noted that some aspects discussed in the following sections, especially the concept of risk and the issue of precaution, are linked to the standard of review, which is investigated in more depth in the next chapter.[1314]

2.5.1. The concepts of science, risk, and risk assessment

In the SPS Agreement, science is the prime arbiter of whether a measure constitutes disguised protectionism or legitimate health protection. Science not only plays a role in connection with the explicit scientific evidence requirements in Art. 5.1 and 2.2 SPS, but it is also of relevance under Art. 5.5 and 5.6 SPS which are not, *prima facie*, written in the language of science. Science is accorded such a crucial role based on the understanding that it is neutral and universal and therefore suitable for separating the wheat from the chaff, or illegitimate protectionist measures from measures

1311 *European Communities – Measures Concerning Meat and Meat Products, WT/DS26/R* 1997, para. 8.67f; the Appellate Body does not take any position on the matter.

1312 For example Wirth 2006, 192 observes that the EU in EC - Biotech Products did not make the point that the Cartagena Protocol on Biosafety was an international standard.

1313 On this topic see Conrad 2007; Peel 2013.

1314 See chapter 3, section 2.1.

genuinely motivated by health concerns.[1315] Other rationales for using science in the SPS Agreement may be contributing to the harmonization of WTO Members' SPS measures as well as reducing trade barriers by requiring that measures be supported by a specific type of rationale.[1316] Which of these functions science ultimately fulfils under the SPS Agreement depends on the way the science-related provisions are interpreted by the WTO adjudicators.[1317] The concept of science adopted by the tribunals, and the way in which they interpret the science-related disciplines, must therefore have a significant impact on how much regulatory leeway WTO Members enjoy, and the extent to which health concerns may triumph over trade, particularly when there is an absence of unequivocal scientific evidence. The same applies to "risks" that science is to assess, according to the conception of the SPS Agreement. It is therefore worth looking at what concepts of science, risk and risk assessment have been adopted by the adjudicators. This has been the subject of no little debate in the literature.

There is little to say about the way the Appellate Body interprets these concepts from a strict legal-dogmatic point of view. After all, while the SPS Agreement gives a definition of risk assessment, neither science or risk are defined in the SPS Agreement nor are they established legal concepts. Nonetheless, given the centrality of these concepts in ascertaining the legal status of WTO Members' SPS measures, it is worth summarizing and discussing the Appellate Body's understanding of these concepts, as evident from the case law. There are some aspects of the Appellate Body's findings on the science-related disciplines in the SPS Agreement that reflect a broad understanding of science and risk. The Appellate Body has acknowledged the following:

- Science does not necessarily produce monolithic conclusions. There may be a majority opinion, but equally well-founded minority opinions that a WTO Member could base its measures on

1315 On the "trans-legal" character of scientific knowledge, see generally Joerges 1997, 297; Hoekman, Bernard and Trachtman, Joel 2010 discuss whether the SPS Agreement is also to enhance the quality of national regulatory decision-making, in addition to being aimed at eliminating discrimination. They answer the question in the negative.

1316 For a brief overview of these different rationales, see Gruszczynski 2006, 25f.

1317 For example Winickoff et al. 2005, 91 note that the "SPS Agreement text is ambiguous about how the goals of harmonization and nondiscrimination should be balanced".

- Science uses a variety of methods, both quantitative and qualitative in nature
- The risks that are relevant for policy-making can not necessarily be ascertained by laboratory methods only; risks stemming from improper handling, i.e. real-world risks, can and should be taken into account
- Scientists cannot make statements with absolute certainty and a risk assessment is not required to produce such findings
- Scientific knowledge evolves over time.

Moreover, it was recognized in *Hormones II* that the chosen level of protection may not only influence how a risk assessment is conducted but also whether scientific evidence is insufficient in the sense of Art. 5.7 SPS. These aspects of the case law, to be found predominantly in appellate reports and reflecting a broad and informed understanding of science,[1318] have been positively received by many observers.[1319]

However, there are also more problematic aspects of the case law. One point is that it is doubtful whether there is sufficient acknowledgment of the fact that risk assessments are infused with the kind of value-driven decisions usually found in the sphere of risk management; science and values usually interact in a process of risk assessment.[1320] Values may influence, for example, the methods chosen to ascertain risk. Whether or not animal testing can be used to assess the risks from a certain pharmaceutical or cosmetic product is an obvious example; generally, choices and assumptions made in the course of a risk assessment depend upon the scientists carrying out the assessment and their beliefs and values. Risk assessment processes are also shaped by cultural preferences; as a consequence their results are not easily transferable from one regulatory system to another.[1321]

The insight that risk assessments are not an assumption- and value-free exercise is recognized in various international documents. A very relevant

---

1318 See for example with regard to the *Hormones I* decision Perez 1998, 572.

1319 See for example Du 2010a, 1083; Gruszczynski 2006, 27; Howse 2001, 65; Scott and Vos 2002, 275; however, some legal commentators close to industry considered the Appellate Body's approach too broad Quick and Blüthner 1999; Cho 2009a is also critical of some aspects of the Appellate Body's findings that others observers praise - for example, Cho criticizes the finding in *Hormones II* that a Member's level of protection could also inform scientific risk assessments as "enmeshing an objective scientific investigation with a subjective policy determination".

1320 Green and Epps 2007, 305; Foster 2008, 443; Gruszczynski 2006, 5; Herwig 2008, 830; Winickoff et al. 2005, 94.

1321 Winickoff et al. 2005, 106.

example in the WTO context are the Codex Alimentarius Commission's "Working principles for Risk Analysis"[1322]. The document states that a risk assessment report "should indicate any constraints, uncertainties, assumptions and their impact on the risk assessment. Minority opinions should also be recorded [...]".[1323] Similarly, the US Environmental Protection Agency (EPA) explicitly requires risk assessors to discuss uncertainties underlying the various steps in a risk assessment.[1324] In some jurisdictions, the insight that risk assessments are not value-free exercises and therefore need to be steered by bodies competent to make value and policy judgements has led to the adoption of what has been labelled "science policy" guidelines. Such guidelines require or permit risk assessors to use certain default assumptions, for example that a chemical substance that can cause cancer in laboratory animals can also do so in humans.[1325] Adopting a certain science policy may have implications for the level of protection chosen in the end: when uncertainties are bridged by assumptions that make the risk appear larger, a higher level of protection is likely to be adopted as a consequence than in case of a risk assessed as less significant.[1326]

WTO case law has for some time failed to acknowledge in anything other than a limited manner that risk assessments are not value-free exercises, a fact that has met with repeated criticism.[1327] For example, legal commentators have expressed disagreement Panel's statement in *EC – Biotech Products* that regulatory purposes do not matter for risk assessments.[1328] The Appellate Body's decision in *Hormones II,* recognizing that the choice of level of protection may influence a risk assessment, is a tentative move away from this narrow understanding; this move has been welcomed by most academic commentators as enhancing the regulatory autonomy of WTO Members.[1329] Some also consider that the Appellate Body's findings in this area, namely that risks can be assessed qualitatively and real-life

1322 Codex Alimentarius Commission, Working Principles for Risk Analysis for Application in the Framework of the Codex Alimentarius, online at http://www.fao.org/docrep/006/y4800e/y4800e0o.htm.

1323 Ibid., para. 25.

1324 Walker 1998, 260.

1325 On the use of science policy and also for the example, see ibid., 259ff.

1326 On this aspect, see also ibid., 270.

1327 Foster 2008, 456.

1328 Herwig 2008, 834.f.

1329 See for example Arcuri 2013, 172ff; by contrast, Cho 2009b, 302ff criticizes the decision for not being stringent enough in its approach to reviewing scientific evidence and therefore undermining the scientific evidence requirements of the SPS Agreement.

risks can be taken into account, open the door for more normative considerations to be taken into account as part of risk assessments.[1330]

Collective, public perceptions of risks play at best a minor role in the Appellate Body's understanding of risk and risk assessments. This choice is not textually compelling. There are indeed different understandings of what the term "risk" means; some strands in risk perception research stress the large differences in risk perception seen indifferent actors.[1331] However, if what constitutes a risk is, to a significant extent, in the eye of the beholder, there is no compelling reason why risk assessments that are based on the risk perception in a given society should not be considered to satisfy the science-related disciplines of the SPS Agreement.

How broadly or narrowly the adjudicators interpret the requirements of Art. 5.1 SPS is also related to broader considerations of the roles of risk assessment and risk management under the SPS Agreement. As indicated above, the Appellate Body has twice held that given that the term "risk management" is not contained in the SPS Agreement, the distinction between risk assessment and risk management cannot be used for justifying a narrow understanding of risk assessment under the SPS Agreement. Some have interpreted the Appellate Body's statement to mean that risk management considerations and the value judgements that risk management normally entails can also be accepted as relevant for judging what is a risk assessment by standards of the SPS Agreement and what is not.[1332] In my view, what precisely the Appellate Body's statement means for the acceptability of WTO Members' risk assessment is not clear. Maybe this is also why the Panel in *Hormones II* misinterpreted what the Appellate Body had said or intended to say on the matter in *Hormones I*. All in all, it is too early to say what line the WTO judges will ultimately adopt.

Another critical point is that the adjudicators, despite showing some insight into the limits of science, may still misunderstand how scientific risk assessments function. In current science theory, it is recognized that empirical natural science cannot make statements about any kind of phenomena with absolute certainty; what it is capable of delivering are rather statements about probabilities.[1333] Hence, scientific risk assessments often have

---

1330 Peel 2004, 65ff.

1331 For an overview of different definitions of risk, see Gruszczynski 2006, 2f.

1332 Arcuri 2013, 172f; Du 2010a, 1082; Gruszczynski 2006, 13; Winickoff et al. 2005, 96.

1333 See for example Landwehr 2000, 65; Silbergeld 1991, 100f.

to deal with scientific uncertainty;[1334] indeed, conducting a risk assessment may precisely involve mapping the limits of scientific knowledge on a certain matter.[1335] If, the course of a risk assessment, a scientist discovers that uncertainty prevails, this will not normally stop him or her from calling the study he or she produces a risk assessment.[1336] Scientific uncertainty is particularly widespread when new technologies are introduced.[1337]

These insights on the pervasive nature of scientific uncertainty, and of how it can be an integral part of a risk assessment, do not seem to be adequately reflected in the understanding of risk assessment that prevails in WTO case law.[1338] Adjudicators do recognize that a risk assessment may involve divergent conclusions or some measure of scientific uncertainty. At the same time, the adjudicators' notion of risk assessment does not seem to encompass the idea that a document entitled "risk assessment" may actually suggest that risks are not yet known or that "a significant amount of scientific uncertainty underlies most risk assessments".[1339] In fact, a scientific risk assessment may conclude that there is scientific uncertainty and the likelihood of a certain risk materializing simply cannot be evaluated with any degree of robustness. The adjudicators may be underestimating the fact that "the scientific endeavour is by its very nature incomplete".[1340] The problem facing the law may not actually be distinguishing between full and insufficient knowledge, but between different levels of insufficiency.[1341] This uncertainty also means that the outcome of a risk assessment is not independent of who does it.

One example of how the adjudicators overestimate the potential of science and do not give appropriate importance to scientific uncertainty is

1334 For a comprehensive description of the various steps of a risk assessment and inherent problems leading to uncertainty, see Gelbert 2001, 217; another account is provided by Epps 2008, 157ff. Different types of scientific uncertainty prevailing in risk assessments are mentioned by Walker 1998, 258: measurement uncertainty, uncertainty associated with the use of scientific models and data gaps; in another article the same author identifies the following five types of uncertainty in risk determinations: conceptual, measurement, sampling, modeling, and causal uncertainty Walker 2003, 204ff. Schropp 2012, 196ff also discusses different types of "incertitude" in risk assessments.

1335 Howse and Horn 2009, 81.

1336 See Herwig 2008, 836.

1337 Winickoff et al. 2005, 105.

1338 See also Walker 2003, 303ff with regard to the *Hormones I* case.

1339 Winickoff et al. 2005, 94.

1340 Perez 2007, 275.

1341 Ibid.

with regard to the specificity requirement. As described, the Appellate Body requires scientific risk assessments to be specific to the risk and substance at hand. Commentators have pointed out that risk assessments at the level of specificity prescribed by the Appellate Body may simply not be feasible in cases of scientific controversy (and hence uncertainty); this applies in particular when a WTO Member wishes to base a measure on a minority scientific opinion or when low risks are involved.[1342] One reason is that minority scientific opinions are often based on general assumptions and inferences rather than specific empirical research.[1343]

An inadequate understanding of science has also been found to be reflected in the Appellate Body's analysis of Art. 5.6 SPS in *Australia – Apples*. Schropp criticizes as too simplistic the Appellate Body's assumption that complainants could make a substantiated claim that proposed alternative measures would reach the level of protection of the defendant and that Panels could meaningfully assess such claims. She maintains that risk assessments are highly subjective exercises, permeated by various type of uncertainty; as a consequence, complainants and Panels would be better to rely on a defending Member's own risk assessment (under Art. 5.1, 5.2 SPS) to ascertain whether alternative measures would also reach the defending Member's level of protection.[1344]

That adjudicators may not have taken the nature of scientific inquiry fully into account in at least some of the cases decided so far is also evident in the way the relationship between Art. 5.1 and 5.7 SPS is construed. To recap, the term "insufficient" was interpreted in *Japan – Apples* by the adjudicators in relation to Art. 5.1 SPS. Evidence was considered insufficient if it was not enough – in a qualitative or quantitative sense – to conduct the risk assessment required by Art. 5.1 SPS. The Panel in *EC – Biotech Products* adopted what seems to be an even narrower approach to Art. 5.7 SPS which has been read to state that a WTO Member could not resort to Art. 5.7 SPS when a risk assessment existed.[1345] In *Hormones II*, however, the Appellate Body chose a different route. It explained that even if a risk assessment existed – in this case the risk assessment preceding the adoption of an international Codex Alimentarius standard – Art. 5.7 SPS could still apply as scientific evidence could evolve over time.

1342 Sykes 2002, 363ff; Gruszczynski 2006, 17.
1343 Peel 2004, 71.
1344 Schropp 2012, 219.
1345 Henckels 2006, 294; Howse and Horn 2009, 81.

The narrower interpretations, i.e. that once a risk assessment has been conducted, Art. 5.7 SPS can no longer be invoked by the defending WTO Member, are problematic in light of the underlying view on how scientific discovery functions. They mean that in situations where a risk assessment has at some stage been conducted, but where doubts are raised regarding the robustness of its outcome by scientific studies, whether subsequent or extant, the defendant could not rely on Art. 5.7 SPS in defence of a measure. It is not unlikely that new or diverging scientific evidence may become available once a risk assessment has been conducted. One may argue that there is scientific uncertainty inherent in any situation which formal risk assessments or other scientific studies produce diverging conclusions. It could further be argued that where such scientific uncertainty obtains the initial, formal risk assessment is not conclusive enough to base measures on, and hence it is a situation that should be covered by Art. 5.7 SPS. Yet this is not the position adopted by the Panel in *EC – Biotech Products*, for example. The Panel disqualified as risk assessments certain scientific studies that put into doubt the results of the "official" risk assessment; as a consequence, the Panel did not take these studies into account. At the same time, however, Art. 5.7 SPS could not be invoked because a risk assessment existed. The narrow understanding of risk assessments by the Panel in *EC – Biotech Products* is thus related to a narrow interpretation of Art. 5.7 SPS as well. The Appellate Body's position on Art. 5.7 SPS in *Hormones II* seems to reflect the reality of scientific inquiry better: it admitted that scientific evidence used in the development of an international standard could become outdated.

An overly static understanding of how science works also creates another problem at the intersection of Art. 5.1 and 5.7 SPS. Under Art. 5.1 SPS, a WTO Member does not need to have conducted a risk assessment itself to base a measure on it. WTO Members may use a risk assessment conducted by another WTO Member, for example. As a corollary, it can be assumed that a risk assessment not conducted by the defending Member itself could also be taken as evidence under Art. 5.7 SPS that it was possible to conduct a risk assessment on a certain issue. Depending on how narrowly Art. 5.7 SPS is interpreted, this would bar recourse to that article for the defending Member. This is problematic if one assumes, for the reasons discussed above, that risk assessments are not value-free exercises, that regulatory purpose and ambitions matter for the results of a risk assessment, and that there may in consequence be substantial differences between risk assessments commissioned by different WTO Members.[1346] Indeed, it has been argued that the sufficiency of scientific evidence can only be meaningfully assessed against risks considered relevant by a certain community.[1347] Against this background, most observers indeed appear critical of narrow interpretations of Art. 5.7 SPS and consider them overly restrictive of Member's regulatory sovereignty.[1348] For example, the interpretation of the clause in *EC – Biotech Products* has been criticized as a "formalistic delineation of Articles 5.1 and 5.7"[1349] SPS. Again, the *Hormones II* Appellate Body report here gives less reason for concern than other reports.[1350]

Another issue, raised by *EC – Biotech Products* in particular, is whether a risk assessment conducted at one governance level can be used to question opposing conclusions in a risk assessment carried out or commissioned by authorities at a different governance level.[1351] That this question can become relevant is shown by *EC – Biotech Products*. In this case, both the competent bodies of the EU and the "competent authorities" in the Member State, both of which had initially received requests to approve marketing of GMOs, had produced risk assessments finding no relevant risk associated to the use of GMOs. Several EU Member States, however, banned the use of GMOs, citing scientific risk assessments as evidence. The Member States' measures were subsequently found to be in violation of Art. 5.1 SPS because they were not "based on" risk assessments. This was mainly due to the fact that the Panel did not consider the studies invoked in defence of Member States' restrictions to constitute risk assessments.[1352] Yet, if the scientific studies on which the Member States relied had been recognized as risk assessments and come to a different conclusion than the risk assessments conducted at EU level, what then would be the consequence? In light of the insight above that *who* does a risk assessment and on the basis of which parameters matters for the outcome, it would be

1346 See Gruszczynski 2008, 120f.
1347 Winickoff et al. 2005, 113.
1348 Arcuri 2013, 175; Eliason, Antonia 2009, 372ff.
1349 Herwig and Joerges 2013, 33.
1350 Arcuri 2013, 176; Herwig and Joerges 2013, 33.4f.
1351 This point is raised by Peel 2012, 439.
1352 See *European Communities – Measures Affecting the Approval and Marketing of Biotech Products, WT/DS291/R, WT/DS292/R, WT/DS293/R* 2006, para. 7.3035ff, 7.3073ff and 7.3090ff for Austrian measures, para. 7.3111ff and 7.3132ff for French measures, 7.3142ff for a German measure, 7.3162ff for a Greek measure, 7.3182ff for an Italian measure, para. 7.3201 for the measure adopted by Luxemburg.

problematic if the risk assessment conducted by the authority adopting a certain SPS measure was given less importance than a risk assessment conducted by a different body of the same WTO Member.

Another issue with the case law is how the broad lines identified above are applied within it, as they do not always appear to be meticulously followed in practice. Legal commentators have been quite critical of the Panel's decision in *EC – Biotech Products*, with Herwig, for example, arguing that the Panel's understanding that regulatory purposes do not matter for a risk assessment results from a selective reading of the Appellate Body report in *Hormones I*.[1353]

2.5.2. Problems with the "appropriate level of protection"

Besides science, the "appropriate level of protection" is another core concept of both the SPS Agreement and WTO law more broadly. It is explicit in Art. 5.5 SPS, but has also come to play a role in the interpretation of other norms. There are parallels between the roles of a Member's appropriate level of protection under the SPS Agreement on the one hand and Art. XX GATT and the TBT Agreement on the other.

Yet there is an important difference between the SPS agreement and the other two agreements. Art. XX GATT does not refer explicitly to the level of protection; the TBT Agreement mentions it only in a provision in the Annex that deals with (non-binding) standards and is thus not a very central norm of the TBT Agreement.[1354] Art. 5.5 SPS, however, mandates that "each Member shall avoid arbitrary or unjustifiable distinctions in the levels it *considers to be appropriate*" [emphasis added]. This is a very clear statement that Members are free to determine their level of protection without judicial interference, just so long as they are consistent in doing so.[1355] Legal commentators have observed that this clause would seem to prohibit balancing by the judicial bodies, in the sense of weighing the importance of the objective pursued against other objectives and thereby judicially down-scaling the regulatory ambition of the respective WTO Members.[1356]

1353 Herwig 2008, 835.

1354 See Annex III F TBT Agreement.

1355 See Andenas and Zleptnig 2007, 417; Kapterian 2010, 113.

1356 Andenas and Zleptnig 2007, 417; Pauwelyn 2003b, 176.

Indeed, while the Appellate Body has stated repeatedly that Members are free to set their appropriate level of protection as they wish,[1357] it is also clear in its opinion that this right is neither absolute nor unqualified,[1358] but subject to the rules governing the adoption of SPS measures by WTO Members. This creates some problems.

At the conceptual level, it is certainly possible to distinguish between a level of protection and measures taken to achieve it. Yet it is subject to debate whether distinguishing between the choice of a level of protection (which is not subject to judicial modification) and measures to attain it (which are) is also meaningful for more practical purposes. That the assumption that the right to choose a level of protection can be regarded as being separate from the measures taken to attain it is problematic is perhaps made clearer when considering these two statements:

(1) "We choose a level of protection X and hence we will take measure Y."

(2) "We choose level of protection X. X is the level of protection incorporated in our measure Y." For example, a Member could formulate the following: "We want to absolutely protect our population against the risk associated to the use of substance A. Absolute protection means for us that we do want to exclude any risk of damage, even the smallest one, resulting from the use of A, even though there is no absolute scientific certainty on whether A is actually dangerous. Zero risk is the level of protection that we reach when completely banning the use and imports of A."

In the practice of WTO dispute settlement, the basic understanding of how the SPS Agreement functions seems to be (1); this idea is also shared in the literature.[1359] For example, the Appellate Body in *Australia – Salmon* clearly distinguished the level of protection from measures taken to achieve it, when stating that

> "[t]he 'appropriate level of protection' established by a Member and the 'SPS measure' have to be clearly distinguished. They are not one

1357 *Australia – Measures Affecting Importation of Salmon, WT/DS18/AB/R* 1998, para. 199.

1358 *European Communities – Measures Concerning Meat and Meat Products, WT/DS26/AB/R, WT/DS48/AB/R* 1998, para. 173.

1359 See Atik 2013, 122.

> and the same thing. The first is an *objective*, the second is an *instrument* chosen to attain or implement that objective."[1360]

Yet, because of practical difficulties with identifying the level of protection applied in a given situation, Panels have needed to rely on measures to identify levels of protection, and in practice concept (2). The Panel in *Australia – Apples* has succinctly summarized the state of affairs so far:

> "Previous panels have also recognised the close link between a Member's SPS measures and the ALOP such measures serve to implement. The panel in *EC – Hormones* stated that, in contrast to Article 2.3 of the SPS Agreement, 'Article 5.5 [...] deals more specifically with *distinctions in levels of protection* (which *will normally be reflected in one or more sanitary measures*) [...].' Likewise, the panel in *Australia – Salmon* found that 'any sanitary measure applied to a given situation inherently reflects and achieves a certain level of protection', and reiterated that 'the appropriate level of sanitary protection will normally be reflected in the sanitary measures imposed for a specific situation.' Further, the panel in *EC – Biotech* held that 'although Article 5.5 does not explicitly refer to 'SPS measures'', this provision 'implies a reference to 'SPS measures'.' The same panel quoted paragraph B.1 of the Guidelines to Further the Practical Implementation of Article 5.5, which provides that 'the concept of appropriate level of protection is applied in practice through sanitary or phytosanitary measures.' The panel confirmed that this guidance 'is consistent with relevant Appellate Body jurisprudence', and quoted the Appellate Body's reference in *EC – Hormones* to a '*measure* embodying or implementing a particular level of protection.'
>
> Yet [...] a Member's ALOP in a specific situation cannot be deduced solely from the SPS measures the Member applies."[1361] [footnotes omitted]

Thus, there is, in the case law, an oscillation between (1) and (2). Commentators have stated that the Appellate Body has sometimes "struggled" to distinguish between the level of protection and the measures taken to attain it.[1362]

1360 *Australia – Measures Affecting Importation of Salmon, WT/DS18/AB/R* 1998, para. 200.

1361 *Australia – Measures Affecting the Importation of Apples from New Zealand, WT/DS367/R* 2010, para. 7.975f.

1362 Magnuson 2010, 133 with regard to *Japan – Apples*.

For practical purposes, concept (1) has been called "largely a fiction" and "wishful thinking".[1363] In real-world policy processes, regulators adopt certain measures, guided by factors such as cost, pressure from interest groups, ideology, or enforceability; a level of protection formulated in quantitative or qualitative terms is rarely the main driving factor. When subject to a challenge at the WTO, a measure will then be defended *ex post* by inferring from it a certain level of protection, rather than a level of protection having been identified before the measure was taken.[1364] In practice, the situation reflected in statement (2) is likely to be the normal case. However, if a WTO Member is forced in a type (2) situation to alter its measure, this is likely to entail a change to the level of protection, too. There are, in other words, very likely many real-world situations in which there is only one measure that reaches the desired level of protection. This is particularly likely when the objective is zero-risk; in such cases, total prohibition of the use of certain dangerous or potentially dangerous products is often the only solution. When a member is prohibited from taking the only measure that is suitable (e.g. an import ban), the implication is that it may not, in practice, choose the level of protection (e.g. zero-risk). Moreover, it also means that WTO Members' assessments of how a level of protection can best be attained are questioned.

One might argue that in a situation where a country can only reach its chosen level of protection through one specific measure, the SPS Agreement as interpreted by the dispute settlement bodies would not prevent a country from taking "the one and only" measure. Yet this is only true *if* there is both scientific justification for it and the same level of protection is sought in similar situations. These latter qualifications are important: the case law so far shows that it is not at all easy for Members to demonstrate that the science-related disciplines of the SPS Agreement are fulfilled. The problem is exacerbated by the fact that it is as yet unclear to what extent the adjudicators accept that certain decisions pertaining to risk management and that are likely to influence the level of protection chosen, such as adopting certain science policies, are a legitimate part of a risk assessment in the sense of Art. 5.1 SPS. If it is not accepted that such decisions can be part of a risk assessment in the sense of the SPS Agreement, then the right

1363 Atik 2013, 133.
1364 Ibid., 122f; Pauwelyn 2003b, 185.

to choose the appropriate level of protection is also impaired and WTO Members' discretion curtailed.[1365]

Moreover, if a WTO Member chooses a level of protection either partially or entirely for reasons other than scientific ones – consumer preferences, ethical considerations – little remains of that Member's right to choose its level of protection. The requirement in Art. 5.5 SPS that levels of protection need to be consistent in comparable situations is also likely to be at odds with the Member's freedom to choose a level of protection. While a WTO Member may disagree with the adjudicators' qualification of two situations as comparable, it will nevertheless be prevented from maintaining the level of protection chosen for each situation, and instead must settle for an equal level of protection for both – again little remains of the right to choose. Moreover, if the regulator aims at a situation of zero risk in one situation, the same level would be required in any similar situation; achieving zero risk in several situations may entail prohibitive costs.[1366] Whether high costs for achieving a similar level of protection in several situations would in itself lead to these situations being deemed not comparable or for differences in levels of protection not to be considered arbitrary or unjustifiable under Art. 5.5 SPS is not yet clear.

Another problem relating to the level of protection in the SPS Agreement, exacerbating the problem identified above, is describing the level of protection and then working with this description for purposes of comparison. The concept of "appropriate level of protection" is of most relevance within the contexts of Art. 5.5 and 5.6 SPS, both of which require a comparison between different levels of protection or the levels of protection reached by different measures at the national level: Art. 5.5 SPS requires a comparison between different levels of protection, while Art. 5.6 SPS requires a comparison between different measures reaching the same level of protection. In both instances, more than one level of protection needs to be identified: under Art. 5.5 SPS the different levels of protection applied in different situations and in Art. 5.6 SPS the level of protection reached by both the measure in dispute and by the feasible alternative measures. In addition, Art. 3 SPS makes it necessary to compare the level of protection

1365 This point is based on the argument by Walker 1998, 276 that "adoption of particular science policies to use in risk assessment should be viewed as an aspect of selecting an appropriate level of protection".

1366 Du 2010a, 1084.

achieved by a domestic measure with the any incorporated in international standards.[1367]

The Appellate Body has held that where a Member provides a description of the level of protection actually pursued, the Panel deciding the matter must base its finding on this description.[1368] The Appellate Body has even construed an obligation of Members to determine their level of protection with sufficient precision.[1369] As a result of this, the Appellate Body uses several connotations of the word "determine": on the one hand meaning to "choose" or "decide", and to "identify" on the other. Both actions are a prerogative of WTO Members with regard to the appropriate level of protection chosen. The adjudicators are only allowed to rely on the level of protection as reflected in the relevant SPS measure when a country has failed to describe its level of protection.[1370] Yet, in practice, the descriptions of their level of protection offered by WTO Members are not always very detailed. In at least one case the Appellate Body has qualified a Member's describing its level of protection as "high" and "conservative" as being sufficiently precise.[1371] A direct description by Members of their level of protection seems to be the exception, rather than the norm.[1372]

Moreover, the adjudicators' obligation to use a WTO Member's description of the appropriate level of protection as a basis for their findings does not extend to the identification of the level of protection that could be reached by alternative measures under Art. 5.6 SPS or applied in comparable situations under Art. 5.5 SPS. For these measures, a Panel may infer the level of protection from the measures applied or suggested. This construction is problematic, particularly when combined with the Appellate Body's acceptance of descriptions of a level of protection as "high" as sufficiently precise. Two levels of protection will be compared, based on the description by two different actors. For example, in the case of Art. 5.6 SPS, the

1367 For an overview of different comparisons to be carried out under the SPS Agreement and a criticism similar to the one presented here, see Atik 2013, in particular at 135ff.

1368 *Australia – Measures Affecting Importation of Salmon, WT/DS18/AB/R* 1998, para. 199, 204.

1369 Ibid., para. 206.

1370 Ibid., para. 207.

1371 Ibid.

1372 Schebesta and Sinopoli 2018, 134 observe that in the nine SPS disputes covered in their article,"the ALOP was clearly indicated in one, it was not evaluated due to a lack of information in three, and in the five others, it had to be inferred, to varying degrees, from the information submitted by the parties and from expert advice".

level of protection actually in place must be described by the defending WTO Member while the level of protection that an alternative measure would reach is to be identified by the adjudicators. A Panel may have a different understanding of what constitutes a "high" level of protection than a WTO Member, however. In other words, the basis on which the comparison takes place is both fragile and open to question. There is a real risk that any finding on the dis/similarity of the levels of protection applied in different situations is more reflective of a choice of words than of the levels of protection actually present: adjudicators might also be tempted or indeed be forced to base their findings on their own assumptions of what constitutes, for example, a "high" or "conservative" level of protection. One observer even states that it is "largely fiction" to assume that there is a specific level of protection and adjudicators will inevitably come to a conclusion of their own regarding any WTO Member's particular level.[1373] Indeed, Panels themselves have sometimes pointed to difficulties inworking with the level of protection as construed by the Appellate Body. For example, the Panel in *Australia – Apples* found in its analysis of Art. 5.5 SPS that Australia had only stated very generically that it aimed at a high-level of protection for all comparable situations, but not at zero risk.[1374] The Panel then went on to state that the defendant should not be allowed to "hide" behind such a generic statement, as this would "diminish" Art. 5.5 SPS.[1375] It then reviewed the level of protection actually in place, apparently ready to replace Australia's characterization with its own. Similar problems with identifying and comparing levels of protection have also been noticed in cases under GATT[1376] and the TBT; yet in a case under the TBT Agreement, the Appellate Body has indicated that Panels need not identify a level of protection in the abstract, but a may only look at the measures instead.[1377]

In some cases, the Appellate Body found a way to avoid the problems resulting from vague characterizations of the appropriate level of protec-

---

1373 Eeckhout 2010, 19.

1374 *Australia – Measures Affecting the Importation of Apples from New Zealand, WT/DS367/R* 2010, para. 7.963.

1375 Ibid., para. 7.970f.

1376 For example, in EC - Seal Products, such problems seemed to occur in connection with ill-defined alternative measures, see *European Communities – Measures Prohibiting the Importation and Marketing of Seal Products, WT/DS400/AB/R, WT/DS401/AB/R* 2014, para. 5.269f.

1377 *United States – Certain Country of Origin Labelling (COOL) Requirements, WT/DS384/AB/R, WT/DS/386/AB/R* 2012, para. 390.

tion. In *Australia – Salmon*, for example, the defendant Member had characterized its own level of protection for one product (for which an import ban existed) as "conservative", but had not described the level of protection for a second, comparable product (the import of which was allowed under certain conditions).[1378] The Appellate Body came to the conclusion that the level of protection accorded to the second product, the importing of which was generally allowed, was *not* "conservative", and that the levels of protection were thus different for the two, comparable, products. The only reason it gave for this conclusion (and possibly could give) was that the import of this product was allowed whereas the importation of the other product was not. In other words, the Appellate Body did not offer an independent characterization of the underlying level of protection with regard to the second product, but rather used the characterization of the level of protection employed by the defendant Member as a yardstick. In this way, it avoided a comparison that could only have been made on the basis of vague qualitative descriptions of the respective levels of protection. However, this solution is not necessarily replicable in other cases. The case involved an import ban, clearly a very trade restrictive and highly risk-preventive measure, as compared to an alternative measure that was no such ban. This facilitated the task of the Appellate Body. Generally, comparing the level of protection in place with a level of protection a hypothetical alternative measure would reach presents a "substantial challenge for a Panel, involving a complex (and highly speculative) assessment".[1379]

Taken in context, therefore, the right of Members to choose their appropriate level of protection appears of limited practical significance, an outcome due at least partially to the way that the adjudicators have interpreted and applied the SPS Agreement. For example, Peel observes:

> "The substantive standard required for risk assessment, the need for scientific evidence relied upon by Member to be 'specific' in nature and for assessed risks to be more than theoretical, together with the trend for panels to examine the scientific basis of Members' SPS measures with increasing stringency, all raise questions about the real scope of a Member's ability to determine autonomously the level of SPS protection its pursues […]".[1380]

1378 *Australia – Measures Affecting Importation of Salmon, WT/DS18/AB/R* 1998, para. 231f.
1379 As rightly noted by Atik 2013, 130.
1380 Peel 2004, 81.

Others have also observed that the Members' right to set their level of protection is significantly limited by the subjection of WTO Members' scientific assessments to judicial review.[1381]

Not everyone shares this rather pessimistic view about the reality of the WTO Members' right to set levels of protection, however. For example, while recognizing that the autonomy in setting the level of protection and the other disciplines of the SPS Agreement are in a "constant state of tension",[1382] Du argues that the level of protection chosen by Members has actually informed the assessment of WTO Members' measures under the SPS Agreement. He maintains that the Appellate Body has shown "sensitivity and deference" to Members' levels of protection when interpreting Art. 5.5 and 5.6 SPS.[1383] In particular, he points to the Appellate Body report in *Hormones II* where it decided that the chosen level of protection could influence risk assessments and the standard of insufficiency under Art. 5.7 SPS; he also mentions the relatively permissive interpretation of Art. 5.5 SPS and a cautious attitude of the adjudicators towards assuming that alternative measures would reach the chosen level of protection of a WTO Member under Art. 5.6 SPS. But *Hormones II* is just one case amongst several; at least some see the later *Australia – Apples* case as rather restrictive of WTO Members' regulatory freedom despite the findings in *Hormones II*.[1384]

In conclusion, the limitations that are imposed by the SPS Agreement as interpreted by the WTO tribunals in regard to setting a level of protection seem to outweigh the limited openings offered by some of the case law. Despite the rhetoric of the Appellate Body, it is difficult for Members to choose a level of protection and then successfully defend it in WTO dispute settlement: the right of the WTO Members to define their level of protection and the limited role of the adjudicators in reviewing it may be highlighted, but the limitations of WTO Members' regulatory freedom are neglected. A speculative but not implausible conclusion is that the Appellate Body's emphasis on the right of WTO Members to choose a level of protection is aimed at certain effect: assuaging fears that the WTO could intrude too much into the sphere of regulatory sovereignty of WTO Mem-

1381 Maybe the most pessimistic view is expressed by Sykes 2002, 355 who writes that "meaningful scientific evidence requirements fundamentally conflict with regulatory sovereignty in all cases of serious scientific uncertainty". Skepticism is also voiced by Cass 2005, 216; Gruszczynski 2006, 28ff.

1382 Du 2010a, 1079.

1383 Ibid.

1384 See Peel 2012, 428f.

bers.[1385] This is supported by the fact that the Appellate Body's emphasis on the right to choose the level of protection is taken, in part at least, from a source that does not seem to consider that such a right exists: Art. 3.3 SPS, which the Appellate Body quotes as embodying WTO Members' right to define their level of protection, actually limits that right.[1386] In other words, there is simply no unfettered right of WTO Members to choose a level of protection under the SPS Agreement.

2.5.3. The role of precaution

Another relevant aspect is the degree to which the SPS Agreement, as interpreted by the WTO dispute settlement bodies, allows precautionary measures by WTO Members, and is, in this sense, precaution-friendly.[1387] The issue of precaution in the SPS Agreement has received quite a lot of attention in the literature.[1388] A brief summary is therefore sufficient here.

To start, the Appellate Body has not taken a position on the existence of a principle of precaution in international customary law or as a general principle of law. What is more, it has stated that even if such a principle existed it could not override the explicit treaty provisions. The Appellate Body's approach to the role and status of non-WTO international law in WTO dispute settlement is discussed more in-depth in the next chapter.[1389] Here, it should be noted that not everyone agrees with the Appellate Body's reticence regarding the recognition of the precautionary principle as a general or customary principle of international law. It has been claimed that in the area of health, the precautionary principle is a general legal principle.[1390] Hey suggests that the Appellate Body ought to have investigated the status of the precautionary principle in international law and, if it recognized that such a principle existed indeed, it should have interpreted Art. 5.1 and 5.2 SPS accordingly.[1391] Howse argues that the Ap-

1385 A similar point is made by Knox 2004, 54.

1386 The point is made by ibid., 53.

1387 For an explanation of what I mean by precaution-friendly, see above section 1.5.5.

1388 See for example Eggers 2001; Cheyne 2007; Cheyne 2006; Bohanes 2002; Gehring and Cordonier Segger 2003; Gerstetter and Maier 2005; Kogan 2004; Richieri Hanania 2009; Scott and Vos 2002.

1389 See chapter 3, section 1.6.

1390 Godt 1998, 205.

1391 Hey 2000, 247.

pellate Body should have clarified whether the WTO provisions in question

> "reflected the intention of the parties to modify, by treaty, customary norms. If so, the treaty text, as interpreted in accordance with the normal rules of interpretation, would prevail. But if not, then customary norms [including the precautionary principle, C. G.] might indeed be a legally binding constraint on the range of permissible interpretations of the treaty provision in question".[1392]

Kulovesi also supports this view.[1393] A similar point has been made with regard to the *EC – Biotech Products* Panel that also failed to take the precautionary principle into account.[1394] From a technical-legal point of view, the Appellate Body's approach does not appear to be the only one that could have been pursued; quite to the contrary, there are appear to be good legal reasons why the adjudicators should have said something on the status of the precautionary principle.

Even though the Appellate Body did not accept the proposition that the precautionary principle could override explicit provisions of the SPS Agreement, it nonetheless stated in its *Hormones I* report that some aspects of precaution were reflected in the SPS Agreement.[1395]

First, the Appellate Body considered Art. 5.7 SPS to be an aspect of precaution in the SPS Agreement: this idea is widely shared in the literature.[1396] A second aspect of precaution, identified by both the Appellate Body and commentators,[1397] is the WTO Members' right to choose the appropriate level of protection mentioned in Art. 3.3 SPS and the agreement's preamble. A third element of precaution identified by the Appellate Body and in the literature[1398] is that a Panel assessing whether sufficient scientific evidence exists for a Member to maintain a certain SPS measure may and should bear in mind

---

1392 Howse 2008, 640.
1393 Kulovesi 2011, 164ff.
1394 Henckels 2006, 301f.
1395 *European Communities – Measures Concerning Meat and Meat Products, WT/DS26/AB/R, WT/DS48/AB/R* 1998, para. 124.
1396 See for example Slotboom 2003, 574.
1397 Cheyne 2007, 162f.
1398 Herwig and Joerges 2013, 32; Gruszczynski 2006, 10; Foster 2009, 51.

> "that responsible, representative government commonly act from perspectives of prudence and precaution where risks of irreversible [...] damage to human health are concerned."

I will briefly consider these elements in turn.

First, Art. 5.7 SPS. There is wide agreement that the norm is indeed a formulation of a precautionary approach, albeit a weak one.[1399] Art. 5.7 SPS is the only explicit reflection of precaution in the SPS Agreement and has been called a "safe harbor".[1400] The interpretation of this norm and some of the shortcomings of a narrow understanding of what constitutes "insufficient" scientific evidence contained in some of the dispute settlement reports have already been discussed.[1401] The narrow interpretation of insufficiency of scientific evidence adopted at least in some cases has been described rather drastically as a "nail in the coffin of the precautionary principle under the SPS Agreement",[1402] and there is no shortage of critical comments on it.[1403] By way of contrast, the broader interpretation of the norm in *Hormones II* has been welcomed as opening the door more widely to precautionary regulation and enhancing WTO Members' scope for regulatory action in general.[1404]

The second aspect of precaution, the right of WTO Members to choose an appropriate level of protection, was discussed in the previous section. This right would indeed amount to something like a *carte blanche* for applying precautionary measures, if it could be exercised without further qualification or limits. In this case, a Member could even set a level of protection at zero risk in a situation where scientific uncertainties concerning causality and/or the magnitude of the risk existed. Considering this in the light of the elements of the precautionary principle described above,[1405] this would clearly be a precautionary approach.[1406] However, as explained in the previous section, this is not the situation under the SPS Agreement; rather the right of governments to choose a level of protection is *ab initio* subject to the disciplines of the SPS Agreement.

1399 See for example Cheyne 2007, 162; Laowonsiri, Akawat 2010, 577.
1400 Winickoff et al. 2005, 116.
1401 See above section 2.5.1.
1402 Foster 2009, 52.
1403 See for example Henckels 2006, 293ff.
1404 See above section 2.5.1.
1405 See above section 1.5.5.
1406 This point was in fact made by Japan in *Japan – Measures Affecting the Importation of Apples, WT/DS245/AB/R* 2003, para. 36 albeit in the context of Art. 5.7 SPS.

A third aspect is the standard of sufficiency of scientific evidence under Art. 2.2 SPS and 5.1 SPS. The formulation in *Hormones I*, quoted above and re-iterated in *Japan – Apples*,[1407] is rather strong, because the Appellate Body stated that Panels "should", rather than "may", bear in mind that "responsible, representative governments commonly act from perspectives of prudence and precaution" in the case of grave risks to human health.[1408] The formulation remains somewhat enigmatic, however, because it tells Panels what behaviour to expect from governments without indicating clearly what this means for the Panels in practice. For example, are there governments that are not to be considered as "responsible and representative", and are their measures to be judged differently? Generally, the Appellate Body's statement seems to indicate that a Panel may lower the standard of what it regards as "sufficient" evidence if a risk is sufficiently severe. Such a finding could indeed be regarded as an aspect of precaution. Accepting less evidence as sufficient for permitting action implies acceptance of a lesser degree of scientific certainty as justification for the adoption of measures. The same logic is inherent to the precautionary principle, but the Appellate Body does not recognize the precautionary principle as such and does not make clear on what other legal basis it has formulated the above guidance to Panels. Moreover, the degree to which Panels review scientific evidence induced by parties in support of their measures, as discussed more in detail below in the section on the standard of review, varies widely in the case law.[1409] When the judicial review of scientific evidence that a WTO Member seeks to rely on to justify a measure is very intense, little space is left for precaution from the side of the WTO Members.

There is one related, but still different, aspect of precaution that the Appellate Body has not explicitly mentioned as such. This is the Appellate Body's acknowledgment that a measure could still be "based on" a risk assessment if the latter only represents a minority scientific view. This once more implies a lowering of the degree of scientific certainty that needs to exist before a measure can be enacted, and hence an element of precaution. It is therefore identified in the literature as an aspect of precaution present in WTO case law.[1410]

1407 *Japan – Measures Affecting the Importation of Apples, WT/DS245/R* 2003, para. 8.105.

1408 See Howse 2008, 641.

1409 See chapter 3, section 2.1.

1410 See also Eggers 2001, 141; Herwig and Joerges 2013, 32.

While certain aspects of precaution are contained in the SPS Agreement, there are also examples where parties to an SPS dispute have invoked the precautionary principle to support their position, but the Appellate Body has not followed their arguments. In the *Australia – Salmon* appellate review, Australia argued – in the context of Art. 5.5 SPS – that a Member had a right "to a cautious approach to determine its own appropriate level of protection."[1411] While Australia's statement was quite general in formulation, relating to several norms of the SPS Agreement, the specific point it wished to make was related to Art. 5.5 SPS. It argued that the comparison that takes place under Art. 5.5 SPS – which can only take place where situations are comparable either with a view to the risk or the consequences involved – should include certain diseases even though it was not clear that the animals in question were susceptible to these diseases. It claimed that as the Panel failed to include diseases not positively detected into its comparisons, it had committed an error of law. The Appellate Body did not refer explicitly to the "cautious approach" that Australia claimed was its right, but dealt with the Australian argument in substance. It found that the Panel had included some diseases not positively detected in its analysis and was had rightly neglected others, because including them all would have been "highly speculative" as reliable scientific evidence was lacking.[1412] This seems to signal that the Appellate Body is rather reluctant to refer to terms such as caution, and is careful not to disconnect its findings from a science-based standard.

As WTO Members are given incentives to use international standards under the SPS Agreement, another entry point for precaution into the SPS Agreement could be through such standards, if they are themselves precautionary in character.[1413] However, this aspect has not played any role in WTO dispute settlement so far.

1411 *Australia – Measures Affecting Importation of Salmon, WT/DS18/AB/R* 1998, para. 150; the paragraph is not a model of sound and conclusive legal reasoning. As the parties' submissions are not published, it is hard to say whether the blame is to be put on Australia or the Appellate Body summarized the arguments in a rather unfortunate way.

1412 Ibid., para. 157.

1413 Herwig and Joerges 2013, 22f.

2.6. Assessment

This section is dedicated, again, not to the discussion of legal-doctrinal matters, but to a normative-political assessment of the case law concerning how much it restricts WTO Members' freedom to take regulatory measures and where it is positioned between the poles of health protection and/or trade.

A first important aspect has been discussed above: the understanding of science, risk and risk assessments prevailing in WTO case law. As described, some aspects of the WTO case law show that the Appellate Body's understanding of science is mostly broader than that of the Panels. In particular, the Appellate Body does not pretend that science always produces unequivocal results: such a statement would be subject to much criticism. It allows reliance on minority opinions, even though the conditions under which this can be done are not necessarily entirely settled. It also permits the use of various scientific methods and adopts a realistic view of the risks that exist in the real word. It acknowledges that a scientific risk assessment involves certain judgements and choices by the risk assessors, but that these judgements do not damage its status as a scientific risk assessment. Through these findings, the Appellate Body seems to avoid or at least mitigate some of the problems entailed by the SPS Agreement's reliance on science as an allegedly neutral arbiter.[1414] For example, Members are not forced to rely only on mainstream science. All in all, the Appellate Body has reached many of its decisions by overruling Panel decisions that would have restricted the regulatory freedom of WTO Members more strongly.[1415]

While the Appellate Body's general guidelines on what constitutes a risk assessment tend to give WTO Members certain leeway in conducting them, the way that the dispute settlement bodies actually deal with Members' scientific risk assessments has, in some cases, been quite intrusive. Generally, this is a question of the standard of review and is therefore discussed in more depth in the next chapter. The ability of WTO Members to justify measures under Art. 5.1 SPS has been significantly restricted by the intensive scrutiny that the WTO Members' risk assessments have been subjected to by the adjudicators, i.e. the way that the adjudicators apply their self-formulated rules. It should be noted that it is unclear whether such intensive scrutiny will continue to be applied in future SPS cases; many ob-

1414 On these problems see for example Bogdandy 2001, 642.
1415 Knox 2004, 42.

servers read the Appellate Body's finding in *Hormones II* as a step back from too intrusive a standard of review.[1416]

Intensive scrutiny of WTO Members' risk assessments or strict interpretations of the science-related disciplines of the SPS Agreement narrow the space in which WTO Members might pursue public policy goals at the national level. Holding WTO Members to a narrowly construed concept of science is problematic, because science cannot solve normative controversies, e.g. about new technologies[1417] or decide on the trade-offs between different policy objectives.

Moreover, there are some general problems with judges who are not scientific experts making decisions on the validity of scientific claims. This problem is not restricted to WTO dispute settlement, but concerns judicial decision-making on scientific evidence generally.[1418] The rationalities of legal decisions and scientific inquiry are fundamentally different: Science is, in principle, an open-ended endeavour where each finding generates a need for more research. Law, however, requires definite answers of the either/or type, allowing conclusions on whether the requirements in a legal norm are fulfilled or not.[1419] This is one of the reasons why it has been argued that evidentiary standards brought to bear on scientific evidence should be different from ones for other forms of evidence.[1420] These problems would seem to suggest that, when in doubt, judicial decision-makers at the WTO and elsewhere should rather lean towards deference when assessing scientific evidence, something the WTO adjudicators have not always done.

A mixed picture can also be drawn with regard to the way that requirements in the SPS Agreement other than the science-related clauses have been interpreted. Requirements that the Appellate Body has interpreted in such a way as to give WTO Members relatively more freedom than other possible interpretations include the following:[1421]

1416 See below chapter 3, section 2.4.1.

1417 This has been stressed by many commentators, see only Joerges 2009, 77.

1418 For an in-depth discussion of this issue, see Brewer 1998.

1419 This point is (I think) made by Herwig and Joerges 2013, 17f; on the different modi of judicial and scientific decision-making, see also Epps 2008, 145; Eliason, Antonia 2009, 352ff.

1420 For an overview of different reasons given in the literature on why the WTO adjudicators should adopt a deferential standard of review see chapter 3, section 2.5.

1421 For an overview of instances of broad and narrow interpretations of the requirements of the SPS Agreement, see also Herwig and Joerges 2013, 15f.

The interpretation offered by the Appellate Body on Art. 3 SPS makes it easier for Members to adopt SPS measures than, for example, the Panel's approach in *Hormones I* would have done. To recap, the Appellate Body stated that the terms "base on" and "conform to" in Art. 3.1 SPS and 3.2 SPS needed to be interpreted differently, and that Art. 3.3 SPS was an autonomous right, rather than an exception (with implications for the burden of proof). The Appellate Body's approach to interpreting Art. 3 SPS and by implication the role of international standards in the SPS Agreement has been valued as far-sighted[1422] and legally more correct than the Panel's.[1423] This is sometimes linked to criticism of the relevant international standard-setting organizations. For example, the Codex Alimentarius Commission has been described as being dominated by lobbyists[1424] and its decision-making procedures have been characterized as lacking democratic legitimacy.[1425]

Still, the Appellate Body's interpretation of Art. 3.3 SPS basically invalidated one of the alternatives contained in the article, though the Appellate Body claimed the poor drafting of the article left it with no choice in the matter. Some agree that the Appellate Body chose the only possible way of interpreting the norm.[1426] Others have described the Appellate Body's interpretation as narrow[1427] and criticized the Appellate Body for disregarding the text of the agreement[1428] or the interpretive principle of *effet utile*.[1429]

Moreover, observers also view the interpretation of Art. 5.5 SPS as relatively lenient and preserving regulatory discretion.[1430] Initially, the notion

---

1422 Bogdandy 2001, 635.

1423 See for example Quick and Blüthner 1999, 612; by contrast, Cho 2009a, 697 seems to be critical of the Appellate Body's interpretation, arguing that the Panel's position was "literally plausible".

1424 Bogdandy 2001, 637; Maier 2017, 109ff draws a more nuanced picture, highlighting that while indeed business representatives participate far more frequently in Codex meetings than representatives of civil society organizations, the actual influence of either of these groups on the Codex standard-setting can only be meaningfully assessed, if the decision-making processes at the national level leading states to formulate their position for the Codex negotiations are also taken into account. Yet according to Maier not much research has been done on the latter aspect.

1425 Godt 1998, 204.

1426 Notaro 2003, 181.

1427 Quick and Blüthner 1999, 615.

1428 Gruszczynski 2006, 7.

1429 Arcuri 2013, 172; Gruszczynski 2006, 12.

1430 Du 2010a, 1087; Herwig and Joerges 2013, 15f.

of what constitutes a comparable situation as adopted in WTO dispute settlement is relatively broad, i.e. many situations could be comparable under Art. 5.5 SPS.[1431] This would tend to restrict the regulatory freedom of WTO Members. Yet the Appellate Body has recognized various grounds for why differences in levels of protection in comparable situations are neither arbitrary nor unjustifiable. For example, there are indications in the appellate decision in *Hormones I* that if the public has divergent perception of different risks, this can justify a distinction in levels of protection. Therefore, while many situations may initially seem comparable under Art. 5.5 SPS, it does not appear to be exceedingly difficult for WTO Members to justify treating such apparently comparable situations differently.

The interpretation of the term "based on" in Art. 5.1 SPS that the Appellate Body has embraced gives WTO Members broader space for SPS measures than, for example, the Panel's approach in *Hormones I* would have done. The Appellate Body has done away with the additional procedural or subjective requirement that the risk assessment must actually have been taken into account by the WTO Member adopting a measure, and embraced a more objective reading. Several scholars consider this objective requirement easier to satisfy.[1432] Nonetheless, the Appellate Body's approach has still been criticized for requiring that for a measure to be "based on" a scientific risk assessment, the scientific evidence must be specific to the risk analysed, bringing the "based on" test close to a causation analysis.[1433] Moreover, if the Appellate Body had interpreted "based on" *only* as a procedural requirement, this would have been a more lenient standard for WTO Members than the current line of interpretation.[1434] Some commentators consider such a procedural approach to international judicial review of certain national risk regulation decisions to be appropriate,[1435] while others support the Appellate Body's interpretation.[1436] Here, the Appellate Body has taken neither the most restrictive nor most permissive stance feasible.

Examples can also be given of the adjudicators interpreting SPS norms in a way that restricts the decision-making space of WTO Members, how-

---

1431 See for example Pauwelyn 1999, 654.

1432 See for a brief overview of the literature Gruszczynski 2006, 19.

1433 Herwig and Joerges 2013, 16.

1434 In this direction Peel 2004, 60.

1435 See Arcuri 2013, 195.

1436 For example Gruszczynski 2006, 18 points out that a procedural reading might result in an exclusion of scientific evidence that becomes available after a measure has been adopted.

ever. An interpretation that has been criticized as too narrow is the one of Art. 5.7 SPS, at least in the version offered by the *EC – Biotech Products* Panel, or the Appellate Body in *Japan – Apples*. Narrow interpretations of Art. 5.7 SPS make it very difficult for WTO Members to rely on Art. 5.7 SPS for all practical purposes.[1437] By way of contrast, the Appellate Body's findings in *Hormones II* have been welcomed as broadening the regulatory space for WTO Members.

The degree to which the adjudicators have provided WTO Members space for regulatory decision-making and enabled them to adopt a precautionary stance also varies between cases, making any generalized statement difficult. With regard to variations between cases, many consider that there is a stark contrast between what the Panel did in *EC – Biotech Products* and what the Appellate Body did in *Hormones II*.[1438] Observers seem to agree that the Appellate Body has chosen neither the most restrictive nor permissive interpretations conceivable. One commentator, for example, concludes that the Appellate Body has adopted a "rather sensitive approach to WTO disputes, addressing most of the issues in a reasonable way".[1439] However, when looking at the details of the case law, the evaluations diverge.

To put things into perspective, it must be noted that some of the aspects that could be seen as unsatisfactory in the case law on the SPS Agreement stem rather from the way that the agreement itself is worded than from inadequacies in interpreting it. For example, the assumption underlying the agreement that governments define a level of protection and then adopt measures to attain it is rather simplistic and does not reflect the reality of risk regulation very well. Moreover, the level of protection is a concept notoriously difficult to apply, in particular where levels of protection are described in qualitative ways by different actors – and often they can only be described in that manner. In addition, "meetings" between law and science tend to create difficulties everywhere, not only in the WTO.[1440] Judicial decision-makers are not scientific experts – and yet they need to decide whether a certain piece of scientific evidence warrants a measure.[1441] More-

1437 For a critical discussion of this aspect, see Foster 2009, 55; Notaro 2003, 255; Herwig 2008, 835f.

1438 Herwig and Joerges 2013, 31ff; Howse and Horn 2009, 49.

1439 Gruszczynski 2006, 2.

1440 Herwig 2008, 828 discusses how different academic commentators view the role accorded to science in the SPS Agreement.

1441 For an in-depth discussion of this issue and possible consequences, see Brewer 1998.

over, as discussed above, uncertainty is inherent to science – but the law is formulated with the intent of providing definitive, either/or answers. In this sense, scientific discovery and judicial decision-making follow rather different rationalities. The difficulties that arise when judges have to deal with competing scientific claims have led the ICJ, for example, to avoid scientific controversies, instead "substituting legal reasoning for a scientific assessment of the facts of the case".[1442] Such a strategy would be rather difficult to justify in WTO dispute settlement, given the language of the SPS Agreement. Moreover, given the explicit science-focused language of the SPS Agreement, it would be rather difficult to argue that a WTO Member under the SPS Agreement should be able to justify an SPS measure based on the fact alone that the measure is in line with preferences of the majority of its population; for such public preferences or perceptions to play a larger role the agreement would arguably have to be changed.[1443] It is not the adjudicators' task to remedy such problematic aspects inherent to the SPS Agreement.

Thus, like any judges, the WTO dispute settlement bodies have some, but not unlimited decision-making space. Generally, the outcomes in SPS cases often depend to a significant extent on how the science-related provisions of the agreement are interpreted and how much deference is afforded to the scientific assessments presented by defendants. It has even been suggested that given that the SPS Agreement establishes some of the most exacting legal obligations in the WTO universe, any ambiguity in the SPS Agreement should be dealt with in a way that restricts rather than expands the reach of these provisions.[1444] This is certainly a standard that the WTO case law does not always meet.

3. TBT Agreement

The Agreement on Technical Barriers to Trade (TBT) is akin to the SPS Agreement inasmuch as it sets out detailed positive obligations that WTO Members need to take, rather than focusing on non-discrimination provisions like the GATT.[1445] Unlike the SPS Agreement, the TBT applies to Members' measures irrespective of their purpose. As a consequence, some

1442 D'Aspremont and Mbengue 2014, 253ff.
1443 For a similar position, see Gruszczynski 2006, 16f.
1444 Wirth 2006, 191.
1445 See for example Howse and Tuerk 2001, 308ff.

of the cases decided so far under the TBT Agreement do not primarily concern measures taken for non-trade regulatory purposes. Nevertheless, like under the GATT, it is important to take into account all case law interpreting the relevant norms, as the interpretation of these norms will have a bearing on future "trade and..." cases. An important norm in the context of this work is Art. 2.2 TBT. It reads:

> "Members shall ensure that technical regulations are not prepared, adopted or applied with a view to or with the effect of creating unnecessary obstacles to international trade. For this purpose, technical regulations shall not be more trade-restrictive than necessary to fulfil a legitimate objective, taking account of the risks non-fulfilment would create. Such legitimate objectives are, inter alia: national security requirements; the prevention of deceptive practices; protection of human health or safety, animal or plant life or health, or the environment. In assessing such risks, relevant elements of consideration are, inter alia: available scientific and technical information, related processing technology or intended end-uses of products."

Art. 2.2 TBT is not an exception norm like Art. XX GATT even though it contains similar language. Rather, it sets forth requirements that a technical regulation or standard needs to fulfil. In this respect, it is similar to Art. 5.6 SPS.

There is another norm in the TBT Agreement that fulfils a similar function: Art. 2.4 TBT. This article says:

> "Where technical regulations are required and relevant international standards exist or their completion is imminent, Members shall use them, or the relevant parts of them, as a basis for their technical regulations except when such international standards or relevant parts would be an ineffective or inappropriate means for the fulfilment of the legitimate objectives pursued, for instance because of fundamental climatic or geographical factors or fundamental technological problems."

This norm is the parallel norm to Art. 3.3 SPS.

As with the other agreements, there are also certain issues concerning the interpretation of the TBT Agreement that I will not discuss in this work. An important one is the definition of "technical regulation" in Annex 1.1 and "standard" in 1.2 TBT; whether a measure is a technical regulation or standard determines the applicability of the TBT Agreement. Whether a certain measure came within the purview of the agreement was contentious in several cases.[1446] Yet whether a measure comes within the purview of the TBT Agreement is unlikely to depend largely on whether it serves a non-economic or a trade-related goal. Therefore – and for reasons of necessary limitations – this issue is not pursued here any further. Art. 2.1 GATT is not discussed, either; while its interpretation is also likely to be relevant to non-trade cases, it is no primarily or only relevant in these cases.

In the following, I will discuss Art. 2.2 TBT (section 3.1) and 2.4 TBT (section 3.2). The section concludes with a discussion and assessment of the case law (section 3.3).

3.1. Art. 2.2 TBT

Art. 2.2 TBT was discussed by the Appellate Body for the first time in 2012, in *United States – Tuna Labelling*. At issue were certain US measures that allowed the use of a "dolphin-safe" label only if certain conditions were met at the time the respective tuna were caught. The Panel decided that as an alternative, less trade-restrictive measure was available, the measure was more trade-restrictive than necessary, and hence not compliant with Art. 2.2 TBT.[1447] A second case where Art. 2.2 TBT was at issue is *United States – COOL Requirements*.[1448] In this case, the Panel also concluded that the measure at issue – regulating the labelling of meat products to inform consumers of the origin of the meat – was not compliant with Art. 2.2 TBT, because it was trade-restrictive and did not fulfil its (legitimate) objective of providing consumers with information on the origin of meat products.[1449] Finally, Art. 2.2 TBT also played a role in *EC – Seal Products*. In this case, only the Panel dealt extensively with Art. 2.2 TBT, having

1446 *European Communities – Measures Prohibiting the Importation and Marketing of Seal Products, WT/DS400/AB/R, WT/DS401/AB/R* 2014, para. 5.1ff; *European Communities – Measures Affecting Asbestos and Products Containing Asbestos, WT/DS135/AB/R* 2001, para. 59ff; *European Communities – Trade Description of Sardines, WT/DS231/AB/R* 2002, para. 171ff; *United States – Measures Concerning the Importation, Marketing and Sale of Tuna and Tuna Products, WT/DS381/AB/R* 2012, para. 183ff.

1447 *United States – Measures Concerning the Importation, Marketing and Sale of Tuna and Tuna Products, WT/DS381/AB/R* 2012.

1448 *United States –Certain Country of Origin Labelling (COOL) Requirements, WT/DS384/AB/R, WT/DS/386/AB/R* 2012.

1449 See the summary of the Panel's decision in ibid., para. 351, 357ff.

characterized the controversial measures as "technical regulation". The Appellate Body did not accept the Panel's qualification of the underlying measures as "technical regulation" and consequently did not discuss any claims under the TBT.[1450]

A first important question concerning the interpretation of Art. 2.2 TBT is how the adjudicators identify the objective a measure pursues and what constitutes a "legitimate objective" of a measure.[1451]

Concerning the first aspect, namely how the adjudicators are to identify the objectives pursued by a measure, the Appellate Body in *United States – Tuna Labelling* supported the Panel's approach. The Panel had stated that whether a technical regulation pursued a legitimate objective had to be assessed objectively. A Panel is, according to the Appellate Body, not bound by the characterization of the measure's objective offered by the respective WTO Member. It may take into account the text of legal norms, legislative history and the structure and operation of the measure.[1452] The Appellate Body confirmed this finding in the later *United States – COOL Requirements* case.[1453] In that case, the Panel had used the notification of the measure by the US to the TBT Committee, the US submission during the dispute settlement proceedings, and the text of the measures and statements made during the legislative process to identify the objective of the measure.[1454] This approach towards identifying the objective of a measure was appealed by the original complainants, who maintained that the Panel should have relied less heavily on the way that the United States characterized their own measure.[1455] The Appellate Body in this case concurred with the appellants that if the Panel had relied solely on the verbal characterization of the objective of the measure by the United States, this would not have been sufficient, but found that the Panel actually had also taken into account

---

1450 *European Communities – Measures Prohibiting the Importation and Marketing of Seal Products, WT/DS400/AB/R, WT/DS401/AB/R* 2014, para. 5.70.

1451 This is one of the aspects where the SPS and TBT Agreements differ; in the SPS Agreement there is only one recognized legitimate objective, the protection of human, animal or plant life or health.

1452 *United States – Measures Concerning the Importation, Marketing and Sale of Tuna and Tuna Products, WT/DS381/AB/R* 2012, para. 314.

1453 *United States – Certain Country of Origin Labelling (COOL) Requirements, WT/DS384/AB/R, WT/DS/386/AB/R* 2012, para. 371, 395.

1454 Ibid., para. 360, 362, 384.

1455 Ibid., para. 392.

> "evidence and arguments presented by the parties relating to the measure's text, design, architecture, structure and legislative history, as well as its operation".[1456]

It also clarified that Panels did not have to discern "in the abstract, the level at which a responding Member wishes or aims to achieve that objective".[1457]

As to the second of the above-mentioned aspects, namely what is a legitimate objective, the Appellate Body has stated twice that a legitimate objective is an objective that is "lawful, justifiable or proper". It also has made clear that the list of legitimate objectives in Art. 2.2 TBT is not a closed one, given that the article uses the words "*inter alia*" when referring to these objectives.[1458]

Whether an objective is "legitimate" is a justiciable matter: where the objective of a measure is not among those explicitly listed in Art. 2.2 TBT, the adjudicators have to pass judgement on this issue.[1459] The burden of proof rests on the complainant, who must show that an objective is *not* legitimate, rather than the defendant having to demonstrate that its objective *is* legitimate.[1460] In *United States – COOL Requirements*, the Panel's finding on the legitimacy of a certain regulatory objective was actually appealed by a party. In this case, Canada maintained that the objective of the controversial US measure as identified by the Panel – providing consumers with certain information on the origin of products – was not a legitimate one in the sense of the TBT Agreement, as it was not named as a privileged objective in any of the WTO agreements and was not similar to the regulatory objectives explicitly mentioned in the TBT Agreement and e.g. Art. XX GATT.[1461] The Panel concluded that the objective was legitimate, *inter alia*, on the basis of the factual finding that more than 70 WTO Members maintained some form of mandatory country of origin labelling requirements.[1462] The Panel also referred to the "policy space" that WTO

1456 Ibid., para. 395f.

1457 Ibid., para. 390.

1458 *United States – Measures Relating to Shrimp from Thailand, WT/DS343/AB/R* 2008, para. 313; *United States – Certain Country of Origin Labelling (COOL) Requirements, WT/DS384/AB/R, WT/DS/386/AB/R* 2012, para. 370.

1459 *United States – Certain Country of Origin Labelling (COOL) Requirements, WT/DS384/AB/R, WT/DS/386/AB/R* 2012, para. 372.

1460 Ibid., para. 449.

1461 Ibid., para. 435.

1462 Ibid., para. 438.

Members enjoyed in deciding on regulatory objectives[1463] and observed that consumers could be assumed to be interested in information on the country of origin. The Appellate Body concurred with the Panel decision, stating, *inter alia*, that the objective of keeping consumers informed bore some similarity to the objective of preventing deceptive practices mentioned in Art. 2.2 TBT and Art. XX (d) GATT. It also related to Art. IX GATT which allows WTO Members to require that products carry a "mark of origin".[1464] More generally, the Appellate Body held that a Panel's determination of the legitimacy of a technical regulation could be guided by, amongst other things, whether a certain objective was covered in WTO provisions other than Art. 2.2 TBT.[1465] Nonetheless, the Appellate Body also criticized some aspects of the Panel's analysis of the analysis of the legitimacy of the goal pursued. In particular it expressed some "difficulties" in understanding what the Panel had meant with its references to a "practice in a considerable proportion of WTO Members" and "social norms" in its analysis of the legitimacy of the objectives of the US measure.[1466] This has been read to imply that the Appellate Body prefers references to objectives contained in WTO law in such analysis.[1467]

In *EC – Seal Products*, the Panel had to decide whether the protection of public morals was a legitimate objective in the sense of Art. 2.2 TBT. It found that the GATT and GATS contained exception norms for measures aimed at protecting public morals. Protecting public morals was also a legitimate policy objective under the TBT Agreement, given that in particular, according to the preamble of the TBT Agreement, the agreement is to foster the aims of GATT.[1468]

With regard to the relationship between the technical regulation and the objective it pursues, the Appellate Body stated that the word "fulfil" in Art. 2.2 TBT related to the level to which the technical regulation in dispute contributed to the legitimate objective. It concluded, in light of the fact that Members are allowed by the TBT Agreement to take measures necessary to achieve their objectives at the level they consider appropriate,

1463 Ibid., para. 440.
1464 Ibid., para. 445.
1465 Ibid., para. 372.
1466 Ibid., para. 452.
1467 Norpoth 2013, 598.
1468 The findings of the Panel are summarized in *European Communities – Measures Prohibiting the Importation and Marketing of Seal Products, WT/DS400/AB/R, WT/DS401/AB/R* 2014, para. 5.140.

that "fulfil" could not be taken to mean "complete achievement".[1469] Altogether, the situation is similar to the one under Art. XX GATT in which Panels must also assess the contribution of a measure to the end pursued.[1470]

One issue that came up in *United States – Tuna Labelling* was the exact level of protection or objective that a measure needed to attain. The Appellate Body's finding diverged from the Panel's finding in this regard. The Appellate Body required the complainant to show that the proposed alternative reached the level of protection of the defendant relating to tuna conservation in a specific geographical area.[1471] This implies that, under the TBT Agreement, WTO Members can choose different levels of protection even when the underlying situations are to a certain extent similar; the adjudicators must then use such differentiated levels of protection as the basis for the comparisons required under Art. 2.2 TBT.[1472]

Concerning the terms "necessary" and "unnecessary" in Art. 2.2 TBT the Appellate Body in *United States – Tuna Labelling* quoted its finding in *China – Publications and Audiovisual Products* (on Art. XX GATT) that there was a range of degrees of necessity.[1473] It concluded that, in the context of Art. 2.2 TBT, the factors that had to be "evaluated" for the necessity analysis were: the trade-restrictiveness of the technical regulation; the degree of contribution a measure makes to the achievement of a legitimate objective, and the nature of risks and gravity of consequences that non-fulfilment of the objectives pursued would create.[1474] The Appellate Body also mentioned in a footnote that "similarly", as in the context of Art. XX GATT and Art. XIV GATT, different factors had to be weighed and balanced in the context of the necessity analysis.[1475]

1469 *United States – Measures Concerning the Importation, Marketing and Sale of Tuna and Tuna Products, WT/DS381/AB/R* 2012, para. 315f; *United States – Certain Country of Origin Labelling (COOL) Requirements, WT/DS384/AB/R, WT/DS/386/AB/R* 2012, para. 373.

1470 *United States – Measures Concerning the Importation, Marketing and Sale of Tuna and Tuna Products, WT/DS381/AB/R* 2012, para. 316f.

1471 Ibid., para. 329f.

1472 Crowley and Howse 2014, 335ff note, however, that the Appellate Body proceeded on the basis of wrong assumptions on which alternative measure the Panel had assessed.

1473 *United States – Measures Concerning the Importation, Marketing and Sale of Tuna and Tuna Products, WT/DS381/AB/R* 2012, para. 318.

1474 Ibid., para. 318, 322.

1475 *United States – Measures Concerning the Importation, Marketing and Sale of Tuna and Tuna Products, WT/DS381/AB/R* 2012, footnote 643.

The Appellate Body then added complexity by turning to an analysis of what the phrase "more ... than" meant. It concluded:

> "In most cases, this would involve a comparison of the trade-restrictiveness and the degree of achievement of the objective by the measure at issue with that of possible alternative measures that may be reasonably available and less trade restrictive than the challenged measure, taking account of the risks non-fulfilment would create."[1476]

Again, it referred in a footnote accompanying the paragraph to the similarity of this analysis with the one under Art. XX GATT and XIV GATS where reasonably available, less trade-restrictive alternative measures are also investigated.

Turning, finally, to the next element of Art. 2.2 TBT, the Appellate Body observed that

> "the obligation to consider 'the risks non-fulfilment would create' suggests that the comparison of the challenged measure with a possible alternative measure should be made in the light of the nature of the risks at issue and the gravity of the consequences that would arise from non-fulfilment of the legitimate objective. This suggests *a further element of weighing and balancing* in the determination of whether the trade-restrictiveness of a technical regulation is "necessary" or, alternatively, whether a possible alternative measure [...] would be reasonably available."[1477] [emphasis added, footnote omitted]

The Appellate Body then summarized its own findings by stating that the analysis of whether a measure was "more trade-restrictive than necessary" within the meaning of Art. 2.2 TBT

> "involves an evaluation of a number of factors. A panel should begin by considering factors that include: (i) the degree of contribution made by the measure to the legitimate objective at issue; (ii) the trade-restrictiveness of the measure; and (iii) the nature of the risks at issue and the gravity of *consequences* that would arise from non-fulfilment of the objective(s) pursued by the Member through the measure. In most cases, a comparison of the challenged measure and possible alternative measures should be undertaken. In particular, it may be relevant for the purpose of this comparison to consider whether the pro-

1476 Ibid., para. 320.
1477 Ibid., para. 321.

> posed alternative is less trade restrictive, whether it would make an equivalent contribution to the relevant legitimate objective, taking account of the risks non-fulfilment would create, and whether it is reasonably available."[1478] [footnote omitted]

In another footnote, the Appellate Body also mentioned two types of measures for which an analysis of alternative measures was not required: measures that are not all trade-restrictive and measures that make no contribution at all to the aim pursued.[1479] Presumably, the former category of measures would in any case conform to Art. 2.2 TBT, the second one never. In summation, the Appellate Body here suggested that balancing needed to occur twice: once with regard to the necessity of the original measures and also when assessing potential alternatives.

Concerning the application of these yardsticks to the facts of *United States – Tuna Labelling*, the Appellate Body only had to review whether an alternative measure accepted by the Panel indeed made the challenged measures unnecessary. Its conclusion, that the Panel had compared the wrong measures with each other, was greatly dependent on the circumstances of the case.[1480]

The above findings were quoted and re-iterated by the Appellate Body in *United States – COOL Requirements*.[1481] In this case, the Appellate Body reversed the Panel's finding that a certain measure was not consistent with Art. 2.2 TBT Agreement because it "fell short" of the legitimate objective. The Appellate Body rejected this finding, stating that there was no "threshold" that a measure needed to fulfil under Art. 2.2 TBT. Rather, a Panel needed to ascertain "the degree of contribution achieved by the measure."[1482] The Appellate Body in this case found that the measure at issue

> "makes some contribution to the objective of providing consumers with information on origin; that it has a considerable degree of trade-restrictiveness; and that the consequences that may arise from non-fulfilment of the objective would not be particularly grave."[1483]

1478 Ibid., para. 322.

1479 *United States – Measures Concerning the Importation, Marketing and Sale of Tuna and Tuna Products, WT/DS381/AB/R* 2012, footnote 667.

1480 See ibid., para. 328–331.

1481 *United States – Certain Country of Origin Labelling (COOL) Requirements, WT/DS384/AB/R, WT/DS/386/AB/R* 2012, para. 374–378, 461, 471.

1482 Ibid., para. 468.

1483 Ibid., para. 479.

It then proceeded to compare this situation to four alternative measures proposed by one of the complainants, concluding ultimately that it was not in a position to complete its analysis, as the Panel had not clarified the factual basis sufficiently for such a finding.[1484]

The Appellate Body also re-iterated in both cases the finding on the burden of proof familiar from GATT cases under which the complainant must prove its position that the measure at issue creates an unnecessary obstacle to trade; it may suggest alternative, less trade-restrictive measures to that end. It is upon the defendant then, then, to rebut the claim by showing, for example, that the alternative measure suggested is not in fact reasonably available.[1485]

In *EC – Seal Products*, the Appellate Body did not deal with the TBT Agreement. However, an important aspect of the Appellate Body's analysis in *EC – Seal Products* is that it appears to have approved of the Panel's approach of relying in its analysis under Art. 2.2 TBT for the interpretation of the "necessary" clause in Art. XX GATT.[1486] This means that the two terms can (or might need to be) interpreted in the same way under Art. XX GATT and Art. 2.2 TBT.

3.2. Art. 2.4 TBT

The first time the Appellate Body had to deal with Art. 2.4 TBT was *EC – Sardines*.[1487] The only other case in which Art. 2.4 TBT has played a role is *United States – Tuna Labelling.*[1488]

1484 Ibid., para. 480–491.

1485 *United States – Measures Concerning the Importation, Marketing and Sale of Tuna and Tuna Products, WT/DS381/AB/R* 2012, para. 323; *United States – Certain Country of Origin Labelling (COOL) Requirements, WT/DS384/AB/R, WT/DS/386/AB/R* 2012, para. 379.

1486 *European Communities – Measures Prohibiting the Importation and Marketing of Seal Products, WT/DS400/AB/R, WT/DS401/AB/R* 2014, para. 5.204ff.

1487 *European Communities – Trade Description of Sardines, WT/DS231/AB/R* 2002.

1488 *United States – Measures Concerning the Importation, Marketing and Sale of Tuna and Tuna Products, WT/DS381/AB/R* 2012.

Art. 2.4 TBT contains three elements:[1489]

1) the existence or imminent completion of a relevant international standard;
2) whether the international standard has been used as a basis for the technical regulation; and
3) whether the international standard is an ineffective or inappropriate means for the fulfilment of the legitimate objectives pursued, taking into account fundamental climatic or geographical factors or fundamental technological problems.

The first element, the existence of an international standard, played a role in both of the cases that have so far involved Art. 2.4 TBT.

In *EC – Sardines* the question was raised whether only such standards adopted by an international organization by consensus were standards in the sense of the TBT Agreement, an issue touched upon in the Explanatory Note on the definition of "standard" in Annex 1.2 TBT Agreement. It reads, at the end:

> "Standards prepared by the international standardization community are based on consensus. This Agreement covers also documents that are not based on consensus."

The Panel held that the second of these sentences meant that standards in the sense of the TBT Agreement did not necessarily have to be adopted by consensus and the Appellate Body approved that interpretation.[1490]

In *United States – Tuna Labelling*, it was controversial whether a certification scheme under the Agreement on the International Dolphin Conservation Program (AIDCP) counted as an international standard in the sense of the TBT Agreement. The AIDCP is an agreement to which some states that are also WTO Members are parties;[1491] its geographical scope is limited to a certain area of the East Pacific Ocean. Other states can join the AIDCP, according to its Art. XXVI, when situated in the region covered by the AIDCP, having vessels fishing there or by invitation following a decision by the parties. When discussing whether the AIDCP constituted an "international standard", the Appellate Body embarked on a rather lengthy

---

1489 *United States – Measures Concerning the Importation, Marketing and Sale of Tuna and Tuna Products, WT/DS381/R* 2011, para. 7.627.

1490 *European Communities – Trade Description of Sardines, WT/DS231/AB/R* 2002, para. 222.

1491 A list of states that have ratified or acceded to the agreement can be found at http://www.iattc.org/IDCPENG.htm.

discussion of the terms “international standard”, “international body” and “standards/standardizing organization” as defined in Annex 1 TBT Agreement and the ISO/IEC guide on terms and definitions. This guide shall also apply under the TBT Agreement according to the introductory clause of Annex 1 TBT Agreement, unless there is a different definition in the TBT Agreement.[1492] The Appellate Body found that the definitions of standards/standardizing “organizations” and “bodies” in both sets of norms were not contradictory, but rather could apply cumulatively. The Appellate Body concluded that both require in one way or another that “standards” must be adopted by a “recognized” body and that a standard is only “international” where the entity adopting is open to at least all WTO Members.[1493] In this context, the Appellate Body also relied on the principle contained in the TBT Committee Decision on the Principles for the Development of International Standards, Guides and Recommendations with Relation to Art. 2, 5 and Annex 3 to the Agreement[1494] that membership in international standardizing bodies should be open to at least all WTO Members on a non-discriminatory basis.[1495] The Appellate Body also relied on the principle of “Impartiality and Consensus”, stipulating that all WTO Members should be provided with meaningful opportunities to contribute to the elaboration of an international standard and the standard development process should not privilege the interests of certain Members.[1496] Moreover, it also drew on the TBT Committee Decision in order to ascertain whether the AIDCP was “recognized” by WTO Members. It noted that "recognition" had a factual and a normative dimension. In a factual respect, it observed that if a standardizing body disseminated information about its activities as envisaged by the transparency principle of the TBT Decision, the standards of such a body would presumably be acknowledged and noticed, and hence recognized by WTO Members. In a normative vein, the Appellate Body held that

> “to the extent that a standardizing body complies with the principles and procedures that WTO Members have decided ‘should be observed’

1492 *United States – Measures Concerning the Importation, Marketing and Sale of Tuna and Tuna Products, WT/DS381/AB/R* 2012, para. 353f.

1493 Ibid., para. 357–359.

1494 Contained in document G/TBT/1/Rev. 10 of 9 June 2011, at 46 – 48.

1495 *United States – Measures Concerning the Importation, Marketing and Sale of Tuna and Tuna Products, WT/DS381/AB/R* 2012, para. 373f.

1496 Ibid., para. 384f.

> in the development of international standards, it would be easier to find that the body has 'recognized activities in standardization".[1497]

With regard to the AIDCP, the Appellate Body found on the basis of these interpretive clarifications that, since states could only join the AIDCP in the event of prior consensus by the parties to the AIDCP – a decision that was hence more than a mere formality – the Agreement was not open to all WTO Members and therefore not an international standard.[1498]

The second requirement in Art. 2.4 TBT is that international standards be used "as a basis" for technical regulations. For interpreting this requirement, the Appellate Body in *EC – Sardines* drew on its earlier interpretation of Art. 3.1 SPS, which contains a similar requirement to that in Art. 2.4 TBT. It concurred with the Panel that an international standard is used "as a basis" for when

> "it is used as the principal constituent or fundamental principle for the purpose of enacting the technical regulation".[1499]

It stressed, moreover, that considering a textual analysis of the term "basis" there had to be "a very strong and very close relationship between two things"[1500] in order for one to be considered the basis of the other. *In casu*, the Appellate Body found a contradiction between the international standard and the EU regulation in dispute, and in consequence concluded that the former was not used as a basis for the latter.[1501] Therefore, the Appellate Body's interpretation of "as a basis for" has been described as an *obiter dictum*:[1502] it needs no refined elaboration of the term "as a basis for" to observe that where a WTO Member's measure contradicts an international standard, it is not based on that standard.

Finally, in *EC – Sardines* the Appellate Body also discussed the third requirement in Art. 2.4 TBT which allows a WTO Member not to base its technical regulation on an international standard if it would be an "ineffective or inappropriate means for the fulfilment of the legitimate objectives pursued".

1497 Ibid., para. 376.
1498 Ibid., para. 398.
1499 *European Communities – Trade Description of Sardines, WT/DS231/AB/R* 2002, para. 243.
1500 Ibid., para. 245.
1501 Ibid., para. 257.
1502 Howse 2002c, 251.

First, the Appellate Body decided that the burden of proof in this case was the same as in the case of Art. 3.1 SPS, given that Art. 2.4 TBT was structurally similar to Art. 3.1 and 3.3 SPS Agreement. Accordingly, Art. 2.4, second part TBT does not contain an exception to a general rule in the first part of this article, but

> "the circumstances envisaged in the second part of Article 2.4 are excluded from the scope of application of the first part of Article 2.4."[1503]

That means that the complainant must not only establish that the impugned measure is not on the basis of a relevant international standard, but also that the relevant international standard is effective and appropriate to fulfil the legitimate objectives of the defendant.[1504] As pointed out by the Panel in the case, this means that the complainant has to make substantiated statements about the regulatory goals that another government pursues through its measures; this could be difficult.

The Appellate Body did not share the concerns that the Panel had voiced in this regard. It maintained that WTO Members could obtain information on regulatory objectives of measures under Art. 2.5 TBT, which establishes an obligation for WTO Members to "explain the justification" for a technical regulation to another Member at that Member's request. The Appellate Body was not convinced by the doubts expressed by one of the parties to the case that the mechanism might not be effective, because WTO Members could fail to fully or adequately respond to such a request for information. The Appellate Body stated that it had to

> "assume that Members of the WTO will abide by their treaty obligations in good faith, as required by the principle of *pacta sunt servanda* articulated in Article 26 of the *Vienna Convention*".[1505]

Moreover, the Appellate Body also pointed to other possible ways in which WTO Members could acquire information about the measures taken by other WTO Members, including the inquiry point provided for in Art. 10.1 TBT and the consultation stage and submissions during the dispute settlement process itself.

1503 *European Communities – Trade Description of Sardines, WT/DS231/AB/R* 2002, para. 275.

1504 Ibid.

1505 Ibid., para. 278.

Second, the Appellate Body had to decide on the substantive interpretation of the norm. The Appellate Body supported the Panel's literal interpretation according to which

> "in the context of Article 2.4, an ineffective means is a means which does not have the function of accomplishing the legitimate objective pursued, whereas an inappropriate means is a means which is not specially suitable for the fulfilment of the legitimate objective pursued. [...] The question of effectiveness bears upon the results of the means employed, whereas the question of appropriateness relates more to the *nature* of the means employed."[1506]

The Appellate Body stated, moreover, that the international standard in question would be effective for the legitimate objectives pursued if it had the capacity to accomplish these objectives, and appropriate if it was suitable for fulfilling all of them.[1507]

3.3. Discussion and assessment

The case law on the TBT Agreement on the questions discussed here and in the time period covered by this work is comparatively limited. The following discussion and assessment, both from a legal-technical and more normative-political point of view, are therefore brief.

An issue that has received some attention in the literature is whether the legitimacy of an objective under Art. 2.2 TBT should actually be subject to judicial review, i.e. is it a justiciable matter? Some have indicated that Art. 2.2 TBT does not give adjudicators the power to review this matter.[1508] In support of this position, for example, it is argued that if WTO Members have the right to choose their level of protection, as the preamble to the TBT Agreement indicates, this should include the right to define which objective is legitimate.[1509] A counter-argument is that the TBT Agreement refers to specific policy objectives, both in Art. 2.4 TBT and in the sixth recital of its preamble. Being allowed to set a level of protection in pursuit of specifically defined or qualified objectives – with the term legitimate being such a qualification – is not the same as choosing *ad libidum* policy ob-

1506 Ibid., para. 285.
1507 Ibid., para. 288.
1508 Neumann and Tuerk 2003, 219.
1509 Ibid.

jectives. There is no reason why "legitimate" should not, in principle, be a justiciable term,[1510] particularly as the WTO legal order defines certain objectives that the WTO Members recognize as legitimate. How intensive scrutiny of WTO Members' statements on their objectives is then applied in practice is an aspect of the standard of review, which is discussed in chapter 3.[1511]

Another issue with regard to Art. 2.2 TBT is the question, already familiar from the analysis of Art. XX GATT, of what "necessary" means. Some scholars read the Appellate Body as not applying a balancing test under Art. 2.2 TBT, and welcome this as being in line with the Appellate Body's mandate.[1512] However, as noted above, the Appellate Body has referred to balancing in the context of Art. 2.2 TBT, even if only in a footnote. Altogether, a certain lack of clarity not only exists with regard to the necessity test under the GATT and GATS, but also under the TBT. Furthermore, and also with regard to Art. 2.2 TBT, scholars have supported the WTO's approach of recognizing that a measure may fulfil its objective only to some extent, but still be aimed at the objective. The contrary position would have reduced WTO Members' regulatory scope, and would probably be unrealistic in terms of the fact that real-world policy measures often involve trade-offs between different policy objectives.[1513]

Some criticism has also been voiced against the adjudicators not accepting the AIDCP as an international standard in *United States – Tuna Labelling*. Shaffer, for example, notes that the requirement that an organization be open to all WTO Members in order to be able to produce international standards may be too strict given that there is at least one WTO Member – Taiwan – that is not a UN Member and in consequence barred from accessing many international organizations.[1514] On the other hand, Crowley and Howse note that in other respects the Appellate Body's approach to ascertaining what an international standard is appropriately lenient: the Appellate Body includes entities that are not principally occupied with standardization in the notion of "standardizing body". According to Crowley and Howse, this opens the door to a broader array of international standards being recognized as international standards in the sense

---

1510 A similar position is expressed by Andenas and Zleptnig 2007, 418; Lowe 2014, 613 described as not favouring a too intensive cross-examination of WTO Members' statements on their regulatory goals.

1511 Lowe 2014, 613.

1512 Mavroidis 2013, 522.

1513 Crowley and Howse 2014, 338.

1514 Shaffer 2012, 8.

of WTO law, including environmental and sustainability standards adopted by private organizations.[1515] Yet it should also be noted that bringing more international standards within the purview of the TBT Agreement means decreasing the regulatory autonomy of WTO Members; only where an international standard in the sense of the TBT Agreement exists (or its completion is imminent) does a WTO Member have to base its measure on it.

Since the case law on the provisions discussed here is relatively sparse, it is useful to slightly extend the analysis and include a brief summary of the literature on the interpretation of the TBT Agreement more broadly.

With regards to the legal-technical discussion of the case law so far, Mavroidis criticizes how the Appellate Body conceives of the relationship between Art. 2.1 and 2.2 TBT and the order in which both are investigated.[1516] Other authors are critical of the definition of "technical regulation" in *United States – Tuna Labelling*, arguing that the Appellate Body has unduly extended the scope of the definition to include measures that were at most only partially compulsory.[1517]

With regards to an assessment of how restrictive the case law is on WTO Members' regulatory freedom, the Appellate Body's interpretation of Art. 2.1 TBT has been observed to build a certain policy space into the provision by requiring a consideration of the regulatory purpose of a measure when assessing that measure's conformity with Art. 2.1 TBT.[1518]

It has also been observed that in all of the three TBT cases mentioned above, the Appellate Body found a violation of Art. 2.1 TBT and none of Article 2.2 TBT. This is read as an indication that it will be difficult for WTO Members to successfully claim that another WTO Member has violated that provision.[1519] More generally, Howse observes that while textually some of the "post-discriminatory" provisions of the TBT Agreement contain more stringent requirements for WTO Members than the old GATT did, the Appellate Body has interpreted various provisions of the TBT Agreement in a way that makes it

1515 Crowley and Howse 2014, 340f.
1516 Mavroidis 2013, 515ff.
1517 Crowley and Howse 2014, 323ff; Norpoth 2013, 583ff; Mavroidis 2013, 522f.
1518 Shlomo-Agon 2015, 572f; Marín Durán 2016, 482.
1519 Carlone 2014, 130f.

> "at least very unlikely to succeed with a claim under the TBT Agreement that would not also succeed under GATT."[1520]

The observed outcome on Art. 2.1 and 2.2 TBT has been presumed to occur, because the Appellate Body is

> "more comfortable finding a violation using non-discrimination, which is widely recognized as the WTO's core function, rather than necessity"[1521].

It has also been welcomed by at least some observers as appropriately respectful of WTO Members regulatory autonomy.[1522] However, the opposite – that the Appellate Body's decisions on the TBT Agreement have narrowed the policy-making space of WTO Members – has also been observed.[1523]

In summation, while there are comparatively few TBT cases, the Appellate Body appears to again have not chosen the most "pro-trade" interpretation nor its opposite.

4. Conclusions

In this chapter, the interpretation of the justification norms contained in various WTO agreements by the WTO adjudicators has been described, discussed from a legal-technical point of view, and been evaluated with a view to whether these interpretations have restricted, broadened, or maintained the regulatory space available for WTO Members intaking measures for non-trade objectives.

Before relating these findings to the broader discussion in the literature on the outcome that the WTO dispute settlement system has produced and relating the findings back to the conceptual framework of chapter 1, it is worth summarizing the core findings of the present chapter. I will do so in section 4.1. I will then relate my own findings to existing research describing where the Appellate Body positions itself on a continuum of pro-trade/ expansionist reading of WTO norm and pro regulatory freedom of WTO

1520 Howse 2016b, 56; by contrast Conconi and Voon 2016, 218 point to and criticies differences in the non-discrimination standards applied by the Appellate Body under the TBT Agreement and GATT.

1521 Carlone 2014, 127 and also 131.

1522 Ibid., 127.

1523 Conconi and Voon 2016, 219.

Members/deference to WTO Members (section 4.2). Finally, I will link my insights back to the theories on factors influencing the outcome of judicial deliberations presented in chapter 1 (section 4.3).

4.1. Summary of the findings

In this section, I will briefly summarize the central findings on the outcome of WTO judicial decisions in "trade and ..." cases.

First, for all of the agreements reviewed, the outcome of the dispute settlement cases in terms of the interpretations of WTO law they contain is quite mixed. The Appellate Body has visibly moved away from understandings prevailing in earlier GATT jurisprudence that favoured trade at the expense of other interests. With regard to both the GATT and the WTO agreements negotiated as part of the Uruguay Round, clear examples can be given of interpretations that are more permissive of WTO Members' regulatory measures than have been adopted by Panels or suggested by WTO Members or legal commentators. Examples include the interpretation of Art. XX (g) GATT to include living "resources", the refusal to automatically interpret exception provisions narrowly, the recognition that a measure may be "based on" minority scientific opinions, the recognition that alternative measures must be "reasonably" available (i.e. not impose excessive burdens on the WTO Member expected to take them), and a willingness to recognize a variety of reasons as justification for treating similar situations differently under Art. 5.5 SPS. However, there is no consistent track record to this end; in other cases, the adjudicators have also favoured restrictive interpretations. Examples include what are the in some cases quite exacting standards of what constitutes a valid risk assessment under Art. 5.1 SPS, the interpretation of what "insufficient" means in Art. 5.7 SPS (in some of the cases), and the interpretation of Art. XX GATT chapeau.

On some other aspects which are also quite central, the case law is not clear. One reason is that for some there are a limited number of cases and in these the adjudicators did not make the meaning of specific terms very clear; hence, broad guidelines are missing. This is sometimes related to an emphasis on the case-by-case character of a certain decision, e.g. the changing line of equilibrium in the chapeau interpretation. Another reason for a lack of clarity on certain issues is that various statements offered by the Appellate Body appear to be contradictory and the case law on certain matters is not uniform. The most important example here is the "necessity" test and the relationship between the Appellate Body's balancing formula and the "alternative measure reasonably available" test. Finally, on some aspects – e.g. the understanding of risk assessment under the SPS Agreement – there are also variations in the case law over time which make an overall assessment difficult.

Another recurring issue in the case law is the gap or mismatch between rhetoric and reality. A notable example is the emphasis put on the right of Members to define their level of protection. Neither under the justification norms of GATT/GATS and its related balancing formula, nor the SPS Agreement with its science disciplines, is it clear to what extent the right to define the level of protection has a real, practical value for WTO Members when trying to justify their measures. In any case, the practical importance is less pronounced than the quite emphatic references of the Appellate Body to the Members' right to choose their level of protection suggest.

Moreover, there is also a mismatch between the interpretation of norms and the application of the interpretations. Notable examples can be given from the case law on the SPS Agreement. There are quite a few statements from the Appellate Body signalling that WTO Members have a certain leeway when conducting a risk assessment. Yet in the practice of WTO dispute settlement intensive scrutiny is applied to WTO Members' risk assessments, leading to a situation where the risk assessments have so far more or less consistently been held to fall short of the requirements of Art. 5.1 SPS. Other authors have identified examples of a mismatch between interpretations adopted and how these are applied. For example, Alvarez notes that while the Appellate Body has in principle accepted non-violation complaints, very few such claims have been successful.[1524] What is common to all these examples is a pattern whereby the legal rules formulated by the Appellate Body are relatively permissive on states, but when applied in a concrete case, they do restrict WTO Members' behaviour quite significantly.

Third, a further aspect is that the Appellate Body's reasoning is not always exemplary in terms of consistency and predictability. This is made plain by the fact that the Appellate Body has not pointed out the apparent frictions between the different parts of the necessity analysis, that earlier dispute settlement reports have been cited for interpretations the reports have hardly embraced (without making the deviations visible) and that some its central findings have either been produced out of virtually nothing (such as the various requirements that the Appellate Body links to the

1524 Alvarez in Abi-Saab 2008, 712.

chapeau of Art. XX GATT), or have come packaged solely with some (dubious) precedents as support (as is the case with the balancing formula).

Finally, another important aspect is that some of the Appellate Body's findings entail maintaining or even enlarging the decision-making space for the adjudicators in future cases. Whenever the adjudicators stress the case-by-case character of certain decisions and do not clarify the criteria by which a decision is to be taken, they effectively grant themselves a large degree of freedom in deciding subsequent cases. An important example of such an interpretation is the case law on the changing line of equilibrium contained in chapeau. Various authors have stressed that this line of interpretation has the effect of bestowing the adjudicators with broad powers to accept or strike down a measure, making the outcome of cases rather unpredictable.[1525] Other examples are the balancing formula used to ascertain whether a measure is necessary and the Appellate Body's statement that whether a measure is "based on" a risk assessment in the sense of Art. 5.1 SPS is a case-by-case decision, and dependent on the particular circumstances of the case. Even despite its lip-service to the letter of the law, the Appellate Body has provided itself with considerable discretion and adjudicative authority.[1526]

To summarize the findings in a short, somewhat simplistic manner: The interpretations found in the Appellate Body's decisions in which different interpretations can be chosen are neither uniformly pro-trade nor uniformly pro-regulatory freedom. Many central issues have yet to be decided or, at least, not in a clear manner. On some central questions, the Appellate Body has stressed the case-by-case character of certain decisions, thereby preserving its own decision-making space for future cases. The rhetoric of regulatory autonomy of the WTO Members that the Appellate Body adopts does not always translate readily into real-world decision-making space of WTO Members, and not all of the central findings in WTO case law are supported by sound legal reasoning.

4.2. Relating the results to existing research

In this section, I will relate the above findings – in particular those on the "pro-trade" vs. "non-trade"/pro-regulatory space outcome of the case law – to existing predominantly legal scholarship on WTO dispute settlement.

1525 See for example Knox 2004, 37.
1526 Charnovitz 2007, 702.

The reception of the case law of the WTO among legal observers has been somewhat mixed.[1527] This is likely attributable at least partly to the fact that it is virtually impossible for any observer, myself being no exception, to know and appreciate each and every aspect of the WTO jurisprudence in depth. Given that different decisions vary quite strongly concerning the degree to which they restrict the freedom of WTO Members to regulate, observers are likely to come to divergent conclusions regarding how the dispute settlement bodies have fared with regard to the substantive interpretations they have offered.[1528] For example, Kulovesi writes that

> "[…] while there have been positive developments […] WTO jurisprudence regarding trade and environment is not consistent and does not therefore form a solid basis for constructive interaction between the international trade and environmental regimes".[1529]

Moreover, assessments are also undoubtedly influenced by commentators' normative positions on which approach they would like the WTO tribunals to take.

The view apparently held by what is probably the larger group of commentators is that the WTO dispute settlement, and in particular the Appellate Body, have performed quite well from both a legal-technical and more normative point of view (though with a few caveats).[1530] Some point to both expansionist and narrow interpretations in the case law and the careful balance struck by the Appellate Body between different policy objectives.[1531] They argue that the WTO dispute settlement bodies do not exhibit a pro-trade bias, have been mindful of WTO Members' sovereignty,[1532] and have taken non-trade concerns (such as environmental protection) into account in a satisfactory manner[1533]. There is also a certain tangibility to the relief that WTO jurisprudence has moved away from some of the questionable GATT case law on environment and health-related measures.[1534] The observation that some of the WTO's judicial decisions must be under-

---

1527 This has also been noted by other authors, see for example Du 2010a, 1078 providing references for different assessments.

1528 See also Krüger 2013, 96.

1529 Kulovesi 2011, 81f.

1530 See for example van den Bossche 2006, 320ff; Picker 2020.

1531 Eeckhout 2010, 9f; Footer and Saman Zia-Zarifi 2002, 141 with regard to *EC – Asbestos*; Howse 2002a, 109ff; van den Bossche 2006, 320ff.

1532 This view seems to be shared for example by Afilalo and Foster 2003, 660.

1533 Knox 2004, 3.

1534 See for example Henckels 2006, 282.

stood as astute and politically responsive judicial drafting that does not favour any of the two sides too much and avoids issues that could be too controversial is made with a certain regularity.[1535] For example, with regard to *EC – Biotech Products*, the Panel's approach of not considering the EU's GMO moratorium an SPS "measure" and thus not reviewing it under the SPS Agreement's science-related disciplines has been interpreted as a deliberate move to eschew scientifically and politically controversial issues.[1536] Similarly, it has been observed that the fact that the Appellate Body found violations of the non-discrimination provision in Art. 2.1 TBT in three cases, and none of the necessity provision in Art. 2.2 TBT can be attributed to hesitancy on part of the Appellate Body to declare national measures as unnecessary.[1537]

A somewhat different, but related account is that the WTO dispute settlement bodies, at least in some cases, have opted for a "procedural" approach, i.e. deciding a case on other grounds than finding a violation of a substantive obligation.[1538] Procedural "solutions" to WTO controversies are in general likely to provoke less controversy than cases revolving around a finding of a substantive violation; a measure's procedural flaws can often be remedied without modifying its essence. Indeed, some authors argue that the dispute settlement bodies should better adopt a procedural approach to interpreting WTO law.[1539]

A group of observers that seems to be smaller in numbers identifies a pro-trade bias in WTO case law.[1540]

From a different angle, others criticize the WTO dispute settlement bodies for judicial creativity, over-reaching,[1541] intruding (too) far into WTO Members' sphere of sovereign decision-making,[1542] taking decisions on the

1535 For statements coming in this category see Howse 2016b; Lieberman and Gray 2008, 48 on *EC – Biotech Products*; Picciotto 2005, 13 on *Hormones I*; Thomison 2007, 297 for *EC – Biotech Products*; Winham 2003, 140 on *Hormones I*.

1536 Herwig 2008, 834.

1537 Carlone 2014, 131.

1538 See for example Shaffer 2009, 35 with regard to the Panel's *EC – Biotech Products* decision; Hoekman, Bernard and Trachtman, Joel 2010, 160 for the *Homones II* case.

1539 For SPS cases, see Winickoff et al. 2005, 85.

1540 Goldstein and Steinberg 2007, 15, 27f; with regard to the *Shrimp – Turtles* decision Gaines 2001, 743.

1541 Mavroidis 2006, 355.

1542 Magnuson 2010, 130ff.

validity of scientific claims that they should not take,[1543] law-making[1544] or judicial activism[1545]. The criticism of judicial law-making, activism or overreaching appears to be made most regularly with regard to trade-remedy cases which have not been investigated in the present study.[1546] It has also been stated that the Appellate Body regularly violates Art. 3.2 forbidding it from modifying the rights and obligations of Members[1547] or has imposed "unrealistic standards" for WTO Members regulation[1548]. By way of contrast, there seems to be no identifiable group of people holding the view that the WTO dispute settlement bodies have been consistently too lenient and afforded WTO Members too much space when interpreting WTO law,[1549] even though such criticism has been voiced on certain individual cases.[1550]

Furthermore, quite a number of observers are also critical of what they perceive as a lack of clarity in the reasoning of the Appellate Body on several core matters of WTO law.[1551]

The analysis of the case law on justification norms offered in the present chapter has yielded results closer to those arguing that the WTO dispute settlement system has so far not exhibited a pro-trade bias. It is thus worth taking a look at the contributions that contradict this finding and identify a pro-trade bias in order to ascertain what might be the reason for this divergence of conclusions.

An important work in this regard is the one by Colares.[1552] It is noteworthy, among others, because it analyses *all* decisions by the Appellate Body in a certain time period (1995 - 2007). In consequence, the results of Colares' study can be taken to have *prima facie* more weight than case

---

1543 Cho 2009a, 716 and passim.

1544 Goldstein and Steinberg 2007, 3; however, they also clarify that they do not claim the Appellate Body to be "irresponsibly 'activist'", at 23; Babu 2020.

1545 Condon 2018.

1546 Krüger 2013, 215 with further references at 35; Cartland, Depayre, and Woznowski 2012, 991ff formulate a general criticism of the Appellate Body being "activist", but rely in large part on a case decided under the SCM in support; Cunningham and Cribb 2003.

1547 Cartland, Depayre, and Woznowski 2012, 989ff.

1548 Lydgate 2017, 562.

1549 However, Cho 2009a, 711ff criticizes the Appellate Body's jurisprudence both for "overregulation" and "underregulation".

1550 See Cho 2009b with regard to the Appellate Body decision in *Hormones II*.

1551 Mavroidis 2016; with regards to the chapeau of Art. XX GATT and XIV GATS Bartels 2015, 96.

1552 Colares 2009.

notes or studies investigating a limited number of cases. On the basis of his statistical analysis, Colares observes a

> "sustained pattern of Complainant success across all categories of disputes (e.g., trade remedy and non-trade remedy), regardless of Complainant-specific characteristics (e.g., country identity, and level of income) or product-type (e.g., commodities and non-commodities)".[1553]

In a later article, Colares finds a similar pattern in compliance disputes.[1554] The result is based on the following methodology:[1555] Colares looks at all cases in the period investigated where at the very least a request for the establishment of a Panel has been filed. The rate of litigants' success is calculated from the overall number of adopted Panel and Appellate Body reports. A complainant is considered as "winning" a case whenever the defendant's measure is considered not to be in compliance with WTO obligations; a finding that a measure of the respondent impairs or nullifies the complainants' rights is coded as the defendant losing the case. Based on this methodology Colares finds that complainants win between 83 % and 91 % of all cases, depending on the type of case.[1556]

Colares concludes that the observed high rate of complainant success is independent of a number of possible explanatory factors, such as the identity or income level of the complainant, the agreement covered, or the type of dispute. He discusses several possible explanations for the pattern discerned, including e.g. that defendants' cases are weak from a legal point of view. After discarding all of them for different reasons, he concludes that the WTO dispute settlement bodies are engaged in what he calls "biased rule development", i.e. WTO adjudicators' decisions are permeated by a pro-complainant decisional pattern.[1557] In cases, where non-trade regulatory measures are the subject of a WTO challenge, a pro-complainant bias equals a pro-trade bias.

As observed above, Colares is not the only author identifying a pro-trade bias in WTO dispute settlement. Other authors have made a similar point, arguing that the Appellate Body tends to favour trade-liberalizing argu-

1553 Ibid., 387; in Colares 2011 these findings are confirmed also for compliance disputes.
1554 Colares 2011.
1555 Colares 2009, 398ff.
1556 Ibid., 402f; Colares distinguishes between different types of trade remedy cases and cases not concerned with trade remedies.
1557 Ibid., 422f.

ments.[1558] Greenwald states that the Appellate Body has constantly read the relevant norms in trade-remedy cases in a pro-complainant way, against the wording of the law and following its own preferences.[1559] Krüger also maintains that the Panels and the Appellate Body follow a "dogma of free trade enshrined in the founding treaties of the WTO" and exhibit a free-trade bias which means that where conflicts between free trade and regulatory goals emerge, free trade tends to prevail.[1560]

Some other authors have also pointed to a high rate of complainant success in terms of the overall percentage of cases in which the defendants have been found to have acted inconsistently with WTO law.[1561] Maton and Maton look at how often a complainant wins on a specific claim that a respondent acts inconsistently with its obligations, rather than looking at who wins an overall dispute. They conclude that measured in these terms, complainants won over 80 % of all complaints between 1995 and 2004.[1562] Turk summarizes the available literature on complainants' rate of success by stating that

> "while statistical studies of WTO outcomes use a variety of methods, their results are all substantially the same: the complainant almost always wins."[1563]

In order that these findings have some context, it is useful to relate them to observations on the behaviour of other international courts. For example, Wessel notes that historically, international courts have engaged in law-making in a way that extends rather than restricts the international legal obligations of states.[1564] He observes a similar tendency in the ICC. Pair also notes that when no clear legal text existed, the ICJ has been quite active in creating law.[1565] While these findings suggest that the pattern of outcome of WTO cases is not entirely unusual in the world of international tribunals, the pattern of outcome in WTO dispute settlement is ultimately different from that of other international courts: before other international tribunals the success rate of complainants is much closer to the

1558 Goldstein and Steinberg 2007, 27f..
1559 Greenwald 2003, 115.
1560 Krüger 2013, 214.
1561 Sweet and Brunell 2013, 82 put the rate of the defendants losing at almost 90 %; the same rate is calculated by Iida 2003, 2f.
1562 Maton and Maton 2007, 326ff.
1563 Turk 2011, 394.
1564 Wessel 2006, 404.
1565 Pair 2001, 218.

50 % expected as the "normal" outcome pattern of judicial procedures.[1566] Hence, the high rate of complainant success in WTO dispute is unusual – and also seems to contradict my own conclusion that the interpretations adopted by the adjudicators are sometimes "pro trade" and sometimes "pro regulatory freedom", with no pattern of trade interests always being favoured. Can this divergence be explained, and if so how?

A first explanation may relate to what the respective authors look at and how comprehensively they do so. As stressed throughout this work, I have looked at "trade and ..." cases and not at all cases decided in WTO dispute settlement so far. For example, I have left out trade remedy cases where at least some observers find the "activism" of the Appellate Body most marked. Yet the circa two dozen cases I have looked at in depth constitute too large a proportion of the overall number of cases decided to be statistically insignificant.[1567] Moreover, many of them feature amongst those cases considered to be iconic or landmark in WTO dispute settlement to date. It is unlikely that these cases would all exhibit an outcome pattern that is not only somewhat, but categorically different from the remainder of the cases decided.

A second, probably more important question is on what basis one makes a statement that a certain judicial decision is e.g. "pro-trade". If one looks at the outcome of judicial cases through a victory/defeat binary lens as Colares did, something gets lost: the arguments with which the judicial decision-makers support their decisions and the manner in which they interpret a legal norm. If a WTO Member loses a case over an environment-related measure, this does not mean necessarily that the *interpretation* of the relevant norm is "pro-trade" and "anti-environment". This is illustrated by the *Shrimp – Turtles* case, where the US environmental measure was found to be inconsistent with WTO law, while at the same time the decision was widely welcomed as not unduly restricting environmental protection measures at the national level and while in the second round, the compliance proceedings, the environmental measure was upheld. In other words, not every case where a non-trade measure is deemed to be WTO-incompatible inevitably involves a pro-trade interpretation of WTO norms. An observa-

1566 Turk 2011, 395.

1567 According to the WTO, 197 Panel and 123 Appellate Body reports had been adopted by the end of 2020 (excluding cases according to Art. 21.5 DSU, Art. 21. 3 c) DSU and Art. 22.6 DSU), see WTO, Dispute settlement activity – some figures, Table 1, https://www.wto.org/english/tratop_e/dispu_e/dispustats_e.htm.

tion by Flett sheds some more light at the phenomenon: Flett, on the basis of his litigation experience in the WTO and elsewhere, observes that if a (biased) judge is seeking to "stitch up" one party, this would mostly *not* be done through offering interpretations going against that party's interests, but rather in other parts of the process of judicial decision-making.[1568] In other words, pro-complainant outcomes of cases need not entail pro-trade interpretations of the law; it could also be down to the way that the evidence is used by the court, for example. If such outcomes evolve into a pattern, then this pattern would warrant both a statement of a "pro-trade" bias (based on who wins or loses the overall case) or no such bias (based on the interpretations of the law offered). As discussed above, some of the formulas used by the Appellate Body to interpret justification norms in WTO law are very open-ended, e.g. the balancing formula used in the interpretation of "necessary". The formula is not "pro-trade" or "anti-trade" – but it can be applied in either of these manners. While there is no "pro-trade" interpretation of the law involved here, there may be a "pro-complainant" pattern of success.

Admittedly, most of the commentators that offer a diagnosis of some kind of pro-trade leaning in WTO dispute settlement support their conclusion with at least some exegesis of the case law and reference to the interpretation of certain provisions. But here, the first explanation given above may play a role: As long as one does not do such an analysis comprehensively, one can be almost sure to find both "pro-trade" interpretations by the Appellate Body and their opposite.

Finally, what constitutes a "pro-trade" interpretation, and what does not, is a highly qualitative judgement. Compared to earlier GATT jurisprudence, the Appellate Body's stance offers more leeway for WTO Members' non-trade regulatory measures in several important respects – in this sense, the Appellate Body's leanings cannot be described as "pro-trade". On the other hand, if one takes as a yardstick the outer limit of what would still be a textually defensible interpretation of a certain provision and holds the view that the Appellate Body should fully exploit this space in order to safeguard WTO Members' regulatory freedom, then any interpretation falling short of that can be considered a "pro-trade" interpretation. And certain examples for such interpretations exist in the WTO case law. For example, if the adjudicators had applied a more deferential standard of review in health cases, some of the adjudicated SPS measures might have been spared a verdict of WTO incompatibility. In conclusion, the two

1568 Flett 2011, 19.

statements that there is a consistent pattern of complainant success and that the WTO adjudicators do not consistently embrace pro-trade *interpretations* of WTO law are not necessarily incompatible – as odd as this may seem at first glance.

In addition, some other explanations for the observed pattern other than a trade-liberalization bias of the WTO adjudicators have been offered in the literature. One such explanation for the high rate of complainant success is that defendants decide to defend cases that they are likely to lose rather than settling because of domestic constraints. Iida explains that while vested interests relating to trade disputes exist on both sides of the disputes, they are likely to be more constraining on the defending Member. After all, the complaining Member is seeking to change an existing status quo (which so far everyone has managed to live with); the effects of such change are likely to be more direct for economic actors in the defending Member than in the complaining Member.[1569] Therefore, a defending Member is unlikely to settle even in a legal situation in which it appears likely to lose. Guzman and Simmons conclude that the WTO Members' ability to reach a settlement is particularly constrained where the subject matter has an "all-or-nothing" character and leaves little room for compromise; they give health and safety regulations as an example. They find that WTO Members do not normally resort to an option that adversaries within the domestic system often make use of – some form of transfer payment in cash.[1570] Again, this may put defending WTO Members in a position where they have no strong legal case, but still do not settle.

Besides this research, there is some more anecdotal evidence of such behaviour by WTO Members. Flett, an observer with an inside perspective of the machinations of the WTO dispute settlement system, suggests that whether a dispute actually proceeds to the stage of appellate review has much to do with domestic political constraints:

> "[…] often cases do not come to litigation because both parties are convinced of the correctness of their positions, but rather because an internal domestic rigidity demands adjudication before ceding. Those close to the litigation or informed observers generally know in advance what the outcome will be, the quip being that there are only two kinds of WTO cases: those that are a foregone conclusion and those that shouldn't be there (because they properly belong to another fo-

1569 Iida 2003, 5ff.
1570 Guzman and Simmons 2002, 206.

rum). Thus, a visit to the Appellate Body has less to do with closing gaps between Members, and more to do with closing gaps between domestic constituencies."[1571]

He indicates that a WTO Member's behaviour may sometimes be due to the lack of familiarity with WTO law on the part of the competent authorities in combination with pressure from domestic interest groups.[1572] As a result, there may be cases where a defendant has a weak position and knows it, but still does not settle. For example, it would likely have been very difficult for the EU to settle in any of the landmark environmental and health cases it was involved in so far – on GMOs, hormone-treated beef, asbestos, and seals. These were all cases where strong preferences existed among the EU public as well as among at least some political actors. In such a situation, opting for a settled solution that would have "sacrificed" a part of the EU's environmental or health measures for trade interests would been likely to have put the EU political institutions in a very difficult situation. Moreover, there are sometimes divergent positions among actors within a certain country which may lead to a situation where "weak" WTO disputes are litigated by defendants. For example, there was an internal EU configuration behind *EC – Biotech Products* in which several EU Member States were very sceptical about GMOs and had national bans in place, while the Commission did not necessarily share the view that these national bans were lawful and appropriate.[1573] The EU's regulatory framework for GMOs was under revision and the public opinion in several Member States about GMOs was very critical. In this situation, it would most likely have been politically difficult for the EU if it had agreed to a settled solution with the US on GMOs involving any compromise on its GMO regulation. Yet the EU's case for defending its moratorium was arguably not very strong from the viewpoint of WTO law. On another case involving the EU as a defendant, *EC – GSP*, Howse observes that both the EU, the defendant in the case, and the US, a third party, came forward with much weaker legal arguments than they could have. He speculates that in the case of the EU this may have been due to the desire to avoid a legal interpretation that would, in certain respects, have been favourable

1571 Flett 2010, 319. Flett is a staff member of the European Commission's Legal Service, WTO Team, and indicates that he frequently represents the European Union in WTO dispute settlement cases.

1572 Flett 2011, 8.

1573 On EU regulation of GMOs and the role of different actors, see for example Weimer 2014, 7ff.

for the US and some aspects of its domestic legal system.[1574] Similarly, in *EC – Seal Products*, the Panel found that the EU measure violated certain provisions of GATT and was not justified under Art. XX GATT, because it did not comply with the terms of the chapeau. Still, it was only the complainants that appealed the Panel's findings on the chapeau; the EU actually defended the Panel's reasoning.[1575] It may be assumed that the EU was rather content with the legal reasoning of the Panel, even though the Panel's approach meant that the EU would lose this particular case.

Colares partially investigates such alternative explanations for the observed pattern of overwhelming complainant success. He discusses whether there are "settlement constraints"[1576] causing a defendant not to agree to an amicable settlement despite having a weak case and being likely to lose. He finds that there is some evidence of constraints on WTO Members' settlement behaviour; this would make them prone to proceed to the adjudication stage even where they do not have a legally sound case. Yet Colares ultimately dismisses these constraints as irrelevant, reasoning that statistically the settlement behaviour of countries is independent of the relevance of trade in their respective economies, while he expects that respondents with a lower trade-dependence would be more likely to accept a settled solution. Consequently, he concludes that

> "although potentially having a settlement-depressing influence, settlement constraints cannot *alone* account for the extreme imbalance between Complainant and Respondent success in litigation".[1577]

Similarly, Turk states that

> "while it is certainly true that WTO rulings may have disproportionate impacts on the parties' domestic politics, in order to explain the 90 percent win-rate this inequality must point overwhelmingly in one direction across all party types and all substantive areas of dispute. It is difficult to construct a believable narrative of domestic politics in which this is always the case."[1578]

Yet this may be an underestimation of the role of such constraints. Colares' methodology does not appear to allow conclusions on whether inter-

1574 Howse 2003b, 399ff.

1575 *European Communities – Measures Prohibiting the Importation and Marketing of Seal Products, WT/DS400/AB/R, WT/DS401/AB/R* 2014, para. 2.146ff.

1576 Colares 2009, 413ff.

1577 Ibid., 415.

1578 Turk 2011, 402.

nal political constraints or other policy considerations, such as avoiding political fallout with another WTO Member, would trump economic rationales when a WTO Member decides whether or not to settle. In other words, a government may know that its economy is not that trade-dependent and a settled solution may therefore not do much economic harm; yet the government but may still fear the political consequences of a settled solution and in consequence not embrace it. Typically, a WTO Member adopting measures for non-trade purposes has already subjected them to an internal assessment with a view to understanding the economic costs of a measure; economic arguments may hence not provide a very strong incentive for settlement in the cases of such measures.

Another alternative explanation for the high rate of complainant success, other than a pro-trade bias in WTO adjudication, may be that environmental and health measures sometimes have a protectionist component. For example, there are a considerable number of schemes supporting the generation of renewable energy that come with some type of in-built local content requirement.[1579] While the overall objective of such schemes is environmental – climate mitigation – the objective behind local content requirements is usually not environmental, or at least not primarily; rather, local content requirements are aimed at building the local economy.[1580] In some cases, local content requirements may be used as an argument by governments to "sell" such schemes to local constituencies. Local content requirements are explicitly prohibited in several provisions of WTO law (e.g. Art. III:5 GATT, or the "Illustrative List" under TRIMS). Whether they could be justified in WTO dispute settlement under e.g. Art. XX GATT is an open question.[1581] Such local content requirements

1579 For an overview of such local content requirements, see Gerstetter et al. 2014, 10ff.

1580 One might argue that environmental benefits are maximized if renewable energy is produced in as many countries of the world as possible, and it hence makes sense to restrict, e.g., they payment of feed-in tariffs to energy produced within a given country. This model was, for example, contained in the German Renewable Energy Act (EEG). However, for other types of local content requirements, requiring for example that components used in solar or wind energy generation be produced domestically, it is difficult to find an environmental rationale. Generally, it will be rather difficult to argue that local content requirements are only adopted for environmental purposes.

1581 For a discussion of local content requirements in support schemes for renewable energy generation and their compatibility with WTO law, see Gerstetter et al. 2014, 77ff; on local content requirements and their WTO compatibility more broadly, see Hestermeyer and Nielsen 2014.

were at issue in several WTO disputes, including and *Canada – Renewable Energy*[1582] *and India – Certain Measures Relating to Solar Cells and Solar Modules*[1583]. In *Canada – Renewable Energy*, the Appellate Body held that the Canadian local content requirements violated Art. III:4 GATT and 2.1 TRIMS; the defendant made no attempt to justify the measures under Art. XX GATT.[1584] In *India – Certain Measures Relating to Solar Cells and Solar Modules* the Panel found a violation of Art. III:4 GATT and 2.1 TRIMS; it also concluded that the measures were not justifiable under Art. XX GATT. The Appellate Body confirmed the findings. The fact that the complainants won these cases constituted, in a sense, a pro-trade outcome. What is struck down is a protectionist component of an environmental scheme; yet it may be difficult for governments to push through such schemes domestically without the protectionist component. Nonetheless, it is doubtful whether a finding that a local content requirement violates WTO law is reflective of a "pro-trade" mission of the WTO adjudicators; it might also be due to a lack of appropriate justification provisions in WTO law (e.g. relating to energy sovereignty or the specifics of the energy market in general).[1585] So the fact that policy measures often have various components that are motivated by different rationales provides yet another explanation of how a certain case may result in an "anti-environment" outcome, without necessarily meaning that there is a pro-trade bias in WTO dispute settlement.

Finally, other commentators have offered alternative explanations for the high rate of complainant success: For example, Turk argues that it results from a "selection effect" by which only meritorious disputes reach a WTO Panel.[1586]

In conclusion, there are explanations for the observed pro-complainant outcome other than a simple pro-trade bias of the adjudicators, and these

---

1582 *Canada – Certain Measures Affecting the Renewable Energy Generation Sector, WT/DS412/AB/R and Canada – Measures Relating to the Feed-in Tariff Program, WT/DS426/AB/R* 2013.

1583 *India – Certain Measures Relating to Solar Cells and Solar Modules, WT/DS456/AB/R* 2016.

1584 See the case summary at http://www.wto.org/english/tratop_e/dispu_e/cases_e/ds412_e.htm. Rather, the defendant argued (unsuccessfully) that the measures came within the purview of Art. Article III:8(a) of the GATT 1994.

1585 Gerstetter et al. 2014, 107.

1586 Turk 2011, 388, 414ff.

explanations have not been refuted in existing research.[1587] By this statement, I do not intend to claim that there may not be some WTO adjudicators who embrace a liberalizing agenda or that such an agenda has not influenced the outcome of some cases. My statement is more limited: I maintain that it has not yet been conclusively and comprehensively demonstrated (through the analysis of all or at least a majority of cases decided) that WTO dispute settlement is dominated by a pervasive pro-trade orientation that leads to concurrent *interpretations* of the law in a clear majority of cases. Thus, I would maintain that my own conclusion – the legal interpretations by the WTO dispute settlement bodies occupy a middle-ground on a scale of "pro-trade" vs. "pro-regulatory freedom"– is not invalidated by studies showing high complainant success rates.[1588]

4.3 Relating the results to the conceptual framework

In this section, I will relate my findings back to the conceptual framework contained in the first chapter of this work. Chapter 1 presented an account of judicial decision-making based on the assumption that the law is frequently indeterminate. As a consequence, judicial decisions often constitute a deliberate choice between different defensible interpretations of the law. Courts have been presented as strategic actors with a certain independence, leeway and discretion in deciding their cases; they have been observed using that "zone of discretion"[1589] for making decisions that avoid trouble with those actors that could take counter-measures (notably non-compliance, changing the mandate of a court, legislative overturn) against the court. Alternatively, judges may use their "zone of discretion" for decisions that correspond to their own preferences.

The assumption that judicial decisions are at least sometimes motivated by non-legal factors has been explained and also held to be plausible within the WTO context. I have argued that the Appellate Body is likely to engage in strategic behaviour as well, in particular with a view to being faced with serious challenges to the legitimacy of the WTO and its being a judicial body in its infancy.

1587 For a more thorough discussion of the findings by Colares and others on the high rate of complainant success, see ibid., 405ff.

1588 Obviously, my conclusion is limited to the cases investigated in this work.

1589 The term is borrowed from Sweet and Brunell 2013, 65.

On this basis, I have formulated the hypothesis that

> "the Appellate Body cannot be expected to exploit its discretion to the maximum and only in a pro-trade way. In light of divergent preferences among WTO Members on how WTO law should be interpreted and in view of the self-description of WTO adjudicators as being very mindful of WTO Members' intentions as enshrined in the WTO agreements, the most plausible scenario is that there will be a mixed picture in terms of substantive outcome, or the Appellate Body will find other ways of avoiding outcomes that would lead to significant opposition from WTO Members."[1590]

The results of the analysis in this chapter are in line with this hypothesis. There is a relatively balanced outcome in terms of substantive interpretations. At the same time, features such as the gap or mismatch between rhetoric and reality and that between the interpretation of norms and the application of the interpretations can contribute to avoiding controversy among WTO Members about outcomes.

In the present study, I have not systematically investigated whether or not the outcomes of certain cases must be seen as a judicial response to external constraints, in the sense of the WTO adjudicators avoiding too controversial issues and one-sided decisions or acting in line with assumed preferences of WTO Members. The relatively balanced approach to the legal interpretation of WTO norms observed in "trade and ..." cases is, however, consistent with the theoretical insights on judicial-decision making and courts' strategic behaviour presented in chapter 1. By way of contrast, my own conclusions are less compatible with claims that other factors, such as an overarching trade-liberalizing philosophy of the WTO adjudicators, are decisive for the outcome of the WTO judicial decisions.

I will revisit these issues in the final chapter of this work, after having looked at additional aspects of the case law in chapter 3.

1590 See chapter 1, section 4.6.

Chapter 3: Judicial style and justification

> *"The juridical canon is like a reserve of authority providing the guarantee for individual juridical acts in the same way a central bank guarantees currency. This explains ...[the] inclination, visible particularly among judges, to prefer the role of lector, or interpreter, who takes refuge behind the appearance of a simple application of the law, and who, when he or she does in fact perform work of judicial creation, tends to dissimulate this fact."*[1591]

The previous chapter dealt with the way that the WTO dispute settlement bodies interpret WTO law in substance. This chapter focuses on what I have called "judicial style" in the first chapter of this work: more or less consistent patterns of reasoning, discernible from the decisions of an individual court. In other words, this chapter is about how the WTO dispute settlement bodies justify their decisions, about a judicial discourse, about certain procedural decisions underlying this discourse, and about rhetoric. The reason for analysing this aspect of WTO settlement is that the legitimacy of judicial decisions depends not only on the substantive outcome in specific cases, but also on what arguments are used in support of a decision.[1592] It is reasonable to assume that judges will use a mode of reasoning acceptable to their constituencies, and will thus seek to avoid, for example, being perceived as too activist.

The numerous WTO dispute settlement decisions taken thus far display many different aspects of judicial style. I will limit my investigation to those that are either particularly central to the judicial style of the WTO or otherwise of particular relevance to the questions underlying this work, namely how judicial decisions get taken and justified in non-trade related cases. The selection of the aspects of the WTO's judicial style that I intend

1591 Bourdieu 1987, 823.
1592 See chapter 1, section 3.

to analyse has been explained in chapter 1 of this work.[1593] To briefly reiterate: I will first analyse certain aspects of the judicial style of the WTO adjudicatory bodies that are, or at least could be, influenced by explicit procedural rules governing WTO dispute settlement. From a lawyer's point of view, the most obvious aspect of the style used by a judicial body is the choice of methods of interpretation that the judicial body uses (section 1). A second aspect (section 2) that reveals much about how the WTO dispute settlement conceives of its role is the standard of review. In WTO law, this term relates to the how intensively the WTO dispute settlement bodies scrutinize certain decisions by the national legislative and executive institutions. As a third aspect (section 3), I discuss to what extent WTO adjudicators rely on precedent, making a WTO judicial decision effectively a decision in an individual case, or whether it produces findings of relevance in other cases, too. A related topic is the extent to which the adjudicators either decide certain aspects of the case before them or avoid to do so. For each of these issues, I will first explain in the respective section why the topic is important and summarize the case law. Each section (with one exception) then contains a subsection entitled "discussion" where I will assess the Appellate Body's approach from a legal-technical point of view, drawing also on existing research. Subsequently, in a section entitled "assessment" I will analyse what Appellate Body's approach means from the perspective of judicial style and legitimizing the judicial decision(s) as well as how the observed features might be explained. Again, relevant literature contributes to this assessment.

In sections 4 and 5 I turn to features which concern rhetoric rather than procedural rules. [1594] Section 4 concerns how WTO dispute settlement bodies engage in balancing, if indeed they do, an aspect closely related to the use of (substantive) principles in WTO dispute settlement. As noted in Chapter 1, a judge who balances projects a different image of her own activity than a judge who deducts. Finally, I discuss some aspects of the WTO dispute settlement rhetoric and style that, while striking, fit into none of the other categories: the length and tone of the reports, the tendency towards verbal appeasement in the direction of the parties, and the extent to which interpretive alternatives are made invisible (section 5). For all of these issues, I will first explain in the respective section why the topic is im-

---

1593 See chapter 1, section 5.3.

1594 Some of them are also about how a case is decided in substance, e.g. the use of principles. However, in this chapter I will focus on the various dimensions of the WTO's judicial style only.

portant and then describe the case law. As these issues are not subject to procedural rules and are hence not procedural issues in a technical sense, the explanation will not be in legal-technical terms. Rather, I will analyse under the heading "assessment" what the approach chosen means from the perspective of judicial style and legitimizing the judicial decision(s) and how the observed features can be explained, drawing also on relevant literature. The discussion and assessment sections feed into an overall final assessment in the last section of this chapter (section 6).

While this chapter is based, like the previous chapter, on the reading of primary sources, namely WTO judicial decisions, it considers different cases from those seen in the previous chapter.[1595] In order to answer the question raised in chapter 2 regarding the position of the adjudicators in the "trade and ..." cases, the discussion of cases where non-trade issues were at stake was sufficient. By contrast, the judicial style of a court can be expected to be largely independent of the substantive issues decided. Strictly speaking, the analysis of a judicial body's style would require the investigation of a representative sample of its decisions and coding salient features which might then be subjected statistical analysis. Given the sheer volume of material this is far beyond the scope this particular work (or even of any individual scholar at this stage of WTO jurisprudential development). Moreover, as pointed out in chapter 1[1596], statistical analysis of judicial decisions has serious limitations as it cannot properly take account of the legal rules that judges must observe.

Methodologically, this chapter will therefore not only draw on a reading of the "trade and ..." cases discussed also in the previous chapter, but also consider the past more than 20 years of scholarly and political debates on WTO dispute settlement. Secondary sources will be used extensively not only in the summary and assessment sections, but also for the actual description of the case law. This literature also provides additional evidence on whether certain observable attributes of the WTO case law indeed constitute recurrent patterns and hence an important aspect of the WTO's judicial style, or are more singular in character.

1595 See chapter 1, sections 5.3 and 5.4.
1596 See chapter 1, section 5.1.

1. *Methods of interpretation*

The Panels and the Appellate Body made clear very early in their history that they consider Art. 31ff VCLT the relevant guidelines for their own interpretative work, by virtue of a reference in Art. 3.2 DSU to "customary methods of interpretation of international law".[1597] In order to show that the methods mentioned in Art. 3.2 DSU had achieved the status of customary international law, the Appellate Body referred to decisions by a number of international courts, including the ICJ, the ECtHR, the Inter-American Commission on Human Rights (IACHR) as well as publications by eminent legal scholars.[1598]

The WTO dispute settlement bodies regularly referred to Art. 31 and 32 VCLT in particular in their earlier cases,[1599] sometimes including the articles verbatim in their reports.[1600] In addition to the VCLT, Art. II:2 WTOA has also been cited as a norm to be observed in the interpretation of WTO law. This article sets forth that the various multilateral trade agreements are an integral part of the WTOA, from which the adjudicators have inferred that these agreements must be interpreted as a whole and in a manner that gives meaning to all of them harmoniously.[1601] In practice, Art. 31 and 32 VLCT are by far more important as interpretative guidelines in WTO case law.

Art. 31.1 VCLT states that a

> "treaty shall be interpreted in good faith in accordance with the ordinary meaning to be given to the terms of the treaty in their context and in the light of its object and purpose".

1597 *United States – Standards for Reformulated and Conventional Gasoline, WT/DS2/AB/R* 1996, sec. III B, at 17.

1598 Ibid., n. 34.

1599 Abi-Saab 2006, 458, himself a former Member of the Appellate Body, notes that Art. 31, 32 VCLT were reproduced or cited at "every breath, whether warranted or unwarranted".

1600 *United States – Standards for Reformulated and Conventional Gasoline, WT/DS2/AB/R* 1996, sec. III B, at 17; *United States – Import Prohibition of Certain Shrimp and Shrimp Products, WT/DS58/AB/R* 1998, para. 157; *Korea – Measures Affecting Imports of Fresh, Chilled and Frozen Beef, WT/DS161/AB/R, WT/DS169/AB/R* 2000, para. 96; *United States – Certain Country of Origin Labelling (COOL) Requirements, WT/DS384/AB/R, WT/DS/386/AB/R* 2012, para. 154.

1601 *United States – Certain Measures Affecting Imports of Poultry from China, WT/DS392/R* 2010, para. 7.466, citing earlier Appellate Body reports.

Thus, the VLCT mandates the use of textual interpretation in combination with systematic and teleological interpretation. Art. 31.2 VLCT specifies in greater detail what is to be considered the "context" of a certain norm, and Art. 31.3 VCLT stipulates:

> "There shall be taken into account, together with the context:
> (a) any subsequent agreement between the parties regarding the interpretation of the treaty or the application of its provisions;
> (b) any subsequent practice in the application of the treaty which establishes the agreement of the parties regarding its interpretation;
> (c) any relevant rules of international law applicable in the relations between the parties."

Art. 32 VCLT defines as "supplementary means of interpretation" the "preparatory work of the treaty and the circumstances of its conclusion". In other words, historic interpretation is only to be used as a secondary method of interpretation in relation to the international legal treaties.

While the reference to Art. 31 and 32 VCLT in the WTO dispute settlement reports brings important clarifications, the VCLT contains different methods of interpretation. Hence, it is necessary to take a closer look at which methods the Appellate Body actually uses. The Appellate Body often makes a noticeable effort at clarifying in the reports which method it is using in a specific passage.

As described above,[1602] different methods of interpretation afford judicial decision-makers different levels of freedom. Among the methods set forth in the VCLT, the strongest commitment to what the parties to a treaty have decided is, of course, inherent in textual or literal interpretation. A purely literal interpretation clarifies the meaning of the law in a deductive manner; afterwards facts are subsumed by means of syllogistic conclusion. Such literalist reasoning corresponds to a traditional conception of the judicial role and conveys an image of neutrality, of the court recognizing, rather than creating the law, of the court keeping away from extralegal considerations or the exercise of discretion.[1603] "I am just clarifying what is already written" is the message when this method is being used. This method of interpretation is the simplest way a judicial body might present itself as an implementing entity rather than an actor either pursuing its own agenda or making a judicial decision inspired by subjective views or preferences. Amongst the established methods of interpretation,

1602 See chapter 1, section 3.1.
1603 Poiares Maduro 1998, 11.

textual interpretation therefore involves the lowest degree of discretion and exercise of judgement by adjudicators.[1604]

The next method that the VCLT mentions, contextual interpretation, provides a greater degree of flexibility in adjudication. Art. 31.2 VCLT gives examples of what is to be considered as the context of a norm (e.g. the preamble and annexes of a treaty); but the more immediate and the wider contexts of a norm do not necessarily point to the same result. Moreover, adjudicators are afforded some leeway in their consideration of what, precisely, constitutes the context of a norm. Thus, contextual interpretation allows judges to occupy a wider argumentative space when applying a norm in its context than does textual interpretation.

This is even more applicable to the third method of interpretation mentioned in the VCLT, the interpretation of a norm according to its object and purpose, i.e. teleological interpretation. Teleological interpretation gives judges a significant extent of leeway.[1605] One former Member of the Appellate Body has referred to teleological interpretation as an

> "approach to interpretation that would enable the members to impose their purely personal views on the meaning of the 'covered agreements'"[1606].

It has also been described as the "most normative" of the three methods of interpretation mentioned in the VCLT.[1607] Teleological interpretation affords judges so much argumentative space because norms often have multiple, conflicting or unclear objectives. When multiple regulatory objectives protected by the law either compete or collide with each other, it is for the adjudicators to decide which of the interests at issue in the case is more relevant.[1608]

The style of a judicial entity is not, however, characterized solely by its preferred method of interpretation, as the manner in which the methods are applied is also relevant. For example, what is seen as the objective of a legal norm in WTO dispute settlement? Is it – similar as in the jurisprudence of the ECJ – the overarching objectives of the WTO legal order and are these assumed to be predominantly trade-related? What is the context

1604 Lo 2010, 434.
1605 For national law, see Koch 1996, 23; for international law in general see Shaw 1991, 656; for WTO law more specifically, see Arup 2003, 913.
1606 Bacchus 2004b, 21.
1607 Mitchell 2007, 806.
1608 Lo 2010, 435.

considered to be of relevance – is it only the WTO agreement in dispute, is it all WTO law or even the wider international law context? All these choices may influence the outcome of a certain case (or at least the way the judges justify that outcome) and merit a closer look.

In the following, I will discuss central aspects[1609] of each of the methods of interpretation mentioned in the VCLT as they are used in WTO dispute settlement – textual interpretation (section 1.1), contextual interpretation (section 1.2), teleological interpretation (section 1.3), and the supplementary means of interpretation (section 1.4). Section 1.5 presents a specific cross-cutting aspect of WTO interpretation, the frequent reference to the intention of WTO Members. Afterwards, I will turn to an overarching question, the use of international law in WTO dispute settlement (section 1.6). This will be followed by a technical-legal discussion (section 1.7) and an assessment (section 1.8).

1.1. Textual interpretation

Literal or textual interpretation is the most prominent of the methods of interpretation used in WTO dispute settlement.[1610] There are many examples in which the WTO adjudicators begin by explaining the literal meaning of a word or phrase.[1611] The adjudicators will not, however, typically cite the text in isolation, declaring instead that they rely on the ordinary meaning of a word or phrase in its context.[1612]

In WTO dispute settlement practice, textual interpretation is often performed with the help of a dictionary, a reference not especially prominent in the judgments of other international courts. Furthermore, a wide range

1609 For a more extensive analysis of the methods of interpretation, see Lennard 2002; van Damme 2009.

1610 *Japan – Taxes on Alcoholic Beverages, WT/DS8/AB/R, WT/DS10/AB/R, WT/DS11/AB/R* 1996, sec. G, at 17f.

1611 See for example *United States – Standards for Reformulated and Conventional Gasoline, WT/DS2/AB/R* 1996, sec. III C, at 20 and n. 40; *Korea – Measures Affecting Imports of Fresh, Chilled and Frozen Beef, WT/DS161/AB/R, WT/DS169/AB/R* 2000, para. 161.

1612 *United States – Import Prohibition of Certain Shrimp and Shrimp Products, WT/DS58/AB/R* 1998, para. 114.

of English language[1613] dictionaries are used, including some online dictionaries of dubious authority, lacking either credentials or quality.[1614]

The Appellate Body sometimes provides lengthy textual interpretations of terms that were neither a point of conflict between the parties nor *prima facie* unclear.[1615] To give an example, in one case the Appellate Body had to interpret section 3 (c) of the GATT Enabling Clause, which mandates that measures taken in favour of developing countries need to respond "positively" to the needs of developing countries.[1616] The Appellate Body cited the dictionary definition of "positive" as "consisting in or characterized by constructive action or attitudes"[1617], concluding therefore that the use of "positive" in the Enabling Clause

> "suggests that the response of a preference-granting country must be taken with a view to *improving* the development, financial or trade situation of a beneficiary country [...]".[1618]

This is not wrong, but the conclusion could have been drawn directly from the term "positive". A few other examples of dictionary definitions the Appellate Body has used are the following:
- "notwithstanding" meant "[i]n spite of, without regard to or prevention by"[1619],
- "accordance" was defined as "conformity"[1620],
- "generalized" schemes had the sense that schemes "apply more generally; [or] become extended in application"[1621],

1613 Even in the French and Spanish versions of the reports it is usually English-language dictionaries that get used. This fact was noticed first – as far as evident – in a French scholarly article, see Canal-Forgues 2001, 20.

1614 For an overview of dictionaries used see Lo 2010, 440, table 1. One of the dictionaries listed by Lo in his overview is http://dictionary.bnet.com/ which at the time of writing this work seemed not to be even online any longer.

1615 See for example the interpretation of "fulfill" in Art. 2.2 TBT in *United States – Measures Concerning the Importation, Marketing and Sale of Tuna and Tuna Products, WT/DS381/AB/R* 2012, para. 315.

1616 See Sec. 3 a) of Decision of 28 November 1979, http://www.wto.org/english/docs_e/legal_e/enabling1979_e.htm.

1617 *European Communities – Conditions for the Granting of Tariff Preferences to Developing Countries, WT/DS246/AB/R* 2004, para. 164.

1618 Ibid.

1619 Ibid., para. 90.

1620 Ibid., para. 145.

1621 Ibid., para. 155.

- the phrase "China's right to regulate trade" was a "reference to China's power to subject international commerce to regulation"[1622],
- a "legitimate objective" is a "target that is lawful, justifiable or proper"[1623],
- a "restriction" is "something that restricts someone or something, a limitation on action, a limiting condition or regulation"[1624],
- competitive means "characterized by competition" and "substitutable" means "able to be substituted"[1625]
- "trade seems to refer, generally, to commerce between nations"[1626]
- "normally" is defined as "under normal or ordinary conditions; as a rule.[1627]
- "competitive" means "characterized by competition" and "substitutable" means "able to be substituted."[1628]

While there is nothing actually wrong with any of these definitions, the explanation of these common and uncontroversial terms is redundant: the definitions fail to yield insights that could not just as easily have been inferred directly from the term itself.

The Appellate Body can be described as being even more committed to the letters of the law than the Panels. In several important instances it has corrected a Panel's findings as the Panel failed to take sufficient account of the text of an agreement. In one case the Appellate Body had to decide whether a certain paragraph of a Ministerial Declaration constituted an "interpretation" in the sense of Art. IX:2 WTOA. The Appellate Body observed that the decision-making procedure defined in Art. XI:2 WTOA had not been followed. According to that norm, any interpretation of a multilateral trade agreement such as the TBT Agreement shall be decided "on the basis of a recommendation by the Council overseeing the functioning of that Agreement". As there was no such recommendation for the deci-

---

1622 *China – Measures Affecting Trading Rights and Distribution Services for Certain Publications and Audiovisual Entertainment Products, WT/DS363/AB/R* 2009, para. 221.

1623 *United States – Measures Concerning the Importation, Marketing and Sale of Tuna and Tuna Products, WT/DS381/AB/R* 2012, para. 313.

1624 Ibid., para. 319.

1625 *Korea – Alcoholic Beverages, WT/DS75AB/R, WT/DS84/AB/R* 1999, para. 116.

1626 *China – Measures Affecting Trading Rights and Distribution Services for Certain Publications and Audiovisual Entertainment Products, WT/DS363/AB/R* 2009, para. 220.

1627 *United States – Measures Affecting the Production and Sale of Clove Cigarettes, WT/DS406/AB/R* 2012, para. 273.

1628 *Korea – Alcoholic Beverages, WT/DS75AB/R, WT/DS84/AB/R* 1999, para. 116.

sion contained in the Ministerial Declaration, the Appellate Body concluded that the respective paragraph of the Declaration did not constitute an interpretation in the sense of Art. IX:2 WTOA. It rejected statements made by the Panel implying that the procedural requirement might be superfluous by pointing to the clarity of the text's wording.[1629] In another case, the Appellate Body rejected a suggestion by one of the parties that an interpretation developed under Art. XX (b) GATT could inform the interpretation of Art. XX (g) GATT, pointing to the differences in wording between both norms by way of explanation.[1630] The interpretation of the term "risk assessment" in the SPS Agreement is another example. Annex A (4) SPS contains two definitions of risk assessment, one referring to the "likelihood" of the materialization of a certain risk, the second one of the "potential" of adverse effects. The Panel in the *Hormones I* case found that a risk assessment had to (1) identify the adverse effects on human health arising from the presence of contaminants in food, beverages or feedstuff and (2) if any such adverse effects existed, evaluate the potential or probability of occurrence of these effects.[1631]

By way of contrast, the Appellate Body stressed the semantic differences between potential and probability by saying that probability implied a higher degree of potentiality.[1632] In the same case, the Appellate Body criticized the Panel for using the term "risk management", a term not contained as such in the SPS Agreement, to support a certain interpretation of the SPS Agreement:

> "The fundamental rule of treaty interpretation requires a treaty interpreter to read and interpret the words actually used by the agreement under examination, and not words which the interpreter may feel should have been used."[1633]

On occasion, the Appellate Body indicated that while an interpretation it offered on the basis of the text of a norm made little sense, it felt compelled to adopt it on the basis of the wording of the norm. For example,

---

1629 *United States – Measures Affecting the Production and Sale of Clove Cigarettes, WT/DS406/AB/R* 2012, para. 253ff.

1630 *China – Measures Related to the Exportation of Rare Earths, Tungsten, and Molybdenum, WT/DS431/AB/R, WT/DS432/AB/R, WT/DS433/AB/R* 2014, para. 5.116.

1631 *European Communities – Measures Concerning Meat and Meat Products, WT/DS26/R* 1997, para. 8.98.

1632 *European Communities – Measures Concerning Meat and Meat Products, WT/DS26/AB/R, WT/DS48/AB/R* 1998, para. 184.

1633 Ibid., para. 181.

when interpreting Art. 3.3 SPS, the Appellate Body in *Hormones I* wrote the following:

> "We are not unaware that this finding [i.e. the one made by the Appellate Body in the same paragraph, C.G.] tends to suggest that the distinction made in Article 3.3 between two situations may have very limited effects and may, to that extent, be more apparent than real. Its involved and layered language actually leaves us with no choice."[1634]

The Appellate Body also sometimes has based its arguments on what a norm does *not* say.[1635] For example, it argued that Art. 2.4 TBT, a central provision of the TBT Agreement, could not be assumed to have a restricted temporal scope of application, as that was not expressed explicitly in the norm. In this context, the Appellate Body observed that if the negotiators had wanted to exempt a large group of technical regulations from the requirements in Art. 2.4 TBT "they would have said so explicitly"[1636]. In another case, the Appellate Body explicitly rejected the idea that Art. XX (g) GATT contained an (unwritten) requirement that conservation measures had to be "primarily aimed at" the conservation of natural resources.[1637] In *China – Raw Materials*, the Appellate Body concluded that the absence of a certain phrase in one article of China's Accession Protocol had to have some meaning as the (absent) phrase appeared in many other provisions.[1638] The Appellate Body also refused to import the standard of review embodied in Art. 17 ADA into the SPS Agreement, arguing that the SPS Agreement gave no indication that WTO Members had wanted that standard to be used there. The Appellate Body rejected the EU's argument that the ADA standard was applicable to all complex factual determinations.[1639] However, the Appellate Body is not consistent in its approach; for example, China in the *China – Rare Earths* dispute quoted a finding by the Appellate Body in an earlier case, according to which the fact that the

1634 Ibid., para. 176.

1635 See also below, section 2.2.

1636 *European Communities – Trade Description of Sardines, WT/DS231/AB/R* 2002, para. 208.

1637 *China – Measures Related to the Exportation of Various Raw Materials, WT/DS394/AB/R, WT/DS395/AB/R, WT/DS398/AB/R* 2012, para. 356.

1638 Ibid., para. 293.

1639 *European Communities – Measures Concerning Meat and Meat Products, WT/DS26/AB/R, WT/DS48/AB/R* 1998, para. 112ff.

legal text was silent on a certain requirement did not exclude the possibility that said requirement "was intended to be included by implication"[1640].

In other instances, the Appellate Body used a technique dubbed "evolutionary interpretation" by observers.[1641] When interpreting the term "exhaustible natural resources" in Art. XX (g) GATT, the Appellate Body observed that these words

> "were actually crafted more than 50 years ago. They must be read by a treaty interpreter in the light of contemporary concerns of the community of nations about the protection and conservation of the environment [...]".[1642]

Relying on the mention of the protection of the environment in the preamble of the WTOA and obligations to conserve natural resources in non-WTO international law, it concluded that this term had to be understood as encompassing living natural resources. The "evolutionary" interpretation of the term exhaustible natural resources was confirmed by the Appellate Body in a later case.[1643] One other example for evolutionary interpretation may be the decision by the Panel in *United States – Gambling*; it held, in a finding not modified by the Appellate Body, that the content of "public morals" as mentioned in Art. XX (a) GATT could "vary in time and space"[1644]. Yet, it is not entirely clear whether this is an instance of evolutionary interpretation of the term "morals" as some claim[1645] or a factual statement that there are empirical variations in what people consider to be a moral issue that are observable across time and space. Evolutionary interpretation has also been used in other WTO dispute settlement cases.[1646]

The Appellate Body has sometimes made use of the different language versions of the WTO agreements. For example, in one instance it inferred from the difference between the term "described" in the English version and the terms "défini" in the French and "define" in the Spanish versions a

---

1640 As quoted by Lim and Senduk 2014, 383.

1641 See for example Conrad 2011, 268.

1642 *United States – Import Prohibition of Certain Shrimp and Shrimp Products, WT/DS58/AB/R* 1998, para. 129.

1643 *China – Measures Related to the Exportation of Rare Earths, Tungsten, and Molybdenum, WT/DS431/AB/R, WT/DS432/AB/R, WT/DS433/AB/R* 2014, para. 5.89.

1644 *United States – Measures Affecting the Cross-Border Supply of Gambling and Betting Services, WT/DS285/R* 2004, para. 6.461.

1645 See Wu 2008, 231.

1646 Marceau 2018, 803ff.

certain interpretation of paragraph 2 (a) of the GATT Enabling Clause.[1647] The Appellate Body has even used different language versions of non-WTO law to help it arrive at a conclusion.[1648] However, as noted by Condon, it was not until 2006 that a Panel conducted an entire hearing in Spanish.[1649] Condon also observes that the Appellate Body has only considered all three official language versions of the WTO texts in about 22 % of all cases, even though Art. 33 VCLT stipulates that when a treaty has been authenticated in more than one language the text is equally authoritative in all of them.[1650] Curiously, one of the reports in which a Panel derived its textual interpretation from different language versions was in the exceptional situation of only the English language version of a WTO text, a schedule of commitments under GATS, being the authoritative version. The Appellate Body expressed some reservations about this Panel's approach.[1651]

While literal interpretation of the English version of the WTO agreements is the mainstay of WTO dispute settlement, the Appellate Body[1652] – and also Panels[1653] – have noted in certain instances that the literal meaning of a text was insufficiently clear to allow for a decision to be made on a specific matter, and that they therefore had to use other methods of interpretation. In *EC – GSP* the Appellate Body stated that a certain norm "on its face" did not explicitly regulate a certain question and consequently went on to investigate the context, and later the purpose of the respective norm.[1654] The Panel in the *Shrimp – Turtles* case tried a literal interpretation of the term "unjustifiable" in the chapeau of Art. XX, but found the term too ambiguous and therefore took into account both the context and

1647 *European Communities – Conditions for the Granting of Tariff Preferences to Developing Countries, WT/DS246/AB/R* 2004, para. 147; for another example where different language versions were used, see *Canada – Certain Measures Affecting the Renewable Energy Generation Sector, WT/DS412/AB/R and Canada – Measures Relating to the Feed-in Tariff Program, WT/DS426/AB/R* 2013, para. 5.67.

1648 In *European Communities – Trade Description of Sardines, WT/DS231/AB/R* 2002, para. 235–239 the Appellate Body used the French version of a Codex standard to arrive at a certain conclusion.

1649 Condon 2010, 191.

1650 Ibid., 193ff; this percentage relates to all Appellate Body reports decided until 7 October 2009, see note 84 of Condon's article.

1651 See Ortino 2006, 124 for the details.

1652 *United States – Import Prohibition of Certain Shrimp and Shrimp Products, WT/DS58/AB/R* 1998, para. 114.

1653 *United States – Import Prohibition of Certain Shrimp and Shrimp Products, WT/DS58/R* 1998, para. 7.34.

1654 *European Communities – Conditions for the Granting of Tariff Preferences to Developing Countries, WT/DS246/AB/R* 2004, para. 154.

the purpose of the norm.[1655] One observer even writes that "occasions on which the Appellate Body considered only the (non)contextualized ordinary meaning are rare"[1656].

There are also a few passages in the case law where the dispute settlement bodies reflect critically on the usefulness of dictionaries.[1657] In *United States – Gambling*, the Appellate Body explicitly said that

> "dictionaries, alone, are not necessarily capable of resolving complex questions of interpretation, as they typically aim to catalogue all meanings of words – be those meanings common or rare, universal or specialized."[1658]

In *EC – Asbestos*, the Appellate Body also observed that "dictionary meanings leave many interpretive questions open"[1659].

Finally, there are also instances where the Appellate Body did not take the wording of a norm all that seriously. For example, Art. 5.5 SPS contains a distinction between discrimination on the one hand and a disguised restriction on international trade on the other. In the relevant reports, it is rarely explicitly stated which of both terms is actually used for testing the contested measures. Similarly, when the Appellate Body interprets Art. XX chapeau, it often fails either to distinguish between "unjustifiable" and "arbitrary" discrimination or to pay much attention to the phrase "between countries where the same conditions prevail".[1660] Moreover, it has been noted that there is a tendency to interpret different terms synonymously, which has been described as an effort "to inject some order into the sometimes chaotic drafting of the covered agreements".[1661] However, if literal interpretation is to be taken seriously, one would expect different words to be interpreted differently.

1655 *United States – Import Prohibition of Certain Shrimp and Shrimp Products, WT/DS58/R* 1998, para. 7.34.

1656 Van Damme 2010, 622.

1657 See for an overview Lo 2010, 442, table 2.

1658 *United States – Measures Affecting the Cross-Border Supply of Gambling and Betting Services, WT/DS285/AB/R* 2005, para. 164.

1659 *European Communities – Measures Affecting Asbestos and Products Containing Asbestos, WT/DS135/AB/R* 2001, para. 92.

1660 See chapter 2, section 1.4.

1661 See Flett 2011, 12 who also provides examples.

1.2. The context in contextual interpretation

Contextual interpretation also plays an important role in WTO dispute settlement. One former Member of the Appellate Body has described it as the second most frequently used method of interpretation.[1662] In this regard, what the Appellate Body considers to be the relevant context is of particular importance. A rare, more abstract statement by the Appellate Body on the matter is the following:

> "'Context' includes all of the text of the treaty [...] and may also extend to 'any agreement relating to the treaty which was made between all the parties in connection with the conclusion of the treaty' and 'any instrument which was made by one or more parties in connection with the conclusion of the treaty and accepted by the other parties as an instrument related to the treaty'. Yet context is relevant for a treaty interpreter to the extent that it may shed light on the interpretative issue to be resolved, such as the meaning of the term or phrase at issue. Thus, for a particular provision, agreement or instrument to serve as relevant context in any given situation, it must not only fall within the scope of the formal boundaries identified in Article 31(2) [VCLT], it must also have some pertinence to the language being interpreted that renders it capable of helping the interpreter to determine the meaning of such language."[1663]

The case law contains a broad range of examples of contextual interpretation. The most immediate context considered relevant is words in the same norm, other paragraphs of the same article, or footnotes accompanying a certain norm[1664]. One example is the interpretation of "relating to" in Art. XX (g) GATT, which according to the Appellate Body, must have a different meaning from the term "necessary" used in other paragraphs of Art. XX GATT. The Panel's identical interpretation of both terms was found to violate Art. 31.1 VCLT.[1665] Next, neighbouring norms or the title of the relevant section of the agreement have also been considered to be

---

1662 Ehlermann 2002, 616.

1663 *China – Measures Affecting Imports of Automobile Parts, WT/DS339/AB/R, WT/DS340/AB/R, WT/DS342/AB/R* 2008, para. 151.

1664 See for example *European Communities – Conditions for the Granting of Tariff Preferences to Developing Countries, WT/DS246/AB/R* 2004, para. 94ff.

1665 *United States – Standards for Reformulated and Conventional Gasoline, WT/DS2/AB/R* 1996, sec. III B, at 16ff.

meaningful context for a norm.[1666] A good example from the Appellate Body case law where different types of context are mentioned is the following:

> "We consider that Article III:8(a) should be interpreted holistically. This requires consideration of the linkages between the different terms used in the provision and the contextual connections to other parts of Article III; as well as to other provisions of the GATT 1994."[1667]

In this regard, it is interesting to note how the Appellate Body conceives of the relationship between norms and exceptions.[1668] The Appellate Body has not subscribed to the view that an exception should *eo ipso* be construed narrowly. It rejected such an understanding explicitly in *Hormones I,* for example.[1669] The Appellate Body's approach towards interpreting the relationship between various norms of the GATT – notably between Art. III and XI GATT on the one hand and Art. XX GATT on the other – as requiring a balance between rights and obligations can also be quoted in this context.[1670] In a situation where rights and obligations are balanced, none of them has *a priori* more weight.

Functionally similar norms of other agreements or norms in other agreements with similar or identical wording have also been considered relevant context for a given provision.[1671] This is particularly evident in the cases on the SPS and TBT Agreements. For example, for a decision on the temporal scope of the TBT Agreement the Appellate Body drew on a prior interpre-

---

1666 See for example *European Communities – Trade Description of Sardines, WT/DS231/AB/R* 2002, para. 211–213; in this case, Art. 2.5 and 2.6 TBT as well as the title of Art. 2 TBT were considered relevant context for the interpretation of Art. 2.4 TBT. In *United States – Measures Concerning the Importation, Marketing and Sale of Tuna and Tuna Products, WT/DS381/AB/R* 2012, para. 212, Art. 2.2 TBT is mentioned as context of Art. 2.1 TBT.

1667 See *Canada – Certain Measures Affecting the Renewable Energy Generation Sector, WT/DS412/AB/R and Canada – Measures Relating to the Feed-in Tariff Program, WT/DS426/AB/R* 2013, para. 5.57.

1668 For a brief overview of the jurisprudence on different types of exceptions, see Marceau 2006, 337ff.

1669 *European Communities – Measures Concerning Meat and Meat Products, WT/DS26/AB/R, WT/DS48/AB/R* 1998, para. 104; this is different from the approach of the ECJ, which interprets exceptions narrowly, see Bogdandy 2001, 665f.

1670 See van den Bossche 2006, 320f.

1671 *European Communities – Trade Description of Sardines, WT/DS231/AB/R* 2002, para. 208.

tation of the temporal scope of the SPS Agreement in *EC – Sardines*.[1672] Similarly, for the interpretation of the "based on" requirement in Art. 2.4 TBT Agreement, the Appellate Body built on its earlier interpretation of Art. 3.1 SPS Agreement, which contains a similar requirement to that in Art. 2.4 TBT Agreement.[1673] The Appellate Body explicitly rejected a finding by the Panel that had set aside earlier findings of the Appellate Body on the burden of proof under Art. 3.1 and 3.3 SPS for the interpretation of Art. 2.4 TBT; in support of its decision the Panel included a footnote in which it casually stated that the Appellate Body's finding on the SPS Agreement had "no direct bearing" on Art. 2.4 TBT, without providing further explanation.[1674] Another example is the parallel interpretation of Art. XIV GATS and Art. XX GATT. When the Appellate Body had to interpret Art. XIV GATS for the first time, it relied on its earlier case law on Art. XX GATT. The Appellate Body justified this approach by saying that both norms were similar in character as exceptions as well as structure and had partially identical wording, such as their use of the term necessary.[1675] Conversely, in later cases Panels and the Appellate Body have drawn on the interpretation of "necessary" under Art. XIV GATS for the interpretation of the same term in Art. XX GATT.[1676]

There are also cases where the SPS and TBT Agreements have been interpreted by resorting to earlier case law on a GATT norm. For example, the Appellate Body in *Australia – Apples* drew on earlier jurisprudence on Art. III GATT in order to decide how the objective of a measure could be identified, and whether, following identification of this objective, the measure would fulfil the definitions in Annex 1 A of the SPS Agreement.[1677] In *EC – Seal Products*, the Panel relied for its analysis of the necessity of a measure under Art. XX (a) GATT on its prior analysis under Art. 2.2 TBT – an approach not repealed by the Appellate Body.[1678]

1672 Ibid., para. 207f.

1673 Ibid., para. 242.

1674 *European Communities – Trade Description of Sardines, WT/DS231/R* 2002, n. 70.

1675 *United States – Measures Affecting the Cross-Border Supply of Gambling and Betting Services, WT/DS285/AB/R* 2005, para. 291.

1676 See for example *China – Measures Related to the Exportation of Various Raw Materials, WT/DS394/R, WT/DS395/R, WT/DS398/R* 2012, para. 7.489.

1677 *Australia – Measures Affecting the Importation of Apples from New Zealand, WT/DS367/AB/R* 2010, para. 173.

1678 See *European Communities – Measures Prohibiting the Importation and Marketing of Seal Products, WT/DS400/AB/R, WT/DS401/AB/R* 2014, para. 5.204ff.

Also, there are instances where the Appellate Body has drawn on the SPS Agreement in order to interpret the GATT. In *EC – Asbestos*, for example, it cited a finding made under the SPS Agreement that Members may base measures on minority scientific opinions.[1679] It has also been observed that the Appellate Body report in *United States – Tuna Labelling* exhibits a "significant amount of cross-fertilization"[1680] between the GATT and the TBT Agreement.

These attempts at harmonious interpretation of different WTO agreements are a particularly noteworthy example of contextual interpretation in WTO dispute settlement. Some observers consider that reading agreements together is the preferred approach of the Appellate Body.[1681] In support, Art. II:2 WTOA is sometimes invoked by the adjudicators. This article sets forth that the various multilateral trade agreements are an integral part of the WTOA, from which the adjudicators have inferred that these agreements must be interpreted as a whole and in a manner that gives meaning to all of them harmoniously.[1682]

Another observer has commented that the dispute settlement bodies seem to apply a "presumption against conflict" between different WTO agreements.[1683]

Nonetheless, the Appellate Body does not always use the case law developed under one WTO agreement for the interpretation of another. For example, the Appellate Body in *Hormones I* rejected using the case law developed under Art. XX GATT for the interpretation of Art. 5.5 SPS, even though both norms are textually quite similar, citing "structural differences" between both norms.[1684] Also, it has yet to draw on its findings – under the SPS Agreement – that WTO Members have to identify their level of protection for its interpretive work relating to Art. XX GATT.[1685] The Appellate Body in *EC – Seal Products* also explicitly rejected the Panel's ap-

---

1679 *European Communities – Measures Affecting Asbestos and Products Containing Asbestos, WT/DS135/AB/R* 2001, para. 178.

1680 Marceau and Trachtman 2014, 379.

1681 Cameron and Gray 2001, 257.

1682 *United States – Certain Measures Affecting Imports of Poultry from China, WT/DS392/R* 2010, para. 7.466, citing earlier Appellate Body reports.

1683 Weiss 2003, 206.

1684 *European Communities – Measures Concerning Meat and Meat Products, WT/DS26/AB/R, WT/DS48/AB/R* 1998, para. 239.

1685 The idea that it would be appropriate to do so is taken from Vranes 2009, 266.

proach of using the test and result of its analysis under Art. 2.1 TBT for conclusions under the chapeau of Art. XX GATT.[1686]

The context considered relevant by the WTO adjudicators is sometimes even broader than the WTO legal order. In an often-quoted formulation, which appeared in one of the first appellate reports and has been referred to in many later ones, the Appellate Body stated that

> "Article 3.2 DSU reflects a measure of recognition that the General Agreement is not to be read in clinical isolation from public international law".[1687]

In consequence, international law has sometimes been used as the context for interpreting a certain norm of WTO law. This is not the only way in which international law has been used, however, as will be discussed in a separate section.[1688]

1.3. The objectives in teleological interpretation

One former Member of the Appellate Body recommended parties to a dispute that they should not

> "bother arguing that the Appellate Body should embrace some 'teleological' approach to interpretation that would enable the members to impose their purely personal views on the meaning of the 'covered agreements', because the Appellate Body Members don't. They won't."[1689]

Nevertheless, teleological interpretation is in practice the third of the methods used by the Appellate Body.[1690] The Appellate Body has stated, albeit only in a footnote, its understanding that according to the VCLT a treaty's "object and purpose" is to be used as a means for "determining the

---

1686 *European Communities – Measures Prohibiting the Importation and Marketing of Seal Products, WT/DS400/AB/R, WT/DS401/AB/R* 2014, para. 5.310ff.

1687 *United States – Standards for Reformulated and Conventional Gasoline, WT/DS2/AB/R* 1996, sec. III B, at 17.

1688 See below section 1.6.

1689 Bacchus 2004b, 21.

1690 For a more extended discussion of the use of teleological interpretation in WTO dispute settlement, see Tomkiewicz 2009.

meaning of the 'terms of the treaty' and not as an independent basis for interpretation".[1691] In another case, the Appellate Body wrote:

> "Where the meaning imparted by the text itself is equivocal or inconclusive, or where confirmation of the correctness of the reading of the text itself is desired, light from the object and purpose of the treaty as a whole may usefully be sought."[1692]

The Appellate Body appears to exercise more caution in using the object and purpose as a means of interpretation than it does when considering the wording of a norm and its context. Sometimes, the Appellate Body is explicit in its use of teleological interpretation, adding "object and purpose" as a distinct subheading to its interpretation of certain norms.[1693] In other instances, references to objectives are less obvious.[1694]

The use of teleological interpretation is particularly interesting when considered in light of what is actually recognized as a *telos* of WTO norms. Is it, for example, the objective of an individual norm such as the protection of the environment as seen in the case of exception norms like Art. XX GATT? Or are the overarching trade-related goals of the WTO legal order to be considered a *telos*? In *EC – Chicken Cuts*, the Appellate Body answered this question in the abstract:

> "It is well accepted that the use of the singular word 'its' preceding the term 'object and purpose' in Article 31(1) of the Vienna Convention indicates that the term refers to the treaty as a whole; had the term 'object and purpose' been preceded by the word 'their', the use of the plural would have indicated a reference to particular 'treaty terms'. Thus, the term 'its object and purpose' makes it clear that the starting point for ascertaining 'object and purpose' is the treaty itself, in its entirety. At the same time, we do not believe that Article 31(1) excludes taking into account the object and purpose of particular treaty terms, if doing so assists the interpreter in determining the treaty's object and purpose on the whole. We do not see why it would be necessary to divorce a treaty's object and purpose from the object and purpose of specific

1691 *Japan – Taxes on Alcoholic Beverages, WT/DS8/AB/R, WT/DS10/AB/R, WT/DS11/AB/R* 1996, n. 20.

1692 *United States – Import Prohibition of Certain Shrimp and Shrimp Products, WT/DS58/AB/R* 1998, para. 114.

1693 See for example *European Communities – Conditions for the Granting of Tariff Preferences to Developing Countries, WT/DS246/AB/R* 2004, para. 90–91.

1694 Tomkiewicz 2009, 244.

treaty provisions, or vice versa. To the extent that one can speak of the 'object and purpose of a treaty provision', it will be informed by, and will be in consonance with, the object and purpose of the entire treaty of which it is but a component."[1695]

In practice, the WTO adjudicators take account of legal objectives at various levels. First, dispute settlement reports can be cited in which the adjudicators looked at the purpose of the individual norms they investigated.[1696] At the second level, the objectives of the respective individual agreement are taken into account.[1697] Finally, the overal*l* objectives of the WTO legal order, as evident from the WTOA preamble, are also considered.

Sometimes the Appellate Body explicitly criticized a Panel for having considered the overall purpose of the multilateral trading system – which the Panel took to be economic and trade-related – rather than the one of specific norms.[1698] The Appellate Body's approach is inconsistent, however, as it can also be seen to observe that GATT was a commercial agreement, concerned with markets, and subsequently base its interpretation of a certain norm – in this case Art. III GATT – on this statement.[1699] In other instances, the Appellate Body relies only on one objective of an agreement – as stated in the preamble – but not on others.[1700]

Moreover, the Appellate Body's understanding of the WTO legal order's objectives sometimes differs from an individual Panel's. In the *Shrimp – Turtles* case, the Appellate Body, like the Panel, emphasized the importance of the preamble to the WTO Agreement. However, it embraced a much broader reading of the underlying purpose of the multilateral trading system than the Panel. The Appellate Body stressed that the preamble referred to the sustainable use of the world's natural resources as one of the

---

1695 *European Communities – Customs Classification of Frozen Boneless Chicken Cuts, WT/DS269, 286/AB/R* 2005, para. 238f.

1696 *European Communities – Measures Concerning Meat and Meat Products, WT/DS26/AB/R, WT/DS48/AB/R* 1998, para. 165.

1697 See for example *European Communities – Trade Description of Sardines, WT/DS231/AB/R* 2002, para. 214ff.

1698 *United States – Import Prohibition of Certain Shrimp and Shrimp Products, WT/DS58/AB/R* 1998, para. 116.

1699 *Japan – Taxes on Alcoholic Beverages, WT/DS8/AB/R, WT/DS10/AB/R, WT/DS11/AB/R* 1996, sec. H 2 a), at 25.

1700 Howse 2002c, 248 criticizes that when discussing the temporal scope of application of Art. 2.4 TBT the Appellate Body only paid attention to the "pro-harmonization goals" of the agreement, but did not consider the recital of the TBT Agreement that refers to the regulatory autonomy of WTO Members.

objectives of the WTO system. The Appellate Body underlined the importance of the negotiators' intention of promoting this goal, which, accordingly, had to inform the interpretation of the agreements annexed to the WTOA.[1701] In another case, the Appellate Body referred to the preamble of the WTOA as requiring positive efforts from WTO Members in favour of developing countries.[1702]

In these examples the preamble serves to illustrate the objective and purpose of certain norms, while it is, in other instances, considered part of the context of a norm.[1703] Contextual and teleological interpretation can sometimes overlap, such as in cases that lack either a preamble (e. g., the Anti-Dumping Agreement) or suitably unequivocal language. In these cases, the Appellate Body has been observed to consider the design and architecture of the relevant agreement instead of a defined *telos*.[1704]

1.4. Supplementary means of interpretation

Art. 32 VCLT mentions supplementary means of interpretation that can be used to confirm the interpretation of the ordinary meaning of the terms of a treaty in their context and in the light of its object and purpose, or can be used where that interpretation leaves the meaning of a treaty ambiguous or obscure or leads to a result which is manifestly absurd or unreasonable. The preparatory work of a treaty is mentioned as one such supplementary means of interpretation in Art. 32 VCLT.

Consistent with the VCLT, the negotiating history of a certain WTO norm is used much less than other methods of interpretation, but when it does get used it is usually after literal interpretation.[1705] In one case, the Appellate Body observed that the negotiating history did not provide evidence of a certain intention of the parties that would have run counter to

1701 *United States – Import Prohibition of Certain Shrimp and Shrimp Products, WT/DS58/AB/R* 1998, para. 152, 153.

1702 *European Communities – Conditions for the Granting of Tariff Preferences to Developing Countries, WT/DS246/AB/R* 2004, para. 92.

1703 Mitchell 2007, 814.

1704 Flett 2011, 14.

1705 See for example *United States – Certain Measures Affecting Imports of Poultry from China, WT/DS392/R* 2010, para. 7.478; *European Communities – Conditions for the Granting of Tariff Preferences to Developing Countries, WT/DS246/AB/R* 2004, para. 107ff; *United States – Import Prohibition of Certain Shrimp and Shrimp Products, WT/DS58/AB/R* 1998, para. 157.

the interpretation preferred by the Appellate Body;[1706] in this case the Appellate Body relied on the negotiating history. By way of contrast, there is at least one case in which the Panel's finding was reversed by the Appellate Body simply because this finding relied on the negotiating history rather than the wording of the norm.[1707] The latter finding shows the secondary relevance of this method of interpretation. It is in line with Art. 32 VCLT, but stands in contrast to how the *travaux* had been used in dispute settlement under GATT.[1708] Indeed, the method of interpretation of GATT has been described as "overly historical" and "basically a game of who had the best archives".[1709]

Further, supplementary means of interpretation include infrequent references to the writings of academic experts[1710] or entities such as the International Law Commission.[1711]

1.5. The role of WTO Members' intention in interpretation

A somewhat peculiar aspect of the Appellate Body's approach to the interpretation of an agreement is that it often invokes the intention of WTO Members.[1712] Referring to the "common intention" of WTO Members has been described as a consistent approach in WTO dispute settlement.[1713] Indeed, the Appellate Body has on several occasions stated that

> "the purpose of treaty interpretation under Articles 31 and 32 of the *Vienna Convention* is to establish the 'common intention' of the parties "[1714].

1706 *United States – Import Prohibition of Certain Shrimp and Shrimp Products, WT/DS58/AB/R* 1998, n. 114 of the Appellate Body report.

1707 Weiss 2003, 186 citing United *States – Section* 211 Omnibus Appropriations Act of 1998, WT/DS176/AB/R, para. 339f.

1708 Howse 2001, 57ff.

1709 Kuijper in Abi-Saab 2008, 722.

1710 See for example Palmeter and Mavroidis 1998, 407.

1711 *United States – Measures Affecting the Production and Sale of Clove Cigarettes, WT/DS406/AB/R* 2012, para. 265; *European Communities and Certain Member States – Large Civil Aircraft, WT/DS316/AB/R* 2011, para. 845.

1712 Van Damme 2010, 622.

1713 Guan 2014, 245.

1714 *China – Measures Affecting Trading Rights and Distribution Services for Certain Publications and Audiovisual Entertainment Products, WT/DS363/AB/R* 2009, para. 405; for a similar statement see *European Communities and Certain Member States – Large Civil Aircraft, WT/DS316/AB/R* 2011, para. 845.

The Appellate Body fails, in either this statement or any other, to state the precise legal basis on which it refers to the intention of WTO Members. Under normal circumstances, the intention of the parties to an international agreement would become relevant as part of historic interpretation and the use of the *travaux préparatoires*. Yet, as discussed, the Appellate Body rarely relies on negotiation documents, and fails to cite the *travaux préparatoires* in any single instance in which it refers to the common intention of WTO Members. References to the common intention of WTO Members are, on different occasions, combined with each of the three methods of interpretation mentioned in Art. 31 VCLT, textual, contextual and teleological.

An example of how textual interpretation is linked to the common intention of WTO Members can be found in the *China – Raw Materials* report. Here, the Appellate Body rejected the applicability of Art. XX GATT to China's commitments under Art. 11.3 of the Chinese Accession Protocol, on the grounds that Art. 11.3 contained no explicit language to this end. The Appellate Body held that "if there had been a common intention" to give China access to the Art. XX GATT defence, such language would have been included. This textual interpretation is combined with a contextual interpretation, i.e. the comparison of Art. 11.3 of China's Accession Protocol with other provisions of that Protocol.[1715]

One example where the Appellate Body links the common intention of WTO Members to contextual interpretation is the discussion of the standard of review to be applied in disputes under the SPS Agreement in *Hormones I*. Here, the Appellate Body concluded that the standard of Art. 17.6 ADA was not applicable because no textual reference to the ADA could be found in the SPS Agreement and consequently the application of the ADA standard would run counter to the intent of the Members.[1716] Obviously, this is a contextual interpretation, because the Appellate Body compares the wording of different agreements, but at the same time it is also an interpretation of the text based on the intention of the WTO Member as identified by the Appellate Body.

The *Hormones I* case also provides an example of how teleological interpretation is combined with the intention of WTO Members. When discussing "the object and purpose" of Art. 3 SPS, the Appellate Body rejected

1715 *China – Measures Related to the Exportation of Various Raw Materials, WT/DS394/AB/R, WT/DS395/AB/R, WT/DS398/AB/R* 2012, para. 293.

1716 *European Communities – Measures Concerning Meat and Meat Products, WT/DS26/AB/R, WT/DS48/AB/R* 1998, para. 114.

an interpretation of the term "based on" that would have transformed international standards in binding norms for the WTO Members. The argument brought forward was that if the Members had wished to impose on themselves such binding obligations, they would have stated so explicitly.[1717] The Appellate Body declined to impose obligations on sovereign states as it was not clear that this was what the states had wanted to do.

In sum, the common intention of WTO Members is an important factor in the Appellate Body's interpretation; the Appellate Body refers to it in the context of all of the three methods of interpretation contained in Art. 31 VLCT. Arguably, this is explained by the Appellate Body's statement that the overall purpose of interpretation is to ascertain the common intention of WTO Members. Nonetheless, the precise legal basis for this aspect of the Appellate Body's approach to interpretation does not become clear from the WTO case law.

1.6. Beyond interpretive methods: The use of international law

Finally, an important overarching aspect of the methods of interpretation used in WTO dispute settlement is the use of international law that exists outside of the WTO legal order: that is, norms of international law that are not referred to explicitly within the WTO legal order.[1718] Referring to and interpreting "external" norms that are explicitly referred to in WTO law poses no particular problems for adjudicators.[1719] Such references can be found in Art. 2.4 TBT, Art. 3 SPS, and Art. XXIV GATT amongst others, and the manner in which they were dealt with by the Appellate Body has already been discussed.[1720] In most of these instances, the Appellate Body appears unwilling to venture too far into the territory of other international agreements (e.g. the discussion of Art. XX (d) GATT in *Mexico – Soft Drinks*) or give them too much of a role (e.g. the discussion of AIDCP in *United States – Tuna Labelling*).

In this section, the focus is on the use of non-WTO international law in cases where there is no such explicit reference to non-WTO international

1717 Ibid., para. 165.

1718 For a brief list of provisions in WTO agreements that refer to international treaties outside WTO law, see Weiss 2003, 194; Canal-Forgues 2001, 12f; Böckenförde 2003, 986ff.

1719 Kleinlein 2012, 274.

1720 See for example chapter 2, sections 2.4.2 and 3.2.

law. The role of non-WTO international law in WTO interpretation may raise controversies. Some WTO Members have expressed, at some stage, that

> "situations in which legal concepts outside the WTO texts have been applied in a WTO dispute settlement proceeding, including asserted principles of international law other than customary international law rules of interpretation (e.g. state responsibility, proportionality)"

are particularly sensitive from their point of view.[1721] In this situation, it appears that what may be perceived as inappropriate use of international law perceived could undermine the acceptance of dispute settlement decision by WTO Members. At the same time, resorting to international law may also foster the perceived legitimacy of WTO dispute settlement decisions, as international law promotes a broader variety of objectives than WTO law.[1722]

In this section, I will deal with non-WTO international law in general, before focusing on the use of (mostly non-WTO) principles.[1723] The section is structured as follows: I will first describe basic aspects of the use of international law in dispute settlement (section 1.6.1). I will then proceed to take a closer look at the sources of international law used in WTO dispute settlement (section 1.6.2). In the two remaining sections I will summarize aspects of the use of international law in WTO dispute settlement that are relatively clear and also uncontroversial (section 1.6.3) and then move to aspects that are less clear and more controversial (section 1.6.4). A concluding section (1.6.5) summarizes the findings.

I do not discuss the question whether non-WTO rules should lead the WTO dispute settlement bodies to decline jurisdiction in certain cases;[1724] since this issue has so far played at most a small role in the practice of WTO dispute settlement.

1721 "Negotiations on improvements and clarifications of the dispute settlement understanding on improving flexibility and member control in WTO dispute settlement", Contribution by Chile and the United States, TN/DS/W/28, 23 December 2002, para. 4.

1722 See Schmid 2001, 23.

1723 See below section 4.1.

1724 For a brief overview see Vranes 2009, 78f; for a more extensive discussion see Marceau 2001, 1108ff.

1.6.1. The basics

The discussion on the applicability of non-WTO international law in WTO dispute settlement stems, at least partially, from the absence in the DSU of a separate and explicit provision on the law applicable in WTO disputes, similar to Art. 38 ICJ Statute.[1725] Nonetheless, adjudicators have situated WTO law within the larger body of international law, and in its very first decision, the Appellate Body stated that Art. 3.2 DSU

> "reflects a measure of recognition that the General Agreement [i.e. GATT, C.G.] is not to be read in clinical isolation from public international law."[1726]

A later Panel stated the following on Art. 3.2 DSU:

> "We take note that Article 3.2 of the DSU requires that we seek within the context of a particular dispute to clarify the existing provisions of the WTO agreements in accordance with customary rules of interpretation of public international law. However, the relationship of the WTO Agreements to customary international law is broader than this. Customary international law applies generally to the economic relations between the WTO Members. Such international law applies to the extent that the WTO treaty agreements do not 'contract out' from it. To put it another way, to the extent there is no conflict or inconsistency, or an expression in a covered WTO agreement that implies differently, we are of the view that the customary rules of international law apply to the WTO treaties and to the process of treaty formation under the WTO."[1727] [footnotes omitted]

In an accompanying footnote, the Panelists also further explained that they could

> "see no basis here for an *e contrario* implication that rules of international law other than rules of interpretation do not apply. The language of 3.2 in this regard applies to a specific problem that had arisen under the GATT to the effect that, among other things, reliance on ne-

---

1725 However, some others see Art. 7 DSU as fulfilling that function in WTO law, see below section 1.7.3.

1726 *United States – Standards for Reformulated and Conventional Gasoline, WT/DS2/AB/R* 1996, sec. III B, at 17.

1727 *Korea – Measures Affecting Government Procurement, WT/DS163/R* 2000, para. 7.96.

> gotiating history was being utilized in a manner arguably inconsistent with the requirements of the rules of treaty interpretation of customary international law."

The same Panel argued that that Art. 7 DSU could not be read to prevent adjudicators from referring to customary international law. Art. 7 DSU stipulates the following:

1. Panels shall have the following terms of reference unless the parties to the dispute agree otherwise [...]:
   "To examine, in the light of the relevant provisions in (name of the covered agreement(s) cited by the parties to the dispute), the matter referred to the DSB by (name of party) in document [...] and to make such findings as will assist the DSB in making the recommendations or in giving the rulings provided for in that/those agreement(s)."
2. Panels shall address the relevant provisions in any covered agreement or agreements cited by the parties to the dispute.
3. In establishing a panel, the DSB may authorize its Chairman to draw up the terms of reference of the panel in consultation with the parties to the dispute, subject to the provisions of paragraph 1. [...]"

The Panel stated, albeit only in a footnote, that

> "The purpose of the terms of reference is to properly identify the claims of the party and therefore the scope of a panel's review. We do not see any basis for arguing that the terms of reference are meant to exclude reference to the broader rules of customary international law in interpreting a claim properly before the Panel."[1728]

As there was no appeal in this case, the Appellate Body neither confirmed nor modified these findings.

The general approach in WTO dispute settlement is that the adjudicators can – or maybe even must – draw on non-WTO substantive international law in certain situations. Both WTO adjudicators and WTO Members regularly draw on international law when arguing their case.[1729] The use of non-WTO international law when interpreting WTO law has become "standard practice"[1730] in WTO dispute settlement. Yet it is less clear

1728 Ibid., n. 755.
1729 Van Damme 2009, 15.
1730 Pauwelyn 2003c, 997.

what purpose, legal basis and type of international law the adjudicators wish to use, and to what lengths they will go to justify it.

The following sections will deal with these questions in more detail.

1.6.2. Sources of international law used and legal basis for using them

In practice, the adjudicators have drawn on every conceivable type of international law outside of the WTO legal order, including treaties, judgments of other international courts and tribunals (in particular the ICJ), general principles of law and customary international law.[1731] References to the law of regional institutions (e.g. decisions by the dispute settlement institutions under NAFTA) have remained infrequent, though.[1732] In terms of frequency of reference to decisions by other international tribunals, the WTO dispute settlement bodies has been ranked between the ICJ, ECJ and ECtHR (low) and the IACHR, ICTY and ITLOS (high).[1733] It has also been observed that the WTO dispute settlement bodies refer to case law by other judicial bodies less frequently than investment tribunals.[1734] The ICJ is the court whose decisions the WTO dispute settlement bodies have referred to most frequently.[1735]

Panels and Appellate Body have often not failed to clarify the legal basis for their use of international law, i.e. which of the different bases for using non-WTO legal instruments and principles contained in the VCLT they are building on.[1736] For example, the Appellate Body in *Shrimp – Turtles* referred to the need for environmental cooperation as recognized, amongst other agreements, in the Agenda 21, the Convention on Biological Diversity, and the Convention on the Conservation of Migratory Species of Wild Animals. From these references to the need for international cooperation in several international environmental agreements, the Appellate Body inferred that, in the case at hand, the US had a duty to cooperate/negotiate with certain countries as it had with others. The Appellate Body, however, failed to explain its citing of the two environmental conventions to which the defendant US is not a party – it might, for example, have referred to

1731 See Hu 2004; Weiss 2003.
1732 Busch 2007, 741.
1733 Miller 2002, 490.
1734 Charlotin 2017, 287.
1735 Ibid., 289.
1736 Mitchell 2007; Marceau 1999, 118; Foltea 2012, 95f.

the VCLT.[1737] When interpreting the clause "exhaustible natural resources" the Appellate Body also referred to non-WTO international legal instruments without making the basis clear. The basis on which the WTO dispute settlement bodies use international law is rarely evident from the reports.[1738] One example is the compliance Panel in *Shrimp – Turtles.* It understood the Appellate Body as saying that the failure of the US as defendant to initiate negotiations with the claimants was unacceptable because of the existence of several international legal instruments and declarations of the WTO CTE that favoured multilateral cooperation in seeking solutions to environmental problems such as the extinction of sea turtles.[1739] The compliance Panel went one step further than the Appellate Body with regard to these international treaties and explicitly mentioned Art. 31.3 c) VCLT as a basis for taking them into account. Art. 31.3 c) VCLT sets forth that in interpreting a treaty other relevant rules of international law "applicable in the relations between the parties" must be taken into account. The Panel stated that the parties to the dispute were also parties to all but one of the relevant non-WTO treaties.[1740] The Panel in the *EC – Biotech Products* case, in a report not appealed, also accepted Art. 31.3 VCLT in principle as forming a basis for the use of non-WTO law in WTO dispute settlement. Moreover, the Panel in this case considered whether it could take non-WTO international law independent of Art. 31.3 c) VCLT into account:

> "In addition to dictionaries, other relevant rules of international law may in some cases aid a treaty interpreter in establishing, or confirming, the ordinary meaning of treaty terms in the specific context in which they are used. Such rules would not be considered because they are legal rules, but rather because they may provide evidence of the ordinary meaning of terms in the same way that dictionaries do. They would be considered for their informative character. It follows that

---

1737 Charnovitz 2007, 704f.

1738 Böckenförde 2003, 994 notes for example, that when Art. 31 VCLT gets cited, it is usually not made clear on which of its many paragraphs the WTO dispute settlement bodies rely.

1739 *United States – Import Prohibition of Certain Shrimp and Shrimp Products, WT/DS58/RW* 2001, para. 5.46-5.56.

1740 Ibid., para. 5.57.

> when a treaty interpreter does not consider another rule of international law to be informative, he or she need not rely on it."[1741]

In sum, the adjudicators do not exclude specific sources of international law *a priori* from consideration in the proceedings, but they are rarely explicit on the basis for using them.

1.6.3. Ways of using international law in WTO dispute settlement – the (relatively) clear part

Some ways in which international law has been used in WTO dispute settlement are relatively clear: to shed light at certain factual aspects, for clarifying procedural matters – often by using certain principles of international law – and for interpreting terms contained in WTO law. These aspects are described in this section, while the following one deals with those aspects of the use of international law that are as yet less clear.

First, international law is sometimes used to shed light on certain factual aspects of a case.[1742] For example, in one case the Appellate Body had to decide whether the mechanism in Art. 2.5 TBT Agreement, which establishes an obligation for WTO Members to "explain the justification" for a technical regulation to another Member at that Member's request, was likely to be effective. The Appellate Body did not share the doubts expressed by both one of the parties to the case and the Panel, namely that the mechanism might not be effective because WTO Members could fail to respond fully or adequately to such a request for information. The Appellate Body stated that it had to

> "assume that Members of the WTO will abide by their treaty obligations in good faith, as required by the principle of *pacta sunt servanda* articulated in Article 26 of the *Vienna Convention*".[1743]

In another case, the Appellate Body observed that the question of whether a developing country had a specific need the sense of paragraph 3 (c) of the GATT Enabling Clause must be assessed by an objective standard, and that, *inter alia*, multilateral agreements adopted by an international organi-

1741 *European Communities – Measures Affecting the Approval and Marketing of Biotech Products, WT/DS291/R, WT/DS292/R, WT/DS293/R* 2006, para. 7.92.

1742 Kulovesi 2011, 147ff.

1743 *European Communities – Trade Description of Sardines, WT/DS231/AB/R* 2002, para. 278.

zation could serve as such as standard.[1744] In the *Shrimp – Turtles* compliance case, the Appellate Body explained that in its original finding it had relied on a specific regional, international agreement, Inter-American Convention for the Protection and Conservation of Sea Turtles (IAC), in two ways: that in the view of the Appellate Body the IAC showed that multilateral procedures were available to pursue as an alternative course of action to the trade measures in place; and that it demonstrated the existence of "unjustifiable discrimination" under the chapeau of Art. XX GATT, because negotiation efforts similar to those that had led to the adoption of the IAC had not been undertaken vis-à-vis other states.[1745] In *Brazil – Tyres*, the Panel referred to the Basel Convention Technical Guidelines on the Management of Used Tyres, i.e. some guidelines under the Basel Convention on the Control of Transboundary Movements of Hazardous Wastes and Their Disposal, a multilateral environmental agreement. It did so in order to establish certain facts on the emissions resulting from the incineration of waste tyres.[1746]

Sometimes a comparative exercise concerning national legislation is one of the adjudicators' fact-finding exercises. In *United States – Gambling*, the Panel related to various national jurisdictions in order to decide whether a certain issue constituted a question of public morals in the sense of Art. XX (a) GATT.[1747] Similarly, the Panel in *United States – COOL Requirements* took the decision that a certain policy objective was "legitimate" in the sense of Art. 2.2 TBT on the basis of the factual finding that more than 70 WTO Members maintained some form of mandatory country of origin labelling requirements.[1748] Equally, in *EC – Seal Products* the Panel accepted animal welfare legislation from various countries as evidence that a controversial EU measure banning seal products from the EU was indeed connected to public moral concerns within the EU.[1749]

1744 *European Communities – Conditions for the Granting of Tariff Preferences to Developing Countries, WT/DS246/AB/R* 2004, para. 163.

1745 *United States – Import Prohibition of Certain Shrimp and Shrimp Products, WT/DS58/AB/RW* 2001, para. 128.

1746 *Brazil – Measures Affecting Imports of Retreaded Tyres, WT/DS332/R* 2007, para. 7.191.

1747 *United States – Measures Affecting the Cross-Border Supply of Gambling and Betting Services, WT/DS285/R* 2004, para. 6.471ff.

1748 See the summary of the Panel's reasoning in *United States – Certain Country of Origin Labelling (COOL) Requirements, WT/DS384/AB/R, WT/DS/386/AB/R* 2012, para. 438.

1749 *European Communities – Measures Prohibiting the Importation and Marketing of Seal Products, WT/DS400/R, WT/DS401/R* 2013, para. 7.407ff.

Second, international law is regularly used to clarify certain procedural matters. Burden of proof, standing, and the representation of parties before Panels are all matters that have been decided by resorting to non-WTO international law[1750], mainly general principles of law[1751]. Panels and the Appellate Body often utilize legal principles for addressing procedural issues rather than for resolving matters of substantive law.[1752]

A third way in which international law is sometimes used in WTO dispute settlement is as support for a certain interpretation of WTO law. Some of the principles used are not codified in the VCLT.[1753] Both international legal principles (both general principles of international law and customary law principles) and non-WTO treaty law play a role in WTO dispute settlement.

With regard to general principles of international law the Appellate Body in *Shrimp – Turtles* stated, albeit in a relatively casual manner (in a footnote), that they could be considered "law applicable in the relations between the parties" that shall be taken into account in interpreting WTO law according to Art. 31.3 c) VLCT.[1754] One principle that the WTO adjudicators regularly refer to and that is closely connected to reliance on the wording of the law is the principle of *effet utile* or effective treaty interpretation.[1755] The Appellate Body has referred to ICJ reports as a source of this principle.[1756] The principle says, in the words of the Appellate Body, that "interpretation must give meaning and effect to all the terms of a treaty."[1757] In some instances, the WTO adjudicators have followed this principle without explicitly referring to it. For example, in *Shrimp – Turtles,* the Appellate Body observed that an interpretation by the Panel would have rendered

1750 See Pauwelyn 2003c, 998; Cameron and Gray 2001.

1751 Petersmann 2006, 99f.

1752 Weiss 2003, 200.

1753 Van Damme 2009, 56.

1754 *United States – Import Prohibition of Certain Shrimp and Shrimp Products, WT/DS58/AB/R* 1998 para. 158, n. 157.

1755 For a detailed discussion of the use of this principle see van Damme 2010, 636.

1756 *United States – Standards for Reformulated and Conventional Gasoline, WT/DS2/AB/R* 1996, n. 45.

1757 Ibid., sec. IV, at 23.

> "most, if not all, of the specific exceptions of Article XX inutile, a result abhorrent to the principles of interpretation we are bound to apply".[1758]

In other instances, the principle has been mentioned explicitly.[1759] Conversely, there are also some cases where commentators have criticized the adjudicators for allegedly not observing the principle.[1760]

Another principle used is *in dubio mitius*. The principle was introduced by the Appellate Body when interpreting the expression "based on" in Art. 3.1 SPS. In this case, the Appellate Body stated that "based on" must be read as carrying a different meaning from "conform to" and based this finding, inter alia, on the *in dubio mitius prin*ciple.[1761] It quoted the principle as follows:

> "If the meaning of a term is ambiguous, that meaning is to be preferred which is less onerous to the party assuming an obligation, or which interferes less with the territorial and personal supremacy of a party, or involves less general restrictions upon the parties."[1762]

In support of the principle, the Appellate Body referred to various international law textbooks as well as to several reports of the ICJ and the PCIJ.[1763]

Legal scholars have seen the principle at work in a series of other interpretations.[1764] However, in a publication from 2009, van Damme also noted that the Appellate Body had failed to take up the principle in subsequent disputes, even though parties relied on it.[1765] She suggests that this

---

1758 *United States – Import Prohibition of Certain Shrimp and Shrimp Products, WT/DS58/AB/R* 1998, para. 121.

1759 *Brazil – Measures Affecting Imports of Retreaded Tyres, WT/DS332/AB/R* 2007, para. 220.

1760 Appleton 1999, 483.

1761 *European Communities – Measures Concerning Meat and Meat Products, WT/DS26/AB/R, WT/DS48/AB/R* 1998, para. 165.

1762 Ibid., n. 154.

1763 Ibid.; van Damme 2009, 63 notes that the Appellate Body may not have been entirely right in considering that the principle was widely recognized as a means of supplementary interpretation in international law; Lennard 2002, 62f also questions whether the Appellate Body is right in relying on the ICJ decisions.

1764 Eggers 2001, 217; Hilf 2001, 118.

1765 One example is *Korea – Alcoholic Beverages, WT/DS75AB/R, WT/DS84/AB/R* 1999, para. 5 where Korea invoked the principle without the Appellate Body taking up this argument.

silence may be indicative of an adjustment in the Appellate Body's position after *Hormones I*.[1766] In a later case, however, the WTO adjudicators state explicitly that they came to a certain interpretation because if they had not done so, they "would effectively impose an unwanted choice on the Member concerned".[1767] While this is not a direct reference to *in dubio mitius*, the statement follows a similar rationale, i.e. not imposing heavier obligations on states than necessary. In some instances, adjudicators have also referred to a "policy space" that WTO Members enjoy in deciding on regulatory objectives[1768]; yet such references are infrequent. Another interpretive principle invoked is *"iura novit curia"*, which is also contained in ICJ judgments.[1769] Also, there are frequent references to rules contained in the VCLT, other than the methods of interpretation.[1770]

Another important principle of international law recognized in WTO dispute settlement is the principle of good faith.[1771] As one author concludes, it has been referred to in practically all Panel and Appellate Body reports[1772] and has even been described as dominating WTO interpretation.[1773] For example, in *Shrimp – Turtles* the Appellate Body described the chapeau of Art. XX GATT as "but one expression of the principle of good faith". This principle is a general principle both of domestic and international law; in the view of the Appellate Body it mandates that parties to a treaty exert their rights reasonably where the exercise of said rights impinges upon the rights of another party.[1774] One inference that the Appellate Body has drawn from this principle is that the adjudicators must assume that WTO Members usually act in good faith, and WTO Members

1766 Van Damme 2009, 64.

1767 *European Communities – Measures Affecting the Approval and Marketing of Biotech Products, WT/DS291/R, WT/DS292/R, WT/DS293/R* 2006, para. 7.170.

1768 See the Appellate Body's summary of the Panel decision in *United States – Certain Country of Origin Labelling (COOL) Requirements, WT/DS384/AB/R, WT/DS/386/AB/R* 2012, para. 440.

1769 *European Communities – Conditions for the Granting of Tariff Preferences to Developing Countries, WT/DS246/AB/R* 2004, para. 105.

1770 For some examples see Lindroos and Mehling 2006, 869ff.

1771 See for example *United States – Continued Suspension of Obligations in the EC – Hormones Dispute, WT/DS320/AB/R* 2008, para. 314; *United States – Import Prohibition of Certain Shrimp and Shrimp Products, WT/DS58/AB/R* 1998, para. 158.

1772 Zeitler 2005, 722 who also provides a more in-depth discussion of the use of the principle in WTO case law.

1773 Canal-Forgues 2001, 8.

1774 *United States – Import Prohibition of Certain Shrimp and Shrimp Products, WT/DS58/AB/R* 1998, para. 157.

must extend the same assumption to other WTO Members.[1775] The Appellate Body has described "good faith" as "a general principle of law and a general principle of international law" that "controls the exercise of rights by states.[1776] As "one application of this general principle", the Appellate Body has also referred to the "doctrine" of *abus de droit*, which forbids the abusive exercise of a state's rights. The Appellate Body has also presented this principle as an established principle of international law, quoting ICJ reports as well as the writing of eminent legal commentators.[1777]

A related[1778] principle of international law used in WTO dispute settlement is the protection of legitimate expectations.[1779] This principle says that rules must be interpreted in such a way as to protect any expectations of a WTO Member that were formed because it had to believe, based on an action (including statements) by another WTO Member, that a situation would not change in a certain way.[1780] Other principles of international law that WTO adjudicators have invoked are the principles of *estoppel* and state responsibility.[1781] Also, the Appellate Body in *EC – Sardines* used Art. 28 VCLT concerning the non-retroactivity of treaties for the interpretation of Art. 2.4 TBT.[1782]

Non-WTO treaty law has been used in a couple of instances for interpreting terms of WTO law. One example can be found in the Appellate Body report in the *Shrimp – Turtles* case. Here, the Appellate Body interpreted the term "exhaustible natural resources" in light of "contemporary concerns of the community of nations about the protection and conservation of the environment"[1783]. It inferred from international legal documents such as UNCLOS and CITES that the term exhaustible natural re-

---

1775 *European Communities – Trade Description of Sardines, WT/DS231/AB/R* 2002, para. 278.

1776 *United States – Import Prohibition of Certain Shrimp and Shrimp Products, WT/DS58/AB/R* 1998, para. 158.

1777 Ibid.

1778 On the relation between the principle of good faith and the protection of legitimate expectations, see Canal-Forgues 2001, 9; Cottier and Schefer 2000, 53f.

1779 See Cameron and Gray 2001, 260f for a discussion of this principle in WTO case law and references.

1780 The definition is based on Cottier and Schefer 2000, 53.

1781 See Cameron and Gray 2001, 292f for references.

1782 *European Communities – Trade Description of Sardines, WT/DS231/AB/R* 2002, para. 200.

1783 *United States – Import Prohibition of Certain Shrimp and Shrimp Products, WT/DS58/AB/R* 1998, para. 129.

sources also comprised living natural resources, in this case sea turtles.[1784] In this example, non-WTO treaty law was used to impart meaning to a WTO treaty term.[1785] While the Appellate Body did not clarify on which legal basis it referred to these other treaties, it did investigate which of the parties were bound by them.[1786]

A further point to be observed when discussing the role of non-WTO international law in WTO dispute settlement is that the WTO dispute settlement bodies so far have not declined to exercise jurisdiction on the grounds that another international judicial body might be more competent to hear the case or had already done so.[1787] At the same time, the Appellate Body has shown reluctance to venture too far into the domain of other courts (or treaties). In *Mexico – Softdrinks*, Mexico had argued that Art. XX (d) GATT, referring to "laws and regulations" should be read to cover measures that Mexico needed to take in order to comply with its obligations from another trade agreement, NAFTA. The Appellate Body rejected this position, observing that Mexico's position implied that "WTO panels and the Appellate Body would [...] become adjudicators of non-WTO disputes", which was "not the function of panels and the Appellate Body as intended by the DSU".[1788] Mexico had also argued in this case that a prior US action, namely its refusal to agree to the establishment of a NAFTA dispute Panel on the controversial measure, should have led the WTO dispute settlement to refuse hearing the case. The Appellate Body rejected Mexico's position, stating that

> "it would imply that the WTO dispute settlement system could be used to determine rights and obligations outside the covered agreements."[1789]

1784 Ibid., para. 131–133.

1785 See also Foltea 2012, 99; by contrast, Kulovesi 2011, 156 argues that these instruments were used as factual evidence, given that the Appellate Body did not clarify the legal basis for using them. I do not find that a convincing reading of the decision, though; the Appellate Body discussed the WTO term and its meaning, not only the factual question whether turtles were "exhaustible".

1786 See for a summary of the Appellate Body's findings Howse 2008, 645f.

1787 For a more in-depth discussion of this aspect of WTO dispute settlement, see Davey and Sapir 2009, 11ff.

1788 *Mexico – Tax Measures on Soft Drinks and Other Beverages, WT/DS308/AB/R* 2006, para. 78.

1789 Ibid., para. 56.

Interestingly, this finding is made "*arguendo*", i.e. there was no need for the Appellate Body to make it for resolving the dispute.[1790]

Finally, it should also be noted that the Appellate Body has, in certain instances, referred to non-WTO international law even when not strictly necessary.[1791] For example, in *Shrimp – Turtles* the Appellate Body described the chapeau of Art. XX GATT as "but one expression of the principle of good faith". This principle, being a general principle both of domestic and international law, mandates according to the Appellate Body that parties to a treaty have to exert their rights reasonably, where the exercise of the rights impinges upon the rights of another party.[1792] The Appellate Body is in no way compelled by the text to add a reference to international law to its interpretation of the chapeau. The reference to international law adds nothing when applying the chapeau to the factual details of the case, either, and yet the Appellate Body decided to add this reference.[1793]

1.6.4. The role of non-WTO international law – how far do the adjudicators go?[1794]

Some uses of non-WTO international law in the WTO legal order are relatively clear, as the preceding sections have shown. These are either relatively "modest" uses of non-WTO international law – to help answer factual questions, to impart meaning to a certain term of WTO law – or to help clarify procedural issues, in particular where there is a gap in WTO law. This section analyses instances where the use of non-WTO international law is either less clear or more controversial.

The controversies tend to relate to the extent of *application* of non-WTO international law in the WTO legal order. Such application could mean any of the following: filling a gap in WTO law by resorting to non-WTO

1790 For a more in-depth discussion of the "*arguendo*" figure, see section 3.2 below.

1791 Howse 2009, 230 maintains that in *Shrimp – Turtles* the Appellate Body could have resorted to prior case law rather than *non-WTO* legal instruments (to which not all WTO Members were parties) for its interpretation of the term "exhaustible natural resources" in Art. XX (g) GATT; Sykes 2014, 489 makes a similar point.

1792 *United States – Import Prohibition of Certain Shrimp and Shrimp Products, WT/DS58/AB/R* 1998, para. 157.

1793 Gourgourinis 2011, 42 observes that in the WTO case "good faith" is used both as a means of interpretation or a directly applicable, selfstanding norm.

1794 This heading is inspired by the title of the article by Pauwelyn 2001b.

international law; modifying the rights and obligations contained in WTO law in the light of non-WTO international law, or setting aside a WTO provision in light of the rights or obligations of a WTO Member resulting from non-WTO international law.[1795] These questions are different from and more far-reaching than the question of whether the adjudicators use non-WTO international law to impart meaning to terms contained in WTO law; the latter is after all an interpretation of WTO law.[1796] The application of non-WTO international law in the legal order would also mean that the WTO dispute settlement bodies would have to assume competence in the interpretation of non-WTO treaty law. Without such competence, they would not be able to ascertain what the non-WTO international legal norms actually stipulate.

For the purposes of the present study, multilateral environmental agreements (MEAs) are of particular importance as reference points in non-WTO international law. Of course, the issue may not only arise with regard to WTO Members' right and obligations under MEAs, but also under regional/bilateral free trade agreements (FTAs). Given that this work is mainly concerned with the question of how the WTO dispute settlement bodies deal with non-economic regulatory goals, I will not discuss the relationship of WTO law and other free trade agreements systematically.[1797]

It should be noted that what I discuss in this section are not merely cases of legal conflict in the narrow sense. A conflict in the narrow sense of the word occurs where one norm *obliges* a legal subject to do something that is forbidden by another norm governing the same legal subject's behaviour or where there are conflicting obligations. Yet there may be situations where a certain action is *permitted* under a MEA/FTA or other rules of international law, while it is not permitted by WTO law.[1798] In this latter case, there is also the question what influence non-WTO rules would have on the permissibility of the action under WTO law.

There are a number of cases in which the application of non-WTO international law from various sources was discussed in WTO dispute settlement:

The Appellate Body formulated a position on the possibility of justifying a departure from WTO law on the basis of general or customary principles

1795 See the discussion in Kulovesi 2011, 139ff.

1796 See on the distinction between these two issues also Kleinlein 2012, 273.

1797 For an in-depth discussion of the relationship of WTO law and regional trade agreements as interpreted in WTO dispute settlement cases, see Mestral 2013.

1798 See chapter 1, n. 89 for a discussion of different notions of conflict.

of international law in *Hormones I*. In this case, the EU had claimed that, in the interpretation of the SPS Agreement, the precautionary principle needed to be taken into account.[1799] The Appellate Body, reacting to this submission, found several elements of precaution present in the SPS Agreement.[1800] However, it refused to go further and state – as the EU had claimed – that the precautionary principle was a general principle of international law and could guide the Members' risk assessment under Art. 5.1 SPS.[1801] On this occasion, the Appellate Body also found that whatever the status of the precautionary principle in international law was, the principle could not override the explicit obligations contained in the SPS Agreement and consequently could not be used to justify measures otherwise inconsistent with the agreement.[1802] Following this decision by the Appellate Body in *Hormones I*, and based on the observation that controversy continued whether a precautionary principle existed either as a matter of customary international law or as a general principle of international law, the Panel in the later *EC – Biotech Products* case also refused to rely on the precautionary principle to resolve the case set before it.[1803]

With regard to the role of non-WTO *treaty* law, the case law is not as clear. The compliance Panel in *Shrimp – Turtles* in a somewhat casual manner stated its view that certain measures, such as an environmentally motivated import ban on certain products by a WTO Member, could only be justified under Art. XX, if they were taken in line with an MEA.[1804] Yet this statement was not the result of an in-depth discussion of the role of non-WTO treaty law in the WTO legal universe and limited to the situation under Art. XX GATT.

The clearest statement on the role of MEAs came from the Panel in the *EU – Biotech Products* case; the decision was not appealed. In this case, the EU had proposed that the Convention on Biological Diversity (CBD) and the related Cartagena Protocol on Biosafety were of relevance for the reso-

1799 The EU in that case does not seem to have made a statement on whether it considered the precautionary principle customary international law or a general principle of international law.

1800 *European Communities – Measures Concerning Meat and Meat Products, WT/DS26/AB/R, WT/DS48/AB/R* 1998, para. 124.

1801 Ibid., para. 17.

1802 Ibid., para. 123ff.

1803 *European Communities – Measures Affecting the Approval and Marketing of Biotech Products, WT/DS291/R, WT/DS292/R, WT/DS293/R* 2006, para. 7.86ff.

1804 *United States – Import Prohibition of Certain Shrimp and Shrimp Products, WT/DS58/RW* 2001, para. 5.88.

lution of the case. The latter contains rules on risk assessment and the precautionary principle. The Protocol had, at the time of the dispute, been ratified by the defendant (the EU); on the complainant side, Canada and Argentina had signed it, while the US had neither signed nor ratified it, but participated in the Protocol's clearinghouse mechanism.[1805] The EU did not argue that any of the provisions of the Cartagena Protocol would override any WTO clause; rather, it argued that both sets of norms could and should be interpreted harmoniously.[1806] By contrast, both the US and Canada claimed that the Biosafety Protocol was not "law applicable in the relations between the parties" in the sense of Art. 31.3 c) VCLT as the claimants had not ratified the Protocol.[1807] Canada argued that only a treaty ratified by all WTO Members was to be considered applicable law in the sense of Art. 31.3 c) VCLT.[1808] In addition, both Canada and the US argued that the Protocol should not be taken into account in WTO dispute settlement, even if all parties to a dispute had ratified it, because the Protocol stated explicitly that it

> "shall not be interpreted as implying a change in the rights and obligations of a Party under any existing international agreements"[1809].

Like the parties, the Panel considered Art. 31.3 c) VCLT the relevant norm for assessing the legal relevance of the Biosafety Protocol for the dispute. It observed first that the term "international law" in that norm was broad enough to encompass international treaties such as the Cartagena Protocol, international customary law and general principles of international law.[1810] With regard to the interpretation of the terms "the parties" in Art. 31.3 c) VCLT the Panel concluded, on the basis of a textual, contextual and teleological interpretation, the following:

> "It may be inferred [...] that the rules of international law applicable in the relations between 'the parties' are the rules of international law

1805 *European Communities – Measures Affecting the Approval and Marketing of Biotech Products, WT/DS291/R, WT/DS292/R, WT/DS293/R* 2006, para. 7.53.

1806 Ibid., para. 7.55.

1807 Ibid., para. 7.58, 7.63.

1808 Ibid., para. 7.60.

1809 Obviously, there is a logical flaw in this argument. If the Biosafety Protocol is not to be applied in WTO disputes and thus completely disregarded, then the provision on the relationship between the Protocol and WTO dispute settlement cannot be relied on either.

1810 *European Communities – Measures Affecting the Approval and Marketing of Biotech Products, WT/DS291/R, WT/DS292/R, WT/DS293/R* 2006, para. 7.67.

applicable in the relations between the States which have consented to be bound by the treaty which is being interpreted, and for which that treaty is in force. This understanding of the term 'the parties' leads logically to the view that the rules of international law to be taken into account in interpreting the WTO agreements at issue in this dispute are those which are applicable in the relations *between the WTO Members*."[1811] [footnotes omitted, emphasis added]

"Taking account of the fact that Article 31(3)(c) mandates consideration of other applicable rules of international law, and that such consideration may prompt a treaty interpreter to adopt one interpretation rather than another, we think it makes sense to interpret Article 31(3)(c) as requiring consideration of those rules of international law which are applicable in the relations between all parties to the treaty which is being interpreted."[1812]

The Panel here chose a restrictive reading of the norm and gave non-international treaty law a limited role in WTO dispute settlement. In the dispute, the Panel did not apply the Cartagena Protocol as it had not been ratified by all Members of the WTO.

A contrary position had previously been taken by the compliance Panel in the (appealed) *Shrimp – Turtles* report, albeit without an extensive discussion. The Panel held that

"Article 31.3(c) of the Vienna Convention provides that, in interpreting a treaty, there shall be taken into account, together with the context, 'any relevant rule of international law applicable to the relations between the parties'. We note that, with the exception of the Bonn Convention on the Conservation of Migratory Species of Wild Animals (CMS), Malaysia and the United States have accepted or are committed to comply with all of the international instruments referred to by the Appellate Body [...]."[1813] [footnotes omitted]

Here, the Panel implied that the term "the parties" in Art. 31.3 c) VCLT was to be understood to refer only to those WTO Members that were parties to the dispute.

1811 Ibid., para. 7.68.

1812 Ibid., para. 7.70.

1813 *United States – Import Prohibition of Certain Shrimp and Shrimp Products, WT/DS58/RW* 2001, para. 5.57.

In some cases where further light might have been shed on whether a departure from WTO law could be justified by resorting to non-WTO international law, the adjudicators avoided taking a position.[1814] For example, before the Panel in *Shrimp – Turtles,* the US had put forward the argument that multilateral environmental agreements permitted taking precisely the kind of measures that the US had actually taken in pursuit of environmental objectives. In reaction to this argument, the Panel pointed out that there was no concrete rule, either of treaty or customary international law, which permitted precisely the measure that the US had taken in favour of marine turtles.[1815] It did, however, *not* state that the arguments used by the US were not pertinent. Also, as noted above, in *Shrimp – Turtles* the Appellate Body relied on non-WTO international law for a number of interpretive questions, but without a clear discussion of the meaning of Art. 31.3 c) VCLT. Some authors argue that in *Shrimp – Turtles*, the adjudicators' stance towards relying on non-WTO environmental law was more open-minded than it had been, for example, in the later *Hormones I* case.[1816]

Finally, two other cases concerned the role of non-WTO economic agreements in WTO law. In the *Argentina – Footwear* case the defendant had argued that a certain measure constituting a violation of a GATT norm resulted from an obligation it had assumed in relation to the International Monetary Fund (IMF). The Appellate Body discussed at some length whether these other agreements modified Argentina's obligations under WTO law and gave it the right to take the measures in dispute at the WTO. It concluded this not to be the case.[1817]

Another relevant, more recent case is *Brazil – Tyres*. The disputed measure was a Brazilian import ban on re-treaded tyres; an exemption existed for those countries party to the regional trade pact Mercosur. This exemption had been added to the Brazilian legislation subsequent to a ruling by a Mercosur tribunal, which concluded that Brazil had acted inconsistently with a certain Mercosur decision by enacting the import ban. The Panel considered this fact sufficient for not classifying the Mercosur exception an unjustifiable or arbitrary discrimination between Mercosur and non-Mer-

---

1814 Weiss 2003, 199; Böckenförde 2003, 989.

1815 *United States – Import Prohibition of Certain Shrimp and Shrimp Products, WT/DS58/R* 1998, para. 7.49, 7.50, 7.58, 7.59.

1816 Sykes 2014, 486.

1817 *Argentina – Measures Affecting Imports of Footwear, Textiles, Apparel and other Items, WT/DS56/AB/R* 1998, para. 67ff.

cosur countries under the chapeau of Art. XX GATT; in its view Brazil's Mercosur obligations provided a reasonable basis for the ban.[1818] The Appellate Body rejected this finding, because it held that

> "the ruling issued by the MERCOSUR arbitral tribunal is not an acceptable rationale for the discrimination, because it bears no relationship to the legitimate objective pursued by the Import Ban that falls within the purview of Article XX(b) [...]."[1819]

This means that the fact alone that a WTO Member has an international legal obligation from a non-WTO international treaty as stipulated by the judicial entity competent to interpret that other treaty cannot justify a departure from WTO law.[1820] Some observers have argued that the finding implies a supremacy of the WTO dispute settlement vis-à-vis the Mercosur tribunal, because the Appellate Body's finding required Brazil to bring its measure in line with WTO law, even though the disputed measure was a result of Brazil having to ensure that its regulations conformed to Mercosur rules.[1821] In fact, the Appellate Body's finding only means that WTO rules are additional to Mercosur rules and that a country that has signed both agreements needs to comply with both. This does not amount to a statement of hierarchy between the two sets of norms. It simply means that a country has to be careful not to take on contradictory obligations.

In *EC – Large Civil Aircraft*, the Appellate Body also engaged in an intensive discussion of Art. 31.3 c) VCLT. At issue in this case was whether a bilateral agreement between the EC and the US dating from 1992 and containing, amongst other things, rules on subsidies granted for developing large civil aircraft was to be taken into account in the WTO dispute; the dispute concerned the WTO legality of such subsidies under the SCM. The Appellate Body started its discussion of the matter by noting that the interpretation of the term "parties" had "in recent years been the subject of much academic debate" and "been addressed by the ILC".[1822] It further observed that not all WTO Members were also parties to the VCLT, but

---

1818 *Brazil – Measures Affecting Imports of Retreaded Tyres, WT/DS332/R* 2007, para. 7.270ff.

1819 *Brazil – Measures Affecting Imports of Retreaded Tyres, WT/DS332/AB/R* 2007, para. 228.

1820 For a more in-depth discussion of the Panel and Appellate Body decisions, see Brink 2010, 815ff.

1821 Lavranos and Viellard 2008, 315f.

1822 *European Communities and Certain Member States – Large Civil Aircraft, WT/DS316/AB/R* 2011, para. 844.

Art. 31.3 c) VCLT expressed, according to the ILC, the "principle of systemic integration".[1823] From this, it inferred that in the multilateral WTO context

> "a delicate balance must be struck between, on the one hand, taking due account of an individual WTO Member's international obligations and, on the other hand, ensuring a consistent and harmonious approach to the interpretation of WTO law among all WTO Members"[1824].

Subsequently, it declined to clarify what the term "the parties" in Art. 31.3 c) VCLT meant, given that according to this article the legal provision "applicable in the relations between the parties" must also be relevant to the dispute at hand. The Appellate Body assumed, for reasons very specific to the case, that the bilateral agreement was not relevant for the interpretation of WTO law.[1825]

1.6.5. Summary on the use of international law in WTO dispute settlement

In the following, I briefly summarize the above analysis of how the WTO adjudicators use non-WTO international law.

The adjudicators rely on and interpret non-WTO international legal rules that are linked to WTO law by an explicit reference (and in cases where such a reference can be construed). This is the case, e.g. for the rules of interpretation contained in the VCLT or international standards referenced in the SPS and TBT Agreements. What is also relatively clear is that international legal principles are routinely used to clarify procedural matters not explicitly regulated by WTO law. Moreover, international law is also used to impart meaning to certain terms contained in WTO law and to clarify certain factual matters. These findings constitute what can be considered the established jurisprudential *acquis* of the WTO; beyond that lies territory that is at most half-charted. At this juncture no coherent approach to the application of non-WTO international law in WTO dispute settlement is apparent.[1826]

1823 Ibid., para. 845.
1824 Ibid., para. 844.
1825 Ibid., para. 855.
1826 See also Kulovesi 2011, 143.

With regard to the relationship between WTO and non-WTO international law, no case has been put before the Appellate Body in which a Member has sought to and could clearly justify a certain behaviour under a multilateral environmental agreement while being simultaneously considered to be in breach of WTO law. The *EC – Biotech Products* case, where the issue was of most acute relevance among the cases discussed so far, did not proceed to appellate stage. Moreover, the EU had actually not claimed that provisions of the Cartagena Protocol could justify a departure from WTO obligations, but rather that Art. 5.1, 5.2 SPS and other provisions of the SPS Agreement needed to be interpreted in the light of the provisions of the Protocol.[1827]

With regard to the relationship between WTO law and bilateral or regional FTAs, *Brazil – Tyres*, *Argentina – Footwear* and *Mexico – Softdrinks* are the most relevant cases. In the Brazilian case, the Appellate Body rejected the idea that an exception to an import ban in Brazilian law introduced to implement a ruling by a Mercosur tribunal (that is as a result of obligations from a non-WTO international treaty), could be used to justify a breach of WTO law. Some read the Argentinean case in a way that would put it at odds with the Brazilian case. To them, the Appellate Body's detailed investigation of whether the agreements between Argentina and the IMF gave Argentina a right that contradicted its obligations under WTO law means that if Argentina actually had such a right it might have prevailed over WTO law[1828] – a conclusion that the Appellate Body did not reach in *Brazil – Tyres*. Others disagree with this reading of the *Argentina – Footwear* case.[1829] In *Mexico – Softdrinks*, the Appellate Body rejected the idea that Art. XX (d) GATT could be invoked to justify a breach of WTO obligations by resorting to international legal obligations of WTO Members stemming from a non-WTO international treaty. Much remains unclear regarding how far WTO adjudicators are willing to go in their reliance on non-WTO international law and whether the approach in different cases is actually consistent.[1830]

The case law is also not clear on Art. 31.3 c) VCLT, another norm that is of relevance with regard to the relationship of different provisions of inter-

1827 For a summary of the EU's position on the role of the Cartagena Protocol in the *EC – Biotech* Products case, see Howse and Horn 2009, 54f.

1828 Bartels 2002, 508; 143 Kulovesi 2011, 143 with reference to a work of Pauwelyn; Vranes 2009, 81 also reads the decision in this way, but argues that the Appellate Body goes too far in making it.

1829 See Vranes 2009, 80, n. 301 for an overview and references.

1830 For a similar conclusion see ibid., 80.

national law. The Panel in *EC – Biotech Products* embraced a narrow interpretation of the provision when deciding that "parties" in that clause referred to all WTO Members. If that line is followed, it would make it virtually impossible for a non-WTO treaty to ever be considered "law applicable in the relation between the parties" in future dispute settlement cases, given the broad membership of the WTO. However, some see the later appellate decision in *EC – Large Civil Aircraft* as a potential sign of greater openness to a stronger role of non-WTO international law in WTO interpretation.[1831]

In short, many of the most controversial and far-reaching questions concerning the role of non-WTO international law in the WTO legal universe are yet to be given clear and definite answers in WTO dispute settlement.

1.7. Discussion

In the following I will discuss some central characteristics of the use of the different methods of interpretation in WTO dispute settlement from a technical-legal point of view.

1.7.1. Transparency about methods of interpretation

The Appellate Body's use of the methods of interpretation contained in the VCLT is not surprising or inappropriate, given that WTO law is treaty law. Indeed, there has not been much criticism of the Appellate Body's approach of referring to these methods.[1832]

What is more unusual is that the WTO adjudicators aim at transparency regarding their methods of interpretation: not all courts provide details of the methods of interpretation they use and the legal basis for using these methods. For example, the ECJ rarely explains which method of interpretation it uses to arrive at a certain finding[1833] and certainly does not explain the legal basis for using a certain interpretive method. The degree of

1831 See for example Sykes 2014, 487.

1832 Abi-Saab 2006, 463; Francioni 2006, 146. Yet, Guan 2014, 237ff is an exception. He criticizes the Appellate Body for referring to the VLCT as codification of the customary rules of interpretation, arguing that this deviates from a widely shared position and practice of international law (e.g. by the ICJ).

1833 Beck 2012, 281.

"technical adherence" to the rules of the VCLT has been described as going beyond the practice of other international courts.[1834] The degree of attention that the Appellate Body has dedicated to explaining its methods of interpretation has been observed to have prompted other international courts to follow its example.[1835]

The Appellate Body has also clarified what it considers to be the purpose of using the VLCT methods of interpretation: establishing the common intention of the parties to the WTO agreements.

The Appellate Body does not only say which methods it uses and clarify the purpose behind their use, it also frequently stresses the roots of the methods of interpretation it uses in international law. In doing so, it construes the reason for using these methods in a particular way: the statement of the Appellate Body that Art. 3.2 DSU refers to "customary methods of interpretation of international law" that are, in turn, incorporated in Art. 31, 32 VCLT is remarkable. As has been noted by van Damme, the argument of the Appellate Body contains a specific twist. The Appellate Body cannot refer to the VCLT as an agreement to which all or most WTO Members are a part.[1836] While well over 100 states have ratified the VLCT[1837], this number is considerably lower than the total number of WTO Members. Therefore, the Appellate Body portrays Art. 31 and 32 VCLT as reflecting customary methods of interpretation. Such methods arguably bind all states;[1838] at the same time the fact that they are laid down explicitly somewhere makes it rather clear what these methods are and what they are not. The Appellate Body's approach of conceiving of Art. 31-33 VCLT as containing customary methods of interpretation is not unusual at all; others (including the ICJ)[1839] also understand the VCLT articles in this way.[1840] The point that I would like to note here is only that

1834 Zleptnig 2010, 83; Pauwelyn and Elsig 2012, 457.

1835 Sacerdoti 2008, 597f.

1836 Van Damme 2009, 23.

1837 See United Nations Treaty Collection, https://treaties.un.org/Pages/ViewDetailsIII.aspx?src=TREATY&mtdsg_no=XXIII-1&chapter=23&Temp=mtdsg3&clang=_en.

1838 This point is indeed made by a former Member of the Appellate Body, see Bacchus 2005, 504.

1839 On the ICJ's practice see Guillaume 2006, 467f.

1840 Cameron and Gray 2001, 254; Conrad 2011, 251; Lennard 2002, 17; Weiss 2003, 184 citing ICJ, Territorial Dispute (Libyan Arab Jamahiriya v. Chad), para. 41; Zeitler 2005, 726.

the Appellate Body refers to two different sources to justify its use of the methods of interpretation: customary international law and the VCLT.

By way of contrast, the Appellate Body is less meticulous when explaining how and on what legal basis it uses international law: the adjudicators do not always explain the legal basis for using non-WTO international law in a given dispute.[1841] One example given above[1842] is the interpretation of the clause "exhaustible natural resources" in *Shrimp – Turtles*. Vranes states that Art. 31.3 c) VCLT would have been an apposite basis for non-WTO international legal instruments in this context,[1843] while Conrad suggests that the Appellate Body referred to these instruments as part of a textual interpretation.[1844] Howse, in turn, suggests that the Appellate Body, rather than considering whether a norm was actually binding on the parties to a dispute, sought to establish whether it was acceptable as a legitimate standard among the parties to the dispute. In Howse's view, the Appellate Body, rather than seeking to give meaning to treaty terms by reference to non-WTO law, sought to make a statement that environmental norms needed to have some value in the WTO universe, thereby empowering environmental constituencies.[1845] Whether this was actually the case or whether the Appellate Body was keen on avoiding a potentially controversial finding on Art. 31.3 c) VCLT can only be answered with certainty by those involved in the decision. However, these discussions in the literature show clearly that when the adjudicators are imprecise with regards to the legal basis on which they use international law, this will give raise to assumptions and suggestions, rather than to predictability and clarity.

Yet another example is the discussion of the status of the precautionary principle in *Hormones I* where the Appellate Body observed that it was considered by some to be a "general principle of customary international environmental law".[1846] This statement mixes two sources of international law, namely "general principles" of and "customary" international law.[1847] To add to the confusion, a reference is made to "international environmental law", rather than "international law" more generally[1848], and all this in a

1841 For a similar conclusion, see Foltea 2012, 95.
1842 See above section 1.6.2.
1843 Vranes 2009, 264.
1844 Conrad 2011, 253.
1845 Howse 2008, 646f.
1846 *European Communities – Measures Concerning Meat and Meat Products, WT/DS26/AB/R, WT/DS48/AB/R* 1998, para. 123.
1847 Howse 2008, 639.
1848 Ibid.

case that concerns public health rather than environmental issues. Legal commentators are quite critical of this lack of clarity in the WTO case law.[1849]

To summarize, the Appellate Body is generally clear and transparent regarding which methods of interpretation it uses and their legal basis. The use of international law is an important exception; the Appellate Body often fails to clarify the legal basis for using non-WTO international law.

1.7.2. The methods of interpretation used

When considering methods of interpretation, by far the most striking feature of judicial interpretation in WTO case law is a very strong, "almost obsessive"[1850] emphasis on literal interpretation.[1851] This strong textual orientation in WTO dispute settlement is indeed unusual when compared to other international tribunals, which while they also engage in literal interpretation, they do not do so with such painstaking attention to literal meaning of the law.[1852] Other international courts also refer to dictionaries, but they do so less frequently than WTO judges.[1853] Dictionary definitions cited in WTO case law are often neither necessary nor useful, as they either seek to define words that need no definition, or they do so in such a manner as to add no clarity to their meaning within the WTO agreement. Examples for the use of such definitions were quoted above in section 1.1: none of them makes the original text any clearer or yields any new insights on the meaning of the respective norms; none of them adds to the Appellate Body's analysis. Indeed, they are what one observer has called a "regurgitation" of the text of the treaty rather than interpretations.[1854]

It is against the background of this very heavy reliance on the text of the WTO agreements almost ironic that in other instances the adjudicators do not seem to give much importance to the wording of the text at all. For example, the different terms contained in the chapeau of Art. XX GATT have been given scant attention by the adjudicators so far[1855] and the Ap-

1849 See for example Knox 2004, 49.
1850 Bacchus 2005, 511.
1851 See for example Bohanes 2002, 376; Magnuson 2010, 124ff; Steinberg 2004, 261.
1852 Sacerdoti 2006, 46.
1853 For the ICJ, see Pavot 2013, 30, 32.
1854 Magnuson 2010, 127.
1855 See chapter 2, section 1.4.

pellate Body has been criticized for paying insufficient attention to the meaning of some parts of Art. 2.4 TBT has been criticized.[1856]

The literalist tendency in WTO dispute settlement is not unbridled, however, as there are occasional reflections on the method's shortcomings, such as when the Appellate Body acknowledges the limits of dictionary definitions.[1857] Moreover, some observers have also claimed that in recent cases the Appellate Body's rulings are becoming less textual[1858] and that it also regularly uses teleological interpretation[1859]. Nonetheless, its textual orientation is still quite marked.

The strong textualist approach taken by the Appellate Body has several shortcomings. The first problem is that is built on assumptions regarding the drafting of agreements that appear to be flawed. The process of negotiating international agreements, in particular those that include multiple agreements as part of a single undertaking, often leads to situations in which either the drafters fail to appreciate the implications of a certain wording or where negotiators decide to accept unclear wording for the sake of compromise.[1860] For example, it has been suggested that the Appellate Body's different approaches to the applicability of Art. XX (a) GATT in the China-related cases are over-reliant on textual differences in different provisions of China's Accession Protocol which may be more or less accidental.[1861] Holding China to "drafting mistakes" in its Accession Protocol has been called a "deplorable outcome"[1862]. A literalist interpretation accords significant weight to such differences. Obviously the text of the legal norms also matters for the methods of interpretation other than textual; how can a judge understand the purpose of a norm without looking at its text? However, getting the *telos* of a norm more or less correct may be feasible, even if at the end of the day a tired negotiator failed to use precisely the same wording in two articles. Furthermore, when different methods

---

1856 Mavroidis 2013, 523.

1857 This is emphasized for example by Howse 2003c, 12f; van Damme 2010, 621ff.

1858 See for example Ortino 2006, 122 concerning the *United States – Gambling* case. See also the comment by Zdouc in Taniguchi et al. 2008, 402 who observes that the Appellate Body now uses contextual interpretation more frequently; van Damme 2010, 641ff.

1859 Lang 2016, 1101.

1860 See chapter 1, section 1.

1861 Gu 2012, 1017 and passim.

1862 Bronckers and Maskus 2014, 400; they also point to the fact that the WTO obligations of new WTO Members are recorded in "what are really extended meeting minutes: dozens, if not hundreds of pages of working party reports, drawn up during the accession negotiations", at 401.

are accorded a more equal footing, it appears that different arguments for and against a certain interpretation are more likely to be thoroughly considered. WTO law has its fair share of gaps and ambiguities – to interpret WTO provisions primarily through textual interpretation is likely to prove difficult.[1863]

Second, the literalist approach of the Appellate Body also means that on occasion too little weight it accorded to the context of norms. This lack of attention to context is inherently problematic, because the meaning of words changes with their context; in this regard, it has even been proposed that the Oxford English Dictionary and other dictionaries should be thrown away and never used again when drafting an Appellate Body report.[1864] Besides drawing on such more principled objections, one can refer to more concrete examples in WTO case law to show why context should probably matter more than it has done so far in case law. For example, it has been questioned whether the Appellate Body is right in interpreting the term "like products" in an identical manner in both Art. 2.1 TBT and III GATT, given the different contexts of these norms.[1865] Another example is the Appellate Body's approach towards interpreting the term "necessary" in an identical manner in different paragraphs and even agreements. It may well be questioned whether "necessary" should be interpreted in an identical manner in all the sub-paragraphs of Art. XX GATT or in Art. XX GATT and Art. 2.2 TBT[1866]. "Necessary" is textually an inconclusive term and has, as the Appellate Body itself observed, a range of connotations. In such a case, where literal interpretation yields only limited insights, one would expect teleological and contextual interpretation to play a major role. When one term is used in two discrete norms, both the immediate context of its use and the *telos* of the respective norms may differ. For example, Art. XX (d) does not define the objectives that a Member's measure must ultimately serve, while the other sub-paragraphs do.[1867] Similarly, Art. XIV (a) GATS allows measures "necessary to protect public morals or to maintain public order", but comes with a footnote *ad* Art. XIV GATS specifying that

1863 Steinberg 2004, 261.
1864 Mavroidis 2006, 358 with reference to Wittgenstein.
1865 Mavroidis 2013, 518.
1866 See Neumann and Tuerk 2003, 277; Kapterian 2010, 118.
1867 See Kapterian 2010, 102.

> "[t]he public order exception may be invoked only where a genuine and sufficiently serious threat is posed to one of the fundamental interests of society".

A similar footnote is not contained in Art. XX (a) GATT. Yet the adjudicators draw indiscriminately on the interpretation of Art. XIV GATS under Art. XX GATT and *vice versa;* the adjudicators have also opted, unconvincingly, for an identical approach to the interpretation of the term "necessary" in various provisions. One observer has argued that this approach is more conducive to the "predictability" that the WTO dispute settlement system is to provide than if the Appellate Body had chosen a more differentiated interpretation of necessity in different norms.[1868] Given that the way the necessity test is applied is rather unclear at present, this conclusion is quite debatable. The approach taken by the Appellate Body in cases dealing with Art. XX GATT is nonetheless not untypical for WTO judicial decision-making at large. The adjudicators have sought to present their case law as a uniform artefact containing no inconsistencies or differences in interpretation between the cases.

Third, it is also the case that, like every judicial body, and especially every judicial body dealing with norms as indeterminate as WTO law, the Appellate Body makes certain choices that do not result strictly from the wording of the law[1869], and arguably often even not from a combination of all the methods contained in the VCLT. It has even been argued that there is no such thing as an easily discernible "ordinary meaning", that such a meaning "depends on the assumptions of the reader of the text and on other factors that vary with time and place"[1870]. If this is the case, would it not be better to openly acknowledge the limits of the interpretive methods, explain the range of options and then lay open the reasons (that may not be strictly legal) for choosing one particular interpretation from amongst the range of legally defensible interpretations available? In the words of Abi-Saab, a former Member of the Appellate Body: "Would it not be better to shed the camouflage?"[1871] This has indeed been proposed by some commentators. For example, when discussing how the Appellate Body should determine the appropriate standard of review, Guzman argues that

1868 Voon 2009, 714.
1869 See for example Picciotto 2005, 13.
1870 McRae 2006, 367.
1871 Abi-Saab 2006, 462.

> "without guidance from the relevant legal texts, the AB should do what judicial organs the world over (including the AB) do in such situations: base their decisions on relevant policy considerations".[1872]

Going beyond textualism and explaining the methodologies and deeper rationales underlying a decision may also help in providing more guidance to WTO Members.[1873] If the underlying reasons impelling particular WTO judicial decisions were acknowledged more openly and explained better, WTO Members as well as other observers would be in a better position to contest, criticize, or support these decisions on a more realistic basis. Indeed, some legal commentators have complained, for example, that the Panel's decision in *EC – Biotech Products* is difficult to criticize because, its textual reasoning is so opaque.[1874] As discussed in chapter 1 of this work, the legitimacy of judicial decisions rests to a great degree on their being supported by rational, convincing and consistent arguments.[1875] If the rationality of decisions suffers on account of the text alone being unable to carry the burden it is asked to shoulder, judicial decisions are less persuasive than they could and should be.

Concerning the use of other methods of interpretation, a specific feature of the WTO's judicial approach is the reliance on the common intention of parties as a cross-cutting element in different types of interpretation and the statement that ascertaining this intention is the overall purpose of the interpretive process. The latter statement is a debatable proposition. The most notable schools of interpretation in international law are textual, teleological and intention-based respectively.[1876] For example, the ICJ has been observed to base its findings on the objective meaning of a term used in international law.[1877] Using this categorization, the Appellate Body's approach towards interpretation is ambiguous and unusual: on the one hand, it stresses the value of textual interpretation (textual school of interpretation), while on the other it refers to the identification of the common intention of parties as an overarching objective of the interpretive process (intention-based school of interpretation). Moreover, ascertaining the in-

1872 Guzman 2008, 53.
1873 See also Magnuson 2010, 125; Guzman 2008, 53.
1874 Perez 2007, 272.
1875 See chapter 1, section 3.1.
1876 Guan 2014, 250; van Damme 2010, 617f also mentions these three schools, but ultimately questions the practical value of these "general labels".
1877 Weiss 2003, 185.

tention of parties would normally involve using the *travaux préparatoires* of a treaty; yet the Appellate Body rarely relies on these materials.

There are different views on whether what the WTO adjudicators do is in line with the VCLT's rules on interpretation; these differences in view stem partially from the fact that commentators disagree on what interpretive approach the VLCT mandates. For example, it has been argued that the VCLT prescribes a holistic approach whereby different methods are brought to bear upon the text, and only once they have all been used may a conclusion be presented on the meaning of a term.[1878] Against this background, some observers have criticized the Appellate Body's application of the different methods of interpretation as too mechanical.[1879] Others, however, stress that the canon of methods of interpretation in the VCLT is not well-defined and does not yield consistent results.[1880] If this view is correct, any interpretations developed by the Appellate Body's with the help of the VCLT interpretive canon would be presented as being more unequivocal and compelling than is necessarily justified by the VCLT itself. Some commentators even claim that the Appellate Body's

> "aspiration to always have one possible interpretation and the over-reliance on the VCLT may lead to circumvention of the Article 3.2 DSU imperative not to add to rights or obligations and result in a tendency of the Appellate Body to behave more as a lawmaker than as a judge".[1881]

Finally, some also hold that the VCLT mandates a predominantly textual method of interpretation[1882]; from this perspective, the Appellate Body would be in line with the VCLT, maybe with the exception of its use of the common intention of WTO Members.

To summarize, the Appellate Body's reliance on the methods of interpretation enshrined in the VCLT has in principle been widely welcomed. At the same time, the concrete ways in which the Appellate Body has relied on the VCLT, and in particular the overwhelmingly textual nature of its interpretations, has met with objections from legal commentators.

1878 See Lennard 2002, 22f noting also that the VCLT approach is "essentially textual"; McRae 2006, 365; Ortino 2006, 120; Zleptnig 2010, 63.

1879 Ortino 2006, 130f; by contrast, Zdouc 2008, 374 the director of the Appellate Body Secretariat, maintains that the Appellate Body "has perceived the process of interpretation in a "holistic" way."

1880 See the references in chapter 1, n. 57.

1881 Cartland, Depayre, and Woznowski 2012, 988.

1882 Conrad 2011, 251.

1.7.3. Struggling with the role of non-WTO international law

A particularly sensitive and much debated aspect concerning methods of interpretation used in WTO dispute settlement is the role of non-WTO international law. While some aspects have already been clarified, many others are still open. In the following section, I will assess the use of non-WTO international law in WTO dispute settlement from a more technical-legal point of view, while referring to the debates being undertaken in the literature.

There are different ideas on what the dispute settlement bodies actually have and have not said on the role of non-WTO international law in the WTO legal order; the Appellate Body's failure to consistently explain the legal basis on which it uses non-WTO substantive international law in WTO dispute settlement may serve as a partial explanation. For example, some observers read the Appellate Body's findings in *Shrimp – Turtles* on the requirement to negotiate with countries affected by the trade measures in dispute to mean that where all parties to a dispute are parties to a MEA and that MEA authorizes the adoption of certain trade-related measures, the latter measures would likely be accepted by the adjudicators.[1883] This, however, is an accurate reading of the *Shrimp – Turtles* decision. As Howse[1884] has pointed out, the existence of a multilateral agreement was used by the Appellate Body as a benchmark for the existence of alternative courses of action as well as for a finding that different countries were treated differently, a relevant fact when assessing the existence of arbitrary or unjustifiable discrimination. Also, the observation that "the Appellate Body has used other treaties only as evidence on empirical questions"[1885] does not appear to be a correct understanding; at least the VCLT has been used in various other manners. As observed above, commentators also disagree on what has and has not been said in the *Argentina – Footwear* case. Such controversies among legal observers on the relationship between WTO law and other international law complicate a legal-technical assessment of the Appellate Body jurisprudence. Here a brief overview must suffice.

Among observers, it is widely agreed that the WTO adjudicators can and should draw on at least some non-WTO international law to inform their

1883 Yavitz 2001, 225.
1884 Howse 2002b, 505ff.
1885 Kleinlein 2012, 267.

interpretation of WTO law.[1886] They have generally praised the Appellate Body for its finding that WTO law should not be read in "clinical isolation" from other international law. While this and a few other starting points for the discussion on the role of non-WTO international law in interpreting WTO law seem to be widely agreed, many details still prove controversial.[1887] The following positions, while not exhaustive, outline the breadth of opinions on the matter: Several commentators seem to subscribe, though in different words and maybe on the basis of slightly different views, to the broad perspective that WTO is part of international law and therefore the WTO adjudicators apply non-WTO international law in WTO disputes. Vranes states that adjudicators are required to "take account of such non-WTO norms that are invoked as a defence, if the latter have to be regarded as lawful modifications of WTO law and as being meant to prevail over WTO law by the WTO Members bound by them."[1888] Lindross and Mehling claim that

> "no provision in the rules on world trade identifies or limits the law that ultimately should apply to disputes. [...] As with any other treaty, however, it is widely acknowledged that the agreement instituting the WTO was born into the wider body of international law. From this assumption, it would normally follow that the multilateral trading system continues to be governed by the precepts of public international law, at least to the extent that these have not been contracted out, deviated from, or otherwise replaced."[1889]

Similarly, Pauwelyn holds that "falling back" on non-WTO international law is permitted in international law generally, and thus, also in the WTO context, to the extent that WTO Members have not contracted out of international law on specific issues.[1890] Furthermore, he contends that WTO rules must be interpreted in light of, and if possible, consistently with non-WTO rules if the latter fall into one of the categories mentioned in Art. 31, 32 VCLT.[1891] He suggests that the applicable law needs to be determined by general rules on the validity and application of international law in cas-

---

1886 See for example Bartels 2001, 499; Howse and Horn 2009, 58f; Marceau 1999; Pauwelyn 2003c; Study Group of the International Law Commission 2006, para. 134.
1887 For a brief overview of the debate see Lagomarsino 2011, 546f.
1888 Vranes 2009, 77.
1889 Lindroos and Mehling 2006, 861.
1890 Pauwelyn 2003a, 205ff.
1891 Ibid., 252ff.

es of conflict, e.g. *lex specialis* or *lex posterior*[1892]; he recommends that the WTO adjudicators should develop a "built-in reflex" to "look outside the 'four corners' of the WTO treaty for guidance" on how to interpret WTO law.[1893] Lim maintains that the manner in which Article 31.3 c) VCLT may be used and to which extent the WTO dispute settlement bodies can thus rely on non-WTO law "depends upon the substantive WTO norm, and the competing non-WTO norm"[1894]. Howse and Horn maintain that the use of non-WTO norms as interpretative guidance in reading WTO norms is permissible. By contrast, non-WTO international law can, according to them, only be applied for purposes other than interpreting terms of WTO law in the following situations: if the respective norms have achieved the status of *ius cogens*, if they constitute an *inter se* amendment of WTO rights and obligations between some WTO Members, if they are explicitly incorporated into WTO law by way of reference or in cases where there is a conflict with WTO rules, but the non-WTO norms are incorporated in a treaty later in time on the same subject matter, or if WTO norms are in conflict with the UN Charter.[1895] Similarly, Henckels states that Art. 11 DSU means that "external sources of international law should inform the interpretation of WTO agreements"[1896]. Conversely, Hu maintains that in the absence of a clause similar to Art. 38 of the ICJ Statute, the WTO dispute settlement bodies are under no obligation to draw on sources outside the WTO legal order.[1897]

Agreement or at least strong majorities among legal commentators exist in relation to the following aspects: First, a distinction must be made between the jurisdiction of the WTO dispute settlement bodies and the law applicable in the disputes where they have jurisdiction.[1898] Claims can only be based on a violation of the "covered agreements" (or in the form of a non-violation complaint) and the adjudicators only have the competence

---

1892 Ibid., 275ff; for a similar position see Gourgourinis 2016, 71.

1893 Pauwelyn 2003a, 269.

1894 Lim 2017, 110f.

1895 Howse and Horn 2009, 58f.

1896 Henckels 2006, 284.

1897 Hu 2004, 157.

1898 This distinction is in particular highlighted and explained by Bartels 2001, 501ff; other authors and the ILC report on the fragmentation of international law make the distinction as well, see Vranes 2009, 72 with further references; Böckenförde 2003, 976; Sacerdoti 2008, 603; Study Group of the International Law Commission 2006, para. 44f.

to decide on such claims;[1899] this is rather clear from the reference in Art. 1.1 DSU to the "covered agreements".[1900]

Second, there are certain areas in which the use of international law in WTO dispute settlement is by and large uncontested. The use of international law as a source of information on certain factual issues appears to have been mostly accepted among observers. The use of the VCLT – not only its interpretive methods, but also other articles such as Art. 26 VLCT – is not in principle controversial, either; yet there is some criticism of how some of the VCLT provisions (e.g. the ones on interpretation) have been applied.[1901] Indeed, drawing on the VCLT seems appropriate, given that WTO agreements are international treaty law, even if not all WTO Members have ratified the Convention. There have also been few objections to the WTO adjudicators drawing on non-WTO international law to clarify procedural matters not explicitly regulated in WTO law, such as the burden of proof.[1902]

A third area of (conceptual) agreement is that a distinction should be made between using non-WTO international law to inform the interpretation of WTO norms and applying international law as a source of independent rights and obligations of WTO Members that could trump those contained in WTO law.[1903] Unfortunately, not all commentators make clear to which of these two issues they refer when talking about the "application" of international law in WTO dispute settlement.

Generally, a majority of commentators accept that using non-WTO international law to inform the interpretation of WTO law is permissible.[1904] A parallel has been drawn in this regard to the adjudicators' use of dictionaries: if they can draw on an Oxford dictionary to clarify the meaning of a certain WTO legal term, should they not also be able to resort, for example, toa definition contained in an MEA accepted by many WTO Members?[1905] Mostly, the Appellate Body's reliance on international law to inform the interpretation of terms such as "exhaustible natural resources" in

---

1899 See for example Henckels 2006, 284.

1900 See Bartels 2001, 502f; by contrast, Conrad 2011, 121 refers to Art. 3.2 and 7.1 DSU in this regard.

1901 See above section 1.7.2.

1902 See Abi-Saab 2006, 463.

1903 See for example Howse and Horn 2009, 53ff; Henckels 2006, 284ff.

1904 See for example Howse and Horn 2009, 53ff; Henckels 2006, 284ff; Zleptnig 2010, 74.

1905 The question is asked by Pauwelyn 2003a, 262; a similar point seems to be made by the Panel in *European Communities – Measures Affecting the Approval*

Art. XX (g) GATT has been welcomed, but there are also a few critical voices.[1906]

The question of whether international legal rights and obligations originating outside WTO law could take precedence over WTO law is much more controversial; the prevailing answer seems to be negative. In legal terms, the discussion on limits to the use of international law in the WTO context focuses on Art. 3.2, 19.2, 7, and 11 DSU. Another relevant norm in the discussion of the role of international law in WTO adjudication is Art. 31.3 c) VCLT. It is not entirely clear how the relationship between this article and potential restrictions on the use of non-WTO international law in WTO dispute settlement emanating from the cited norms of the DSU is to be construed. The issue has not been decided by the Appellate Body; the following short clarification of the options may be useful for future discussions, however.

One could argue that, as the DSU is WTO law while Art. 31.3 c) VCLT is not, DSU norms would take priority. From such a perspective, the use of non-WTO international law in the WTO legal order would depend on whether one assumes that the DSU imposes any limits in this regard. In other words, only if one holds the view that the DSU norms in principle allow for the use of international law for a certain purpose could the question whether a certain international legal norm is "applicable in the relations between the parties", as required by Art. 31.3 c) VCLT become relevant. However, this would probably not do justice to the fact that Art. 31.3 c) VLCT is a rule of interpretation. If one accepts – as many do – that the VCLT's rules on interpretation can be used in WTO dispute settlement, this would need to extend to Art. 31.3 c) VCLT, too. As a consequence, the relationship between Art. 3.2, 19.2, 11 or 7 DSU on the one hand and Art. 31.3 c) VCLT on the other should be construed in the opposite way: Once it has been established that a certain norm of international law is applicable in the relation between "the parties", it needs to be assessed whether Art. 3.2, 19.2, 11 or 7 DSU impose any limits on the use of that norm within the WTO legal universe. The appropriate order of reviewing these legal norms appears not to have been discussed in the literature. There is no need to resolve the issue here, given that is has not been

and Marketing of Biotech Products, WT/DS291/R, WT/DS292/R, WT/DS293/R 2006, para. 7.92.

1906 For the discussion in the literature on the interpretation of exhaustible natural resources, see chapter 2, section 1.6.2.

discussed by the Appellate Body, either. In the following, I will start with the discussion of Art. 31.3 c) VCLT and then proceed to the DSU norms.

The wording of Art. 31.3 c) VCLT raises the question, amongst others[1907], whether in the phrase "law applicable in the relations between the parties", the term "parties" includes all WTO Members or only those WTO Members that are parties to a given dispute.[1908] In other words, it is controversial whether a non-WTO treaty would only have to be taken into account if all WTO Members are parties to it (as suggested by the Panel in *EC – Biotech Products*), or whether it is sufficient that only the parties to the specific dispute are parties to it. The former position is supported by some[1909], but the latter approach is clearly the more widely taken position among WTO commentators[1910] and has also been embraced by the ILC in its report on the fragmentation of international law.[1911] McGrady identifies a third possible reading:

> "the phrase 'the parties' could refer to the parties to the treaty under interpretation, but the phrase 'applicable in relations between' might be interpreted so as to refer to relations between the parties to the treaty generally. Under this interpretation, the provision does not refer to the extraneous treaty having binding force overall the parties to the treaty under interpretation or overall disputants. Rather, the phrase simply concerns whether the extraneous treaty is applicable [...]".[1912] [footnote omitted]

This reading is closer to the broad reading, i.e. that it is sufficient if the parties to the WTO dispute are parties to a non-WTO treaty. In addition, some other suggestions have been made on how to interpret the norm. For example, it has been suggested that non-WTO law should be taken into account under Art. 31.3 c) VCLT, if it reflects the common intention of all WTO Members; on this basis, it is argued, the Cartagena Protocol should

1907 It has been noted that the article is not clear in many regards, see Study Group of the International Law Commission 2006, para. 423.

1908 For an overview of the academic debate see Conrad 2011, 254ff; McGrady 2008; Zleptnig 2010, 69ff.

1909 See for example Knox 2004, 67.

1910 See Palmeter and Mavroidis 1998, 411f; Weiss 2003, 196; Marceau 1999, 125; Herwig 2008, 837ff; Kleinlein 2012, 275; Franken and Burchardi 2007, 49f; Foltea 2012, 38; Mavroidis 2000, 77, albeit without reference to the VCLT; Howse 2008, 656 also criticizes the Panel's arguments.

1911 Study Group of the International Law Commission 2006, para. 472.

1912 McGrady 2008, 592.

have been taken into account.[1913] Yet another suggestion is that non-WTO rules widely accepted by WTO Members should be applied.[1914] Similarly, it is suggested that only non-WTO agreements or practice that reflect the common intention of all WTO Members can be taken into account under Art. 31.3 c) VCLT, even if WTO Members are not formally bound by a non-WTO legal rule.[1915]

Moreover, it is also not quite agreed what limits Art. 31.3 c) VCLT imposes on the type of non-WTO international law that could be used in WTO dispute settlement. Some argue that it would allow general principles of international law to be applied, unless specifically excluded by WTO treaty provisions, but no other type of international law.[1916] It is beyond the scope of this work to discuss this issue in depth; one of the most convincing arguments against the Panel's approach is that it means that the greater the membership of an international treaty, the less likely it is that other treaties might be taken into account.[1917] In the case of the WTO, hardly any non-WTO treaty could be taken into account.[1918]

Observers also have divergent views on the significance of Art. 3.2 DSU which forbids the adjudicators from adopting an interpretation that would "add to or diminish the rights and obligations provided in the covered agreements" and the parallel clause in Art. 19.2 DSU. The clause has been taken to mean that the WTO dispute settlement bodies do not have the capacity to enforce non-WTO rules, if doing so would add to or diminish WTO rights and obligations.[1919] Other observers have stated that if there is a conflict between WTO law and, for example, a MEA, the adjudicators are prevented under WTO rules from setting aside WTO law.[1920] Yet another position is that Art. 3.2 DSU prohibits an interpretation according to which customary law would supplement or displace WTO law.[1921] Others go further and state that Art. 3.2 DSU categorically forbids adjudicators

---

1913 Lagomarsino 2011, 564f.

1914 Henckels 2006, 285.

1915 Pauwelyn 2003a, 257ff.

1916 Cheyne 2007, 157.

1917 Kleinlein 2012, 275 with further references.

1918 Henckels 2006, 293; Zleptnig 2010, 72.

1919 Marceau and Trachtman 2002, 849; for a similar view see Bartels 2001, 499.

1920 Kleinlein 2012, 281 states this with reference to (unspecified) constitutional rules of WTO law and existing literature; see also Kelly 2002, 365f; Böckenförde 2003, 984; Marceau 2001, 1103ff; probably also Trachtman 1999, 342f.

1921 McGinnis 2003, 266ff.

from resorting to non-WTO substantive international law at all.[1922] Yet others do not share the view that Art. 3.2, 19.2 DSU impose meaningful limitations on the use of non-WTO international law in WTO dispute settlement. In support of this latter position, it is argued, for example, that these articles do not forbid the adjudicators to acknowledge the fact that WTO Members may either have modified their rights and obligations themselves by entering into competing agreements, or to recognize that certain WTO obligations had already been modified by existing rules of customary international law or general (substantive) principles of law at the time the WTO agreements were concluded.[1923]

Yet another norm that is used to make inferences regarding the role of non-WTO international law in WTO dispute settlement is Art. 7 DSU. It mandates the adjudicators to examine the matter in dispute "in the light of the relevant provision cited by the parties". A similar obligation in Art. 11 DSU requires the adjudicators to make an "objective assessment of [...] the applicability of and conformity with the relevant covered agreements". Some view Art. 7.2 DSU as a parallel provision to Art. 38 ICJ Statute,[1924] defining the law applicable in WTO disputes. The prevailing view, however, seems to be that there is no provision in WTO law that deals explicitly with the applicability of non-WTO international law in WTO proceedings.[1925] Yet even those that read Art. 7 DSU as defining the applicability of international law in WTO dispute settlement proceedings disagree on what the norm means.[1926] Some authors have inferred from the reference to the "relevant provisions in any covered agreement" that

---

1922 Colares 2009, 433f; the author on this basis also criticizes the Appellate Body for quoting non-WTO conventions and treaties in its interpretation of Art. XX GATT in *Shrimp – Turtles*. However, contrary to what he suggests, the Appellate Body in that case rather seems to have used the non-WTO declarations and conventions to show a certain fact, i.e. that different countries had been treated differently and a multilateral course of action was open to the defendant; on this later aspect of the Appellate Body report in *Shrimp – Turtles*, see Howse 2002b, 505f.

1923 I take Vranes 2009, 83ff to make this point, even though he phrases it slightly differently; Howse and Horn 2009, 59 also make a similar point, but limited to the interpretation of WTO legal norms in light of other rules of international law, i.e. they argue that WTO law could only be set aside in specific cases.

1924 Palmeter and Mavroidis 1998, 399.

1925 Vranes 2009, 72.

1926 See the references in Bartels 2001, 504 and n. 20 and 21; Vranes 2009, 87.

adjudicators are only to apply WTO agreements.[1927] Other legal commentators opine that the term "in light of the relevant provisions" in Art. 7.1 DSU does not forbid the adjudicators from applying other norms of international law.[1928] It is even argued that adjudicators may have to apply non-WTO international law if this "assists" the DSB in the sense of Art. 7 DSU and that making an assessment without taking into account non-WTO international law would not be "objective" in the sense of Art. 11 DSU.[1929] This is the view that seems to be shared by the adjudicators: as noted above, one Panel had refused to read any limitations on applicable law from this norm, rather considering it to pertain to the scope of the Panel's review. Implicitly, this is also the approach that the Appellate Body has followed; the Appellate Body regularly refers to the VLCT and thus to international law other than the covered agreements referred to in Art. 7 DSU. The approach by the Panels and the Appellate Body merits support: the formulations in Art. 7, 11 DSU are rather weak; for example, the fact that a Panel must "address" relevant provisions in the covered agreement/s does not textually imply that it is forbidden from addressing anything else. It would not be unreasonable to read this as a statement regarding what the Panels must do in a given case, but without any sense that they may not also consider other provisions as they think appropriate.

Altogether, I tend to agree with the general conclusion, which also seems to underlie many of the WTO dispute settlement decisions, that the above cited norms of the DSU are inconclusive on the applicability of non-WTO international law in WTO proceedings.[1930] They do not oblige the adjudicators from applying international law – with the exception of the customary rules of interpretation mentioned in Art. 3.2 DSU – nor do they prevent the adjudicators from doing so. If one supports this conclusion, the relationship between WTO law and non-WTO international law would have to be assessed in each case on the basis of the usual rules of interpretation as well as the general collision norms of international law.[1931]

Finally, some criticism has been voiced regarding the Appellate Body's use of some (alleged) principles of international law in interpretation. For

---

1927 Weiss 2003, 193; Böckenförde 2003, 979ff; probably also Trachtman 1999, 342f; Marceau 1999, 110 is also critical about Palmeter's and Mavroidis' reading of Art. 7.2 DSU.

1928 Bartels 2001, 505; Vranes 2009, 87.

1929 Foltea 2012, 34.

1930 Vranes 2009, 90ff; Lindroos and Mehling 2006, 873f.

1931 Conrad 2011, 128 appears to have a similar position.

example, several commentators have pointed out that the principle *in dubio mitius* that the Appellate Body used in *Hormones I,* drawing on ICJ and PCIJ decisions, is not widely used or recognized in international law. Where it has been used is in the context of unilateral declarations, rather than in the context of a treaty with reciprocal obligations.[1932] In reaction it has been surmised that what has motivated the Appellate Body's recourse to the principle was rather a certain rhetorical effect, i.e. emphasizing to relevant constituencies that the Appellate Body does not unduly restrict WTO Members' sovereignty or overstep the boundaries of its role.[1933] Another principle that the Appellate Body has referred to is the prohibition of *abus de droit*, i.e. the prohibition of the abusive exercise of a state's rights. While the Appellate Body has presented this principle as an established principle of international law, doubts have been expressed as to its existence therein.[1934]

In sum, certain aspects of how the adjudicators use international law are not clear, but there is no uniform position on the matter in the literature, either. There are strong voices suggesting that the adjudicators have – at least in some instances – taken an overly restrictive view on the role of non-WTO international law in the WTO legal universe; fewer commentators seem to believe that they have been too bold.

1.8. Assessment

After the discussion of the approach of the Appellate Body in more legal-doctrinal terms, this section considers the assessment in less technical terms, such as: How can we explain the interpretive choices made by the WTO dispute settlers? What do these choices mean in terms of the legitimacy of findings and the WTO's judicial style? These questions will be discussed both with regards the methods of interpretation chosen in general and also, more specifically, the use of international law in the WTO settlement decisions.

As noted above, it is perfectly reasonable for the WTO dispute settlement bodies to refer to the methods of interpretation contained in the VCLT, given that WTO law is treaty law. It is, however, noteworthy, is the

1932 Flett 2011, 28; Lennard 2002, 65; Zleptnig 2010, 80f.

1933 Lennard 2002, 65.

1934 Ibid., 69 writes that there is no "solid support for the arguments for such principle".

adjudicators' consistent approach of making very clear which methods of interpretation they use. The WTO dispute settlement bodies have done this not once, but in a considerable number of reports. As one former Member of the Appellate Body has remarked, this is in stark contrast to the approach of the ECJ which never explains explicitly which methods of interpretation it uses and why.[1935] Explaining and making transparent judicial approaches can be seen as an attempt to "win over" the audience, to convince it of the correctness of the judicial approach chosen. Or, as one author has put it:

> "The reliance on established 'maxims' of international law adds an extra shine of neutrality and predictability to the Appellate and Panel jurisprudence, even though the selection of those maxims, and how they are used, gives some room to move at the fringes."[1936]

The way that the VCLT methods of interpretation have been applied by the WTO dispute adjudicators is not an automatic result of choosing them; these methods can be used in different ways.[1937] On the basis of Art. 31, 32 VLCT their overall interpretative approach could also be less text-oriented. An eminent observer has stated that no other international judicial body relies on literal interpretation quite as heavily as the Appellate Body[1938], even though other international courts are also guided by the methods of interpretation codified in the VCLT. The textual reliance seen in the Appellate Body decisions is certainly a matter of choice.

Many see the particular way in which the WTO dispute settlement bodies use the established methods of interpretation and then justify their use of these methods as an attempt at generating legitimacy and winning acceptance for their decisions.[1939] I see no reason to disagree with this analysis. It has been observed above[1940] that literal interpretation is generally the method of interpretation allowing a judicial entity to avoid appearing as "activist", and to present itself as an interpreter rather than a creator of law. Textual interpretation has strong legitimatory force, at least in cases where the text is relatively determinate.[1941] Literal interpretation is, there-

---

1935 Ehlermann 2002, 616.
1936 Lennard 2002, 61.
1937 See Abi-Saab 2006, 460.
1938 Ibid., 461.
1939 See for example Henckels 2006, 284; Knox 2004, 48ff; Magnuson 2010, 123f; Shany and Shlomo-Agon 2014, 206.
1940 See chapter 1, section 3.1.
1941 Beck 2012, 149f.

fore, the least risky option for the Appellate Body.[1942] By using it, the adjudicators can appear to adhere to the intention of the WTO treaties and their negotiators.[1943] The use of textual interpretation is a way to project judicial restraint in a legal order which is characterized by the overlap of various agreements and a variety of objectives.[1944] The Appellate Body's textualism, including its heavy use of dictionaries,[1945] is hence a means of generating and maintaining legitimacy and preventing criticism.[1946] An aspect of the Appellate Body's judicial reasoning that supports such a reading is the frequent references to dictionary definitions that fail to add clarity to the original text: If the dictionary definitions are not needed and used to clarify controversial terms, there must be a different rationale for using them so frequently. Legitimizing the judicial decisions taken and with it the judicial entity taking them is clearly a promising explanation for the excessive and unnecessary reference to dictionaries.[1947]

The alternatives – notably teleological interpretation and the use of the negotiating history – can been seen as fraught with risks. With regard to teleological interpretation, given that WTO norms do not always specify their objectives, the judicial decision-makers could easily be accused of getting it wrong – a danger stressed by some former Members of the Appellate Body themselves.[1948] Indeed, the Appellate Body has in some instances been criticized when supporting a certain interpretation with teleological arguments[1949] and some commentators have cautioned against excessive use of teleological interpretation in WTO dispute settlement[1950]. The reluctance to engage in teleological interpretation has also been linked to the compulsory and exclusive character of the Appellate Body's jurisdiction.[1951] The Appellate Body does not seem to be alone in its hesitance to rely on teleological interpretation: the ICJ has also been described as cau-

1942 Ehlermann 2003a, 699.
1943 Ruiz Fabri 2006, 132.
1944 Zdouc 2008, 375.
1945 On this aspect, see in particular Pavot 2013, 32, 39ff who calls dictionaries an "instrument legitimizing the judge's legal discourse" in the WTO context.
1946 Knox 2004, 3; Picciotto 2005, 15; Weiler 2001, 206; van Damme 2010, 641ff.
1947 For a similar point see Pavot 2013, 37f.
1948 Ehlermann 2003a, 699; Bacchus 2005, 515.
1949 Howse 2002c, 248 with regard to the Appellate Body's position on the temporal scope of Art. 2.4 in EC - Sardines.
1950 See or example Lennard 2002, 70.
1951 Sacerdoti 2006, 46.

tious in this regard.[1952] By contrast, human rights tribunals have been described as more teleological in orientation.[1953]

The Appellate Body's reluctance to rely on the negotiating history has been attributed to a lack of reliable records[1954] and ambiguous and contradictory statements of the negotiating parties[1955]. Moreover, it has been pointed out that using documents on the negotiating history, which are sometimes not readily accessible, attracted criticism in cases where it was used against Members that joined the WTO later and as a consequence may not even have known the negotiating documents;[1956] basing interpretations on negotiating history privileges the small community of treaty negotiators over other relevant constituencies.[1957] Generally, relying on the supplementary means of interpretation in Art. 32 VCLT might lead to acceptance problems for the Appellate Body. Resorting to this means of interpretation presupposes a finding that a treaty term remains ambiguous or obscure even after having examined the text, context and object and purpose.[1958] Yet to put things into perspective, it should also be noted that there is generally a tradition of restricting the use of the *travaux préparatoires* in treaty interpretation in international legal practice.[1959]

There has been praise for the Appellate Body's heavy reliance on literal interpretation, describing it as conducive to certainty and predictability, the basic aims of the WTO dispute settlement system.[1960] Others have observed that the interpretative choices the Appellate Body made early in its career, including the reliance on textual interpretation, have contributed to its success.[1961]

At the time and as discussed at some length in the previous section, the approach – which one eminent commentator called a "laughable dictionary hermeneutics" providing false security[1962] – comes with its own prob-

1952 Guillaume 2006, 469.

1953 Study Group of the International Law Commission 2006, para. 130f.

1954 Bacchus 2005, 506; for an example how well/poorly the negotiating history is documented, see the description by Maier 2017, 159ff. He notes that there are no records of (important) informal meetings and even for some of the official meetings there are short or no minutes.

1955 Ehlermann 2002, 616.

1956 Weiss 2003, 186.

1957 Schmid 2001, 23.

1958 See Ortino 2006, 129f.

1959 See Dörr, in Dörr and Schmalenbach 2012 Art. 32, para 5.

1960 Weiss 2003, 192.

1961 Howse and Essermann 2006, 68.

1962 Weiler 2009, 139.

lems. The textualist approach has certainly not isolated the Appellate Body from criticism.[1963] A "growing number of scholars"[1964] criticize the approach in one way or the other,[1965] while one former Member of the Appellate Body indicates that he sees most criticism as related to its approach to interpretation.[1966] In this sense, textualism might, in the longer term, have a de-legitimizing rather than legitimizing effect.[1967]

The regular references made by the Appellate Body to the common intention of the parties – and the statement that identifying this intention is the overall objective of WTO interpretation – can be understood as a way of defusing potential criticism of the judgements and helping to legitimize the WTO judicial decisions. By emphasizing Members' intentions, the judicial outcome is presented not as a decision involving the discretion of the WTO judicial decision-makers, but essentially as clarifying what the WTO Members intend as a collective; this could explain the Appellate Body's reliance on the common intention of WTO Members, which has some legal-technical deficiencies and is not free of ambiguities.[1968]

Having discussed the methods of interpretation more generally, I will now turn to the role of international law. It is not possible at this stage to state exactly where on a continuum of "international law averse" versus "international law friendly" the Appellate Body situates itself. Given the absence of a coherent picture on how the Appellate Body uses non-WTO international law, it is not surprising that different commentators hold different views on the matter. Indeed, some important issues, like the interpretation of the term "the parties" in Art. 31.3 c) VLCT, still await authoritative statements by the Appellate Body. More generally, it has been observed that in some cases the WTO adjudicators did not invoke certain rules of international law to settle controversial issues, even though they could have done so[1969] and that the WTO dispute settlement bodies have been quite restrained concerning the use of international law, with few exceptions.[1970] On the other hand, the Appellate Body has in certain instances referred to non-WTO international law where not strictly neces-

1963 See for example Ortino 2006.
1964 Magnuson 2010, 125.
1965 Picciotto 2005, 18.
1966 Bacchus 2005, 509.
1967 For a similar statement, see Magnuson 2010, 128.
1968 See above section 1.7.2.
1969 Weiss 2003, 199; Böckenförde 2003, 989; Foltea 2012, 99f.
1970 Böckenförde 2003, 992.

sary.[1971] Moreover, the Appellate Body has upheld the idea that WTO law is part of the international legal order and thus appears to be much more open to non-WTO international law than, for example, Panels under the old GATT used to be.

Divergent observations on the current role of non-WTO international law in the WTO legal order may also be attributable to different normative positions on what the role of international law in the WTO system should be. Conflicting views are not only held regarding the appropriate role of WTO dispute settlement in interpreting and applying international law, but also about international law and its legitimacy more broadly.[1972] For example, it has been noted that a broad reading of Art. 31.3 c) VLCT gives the adjudicators more leeway and power, because they can "choose" from a great range of non-WTO treaties that may become relevant in a given case.[1973] The question of whether the granting of such additional power to the WTO dispute settlement bodies is a good thing or not is a contentious one. Moreover, when the Appellate Body relies on substantive non-WTO international law (as opposed to procedural principles), this often means that the adjudicators afford recognition to the non-economic interests protected by non-WTO international law as well as WTO Members' right to take measures in support of such objectives. Again, how much leeway WTO Members should have is politically contested. Some are content with the limited role that international law has so far played in WTO dispute settlement.[1974] Others are generally sceptical about at least some sources of international law (such as customary international law) and therefore argue that its role in the WTO legal order should be limited.[1975] Some have claimed that the adjudicators have sometimes gone too far in their reliance on international law.[1976]

The opposite position is that the WTO would risk its legitimacy by *not* drawing on non-WTO international law which protects a wider set of

1971 See above section 1.6.4.

1972 Kulovesi 2011, 69 offers a similar observation, i.e. that the views that people hold on how the WTO dispute settlement system should deal with linkage issues is related to their view on trade and the WTO more broadly. For an overview and references, see Lagomarsino 2011, 546; Sykes 2014, 487f also provides a good overview of different rationales militating for and against an enhanced role of non-WTO international law in WTO law.

1973 McGrady 2008, 613.

1974 See for example Alvarez 2008, 612.

1975 Examples are Kelly 2002; McGinnis 2003.

1976 Steinberg 2004, 262.

interest and values than the WTO itself does.[1977] Proponents of this view argue that interpreting WTO law in line with international law enhances legal security and consistency in the WTO legal system, the parties' acceptance of adjudication in the WTO, and/or the overall legitimacy of the WTO dispute settlement exercise.[1978] There are also concerns that the narrow interpretation by the *EC – Biotech Products* Panel of Art. 31.3 c) VCLT increases the fragmentation of international law, leading to conflicting obligations for states.[1979] Yet another observation is that the Appellate Body has quite successfully drawn on international law in order to ascertain areas of political consensus between WTO Members, using it as guidance on how to decide cases in substance;[1980] conversely by not drawing on non-WTO international law the adjudicators might lose a valuable source of information that makes it likelier that they issue reports that meet with the approval of at least the majority of WTO Members. A modified version of this argument is that the adjudicators should draw on non-WTO international law to be able to deal with the indeterminacy of WTO law (e.g. the exceptions in Art. XX GATT) in a manner that best fits the "legal doctrine of the WTO community and, by extension, of the international community"[1981]. Finally, it has also been suggested that the WTO adjudicators are likely to be concerned with the impact of their rulings on wider international law, given that the WTO dispute settlement system is by far the most active international judicial mechanism.[1982]

It is beyond the scope of this work to contribute to this larger debate. Yet the kaleidoscope of opinions shows that much of what has been decided on the role of international law in WTO dispute settlement so far (and also what has not been decided) is the result of a deliberate choice, and not the only possible way that the legal questions at issue could have been solved. How can the way that the Appellate Body uses (or refrains from using) non-WTO international law be explained?

1977 See for example Howse and Horn 2009, 53.

1978 Cameron and Gray 2001, 252; Henckels 2006, 280, 288.; Lagomarsino 2011, 566f.

1979 Herwig 2008, 837f.

1980 Knox 2004, 48.

1981 Eeckhout 2010, 22ff referring to Dworkin's theory of judicial decision-making.

1982 Wald in Abi-Saab 2006, 729.

When taken as a whole, the use of international law in WTO dispute settlement presents a rather mixed picture.[1983] This may be the result of a situation where there are reasons both for and against the WTO dispute settlement bodies drawing intensively on non-WTO international law. One eminent scholar explains the use of international law in WTO dispute settlement in the following terms:

> "WTO adjudicators, like other international dispute settlers, feel the pull of a common need to produce reasoned opinions, to respect relevant judicial precedents (especially their own), to feel a part of a global 'invisible college' of international lawyers, and to legitimize their role as judges."[1984]

Kulovesi summarizes the "dilemma" that the adjudicators find themselves in a different way and as follows:

> "Directly applying non-WTO norms of international law would sometimes be necessary to reach a satisfactory substantive outcome, especially in linkage disputes [i.e. dispute where non-trade interests are at stake, C.G.]. [...] Yet the formal competence of the WTO dispute settlement system to engage in such an exercise is subject to debate – and venturing too far into the grey area would almost certainly irritate WTO Members States and surface critique [...]."[1985]

Foltea claims that the "somewhat constraining nature" of Art. 3.2, 19.2 DSU has led to a restrictive approach towards applying non-WTO international law in WTO dispute settlement.[1986] According to Charlotin, the observed pattern could be linked to several factors, including the permanent character of the WTO dispute settlement system, the relative independence of WTO adjudicators, and the fact that WTO law is less indeterminate than some other norms of international law.[1987]

When seen in light of all these textual, strategic and political factors that militate for and against the wider application of non-WTO international law in the WTO context, and when the sharply diverging positions on the matter are considered, that the use of non-WTO international legal norms

1983 See also the observation by Charlotin 2017, 291 that "WTO jurisprudence displays very few external citations" to the case law of other international tribunals (when compared to the practice of other international courts).

1984 Alvarez 2008, 618.

1985 Kulovesi 2011, 136.

1986 Foltea 2012, 132.

1987 Charlotin 2017, 296f.

in WTO dispute settlement should be such a mixed picture is perhaps not too surprising.

It is a plausible explanation for some of the observable aspects of the WTO's jurisprudence (e.g. the very frequent references to the VCLT) in terms of the adjudicators trying to "borrow" legitimacy by referring to international law and hence a corpus of norms that is beyond contention in terms of legitimacy – or, at least, more so than WTO law. A noticed above, the Appellate Body justifies at least some of its references to balancing under Art. XX GATT, i.e. a non-deductive way of reasoning that departs from prior GATT case law, by resorting to the VCLT methods of interpretation and the principle of good faith.[1988] Any decision to depart from textualism and prior GATT case law is likely to be criticized – tying it to an instrument as reputable and consensual as the VCLT might provide the much-needed support and legitimacy. At the same time, it has also been suggested that in cases where resorting to certain rules of international law may have been controversial, the adjudicators have refrained from doing so simply to avoid charges of judicial activism. Examples are the case law on the status of the precautionary principle or the non-use of Art. 31.3 c) VCLT in support of reference to various international legal instruments in *Shrimp – Turtles.*[1989]

To summarize this section, it is reasonable to understand the way that the adjudicators use methods of interpretation and international law as an attempt to gain credibility and acceptance for their decisions and their institution and thus to legitimize them. Much remains to be clarified about the role of international law in WTO dispute settlement. The instances where non-WTO international law has been used so far appear to be primarily ones that would not generate too much controversy. Yet even though the Appellate Body's approach to methods of interpretation and the use of international law can be understood in terms of efforts to prevent criticism and win acceptance, the approach chosen appears not to fully achieve this effect, at least not as far legal commentators are concerned. Notably, the Appellate Body's textual approach has provoked justified criticism.

1988 This is highlighted by Martineau 2007, 1017f.

1989 The latter example is given by Alvarez 2008, 622 who also maintains that drawing on the vague and open-ended language of Art. XX GATT as a basis for interpretation avoided charges of judicial activism that could have resulted from using Art. 31.3 (c) VCLT.

2. Standard of review and deference to decisions taken in the political realm

Another important element of the style of a judicial entity is the way it deals with decisions by the legislative and executive branches of government. In the WTO context, the issue is normally discussed under the heading of "standard of review". In other judicial settings, similar questions are linked to the so-called margin of appreciation doctrine[1990] or other terms[1991].

The extent to which a judicial entity reviews the decisions of executive or legislative bodies and subsequently replaces them with its own is perhaps an important factor in the acceptance and legitimacy accorded decisions made by a court or the WTO dispute settlement.[1992] It is much more than a simple technicality.[1993] At the international level, the issue is compounded by the fact that an international judicial body reviews measures which were originally taken at the national level, often through democratic decision-making processes. Indeed, the standard of review has been used as a way to measure judicial activism[1994]; it has also been called a "touchstone" for balancing the relationship between national sovereignty and the WTO system.[1995]

Generally, adopting a certain standard of review involves a deliberate allocation of power between an authority taking a measure and a judicial body reviewing it.[1996] A court carves out a role for itself, and this is most visible at the point when it adopts a standard of review. Does it put itself "above" or "in the place of" other branches of the government whose democratic legitimacy is – at least in the case of the legislative branch – more direct, and hence potentially stronger than that of a court? Does an international judicial entity, an unelected body, at any point substitute an elected national government's political judgement with its own? These questions do get asked, and if an international court gives the wrong answers, it is unlikely to win over its critics. This is all the more apparent in "trade and ..." cases where the national measures under judicial review are

1990 See on the European Court of Human Rights Gross and Ní Aoláin 2001; and more generally Shany 2005.
1991 Lovric 2010, 60.
1992 Reusch 2007, 47; Oesch 2003, 642; Shany 2005, 909.
1993 Cass 2001, 58.
1994 Yung 2011, 19; Zarbiyev 2012, 4.
1995 Zleptnig 2002, 429.
1996 Oesch 2003, 636; Schropp 2012, 188.

taken for non-trade regulatory purposes, while the WTO legal system is ultimately designed to serve trade interests.

The wider implications of the standard of review have also been noted by the Appellate Body itself:

> "The standard of review appropriately applicable in proceedings under the *SPS Agreement*, of course, must reflect the balance established in that Agreement between the jurisdictional competences conceded by the Members to the WTO and the jurisdictional competences retained by the Members for themselves."[1997] [footnote omitted]

Concerning terminology, "standard of review" in the WTO context normally refers to the way that WTO judicial decision-makers deal with the review of national measures, including fact-finding by national authorities.[1998] In addition, it could also be used to describe the Appellate Body's approach to examining Panel reports.[1999] This later aspect will not be discussed here. Finally, some authors also use "standard of review" to discuss – broadly – the way the dispute settlement bodies interpret WTO law.[2000]

Besides the standard of review, another aspect of how the WTO dispute settlement bodies deal with political decisions is their approach to (potential) gaps in WTO law. If a judicial body fills what is or could be perceived by others as a gap, this can lead to charges of judicial activism or law-making. The respective judicial body could be accused of having created a rule or requirement that is nowhere written in the law. Indeed, some commentators use gap-filling as a measure of judicial law-making or activism.[2001] Some WTO Members observed, at some stage, that

> "situations where the relevant WTO text does not address an issue, leading to concerns over whether an adjudicative body might 'fill the gap' and consequently add to or diminish rights and obligations under the relevant agreement instead of clarifying those rights and obligations"

1997 *European Communities – Measures Concerning Meat and Meat Products, WT/DS26/AB/R, WT/DS48/AB/R* 1998, para. 115; *Australia – Measures Affecting the Importation of Apples from New Zealand, WT/DS367/AB/R* 2010, para. 211.

1998 See for example Oesch 2003.

1999 Zleptnig 2002, 428; Du 2010b, 445ff.

2000 Oesch 2003, 656ff.

2001 For the WTO context, see Goldstein and Steinberg 2007, 19; see also the literature overview in chapter 1, section 5.3.2.

are a sensitive area.[2002] WTO Members have also claimed that in specific instances the Appellate Body had "read words into the text"[2003].

Moreover, the following sections also include a discussion of how the WTO dispute settlement bodies deal with decisions taken by political bodies within the WTO itself after the adoption of the text of the WTO agreements. If the WTO dispute settlement bodies take what is considered the wrong approach by WTO Members or observers, they are likely to face charges of judicial activism.[2004]

The section is structured as follows: First, it analyses the standard of review used in WTO dispute settlement concerning decisions taken by the responsible political bodies and authorities in WTO member states (section 2.1). The focus is on the "trade and ..." cases discussed in this work, rather than on, for example, trade remedy cases, but more general insights are also discussed. The second section deals with the treatment of gaps in WTO dispute settlement (section 2.2). After this the way in which the dispute settlement bodies take account of decisions taken by political bodies of the WTO after the establishment of the WTO (section 2.3) is presented. The final sections again present a legal-technical discussion (2.4) and an assessment (2.5) of the case law.

2.1. Standard of review concerning non-trade measures by WTO Members

Before turning to what standard of review the Panels use, it is important to clarify different dimensions of the standard of review concerning WTO Members' non-trade measures, i.e. measures taken for non-economic purposes. Three main dimensions can be distinguished[2005]: the way that the adjudicators deal with the facts presented by WTO Members and ascertain

2002 "Negotiations on improvements and clarifications of the Dispute Settlement Understanding, Contribution by Chile and the United States on improving flexibility and member control in WTO dispute settlement", TN/DS/W/28, 23 December 2002, para. 4, http://www.ustr.gov/archive/assets/Trade_Agreements/Monitoring_Enforcement/Dispute_Settlement/US_Papers_on_Dispute_Settlement/asset_upload_file567_7701.pdf.

2003 See Dispute Settlement Body, Minutes of Meeting of 11 December 2006, WT/DSB/M/223, statement of the US in para. 5.

2004 For example, Bartels 2004, 877ff discusses cases involving questions of institutional balance as one category of potentially particularly controversial cases.

2005 See for example Oesch 2003; Ruffert 2001; Reusch 2007, 84ff; Ehlermann and Lockhart 2004, 496.

the factual aspects of the case (only of relevance at the Panel stage); the manner in which the adjudicators review the conclusions and judgements, including legal ones, that a WTO Member arrives at on the basis of the facts and, finally, how the adjudicators deal with national laws and a WTO Member's statements on how its own national legislation is applied and to be interpreted.[2006] The first two of these dimensions are closely intertwined and can be hard to distinguish from one another in practice.

While a lack of agreement during negotiations has resulted in the DSU being without an explicit standard of review clause[2007], the Appellate Body has identified Art. 11 DSU as an overarching standard of review for WTO dispute settlement.[2008] Art. 11.2 DSU sets forth that

> "a panel should make an objective assessment of the matter before it, including an objective assessment of the facts of the case and the applicability of and conformity with the relevant covered agreements."

An explicit standard of review clause is contained in Art. 17.6 ADA which provides for a deferential standard of review to be applied in anti-dumping cases. Art. 17.6 ADA reads:

(i) in its assessment of the facts of the matter, the panel shall determine whether the authorities' establishment of the facts was proper and whether their evaluation of those facts was unbiased and objective. If the establishment of the facts was proper and the evaluation was unbiased and objective, even though the panel might have reached a different conclusion, the evaluation shall not be overturned;

(ii) the panel shall interpret the relevant provisions of the Agreement in accordance with customary rules of interpretation of public international law. Where the panel finds that a relevant provision of the Agreement admits of more than one permissible interpretation, the panel shall find the authorities' measure to be in conformity with the Agreement if it rests upon one of those permissible interpretations.

2006 In addition, the question of legal interpretation of WTO rules is also sometimes discussed under the heading of standard of review, see for example Ehlermann and Lockhart 2004, 496; however, given that the question of which standard of review is applied in this regard is not much different from the more general question of what approach the WTO dispute settlement bodies take towards interpreting WTO law generally, this aspect is not discussed in the following any further.

2007 Zleptnig 2002, 430.

2008 *European Communities – Measures Concerning Meat and Meat Products, WT/DS26/AB/R, WT/DS48/AB/R* 1998, para. 115f.

A situation such as the one described in Art. 17.6 (ii), where there is more than one permissible interpretation, does not as yet seem to have been identified in WTO dispute settlement; the Appellate Body has always held that only one interpretation of the Anti-Dumping Agreement is possible.[2009]

In addition, WTO law contains rules on the standard of review to be applied by national authorities in certain other trade remedy cases, e.g. Art. 4.2 of the Agreement on Safeguards, which is not discussed any further here, as trade remedies are not the topic of this work.[2010] Yet other norms indicate by their wording that a certain standard of review is warranted. Lovric gives as an example that a licensing requirement must not be more administratively burdensome than is "absolutely necessary" for administrative purposes in Art. 3.2 of the Licensing Agreement. This clause sets a very demanding standard for governments, but would also seem to call for a quite thorough review by the adjudicators in cases where licensing requirements are in dispute.[2011]

The agreements that have been identified in this work as particularly relevant in "trade and ..." cases do not contain an explicit standard of review clause. Therefore, Art. 11. DSU is the relevant standard of review in these cases. The Appellate Body has inferred from Art. 11.2 DSU that neither a *de novo* review, i.e. a new review that does not consider the findings of national authorities, nor total deference are the appropriate ways to proceed for WTO judicial decision-makers. In support of its position, the Appellate Body argued that Panels are "poorly suited" to engage in a *de novo* review.[2012]

2009 See the WTO Analytical Annex, Anti-Dumping Agreement, para. 928ff, http://www.wto.org/english/res_e/booksp_e/analytic_index_e/anti_dumping_04_e.htm#925.

2010 See Spamann 2004, 522ff for how this clause has been interpreted in WTO case law.

2011 Lovric 2010, 89.

2012 *European Communities – Measures Concerning Meat and Meat Products, WT/DS26/AB/R, WT/DS48/AB/R* 1998, para. 117; *United States – Continued Suspension of Obligations in the EC – Hormones Dispute, WT/DS320/AB/R* 2008, para. 589.

The Appellate Body has stated that Art. 11 DSU requires a Panel to

> "consider all the evidence presented to it, assess its credibility, determine its weight, and ensure that its factual findings have a proper basis in that evidence"[2013].

In other words,

> "[t]he duty to make an objective assessment of the facts is, among other things, an obligation to consider the evidence presented to a panel and to make factual findings on the basis of that evidence"[2014].

The Appellate Body has also set a high threshold for a violation of that standard by Panels by stating that:

> "The deliberate disregard of, or refusal to consider, the evidence submitted to a panel is incompatible with a panel's duty to make an objective assessment of the facts. The wilful distortion or misrepresentation of the evidence put before a panel is similarly inconsistent with an objective assessment of the facts. 'Disregard' and 'distortion' and 'misrepresentation' of the evidence, in their ordinary signification in judicial and quasi-judicial processes, imply not simply an error of judgment in the appreciation of evidence but rather an egregious error that calls into question the good faith of a panel. A claim that a panel disregarded or distorted the evidence submitted to it is, in effect, a claim that the panel, to a greater or lesser degree, denied the party submitting the evidence fundamental fairness, or what in many jurisdictions is known as due process of law or natural justice."[2015]

A Panel may not disregard a piece of evidence before it, even though it is not required to refer explicitly to each and every single piece of evidence in its report.[2016] Moreover, Panels are required actually to evaluate the evi-

---

2013 *Brazil – Measures Affecting Imports of Retreaded Tyres, WT/DS332/AB/R* 2007, para. 185; *United States – Certain Country of Origin Labelling (COOL) Requirements, WT/DS384/AB/R, WT/DS/386/AB/R* 2012, para. 403; *China – Measures Related to the Exportation of Rare Earths, Tungsten, and Molybdenum, WT/DS431/AB/R, WT/DS432/AB/R, WT/DS433/AB/R* 2014, para. 5.178.

2014 *Australia – Measures Affecting the Importation of Apples from New Zealand, WT/DS367/AB/R* 2010, para. 269.

2015 *European Communities – Measures Concerning Meat and Meat Products, WT/DS26/AB/R, WT/DS48/AB/R* 1998, para. 133.

2016 *Australia – Measures Affecting the Importation of Apples from New Zealand, WT/DS367/AB/R* 2010, para. 275.

dence, rather than, for example, simply enumerating various pieces of evidence, following the majority view of experts in a given case or disregarding minority scientific opinions.[2017]

Within these parameters,

> "it is generally within the discretion of the panel to decide which evidence it chooses to utilize in making findings"[2018]

and Panels

> "are not required to accord to factual evidence of the parties the same meaning and weight as do the parties"[2019].

In the *EC – Asbestos* case, the Appellate Body when faced with a challenge by the complainant of the Panel's findings on the existence of a risk, also stated that the

> "Panel enjoyed a margin of discretion in assessing the value of the evidence, and the weight to be ascribed to that evidence"[2020].

The Appellate Body also stated that it would not interfere lightly with a Panel's fact-finding authority and would only acknowledge a violation of Art. 11 DSU where it was convinced that the Panel had exceeded the boundaries of its discretion.[2021] Altogether, Panels are afforded a considerable degree of discretion to assess and employ the evidence before them in the manner they find most probative and useful and to then draw conclusions on this basis.[2022] Nonetheless, a violation of Art. 11 DSU is almost routinely claimed by parties in appellate proceedings,[2023] however, rarely

---

2017 Ibid., para. 274ff.

2018 *European Communities – Measures Concerning Meat and Meat Products, WT/DS26/AB/R, WT/DS48/AB/R* 1998, para. 135.

2019 *Australia – Measures Affecting Importation of Salmon, WT/DS18/AB/R* 1998, para. 267.

2020 *European Communities – Measures Affecting Asbestos and Products Containing Asbestos, WT/DS135/AB/R* 2001, para. 161.

2021 *China – Measures Related to the Exportation of Rare Earths, Tungsten, and Molybdenum, WT/DS431/AB/R, WT/DS432/AB/R, WT/DS433/AB/R* 2014, para. 5.179.

2022 *United States – Certain Country of Origin Labelling (COOL) Requirements, WT/DS384/AB/R, WT/DS/386/AB/R* 2012, para. 416; *Australia – Measures Affecting the Importation of Apples from New Zealand, WT/DS367/AB/R* 2010, para. 271 with further references to case law.

2023 Oesch 2003, 635.

successfully.[2024] A notable exception is *Hormones II*. According to the Appellate Body, the Panel violated Art. 11 DSU by appointing two scientific experts to evaluate the EU's scientific risk assessments who had previously been involved in the development of an international standard from which the EU wished to depart.[2025] The Appellate Body indicated that using the wrong experts could, in principle, lead to the invalidation of all of the Panel's findings concerning the provisions for which the experts had delivered factual evidence[2026]. The Appellate Body later mentioned this finding when coming to the conclusion that the substantive norm at issue, Art. 5.1 SPS, had been violated by the application of the wrong standard of review;[2027] The Appellate Body, however, also identified other flaws in both the Panel's standard of review and its allocation of the burden of proof; it is therefore unclear whether the use of the "wrong" experts alone would have led the Appellate Body to find a that the substantive WTO provisions at issue were violated. In the view of the Appellate Body, the Panel in *Hormones II* also committed an additional violation of Art. 11 DSU by being insufficiently deferential when reviewing the WTO Member's risk assessment.[2028]

With regard to reviewing whether studies presented by the parties can be considered to constitute the scientific risk assessments required by the SPS Agreement, the Appellate Body provided some more detailed instructions on how the Panels should proceed:

> "The panel's task is to review that risk assessment. Where a panel goes beyond this limited mandate and acts as a risk assessor, it would be substituting its own scientific judgement for that of the risk assessor and making a *de novo* review and, consequently, would exceed its functions under Article 11 of the DSU. Therefore, the review power of a panel is not to determine whether the risk assessment undertaken by a WTO Member is correct, but rather to determine whether that risk as-

2024 See for example *European Communities – Trade Description of Sardines, WT/DS231/AB/R* 2002, para. 303; *Brazil – Measures Affecting Imports of Retreaded Tyres, WT/DS332/AB/R* 2007, para. 185–209; *United States – Certain Country of Origin Labelling (COOL) Requirements, WT/DS384/AB/R, WT/DS/386/AB/R* 2012, para. 295–326.

2025 *United States – Continued Suspension of Obligations in the EC – Hormones Dispute, WT/DS320/AB/R* 2008, para. 433ff.

2026 Ibid., para. 484.

2027 Ibid., para. 618.

2028 Ibid., para. 598ff.

> sessment is supported by coherent reasoning and respectable scientific evidence and is, in this sense, objectively justifiable."[2029]

The last part of the formulation was re-iterated by the Appellate Body in *Australia – Apples.*[2030]

Altogether, the Panel should double-check whether the risk assessment comes from a qualified source, its reasoning is objective and coherent, its conclusions are supported by the evidence, and whether a study has the necessary scientific and methodological attributes to be considered "reputable" and "legitimate" science by the standards of the respective scientific community.[2031] The Panel should not determine whether there is a risk.[2032]

The Appellate Body emphasized

> "that a distinction should be drawn between, on the one hand, the scientific evidence relied upon by the risk assessor and, on the other hand, the reasoning employed and the conclusions reached by the risk assessor on the basis of that scientific evidence."[2033]

According to the Appellate Body, the scrutiny of Panels should be more intense concerning the second aspect, because Panelists are not scientists and by implication not in a position to conduct scientific research of their own. Nevertheless, the Appellate Body considered that Panelists could assess whether

> "the conclusions of the risk assessor are based on the scientific evidence relied upon and are, accordingly, objective and coherent."[2034]

The Appellate Body also noted that more intense scrutiny may be necessary when a risk assessment is comprised of minority scientific views.[2035] After finding out the scientific basis on which an SPS measures was adopted

2029 Ibid., para. 590.

2030 *Australia – Measures Affecting the Importation of Apples from New Zealand, WT/DS367/AB/R* 2010, para. 213.

2031 Ibid., para. 214.

2032 *United States – Continued Suspension of Obligations in the EC – Hormones Dispute, WT/DS320/AB/R* 2008, para. 614.

2033 *Australia – Measures Affecting the Importation of Apples from New Zealand, WT/DS367/AB/R* 2010, para. 224.

2034 Ibid., para. 225.

2035 Ibid., para. 221.

> "[...] the panel must then verify that the scientific basis comes from a respected and qualified source. Although the scientific basis need not represent the majority view within the scientific community, it must nevertheless have the necessary scientific and methodological rigour to be considered reputable science. In other words, while the correctness of the views need not have been accepted by the broader scientific community, the views must be considered to be legitimate science according to the standards of the relevant scientific community. A panel should also assess whether the reasoning articulated on the basis of the scientific evidence is objective and coherent. In other words, a panel should review whether the particular conclusions drawn by the Member assessing the risk find sufficient support in the scientific evidence relied upon. Finally, the panel must determine whether the results of the risk assessment 'sufficiently warrant' the SPS measure at issue."[2036]

The Appellate Body added that a Panel could seek the advice of experts on all of these aspects, but

> "should not seek to test whether the experts would have done a risk assessment in the same way and would have reached the same conclusions as the risk assessor."[2037]

The Appellate Body draws a distinction between the standard of review applicable when Panels assess the risk assessment conducted by the defending WTO Member under Art. 5.1 SPS and when deciding whether alternative measures are available under Art. 5.6 SPS:

> "Caution not to conduct a *de novo* review is appropriate where a panel reviews a risk assessment conducted by the importing Member's authorities in the context of Article 5.1. However, the situation is different in the context of an Article 5.6 claim. The legal question under Article 5.6 is not whether the authorities of the importing Member have, in conducting the risk assessment, acted in accordance with the obligations of the SPS Agreement. Rather, the legal question is whether the importing Member could have adopted a less trade-restrictive measure. This requires the panel itself to objectively assess, inter alia, whether

---

2036 *United States – Continued Suspension of Obligations in the EC – Hormones Dispute, WT/DS320/AB/R* 2008, para. 591.

2037 Ibid., para. 592.

the alternative measure proposed by the complainant would achieve the importing Member's appropriate level of protection."[2038]

Here, the Appellate Body distinguishes between a situation in which a Member's own previous fact-finding exercise is under review and that when a Member has not carried out such a formal fact-finding exercise.

When looking at the practical approach of the Panels in establishing the facts of a case, an important initial observation is that the dispute settlement bodies have been quite willing to recognize different types of evidence – both qualitative and quantitative – as relevant and sufficient.[2039]

In some cases, the Panelists appear to have come close to a *de novo* review. One example is the *China – Audiovisual Products* case. In this case, China had claimed that a certain alternative measure suggested by the US was not reasonably available, as it imposed an undue burden upon it. The Appellate Body approved the Panel's rejection of this argument, which was based both on the lack of data on the estimated costs of alternative measures and on other observations by the Panel of the measures already in place.[2040] In *China – Rare Earths*, the Panel also delved deeply into the evidence, assessing the persuasiveness of conflicting economic arguments and expert opinion on the effect of export restrictions on the conservation of exhaustible natural resources.[2041] Panels are also known to conduct quite intensive reviews for disputes decided under the Anti-Dumping Agreement, where there is a rule obliging the judicial decision-makers to adopt a deferential approach.[2042]

Also, in at least some cases where a "necessity" analysis had to be conducted, the adjudicators were quite strict when assessing whether a measure was reasonably available; they did not simply accept a defending Member's statement to this end.[2043] In *EC – Seal Products* the Panel and

2038 *Australia – Measures Affecting the Importation of Apples from New Zealand, WT/DS367/AB/R* 2010, para. 356.

2039 *China – Measures Affecting Trading Rights and Distribution Services for Certain Publications and Audiovisual Entertainment Products, WT/DS363/AB/R* 2009, para. 253.

2040 Ibid., para. 325ff.

2041 For a summary of the Panel's reasoning, see *China – Measures Related to the Exportation of Rare Earths, Tungsten, and Molybdenum, WT/DS431/AB/R, WT/DS432/AB/R, WT/DS433/AB/R* 2014, para. 5.188ff.

2042 Steinberg 2004, 260.

2043 For example, Neumann and Tuerk 2003, 208 observe that the adjudicators were "reluctant" to consider alternatives as not being reasonably available in *United States – Gasoline* and *Korea – Beef*.

(also the Appellate Body) put the practical functioning of an exception clause to the EU's trade ban on seal products to quite intensive scrutiny. They observed that there were ambiguities in the legal requirements of the exception clause and it was unclear how they worked in practice. Rather than accepting the EU's explanation of how the requirements were to be understood and applied, the Appellate Body embraced a view on the functioning of the exception clause that made it unjustifiable under the chapeau of Art. XX GATT.[2044] The Appellate Body's reasoning in *Shrimp – Turtles*[2045] and *Brazil – Tyres*[2046] have also been criticized for a lack of deference. By contrast, the adjudicators' approach to ascertaining the legitimacy and importance of policy objectives is rather deferential.[2047]

It is in health-related cases, most of which are decided under the SPS Agreement, in which the standard of review has been most problematic.[2048] The picture is quite mixed; arguably, a different standard of review has been applied in different cases. Once the factual basis has been established, the adjudicators have in some cases and respects been quite restrained in not replacing parties' conclusions from the evidence with their own. In *Hormones I*, the Appellate Body stated that

> "responsible and representative governments may act in good faith on the basis of what, at a given time, may be a divergent opinion coming from qualified and respected sources."[2049]

In *EC – Asbestos*, the Panel found that the evidence tended to prove the existence of a health risk rather than the opposite and that therefore a decision-maker in the field of health policy could reasonably conclude that a health risk existed.[2050] It stated that, in assessing the evidence, it had to keep in mind that it was a public health measure that was under review.[2051] The Appellate Body in the same case approved the Panel's ap-

2044 *European Communities – Measures Prohibiting the Importation and Marketing of Seal Products, WT/DS400/AB/R, WT/DS401/AB/R* 2014, para. 5.324ff.

2045 Gaines 2001, 790.

2046 Lydgate 2017, 570.

2047 Lovric 2010, 146; with regard to Art. XX (a) GATT, see also Sykes 2014, 473.

2048 While health-related cases have also been decided under the GATT Gruszczynski 2013, 732 observes that these have not required as complex factual assessments as the SPS cases decided so far.

2049 *European Communities – Measures Concerning Meat and Meat Products, WT/DS26/AB/R, WT/DS48/AB/R* 1998, para. 194.

2050 *European Communities – Measures Affecting Asbestos and Products Containing Asbestos, WT/DS135/R* 2000, para. 8.193.

2051 Ibid., para. 8.184.

proach.[2052] This approach is considered by some as an instance of the application or approval of a precautionary approach by the WTO dispute settlement bodies.[2053] The Appellate Body report in *Hormones I* is also relatively deferential, with its recognition of minority scientific opinions and relatively generous approach with respect to when a measure can still be considered to be based on a scientific risk assessment.[2054] Another case where a mostly deferential standard of review is evident is the Appellate Body's report in *Hormones II*.[2055]

On the other hand, there are also cases under the SPS Agreement in which Panels have quite intensively reviewed the scientific evidence presented by the parties. The *Australia – Salmon*, *Japan – Apples* and *Hormones II* Panels are all described as falling into this category.[2056] In *EC – Biotech Products*, the Panel also subjected the details of certain scientific studies to intense scrutiny. For example, it rejected one study as a risk assessment because the study, designed to assess the impact of genetically modified on certain insects, had not been conducted under field conditions and because the insects had been fed a liquid diet containing toxins produced by the plants rather than the genetically modified plants themselves.[2057] In other words, the review was rather intense in this case.[2058] However, as far as the review of the scientific basis for the Member States' national safeguard measures on GMOs was concerned, the Panel was in a very difficult situation, because the EU's own scientific studies diverged from the scientific arguments on which the Member States sought to rely. Thus, the Panel could have been deferential either to the EU's risk assessment or the scientific basis the EU Member States wished to rely on, but not both.[2059] There was no appellate decision in this case.

The *Australia – Apples* Panel case, decided after the deferential *Hormones II*, is also described as not exhibiting a deferential enough standard of re-

2052 *European Communities – Measures Affecting Asbestos and Products Containing Asbestos, WT/DS135/AB/R* 2001, para. 159–163.

2053 Iynedjian 2002, 101.

2054 See for example Schropp 2012, 189.

2055 See Fukunaga 2012, 564f; Du 2010b, 451, 458; Hoekman, Bernard and Trachtman, Joel 2010, 172; Howse and Horn 2009, 49; Gruszczynski 2013, 750ff.

2056 Gruszczynski 2013, 741ff; Schropp 2012, 189f; Peel 2012, 438 who also describes the standard of review applied in these cases as "de facto approach of de novo review", at 446.

2057 *European Communities – Measures Affecting the Approval and Marketing of Biotech Products, WT/DS291/R, WT/DS292/R, WT/DS293/R* 2006, para. 7.3098.

2058 See also Gruszczynski 2013, 742; Herwig 2008, 835ff.

2059 Howse and Horn 2009, 51.

view, in particular when reviewing conclusions made on the basis of scientific evidence.[2060] In *Australia – Apples*, the Panel stressed at various times that it was trying to avoid a *de novo* review.[2061] Nonetheless, the Panel then discussed at quite some length various aspects of studies presented as risk assessments by the defending party, relying on experts' statements during the proceedings. The Panel criticized such details as the methodology used to calculate certain probabilities, the failure to take certain factors into account, an alleged overestimation of the severity of certain risks, and certain other assumptions and qualifications made by the risk assessors.[2062] The Appellate Body approved how the Panel had proceeded.[2063] This raises questions regarding how deferential the standard of review will be in future SPS cases.

Finally, the interpretation of the domestic law of the WTO Members is treated as factual matter, like other factual matters, in WTO dispute settlement.[2064] One Panel observed that in making factual findings on the meaning of a US norm it was not "bound to accept the interpretation by the US", but that

> "any Member can reasonably expect that considerable deference be given to its views on the meaning of its own law."[2065]

By way of contrast, in the *EC – Seal Products* case, the Appellate Body did not accept the way that the EU described the functioning of some of its own legal requirements.[2066]

In conclusion, the Appellate Body uses Art. 11.2 DSU as an overarching standard of review in the absence of an explicit provision in the DSU. For cases decided under the agreements that are of primary relevance for "trade and …" cases Art. 11.2 DSU gets used, as there is no more specific standard of review. Under the general standard of review, which the Appellate Body describes as neither *de novo* review nor total deference, Panels have considerable discretion in dealing with the evidence. Somewhat more detailed

---

2060 Gruszczynski 2013, 752ff.
2061 See the reference in *Australia – Measures Affecting the Importation of Apples from New Zealand, WT/DS367/AB/R* 2010, para. 356.
2062 See the summary of the Panel's analysis in ibid., para. 190ff.
2063 Ibid., para. 222ff.
2064 Oesch 2003, 654.
2065 *United States – Sections 301-310 of the trade act of 1974, WT/DS152/R* 1999, para. 7.19.
2066 See chapter 2, section 1.2.1.

guidance has been given for SPS cases. In practice, the application of the standard of review varies substantially across cases.

2.2. Dealing with gaps in the text

Another aspect of how the WTO dispute settlement system positions itself with regard to the WTO legal texts and the political decisions of WTO Members embodied therein is how it deals with gaps in the text. Indeed, this issue has created a degree of controversy among WTO Members, with some of them accusing the WTO dispute settlement bodies of improper gap-filling.[2067] In this section, I will summarize insights on the extent to which the adjudicators have engaged in gap-filling.[2068]

An analysis of whether gaps in WTO law are filled by the adjudicators is compounded by the fact that it is not easy to differentiate between a "real" gap and a situation in which a matter is simply outside the scope of WTO law, or between a case in which a certain norm was not extended to a specific situation deliberately and one which contains an unintended silence on that situation. In fact, there are several cases in which the Appellate Body has attributed a certain meaning to the fact that a norm was silent on the issue in question, assuming in the process that the silence was intended by negotiators.[2069]

But there are also instances where the Panel and the Appellate Body disagreed on how to interpret the fact that a certain requirement was not mentioned in the text. One example is the following:

> "We believe that [...] the Panel failed to give meaning and legal effect to all the relevant terms of the WTO Agreement, contrary to the principle of effectiveness [...] in the interpretation of treaties. The Panel states that the 'express omission of the criterion of unforeseen developments' in Article XIX:1(a) from the Agreement on Safeguards 'must, in our view, have meaning.' On the contrary, in our view, if they had intended to expressly omit this clause, the Uruguay Round negotiators

---

2067 Van Damme 2009, 118, 122f.

2068 However, I will not discuss what legal norms (e.g. international law) they have resorted when doing so, as this was already discussed in the first section of this chapter.

2069 See above section 1.1.

> would and could have said so in the Agreement on Safeguards. They did not."[2070]

In what is probably the most thorough analysis so far on how the WTO adjudicators have dealt with (alleged) gaps in WTO law, van Damme argues that the Appellate Body has indeed filled gaps in procedural law, often by resorting to general principles of law or the practice of other international courts and tribunals. She mentions, *inter alia,* burden of proof, confidentiality of business information, and the standard of review as examples.[2071] Moreover, she observes that the Appellate Body appears to be more ready to fill procedural gaps than those appearing in substantive law.[2072] Similarly, Pauwelyn observes that the Appellate Body has "fallen back" on general international law for a number of matters on which WTO law is silent, with most of the examples given concerning procedural matters.[2073] Foltea also states that international law has been "commonly applied" by the adjudicators to fill procedural gaps.[2074] Gourgourinis also concludes that the Appellate Body has decided certain procedural questions *praeter legem,* i.e. by filling gaps.[2075]

Maybe the most famous case of procedural gap-filling is the jurisprudence on the admissibility of *amicus curiae* briefs. The Appellate Body in *Shrimp – Turtles* decided it would accept *amicus curiae* briefs, but WTO law contains no explicit provision on *amicus curiae* briefs or, indeed, even mentions the term, and hence a gap on that matter.[2076] The Appellate Body's decision was based on a reading of Art. 13 DSU which stipulates that a Panel

> "shall have the right to seek information and technical advice from any individual or body which it deems appropriate".

2070 *Argentina – Safeguard Measures on Imports of Footwear, WT/DS121/AB/R* 1999, para. 88.

2071 Van Damme 2009, 135f; McRae 2006, 361 also observes that burden of proof, judicial economy, completing the analysis, and *stare decisis* are all "judge-made developments" in WTO law; Goldstein and Steinberg 2007, 20f mention the *amicus curiae* decision and the decision on the admissibility of private legal counsel as examples of filling procedural gaps.

2072 Van Damme 2009, 136.

2073 Pauwelyn 2003a, 207ff.

2074 Foltea 2012, 33.

2075 Gourgourinis 2016, 109ff.

2076 Van Damme 2009, 136.

The Appellate Body concluded, on the basis of a purposive reading, that this clause did not prohibit the acceptance of *amicus curiae* briefs by the judicial bodies. The *amicus curiae* decision was followed by what one observer has called a "firestorm of criticism"[2077], as many WTO Members were unhappy with it.[2078] Some observers cite the decision as an instance in which the Appellate Body "overstepped the bounds".[2079] As a consequence, a former Member of the Appellate Body recommended that, while he considers the decision taken to be legally correct, the issue should be settled through negotiations among Members.[2080] In subsequent cases, the adjudicators admitted the *amicus curiae* briefs in principle while expressing they did not find it necessary to take them into account in their findings.[2081] Altogether, Panels and the Appellate Body have accepted the submission of *amicus curiae* briefs relatively regularly, but actually referred to them very infrequently.[2082]

Concerning (unintended) gaps in substantive law, van Damme observes that the Appellate Body might be more prone to interpreting substantive silences when these concern matters of general international (treaty) law, such as the temporal scope of a treaty that can be solved with reference to the VCLT. By contrast, when the gap relates to substantive trade law, she observes that the Appellate Body's interpretative approach is altogether less consistent and that it is "inclined to offer more justification".[2083] Other authors have identified instances where gaps in substantive law have been filled by the adjudicators.[2084]

2077 McCall Smith 2003, 89.

2078 Goh and Morgan 2007, 487.

2079 Barfield 2001, 13 who also describes the reaction by various actors to the *amicus curiae* decision at 18ff.

2080 Matsushita 2005b, 627.

2081 *European Communities – Measures Affecting the Approval and Marketing of Biotech Products, WT/DS291/R, WT/DS292/R, WT/DS293/R* 2006, para. 7.11; *European Communities – Measures Prohibiting the Importation and Marketing of Seal Products, WT/DS400/AB/R, WT/DS401/AB/R* 2014, para. 1.15.

2082 In a text published in 2016 Charvat 2016 states that Panels and the Appellate Body had accepted 60 *amicus curiae* briefs for consideration, but only referred directly to three of them.

2083 Van Damme 2009, 140.

2084 Zeitler 2005, 754 mentions the Panel report in *Korea – Measures Affecting Government Procurement*, WT/DS163/R as one example, suggesting that the Appellate Body would have reversed the Panel's finding if the case had been appealed.

Yet the Appellate Body has not always been eager either to fill gaps or to explicitly acknowledge their existence in the first place. As Steinberg observed (in 2004), *non liquet* has never been invoked in WTO dispute settlement[2085] and neither has the Appellate Body commented on it.[2086] At the same time, cases in which gaps were acknowledged to exist have been identified.[2087] In some of these cases, the Appellate Body either avoided making a decision on the matter at hand[2088] or declined to provide a remedy because no WTO provision applied *ratione temporis*.[2089]

Altogether, there is evidence for a rather mixed attitude of the Appellate Body to gaps: it is quite confident in filling gaps in procedural law as compared to gaps in substantive law. The existence of gaps in WTO law is admitted in some instances by the adjudicators, but these are rare.

2.3. The use of the decisions of WTO political bodies

The previous section presented insights into how the dispute settlement bodies deal with gaps in the (original) WTO legal texts, i.e. situations where WTO Members have either deliberately or unintentionally left a certain issue open. This section discusses the reverse situation: how do the WTO dispute settlement bodies deal with expressions of the intention or political will of the WTO Members that have become manifest after the entering into force of the WTO agreements? This issue is sometimes discussed under the heading of "institutional balance".[2090]

The WTO dispute settlement bodies have touched upon this issue in general times only a few times. In *India – Quantitative Restrictions*, India claimed that the Appellate Body should recognize and draw on the principle of institutional balance between judicial and political bodies, as developed by the ECJ and contained in the constitutions of modern democracies. India argued that

2085 Steinberg 2004, 260.

2086 Van Damme 2009, 119.

2087 See Pauwelyn 2002, n. 33.

2088 Van Damme 2009, 188 referring to the Appellate Body report in *United States – Anti-Dumping Measures on Certain Hot-Rolled Steel Products from Japan*, WT/DS184/AB/R, para.. 125f; Goh and Morgan 2007, 490f.

2089 Trachtman 1999, 338 citing the Appellate Body report in *Brazil – Measures* Affecting Desiccated Coconut, WT/DS22/AB/R.

2090 Roessler 2000.

> "an organ of the WTO cannot determine its jurisdiction in a manner that entails a change in the procedural or substantive rights and obligations of Members. Each organ of the WTO must, in determining the scope of its own powers, proceed with due regard to the powers of the other organs of the WTO, and with due regard for the rights and obligations of Members."[2091]

Accordingly, reviewing a certain matter under the GATT was, in India's view, outside the competence of the Panel; rather, according to India, the matter fell within the responsibility of a specific WTO committee.[2092] In its response, the Appellate Body did not recognize any abstract principle of institutional balance. In substance, it accepted that the Panel was competent to comprehensively review the provisions in dispute. It based this decision, *inter alia*, on Art. XXIII GATT which allows recourse to the dispute settlement system to any WTO Member that considers that a benefit accruing to it under the GATT 1994 is being nullified or impaired as a result of the failure of another Member to carry out its obligations. Moreover, the Appellate Body referred to Art. 1.2 DSU, according to which the DSU shall apply to the agreements identified in Appendix 2 to the DSU, of which the GATT is one.[2093] The Appellate Body also supported the Panel's position that the review by Panels of the measures in question did not call into question the competence of the respective committee; the Appellate Body also concurred with the Panel that the judicial bodies and the respective committee had functions and procedures that differed in nature, scope, timing and type of outcome.[2094]

Some observers read a reference to the Indian case by the Appellate Body in *Turkey – Textiles* as confirming this approach.[2095] At stake in *Turkey – Textiles* was a measure that Turkey indicated it had taken to comply with a decision made under the Turkey – EC Association Agreement. Turkey classified the agreement as a customs union in the sense of Art. XXIV GATT. In the Panel proceedings, Turkey had argued that the WTO Committee on Regional Trade Agreements charged with deciding on the WTO compatibility of regional trade agreements should decide on the compatibility of the Association Agreement with Art. XXIV GATT, be-

---

2091 *India – Quantitative Restrictions on Imports of Agricultural, Textile and Industrial Products, WT/DS90/AB/R* 1999, para. 22.

2092 Ibid., para. 8ff.

2093 Ibid., para. 84ff.

2094 Ibid., para. 104.

2095 Bartels 2004, 879; Roessler 2000, 338.

fore the Panel could take a decision on the legality of the measure.[2096] The Appellate Body rejected the Turkish position, asserting that the WTO judicial bodies possessed full competence to decide on whether a measure falls under Art. XXIV GATT.

There are several norms besides those in these two cases that explicitly define the respective competences of WTO political bodies and judicial organs. Art. IX:3 and XI:4 WTOA on waivers or Art. X WTOA on amendments are examples of norms which, if they were to be interpreted by the WTO dispute settlement bodies, would also be relevant for delineating the relationship between both branches of WTO governance.

Unlike these norms, Art. IX:2 WTOA has been interpreted by the Appellate Body. According to Art. IX:2 WTOA, the Ministerial Conference and the General Council, where all WTO Members are represented, have the "exclusive authority to adopt interpretations" of WTO Agreements. In what seems to be the first case dealing with this norm, the Appellate Body expressed the opinion that interpretations adopted pursuant to Art. IX:2 WTOA are "meant to clarify the meaning of existing obligations, not to modify their content"[2097]. It also observed that

> "a multilateral interpretation pursuant to Article IX:2 of the WTO Agreement can be likened to a subsequent agreement regarding the interpretation of the treaty or the application of its provisions pursuant to Article 31(3)(a) of the Vienna Convention, as far as the interpretation of the WTO agreements is concerned".[2098]

In one relatively recent (2012) case, the Appellate Body discussed whether paragraph 5.2 of the Doha Ministerial Declaration constituted an interpretation in the sense of Art. IX:2 WTOA on a certain article of the TBT Agreement. The Panel had avoided deciding the matter and had stated the following:

> "Although the parties disagree on the categorization of paragraph 5.2 of the Doha Ministerial Decision as an authoritative interpretation under Article IX:2 of the WTO Agreement, this Panel deems that it must be guided by it in its interpretation of the phrase 'reasonable interval', as it was agreed by all WTO Members meeting in the form of Ministe-

---

2096 For the details of the case, see Roessler 2000, 33ff.

2097 *European Communities – Regime for the importation, sale and distribution of bananas, second recourse to Article 21.5 of the DSU by Ecuador, WT/DS27/AB/RW2/ECU* 2008, para. 383.

2098 Ibid.

> rial Conference, the highest ranking body of the WTO. Furthermore, the Panel is of the view that paragraph 5.2 of the Doha Ministerial Decision could be considered as a subsequent agreement of the parties within the meaning of Article 31(3)(a) of the VCLT […]."[2099]

One of the parties to the dispute appealed this finding, stating that the Panel had attributed an incorrect "interpretative value" to the paragraph[2100] and should have considered it, at most, as a supplementary means of interpretation in the sense of the VCLT.[2101] The Appellate Body took the opportunity not only to clarify the status of the quoted paragraph of the Doha Ministerial Declaration, but also to elaborate more broadly on Art. IX:2 WTOA. It stated that the adoption of interpretations according to Art. IX:2 was subject to clearly articulated and strict decision-making procedures because of "the broad legal effect" of such interpretations.[2102] *In casu*, it observed that the decision-making procedure defined in Art. XI:2 WTOA had not been followed. According to this article, an interpretation of a multilateral trade agreement like the TBT Agreement shall be taken "on the basis of a recommendation by the Council overseeing the functioning of that Agreement". As there was no such recommendation for the decision contained in para. 5.2 of the Ministerial Declaration, the Appellate Body concluded that the paragraph did not constitute an interpretation in the sense of Art. IX:2 WTOA. The Appellate Body rejected some statements by the Panel that implied that the procedural requirement might be dispensable, pointing to the clear wording of the text.[2103]

The Appellate Body then considered whether the Declaration constituted "subsequent practice" in the sense of Art. 31.3 a) VCLT. It clarified that even though the procedural requirements of Art. IX:2 WTO were not satisfied, this did not mean that the Declaration could not be taken into account under Art. 31.3 a) VCLT as

> "multilateral interpretations adopted pursuant to Article IX:2 of the WTO Agreement, on the one hand, and subsequent agreements on interpretation within the meaning of Article 31(3)(a) of the Vienna Con-

---

2099 *United States – Measures Affecting the Production and Sale of Clove Cigarettes, WT/DS406/R* 2011, para. 7.576.

2100 *United States – Measures Affecting the Production and Sale of Clove Cigarettes, WT/DS406/AB/R* 2012, para. 240.

2101 Ibid., para. 242.

2102 Ibid., para. 250.

2103 Ibid., para. 253ff.

vention, on the other hand, serve different functions and have different legal effects under WTO law".[2104]

Furthermore, the Appellate Body clarified that for a decision to be considered as subsequent practice in the sense of Art. 31.3 a) VCLT, two requirements needed to be met: that the decision is adopted after the relevant agreement and that the terms and content of the decision express an agreement between WTO Members on the interpretation or application of WTO law.[2105] The Appellate Body found these requirements to be met in the case, using the Ministerial Declaration for the interpretation of the TBT Agreement.[2106]

In another case, the Appellate Body explicitly discussed the legal basis on which a decision by a WTO Committee, in this case the TBT Committee[2107], could be taken into account in WTO dispute settlement. The Appellate Body decided to qualify the decision as subsequent agreement between the parties in the sense of Art. 31.3 a) VCLT, pointing out that the decision had been adopted by consensus and all Members were represented on the TBT Committee.[2108] It also found that the decision referred explicitly to certain articles of the TBT Agreement and was taken with the aim of clarifying certain concepts contained therein, and thus concerned the interpretation of the TBT Agreement.[2109]

The Appellate Body has also sometimes implied that it would welcome an authoritative interpretation by Members of a particular treaty text.[2110] For example, in *Shrimp – Turtles*, the Appellate Body, having noted the ab-

---

2104 Ibid., para. 257.

2105 Ibid.

2106 This case also illustrates that, contrary to what may be expected, WTO Members are not necessarily happy when consensual decisions by WTO Members are taken into account in WTO dispute settlement procedures; the US had in fact objected to the interpretation ultimately adopted by the Appellate Body.

2107 The decision in question was the TBT Committee "Decision on Principles for the Development of International Standards, Guides and Recommendations with Relation to Articles 2, 5, and Annex 3 to the Agreement", contained in WTO document G/TBT/1/Rev.10, Decisions and Recommendations adopted by the WTO Committee on Technical Barriers to Trade since 1 January 1995, 9 June 2011, 46-48, http://www.wto.org/english/tratop_e/tbt_e/tbt_work_docs_e.htm.

2108 *United States – Measures Concerning the Importation, Marketing and Sale of Tuna and Tuna Products, WT/DS381/AB/R* 2012, para. 371.

2109 Ibid., para. 372.

2110 Van Damme 2010, 611.

sence of any specific decision or recommendation of any WTO body that would alter any of the agreements relevant to the case, stated:

> "Pending any specific recommendations by the CTE to WTO Members on the issues raised in its terms of reference, and in the absence up to now of any agreed amendments or modifications to the substantive provisions of the GATT 1994 and the WTO Agreement generally, we must fulfill our responsibility in this specific case, which is to interpret the existing language of the chapeau of Article XX by examining its ordinary meaning, in light of its context and object and purpose."[2111]

Although the Appellate Body found no additional legal documents it could rely on in the concrete case besides the original agreements, the reference to the WTO Committee on Trade and Environment (CTE) recommendations indicates that the Appellate Body would have been willing to take into account such a decision in principle.

All in all, there is a quite mixed record on how the WTO dispute settlement bodies deal with decisions either taken or to be taken by the political bodies of the WTO. Where there are explicit and specific decisions by a political committee on a certain agreement, these tend to be taken into account. However, the Appellate Body does not recognize any principle of institutional balance or assume that it is improper for the WTO judicial decision-makers to review certain measures when WTO committees could also do so.

2.4. Discussion

In the following I will discuss the case law from a more legal-technical point of view. This process is complicated by the fact that few of the questions discussed so far are explicitly regulated in the text of WTO law, rendering it impossible to carry out an analysis informed by positive law. The Appellate Body has also failed to formulate a clearly articulated overarching approach on how it will deal with these questions. For some of the questions, this is quite reasonable. For example, manifestations of the will of WTO Members will be manifold – and so must their judicial assessment. The Appellate Body's reluctance to provide overarching guidance is, however, less understandable in other respects, notably regarding how ad-

2111 *United States – Import Prohibition of Certain Shrimp and Shrimp Products, WT/DS58/AB/R* 1998, para. 155.

judicators are to deal with gaps or what standard of review is to be employed by the WTO adjudicators.

In the following, I will consider the three issues that have attracted most attention in a sub-section each: the standard of review (section 2.1) and how the Appellate Body deals with gaps in the WTO agreements (section 2.2) and decisions by WTO political bodies (section 2.3). Again, this is complemented by a discussion (section 2.4) and assessment (2.5) of the case law.

2.4.1. Standard of review

Among the various issues discussed in this section, the standard of review is most widely discussed. As mentioned above, the Appellate Body conceives of Art. 11 DSU as the embodiment of the standard of review in WTO law, an approach that is not without its critics.[2112] Yet there are more troubling aspects of the Appellate Body's articulation of the standard of review, notably, and given its systemic importance, it is both surprising and unsatisfactory that the Appellate Body has provided so little in the way of guidance.[2113]

The discussion of whether an alternative measure is reasonably available and hence the measure in place unnecessary under the sub-paragraphs of Art. XX GATT is an example. Legal commentators have pointed out that the Appellate Body seemed to accord less weight to the defending Member's claim that proposed alternatives would not reach the desired level of protection in two cases involving Art. XX (d) GATT and policy goals such as preventing fraud or smuggling than it did in cases where health issues were at stake.[2114] This may either have been a result of the balancing exercise that the Appellate Body conducts as part of the necessity analysis under Art. XX GATT, where the importance of the regulatory objective constitutes one of the factors to be balanced, or it may be a result of less intensive judicial scrutiny being applied where the regulatory objective is considered to be of particular importance.[2115] By way of comparison, one com-

2112 Spamann 2004, 529; Gruszczynski 2013, 737.

2113 Schropp 2012, 189.

2114 See chapter 2, section 1.5.1.

2115 Cho 2009a, 714 suggests that less intensive scrutiny is applied when measures of more powerful WTO Members are at stake. I do not find this very plausible, among others, because in some of the cases he quotes in support, e.g. the Hormones case, powerful WTO Members are on both sides of the dispute.

mentator has observed that in the context of the TBT Agreement the Appellate Body appears to apply "diligent scrutiny" to the effectiveness of alternative measures available for reaching a Member's objectives, i.e. it does not appear predisposed to accepting such alternative measures easily.[2116]

The Appellate Body has given few indications of what could influence the standard of review in a given case. Notably it has stated that where serious risks are at issue, such as those to human health and life, Panels may assume that governments act prudently when assessing the evidence. This is an indication that in such cases Panels are to tread more lightly in their own assessment.[2117] Remarkably, this has rarely been discussed under the explicit heading of "standard of review" which makes the systematic accounting of such indications difficult. Some guidance has also been provided by the Appellate Body in *Hormones II* on how Panels need to deal with scientific evidence, including in situations where a Member wishes to rely on a minority scientific opinion, but such clarifications remain scarce. The current jurisprudence on the matter has been described as ambiguous and conducive to further controversies in WTO disputes.[2118] Indeed, the Appellate Body seems to have mostly circumscribed what is *not* the appropriate standard of review.[2119] Observers have called for more clarity on the matter.[2120]

Admittedly, Art. 11 DSU offers limited textual guidance as to the standard of review that WTO dispute settlement bodies are to observe.[2121] It has been described as "enigmatic" and "singularly unhelpful" in providing guidance on the nature and intensity of scrutiny Panels are to apply.[2122] As noted above[2123], Art. 11.2 DSU states the more or less obvious – no one would expect or request a judicial entity to perform a non-objective assessment of any matter before it. Objectivity is, however, insufficient in itself to constitute a meaningful or consistent standard of review.[2124] Indeed, both highly deferential or less deferential standards of review can be con-

2116 Norpoth 2013, 599.
2117 See chapter 2, section 2.1.1.
2118 Gruszczynski 2013, 731; a more positive evaluation comes from Zdouc 2008, 378 who is the head of the Appellate Body Secretariat.
2119 Ehlermann and Lockhart 2004, 501.
2120 Lovric 2010, 95; Schropp 2012, 214 in relation to the Appellate Body decision in *Hormones II*.
2121 Reusch 2007, 269.
2122 Du 2011, 669.
2123 See chapter 1, section 4.3.2.
2124 Guzman 2008, 51.

sidered "objective";[2125] interestingly, this idea is also held by a former Member of the Appellate Body.[2126] A comparison between Art. 11 and 17.6 DSU allows at least the inference that Art. 11 DSU does not promote judicial restraint.[2127]

Arguably, it is difficult for a judicial body to formulate a general standard that would apply to judicial reviews of different agreements and to the wide variety of measures taken by countries worldwide on the basis of a norm as vague as Art. 11 DSU. Nevertheless, there are two ways in which the outcome of cases might be made a little more predictable: if factors to take into consideration for determining the appropriate standard of a review in a given instance were presented in a systematic matter in one Appellate Body report, and if the adjudicators were more explicit about the policy considerations that were behind the adoption of a particular standard of review in a given case. Suggestions that have been made in the literature on factors that should determine the intensity of judicial review include the following: the type of regulatory issues at stake[2128], the importance of the regulatory goal at stake as expressed by the WTO Member[2129], whether a formal investigation by national authorities is mandated in WTO (i.e. whether a Panel would be the first body to thoroughly investigate the validity of a certain factual justification of a measure[2130]), the degree of determinacy of the legal norm on which the dispute is based[2131], and the degree of scientific uncertainty and socio-political disagreement on a certain topic[2132].

The above considerations relate to the way that the standard of review has (or rather has not) been formulated in the case law today. Yet another matter is how the few guidelines that the Appellate Body has formulated have actually been *applied* in the case law. Quantifying or even just describing with any degree of accuracy how deferential or intrusive the standard of review used by a certain judicial entity is, presents, of course, a difficult

2125 Du 2010b, 444.
2126 Ehlermann and Lockhart 2004, 495.
2127 Oesch 2003, 647.
2128 See for example Ehlermann and Lockhart 2004, 503; Howse and Langille 2011, 417 that in Art. XX (a) GATT cases scrutiny should be "higher where a measure looks like some kind of commercial restriction than the kind of sanction usually associated with an expression of moral disapprobation".
2129 Regan 2007, 352.
2130 Ehlermann and Lockhart 2004, 513f; Andenas and Zleptnig 2007, 395.
2131 Shany 2005, 913, but not with regard to the WTO specifically.
2132 Peel 2012, 444ff.

task; there is no agreed, clear scale for measurement. The fact that a violation of the standard of review is almost routinely claimed in appellate cases, but rarely successfully, may be indicative of how underspecified the standard of review is. Nonetheless, some observers have alleged that in certain cases the Appellate Body has undermined its own understanding of Art. 11 DSU.[2133]

The case law today warrants at least one barely contestable observation: the standard of review applied in WTO proceedings varies from issue to issue.[2134] The standard of review has become particularly salient in cases under the SPS Agreement where complex factual assessments on risks need to be made. What is the standard of review in these cases? As has been shown, the picture here is also quite mixed; it is largely agreed that a different standard of review has been applied in different cases.[2135] Observers hold no uniform view on how deferential the standard of review in the SPS cases was in practice, beyond abstract statements, however.[2136]

Several authors have concluded that the Panels have often scrutinized the facts presented by a WTO Member in dispute settlement proceedings quite intensively[2137], including for example whether all relevant facts have been gathered.[2138] Panels have also come close to a *de novo* review, if some observers are to be believed, and the margin left to national authorities in evaluating the facts has, across all types of cases, been generally quite small.[2139] Guzman writes that "the evaluation of science is subject to a significant review".[2140] Du notes that even though the Appellate Body has rejected *de novo* as the proper standard of review, the Panels in SPS cases come close to applying this standard by leaning heavily on the testimonies of experts rather than checking whether the scientific conclusions as laid out by the defending WTO Member were reasonable and defensible.[2141] He claims that the standard of review adopted by Panels in science-related

2133 Guzman 2008, 50f citing the *China – Agricultural Products* and *United States – Hot Rolled Steel* cases.
2134 Ibid., 51f; Kapterian 2010, 99; Schropp 2012, 189.
2135 See for example Gruszczynski 2013, but also section 2.1 above.
2136 See also Schropp 2012, 191f who notes that observers disagree on how deferential the standard of review adopted by the Appellate Body in *Hormones II* actually is.
2137 Bloche 2002, 831f.
2138 Ruffert 2001, 308.
2139 Oesch 2003, 650f; Fukunaga 2012, 564.
2140 Guzman 2008, 70.
2141 Du 2010b, 448ff.

cases has become so stringent that in certain circumstances it is "practically impossible" for WTO Members to successfully defend SPS measures.[2142] Cho identifies several instances in which the Appellate Body endorsed one specific scientific position amongst several ones, rather than just reviewing the plausibility of the various scientific claims.[2143] Peel maintains that there is an "overall trend in the SPS jurisprudence towards a more stringent review" of the scientific evidence that risk-related regulatory decisions are based on.[2144] Norpoth writes that in recent TBT cases the Appellate Body "clearly, did not follow a concept of policy space based on full deference to national regulations".[2145]

While this first group of commentators identify a tendency of the adjudicators to subject scientific evidence introduced by parties to quite intensive scrutiny, others observe that Panels do accord deference to the conclusions drawn from the facts by WTO Members and the policy choices made[2146], particularly in health-related cases.[2147] One observer states that if a WTO Member's conclusion is reasonable and, in the case of a scientific assessment, based on a qualified and respected opinion, it is not usually reversed by the Panel.[2148] Others, however, point to instances where the Appellate Body overruled findings by a Panel that would have restricted WTO Members' regulatory freedom to a greater extent.[2149]

Many also see indications of a move towards more deference in more recent cases, in particular the *Hormones II* case.[2150] It has been described as a "revolutionary shift" in WTO case history[2151] and a reaction to earlier cases in which Panels applied intensive scrutiny to the evidence presented by a defending Member[2152]. Others have a more guarded view of this decision, though. For example, Peel agrees that there are some indications in the decision that the Appellate Body "favoured a more deferential approach" to-

---

2142 Du 2011, 652.

2143 Cho 2009a, 683. However, it should be noted that Cho does not consider this as an instance of a too intrusive standard of review, but rather as too much deference having been accorded to one party.

2144 Peel 2012, 438.

2145 Norpoth 2013, 599.

2146 Ehlermann and Lockhart 2004, 517.

2147 Bloche 2002; Goh and Morgan 2007, 496; Mavroidis 2016, 1109.

2148 Oesch 2003, 653.

2149 Knox 2004, 42.

2150 See for example Kapterian 2010, 125; Du 2011, 655.; Herwig and Joerges 2013, 16 also seem to adopt this view.

2151 Gruszczynski 2013, 749.

2152 Schropp 2012, 190.

wards reviewing scientific evidence than had been employed in previous case law. At the same time, she expresses reservations towards considering the case a "turning point" in the WTO approach to the standard of review in SPS cases, pointing to the fact that the Appellate Body still puts considerable emphasis on the robustness of scientific evidence.[2153]

A comparison with the practice of the EU and US courts and investment tribunals when assessing science-based measures, in particular SPS measures, helps to shed some more light on whether the standard of review used in WTO dispute settlement is to be characterized as more or less intrusive or deferential. Generally, environmental and health measures are subject to similar disciplines in WTO law and (primary) EU law,[2154] and the issue of how to review risk-related decisions also exists in the US (like in any jurisdiction). US and EU courts have been described as adopting a standard for the review of scientific assessments made by regulators that is somewhere between a *de novo* review and full deference.[2155] In the EU, there is stronger deference to measures taken by EU institutions than there is for the measures of Members States;[2156] the ECJ has in some cases subjected the scientific basis of a Member State's measure to intense scrutiny.[2157] The WTO approach has been described as less deferential than that taken by US and EU courts.[2158] Also, it has been observed that at least some national courts are rather deferential to decisions taken by policy makers in the area of external economic relations.[2159] Finally, there are also examples in international investment arbitrations where tribunals have applied a clearly deferential standard of review; their language when dealing

2153 Peel 2012, 447f.

2154 For SPS measures, see Slotboom 2003; for environmental and health measures, see Notaro 2003, 253ff who observes that "overall domestic environmental and health measures stand a better chance to be accepted [...] under the EC than under the WTO dispute settlement mechanism".

2155 Peel 2012, 435ff; Peel 2004, 7, 48, 73; the author herself questions whether it is advisable to transpose the approach to the review of science-based risk decisions found at the national level to the WTO context, see at 9.

2156 Slotboom 2003; Neumann and Tuerk 2003, 202; Peel 2004, 48 indicates as a reason for the more stringent review of Member States' measures that countervailing internal market considerations are less strong in the case of EU measures.

2157 See the discussion by McNelis 2001, 203ff of the German Beer case of the ECJ (Case C-178/84, Commission vs. Germany).

2158 Peel 2004, 73; by contrast, Slotboom 2003, 585f offered a tentative conclusion that the standards of review in the EU and the WTO were similar after *Hormones I*.

2159 Oesch 2003, 289ff.

with scientific evidence by the parties differs remarkably from that of WTO Panels.[2160]

Of course, making such a comparison does not mean that the WTO should necessarily adopt the same standard of review as national or EU courts or international investment tribunals. McNelis, for example, suggests that the standard EU courts have adopted for reviewing EU measures may be too deferential for the WTO; in contrast to WTO Members, EU institutions are unlikely to harbour any protectionist intentions. At the same time she also suggests that the Appellate Body should not scrutinize WTO Members' measures as intensively as the EU courts do with EU Members' measures, because the EU is a more homogenous community and the European courts have more legitimacy than the Appellate Body.[2161] Moreover, considerations of balance of powers, which are an important rationale when it comes to the standard of review applied by domestic courts, do not necessarily apply in an identical manner when an international court reviews a national measure.[2162] These are all important arguments. Yet the point I wish to make here by referring to the standard of review employed at the national and EU level as well as by investment tribunals is more limited than suggesting that the WTO should employ the same standard: if it can be shown that the WTO dispute settlement bodies are less deferential than several other judicial institutions that deal with similar issues as the WTO dispute settlement bodies do, this is a good basis on which to make the statement that they are in fact not very deferential.

Another important aspect to note is that the way the Appellate Body has interpreted Art. 11 DSU gives Panels a lot of leeway in deciding how to deal with evidence. Only deliberate misrepresentations or disregard of the evidence constitute a violation of that article.

2.4.2. Dealing with gaps and political decisions by WTO political bodies

The way that the adjudicators deal with gaps is another sensitive topic in WTO dispute settlement: judicial gap-filling is very controversial from a doctrinal point of view in international law and also in WTO law more specifically. The Appellate Body has no publicly articulated theory on gap-filling, if indeed it has one at all. It has neither made explicit its position

2160 See the examples given in Fukunaga 2012, 571ff.
2161 McNelis 2001, 202ff.
2162 Oesch 2003, 296.

regarding the possibility of there being gaps in WTO law nor has it stated how, should they be discovered, they should be dealt with by the adjudicators and what legal reasons lie behind this.

The prevailing view in international law seems to be that there is no room for gaps and hence a *non liquet* statement from a court.[2163] Two different reasons are mentioned: First, the principle of state sovereignty stipulates that whatever is not forbidden to a state by international law is permitted. Hence, there is always a default rule governing a state's behaviour. Second, because wherever something is not regulated by treaty law or custom, general principles of international law still apply.[2164] With regard to WTO law, many observers concur that gaps do occur.[2165] This may be related to the fact that WTO law is a distinct and relatively densely structured legal (sub)-order; the notion that there may be identifiable gaps within such a structure appears intuitively more plausible than in the more diffuse wider international legal system with its variety of sources of law.

Yet the notion that there are gaps in WTO law does not mean that the legal commentators expect the WTO dispute settlement bodies to produce *non liquet* statements. Notably, Pauwelyn maintains that as the dispute settlement bodies only are competent to decide on whether a specific agreement was violated, it is logically impossible for them to find themselves facing a gap in applicable law. Where there is no claim of a specific WTO norm being violated, the dispute settlement bodies have no jurisdiction and cannot rule against a defendant.[2166] Similarly, another eminent observer, Davey, maintains that if a party cannot support its claim by reference to a specific WTO norm, it will simply lose the case, with no need for the dispute settlement bodies to state a *non liquet*.[2167] This issue ultimately does not need to be resolved here; it is enough to note that WTO Members are concerned about potential gaps in WTO law and the fact that the adjudicators, on occasion, fill them.

2163 This is stated by Alvarez 2008, 617; for a detailed discussion of whether a non liquet is permissible in international law, see Fastenrath 1991, 272ff. Fastenrath himself holds the view that a *non liquet* is neither mandated nor prohibited in international law, see at 284 and 281 respectively.

2164 See Trachtman 1999, 341; Pauwelyn 2003a, 438 seems to hold a similar view when stressing that situations where adjudicators must declare a non liquet, because it is not clear which legal norm must be applied, are the exception.

2165 See for example Kelly 2002, 386; Trachtman 1999, 341.

2166 Pauwelyn 2003a, 152f; Pauwelyn 2002, 72.

2167 Davey 2003, 68.

The next question, therefore, is whether filling gaps is an appropriate task for the WTO adjudicators – or whether they are even obliged do so. The dominant view, also shared by some former Members of the Appellate Body, seems to be that the DSU leaves the adjudicators with no choice but to fill such gaps when necessary for settling the dispute.[2168] A former Member of the Appellate Body has referred to Art. 17.12 DSU in support of the position that the Appellate Body must decide all matters brought before it;[2169] the provision mandates that the Appellate Body is to "address each of the issues" raised on appeal. Such an understanding of its mandate might explain why the Appellate Body sometimes engages in gap-filling. However, as Bartels points out, it is unclear whether the norm can actually be taken to support such a far-reaching conclusion on the role of the Appellate Body in filling gaps.[2170] The requirement to "address each of the issues" is rather weak; merely stating that there is a gap could be seen as already fulfilling it. At the same time, the position that the dispute settlement bodies cannot decide not to decide or will never be in a situation of "no law" is far from uncontroversial;[2171] some maintain that in such cases the adjudicators should declare a *non liquet* and defer to a decision by the WTO Members.[2172] Indeed, the Appellate Body is apparently unfazed by any (alleged) restrictions imposed by Art. 17.12 DSU in this regard, and frequently uses certain "techniques", notably judicial economy, in order to avoid deciding an issue.[2173] Any response to a gap in WTO rules, therefore, is not predetermined by the DSU rules or any other WTO provisions: it is a matter for the adjudicators to choose.

With regard to the way that the Appellate Body has taken decisions by political bodies of the WTO into account, the existing cases are too varied for a conclusive statement on the matter. Those few commentators that have investigated the limited case law seem to be quite satisfied with the Appellate Body's decisions in these cases.[2174] The Appellate Body's approach in refusing to adopt the suggestion that it should recognize an overarching principle of institutional balance does seem appropriate, however

2168 Ehlermann 2002, 633; Bacchus 2003, 439; Bacchus 2005, 507; Abi-Saab 2006, 47; Sacerdoti 2006, 47; Iida 2004, 221.

2169 Bacchus 2003, 439.

2170 See for these arguments Bartels 2004, 874ff.

2171 See for a discussion of different positions Steinberg 2004, 258ff; Reusch 2007, 266.

2172 See Bartels 2004, 894; Kelly 2002, 386.

2173 See below section 3.2.

2174 See Bogdandy 2001, 631f; Howse 2003c, 32ff.

– after all, it is likely that the content of such a principle would be very vague. It is unclear what (if anything) it would add to the explicit provisions on the respective competences of the different entities within the WTO institutional structure, notably those contained in the WTOA and the DSU.

2.5. Assessment

In this section, I will, again assess the judicial style implicit in the case law of the WTO dispute settlement bodies along more normative-political lines and with a view to what they mean for the legitimacy of the WTO judicial decision-making. I will focus on the two more prominent issues: standard of review and dealing with gaps.

With regards to the standard of review, it is clear that the more intensively the adjudicators scrutinize measures taken by WTO Members, the more they restrict the regulatory freedom of WTO Members.[2175] As things stand, the Appellate Body's piecemeal, case-by-case approach allows the Panels great flexibility in the approach they choose, including a deferential approach'. This flexibility notwithstanding, deferential standards of review have rarely been used in the WTO's "trade and ..." cases.

By way of contrast to the approach taken by the dispute settlement bodies, many observers have expressed a preference for WTO dispute settlements to use a deferential standard of review[2176], at least in cases where health and safety issues are at stake and there are competing scientific claims.[2177] It has been suggested that Panels should restrict themselves to checking whether scientific claims are reasonable or plausible.[2178] Some arguments put forward in favour of such a deferential standard of review are as follows:

Health matters are a core part of WTO Members' sovereignty, while WTO Members have given up part of their sovereignty over trade matters through WTO law. Therefore, a judicial examination of, for example,

2175 See for example Gruszczynski 2013, 733.

2176 See for example Lovric 2010, 2; Schropp 2012, 206ff.

2177 See for example Trebilcock and Soloway 2002, 543; Epps 2008, 278; Winickoff et al. 2005, 117ff; Howse and Horn 2009, 72; Fukunaga 2012, 567ff.

2178 Herwig 2008, 842ff; Walker 1998, 281ff.

whether states have selected the least trade-restrictive available measure, is less problematic than double-checking health-related assessments.[2179]

- Countries should be allowed to choose from amongst the policy options that have a reasonable scientific basis those that best protect humans against risks.[2180]
- WTO Panels do not have the institutional capacity to decide between scientifically plausible alternatives.[2181]
- An international court is much less well-placed than national legislators to make judgements about the perceptions of the population.[2182]
- Risk assessments are a value-infused exercise which WTO Members are more competent to judge than the WTO dispute settlement bodies.[2183]

When these suggestions or models are used as a yardstick, at least some of the SPS-related case law is clearly more restrictive of WTO Members' regulatory freedom than required under the SPS Agreement. Few scholars argue that the WTO agreements do not allow a consistently deferential approach in textual terms, however.[2184] More generally, there are a wide variety of views in the literature regarding how international courts should deal with scientific evidence.[2185]

Another problematic issue with the standard of review as formulated by the Appellate Body is that it makes it very difficult for a party to successfully claim a violation of that standard.[2186] It would hardly be possible for a party to prove a wilful distortion of facts by the Panel, as is required by the Appellate Body to constitute a violation of Art. 11 DSU. Indeed, claims based on Art. 11 DSU were successful at the appellate stage in only a very few cases. It is reasonable to believe that this being the case, Panelists will typically take less care with the facts presented by the parties than if they felt that an inappropriately intrusive approach towards the facts of the case might lead to their decision being overturned by the Appellate Body. The Appellate Body's stance in this area thus broadens the decision-making space of the adjudicators.

2179 Guzman 2008, 52.
2180 Walker 1998, 282.
2181 Ibid. who also gives several more reasons in favour of deference.
2182 Lovric 2010, 2.
2183 Gruszczynski 2013, 746; he also discusses some other arguments for deference at 743ff; Fukunaga 2012, 567f.
2184 Zleptnig 2010, 359; Cottier and Oesch 2003, 297.
2185 For an overview, see D'Aspremont and Mbengue 2014, 265ff.
2186 See Christoforou 2000, 646; Du 2010b, 436.

With regard to gap-filling, the observed tendency of the adjudicators to be relatively bold in filling procedural gaps (often by resorting to the VCLT or international law more generally) while being quite reluctant to even acknowledge gaps in substantive law can be linked to the degree to which either of these types of activities might prove controversial. The Appellate Body's crafting of procedural rules is unlikely to be perceived as an overstepping of the boundaries of judicial competence; after all, judicial procedures are the domain of a court and it needs to have rules to work by in order to function.[2187] Indeed, it has been observed that other international courts may be "all the more creative with regard to developments in procedural law and their genuine competences"[2188] than with regard to substantive law. Letting courts write procedural law is probably expedient from a governmental viewpoint;[2189] after all, it is the court that must handle judicial proceedings and negotiating these procedures between states may involve high negotiating costs.[2190] This suggests that episodes such as the fierce protest by WTO Members over the Appellate Body's handling of the admissibility of *amicus curiae* briefs, amongst other controversial issues, must rather be seen as exceptions to the implicit agreement between Members that the rules of the judicial game be developed by the judicial bodies.

The same does not apply to filling gaps in substantive law, which can and has provoked antagonism from WTO Members. This is a plausible explanation for why the adjudicators have generally been more hesitant in this regard. However, it has been observed that they have become somewhat bolder in this regard over time.[2191]

3. *To decide or not to decide – precedents and avoidance techniques*

Another feature of the WTO dispute settlement reports that warrants attention is the extent to which the judicial decision-makers avoid deciding upon certain aspects that are well within their power in a given case. This is related to a second question: If the WTO dispute settlement bodies take a decision on a certain matter, do they decide only the concrete case at

2187 See for example Abi-Saab 2006, 463; van Damme 2009, 136; Bacchus 2005, 518.
2188 Bogdandy and Venzke 2012, 23.
2189 See Terris, Romano, and Swigart 2007, 112.
2190 See Kelly 2002, 382f.
2191 Pauwelyn and Elsig 2012, 455.

hand or do their decisions create a precedent? In other words, do decisions in a given case restrain the scope for WTO judicial decision-making in future cases?

This issue is of relevance in the context of this work as it has an impact on whether a court's decision is perceived as legitimate and why. Certainly, continuity and consistency, and by extension certainty and predictability, are important sources of legitimacy for any adjudicator.[2192] Reference to an existing body of recognized judicial decisions "legitimizes the decision by making it seem the result of neutral and objective application of specifically juridical procedures"[2193]. Moreover, treating like cases alike regardless of the parties involved is a matter of justice[2194] as well as of "equality, fairness, unity, stability, continuity, legal certainty, and the protection of legitimate expectations"[2195]. These are important considerations in a judicial system that, according to the explicit statement in Art. 3.2 DSU, aims to provide security and predictability to the multilateral trading system. Indeed, the role of precedents in WTO law is occasionally discussed against the background of Art. 3.2 DSU.[2196] Inconsistency across decisions would, by contrast, entail a serious risk of undermining the credibility and acceptance of a judicial entity.[2197]

It is also the case, however, that by either adopting a case-specific approach or avoiding a decision on a certain issue in a given case, a judicial body preserves scope for future decisions that may be particularly suitable to that case or may enable it to respond to political pressure in a future case, thereby avoiding criticism of its jurisprudence.[2198] A court that creates precedents is also more likely to be considered activist and law-making,[2199] while judicial economy allows for an amount of judicial self-restraint.[2200] Altogether, a judicial entity's position on a continuum from avoiding a decision in a given case at one pole, through very clearly deciding only the case at hand, to making a decision of (potential) legal rele-

---

2192 Palmeter and Mavroidis 1998, 402; Howse 2001, 51, 60f; Foltea 2012, 139f.

2193 Bourdieu 1987, 832.

2194 Watson 2013, 65; Scully-Hill and Mahncke 2009, 137 who also highlight legal certainty as the other rationale behind *stare decisis*.

2195 Jacob 2012, 51.

2196 See Scully-Hill and Mahncke 2009, 146ff; Bhala 1999a, 878ff.

2197 Chua 1998, 173.

2198 This point is made in particular by McCall Smith 2003.

2199 See Zarbiyev 2012, 8; Bhala 1999a, 848f.

2200 Bhala 1999b, 51.

vance for later cases at the other pole, is closely linked to how it generates acceptance for its decisions.

I will look at several sub-dimensions of this question: The first one (section 3.1) is the extent to which WTO dispute settlement bodies are bound by and refer to earlier case law as precedents in the absence of a formal *stare decisis* rule in WTO dispute settlement. If a decision taken in a certain case has any kind of precedential value, it will do more than merely resolve the concrete matter at hand; it will also refine the existing rules on how matters are to be treated in future disputes. In other words, precedents create "redistribute argumentative burdens in legal discourse in a way that is hard, if not impossible, to escape."[2201]

The second dimension is the extent to which the WTO dispute settlement bodies use "avoidance techniques". The term is taken from Davey, who uses the term "issue avoidance techniques" for techniques that courts have developed to "dispose of issues within cases where a decision seems unnecessary, inappropriate or perhaps simply too controversial".[2202] Such techniques are relevant to the present context, as their use by WTO dispute settlement bodies could be considered an instance of judicial restraint.[2203] If the dispute settlement bodies deliberately refrain from pronouncing themselves and "making law" on certain matters, they also avoid potentially controversial issues.[2204] Avoidance techniques may make it easier to achieve compliance from the losing party[2205] – a party will have lost with regards certain legal questions, but still has a chance of prevailing, in another case, on those not yet decided. In this manner, avoidance techniques may also serve to avoid antagonism or hostile reactions towards the WTO dispute settlement system.

Generally, there are several issues that could be discussed under the heading of avoidance techniques. Davey discusses four of them: limitations on who has standing, restrictions limiting the time at which an action may be brought, categorization of an action as inappropriate for judicial decisions (e.g. because of their political nature), and exercise of judicial economy.[2206] Steinberg mentions a few others such as non-justiciability, *in dubio*

2201 Bogdandy and Venzke 2012, 18.

2202 Davey 2003, 58.

2203 McCall Smith 2003, 95 explicitly states that judicial economy is essentially a "principle of self-restraint".

2204 Steinberg 2004, 269.

2205 This possibility is mentioned, even if not fully supported by Busch and Pelc 2010, 258.

2206 Davey 2003, 59.

mitius, and *non liquet*.[2207] For many tribunals, decisions on justiciability are a very important way of avoiding a decision. By contrast, as described above[2208], the WTO dispute settlement system has compulsory jurisdiction and thus little leeway to avoid judging on a case brought before it. Hence, a negative ruling on justiciability is not a tool readily available to the WTO adjudicators to avoid a decision on a matter. In other words, not all of the avoidance techniques discussed in the literature appear to have *prima facie* relevance in the WTO context. Therefore, I will focus on those avoidance techniques that seem to have been most relevant in WTO dispute settlement so far: the use of judicial economy, discussing a certain matter *arguendo*, and stressing the case-by-case character of certain decisions (3.2). Again, the section concludes with a legal-technical discussion of the case law (3.3) and a more normative-political assessment (3.4).

3.1. Precedents

The Appellate Body has stated repeatedly that the interpretations developed in WTO case law are binding only on the parties to a particular dispute.[2209] Like in international law in general, there is hence no formal rule of *stare decisis* in WTO law.[2210] Nevertheless, the practice of the WTO dispute settlement bodies has been described as "*de facto stare decisis*", the absence of a *stare decisis* rule therefore becoming a "myth".[2211] According to some observers, earlier dispute settlement decisions have "persuasive power", a "tempered type of precedents" has been identified in WTO dispute settlement[2212], and Appellate Body reports have been described as having almost the same "stature" as precedents in common law[2213] or amounting to *de facto* precedents[2214]. It has even been stated that apart from the text of the agreement, the most important source of law in WTO

2207 Steinberg 2004, 269.

2208 See chapter 1, section 4.3.2.

2209 See for example *United States – Measures Affecting the Production and Sale of Clove Cigarettes, WT/DS406/AB/R* 2012, para. 258 with references to earlier reports.

2210 Terris, Romano, and Swigart 2007, 117; Watson 2013, 64.

2211 Bhala 1999a, 849 and passim; Pauwelyn 2016a, 143ff also confirms a "de facto rule of precedent" in the practice of the Appellate Body.

2212 Van Damme 2010, 614.

2213 Pauwelyn 2003d, 125.

2214 Condon 2018, 544.

dispute settlement[2215] is prior dispute settlement decisions, and that few, if any, dispute settlement decisions do not refer back to prior reports[2216]. Bhala observes that the Appellate Body cites precedents when it "seems uncertain of itself",[2217] even when the law being considered is relatively clear. Indeed, the Appellate Body observed the following:

> "Dispute settlement practice demonstrates that WTO Members attach significance to reasoning provided in previous panel and Appellate Body reports. Adopted panel and Appellate Body reports are often cited by parties in support of legal arguments in dispute settlement proceedings, and are relied upon by panels and the Appellate Body in subsequent disputes. In addition, when enacting or modifying laws and national regulations pertaining to international trade matters, WTO Members take into account the legal interpretation of the covered agreements developed in adopted panel and Appellate Body reports. Thus, the legal interpretation embodied in adopted panel and Appellate Body reports becomes part and parcel of the *acquis* of the WTO dispute settlement system. Ensuring 'security and predictability' in the dispute settlement system, as contemplated in Article 3.2 of the DSU, implies that, absent cogent reasons, an adjudicatory body will resolve the same legal question in the same way in a subsequent case."[2218] [footnotes omitted]

The Appellate Body clarified its position on the legal status of previous dispute settlement reports very early in its existence. For adopted GATT reports the Appellate Body stated in one of its first reports:

> "Adopted [GATT] panel reports are an important part of the GATT *acquis.* They are often considered by subsequent panels. They create legitimate expectations among WTO Members, and, therefore, should be taken into account where they are relevant to any dispute. However, they are not binding, except with respect to resolving the particular dispute between the parties to that dispute."[2219]

2215 Palmeter and Mavroidis 1998, 400.

2216 Bhala 1999b, 8.

2217 Ibid.

2218 *United States – Final Anti-Dumping Measures on Stainless Steel from Mexico, WT/DS344/AB/R* 2008, para. 160.

2219 *Japan – Taxes on Alcoholic Beverages, WT/DS8/AB/R, WT/DS10/AB/R, WT/DS11/AB/R* 1996, sec. E, at 14.

In the same case, the Appellate Body also rejected the finding of the Panel that dispute settlement reports constituted "subsequent practice" in the sense of Art. 31.3 b) VLCT, arguing that in this respect a "concordant, common and consistent sequence of acts or pronouncements" was required. By contrast, the GATT Panel reports were, by agreement of the Contracting Parties under GATT, only binding upon the parties to a dispute.[2220] With regard to un-adopted Panel reports, the Appellate Body stated that while they had no legal status in the WTO legal system, they could still serve as useful guidance.[2221] The Appellate Body also made its position clear on why it required Panels to take earlier Appellate Body reports into account:

> "The creation of the Appellate Body by WTO Members to review legal interpretations developed by panels shows that Members recognized the importance of consistency and stability in the interpretation of their rights and obligations under the covered agreements. This is essential to promote 'security and predictability' in the dispute settlement system, and to ensure the 'prompt settlement' of disputes. The Panel's failure to follow previously adopted Appellate Body reports addressing the same issues undermines the development of a coherent and predictable body of jurisprudence clarifying Members' rights and obligations under the covered agreements as contemplated under the DSU. Clarification, as envisaged in Article 3.2 of the DSU, elucidates the scope and meaning of the provisions of the covered agreements in accordance with customary rules of interpretation of public international law."[2222]

Generally, Appellate Body reports are cited more frequently than Panel reports.[2223] Panels have been observed to rely on and conform to Appellate Body reports regularly.[2224] The Appellate Body appears less than amused when a Panel tries to stray from prior case law.[2225] Only in a few cases have

---

2220 Ibid., sec. E, at 13.

2221 Ibid., sec. E, at 14f.

2222 *United States – Final Anti-Dumping Measures on Stainless Steel from Mexico, WT/DS344/AB/R* 2008, para. 160.

2223 Lanye 2003, 231.

2224 Sacerdoti 2006, 49; Hughes 2009, 289.

2225 A good overview of cases where Panels departed from prior Appellate Body cases is provided by Hughes 2009289ff; some examples of particular strong wording of the Appellate Body are given by Lavranos and Viellard 2008, 317; Venzke 2012, 195.

Panels deviated from existing Appellate Body case law without a finding that the cases were different.[2226] In more recent case law, Panels and parties appear to use certain formulations coined by the Appellate Body almost as if they were legal rules. For example, in *EU – Seal Products* the Panel argued that, in the case of trade-restrictive measures, the contribution of a measure to the end pursued needed to be at least "apt" to make a "material" contribution in order to be justified under Art. XX (a) GATT.[2227] With this, it took up an earlier similar formulation from the Appellate Body's *Brazil – Tyres* report. The Appellate Body rejected this approach, indicating that its earlier formulation had been rather soft and a result of the specific circumstances of the case and that it was therefore not to be taken as a generally applicable standard.[2228]

Earlier GATT Panel reports sometimes play a role: One prominent example where an earlier adopted GATT report is cited in a WTO dispute settlement report is the *Shrimp – Turtles* case, where the Appellate Body justified its interpretation of the term "exhaustible natural resources", *inter alia*, by observing that two adopted GATT 1947 Panel reports had found fish to be an "exhaustible natural resource" within the meaning of Art. XX (g).[2229] With regard to unadopted Panel reports it is observed that while they play a somewhat less important role in later cases than adopted ones, they still remain relevant.[2230]

The most puzzling aspect of the use of precedents in WTO case law is how they are used, not the fact that they are, or how often. In some cases, the very fact that a past WTO dispute settlement decision contains a certain interpretation of WTO law seems to be enough for the WTO judicial

---

2226 In a 2008 publication, Zdouc 2008, 373 states that this had in fact only happened in two cases.

2227 *European Communities – Measures Prohibiting the Importation and Marketing of Seal Products, WT/DS400/R, WT/DS401/R* 2013, para. 7.635f.

2228 *European Communities – Measures Prohibiting the Importation and Marketing of Seal Products, WT/DS400/AB/R, WT/DS401/AB/R* 2014, para. 5.213. The earlier formulation by the Appellate Body was: "it appears to us that it would be difficult for a panel to find that measure necessary unless it is satisfied that the measure is apt to make a material contribution to the achievement of its objective".

2229 *United States – Import Prohibition of Certain Shrimp and Shrimp Products, WT/DS58/AB/R* 1998, para. 131 quoting United States – Prohibition of Imports of Tuna and Tuna Products from Canada, adopted 22 February 1982, BISD 29S/91, para. 4.9; *Canada – Measures Affecting Exports of Unprocessed Herring and Salmon*, adopted 22 March 1988, BISD 35S/98, para. 4.4.

2230 Palmeter and Mavroidis 1998, 402.

decision-makers to cite it as a justification for their decision – even if the earlier case does not actually support the finding for which it is invoked in support. Some examples from the case law on Art. XX GATT have already been given above.[2231] For example, in *Korea – Beef* almost the only way that the Appellate Body justified its way of interpreting the necessity requirement in Art. XX (d) GATT was presenting it as being nothing more than an explicit formulation of what was already built into an earlier (GATT) formula from the *Section 337* case.[2232] That an earlier precedent has to bear the burden of justifying what later becomes an entire line of interpretation of one of the central elements of WTO law almost single-handedly is quite astonishing. The picture becomes even more puzzling when one considers that the *Section 337* findings were much less refined than those the Appellate Body proposes in *Korea – Beef* and did not involve any explicit "weighing and balancing" of different factors, contrary to the Appellate Body's implications.[2233] The Appellate Body's reliance on the *Section 337* case to support its weighing and balancing formula in *Korea – Beef* has therefore been described quite correctly as a "far stretch and valiant claim"[2234].

There are other cases where doubts exist (to say the least) on whether a finding that was presented as having been contained in an earlier report actually existed in the way it was quoted. For example, in *China – Raw Materials*, the Appellate Body presented its interpretation of Art. XX (g) GATT, as if it had already been contained in one of its earlier decisions. It stated that in *United States – Gasoline*

> "the Appellate Body did not consider that, in order to be justified under Article XX(g), measures 'relating to the conservation of exhaustible natural resources' must be primarily aimed at rendering effective restrictions on domestic production or consumption. Instead, the Appellate Body read the terms 'in conjunction with', 'quite plainly', as 'together with' or 'jointly with', and found no additional requirement that the conservation measure be primarily aimed at making effective

2231 See chapter 2, section 1.5.3.

2232 *Korea – Measures Affecting Imports of Fresh, Chilled and Frozen Beef, WT/DS161/AB/R, WT/DS169/AB/R* 2000, para. 166.

2233 See chapter 2, section 1.5.1.

2234 Venzke 2012, 205; for a critical position on the Appellate Body's incorrect use of the earlier GATT case, see also Kulovesi 2011, 188.

> certain restrictions on domestic production or consumption"[2235]. [footnotes omitted]

This is, at best, an ambitious reading of the earlier Appellate Body decision; as described above[2236] the Appellate Body had explicitly left the Panel's finding in the *United States – Gasoline* case that measures needed to be "primarily aimed at" conservation unrevised, as the parties had not appealed the finding. Instead, the Appellate Body in the earlier case had simply made a casual statement that the

> "phrase 'primarily aimed at' is not itself treaty language and was not designed as a simple litmus test for inclusion or exclusion from Article XX(g)"[2237].

Indeed, the Panel in the *China – Raw Materials* case had taken the Appellate Body in the *United States – Gasoline* case to have ruled

> "that a measure was 'relate[d] to' conservation if there was a substantial relationship between the export measures and conservation, and 'that a measure must be *'primarily aimed at'* the conservation of exhaustible natural resources in order to fall within the scope of Article XX(g)[2238]".[2239]

In other words, the Panel and the Appellate Body in the *China – Raw Materials* case read the earlier report on *United States – Gasoline* by the Appellate Body quite differently from one another.

Another example is the *EC – Biotech Products* Panel's characterization of Art. 5.7 SPS. The Panel discussed at quite some length whether the norm was an exception in relation to Art. 5.1, 2.2 SPS or an "autonomous right". The Panel opted for the latter. It did so cognizant of an earlier finding of the Appellate Body that had described Art. 5.7 SPS as a "qualified exemption", albeit without an in-depth deliberation of the matter. The Panel,

---

2235 *China – Measures Related to the Exportation of Various Raw Materials, WT/DS394/AB/R, WT/DS395/AB/R, WT/DS398/AB/R* 2012, para. 358.

2236 See chapter 2, section 1.2.4.

2237 *United States – Standards for Reformulated and Conventional Gasoline, WT/DS2/AB/R* 1996, sec. III B, at 18.

2238 The original footnote in the Panel report is: "Appellate Body Report, *US – Gasoline*, p. 18, DSR 1996:I, 3, at p. 17 (emphasis added)".

2239 *China – Measures Related to the Exportation of Various Raw Materials, WT/DS394/R, WT/DS395/R, WT/DS398/R* 2012, para. 7.370. However, the Panel in turn omitted from its quote the part where the Appellate Body said that the phrase "primarily aimed at" was not itself treaty language.

rather than simply explaining that and why it disagreed with the Appellate Body's casual statement, embarked instead on something of a discursive high wire act. Its argument rested on a claim that the terms "exemption" and "exception" were semantically different from one another, and that the Appellate Body would certainly have spoken about "exception" if, unlike the Panel, it had considered Art. 5.7 SPS to be an exception rather than an autonomous right.[2240] Also, it has been noted that the Panel's reliance on an allegedly established distinction between rules, exceptions and qualified exemptions/autonomous rights – on which it bases its position on the relationship between Art. 5.1 and 5.7 SPS – was a misreading of the piecemeal earlier case law.[2241] The Panel in the *EC – Biotech Products* case is also likely to have mis-read earlier case law in other respects. Herwig argues that the Panel in *EC – Biotech Products* adopted a narrower conception of science than warranted by earlier case law on the SPS Agreement. In this case, the Panel rejected the EU's argument that the purpose of a measure matters when judging whether the scientific evidence was sufficient for risk assessment purposes. Herwig argues that this position seems to be based on a selective reception of prior SPS dispute settlement reports. In particular, she points to the Appellate Body's statement in *Hormones I* that Panels reviewing the scientific basis of a measure should bear in mind that governments act on the basis of prudence and caution when irreversible risks are concerned.[2242]

The fact that the WTO dispute settlement bodies seem, at least in some instances, to make precedents fit for their purposes and seek to avoid any appearance of being out of line with an earlier Appellate Body finding, shows how much weight precedents are given in WTO dispute settlement. Several other aspects of the practice of the WTO dispute settlement bodies corroborate that both the bodies themselves and the Members accord a legal value to the settlement reports that reaches beyond the settlement of the case in hand.[2243] First, rather than reverse the ultimate findings and recommendations of a Panel, the Appellate Body is regularly seen to amend the legal analysis and reverse part of the conclusions in a Panel report.[2244] This only makes sense if a dispute settlement report does more

2240 *European Communities – Measures Affecting the Approval and Marketing of Biotech Products, WT/DS291/R, WT/DS292/R, WT/DS293/R* 2006, para. 7.2972.

2241 Broude 2006, 12.

2242 Herwig 2008, 835.

2243 See Lanye 2003, 232ff.

2244 Van Damme 2010, 614.

than settle the dispute at hand. In some instances, parties will not appeal a Panel's ultimate findings, merely some of the intermediate ones. For example, in *EC – Seal Products*, the Panel found that an EU measure provisionally justified under Art. XX (a) GATT violated the terms of the chapeau.[2245] The complainants accepted the overall conclusion, but appealed certain parts of the Panel's findings, notably that the Panel used the same test under Art. 2.1 TBT and the chapeau.[2246] Moreover, the frequent involvement of third parties in the dispute settlement proceedings also shows that WTO Members attribute a value to them that goes beyond the settlement of individual cases; otherwise they would not need to get involved in cases regarding measures they have neither taken themselves nor consider disturbing enough to file a complaint against. Also, the fact that in some cases the winning parties have appealed the decisors' findings[2247] indicates that they on occasion attribute them a significance transcending the individual case.

Courts can use two main strategies when they wish to avoid the decision taken in an earlier case that is *prima facie* similar enough to the case at hand to be considered a precedent: differentiating between the cases, i.e. pointing out why the prior case is in fact not relevant for the later, and departing from or overruling precedents.[2248]

It does not appear that the Appellate Body has yet modified one of its earlier interpretations, that is, it has neither departed from nor overruled precedents, at least not explicitly. There are, however, a few cases in which discussions were had regarding whether a later case was sufficiently different from an earlier case to warrant departure from the earlier line of reasoning. These cases have mostly been relatively recent. In *Hormones I,* for example, the Appellate Body rejected the Panel's reliance on the Appellate Body's interpretation of the chapeau for interpreting Art. 5.5 SPS "in view of the structural differences" between the legal provisions. In the same case, it also clarified that an earlier appellate decision taken under Art. III:2 GATT could not be used for inferences under the chapeau in another case.[2249] Another example is the *China – Rare Earths* case. Like the earlier *China – Raw Materials* case, it dealt with export restrictions on certain raw

2245 *European Communities – Measures Prohibiting the Importation and Marketing of Seal Products, WT/DS400/R, WT/DS401/R* 2013, para. 7.644.

2246 *European Communities – Measures Prohibiting the Importation and Marketing of Seal Products, WT/DS400/AB/R, WT/DS401/AB/R* 2014, para. 2.146ff.

2247 For examples see Weiler 2009, 141.

2248 Jacob 2012, 64f.

2249 *European Communities – Measures Concerning Meat and Meat Products, WT/DS26/AB/R, WT/DS48/AB/R* 1998, para. 239.

materials and a certain provision in China's Accession Protocol. Even though it had been decided in the earlier *Raw Materials* case that China could not invoke Art. XX GATT as justification for a breach of the respective provision in its Accession Protocol, China raised this issue again in the later *Rare Earths* case. China put forward new arguments that, it said, had not been asserted or addressed earlier.[2250] In considering China's new arguments, the Panel concluded that China had not presented any "cogent reason" for departing from the decision in the earlier case. Here, it relied on an earlier finding by the Appellate Body in the *United States – Stainless Steel* case that cogent reasons were required for departing from precedent. Interestingly, a dissenting opinion within the Panel argued that China should be allowed to rely on Art. XX GATT for justifying a breach of the controversial norms in its Accession Protocol.[2251] China's appeal on the matter was limited, extending only to a rejection of one of its "new" arguments for the applicability of Art. XX GATT to the relevant provision of China's Accession Protocol. In response, the Appellate Body did not explicitly ascertain the existence of "cogent reasons" for departing from its earlier decisions; yet it did approve the way that the Panel had dealt with China's arguments. Hence, the Appellate Body upheld both the Panel's findings in the current case and the earlier precedent.[2252] In *EC – Seal Products*, the Appellate Body discussed whether the measures at issue in this case and the earlier *EC – Asbestos* case were structurally similar enough to warrant a similar decision on the applicability of the TBT Agreement in the later case. The Appellate Body decided against it.[2253] In the same case, it also held that the approach in earlier case law towards ascertaining whether a measure was to "protect" health in the sense of Art. XX (b) GATT was not pertinent for finding out whether a measure protected public morals under Art. XX (a) GATT; the Appellate Body considered the two regulatory goals as being too different in character.[2254]

In sum, there is a marked reliance on precedents in the WTO case law, i.e. the Appellate Body presents and justifies its decisions as being embedded in existing case law; the Appellate Body's approach has therefore been

---

2250 China's arguments are summarized in *China – Measures Related to the Exportation of Rare Earths, Tungsten, and Molybdenum, WT/DS431/AB/R, WT/DS432/AB/R, WT/DS433/AB/R* 2014, para. 5.4ff.

2251 Finding of the Panel as summarized in ibid., para. 1.13, 5.7.

2252 Ibid., para. 5.8–5.74.

2253 *European Communities – Measures Prohibiting the Importation and Marketing of Seal Products, WT/DS400/AB/R, WT/DS401/AB/R* 2014, para. 5.41ff.

2254 Ibid., para. 5.197f.

characterized as "*de facto stare decisis*". Yet in practice, the Appellate Body often does not always use the existing cases as proper precedents.

3.2. Avoidance techniques (and their opposites)

In the following section I will focus my discussion on two avoidance techniques: judicial economy and taking a decision based on an argument *arguendo*. While both techniques are regularly used in WTO dispute settlement to avoid making a decision, there are occasions in which the adjudicators do the opposite – they decide on matters that are not strictly necessary to settle the dispute in hand. I will also consider this aspect of WTO settlement behaviour.

The Appellate Body has indicated that WTO adjudicators should avoid deciding too much, and their statement to this end is a useful starting point for discussing these aspects of WTO case law:

> "[g]iven the explicit aim of dispute settlement that permeates the DSU, we do not consider that Article 3.2 of the DSU is meant to encourage either panels or the Appellate Body to 'make law' by clarifying existing provisions of the WTO Agreement outside the context of resolving a particular dispute. A panel need only address those claims which must be addressed in order to resolve the matter in issue in the dispute."[2255]

Given that parties often bring more arguments and claims than are needed to find that a measure is inconsistent with WTO law, it suggests, the WTO dispute settlement bodies need ways of legitimately dodging such "superfluous" claims.

Judicial economy is one such way. Generally, judicial economy has been defined as an approach whereby a judicial entity attempts to "settle as many issues as possible in a single proceeding".[2256] WTO proceedings, however, use the term in a different manner, namely to refer to the practice of the WTO dispute settlement bodies to "rule not to rule on certain of the litigants' legal arguments, deeming these unnecessary to solving the

2255 *United States – Measures Affecting Imports of Woven Wool Shirts and Blouses from India, WT/DS33/AB/R* 1997, sec. VI, at 19.

2256 Cameron and Gray 2001, 281f.

dispute at hand".[2257] Judicial economy is not mentioned explicitly in any WTO provision.[2258]

The Appellate Body has condoned the use of judicial economy in principle by stating that Panels are not required to address all arguments of parties, but only those necessary to resolve a claim.[2259] This finding has been cited by subsequent Panels.[2260] The Appellate Body has also called judicial economy a "prudential dictate" in one case.[2261] While merely one amongst many avoidance techniques, judicial economy is the most frequently used;[2262] it was used in 41 % of the Panel cases decided between 1995 and 2005.[2263]

Some examples of how Panels have used judicial economy are the following: In *EC – Asbestos*, certain claims under the TBT Agreement were not decided by the Panel, because a violation of GATT and lack of justification under Art. XX had already been found.[2264] In *EC – Biotech Products*, the Panel observed that it did not have to take into account a non-WTO international treaty that was inapplicable to all parties of the dispute. It then went on to state that

> "the present case is not one in which relevant rules of international law are applicable in the relations between all parties to the dispute, but not between all WTO Members, and in which all parties to the dispute argue that a multilateral WTO agreement should be interpreted in the light of these other rules of international law. Therefore, we need not, and do not, take a position on whether in such a situation we would be entitled to take the relevant other rules of international law into account."[2265]

2257 Busch and Pelc 2010, 257.

2258 Pauwelyn 2003a, 208.

2259 See for example *European Communities – Measures Affecting the Importation of Certain Poultry Products, WT/DS69/AB/R* 1998, para. 135.

2260 *Mexico – Tax Measures on Soft Drinks and Other Beverages, WT/DS308/R* 2005, para. 8.143.

2261 *European Communities – Measures Concerning Meat and Meat Products, WT/DS26/AB/R, WT/DS48/AB/R* 1998, para. 251.

2262 Busch and Pelc 2010, 260.

2263 Ibid., 257.

2264 *European Communities – Measures Affecting Asbestos and Products Containing Asbestos, WT/DS135/R* 2000, para. 6.43.

2265 *European Communities – Measures Affecting the Approval and Marketing of Biotech Products, WT/DS291/R, WT/DS292/R, WT/DS293/R* 2006, para. 7.72.

The Panel could also have resolved the matter by taking such a position and thus contributing to the clarification of this important and often disputed legal issue. However, it chose not to. In the *EC – Biotech Products* case the Panel seems to have resorted to judicial economy concerning most of the violation claims brought before it. The Panel did not decide on a violation of Art. III:4 and XI GATT after it had already found a violation of certain procedural rules of the SPS Agreement.[2266] A finding on Art. III:4 GATT might have been quite controversial as it would have required a statement on whether genetically modified products were "like" their conventional counterparts.[2267] Moreover, the Panel did not decide on a violation of Art. 5.6, 5.5 SPS, and the first requirements of Art. 2.2. and 2.3 SPS, either, after a violation of Art. 5.1 SPS had already been found.[2268]

In some cases, the Appellate Body quite deliberately held a Panel to deciding only that which strictly needed to be decided in a certain case. In *EC – Sardines*, the Panel made a finding on the trade-restrictiveness of a certain measure, but did not make any finding on Art. 2.2 TBT, the article which needed this particular finding. The Appellate Body consequently declared the Panel's finding on trade-restrictiveness moot and without legal effect.[2269] In other words, the Panel did not exercise judicial economy and the Appellate Body reversed its finding. James Bacchus, a former Appellate Body Member, rejects general criticism of an alleged "overreaching" by the Appellate Body by pointing to the fact that time and again, the Appellate Body has trimmed

> "the legal reasoning of panels and tempered the legal rulings of panels when the reasoning or the rulings were not needed to reach a 'positive solution' in a particular dispute? Literally hundreds of pages of panel reports have been erased by the Appellate Body on appeal for that reason."[2270]

2266 Ibid., para. 7.2505, 7.3422, 7.3429.

2267 Goh and Morgan 2007, 482.

2268 See *European Communities – Measures Affecting the Approval and Marketing of Biotech Products, WT/DS291/R, WT/DS292/R, WT/DS293/R* 2006, para. 7.3377, 7.3384, 7.3393f and 7.3405 respectively.

2269 *European Communities – Trade Description of Sardines, WT/DS231/AB/R* 2002, para. 311.

2270 Bacchus 2005, 508.

However, the Appellate Body appears to have shifted its approach towards the exercise of judicial economy by Panels: where initially it promoted its use, in later case law it is less active in such encouragement.[2271]

The Appellate Body has itself also resorted to judicial economy, such as in *United States – Gasoline.* [2272] Here, the question was whether the reference in the chapeau to "countries where the same conditions prevail" referred to conditions in exporting as compared to importing countries or to conditions in different exporting countries. The Appellate Body did not decide the issue as none of the parties had contested the applicability of Art. XX GATT in the case of a violation of Art. III:4 GATT, the national treatment obligation, where an importing and exporting countries are always involved. The Appellate Body found some support in the GATT for the position of the parties, but ultimately concluded there was

> "no need to decide the matter of the field of application of the standards set forth in the chapeau nor to make a ruling at variance with the common understanding of the participants".[2273]

In *United States – Gambling*, the Appellate Body decided not to make a finding on the necessity of the US measures under Art. XIV (c) GATS having found that they came under Art. XIV (a) GATS.[2274]

A second avoidance technique occasionally used in WTO dispute settlement is an argumentation *"arguendo"*. *"Arguendo"* means literally "for the sake of an argument". It denotes situations where one side agrees on a hypothetical basis to accept certain factual or legal points made by another party in order to construe, on this basis, an argument, mostly for the purpose of refuting the opponent's view. In *Shrimp – Turtles*, the Appellate Body observed that *if* a territorial nexus between the state taking the measure and the resources protected was required by Art. XX (g) GATT, it was, in any event, present, given the migratory habits of sea turtles; the Appellate Body did not elaborate on whether a territorial nexus was indeed required.[2275] In another case, the issue was whether Art. XX (d) GATT was available as a justification for breaching a norm of the Anti-Dumping

2271 Alvarez-Jiménez 2009b, 396ff.

2272 For more examples see ibid., 400ff.

2273 *United States – Standards for Reformulated and Conventional Gasoline, WT/DS2/AB/R* 1996, sec. IV, at 24.

2274 *United States – Measures Affecting the Cross-Border Supply of Gambling and Betting Services, WT/DS285/AB/R* 2005, para. 335–337.

2275 *United States – Import Prohibition of Certain Shrimp and Shrimp Products, WT/DS58/AB/R* 1998, para. 133.

Agreement. Instead of answering the primary question of the applicability of Art. XX (d) GATT, the Appellate Body first looked "*arguendo*" at whether the measure at issue was "necessary" in the sense of Art. XX (d) GATT. Having answered this question in the negative, it did not deal with the logically primary question of whether Art. XX (d) GATT could be invoked at all for justifying a violation of anti-dumping disciplines.[2276]

However, the Appellate Body has put some limits to the use of the *arguendo* technique and stated that

> "reliance upon an assumption arguendo is a legal technique that an adjudicator may use in order to enhance simplicity and efficiency in decision-making. Although panels and the Appellate Body may choose to employ this technique in particular circumstances, it may not always provide a solid foundation upon which to rest legal conclusions. Use of the technique may detract from a clear enunciation of the relevant WTO law and create difficulties for implementation. Recourse to this technique may also be problematic for certain types of legal issues, for example, issues that go to the jurisdiction of a panel or preliminary questions on which the substance of a subsequent analysis depends. The purpose of WTO dispute settlement is to resolve disputes in a manner that preserves the rights and obligations of WTO Members and clarifies existing provisions of the covered agreements in accordance with the customary rules of interpretation of public international law. In doing so, panels and the Appellate Body are not bound to favor the most expedient approach or that suggested by one or more of the parties to the dispute."[2277] [footnotes omitted]

There are some instances, where, by these standards, the Appellate Body found that a Panel should not have proceeded *arguendo*. The Appellate Body did not accept, for example, that in *China – Audiovisual Products* a Panel had assumed *arguendo* that a deviation from China's Accession Protocol could be justified, in principle, under Art. XX (a) GATT. The Panel had then found that the conditions of Art. XX (a) GATT were not met, relieving it of the necessity to pronounce itself on the matter whether

2276 *United States – Measures Relating to Shrimp from Thailand, WT/DS343/AB/R* 2008, para. 310.

2277 *China – Measures Affecting Trading Rights and Distribution Services for Certain Publications and Audiovisual Entertainment Products, WT/DS363/AB/R* 2009, para. 213f.

Art. XX (a) GATT was actually available as a defence to China.[2278] The Appellate Body did not approve of this approach, saying that

> "the Panel's analysis rest upon an uncertain foundation as a result of the absence of a ruling on the applicability of Article XX(a) in this case. In addition, the absence of clarity on the issue of whether China may rely on Article XX(a) as a defence to a violation of paragraph 5.1 of its Accession Protocol may leave the participants uncertain as to the regulatory scope that China enjoys in implementation and as to whether any implementing measure is, in fact, consistent with China's WTO obligations or susceptible to further challenge in proceedings under Article 21.5 of the DSU."[2279]

This argument is somewhat surprising; as just described above, the Appellate Body had indeed proceeded in a manner similar to the Panel in an earlier case.

Besides judicial economy and *arguendo*, the dispute settlement bodies have sometimes used other justifications for not deciding a certain matter.[2280] In *EC – Asbestos*, the Appellate Body declined to decide on the applicability of the TBT Agreement on a variety of grounds, including that the case presented novel issues not previously decided in WTO case law.[2281] At least one eminent scholar has criticized this decision of the Appellate Body as legally non-defensible.[2282] In the *EC – Biotech Products* case, the complainants had asked the Panel to decide on the EU's decision not to process certain requests for the approval of marketing of GMOs within the EU over an extended period of time. Some of these requests had already been withdrawn at the time of the Panel's establishment. The parties disagreed whether the Panel should still decide on the matter. The Panel decided that its decision would not be required to "secure a positive solution of the dispute", as set forth in Art. 3.7, second sentence DSU as an ob-

2278 *China – Measures Affecting Trading Rights and Distribution Services for Certain Publications and Audiovisual Entertainment Products, WT/DS363/R* 2009, para. 8.2(a)(ii).

2279 *China – Measures Affecting Trading Rights and Distribution Services for Certain Publications and Audiovisual Entertainment Products, WT/DS363/AB/R* 2009, para. 215.

2280 For more examples *see* Howse 2016b, 66ff; Lang 2016, 1101f.

2281 *European Communities – Measures Affecting Asbestos and Products Containing Asbestos, WT/DS135/AB/R* 2001, para. 78–83.

2282 Pauwelyn 2002.

jective of the WTO's dispute settlement system.[2283] Hence it did not decide on these claims. On the other hand, the Panel in *EC – Biotech Products* did – like other Panels before it – decide on measures that had ceased to exist after its establishment, but before its actual decision.[2284]

Finally, the adjudicators have sometimes declined to decide on a matter, because there was a consensus among the parties. For example, in *United States – Gasoline*, one of the first cases decided after the WTO's establishment, the term "relating to" in Art. XX (g) GATT played a role; the Appellate Body noted that both opponents accepted the interpretation that this clause meant "directly aimed" and consequently did not examine the matter in more depth.[2285] Only in later cases did it revise that interpretation that dated back to the old GATT times. Another, somewhat curious instance where a Panel simply decided not to decide is the following discussion of Art. 5.6 SPS in *Australia – Salmon*:

> "We referred above to several options without deciding that one of these would necessarily meet Australia's ALOP. We have been convinced, however, that there are other measures available [...] that would achieve Australia's ALOP. We leave it up to Australia, preferably in a close cooperation with Canada and other trading partners, to select and identify the details of such other measures."[2286]

Here, the Panel's argument is very vague, as it does not even clearly identify a specific, less trade-restrictive measure that would lead to a statement of violation of Art. 5.6 SPS.

In some cases, the Appellate Body stated explicitly that taking a decision on a certain matter was not "prudent" in light of, for example, the politically or legally controversial nature of a certain issue. For example, both the Appellate Body in the *Hormones I* case and the Panel in the *EC – Biotech Products* case considered that it would not be "prudent" for them to make a statement on the status of the precautionary principle in international law, in light of ongoing debates on that matter.[2287]

2283 *European Communities – Measures Affecting the Approval and Marketing of Biotech Products, WT/DS291/R, WT/DS292/R, WT/DS293/R* 2006, para. 7.1647ff.

2284 See ibid., para. 7.1668ff including references to earlier case law.

2285 *United States – Standards for Reformulated and Conventional Gasoline, WT/DS2/AB/R* 1996, sec. III B, at 18.

2286 *Australia – Measures Affecting Importation of Salmon, WT/DS18/R* 1998, para. 7.144.

2287 *European Communities – Measures Affecting the Approval and Marketing of Biotech Products, WT/DS291/R, WT/DS292/R, WT/DS293/R* 2006, para. 7.89;

In other instances, the adjudicators simply seem to avoid certain potentially controversial findings – without explicitly making use of judicial economy, *arguendo*, or stating that they have deliberately avoided taking an "imprudent" decision. For example, the Appellate Body has never described any policy goal of a WTO Member as unimportant in the balancing exercises under Art. XX GATT or XIV GATS. Rather, it has struck down measures, because alternative measures were reasonably available.[2288] Obviously, the latter is a much less normative, superficially facts-based assessment and hence likely to be less controversial than calling a policy goal pursued by a sovereign state "unimportant". It has also been observed that while Panels have sometimes stated that a WTO Member's measures did not serve the objective of compliance in the sense of Art. XX (d) GATT, contrary to the claims of the respective Member, there is no similar statement, for example, on Art. XX (b) GATT. Fontanelli argues that this is because it is (politically) more difficult for a Panel to state that a measure does not protect health purposes than it is to state that the measure does not serve compliance.[2289] Moreover, sometimes a case is decided on the basis of the fact that a WTO Member has not discharged its burden of proof (e.g. when invoking a justification norm) – rather than on the basis of a finding that a Member violated WTO law. A finding based on the burden of proof is less severe for the losing party, as it can still make a similar claim in a future case that is built on better evidence.[2290] Yet another example is that in recent cases involving the TBT Agreement measures were struck down for being incompatible with Art. 2.1 TBT (because of being discriminatory) rather than for being incompatible with Art. 2.2 TBT (because of being unnecessary); this has been attributed to the fact that the Appellate Body may be more comfortable with assessing the discriminatory nature of a measure rather than its necessity for certain public policy goals.[2291] The Appellate Body's decision in *EC – Large Civil Aircrafts* can also be mentioned in this regard. In this case, the Appellate Body decided it did not need to interpret the term "the parties" in Art. 31.3 c) VCLT, because irrespective of whether a certain EU-US bilateral agreement was to be considered "law applicable between the parties" in

European Communities – Measures Concerning Meat and Meat Products, WT/DS26/AB/R, WT/DS48/AB/R 1998, para. 123.

2288 Lovric 2010, 145f.

2289 Fontanelli 2012, 44.

2290 This point is made by Cho 2009a, 699.

2291 Shaffer 2012, 6.

the sense of this norm, it was not relevant in this case.[2292] How the term "the parties" in Art. 31.3 c) VCLT is to be interpreted is an issue of huge systemic significance for the relationship between WTO law and non-WTO international law, and potentially even for the relationship between different international legal instruments beyond the WTO universe. Deciding, as the Appellate Body did, whether a certain provision of a bilateral agreement between the EU and the US concerning subsidies for the development of aircrafts was of relevance for the interpretation of one word in one of provision of the SCM is an issue of much less overall legal and political significance – and therefore likely to be much less controversial among the WTO membership at large. Yet another example is the *EC – Biotech Products* Panel report. The Panel discussed whether in interpreting certain terms of WTO law, certain non-WTO treaties needed to be taken into account. The Panel, when dismissing these other treaties as irrelevant to the interpretation of WTO law, stated that the EU, which had argued in favour of taking the non-WTO treaties into account, had not explained how the non-WTO provisions were relevant to the interpretation of the WTO provisions at issue in the dispute.[2293] Yet, as Howse points out[2294], the relevance of the non-WTO norms is very evident from the pleadings of the EU; the Panel nonetheless fails to explain why it does not consider these norms relevant. Here, the Panel's avoidance technique seems to consist in somehow mis-representing what a party had said or simply ignoring the rather obvious.[2295]

Examples can also be given where the legal interpretations embraced by the adjudicators are relatively protective of WTO Members' regulatory freedom, but the latter application of the rules, as interpreted in WTO dispute settlement, is not. Typically, the interpretation of a certain norm contrary to the wishes of relevant constituencies is liable to provoke criticism either in greater quantities or of a fiercer nature than if a norm is applied in a questionable manner. This is because while a norm might be applied differently in a future case, its interpretation could be taken as a precedent. Hence, a judicial decision-maker who wishes to avoid antagonizing the audience might be well advised to reach a certain outcome by drawing on

2292 *European Communities and Certain Member States – Large Civil Aircraft, WT/DS316/AB/R* 2011, para. 844ff.

2293 *European Communities – Measures Affecting the Approval and Marketing of Biotech Products, WT/DS291/R, WT/DS292/R, WT/DS293/R* 2006, para. 7.95.

2294 Howse 2008, 658.

2295 Ibid., 658.

factual particularities of the case, rather than by indulging in potentially far-reaching interpretations.

Example can be found in SPS case law. There are several statements made by the Appellate Body signalling that WTO Members have a certain leeway when conducting a risk assessment. It appears, however, that in practice WTO Members' risk assessments are subject to significant scrutiny. WTO Members' risk assessments have, as a result, been consistently held as falling short of the requirements of Art. 5.1 SPS. Another example, relating to an aspect of WTO dispute settlement not discussed in this work, are non-violation complaints. Alvarez notes that while the Appellate Body has in principle accepted non-violation complaints, very few such complaints have been successful.[2296] What is common to these examples is that while the legal rules formulated by the Appellate Body are relatively permissive on states, they quite significantly restrict WTO Members' regulatory behaviour when applied in a concrete case.

Avoidance techniques are not only a means of avoiding potentially controversial issues. They are also a means of keeping the future decision space for the WTO dispute settlement bodies open, thereby allowing them to react flexibly to the circumstances of future cases, including political sensitivities.[2297] Dispute settlement bodies effectively employ another "technique" for this purpose when they stress that certain decisions can only be made on a case-by-case basis. One example, relating to the interpretation of Art. III GATT, is the following:

> "WTO rules are reliable, comprehensible and enforceable. WTO rules are not so rigid or so inflexible as not to leave room for reasoned judgments in confronting the endless and ever-changing ebb and flow of real facts in real cases in the real world. They will serve the multilateral trading system best if they are interpreted with that in mind. In that way, we will achieve the 'security and predictability' sought for the multilateral trading system by the Members of the WTO through the establishment of the dispute settlement system."[2298]

In other words, the Appellate Body here says that "security and predictability" will be attained on an individual, case-by-case basis – somewhat unusual, slightly Orwellian approach towards seeking these objectives. Moreover,

2296 Alvarez in Abi-Saab 2008, 712.

2297 McCall Smith 2003, 79.

2298 *Japan – Taxes on Alcoholic Beverages, WT/DS8/AB/R, WT/DS10/AB/R, WT/DS11/AB/R* 1996, sec. H 2 c, at 31.

the statement makes it sound as if the Appellate Body considers that the interpretation of WTO law always warrants a case-by-case approach.

Some other examples of where a flexible, case-by-case approach to interpreting central provisions of WTO law has been used are the following:

For the interpretation of whether two products are "like", WTO jurisprudence has identified four criteria to be taken into account. Whether these lead to the conclusion, in a concrete case, that two products are "like" is a highly case-specific decision, involving, in the words of the Appellate Body in *Japan – Alcoholic Beverages*, "an unavoidable element of individual, discretionary judgement"[2299] or, in the words of the *EC – Asbestos* Panel, a "degree of discretionary judgement".[2300] In this case, the Panel also rejected a certain interpretation that had been suggested by one party because that interpretation would not have been consistent with the flexibility given to Panels and the Appellate Body when examining the issue of likeness.[2301] The Appellate Body in *United States – Gasoline* also stated that the relationship between Art. I, III, XI and XX GATT could only be given meaning on a case-by-case basis.[2302] Similarly, according to the Appellate Body, Art. 5.5 SPS warrants a case-by-case approach. Several factors, warning signals or indicators may cumulate in the finding of a violation of Art. 5.5 SPS.[2303] Equally, the Appellate Body's approach to interpreting the chapeau of Art. XX GATT has been described as involving flexibility;[2304] the Appellate Body here stresses that the "line of equilibrium" contained in that article needs to be fixed on a case-by-case basis.[2305]

Yet the adjudicators do not always avoid deciding matters they need not decide when resolving a dispute. For example, in *China – Measures Affecting Imports of Automobile Parts,* the Panel investigated the Chinese measures under Art. XX (d) GATT. Having concluded that the controversial Chinese measure did not satisfy the first requirement contained in Art. XX (d) GATT, namely that measures needed to be designed to ensure compliance with certain laws or regulations, it still went on to investigate

2299 Ibid., sec. H 1 a, at 20f.

2300 *European Communities – Measures Affecting Asbestos and Products Containing Asbestos, WT/DS135/R* 2000, para. 8.114.

2301 Ibid., para. 8.123.

2302 *United States – Standards for Reformulated and Conventional Gasoline, WT/DS2/AB/R* 1996, sec. III B, at 18.

2303 *European Communities – Measures Concerning Meat and Meat Products, WT/DS26/AB/R, WT/DS48/AB/R* 1998, para. 240.

2304 Ortino 2004, 244f.

2305 See Venzke 2012, 202.

whether the measure was "necessary" to this end.[2306] In *China – Audiovisual Products*, China had claimed that its measures were taken to protect public morals in line with Art. XX (a) GATT, and this was not contested by the other party.[2307] Still, the Panel elaborated on the meaning of the phrase "to protect public morals",[2308] only to conclude that given that neither of the parties disputed that the controversial measures protected public morals, it could proceed with its analysis of the remainder of Art. XX (a) GATT *under the assumption* that the measure did, indeed, protect public morals. The Appellate Body has also welcomed this approach as expedient.[2309]

By contrast, the Appellate Body has been described as reluctant to formulate *obiter dicta*,[2310] i.e. statements that are not necessary for resolving the dispute at hand. Yet there are some examples where the Appellate Body makes statements not necessary for deciding a case. For example, in *EC – Asbestos*, the Appellate Body arrived at the conclusion that the measures in dispute did not violate Art. III:4 GATT (or any other rule of the GATT). Nonetheless, it still investigated whether the conditions of Art. XX GATT were met. In a different case, the Appellate Body had found that it did not need to consider certain arguments by a party concerning an alleged misinterpretation of a certain norm by the Panel, because it had already found a flaw in the Panel's analysis. Nevertheless, it went on to address both some of the arguments raised and certain aspects of the Panel's finding, using the opportunity to clarify to which extent it agreed with the arguments brought forward by the party.[2311] It has also been claimed that the discussion by the Appellate Body in the original *Shrimp – Turtles* decision on an alleged territorial limitation inherent to Art. XX GATT was not necessary for deciding the case.[2312] Indeed, the Appellate Body left the

---

2306 *China – Measures Affecting Imports of Automobile Parts, WT/DS339/AB/R, WT/DS340/AB/R, WT/DS342/AB/R* 2008, para. 7.348.

2307 *China – Measures Affecting Trading Rights and Distribution Services for Certain Publications and Audiovisual Entertainment Products, WT/DS363/R* 2009, para. 7.756.

2308 Ibid., para. 7.757ff.

2309 *United States – Measures Affecting the Cross-Border Supply of Gambling and Betting Services, WT/DS285/AB/R* 2005, para. 344.

2310 See for example Ruiz Fabri 2006, 131.

2311 *Australia – Measures Affecting the Importation of Apples from New Zealand, WT/DS367/AB/R* 2010, para. 403ff.

2312 Venzke 2012, 199ff.

question open in that case – but then it would not have needed to touch upon it at all.

By way of summary, there are several manners in which the adjudicators avoid deciding matters in any given case, and while it would be incorrect to suggest that they employ them whenever possible, it is certainly common.

3.3. Discussion

In this section I will summarize the insights taken from the above analysis, with a focus on legal-doctrinal matters as relate to both precedents and judicial economy respectively.

The Appellate Body's approach to precedents is not, on the surface, categorically different from that of other international judicial bodies. Precedents in the purest form of a *stare decisis* rule exist in common law systems but international law is no such system: it has been argued that it is closer to civil law.[2313] The rationales for using precedents as discussed are, however, also valid in international law – that is, to assure not only equity and predictability, but also coherence and consistent legal reasoning.

This is probably why relying on precedents has become a "general and omnipresent" concept in international judicial decision-making[2314], despite the absence of positive legal provisions on the matter. A soft, non-binding form of precedent, described sometimes as "persuasive precedent", exists, for example, in the ICJ's case law[2315] – even though Art. 59 of the ICJ Statute explicitly stipulates that ICJ decisions only have binding force between the parties to a dispute.[2316] In this respect, the WTO's approach to precedents has been observed to be similar to that of the ICJ.[2317] Some find

2313 For a discussion of the roles of precedents in different legal systems, see Blackmore 2004, 496ff.

2314 Jacob 2012, 36.

2315 The legal starting point for the ICJ is somewhat different from that of the WTO dispute settlement bodies, though. Art. 38.1 (d) of the ICJ Statute stipulate that judicial decisions may be taken into account as a supplementary means of interpretation. This is subject to the provision in Art. 59 ICJ Statute, though, according to which an ICJ decision only has binding force between the parties to the particular dispute.

2316 See *United States – Final Anti-Dumping Measures on Stainless Steel from Mexico, WT/DS344/AB/R* 2008, n. 308 referring to the earlier *Japan – Alcoholic Beverages* case.

2317 Chua 1998, 183.

the idea of a non-binding precedent as apparently embraced by the Appellate Body illogical; for example, Bhala argues that what makes a precedent a precedent is the very idea that it would bind a court in a later similar case.[2318] However, not everyone agrees. Jacobs, for example, maintains that "a crude binary understanding of a case's normativity ('binding or not')" is too simplistic and does not adequately describe how precedents are used in practice.[2319] This question is not, however, specific to WTO dispute settlement.

What is perhaps more specific to WTO dispute settlement is how explicit the relevant bodies have been on their assessment of the status of prior decisions. Just as they make transparent both the interpretive methods they use and their reasons for using them, so they are clear and explicit about the legal status of precedents in the WTO legal order. Given the logical problems with a notion of non-binding precedent, it would not have been a surprise had the adjudicators quietly integrated the occasional reference to prior case law into their findings. Instead, they made a point of stating that prior decisions created legitimate expectations.

There is on particular critical aspect about the WTO adjudicators' approach to precedents: they often and on very central issues seem to misquote earlier cases or at least are silent on smaller or larger shifts in their jurisprudence while they could (and probably should) have explicitly departed from an earlier case or have indicated why a later case was unlike the former. Others have noted that in certain instances there are tensions between the approaches of the Appellate Body in different cases.[2320] While it is difficult to identify any single legal norm in WTO law or outside of it that mandates that precedents be used correctly, the rationales behind the use of precedents require that precedents be used correctly. For example, if precedents are used to ensure equality before the law, using false precedents would lead to different situations and individuals being treated alike before the law – thus failing to meet the standard of equality before the law. In conclusion, the notion that precedents are to be used in a manner that is faithful to the case in which they were set is inherent in the concept of precedents – but the WTO adjudicators do not always use precedents in this way.

The WTO approach here appears to be different from that of the ICJ, for example. The ICJ seldom departs from precedent, but on those occasions

---

2318 Bhala 1999a, 917ff.

2319 Jacob 2012, 49.

2320 Howse and Essermann 2006, 65; Howse 2016b, 13.

that it does it presents its reasons for doing so.[2321] The Appellate Body, however, appears not to have explicitly departed from one of its own earlier decisions. Not only does it not explicitly depart from earlier decisions, it very rarely distinguishes a later case from an earlier one in order that it might avoid following a precedent. There are a few cases, in particular more recent ones, where the Appellate did explicitly decline to rely on earlier case law on the grounds that the cases were dissimilar. The ICJ, on the other hand, seems to resort to such distinctions more frequently in order that it is not compelled to follow the line of reasoning adopted in earlier cases.[2322] However, the need for departing from prior case law or distinguishing between cases may also become more pronounced at a later stage of the existence of the WTO dispute settlement system, when more cases have been decided.[2323]

I will now turn to the second issue: judicial economy. It is a technique also used by other judicial bodies. Cass considers judicial economy to be a "staple tool of constitutional interpretation"[2324] and international judicial bodies use judicial economy, too.[2325] Others hold that issues related to judicial economy are particularly common in WTO dispute settlement.[2326] This may, of course, be due to the fact that other international courts have a wider array of instruments at their disposal to avoid decisions on certain issues, notably the declaration of certain claims as inadmissible.[2327]

Generally, the Appellate Body gives Panels a lot of latitude regarding if and when they might exercise judicial economy.[2328] Two main situations have been identified in which the Appellate Body itself exercises judicial economy: when assessing a certain question of substantive law that does not have to be decided to solve the dispute at large, and when a case does not appear an appropriate occasion to make a very important ruling, given the details of the case.[2329]

2321 Watson 2013, 78f; see also Jacob 2012, 66.

2322 Jacob 2012, 64.

2323 See also Bhala 1999b, 128.

2324 Cass 2001, 63.

2325 Alvarez-Jiménez 2009b, 409.

2326 Bohanes and Sennekamp 2006, 425.

2327 For example, Slaughter and Helfer 1997, 313f observe that both the ECtHR and the ECJ sometimes have declined to decide on the merits of a case, declaring it inadmissible.

2328 Busch and Pelc 2010, 258.

2329 Alvarez-Jiménez 2009b, 403.

Occasionally, observers have claimed that the use of judicial economy or other avoidance techniques by the dispute settlement bodies were inappropriate for a given case.[2330] A legal argument that could be made in favour of such a position is that according to Art. 3.4 DSU, the dispute settlement bodies are to aim at "a satisfactory settlement of the matter in accordance with the rights and obligations" resulting from WTO law. If avoiding a decision on a certain issue does not lead to the resolution of the dispute in question, then use of judicial economy or any other such technique constitutes a violation of that norm. In the cases discussed here, however, avoidance techniques have only been used after a violation of a WTO norm had already been found and it was therefore clear that the defending Member needed to bring its laws or practice in conformity with WTO law. This can be considered as sufficient for satisfactorily settling a dispute in the sense of Art. 3.4 DSU.

Moreover, one might argue that not deciding on matters that could have been decided amounts to a violation of Art. 3.2 DSU, which holds that the dispute settlement system is a central element in providing security and predictability to the multilateral trading system. Decisions on legal issues not indispensable for solving the dispute at hand may indeed be of interest to the parties involved in a dispute or the wider WTO membership and could make the interpretation and application of WTO law more predictable. Nevertheless, Art. 3.2 DSU does not give WTO Members a right to obtain a judicial decision on any matter not required for solving the dispute at hand; the DSU does not provide WTO Members with the option of soliciting something akin to advisory opinions of the ICJ. Thus, it is not evident that the use of judicial economy or other avoidance techniques would violate Art. 3.2 DSU. It has been claimed that the Appellate Body's using of judicial economy is hardly consistent with Art. 17.12 DSU, which requires that the Appellate Body "address each of the issues raised during the appellate proceedings".[2331] What, however, is an "issue" – any individual claim raised? Or might it be a situation where a certain measure was taken whose overall WTO compatibility needs to be ascertained, but without the need to review each and every legal issue that the situation raises? Both appear to be plausible readings, suggesting that there is nothing wrong

2330 See for example Delimatsis 2011, 283 with regard to the Panel's discussion of Art. XX GATT in *China – Audiovisual Products*; Cho 1998, 8 with regard to the Appellate Body's decision in EC-Asbestos not to discuss claim under the TBT.

2331 Flett 2011, 31; for some other statements to the end that the Appellate Body may not resort to judicial economy see Alvarez-Jiménez 2009a, 393f.

with the Appellate Body's approach from a legal-doctrinal point: other courts have also been seen to exercise judicial economy.

When taken as a whole, the strong reliance on precedents when combined with a toolbox of avoidance techniques and the insistence that some issues can only be decided on a case-by-case basis, in effect gives the WTO dispute settlement bodies great flexibility on which matters to decide in a given case (and with effect for future cases) and which matters to leave undecided.

3.4. Assessment

This section is about how the observed approach towards precedents and avoidance techniques taken by the WTO dispute settlement bodies, and in particular the Appellate Body, can be explained and what this means in terms of justifying and legitimizing its decisions.

The picture presented thus far may appear puzzling at first sight. On the one hand, the Appellate Body appears to be very committed to precedents and sometimes decides on more than is strictly necessary. On the other hand, the adjudicators also resort to judicial economy quite frequently. The Appellate Body regularly avoids deciding on controversial issues or maintains flexibility for future cases by insisting on the case-by-case character of a certain decision. In other words, while there is an approach of generating interpretations that transcend individual cases, sometimes in cases where these interpretations are not needed for settling the individual case at hand, and relying on these interpretations in later cases, it is also true that attempts are made simply to avoid such case-transcendent findings.

This picture is probably the result of the fact that both the consistent use of precedents and the avoidance of certain, potentially controversial findings can help legitimize a judicial decision.

Let us first take a look at precedents. Precedents provide a formal legal argument that a judicial decision-maker can rely on. Using them allows a judge to appear compelled to abide by existing legal rules and thus avoid giving the impression of creating new legal rules. Not openly acknowledging frictions and turns in the case law – as the Appellate Body does – makes sense, if constructing a uniform and consistent body of law is an important part of a strategy of generating acceptance for judicial decisions by adding authority and credibility to the adjudicators' new decisions.[2332] Or,

---

2332 See Bhala 1999a, 940.

to quote Venzke's more elegant phrasing relating to an instance where the Appellate Body quoted an earlier report for what the report had not said:

> "If nothing else, it testifies to the Appellate Body's endeavor to connect its interpretations to precedents and to instantiate new meanings within prevalent discursive structures."[2333]

However, in other instances, the creation of a precedent may not be opportune in first place. This thinking is evident from statements by two formers Members of the Appellate Body. The first statement is by James Bacchus:

> "[...] *more* [reasoning] is sometimes *less* in treaty interpretation. The Appellate Body is ever mindful that the words of sentences that are included in appellate reasoning in one case can have a way of taking on life of their own in later cases. [...] It is for this reason that examples of *obiter dicta* are rare in Appellate Body."[2334] [italics in original]

Claus-Dieter Ehlermann states:

> "A more principled, less case-specific, approach would certainly carry the risk that the Appellate Body would have to correct its reasoning in future appeals. I recognize that, to a certain degree, this process of refining and adapting existing administrative practice and jurisprudence to new situations is inherent in the application of general rules by administrators and judges, and therefore unavoidable. I do not believe however that the Appellate Body should increase the likelihood of being obliged to correct the reasoning set out in one of its earlier reports. Such corrections would do even greater harm to the 'security and predictability of the multilateral trading system', than the questions that the Appellate Body leaves open today in following its rather narrow, case-specific approach. In addition, such corrections would probably be detrimental to the credibility of the Appellate Body and thus affect its legitimacy."[2335]

These statements lend plausibility to observations in the literature that techniques such as judicial economy are used in WTO dispute settlement to avoid (potentially) controversial findings.[2336] The only academics to have investigated the use of judicial economy (by Panels) in depth and

2333 Venzke 2012, 205.
2334 Bacchus 2005, 514.
2335 Ehlermann 2002, 638.
2336 For such an observation, see Shany and Shlomo-Agon 2014, 207.

from a sound empirical basis are Busch and Pelc.[2337] They maintain that whether or not judicial economy is exercised by a Panel is a function of the positions of third parties in a dispute and their preferences. In particular, they claim, Panels rely on so called mixed submissions, where third parties side with each of the parties on some arguments or comment on the interpretation of WTO law more broadly. Busch and Pelc argue that such submissions act as signals to the Panelists identifying the prevailing controversies among WTO Members and by implication on political consequences of setting certain precedents that should be avoided – signals the Panelists then follow.[2338] They do so, because they would prefer to

> "gain litigants' compliance, avoid appeal, or, in the alternative have their findings upheld by the Appellate Body [...]. Since verdicts become part of the jurisprudence that governs dispute settlement, panels have to consider the broader ramifications of ruling on all of the litigants' arguments in establishing a broader or narrower precedent, not least because the AB has incentive to be politically savvy as well."[2339]

Busch and Pelc also conclude, on the basis of their statistical analysis, that health and safety disputes are more likely to involve a reliance on judicial economy, a finding they relate to the fact that scientific findings change and Panels would therefore want to avoid setting precedents.[2340] They also find that statistically speaking, judicial economy is more likely to be exercised when the US or the EU are in the defendant role.[2341] The idea that the Appellate Body uses judicial economy strategically is also confirmed by the fact that it sometimes consults with parties during proceedings to understand whether they desire a decision on a specific aspect or whether the exercising of judicial economy is feasible.[2342] However, there are also competing explanations in the literature. For example, Alvarez-Jiménez states that not deciding a certain issue is also a way of dealing with internal disagreement among the judicial decision-makers on a certain issue.[2343] Bohanes and Sennekamp, however, contend that judicial economy comes up

2337 Busch and Pelc 2010; their study is based on a statistical analysis of all (105) Panel reports between 1995 and 2005, looking at how the use of judicial economy is linked to third-party participation, see 268ff.
2338 Ibid., 259.
2339 Ibid., 264.
2340 Ibid., 274.
2341 Ibid., 274f.
2342 Alvarez-Jiménez 2009a, 413.
2343 Ibid., 311.

so frequently in WTO dispute settlement because there is often overlap between the multiple WTO agreements and WTO Members therefore tend to bring numerous claims at once.[2344] The fail to control for whether fewer claims are brought by parties in other judicial forums where judicial economy is exercised less frequently.

It is also worth noting that the use of precedents and avoidance techniques are interrelated: not deciding on legally or politically controversial issues in a given case may become a more important approach where there is a strong reliance on precedents in a system.[2345] Indeed, some observers see the wide use of judicial economy in WTO dispute settlement as a strategy to narrow precedents.[2346] A similar perspective can also be garnered from two statements by former Members of the Appellate Body.

Altogether, the evidence that the adjudicators use "judicial economy" strategically consists of published statements by former Appellate Body Members and the comprehensive statistical analysis by Busch and Pelc which covers all the cases decided by Panels over a certain period. At the same time, adjudicators do not go so far as to leave undecided matters that must be decided upon in order that the dispute in question might be resolved. The existence of an appellate stage means that Panels may want to create an alternative legal basis for their findings, in case the Appellate Body rejects a particular conclusion.[2347] They may also seek to establish a factual record sufficient for the Appellate Body to be able to proceed on a different legal basis from that considered relevant in the Panel report. Indeed, instances have been identified where Panels have actively reacted to this risk by indicating that on some claims they could have exercised judicial economy, but did not do so in order that they might give the Appellate Body an established factual basis in case of appeal.[2348] The Appellate Body in its turn has not dodged complex issues whenever a ruling was needed to resolve a certain dispute.[2349] Taken together, the adjudicators appear to be careful about when and on what issues they create precedents, but once the precedents have been created, they become a central part of the adjudicators' strategy of legitimation.

2344 Bohanes and Sennekamp 2006, 441f.
2345 Bhala 1999b, 48.
2346 Busch and Pelc 2010, 258; Ruiz Fabri 2006, 131f.
2347 Davey 2003, 70.
2348 See Bohanes and Sennekamp 2006, 442ff; Busch and Pelc 2010, 261.
2349 Alvarez-Jiménez 2009b, 413.

Generally, there is no agreement on which is better, a case-transcendent, strongly precedent-based judicial system or one with flexible case-by-case decisions (leaving open here by what standards "good" or "bad" are defined). Not only do individual observers disagree on the matter, but different legal systems have different fundamental approaches: representatives of common law systems, where individual cases have a central role, may tend to emphasize the gains in efficiency, effectiveness and contextual sensitivity that a more case-oriented approach brings. Lawyers from other systems may harbour reservations on that score.[2350] In WTO law, the picture is equally divided: some claim that the Appellate Body's presentation of an interpretation not strictly needed to settle the case at hand is (inappropriate) judicial policymaking.[2351] Others, conversely, have chided the Appellate Body for avoiding to decide issues that it could have decided, claiming this has led to a lack of clarity, transparency and predictability[2352] or have called for transforming the *de facto stare decisis* approach into a *de jure stare decisis* rule[2353]. Similarly, there are also widely divergent views on the use of judicial economy in WTO dispute settlement: while some would like to see more judicial economy, others would like to see less.[2354]

All in all, the judicial approaches and techniques discussed in this section – namely the construction, usage and avoidance of precedents and the circumventing of controversial issues through such techniques as judicial economy, *arguendo* and stressing the case-by-case character of a certain decision – give the adjudicators considerable flexibility on what issues to decide in which case and which they might better leave aside. It is reasonable to assume that the adjudicators have used these tools quite deliberately to avoid producing judgements that might prove too controversial. At the same time, they appear to have sought to establish for themselves and the judicial mechanism they serve a reputation of producing defensible, methodologically sound judicial decisions – and precedents contribute to this purpose. Behind the creation and use of precedents loom larger issues of whether a court engages in (inappropriate) judicial law-making – and

---

2350 See Jacob 2012, 40.

2351 See for example with regard to the Appellate Body's report in *EC – Asbestos* Yavitz 2002, 64.

2352 Cho 1998, sec. II C.

2353 Bhala 1999a, 850.

2354 For sources on both positions, see Busch and Pelc 2010, 258. For the latter position, see Quick and Blüthner 1999, 635 who call the Appellate Body's use of judicial economy on some of the claims in dispute in *EC – Hormones* "surprising, if not legally shocking"; Cho 1998, 8 of the online text.

this is an impression that the WTO adjudicators have, so far as such a conclusion is possible based on published records, been keen to avoid.[2355]

4. The use of substantive principles and balancing

The next aspect of the WTO case law that I turn to is the use of substantive principles, including the proportionality principle, and balancing by the WTO dispute settlement.

In chapter 1, I elaborated on the reasons why it is significant whether a court uses balancing to substantiate its decisions or whether it does not. When balancing, a court moves away from the formalist, deductive method of interpretation that presents the judge as interpreter rather than the maker of the law. Balancing generally shifts the power from legislator to court, the consequences of which depends on how the courts choose to exercise this power.

It is nonetheless widely recognized that balancing is, in principle, a legitimate way of arriving at a judicial decision in situations where the law is indeterminate. Still, a court that engages intensively in balancing is more vulnerable to charges of judicial activism than one that does not; in the words of two observers, the "idea of balancing tests in contexts where domestic regulation is subject to international scrutiny has been anathema to judicial restraint and national sovereignty" to many.[2356] Therefore, this chapter explores whether the WTO dispute settlement bodies engage openly in balancing, i.e. whether they actually use the term balancing or at least terms reminiscent of a balancing exercise. In line with the overarching subject of this chapter, this discussion is not concerned with the *substantive* balance struck between economic and other interests at the end of a case, but with the *reasoning* used.

Balancing may be performed in different situations. In particular, judges resort to it when the law uses normatively tainted and relatively vague terms such as "appropriate", "equity" or "justifiable". Indeed, balancing seems to be more widely accepted in such situations than when the language of the law is less vague and normative.[2357]

2355 For example, Ruiz Fabri 2006, 131 sees a reason for the "casuistic approach" of the Appellate Body in an attempt to not appear as making law.
2356 Bown and Trachtman 2009, 119.
2357 See chapter 1, section 3.1.

Judges may engage in balancing in different ways. For example, the US Supreme Court has been described as looking for societal and political values existing in society, when engaging in balancing, rather than basing its decision on values which would appear as the judges' personal ones. In other words, its balancing could be seen as primarily descriptive or empirical; this approach to balancing has immunized the Court against charges of judicial activism.[2358] Another interesting aspect is whether or not the values and interests that the respective court uses in balancing have a textual foundation or not (e.g. a state's interest in the effective functioning of a certain institution will usually not be mentioned explicitly in the text of law). A court that refers in its balancing exercise to interests that are not explicitly mentioned in an international treaty or a national law is likely to be seen as more "activist" than one that does not. As a corollary, for a complete picture of balancing in the WTO dispute settlement, it is not only important to notice if any explicit balancing occurs, but also in which textual situations and in what way it is carried out.

Balancing is often seen as being closely related to the use of principles, as opposed to the application of rules. As discussed above[2359], the distinction between principles and rules is often made along the following lines: Typically, principles are seen as general, basic or underlying assumptions or precepts and embody fundamental regulatory purposes or values.[2360] Rules, however, are based on an "if ... then" structure. As a corollary, principles and rules function differently in collision cases. Robert Alexy describes the difference as follows: Where the "... then" parts of two rules mandate different things in a certain factual situation, one of those rules must be invalid or inapplicable: the decision to be made is which rule to ignore. Principles work differently as they provide certain aspects that must always be taken into account when a case is decided. Where two principles collide, the judicial decision-maker must take each into consideration. Where two principles contradict each other, she will have to decide which of them is more important in the case at hand and take the decision accordingly; this does not mean that the either principle is invalid, just that one is less weighty than the other in the concrete case.[2361] In other

2358 Aleinikoff 1987, 963.
2359 See chapter 1, section 1.
2360 Mitchell 2007, 797; Hilf 2001, 112; Andenas and Zleptnig 2007, 376f.
2361 Alexy 1995, 216–219; Dworkin 1981, 24–28.

words, various principles need to be balanced against each other.[2362] Balancing and principles are related.

Whether or not principles are given a prominent role in a judicial entity's decision-making process says something about the role that the entity assumes for itself. While rules are normally made by the legislator, judges often decide on the existence and application of principles.[2363] The use of broad principles has been linked to a risk of judicial activism.[2364] Principles are a means of clarifying provisions that are ambiguous or contradictory, or of dealing with gaps,[2365] all quite sensitive judicial activities. Moreover, it has also been noted that among the established methods of interpretation, the teleological approach provides the strongest support for using principles;[2366] as explained above,[2367] teleological interpretation affords judges more discretion than other methods.

The focus in the present context is on the use of substantive principles rather than procedural ones. As has been shown above,[2368] procedural principles of international law are used quite regularly in WTO dispute settlement. With few exceptions, the use of such principles has been relatively uncontroversial given that judicial procedures are the original domain of a court.[2369] Moreover, it should be noted that it is not those principles contained explicitly in a certain WTO agreement that are of interest here. Undoubtedly, a WTO dispute settlement organ could draw on any such explicit principle. The more interesting question is whether the WTO dispute settlement bodies identify or create unwritten principles underlying the WTO legal order upon which they subsequently base any substantive findings. An example from a different jurisdiction is the ECJ's use of the proportionality principle as general principle,[2370] which had not been en-

2362 Mitchell 2007, 798; Hilf 2001, 116.

2363 Trachtman 1999, 353 speaks of "standards" rather than principles, but the way he defines "standards" is quite similar to the way that "principles" are usually defined.

2364 Zeitler 2005, 753.

2365 Mitchell 2007, 796; Hilf and Goettsche 2003, 11f.

2366 Mitchell 2007, 802.

2367 See chapter 1, section 3.1.

2368 See above section 1.6.3.

2369 This is the same rationale for why the WTO adjudicators appear to be less reluctant to fill gaps in procedural law in first place, see above section 2.5.

2370 For the proportionality principle see Neumann and Tuerk 2003, 202.

shrined explicitly in EU primary law when it was first used in the ECJ's jurisprudence.[2371]

The principle of proportionality is particularly important in the present context, as it is closely related to balancing – indeed its very purpose is to assist in decisions on trade-offs between different interests. How the proportionality principle is used, tells us much about "the nature, if not the maturity of a particular legal system"[2372]. As has been described in more depth above[2373], balancing is the final step of a three-pronged proportionality test in some legal orders like the EU legal order or German public law. What has been said about balancing is also true for the use of the proportionality principle: It gives judges an apparently active role[2374] in deciding a case, and therefore carries the risk of charges of judicial activism resulting from this type of judicial decision-making.

The section is structured as follows: I will first discuss the use of unwritten substantive principles in WTO dispute settlement, including a general discussion and a more in-depth discussion of the proportionality principle in WTO law (section 4.1). After this, I will discuss if and how the dispute settlement bodies engage in balancing, above and beyond the use of principles (section 4.2). The results of the analysis will then be assessed with regard to what it means for the dispute settlement judicial style (section 4.3).

4.1. The use of unwritten (substantive) principles

To make the scope of the analysis clearer, it should first be noted that the WTO legal order does occasionally feature the word "principle". For example, the preamble of the WTOA refers broadly to the "basic principles" of the WTO legal order.

One example is contained in Art. III:2 GATT which refers to "the principles set forth in paragraph 1"; from this it can be concluded that Art. III:1 GATT, which sets forth a national treatment rule, contains a "principle". For example, in the *EC – Asbestos* case, the Appellate Body said

2371 The case usually cited as being the first in which the ECJ recognized the principle of proportionality is case C-11/70 (Internationale Handelsgesellschaft), see Jacobs 1999, 1. In this case, the ECJ, after a thorough review of possible alternatives, found that the regulation in dispute was both "necessary and appropriate" for the end pursued (para. 12).

2372 Desmedt 2001, 442.

2373 See chapter 1, section 3.1.

2374 Andenas and Zleptnig 2007, 384.

the following about the term "less favourable treatment" embodied in Art. III:4 of the GATT 1994:

> "The term 'less favourable treatment' expresses the general *principle*, in Article III:1, that internal regulations 'should not be applied [...] so as to afford protection to domestic production'. If there is 'less favourable treatment' of the group of 'like' imported products, there is, conversely, 'protection' of the group of 'like' domestic products."[2375] [emphasis added]

Similarly, in *Canada – Renewables* the Appellate Body wrote that

> "the national treatment *principle* enshrined in Article III has been a cornerstone of the multilateral trading systems since its inception."[2376] [emphasis added]

In terms of the definitions given above, however, Art. ...'Art. III:1 GATT and the subsequent paragraphs have the character of rules rather than principles. This being the case, the reference to principles in the above quotations cannot be considered as reliance on (unwritten) substantive principles in the sense initially described. Similarly, the Appellate Body has also referred to the right of Members to choose their appropriate level of protection as a "principle", apparently using the word without attaching further legal value to it.[2377] Moreover, it could be argued that certain identical ideas or fundamental precepts underlie articles in various agreements. This is true, for example, for non-discrimination (e.g. Art. 2 GATS, Art. III GATT, Art. 5.5 SPS), elements of proportionality (Art. 2.1 and 2.2 TBT, Art. 5.4 and 5.6 SPS, Art. XX GATT, Art. XIV GATS, Art. 9.1 Anti-Dumping Agreement, Art. 22.4 and 22.6 DSU, Art. 5.1 of the Agreement on Safeguards)[2378] or articles regulating certain aspects of transparency and good governance (Art. 7 SPS, Art. 10 TBT). These "principles" come, however, in the form of written norms that are specific and define the legal consequences of a certain behaviour. Reference to such "principles" is not

---

2375 *European Communities – Measures Affecting Asbestos and Products Containing Asbestos, WT/DS135/AB/R* 2001, para. 100.

2376 *Canada – Certain Measures Affecting the Renewable Energy Generation Sector, WT/DS412/AB/R and Canada – Measures Relating to the Feed-in Tariff Program, WT/DS426/AB/R* 2013, para. 5.55.

2377 *Brazil – Measures Affecting Imports of Retreaded Tyres, WT/DS332/AB/R* 2007, para. 210.

2378 These provisions have been described in the literature as proportionality-related, see the references in note 2389 below.

related to a specific mode of judicial reasoning, where judges are particularly creative and decide to which extent certain principles apply. The "principles" appear to have no significance in the WTO case law that goes beyond the interpretation and application of the mentioned specific rules. Thus, when applying the distinction between rules and principles outlined above, they would have to be classified as rules rather than as principles.

The word "principle" moreover appears regularly when the Appellate Body draws on non-WTO international law in deciding a case. The role of international law in WTO dispute settlement has been discussed above.[2379] Some aspects of the above analysis are relevant from the viewpoint of how the Appellate Body uses principles and therefore need to be summarized here: First, the Appellate Body uses non-WTO international legal principles to clarify procedural matters and its own judicial competences. Second, the Appellate Body draws on certain "principles" enshrined in the VCLT, for example "*pacta sunt servanda*" (Art. 26 VCLT) and the non-retroactivity of treaties (Art. 28 VCLT). Again, it is doubtful whether these are really principles in the sense it has been defined above. Neither of these two articles can be applied to a degree or are open-ended, stipulating no clear legal consequences; rather they present clear rules of behaviour for states or conditions for the application of treaties. Again, even though the Appellate Body refers to them as principles, they must rather be classified as rules.[2380] Moreover, references to the VCLT are not unusual for a court interpreting international agreements. Even if some of the provisions of the VLCT could be classified as principles rather than rules, using them would likely not convey a picture of the Appellate Body as being particularly "creative" or "activist".

Yet the Appellate Body also draws on some principles of international law that are neither enshrined in the VCLT as such nor purely procedural in character. Examples given in the analysis of the use of international law above are effective treaty interpretation, *in dubio mitius*, good faith, the

2379 See above, section 1.6.

2380 A reason why the Appellate Body relates to e.g. Art. 26 VCLT as a principle may be that the article codifies what was recognized as a principle of international law before the VCLT was adopted; see on the status of "pacta sunt servanda" as a principle of international law, Schmalenbach in: Dörr and Schmalenbach 2012, Art. 26, para 4. Yet the fact that a norm is called a "principle" of international law does not necessarily mean that it is also a principle as understood here. That a norm is labelled as "principle" rather than as a "rule" in international law may be due to the fact that general "principles" are a recognized source of international law, but "rules" are not.

protection of legitimate expectations, *estoppel* and state responsibility. The Appellate Body has relied on a variety of sources for ascertaining the existence of these principles, including ICJ judgements and the writing of scholars. While the actual existence of these principles in international law is not beyond doubt in all cases,[2381] the Appellate Body presents them as principles whose existence is uncontroversial. Moreover, most of these principles are neutral in the sense that they would not foster a certain substantive outcome of cases. For example, the principle of effective treaty interpretation can be used to strengthen obligations contained in WTO law aimed at preventing WTO Members from erecting trade barriers; at the same time, it can and has been used also to strengthen the role of exceptions in favour of non-trade measures. The Appellate Body appears hesitant regarding the role of international legal principles in the WTO legal order, stating in one case that even if a relevant principle existed it

> "does not, by itself, and without a clear textual directive to that effect, relieve a panel form the duty of applying the normal principles of treaty interpretation in reading the provisions of the agreement".[2382]

In line with this, even though the Appellate Body uses the word "principle" regularly and actually draws on some rather neutral principles of general international law, it is in tendency rather reluctant to rely on substantive principles not explicitly contained in WTO law that are less neutral in content or more controversial in international law.

For example, the Panel in *China – Raw Materials* drew extensively on the principle of sovereignty over natural resources[2383]; however, the Appellate Body did not refer to the principle at all. Similarly, in *China – Raw Materials*, the Appellate Body rejected any overarching "right to regulate trade"[2384] which could justify China's departure from the obligations assumed in its Accession Protocol. As observed above, the Appellate Body has also declined to recognize the existence of a principle of institutional balance within the WTO.[2385] Moreover, the Appellate Body in *Hormones I* did not recognize any general precautionary principle in WTO law (or out-

---

2381 See above section 1.7.3.

2382 *European Communities – Measures Concerning Meat and Meat Products, WT/DS26/AB/R, WT/DS48/AB/R* 1998, para. 124.

2383 *China – Measures Affecting Imports of Automobile Parts, WT/DS339/AB/R, WT/DS340/AB/R, WT/DS342/AB/R* 2008, para. 7.378ff.

2384 *China – Measures Related to the Exportation of Various Raw Materials, WT/DS394/AB/R, WT/DS395/AB/R, WT/DS398/AB/R* 2012, para. 300ff.

2385 See above section 2.3.

side of it), that could inform the interpretation of WTO norms.[2386] Instead, the dispute settlement bodies have only acknowledged that Art. 5.7 SPS "reflects" the precautionary principle. Likewise, the Panel did not examine a claim by the EU in the *EC – Biotech Products* case that its measures were based on the precautionary principle and should be allowed to stand.[2387]

With regard to the proportionality principle, some authors have attempted to frame the substantive requirements of various agreements in terms of a proportionality test[2388], while others have pointed to the presence of certain proportionality elements in various WTO agreements.[2389] However, what is of interest here is not how each of the requirements of these norms has been interpreted – this is discussed at length in the previous chapter. The question here is whether proportionality as an overarching principle or concept has informed the jurisprudence of the WTO dispute settlement system above and beyond what is written.

The WTO dispute settlement bodies have not developed a "binding, unitary proportionality jurisprudence across a multitude of obligations".[2390] An exception to the general statement of the absence of the proportionality principle in WTO law is the area of counter-measures where the Appellate Body has actually referred to the principle of proportionality.[2391] In this regard it has been observed that the proportionality principle as recognized in customary international law is generally less restrictive on a state's countermeasures against the behaviour of another state than WTO law is on trade-related countermeasures, but that relevant WTO rules still have been interpreted so as to conform to the principle as applied in international customary law.[2392] Given that countermeasures are not within the focus of this work, this issue is not discussed any further here.

2386 See above section 1.6.4.

2387 *European Communities – Measures Affecting the Approval and Marketing of Biotech Products, WT/DS291/R, WT/DS292/R, WT/DS293/R* 2006, para. 7.3221.

2388 Neumann and Tuerk 2003, 211f; Desmedt 2001, 454–462; Marceau and Trachtman 2002, 824–832; Neumann 2002, 441–483; Montini 2001, 150–155; Andenas and Zleptnig 2007, 405ff; Osiro 2002; Hilf and Goettsche 2003, 20ff; Epiney 2000, 84; Cheyne 2006, 270f.

2389 Bossis 2001, 346; Cottier et al. 2017, 645ff; Desmedt 2001, 443; Eckert 1995, 373; Lovric 2010, 134ff; Palmeter and Mavroidis 1998, 408; Van den Bossche 2008, 286ff.

2390 Lovric 2010, 137. See also Andenas and Zleptnig 2007, 380; Neumann and Tuerk 2003, 231f.

2391 Hilf and Goettsche 2003, 26ff; Andenas and Zleptnig 2007, 380 with quotes from the case law.

2392 Desmedt 2001, 453.

The fact that the WTO dispute settlement bodies rarely make use of an overarching proportionality principle when interpreting substantive provisions of WTO law does not mean that the WTO adjudicators never use the language or concept of proportionality. Indeed, it has been observed that the Appellate Body's approach under Art. XX GATT "structurally resembles the proportionality analysis in other areas of international law"[2393]. This is not too surprising given that some of the requirements contained in various WTO agreements can be read as elements of proportionality.[2394] For example, when discussing the controversial US measure in *Shrimp – Turtles* under Art. XX (g) the Appellate Body observed the following:

> "In its general design and structure [...] Section 609 is not a simple, blanket prohibition of the importation of shrimp imposed without regard to the consequences (or lack thereof) of the mode of harvesting employed upon the incidental capture and mortality of sea turtles. Focusing on the design of the measure here at stake, it appears to us that Section 609, *cum* implementing guidelines, is not disproportionately wide in its scope and reach in relation to the policy objective of protection and conservation of sea turtle species. The means are, in principle, reasonably related to the ends."[2395] [emphasis added]

Here, whether a measure is proportionate to its aim is discussed in order to assess whether the measure complies with a certain norm of WTO law that does not explicitly refer to proportionality. Reference to "proportionality" here is used as a way of interpreting the term "relating to" in Art. XX (g) GATT and does not constitute reliance on an overarching principle. Similarly, in *Korea – Beef*, the Panel stated when discussing the compatibility of a measure with the necessity criterion under Art. XX (d) GATT that for certain reasons a Korean measure was "disproportionate".[2396] Again, the Panel's use of the language of proportionality here is related to the interpretation of a certain term that can be characterized as "propor-

2393 Andenas and Zleptnig 2007, 412.

2394 This seems to be the reason why Hilf 2001, 210 identifies the proportionality principle as one of the more basic principles of WTO law. However, for the present purpose I am interested in principles in the sense above, i.e. norms that inform WTO case law above and beyond the interpretation of specific articles.

2395 *United States – Import Prohibition of Certain Shrimp and Shrimp Products, WT/DS58/AB/R* 1998, para. 141.

2396 *Korea – Measures Affecting Imports of Fresh, Chilled and Frozen Beef, WT/DS161/R, WT/DS169/R* 2000, para. 674–675.

tionality-related". However, "proportionality" is not as such used consistently by the WTO dispute settlement for interpreting the necessity criterion.

Altogether, the Appellate Body relies on some principles established in international law, but probably employs the word "principle" even more frequently in situations where no principle as the term is understood here is at stake. Indeed, it has been observed that almost every Appellate Body report contains references to principles.[2397] While this is true, it does not mean that each and every claim of legal commentators on the existence of certain substantive principles in WTO law is correct or meaningful, when the term principle is used in the sense employed here. For example, Hilf identifies the following substantive principles in WTO law: trade liberalization, non-discrimination, sovereignty and national deference, sustainable development, cooperation and multilateralism, transparency, rule of law, and proportionality[2398]; he claimed, already in 2001, that the WTO legal system had become "principle-oriented".[2399] While analysing his arguments on each of the principles in detail is beyond the scope of this work, it can generally be observed that some of what he classifies as principles are rather objectives enshrined in the preambles of various WTO agreements (e.g. trade liberalization, sustainable development) or an idea behind several concrete rules of WTO law rather than overarching and independently applied principles in the sense that the term is understood here (e.g. transparency and proportionality). The latter also applies to Bogdandy's reference to the most favoured nation principle and the principle of non-discrimination.[2400] Bloche identified, at an early stage of WTO dispute settlement, an "interpretive principle" of deference to national policy, noting a certain interpretive pattern in the WTO case law.[2401] How Bloche's reading of the case law leads to the inference that there is an interpretive principle of deference is unclear, however, as an observable pattern of outcomes or interpretative approaches is not the same as a legal principle. The author appears to make no claim that the Appellate Body has explicitly recognized such a principle; moreover, it is doubtful whether a pattern of deference to national health measures indeed exists[2402]. Another scholar, Lydgate, main-

2397 Hilf 2001, 116.

2398 Cottier et al. 2017, 654 also maintain that the "general principle of proportionality is implicitly recognised in WTO law".

2399 Hilf 2001, 114ff.

2400 Bogdandy 2001, 641.

2401 Bloche 2002, 831ff., 831ff.

2402 See above sections 2.1 and 2.4.1.

tains that sustainable development is a principle in WTO law, highlighting that the WTO Secretariat shares this view.[2403] While her elaboration of the alleged status of sustainable development as a principle is more comprehensive than Hilf's, as she cites various WTO documents in which sustainable development is mentioned as an important principle, when considering its use in WTO dispute settlement, she points to instances where the reference to sustainable development in the WTOA preamble and other documents has been used to impart meaning to certain WTO terms. But such use of the preamble is standard teleological interpretation and does not provide conclusive evidence for sustainable development being a legal "principle" in WTO law. Lydgate actually states herself that the

> "term's vagueness and breadth, coupled with uncertainty about its legal weight, suggest that it may not seem a particularly important value, if negative trade impacts are its result".[2404]

This undermines the author's claim that sustainable development is a legal principle of WTO law. In any case, it does not appear to be one that has played an important role in WTO dispute settlement.

To summarize the insights on principles: The term principle is regularly used in the WTO case law, reflecting the use of the terms in some WTO provisions itself. It is not always the case that "real" legal principles, in the sense the term is understood here, are at stake. In some of the situations where the Appellate Body refers to principles, what is at actually stake are certain structurally similar legal rules contained in different WTO agreements, or rules in the VLCT. These rules do not have a legal value transcending their own scope of application. In other cases, the Appellate Body relies on what it portrays as established principles of international law, though these principles are generally neutral in character, in the sense that they do not pre-determine a particular outcome. The Appellate Body tends, however, to be more reluctant to rely on substantive principles not explicitly contained in WTO law that are less neutral in content or more controversial in international law, maintaining that they cannot override explicit provisions of WTO law. For example, the Appellate Body has not recognized the existence of the precautionary principle as a principle of international law and has stressed that even if such a principle existed, it would only have a limited function in WTO law. Similarly, no overarching proportionality principle is contained in the WTO agreements and the

2403 Lydgate 2012, 623ff.
2404 Ibid., 636.

WTO dispute settlement bodies have not acknowledged the existence of such a principle or judicially created it. Nonetheless, WTO law contains some elements of proportionality. As a consequence, proportionality is sometimes used as a concept in WTO dispute.

4.2. Balancing

Like the proportionality principle balancing is not an explicit legal requirement in WTO law. Nonetheless, the language of balancing is used in WTO dispute settlement in various ways; in this section I will address how. In the previous chapter I discussed the extent to which the Appellate Body in substance strikes a balance between different interests, the "context of discovery". In this chapter, however, I shall consider balancing in the "context of justification".[2405]

The first situation where balancing language appears is the interpretation of the necessity clause which, according to the *Korea – Beef* formula used in many later cases, requires "weighing and balancing"

> "[…] a series of factors which prominently include the contribution made by the compliance measure to the enforcement of the law or regulation at issue, the importance of the common interests or values protected by that law or regulation, and the accompanying impact of the law or regulation on imports or exports"[2406].

As part of this test, the adjudicators are thus called upon to assess the relative importance of the regulatory interests and values pursued by WTO Members. Another example for the use of quite explicit balancing language is *China – Audiovisual Products*. The Appellate Body writes:

> "[...] if a Member chooses to adopt a very restrictive measure, it will have to ensure that the measure is carefully designed so that the other elements to be taken into account in weighing and balancing the factors relevant to an assessment of the 'necessity' of the measure will 'outweigh' such restrictive effect".[2407]

2405 See for the difference between both Martineau 2007, 994.

2406 *Korea – Measures Affecting Imports of Fresh, Chilled and Frozen Beef, WT/DS161/AB/R, WT/DS169/AB/R* 2000, para. 162–164.

2407 *China – Measures Affecting Trading Rights and Distribution Services for Certain Publications and Audiovisual Entertainment Products, WT/DS363/AB/R* 2009, para. 310.

More broadly, balancing often seems to take place where WTO law relates to a means-end relationship,[2408] even though the term "balancing" does not necessarily appear in the dispute settlement reports. When interpreting Art. XX (g) in the *Shrimp – Turtles* case, the Appellate Body observed that means were "reasonably related to the ends".[2409] The use of the word "reasonable", a normative term requiring the exercise of judgement on what is "reasonable" in a given situation, indicates that here, too, some kind of balancing is at work,[2410] even though the Appellate Body does not use words such as "balancing" or "equilibrium" explicitly. Reference to balancing has also been made by the Appellate Body in the context of the analysis of necessity under Art. 2.2 TBT.[2411]

Outside of these rather limited circumstances, the adjudicators engage in an open balancing of different interests, objectives and values at stake infrequently. In one case, a Panel stated that while a measure's underlying commercial objectives were important, they were not as important as health protection.[2412] Another of the rare examples, where an ethical argument is brought into play by the Appellate Body outside the Art. XX GATT/XIV GATS analysis is in the following:

> "[...] where a substance may be potentially toxic, requiring a WTO Member to evaluate specifically the risks through actual human consumption of the substance would be unethical and would not be 'appropriate to the circumstances' within the meaning of Article 5.1."[2413]

However, such use of policy arguments is the exception, not the norm.[2414] The balancing formula used in the necessity analysis in Art. XX GATT and XIV GATS is almost the only place where the importance of certain policy goals is consistently mentioned. Here, policy rationales are sometimes dis-

2408 Hilf and Puth 2002, 212f.

2409 *United States – Import Prohibition of Certain Shrimp and Shrimp Products, WT/DS58/AB/R* 1998, para. 141.

2410 Hilf and Goettsche 2003, 23.

2411 *United States – Measures Concerning the Importation, Marketing and Sale of Tuna and Tuna Products, WT/DS381/AB/R* 2012, para. 321f; *United States – Certain Country of Origin Labelling (COOL) Requirements, WT/DS384/AB/R, WT/DS/386/AB/R* 2012, para. 377f.

2412 *Canada – Measures Relating to Exports of Wheat and Treatment of Imported Grain, WT/DS276/R* 2004, para. 6.224.

2413 *United States – Continued Suspension of Obligations in the EC – Hormones Dispute, WT/DS320/AB/R* 2008, para. 563.

2414 Another example is given by Bhala 1999b, 64.

cussed quite openly; for example, the Appellate Body *in Brazil –Tyres* stated quite clearly that the necessity clause in Art. XX (b) GATT

> "illustrates the tensions that may exist between, on the one hand, international trade and, on the other hand, public health and environmental concerns arising from the handling of waste generated by a product at the end of its useful life."[2415]

Finally, it should also be noted what the Appellate Body does not balance: the ECJ regularly uses the community/EU/internal market interest as one of the factors in balancing; by contrast, the Appellate Body never refers to any WTO interest in its judgements, but at most to the interests of WTO Members.[2416]

A second constellation where the Appellate Body engages in balancing is concerning competing rights and obligations of WTO Members as enshrined in the WTO agreements. The language of balancing is most openly used by the Appellate Body in the interpretation of the chapeau of Art. XX GATT in the *Shrimp – Turtles* case. The Appellate Body noted that the chapeau

> "embodies the recognition on the part of WTO Members of the need to maintain a balance of rights and obligations between the right of a Member to invoke one or another of the exceptions of Article XX [...] and the substantive rights of the other Members under the GATT 1994 [...]"[2417].

Consequently, the task of interpreting the chapeau involved

> "locating and marking out a line of equilibrium between the right of a Member to invoke an exception under Article XX and the rights of the other Members under varying substantive provisions (e.g., Article XI) of the GATT 1994, so that neither of the competing rights will cancel out the other and thereby distort and nullify or impair the balance of rights and obligations constructed by the Members themselves in that Agreement. The location of the line of equilibrium, as expressed in the chapeau, is not fixed and unchanging; the line moves as the kind and

---

2415 *Brazil – Measures Affecting Imports of Retreaded Tyres, WT/DS332/AB/R* 2007, para. 210.

2416 Bogdandy 2003, 123f.

2417 *United States – Import Prohibition of Certain Shrimp and Shrimp Products, WT/DS58/AB/R* 1998, para. 156.

the shape of the measures at stake vary and as the facts making up specific cases differ."[2418]

In other instances, Panels and the Appellate Body also referred to a "line of equilibrium" that had to be drawn or identified in cases under Art. XX GATT.[2419] Similarly, concerning the relationship between obligations and exceptions, and by implication the rights and obligations of Members, the Appellate Body in *United States – Gasoline* wrote:

> "The chapeau is animated by the principle that while the exceptions of Article XX may be invoked as a matter of legal right, they should not be so applied as to frustrate or defeat the legal obligations of the holder of the right under the substantive rules of the General Agreement. If those exceptions are not to be abused or misused, in other words, the measures falling within the particular exceptions must be applied reasonably, with due regard both to the legal duties of the party claiming the exception and the legal rights of the other parties concerned."[2420]

In *Shrimp – Turtles* (Art. 21.5 Review), the Appellate Body observed:

> "Requiring that an agreement be concluded would mean that any country would in effect have a veto over whether the United States could fulfill its WTO obligations – such requirement would not be reasonable."[2421]

While the Appellate Body does not refer to balancing explicitly in this case, the reference to rights and obligations of different WTO Members and the statement that they need to be in a "reasonable" relationship indicate that adjudicators will balance the rights and obligations of WTO Members when applying the chapeau of Art. XX GATT.

The Appellate Body describes the balancing act as "bringing out" something already in the text and an implementation of the intention of the parties and only way that a decision under Art. XX GATT could possibly be taken.[2422] This is evident from what the Appellate Body says, with re-

2418 Ibid., para. 158.

2419 *United States – Import Prohibition of Certain Shrimp and Shrimp Products, WT/DS58/RW* 2001, para. 5.58f.

2420 *United States – Standards for Reformulated and Conventional Gasoline, WT/DS2/AB/R* 1996, sec. IV, at 22.

2421 *United States – Import Prohibition of Certain Shrimp and Shrimp Products, WT/DS58/AB/RW* 2001, para. 123.

2422 This insight is taken from Martineau 2007, 996f, 1018 who also identifies the following quote in her contribution.

gard to its prior order of analysis of Art. XX GATT in *United States – Gasoline*:

> "The sequence of steps indicated above in the analysis of a claim of justification under Article XX reflects, *not inadvertence or random choice*, but rather the *fundamental structure and logic* of Article XX."[2423] [emphasis added]

Moreover, the Appellate Body also referred to the VCLT rules of interpretation in support of its balancing approach.[2424]

Another instance in which the Appellate Body has referred to a balance of different rights of WTO Members is in reading the preamble of the TBT Agreement in *United States – Clove Cigarettes.* In that case, the Appellate Body observed that the fifth recital of the TBT Agreement's preamble – stating that technical regulations and standards should not create unnecessary obstacles to trade – was "counterbalanced"[2425] by the sixth recital of the Agreement's preamble. The latter says:

> "*Recognizing* that no country should be prevented from taking measures necessary to ensure the quality of its exports, or for the protection of human, animal or plant life or health, of the environment, or for the prevention of deceptive practices, at the levels it considers appropriate, subject to the requirement that they are not applied in a manner which would constitute a means of arbitrary or unjustifiable discrimination between countries where the same conditions prevail or a disguised restriction on international trade, and are otherwise in accordance with the provisions of this Agreement;"

The Appellate Body understood this part of the preamble as a reinforcement of the Members' right to use technical regulations

> "in pursuit of their legitimate objectives, provided that they do so in an even-handed manner and in a manner that is otherwise in accordance with the provisions of the TBT Agreement"[2426].

2423 *United States – Import Prohibition of Certain Shrimp and Shrimp Products, WT/DS58/AB/R* 1998, para. 119.

2424 This is emphasized by Martineau 2007, 1018f; she points to *United States – Standards for Reformulated and Conventional Gasoline, WT/DS2/AB/R* 1996, 18f in this regard.

2425 *United States – Measures Affecting the Production and Sale of Clove Cigarettes, WT/DS406/AB/R* 2012, para. 95.

2426 Ibid., para. 96.

It also noted that Art. 2.1 TBT contained a similar "balance" as the one set out in GATT with its Art. III and XX.[2427] Indeed, the construction of the relationship between Art. III and XX GATT is also an instance in which the Appellate Body apparently sought to put the rights and obligations of Members into an equilibrium by stating that neither Art. III:4 GATT nor Art. XX GATT should be read so broadly as to effectively subvert the respective other norm, without actually using the word "balancing".[2428] Similarly, the Appellate Body observed in *Hormones I* the following for the SPS Agreement:

> "The ultimate goal of the harmonization of SPS measures is to prevent the use of such measures for arbitrary or unjustifiable discrimination between Members or as a disguised restriction on international trade, without preventing Members from adopting or enforcing measures which are both 'necessary to protect' human life or health and 'based on scientific principles', and without requiring them to change their appropriate level of protection. The requirements of a risk assessment under Article 5.1, as well as of 'sufficient scientific evidence' under Article 2.2, are essential for the delicate and carefully negotiated balance in the SPS Agreement between the shared, but sometimes competing, interests of promoting international trade and of protecting the life and health of human beings".[2429]

On this basis, it decided that the Panel's finding that Art. 3.3 SPS required Members also to comply with Art. 5 SPS was correct.[2430] It is also clear that the Appellate Body does not only talk about a balance between rights and obligations of Members in this passage, but also of a balance between substantive interests. Hence, one may even read this as Appellate Body balancing substantive interests rather than Members' rights and obligations. Mostly, however the Appellate Body has only stated openly that it would engage in balancing the rights and obligations of WTO Members, but has not openly balanced substantive interests (e.g. trade vs. environment).

A third type of situation in which the Appellate Body refers to balancing is with regard to the way that a Panel treats the factual evidence before it. For example, in *EC – Asbestos*, the Appellate Body concluded that the Pan-

2427 Ibid., para. 109.

2428 See for the references to case law Marceau and Trachtman 2002, 854.

2429 *European Communities – Measures Concerning Meat and Meat Products, WT/DS26/AB/R, WT/DS48/AB/R* 1998, para. 177.

2430 Ibid.

el should have investigated various pieces of evidence and then should have "weighed" all of the evidence in making an overall determination on the likeness of products under Art. III:4 GATT.[2431] In other cases, Panels themselves have declared that they were "balancing evidence".[2432] This kind of balancing occurs, in particular, when risk-related decisions taken by national governments are reviewed. For example, with regard to the interpretation of the term "sufficient" in Art. 2 SPS, Panels have stated that what is "sufficient" evidence in a case depended on what risk was involved and what damage might result from it.[2433] The amount or quality of evidence here is weighed against the magnitude of risk. There is one other procedural issue that the Appellate Body has framed in terms of a balance: the standard of review. The Appellate Body in *Hormones II* stated that the standard of review had to

> "reflect the balance established in [the SPS Agreement] between the jurisdictional competences conceded by the Members to the WTO and the jurisdictional competences retained by the Members for themselves".[2434]

To summarize, the Appellate Body's use of the language of balancing and references to policy considerations are mainly limited to three different types of constellations: the analysis of the necessity clauses; certain situations where conflicting rights and obligations of WTO Members are identified as being at stake, and finally when weighing different pieces of evidence. The objectives of the WTO legal order are not part of the Appellate Body's balancing exercises, a feature which distinguishes the WTO from the EU judicial setting.

4.3. Assessment

In this part, I will again proceed to assess the WTO case law with the aim of making sense of it from the viewpoint of judicial style and the generation of legitimacy. By contrast, what substantive balance the adjudicators

2431 *European Communities – Measures Affecting Asbestos and Products Containing Asbestos, WT/DS135/AB/R* 2001, para. 110.

2432 *Korea – Alcoholic Beverages, WT/DS75/R, WT/DS84/R* 1998, para. 10.82.

2433 *Japan – Measures Affecting the Importation of Apples, WT/DS245/R* 2003, para. 8.105.

2434 *United States – Continued Suspension of Obligations in the EC – Hormones Dispute, WT/DS320/AB/R* 2008, para. 587.

have in substance struck between different interests at stake has been discussed in chapter 2.

As described above, the Appellate Body is not shy in using the word "principle" or to draw on certain principles that are procedural in nature or firmly established in international law. By way of contrast, the Appellate Body has been more reluctant to recognize or "coin" substantive principles such as the proportionality or precautionary principles. Some commentators have criticized the Appellate Body's understanding of the role of principles in interpreting WTO law as being too narrow. Notably, disagreement has been voiced with regard to the Appellate Body's stance as implied in *Hormones I* that the status of the precautionary principle was irrelevant to the outcome of the dispute, which was replicated by the Panel in *EC – Biotech Products*.[2435]

While there is some criticism of the Appellate Body's approach towards principles, observers have at the same time expressed a lack of surprise at this approach and see it as indicative of the effort of the WTO dispute settlement bodies to appear as the "mouthpieces"[2436] of a member-driven organization. Indeed, given that the precise nature of substantive principles of international law is often contested, the approach taken by the Appellate Body makes it appear both prudent and not unduly activist. It is also no surprise that the Appellate Body would be more daring when drawing on unwritten procedural principles regarding such issues as burden of proof; procedural issues are very much the domain of a court and if a court clarifies such matters drawing on principles, this is unlikely to lead to charges of inappropriate judicial behaviour.[2437] And to put things into perspective, it should be noted that other courts have also on occasion been hesitant to recognize substantive principles of international law. For example, the ICJ and ITLOS in judicial decisions taken in the 1990s – like the Appellate Body – did not recognize the precautionary principle as an established principle of international law, and at most indicated it might be emerging as such.[2438]

Let us then turn to the use of balancing by the adjudicators. To recap, I have identified three types of situations in which the language of balancing is used: (1) the requirement of assessing the importance of the regulatory goal at stake in the "necessity" analysis under Art. XX GATT/XIV GATS;

2435 Kulovesi 2011, 164f, 175f.
2436 Desmedt 2001, 443.
2437 See on the role of courts in crafting procedural rules also above section 2.5.
2438 Kulovesi 2011, 163f.

(2) instances and balancing more broadly the rights and obligations of various WTO Members enshrined in the WTO agreements, and (3) weighing and balancing different pieces of evidence by the adjudicators. These situations merit closer scrutiny with regard to how, precisely, the adjudicators use the language of balancing to justify their decisions and what consequences their approach has for the acceptance of these decisions.

To start with the least controversial part, situation (3): the weighing and balancing of evidence. That Panelists 'weigh' pieces of evidence is not a particularly noteworthy aspect of the WTO's specific judicial style. Dealing with evidence is at the very heart of the judicial function: weighing it an integral part of the judicial decision-making process.[2439] Fundamental questions concerning judicial reasoning are not raised when adjudicators balance pieces of evidence against each other and determine their overall probative weight. This does not, in principle, limit the regulatory freedom of WTO Members, for as has already been observed with regard to procedural issues more broadly, it is unlikely to lead to a court being perceived as "activist".

By way of contrast, referring to a "balance" and "equilibrium" of rights and obligations of WTO Members contained in the agreements (situation 2) may provoke more controversy concerning the role of the WTO adjudicators. Generally, one could argue that any interpretation of WTO law amounts to balancing rights and obligations, as each interpretation favours one WTO Member in a concrete dispute over the other. This does not, however, concern the judicial style of the adjudicators, i.e. the question of how they justify their decision. There is no need to refer to the language of balancing in making decisions on the interpretation of WTO law that strike a certain substantive balance between the rights and obligations of WTO Members. Instead of interpreting the chapeau and some other provisions with reference to a balance of rights and obligations of WTO Members, the Appellate Body could have approached the interpretation of these provisions in a more deductive way, presenting findings as a syllogistic conclusion from the letter of the law.

One explanation why it has not done so and instead opted for balancing, could be that by using the language of balancing the adjudicators arrive at a substantive outcome that would have been more difficult to "sell" if a more deductive, textual approach had been used. Martineau makes the point that for avoiding a consistent pro-trade outcome the Appellate Body needed to depart from earlier Panels' more restrictive interpretation of the

2439 D'Aspremont and Mbengue 2014, 244.

exceptions contained in Art. XX GATT/XIV GATS; as a consequence, the Appellate Body needed to elevate them to the same status as the rights resulting from WTO provisions that oblige states to remove trade barriers. Once there are several conflicting rights of *ex ante* equal status or importance, balancing becomes the appropriate mode of reasoning.[2440] Indeed, some of the (substantive) requirements that the Appellate Body finds in the chapeau can be related to the idea that some kind of balancing of conflicting interests of Members needs to occur. For example, there appears to be a tendency under the chapeau to favour multilateral and negotiated approaches; negotiations are, as McRae puts it, "by definition solutions, where the parties have balanced their interests".[2441] At the same time, it is neither easy to connect these requirements to the actual text of the chapeau nor does the Appellate Body make the connection very clear in its reports, suggesting that it might have been difficult to justify the same outcome in a merely deductive exercise.

An additional rationale for the use of balancing in the interpretation of the chapeau may be that the language of the chapeau is rather indeterminate, rendering an entirely textual interpretation difficult. In this situation of textual twilight, using the language of balancing evokes a certain image – one probably desirable from the point of view of the adjudicators – of the judicial decision-makers carefully looking at all of the interests at stake and then taking a wise and moderate decision. Nonetheless, by referring to balancing the adjudicators also run the risk of appearing as overly active judicial decision-makers; the language of balancing signals to WTO Members that the dispute settlement bodies avail themselves openly of an active, creative role and space for decision-making. Indeed, some commentators consider that an element of subjectivity has been inserted into the interpretation of WTO law through the balancing formula.[2442] Attempting to avoid this impression could explain why the Appellate Body is very careful to support its relevant decisions by reference to principles of international law as contained in the VLCT as well as by the intention of WTO Members, and why it justifies its balancing approach as resulting inevitably from the text of the WTO agreements. Altogether, there is a visible effort to support and legitimize the potentially controversial "equilibrium jurisprudence" by resorting to accepted international legal principles. A provision that the adjudicators do not appear to have drawn on, but could

2440 See chapter 2, section 1.6.4.
2441 McRae 2000, 231.
2442 See chapter 2, section 1.6.3.

have used to support their approach, is Art. 3.3 DSU.[2443] The provision expresses that maintaining a "proper balance between the rights and obligations of Members" is an essential function of the WTO dispute settlement system. It is therefore somewhat surprising that this reference to a balance of the rights and obligations of WTO Members in the DSU does not seem to have played a major role in justifying the judicial balancing decisions of type (2).[2444]

The part of the Appellate Body's balancing exercises that has provoked most alarm is the fact that the Appellate Body assumes competence to pass judgement on the importance of a regulatory goal at stake in the necessity analysis (situation 1).[2445] This has happened so far mostly under Art. XX GATT and XIV GATS; Art. 2.2 TBT has only recently come to play a major role in the case law, but similar concerns are likely to be relevant here.

The jurisprudence of the Appellate Body has triggered a lively and critical debate in the literature. At a very general level, the Appellate Body's stance is criticized for having at least the potential for inappropriate interference in WTO Members' regulatory freedom.[2446] More specifically, the following WTO-related[2447] arguments against balancing are brought forward, phrased slightly differently by different authors:[2448]

1) A first argument is that balancing should not occur, because it is against the text of the WTO agreements. The very existence of the Art. XX GATT/XIV GATS exceptions for the benefit of certain regulatory goals indicates that the WTO negotiators considered these goals

2443 This thought has been triggered by the reference of Shany and Shlomo-Agon 2014, 194 to Art. 3.3 DSU as an objective of WTO dispute settlement.

2444 According to the WTO Analytical Annex, the adjudicators have referred to various parts of the provision in some cases, but not to the one the balance of rights and obligations, see WTO Analytical Annex, Art. 3 DSU, https://www.wto.org/english/res_e/publications_e/ai17_e/dsu_art3_jur.pdf.

2445 For example, Kulovesi 2011, 99 observes that "balancing rights and obligations of WTO Members under the GATT [...] is arguably less challenging to the legitimacy of the WTO dispute settlement than 'necessity' tests where non-trade policies are balanced against free trade".

2446 McGrady 2009, 162; Buchmüller 2013, 267.

2447 In the following, more general or conceptual problems regarding balancing are not discussed. For an excellent presentation of such arguments see Martineau 2007, but also the discussion on balancing in chapter 1, section 3.1. It should also be noted that some of the arguments presented in the following do not only relate to using balancing as a way of explaining and justifying decisions, but also to how a decision gets "really" taken.

2448 See for example Davies 2009, n. 48; Marceau and Trachtman 2002, 850.

important and there is hence no room for a judicial entity to replace their judgements on the importance of various regulatory goals with its own.[2449] In addition, it has also been claimed that the word "necessary" supports a less-restrictive alternative measure test textually "more naturally" than it supports a balancing approach.[2450] It has also been argued that "necessary" is about a means-end relationship and interpreting it in such a way that this end would be put in question would be an interpretation against the wording of WTO law.[2451]

2) A second strand of arguments relates to the lack of democratic legitimacy of an international court to engage in balancing. There are different aspects of this argument, which are sometimes not clearly separated.
   a) The first version of this argument is that the WTO adjudicators should not engage in balancing, because taking decisions on what interests and policy objectives should prevail is the role of elected legislators and regulators.[2452] Balancing opens the door to judicial activism by the WTO adjudicators.[2453] According to a modified version of this argument, balancing is only acceptable if the body undertaking it has a strong democratic legitimacy – something the WTO dispute settlement system lacks.[2454]
   b) A second version of this argument is that balancing should not occur, because it gives an international body, the WTO, too much power as compared to national decision-makers.[2455] This can be related to the modified version of the previous argument that the WTO does not have the democratic legitimacy necessary for balancing. Indeed, it has been argued that because balancing is very intru-

2449 Buchmüller 2013, 268; Kapterian 2010, 119f; Thomas 2009, 46; Du 2011, 668; Howse and Tuerk 2001, 326 make a similar, but not identical point, arguing that when assessing the importance of the various interests in Art. XX GATT, the Appellate Body must follow the hierarchy of values implicit or explicit in international law more broadly. Thus, they do not claim that the Appellate Body should not undertake any such assessment, but rather question the basis for doing so.

2450 Regan 2007, 366.

2451 Neumann and Tuerk 2003, 213.

2452 Desmedt 2001, 465; see also Regan 2003, 106 in the context of the US Dormant Commerce Clause.

2453 See Neumann and Tuerk 2003, 215.

2454 Kapterian 2010, 126; see also Neumann and Tuerk 2003, 203, 232f.

2455 Van Calster 2008, 135; Kulovesi 2011, 185ff.

sive into national regulatory sovereignty, it can only be done by a constitutional court.[2456]

c) A third version of the argument is that a body firmly linked to one of the substantive interests to be balanced – trade – should not engage in balancing.[2457] A version of this criticism is that the balancing test has actually tipped the scales in favour of trade liberalization.[2458]

3) A third point made is that the WTO dispute settlement bodies do not know enough in factual terms to carry out a legitimate balancing and should therefore refrain from it.[2459] In a sense, this is the empirical version of 2 a) and b) – what judges are seen to be lacking here is not the normative competence to balance, but the factual one.[2460] Legislators are seen as being in a better position for this purpose.[2461]

4) Finally, some observers have suggested that balancing is dispensable, because most of the elements of the Appellate Body's balancing test are also incorporated in the least-restrictive means test.[2462] Another proposition is that the objective of dealing with trade restrictions, even far-reaching ones, can be reached by means less onerous to WTO Mem-

---

2456 Ortino 2004, 472.

2457 For the latter position an example is Delimatsis 2011, 287; Bogdandy and Venzke 2012, 25 describe the mono-thematic orientation of most international agreements and the courts authorized to interpret them as a problem for judicial decision-making at the international level more generally.

2458 Kapterian 2010, 91.

2459 Bown and Trachtman 2009, 133 seem to argue in this direction, but also state, on the other hand, that this is an obstacle that the WTO adjudicators will have to overcome somehow; Lovric 2010, 130.

2460 See Regan 2003, 106.

2461 Lovric 2010, 129f.

2462 It is pertinent to note, for the sake of readers familiar with the interpretation of the Interstate Commerce Clause in the US, that the basis of this statement is in a certain sense an "order of intrusiveness" opposite to that in the interpretation of the Interstate Commerce Clause. When the latter is interpreted, there is a more thorough and hence more intrusive necessity test in cases of discriminatory regulation and a less strict balancing test in cases of non-discriminatory regulation, see Andenas and Zleptnig 2007, 402ff. Thus, here, the necessity/least-discriminatory regulation test is the less "heavy" test as compared to balancing, while in WTO dispute settlement the discussion about the legitimacy of balancing is premised on the reverse assumption, i.e. balancing being the more intrusive, heavy test.

bers' sovereignty than balancing, such as a prohibition on the abuse of rights[2463].

On the other hand, some arguments have also been made in favour of WTO judicial balancing: Balancing could be used to reduce the fragmentation of international law if it incorporates norms outside the legal order.[2464] However, the extent to which non-WTO law can be applied in the WTO legal order is at present unclear and disputed.[2465] Balancing may also be a way of discussing rationally and in a non-camouflaged way the substantive interests at stake in a given case[2466] and a tool to structure the judicial and legal discourse on a matter.[2467]

In the present context, it is not of interest which of these arguments are correct and which are not. What I intended to show here is that the balancing test that the Appellate Body has created to interpret "necessary" in Art. XX GATT/XIV GATS is not at all uncontroversial. In other words, the Appellate Body has not increased its perceived legitimacy by using this test, at least not among academics. I can only speculate why the Appellate Body has chosen the balancing test, rather than staying with the least-restrictive means available test that is more deductive in character.[2468] Obviously, the balancing test gives the adjudicators a lot of leeway and discretion to decide cases – it may be that the adjudicators were willing to pay the price of being criticized for doing what they should not do in exchange for enlarged judicial discretion and flexibility. It is also worth noting that the Appellate Body has hardly ever used the balancing formula in a comprehensive way – no policy objective has ever been described as not important. It is therefore not clear how often the Appellate Body has in substance ever struck a balance between the different interests at stake in the sense of proportionality *sensu stricto*.[2469] Applying the controversial formula in a restrained manner may be an attempt to counter criticism and assuage fears that the adjudicators may be over-reaching. On the other hand, if the formula is not used fully, there is even less point in continuing to endorse it.

2463 This is proposed by Neumann and Tuerk 2003, 233.
2464 On this, see in particular Kleinlein 2012, 272ff.
2465 See above, section 1.7.3.
2466 I read Peel 2012, 452f to make this point.
2467 This is basically the flip-side of the arguments against the Appellate Body's textualist orientation discussed above in section 1.7.2.
2468 Martineau 2007, 1008.
2469 See chapter 2, section 1.5.1.

To summarize this section: The language of balancing is only used in certain constellations; otherwise reference to substantive policy arguments or interests at stake is rare in WTO dispute settlement. The balancing formula used in the "necessity" test constitutes an important departure from the Appellate Body's predominant style of not engaging too openly in the discussion of interests and policy objectives at stake; the reference in the WTO legal texts to such policy objectives in Art. XX GATT/XIV GATS facilitates this approach. The Appellate Body is also reluctant to recognize substantive principles that are not explicitly mentioned in WTO law, would consistently favour a certain substantive outcome of cases (e.g. the precautionary principle), and/or are controversial in international law. This picture can be explained as an attempt by the adjudicators to avoid appearing as too activist or creative. Yet, even the limited use of the language of balancing in the analysis of the necessity clause in Art. XX GATT/XIV GATS by the Appellate Body and particular its use of the importance of the regulatory goal at stake as one of the factors to be balanced has provoked considerable criticism among commentators, showing the limits of the Appellate Body's endeavour to build its legitimacy.

5. *Other stylistic features of the WTO dispute settlement reports*

In this section, I discuss some other remarkable characteristics of WTO dispute settlement that are all – more or less closely – related to certain parameters of the Summers/Taruffo scheme for assessing whether a court adopts a predominantly formalist or non-formalist style.

The first issue discussed here is the length and tone of the dispute settlement reports (section 5.1); it is directly related to whether a judicial decision is "abbreviated and terse" or "extended and elaborate". The second issue discussed is the use of appeasement techniques addressed at the parties (section 5.2). By "appeasement techniques" I mean instances where the adjudicators verbally re-assure the parties (and the larger public) that their concerns and arguments have been heard without these statements usually having any legal value of their own. The use of appeasement techniques can best be placed in the category of whether a judicial body uses a "magisterial and authoritative" way of reasoning, or an "argumentative and dialogic" one as classified in the Summers/Taruffo scheme. If appeasement is used a lot, this is a sign that a court seeks to enter into a dialogue with its clientele, explain its findings and win consent, but could also mean that it is self-conscious or unsure of its authority. Finally, the extent to which different interpretive options are made visible in a judicial decision is a category of its own in the Summers/Taruffo scheme (section 5.3). Again, the section concludes with an assessment (section 5.4).

5.1. Length and tone of reports

One remarkable feature of the WTO dispute settlement reports – and perhaps the first a newcomer to the WTO dispute settlement world would note – is their length. This is true, in particular, for the Panel reports, which routinely comprise a few hundred pages. These reports reproduce in great detail every aspect of the submissions and oral arguments that the parties to the dispute, including third parties, have made as well as experts' statements, comments on these etc.[2470] The Appellate Body reports are not of a similarly monumental length, which must be considered a result of the Appellate Body's mandate to only decide on matters of law, and not on matters of fact. Still, filling between several dozens and (more frequently) well over a hundred pages, they are longer than, for example, decisions by the ECJ or the ECtHR, even though not necessarily longer than those of all national courts of last instance or constitutional courts.[2471] It has also been observed that the reports have become longer over the years.[2472]

Obviously, the comparison of the length of judicial decisions is only meaningful if the courts concerned fulfil equivalent functions and typically deal with issues of comparable complexity. Some, like the ECtHR, do not deal with subjects similar to those put before the WTO dispute settlement system, while others, such as the ECJ, do. The ECJ often needs to interpret fairly complex and detailed legal rules of EU law and assess whether certain measures are compatible with legislation aimed at safeguarding the functioning of the EU's internal market. There is no reason to assume that the cases the ECJ deals with are generally less complex legally or factually than the ones brought to the WTO. Moreover, there are also often several

---

2470 A good example is the Panel report in *European Communities – Measures Affecting the Approval and Marketing of Biotech Products, WT/DS291/R, WT/DS292/R, WT/DS293/R* 2006; it has more than 1000 pages even without the additional ten annexes comprising an additional 1200 pages.

2471 Summers and Taruffo 1991, 489f conclude on the basis of a comparison of the judicial style of higher courts in 9 countries that the "prevailing practice [...] is to write lengthy opinions in order to justify the interpretation of statues", with the French system being the only major exception.

2472 Meagher 2020, 149.

parties involved in ECJ proceedings that make statements on the case – similar to the third parties in WTO cases. Hence, the length of the WTO dispute settlement reports is a particular feature and does not inevitably result from the type of cases brought or the complexity of legal issues involved.

A few factors that inflate the volume of the dispute settlement reports can be identified. The first is that the positions and individual arguments of all parties involved are summarized scrupulously and in great detail. In fact, they are often summarized both in a general manner and then at some length as the adjudicators present their own findings. The second is that the arguments of the parties are not only summarized, but the adjudicators also try to respond to them at a level of detail other courts do not. For example, it has been observed that the ECJ deals with public policy justifications in EU law in a few paragraphs, while discussions of Art. XX GATT usually extend over several pages.[2473] The third, as noted above in section 1.1 of this chapter, is the tendency to take literal interpretation to extremes that sometimes border on the meaningless. The fourth, as also noted above, is that while the dispute settlement bodies often exercise judicial economy, the Panels – and to a lesser extent also the Appellate Body – in some cases also have taken decisions that were not needed in order for the WTO-legality of a certain measure to be decided.

A different, but related aspect is the tone of the WTO's judicial decisions. There is sometimes a personal tone to the reports, where adjudicators reflect upon their appropriate role or where they express a certain measure of surprise or even indignation in their decision.[2474] For example, the Appellate Body commented in one case that it was "deeply concerned"[2475] about a certain interpretation by a Panel. In another report the Appellate Body expressed it had "some difficulties understanding" a certain view of the Panel.[2476] This is all quite personal, even emotional, everyday non-technical language. According to Bush and Pelc the language of

---

2473 Ortino 2004, 244.

2474 For example Bhala 1999b, 38 writes on a certain report that the "anger of the Appellate Body in defending vigorously its Wool Shirts burden of proof precedent is palpable".

2475 *United States – Final Anti-Dumping Measures on Stainless Steel from Mexico, WT/DS344/AB/R* 2008, para. 162.

2476 *United States – Certain Country of Origin Labelling (COOL) Requirements, WT/DS384/AB/R, WT/DS/386/AB/R* 2012, para. 452.

WTO dispute settlement decisions becomes the more "affect-laden" the more politically sensitive a legal issue is.[2477]

The Appellate also uses the pronoun "we", in phrases such as "we are not persuaded that" or "we are not convinced that", or "we do not agree".[2478] "We" is the standard way how the Appellate Body refers to itself, rather than using a more magisterial formulation, such as referring to itself in the third person as "the Appellate Body" or "the tribunal" or "the division". Finally, reports are also signed by individuals, i.e. judgements are not presented in the name of a faceless institution, but potentially fallible individuals appear as its authors.

5.2. Appeasement techniques

Dispute settlement reports also make regular use of appeasement techniques, that is, statements of no intrinsic legal value through which the adjudicators verbally re-assure the parties (and the larger public) that their concerns and arguments have been heard and that proper account has been taken of their interests.

A first appeasement technique is that Panels and the Appellate Body regularly state very explicitly what they have or – more frequently – have not concluded and decided. For example, the Panel in *China – Raw Materials* observed that it was not "asked to discuss the appropriateness of the WTO rules at issue in the present dispute".[2479] Similarly, the Panel in *EU – Biotech Products* presented a rather long list of issues it had not decided at the end of its report, before stating what it actually *had* decided.[2480] Among the issues that the Panel stressed it had not decided were controversial ones such as whether biotech products in general were safe or not, or whether the biotech products at issue in the dispute were "like" their

2477 Busch and Pelc 2019, 465ff.

2478 For example, doing an automatic search for the word "we" in the *Hormones II* Appellate Body report and replacing it with a symbol, led to 344 replacements according to the automatic replacement function of the Word program.

2479 *China – Measures Related to the Exportation of Various Raw Materials, WT/DS394/R, WT/DS395/R, WT/DS398/R* 2012, para. 7.588.

2480 *European Communities – Measures Affecting the Approval and Marketing of Biotech Products, WT/DS291/R, WT/DS292/R, WT/DS293/R* 2006, para. 8.3.

conventional counterparts.[2481] In other cases, the dispute settlement bodies underlined their opinion that certain findings applied to a specific measure in a given case, but could not be taken as a more general statement on the compatibility of a certain type of measures with WTO law. In *Shrimp – Turtles*, the Panel emphasized that its findings did not question the legitimacy of environmental protection as such.[2482] In the same case, the Appellate Body stated that it had *not* decided certain issues, notably that the "sovereign Members of the WTO might not adopt measures to protect endangered species" or that "states could not act together bilaterally".[2483] Similarly, in *Brazil – Tyres*, the Appellate Body noted

> "that the participants do not dispute that it is within the authority of a WTO Member to set the public health or environmental objectives it seeks to achieve, as well as the level of protection that it wants to obtain, through the measure or the policy it chooses to adopt."[2484] [footnotes omitted]

In *United States – Clove Cigarettes*, the Appellate Body also dedicated more than one paragraph to saying that even though a US trade-restrictive measure relating to clove cigarettes was found to violate certain WTO provisions, it did not wish to state that Members could not take tobacco control and anti-smoking measures; the Appellate Body also explicitly recognized the importance of WHO efforts on tobacco control.[2485] There are numerous other examples where the Appellate Body made clear what it did not decide in a certain case.[2486] Sometimes such disclaimers even relate to fac-

---

2481 Joerges 2009, 79 also points to these statements by the Panel, but then notes that "the intended (quasi-)judicial self-restraint was not achieved in practice. The panel adopted partisan positions, albeit partly indirectly and implicitly.".

2482 *United States – Import Prohibition of Certain Shrimp and Shrimp Products, WT/DS58/R* 1998, para. 7.60.

2483 *United States – Import Prohibition of Certain Shrimp and Shrimp Products, WT/DS58/AB/R* 1998, para. 185.

2484 *Brazil – Measures Affecting Imports of Retreaded Tyres, WT/DS332/AB/R* 2007, para. 140.

2485 *United States – Measures Affecting the Production and Sale of Clove Cigarettes, WT/DS406/AB/R* 2012, para. 235.

2486 *European Communities – Conditions for the Granting of Tariff Preferences to Developing Countries, WT/DS246/AB/R* 2004, para. 128–130; *China – Measures Affecting Trading Rights and Distribution Services for Certain Publications and Audiovisual Entertainment Products, WT/DS363/AB/R* 2009, para. 335; *Korea – Measures Affecting Imports of Fresh, Chilled and Frozen Beef, WT/DS161/AB/R,*

tual matters; for example in *Canada – Renewables*, the Appellate Body stated:

> "We note that some of the panel's factual findings seem to refer generally to electricity markets, while others seem to refer to the Ontario electricity market in particular. To the extent we reproduce the Panel's statements that seem to relate generally to electricity markets, we do so because we consider them to be of particular application to the circumstances of these disputes and not necessarily because we are of the view that they necessarily reflect the characteristics of all electricity markets."[2487]

In the *EC – Biotech Products* case, the Panel even went so far as to write a letter explaining its findings.[2488]

Another instance of appeasement is the quite frequent reference to the principle of good faith. Assuming that each and every WTO Member acts in good faith is also a kind of verbal genuflection in the direction of the WTO Members. Zeitler observes that even where the Panels or the Appellate Body considered that in a particular case Members had violated certain obligations that were based on good faith, these findings were never linked to an explicit assumption of "bad faith" in the particular case.[2489] In another instance, Panelists paid a verbal tribute to

> "the breadth and depth of China's environmental actions and the regulatory potential in the light of the various stated policy goals"

and explained they were "impressed" by it.[2490] While they may have been impressed with this aspect of China's actions, this did not prevent them from ruling that certain Chinese measures were not consistent with WTO

WT/DS169/AB/R 2000, para. 149; *European Communities – Measures Affecting the Approval and Marketing of Biotech Products, WT/DS291/R, WT/DS292/R, WT/DS293/R* 2006, para. 8.1–8.3.

2487 *Canada – Certain Measures Affecting the Renewable Energy Generation Sector, WT/DS412/AB/R and Canada – Measures Relating to the Feed-in Tariff Program, WT/DS426/AB/R* 2013, para. 4.1.

2488 The letter is contained in Annex K of *European Communities – Measures Affecting the Approval and Marketing of Biotech Products, WT/DS291/R, WT/DS292/R, WT/DS293/R* 2006. The background to this letter was that a draft version of the interim report had been leaked by one of the parties, leading to discussions in the public of the Panel's findings, which were only preliminary at that stage.

2489 Zeitler 2005, 724.

2490 *China – Measures Related to the Exportation of Various Raw Materials, WT/DS394/R, WT/DS395/R, WT/DS398/R* 2012, 7.583.

law. Sometimes, the Appellate Body will express a finding against a WTO Member in very cautious terms. Take, for example, the following paragraph from *Korea – Beef*:

> "We think it unlikely that Korea intended to establish a level of protection that *totally eliminates* fraud with respect to the origin of beef (domestic or foreign) sold by retailers. The total elimination of fraud would probably require a total ban of imports. Consequently, we assume that in effect Korea intended to *reduce considerably* the number of cases of fraud occurring with respect to the origin of beef sold by retailers."[2491] [underlining added, italics in original]

In substance, the Appellate Body here took quite a harsh decision; it stated that in its view Korea mis-presented (one could also say: strategically lied about) its own level of protection. While basing their decision on this statement, the adjudicators still presented their finding in a tone that suggests they could be wrong. After all, they made "assumptions" rather than arriving at firm conclusions, and considered probabilities rather than stating facts.

Similarly, in *Hormones I*, the Appellate Body made the following statement when interpreting Art. 3.3 SPS:

> "We *are not unaware* that this finding [i.e. the one made by the Appellate Body in the same paragraph, C.G.] *tends to suggest* that the distinction made in Article 3.3 between two situations *may have very limited effects and may*, to that extent, be more apparent than real. Its involved and layered language actually leaves us with *no choice*."[2492] [emphasis added]

In substance, the interpretation adopted by the Appellate Body in this case clearly nullified a distinction contained in the wording of the norm. The Appellate Body acknowledged that its interpretation did away with a distinction *prima facie* contained in the legal text, thus acknowledging its own agency in dealing with the legal text. At the same time, the Appellate Body's statement is phrased in terms much less determined and resolute than its actual substantive finding; the Appellate Body ultimately says it has "no choice".

2491 *Korea – Measures Affecting Imports of Fresh, Chilled and Frozen Beef, WT/DS161/AB/R, WT/DS169/AB/R* 2000, para. 178.

2492 *European Communities – Measures Concerning Meat and Meat Products, WT/DS26/AB/R, WT/DS48/AB/R* 1998, para. 176.

There are also a number of instances where the Appellate Body's ultimate decision allowed both parties to claim that their own legal interpretation was either not at all or at least not entirely wrong. For example, in the *EC – GSP* dispute the Appellate Body observed that according to one party, India, the term "non-discrimination" in footnote 3 to paragraph 2(a) of the GATT Enabling Clause conveyed a "*neutral* meaning of making a distinction". By contrast the other party, the EU, held that it conveyed a "*negative* meaning carrying the connotation of a distinction that is unjust or prejudicial." The Appellate Body confirmed that both definitions "can be considered as reflecting the ordinary meaning of the term".[2493] Over the further course of its reasoning, however, the Appellate Body made no statement that suggested that it considered either of these interpretations to be the correct one in light of systematic or teleological considerations. Instead, it concluded that both parties agreed that distinguishing between similarly situated beneficiaries was discriminatory, and they only disagreed as to the basis for determining whether beneficiaries were similarly situated.[2494] It was only the latter point that the Appellate Body then went on to investigate more in-depth. The adjudicators have sometimes even shown sensitivity at the purely terminological level. In *EC – Biotech Products,* the Panel used a variety of terms to refer to the product under dispute – GMOs, GM products or biotech products – reflecting the different preferences in wording by the parties.[2495] In what can be read as a pre-emptive defence against charges of judicial intrusion in the regulatory sovereignty of WTO Members, the Panel in *United States – Gambling* stated that it was

> "well aware that there may be sensitivities associated with the interpretation of the terms 'public morals' and 'public order' in the context of Article XIV".[2496]

Moreover, the rhetoric of the Appellate Body used to support a certain interpretation is not always consistent with the real importance of that interpretation. A notable example of the mismatch between rhetoric and reality is the emphasis that the adjudicators put on the level of protection. It is unclear to what extent the right to choose the level of protection has a real,

---

2493 *European Communities – Conditions for the Granting of Tariff Preferences to Developing Countries, WT/DS246/AB/R* 2004, para. 152.

2494 Ibid., para. 153.

2495 *European Communities – Measures Affecting the Approval and Marketing of Biotech Products, WT/DS291/R, WT/DS292/R, WT/DS293/R* 2006, para. 7.2.

2496 *United States – Measures Affecting the Cross-Border Supply of Gambling and Betting Services, WT/DS285/R* 2004, para. 5.17.

practical value for WTO Members when trying to justify their measures under either the justification norms under GATT/GATS and the related balancing formula or the SPS Agreement with its science disciplines. In any case, the practical importance is less pronounced than the quite emphatic references of the Appellate Body to the Members' right to choose their level of protection suggest.[2497]

All in all, the adjudicators regularly seek to verbally reassure the parties that nothing untoward is happening in WTO dispute settlement.

5.3. Making different interpretive options invisible

Courts have different practices regarding the extent to which they make different possible interpretations visible in their judgements, discuss the alternatives and then pick the one that is supported by the best arguments. A comparative study of the reasoning used by higher courts in nine different countries has concluded that only some of them follow what has been called a model of "alternative discursive justification"[2498]. Following this model, US and UK common-law courts present conflicting arguments and potential interpretations in their decisions, discussing them openly before choosing one interpretation. Other courts, with the French *Court de Cassation* being the most pronounced example, do not routinely acknowledge competing possible interpretations or arguments.[2499] In the following, this dimension is analysed for WTO dispute settlement.

It is relatively easy to discern the extent to which individual opinions, and particularly those which dissent, are made public by a judicial entity; the way a court approaches this matter may help it justify and legitimize its decision. For example, the ECJ's practice of not publishing opinions by individual judges and speaking "as quasi-mystical voice of the law" has been described as a strategy for insulating individual judges against criticism.[2500] Flett summarizes the pros and cons of individual opinions as follows:

> "The actual exercise of the right to express dissent is said to have the following advantages: constituting a per se virtuous incidence of the right to freedom of expression; being correct; increasing clarity of the

---

2497 See chapter 2, section 2.5.2.

2498 Summers and Taruffo 1991, 493.

2499 Ibid., 481f, 493 the authors observe "some trend away from deductive demonstration to discursive justification", at 494.

2500 Slaughter and Helfer 1997, 327.

majority report; clearly setting out an alternative view; flagging a controversial issue for appeal; acting as markers for future litigation; and acting as spurs for political action. On the other hand, it is said to have the following disadvantages: diminishing the authority of the court; creating legal uncertainty; and drawing the focus towards individuals and their motivations rather than the merits of legal reasoning."[2501] [footnotes omitted]

What is probably missing from the list of arguments above in relation to international courts is that dissenting opinions may also be a way of responding both to prevailing uncertainty in the law and to divergent preferences among the states subject to the jurisdiction of an international court; through a dissenting opinion, a court may avoid establishing unequivocal precedent on a matter.[2502]

What is the approach to individual opinions in WTO dispute settlement? For the appellate stage a marked orientation towards consensus is also enshrined in the Appellate Body's (self-chosen) Procedural Rules. As described in chapter 1 above, Rule 3.2 of the Working Procedures sets forth that

> "[t]he Appellate Body and its divisions shall make every effort to take their decisions by consensus. Where, nevertheless, a decision cannot be arrived at by consensus, the matter at issue shall be decided by a majority vote."

This clause does not forbid individual opinions[2503], but it does discourage them. This may help to explain why the number of individual opinions apparent in the decisions made by the Appellate Body has been "extremely rare"[2504] and is lower for the Appellate Body than for Panels Generally, the decision-making process of the Appellate Body is heavily consensus-oriented.[2505] This is not only manifest from the low number of cases in which a dissenting opinion was actually published, but also by the participation of all Members of a division hearing a case in the drafting of the report.

2501 Flett 2010, 312f.

2502 This is the reason why, for example, Greenwald 2003, 124 argues that dissenting opinions should be more widely used in WTO dispute settlement.

2503 See Flett 2010, 309f; Ehlermann 2003a, 696.

2504 See for this statement and figures Dunoff and Pollack 2017, 50. A list with individual opinions in appellate proceedings can be found in the WTO Analytical Annex, Art. 17.11 DSU at https://www.wto.org/english/res_e/publications_e/ai17_e/dsu_art17_jur.pdf.

2505 Bacchus 2002, 1029; Alvarez-Jiménez 2009a, 311.

Among the cases investigated in this work, there are only a handful in which dissenting opinions have been published, including the *EC – Asbestos* appellate case[2506] as well as the *United States – Tuna Labelling*[2507], the *Canada – Renewables*[2508] and *the China – Rare Earth*[2509] Panel reports.[2510] Moreover, there have been dissenting opinions in some other reports concerning trade-remedies.[2511] The dissenting voices made themselves heard concerning matters that had not yet been decided and were also quite controversial in the academic debate. They are almost "hidden" in the larger body of the respective reports and not given a separate heading. In the few cases in which individual opinions were produced, they were published anonymously. Nonetheless, these anonymous authors are known in "WTO litigation circles", according to one insider.[2512]

Another aspect of the WTO case law indicating a tendency to avoid highlighting the possible existence of different yet equally plausible interpretations of WTO law in a given case is the fact that the adjudicators have never relied on Art. 17.6 ADA (ii) in any of the dispute settlement reports. Applying this article would require an admission that there is more than one defensible interpretation of WTO law in a given case – an admission that the WTO adjudicators seem to be reluctant to make.[2513] Another explanation offered for the non-use of this provision in WTO dispute settlement is that there may be hardly any situations in which there are two equally convincing interpretations of a norm.[2514]

In addition, there are other aspects of the reasoning of the WTO adjudicators that are more difficult to analyse systematically, but that are also indicative of the tendency to make the possibility of different interpretations

2506 *European Communities – Measures Affecting Asbestos and Products Containing Asbestos, WT/DS135/AB/R* 2001, para. 149ff; for a summary of the dissenting opinion in this case, see Wiers and Mathis 2001, 220f.

2507 *United States – Measures Concerning the Importation, Marketing and Sale of Tuna and Tuna Products, WT/DS381/R* 2011, para. 7.146–7.190.

2508 *Canada – Certain Measures Affecting the Renewable Energy Generation Sector, WT/DS412/R and Canada – Measures Relating to the Feed-in Tariff Program, WT/DS426/R* 2012, sec. IX.

2509 Finding of the Panel as summarized in *China – Measures Related to the Exportation of Rare Earths, Tungsten, and Molybdenum, WT/DS431/AB/R, WT/DS432/AB/R, WT/DS433/AB/R* 2014, para. 1.13.

2510 For a brief discussion of some of the dissenting opinions, see Flett 2010.

2511 Elsig and Pollack 2012, n. 45.

2512 Flett 2010, 306.

2513 Spamann 2004, 517; van Damme 2010, 610.

2514 Flett 2010, 306.

invisible in WTO judicial-decision making. A first one is that the adjudicators do not normally discuss the pros and cons of different interpretations and on this basis arrive at a conclusion of what is the best interpretation in light of all arguments considered.[2515] Rather, the adjudicators tend to provide various arguments that support the interpretation they favour.[2516] Admittedly, the opposing arguments by the parties are presented in great detail and often repeated various times in the reports, making the different interpretations embraced by the parties visible. These views are not, however, presented as arguments that the WTO dispute settlement bodies themselves might subscribe to – judicially, only one solution is presented as possible.[2517] The solution presented is supported by different arguments. For example, as Bhala observes, the Appellate Body cites precedents even in cases where the law is relatively clear, and indicates that this happens where "the Appellate Body seems uncertain of itself".[2518] In relying on both text and on precedents, the Appellate Body presents two different arguments in support of a certain interpretation. Another example is the justification of the Appellate Body's interpretation of Art. XX GATT as containing a balance of rights and obligations of WTO Members; this interpretation is justified both by reference to international law, as it states that the interpretation results compellingly from the legal provision itself and also by pointing to the common intention of the parties.[2519]

Another aspect of how the adjudicators hide the possibility that there might be other options (as already described above[2520]), is the way in which they deal with precedents. Adjudicators will sometimes use precedents that do not really support a certain finding rather than acknowledging ruptures or discontinuities between different decisions which may suggest the possibility of different interpretations.

In sum, the absence of individual decisions, the lack of use of Art. 17.6 ADA, and the reluctance to explicitly depart from prior case law all allow the adjudicators to avoid having to choose from between several

2515 Summers and Taruffo call this pattern of justification "conflict settling" and find it, in particular, in the decisions of the higher courts in Argentina, Sweden, the UK, and the USA, see Summers and Taruffo 1991, 480f.

2516 Ibid., 479f call this a "cumulative pattern of justification".

2517 This view seems to be shared by Cartland, Depayre, and Woznowski 2012, 987 who critically refer to the Appellate Body's heavy reliance on the VCLT in this regard.

2518 Bhala 1999b, 8.

2519 See section 4.2 in this chapter.

2520 See section 3.3 in this chapter.

interpretations that are either presented as or appear to be *prima facie* equally plausible.

5.4. Assessment

None of the characteristics of the WTO case law discussed in this section is a doctrinal feature in the strict sense of the word; rather, they are rhetorical ways of arriving at and presenting findings. With the exception of the publication of individual opinions, there are no provisions on any of these issues in the DSU or other WTO agreements. This is why I do not present a discussion from a legal-technical point of view here as I have done for the other aspects of the WTO's judicial style discussed in this chapter, but proceed directly to the assessment.

Each of the three features of the WTO dispute settlement reports presented in this section contribute to the same effect: making the acceptance of the decisions more likely.

Concerning the length of reports, the Appellate Body's decisions are not always longer than those of *all* other international courts, but they are certainly longer than, for example, the ECJ's. An important factor contributing to their length is the detailed and often repetitious reporting of each of the arguments of the parties that is carried out before they are dealt with. This is a way of re-assuring the parties that all of their concerns have been heard, even if they ultimately do not prevail or the dispute settlement bodies ultimately do not decide on their claims by exercising judicial economy. This can clearly be seen as an attempt to convince the parties to accept the findings. Moreover, the length of the reports may also be linked to the rather banal insight that law and legal justifications are about words; it has been argued that "the more fully a point is argued, the more likely it will be successful"[2521] – one might easily add the clause "in convincing relevant audiences that the Appellate Body is right" to this statement.

Conversely, the length of the reports is also sometimes seen as a problem. For example, commentators have questioned whether it is possible to communicate concisely the central legal interpretations and the judicial approach to dealing with the facts in a report of about 1000 pages (plus another 1000 pages of annexes), such as the one by the *EC – Biotech Products* Panel.[2522] In part, the length of these reports may be attributable to the fact

2521 Jacob 2012, 60.
2522 Howse and Horn 2009, 50.

that the adjudicators ultimately need to cater to different audiences. In a seminal article, Weiler observed that the adjudicators need to address and win the support of two audiences – the wider public and the insider world of the Geneva trade communities.[2523] A level of detail and technicality that may work for "insiders" – the people involved to various degrees in WTO dispute settlement in Geneva – is likely to work less well for "outside" legal commentators and will often constitute an insurmountable hurdle to people who are not trade lawyers.[2524] Moreover, it is probably also more difficult to maintain the consistency of findings and formulations in a longer report than in a shorter one. In conclusion, what at first sight seems to be a very reasonable approach to winning over an audience – explaining, explaining and explaining even more – may in the end achieve quite the opposite: creating inconsistencies in the case law and leaving observers overwhelmed and puzzled.

The kind of verbal appeasement that the dispute settlement bodies sometimes engage in can also be taken as an attempt to "win over" both the parties to a dispute and the wider WTO membership, a kind of judicial diplomatic effort. At least some of these attempts are quite unusual – certainly, courts do not usually write accompanying letters to the parties explaining alleged misunderstandings of their findings, as the Panel did in the *EC – Biotech Products* case. Other courts also employ such rhetorical strategies, however. For example, de Visser notes that European constitutional courts are usually careful to emphasize that they need to be deferential to choices made by the elected legislators; he concludes that "judicial restraint must not only be done, it must also be *seen* to be done".[2525]

Turning to the third of the aspects discussed in this section, a plausible explanation for the observed tendency of obscuring the possibility of different opinions is that the judicial bodies wish to create the impression among readers that a certain interpretation results inevitably and by necessity from the text of the law. The creative, law-making, choice-making function of the adjudicators is thereby hidden. Generally, international courts follow different practices when publishing individual opinions. For example, the ICJ's case law has been described as "being burdened by mul-

---

2523 Weiler 2001.

2524 Indeed, some researchers coming e.g. from political science have complained about the inaccessibility of the judicial reports, see for example Krüger 2013, 28; but lawyers have also negatively commented on the technical language of WTO rulings, see Eeckhout 2010, 5f.

2525 De Visser 2013, 200f.

tiple concurring and dissenting opinions of different judges"[2526] and extended separate and dissenting opinions have been described as the ICJ norm[2527]. Indeed, there are certain cases with several individual opinions.[2528] By way of contrast, the ECJ follows the self-imposed rule of never publishing such opinions[2529] – though it does publish the ones by the Advocates General (which it does not always follow). The ECtHR also admits individual opinions.[2530] Generally, the number of individual opinions in WTO dispute settlement is considerably lower than for other international courts.[2531]

As described, the self-imposed procedural rules of the Appellate Body encourage consensus among Appellate Body Members. The decision of the Appellate Body to adopt this rule was, in the words of one former Member of the Appellate Body, geared towards projecting an image of legal and technical consistency and thus to strengthen the legitimacy of the organ.[2532] The Appellate Body's self-imposed procedural rules are aimed at collegial and consensus-oriented decision-making and not at fostering individual opinions. They do not, however, forbid individual opinions.

One can therefore understand the practice of the Appellate Body as a deliberate approach; it is a plausible assumption that the Appellate Body presents a coherent decision, delivered in one authoritative voice as the one and only correct interpretation of the law, to both win support for its decisions and to avoid a situation in which this effort is undermined by a dissenting voice.

Making disagreement public might have compromised the Appellate Body's position as an authoritative arbiter of WTO law, in particular in its infancy,[2533] just as other courts also sought to avoid the publication of dis-

2526 Howse and Essermann 2006, 66; for a similar observation see Hughes 2009, 285.

2527 Hughes 2009, 285.

2528 For example in the case International Court of Justice, 6 November 2003, Case Concerning Oil Platforms (Islamic Republic of Iran v. United States) there were no less than nine separate and dissenting opinions by individual judges on various aspects of the case.

2529 Slaughter and Helfer 1997, 326.

2530 Ibid.

2531 Kolsky Lewis 2006, 901f makes the observation in particular for the ICJ, the UNCLOS tribunal and NAFTA panels; see also Flett 2010, 310ff.

2532 Lacarte Muró 2007; as cited by Costa 2011, 8.

2533 Not all WTO Members have always been happy with this approach, though. Some least developed country (LDC) members in 2002 stated: "Often, and as

senting views during their early years.[2534] Indeed, a former director of the Appellate Body Secretariat observes that

> "a record of solid decisions, especially in the nascent years of an institution like the WTO, serves to contribute to clarity in the law and the establishment of a well-respected and authoritative institution. Frequent dissent in the early years would have eroded any authority the Appellate Body might have achieved. Moreover in the early years, it was especially important that delegations not speculate about or seek to exploit opposing doctrinal views of individual Appellate Body members."[2535]

A former Member of the Appellate Body attributes the relative paucity of individual opinions to the wish of the Members of the Appellate Body to contribute to the building of the new judicial institution, to establish its reputation for independent decision-making, and to gain credibility, acceptability and legitimacy.[2536] In this regard, he points out that publishing individual opinions might be viewed negatively in countries where individual judicial opinions are not usually published.[2537] Another WTO insider also considers the limited use of individual opinions in WTO dispute settlement to result from a "deliberate choice of the first generation of Appellate Body Members to swallow their ego and work on institution-building"[2538]. Also, the lack of individual opinions has been attributed to a wish of the Appellate Body Members to retain their independence from WTO Members by minimising the risk of pressure on or measures by WTO Members against individual Members of the Appellate Body.[2539]

---

demonstrated by judicial practice at the International Court of Justice, and in certain national court systems, dissenting judgments may bring to the fore usually unheard concerns which may in the long run shape the evolution of the system." They also criticized the Panels and the Appellate Body for an „excessively sanitized concern with legalisms", see "Negotiations On The Dispute Settlement Understanding- Proposal by the LDC Group", TN/DS/W/17, 9 October 2002, para. 5.

2534 McCall Smith 2003, 81.

2535 Hughes 2009, 285.

2536 Ehlermann 2003a, 695ff; for futher references see Dunoff and Pollack 2017, 50f.

2537 Ehlermann 2003a, 697.

2538 See comment by Zdouc, the director of the Appellate Body Secretariat, in Taniguchi et al. 2008, 402.

2539 Dunoff and Pollack 2017, 51ff.

By way of contrast, the former director of the Appellate Body Secretariat observes:

> "Former Appellate Body members maintain that regularly achieving consensus was more coincidence than design, and was always the result of frank and thorough discussions."[2540]

In this context it may be of relevance that in the initial years of the WTO countries sought to appoint Appellate Body Members not inclined to produce dissenting opinions, while in later years at least some players (such as the US) endorsed candidates that might publish such opinions.[2541]

A further point is noteworthy in this aspect: the Appellate Body is parsimonious concerning separate opinions, and at the same it does not very often deliver *obiter dicta.* This combination is remarkable as for other courts *obiter dicta* have been described as a means to deal with disagreement among judges sharing a bench.[2542] As Alvarez-Jimenez writes: The

> "use of obiter dicta allows the collegial judicial body not to leave dissenters with empty hands by permitting them to put their imprint on the decisions."[2543]

The WTO judicial approach is cautious with regard to both of those channels for articulating internal dissent – individual opinions and including an *obiter dictum*.

Disagreement persists about whether the Appellate Body's approach is right or not: some observers would like to see more individual opinions[2544]; others would like to see even fewer.[2545] In general, however, observers have concluded that the consensual practice of the Appellate Body has "contributed significantly to the impression of consistency, continuity, and coherence"[2546].

In conclusion, all of the stylistic traits of the dispute settlement reports and the described approaches of the Appellate Body can be explained as an attempt to win the acceptance of relevant constituencies and as attempts at legitimizing the WTO's judicial decisions.

2540 Hughes 2009, 285.

2541 Elsig and Pollack 2012, 17.

2542 Craig and Búrca 2011, 63 observe this for the ECJ where there are generally no individual opinions.

2543 Alvarez-Jiménez 2009a, 312f.

2544 Greenwald 2003, 123; Kolsky Lewis 2006.

2545 Flett 2010.

2546 Howse and Essermann 2006, 66.

6. *Conclusion: Judicial style of the WTO dispute settlement bodies*

In conclusion, how can the distinctive style of the WTO dispute settlement bodies and the Appellate Body in particular be described and explained?[2547]

I will focus in this section on a few overarching points, reflecting on the initial question of how the WTO judicial decision-makers justify their decisions; what is, hence, their judicial style. In section 6.1, I will describe the WTO's judicial style by using the Summers/Taruffo's table, presented in chapter 1, in which they set out the characteristics of the reasoning of other courts.[2548] In addition, I will summarize the findings on the aspects of the judicial style of the WTO that go beyond the rhetorical aspects discussed by Summers/Taruffo. In section 6.2, I will relate my insights on the WTO's judicial style back to the existing research on judicial styles discussed in the first chapter as well as the hypothesis developed there.

6.1. Characterizing the judicial style of the WTO dispute settlement bodies

The WTO dispute settlement bodies have, like other judicial bodies, their own judicial style. This is not surprising, but still an important observation.

6.1.1. Using the (adapted) Summers/Taruffo table

As careful readers will have noted, I have not directly assessed how the WTO dispute settlement is to be characterized with regard to each of the aspects summarized in the Summers/Taruffo table. To recap, sections 1 to 3 of this chapter considered aspects of the judicial style of the WTO dispute settlement bodies that are subject to codified or judicially construed procedural rules. Yet the issues discussed in these sections are not only legal-procedural in character; they also have a rhetorical dimension and are

2547 While I have focussed mostly on an analysis of Appellate Body reports, it has been observed that the Panels and the Appellate Body have a "broadly similar" style, see Meagher 2020, 142.

2548 See chapter, 1, 3.1.

therefore relevant for the Summers/Taruffo table. The remaining sections 4 and 5 were concerned with rhetorical issues in a narrow sense.

Before proceeding to apply the Summers/Taruffo scheme, a methodological *caveat* must be made in this regard: Given the length and number of dispute settlement reports, analysing each and every argument used by the Appellate Body with regard to its formalist/non-formalist orientation was not feasible. Moreover, putting arguments used by the adjudicators in any of the categories is likely to involve some subjective judgement. However, others, including Summers/Taruffo, must have faced the same issue of classifying the reasoning of different courts. In similar fashion to this study, they seem to have done so on the basis of existing, qualitative descriptions of the style of reasoning of different courts.[2549] This shows that such a classification of the WTO's judicial style is a feasible and meaningful exercise and valid research method.

The results of the assessment of the WTO dispute settlement bodies' judicial style, using the parameters of the modified Summers/Taruffo scheme, are presented in the following table:[2550]

2549 Lasser 2004 also uses a similar approach.

2550 Where possible, readers are referred to the sections of this work, where the respective features are discussed. In cases, where this was not possible, because the respective aspects have not been analyzed in a distinct section, examples or references will be provided in the narrative explanation following the table.

Table 3: Assessment of the style of reasoning/rhetoric of the WTO Appellate Body[2551]

	Formalist rhetoric or reasoning	Non-formalist/ less formalist rhetoric or reasoning	WTO dispute settlement	Predominantly formalist/ non formalist
1	Genuine issues of interpretation not openly acknowledged Only one answer possible	Open acknowledgment of alternative readings of statute More than one possible answer	Genuine issues of interpretation not openly acknowledged and only one answer possible – Different possible interpretations mainly acknowledged through replication of arguments of parties and Panels (see section 5.3) – ADA standard of review, which refers to the possibility of more than one defensible interpretation, never used (see section 5.3) – Individual opinions rare (see section 5.3) – No explicit departure from precedents (see section 3.1)	Predominantly formalist
2	High proportion of legalistic, technical and bureaucratic language in the opinion	Lower proportion of legalistic and technical language in the opinion	Non-legalistic and non-technical language in the opinion – Frequent reference to standard dictionaries, i.e. everyday language used (see section 1.1) – Use of everyday language, e.g. to relate to Panel reports (see section 5.1) Legalistic and technical language in opinion – Occasional use of legal terms in Latin (e.g. *arguendo, in dubio mitius*) or technical legal terms ("good faith") (see section 5.1) – Occasional "complaints" by non-lawyers on lack of accessibility of reports (see section 5.4)	Elements of both types of reasoning
3	Abbreviated and terse opinion	Extended and elaborate opinion	Extended and elaborate opinion – Long decisions with a lot of explanation (see section 5.1) – Explanations on what has not been said in a report (see section 5.2)	Predominantly non-formalist

	Formalist rhetoric or reasoning	Non-formalist/ less formalist rhetoric or reasoning	WTO dispute settlement	Predominantly formalist/ non formalist
4	Implicit model of rationality is logico-deductive, i.e. syllogistic subsumption Evaluative and creative role (of courts, CG) not recognized, decision process viewed as essentially one of cognitive ascertainment and application of the law that "is"	Implicit model of rationality is not deductive but discursive – open choice Acknowledgment of some evaluative and creative role	Implicit model of rationality is logico-deductive, i.e. syllogistic subsumption: – Preferred method of interpretation is textual interpretation (see section 1.1) – Explicit statement of Appellate Body that role of adjudicators is not to "make law" – Limited role of substantive principles, including proportionality principle (see section 4.1) – Balancing takes place only in limited circumstances and does not normally include balancing of substantive interests, reference to established legal principles or common intention of WTO Members in justification (see sections 4.2, 4.3) – Adjudicators stress that the interpretation they choose is in line with the common intention of WTO Members, they have no choice, cannot add to or diminish the rights of the parties (see section 1.5) – Infrequent acknowledgement of gaps (see section 2.2) – Decisions are presented as resulting from precedents (see sections 3.1, 3.4)	Predominantly formalist

2551 Sections mentioned in this table are sections in this chapter.

	Formalist rhetoric or reasoning	Non-formalist/ less formalist rhetoric or reasoning	WTO dispute settlement	Predominantly formalist/ non formalist
5	Higher proportion of formal rather than substantive reasons	Lower proportion of formal rather than substantive reasons	High proportion of formal rather than substantive reasons – Only rarely explicit policy considerations outside of Art. XX GATT, XIV GATS, which refer to such policy objectives; few moral, political, economic arguments used (see section 4.2) – Frequent references to VCLT (see section 1.7.1) – Reference to principles of international law, even where their status in international law is doubtful (e.g. in dubio mitius) (see sections 1.7.3) – Reference to precedents even if they do not support a certain reasoning or decision (see section 3.1 and chapter 2, section 1.5.3 – Teleological interpretation has no central role (see sections 1.7.2, 1.3)	Predominantly formalist
6	Magisterial and authoritative	Argumentative and dialogic	Magisterial and authoritative – Very rare individual opinions (see section 5.3) – Interpretations presented as only possible interpretation (see above, row 1) Argumentative and dialogic: – Length of reports (see section 5.1) – Careful repetition of arguments of parties (see section 5.1) – Transparency on methods of interpretation (see section 1.7.1) and reference to VCLT – Use of appeasement techniques (see section 5.2) – Attempts at dialogue with parties (e.g. letter of Panel in GMO case) (see section 5.2) – Reports signed by individuals (see section 5.1) – Sometimes personal tone to reasoning of Appellate Body, expressing astonishment or indignation, use of "we" (see section 5.1)	Elements of both types of reasoning, but more non-formalist aspects

With regard to the characteristics in row 1, the extent to which different interpretations of WTO law may be possible is acknowledged, the style of the Appellate Body is predominantly formalist. It is rarely acknowledged that more than one solution to a certain interpretive question can be justified. The adjudicators do not generally discuss arguments favouring different interpretations, but predominantly those favouring the interpretation they adopt in the end. The situation to which Art. 17.6 (ii) ADA refers, i.e. the possibility that a provision admits more than one permissible interpretation, has never been acknowledged to exist in WTO dispute settlement. Individual opinions, which indicate that judges may hold different views on how the law is to be interpreted and thus that different interpretations are defensible, are rare. The consensus-oriented decision-making creates an image of the interpretation adopted being the only possible and defensible interpretation. Finally, the heavy reliance on prior case law, including tenuous precedents, creates a (seemingly) consistent body of law that the decision-makers in later cases are effectively "forced" to follow.

With regard to the characteristics in row 2, only a summary assessment can be given here. For a more in-depth analysis, a statistical linguistic assessment of the degree to which technical vs. non-technical language is used by WTO adjudicators would be required. This is beyond the scope of what is possible in this work. Summers and Taruffo provide little guidance on what they mean by technical vs. non-technical language; they only sometimes use "technical" as opposed to "ordinary" language.[2552] This implies that "technical" language refers to terms that are used in a specific legal sense, deviating from everyday use of the terms. If "technical" is understood in this sense, the general impression is that there is technical language in the reports, but often non-technical, ordinary language is also used: the latter being probably the more widely used. There are regular references to, for example, legal terms in Latin (such as *in dubio mitius*, *arguendo*) or technical terms (e.g. good faith) that a non-lawyer would not normally be familiar with. Indeed, some non-lawyers have complained about the reports being too technical and hardly accessible for non-specialists.[2553] On the other hand, when seeking to identify the meaning of a certain term, the adjudicators do not resort primarily to legal definitions, but to standard dictionaries. Also, the Appellate Body sometimes uses a quite personal, even emotional tone and everyday non-technical language. However, the assessment that such non-technical language is quite widely used and thus the Appellate Body leans more to the non-formalist side in this

2552 Basically, they do not explain at all what precisely they mean by it, see Summers and Taruffo 1991, 481ff.

2553 See above, n. 2524.

regard is obviously subjective. Moreover, it comes from a lawyer familiar with legal language; a non-lawyer may come to a different assessment.

With regard to the characteristics in row 3, the reports are extended and elaborate, rather than abbreviated and terse – as shown already by their length. Arguments of the parties as well as facts are explained in detail. The Appellate Body sometimes discusses at great length the dictionary definitions of words, even where the definitions do not add much to the understanding of the term. The adjudicators often stress what they have not decided – namely that which adds nothing to the decision or interpretation of the law and is from a strict legal point of view superfluous. The adjudicators use many words, not few.

Concerning row 4, the model of rationality implied in the reports as well as the degree to which they acknowledge an evaluative and creative role of the WTO dispute settlement bodies, the Appellate Body is predominantly formalist in orientation. Textual interpretation, i.e. a method of deducting in a logical way the meaning of the text and drawing syllogistic conclusions on whether a certain situation fulfils the predicates of a norm, prevails. There is a limited role for methods of reasoning that are non-deductive, i.e. balancing and resorting to principles. Where balancing is used, there is a tendency to present the balancing exercise as a requirement resulting from the text of the law. Martineau notes that the Appellate Body's interpretation of Art. XX GATT as involving a balancing of rights and obligations and WTO Members and establishing an equilibrium is presented as a logical imperative resulting from the text of the agreement;[2554] moreover, it is also justified by reference to established international legal principles. Describing balancing – which is normally a judicially-created tool, giving judicial decision-makers considerable leeway – as an inevitable deduction from a text that contains no reference to it and had not been interpreted as containing a balancing requirement in previous jurisprudence is unexpected, to say the least. The emphasis on textual interpretation also signals that the WTO dispute settlement bodies do not depart from the classical judicial role of interpreting rather than making law. The adjudicators have occasionally stressed that their interpretation is in line with the intention of parties, going so far as to state explicitly that they have "no choice" with regard to a certain interpretation as in the *Hormones I* case.[2555] There are also explicit statements by the Appellate Body that its own role is

2554 Martineau 2007, 1002.
2555 See above, section 1.1.

not to make law as in *India – Wool Shirts*[2556]. Gaps are hardly acknowledged to exist; by implication, there is no apparent creative role for the adjudicators in filling them.

With regard to row 5, the degree of formal versus substantive reasons being induced for a decision, there is also a predominantly formalist orientation of the Appellate Body. Teleological interpretation, where political objectives motivating certain norms are more important, does not play a huge role in WTO dispute settlement. Almost every interpretation is justified by resorting to a formal legal reason, i.e. either a method of interpretation mentioned in the VCLT, an allegedly established principle of international law (which may not be that established after all, such as the *in dubio mitius* principle), or a precedent (which may not be that suitable in some cases). What is mostly absent from the WTO judicial style are policy-related arguments, which, according to the accounts of both Lasser and Kennedy[2557], are very prominent in the US judicial discourse. The interests and policy choices behind a certain norm are rarely discussed[2558] and the Appellate Body rarely uses the language of morals or economics (unless explicitly required by a norm).

The balancing formula used in the necessity analysis in Art. XX GATT and XIV GATS is almost the only place where the importance of certain policy goals is consistently mentioned. In the context of the GATT and GATS exception norms those interpreting the agreement can hardly avoid referring to policy considerations, given that the text of the WTO agreements refers to distinct policy objectives. And even in this context, the Appellate Body's stance is so careful that it is not clear whether the Appellate Body actually engages in a full-fledged balancing of the interests at stake or not, whether it decides a case on the bases of policy considerations or it does not.[2559] Normally, the Appellate Body claims that it is the WTO Members' prerogative to decide on policies (as long as they act consistently with WTO law).

With regard to row 6, the reports contain magisterial and authoritative as well as argumentative and dialogic elements, with the latter probably being somewhat more widespread. Among the magisterial and authoritative features is the inclination to present a particular interpretation as the only one possible, as identified in the discussion of the elements in row 1

2556 See above, section 3.2.
2557 See chapter 1, section 3.2.
2558 See also Picciotto 2005, 13.
2559 See chapter 2, section 1.5.1.

above. Another magisterial element is the paucity of individual opinions, and the Appellate Body's attempt to speak in one voice. But there are also many instances where the Appellate Body appears to try and convince readers rather than simply handing down an opinion. Among the argumentative and dialogic elements in the reasoning of the Appellate Body is the length of the reports; someone who makes no attempt at convincing would likely not need to write so many pages. The length of judgements signals to the audience that every possible argument has been thoroughly considered and to the parties that they have been listened to. A contributing factor here is the extent to which the arguments of the respective parties to a dispute are related in the reports and dealt with by the adjudicators. The transparency regarding the methods of interpretation also must be understood as a way to convince parties; not all courts explain their methods of interpretation to their readership. Resorting to the established methods of interpretation of international law, which are widely accepted and even codified in an international agreement, amounts to an assurance that the tools used to wield a decision are proper and acceptable.

There are other ways through which the adjudicators try to convince the audience that they are right. They use appeasement techniques that contribute nothing to the legal findings but to send certain signals to a chosen audience. Verbal deference to the right of Members to decide certain issues, to determine their appropriate level of protection, pointing to what is not decided in a certain decision or to the case-by-case character of a certain decision are ways of assuaging fears over the impact of a certain decision in the future, while giving the adjudicators scope for deciding future cases in a suitable manner. Both the sometimes personal tone of the decisions as described above as well as the fact that the Appellate Body Members use the pronoun "we" and sign decisions by name are also argumentative and dialogic rather than magisterial and authoritative elements of judicial style.

In sum, having considered all of the dimensions included above, the WTO adjudicators and the Appellate Body are predominantly formalist in style.[2560] At the same time, there are important non-formalist elements, in particular the explicit attempts the adjudicators make to convince their audience of the correctness of their findings, rather than simply handing them down in an authoritative tone. Like many other courts the WTO dispute settlement bodies have adopted a judicial style that is between the

2560 For a similar conclusion, see Picciotto 2005, 13.

two extreme poles identified by Summers/Taruffo, the formalist French way of reasoning and the non-formalist US rhetoric.[2561]

6.1.2. Other aspects of judicial style

The WTO's judicial style has additional features, such as the standard of review applied and avoidance techniques, that do not fit easily into the categories above, mostly because they do not concern judicial reasoning or rhetoric in a narrow sense. These aspects of the judicial style of the WTO dispute settlement bodies are discussed in the present section, again with a view to explaining how they contribute to enhancing the perceived legitimacy of WTO dispute settlement decisions and to avoiding criticism.

The standard of review to be applied in WTO dispute settlement is, as described above, only circumscribed in a rather general manner by the adjudicators, giving Panels significant leeway on how to deal with the facts of a case. The only area where some more finely-grained rules are starting to appear is with regard to cases under the SPS Agreement. The application of the formulated rules to the facts of the case does not seem to be uniform, and it is not entirely clear which factors determine the intensity of scrutiny. Again, a potential exception is the SPS Agreement where in recent cases a standard of review somewhat more deferential than previously used was applied, though it is not clear whether these are outliers or represent a future trend. The standard of review is a sensitive issue and when the adjudicators "get it wrong", they risk accusations of activism. It is, therefore, difficult to understand why the adjudicators have been hesitant to commit explicitly to a uniformly deferential standard of review. The only apparent rationale is that keeping the standard of review rather vague gives them more discretion and decision-making space in future cases.

Another issue not easily captured in the formalist/non-formalist table is the use of avoidance techniques by the WTO adjudicators. Avoiding a decision on certain issues avoids creating potentially unwanted precedents, it may make it easier for a defending party to accept a decision (as it is not losing on all points and may bring them up again in a future case), and it pre-empts potential critical reactions. Therefore, this feature is best explained in terms of seeking to gain acceptance for judicial decisions from WTO Members.

2561 Summers and Taruffo 1991, 506f.

A final point that also fails to fit easily in the Summers/Taruffo scheme above is that the adjudicators seem to be bolder concerning procedural than substantive matters; while they have resorted to international law to clarify procedural measures and for gap-filling, they have been much more hesitant to do so with regard to issues of substantive law. Some have described the Appellate Body as being "activist" with regard to procedural matters.[2562] A former Member of the Appellate Body also observed it to be particularly cautious in following textual meaning when substantive obligations were at stake.[2563] As noted above, if a court takes a more active role in deciding procedural matters – using principles, filling gaps, drawing on non-WTO international law – it is less likely to provoke antagonism than if it were to do so on substantive provisions. Deciding procedural matters is the very function of a court.[2564] Hence, the observed pattern that the adjudicators are relatively more cautious with substantive interpretations can be understood in terms of efforts by the adjudicators to legitimize their judgements, to project a role of the "voice of the law" in the more sensitive area of interpreting substantive provisions, and to be mindful of the likely preferences of WTO Members.

6.1.3. Assessments of the WTO judicial style in the literature

Given how hard the adjudicators seek to present any findings as resulting from the text of the WTO agreements, it is not surprising that the literature on WTO dispute settlement features occasional references to Dworkin's Hercules – an omnipotent judge that discerns or detects, but never makes law.[2565]

On this basis, a majority of academic observers appears to be generally quite satisfied with the judicial decision-making in the WTO so far.[2566] Since contributions oftentimes cover both certain aspects of the judicial style and the outcome, it is somewhat difficult to gauge what exactly observers are satisfied with; however, there appears to be quite some satisfaction with the WTO's judicial style among academic observers.

2562 McCall Smith 2003, 67.

2563 Ehlermann 2003a, 700.

2564 See on the role of courts in crafting procedural rules also above section 2.5.

2565 Cho 2009a; Martineau 2007, 1003.

2566 See above in the assessment sections of this chapter, but also chapter 2, section 4.2.

Nonetheless, Hercules is not liked by everyone. The judicial style adopted by the Appellate Body, while aimed at generating acceptance of the judicial decisions, has also produced friction. Even though the adjudicators have not openly embraced the idea that they are fulfilling a creative role, they have not been spared from criticism of being activist. Steinberg for example concludes that the Appellate Body has

> "leaned toward the less deferential approach in deciding whether to interpret WTO agreements, favoring gap filling, ambiguity clarification, and dynamism".[2567]

Similarly, Guan states that by its choice of interpretive methods the Appellate Body exhibits a "clear tendency of 'judicial activism'".[2568] WTO dispute settlement has also been called an "exercise in trade legislation"[2569]. Others have phrased similar statements in less general terms and pointed to specific instances where they consider the adjudicators to have adopted an "activist" approach.[2570] For example, the Appellate Body's interpretation of the term exhaustible natural resources in Art. XX (g) GATT, which was partially drawn from non-WTO international legal norms, has been described as (inappropriately) activist.[2571] Similarly, the Appellate Body has been described as "backing away from its mandate" with the *Korea – Beef* "balancing approach", as WTO Members could not have expected such an interpretation in light of GATT precedents.[2572] Others have made the opposite contention and stated that adjudicators have not assumed an overly active role in interpreting the open-textured and ambiguous norms of WTO law[2573] and that the Appellate Body has, in various instances, shown considerable judicial restraint[2574].

The choosing of one position over the other is likely a function of the concrete cases which have been read; at this stage of the development of WTO case law it is unlikely that anyone might have read and digested each and every decision fully. Positions may also be dependent on their time of formation; for example, a reader of the WTO case law may have come to a

2567 Steinberg 2004, 260.

2568 Guan 2014, 243.

2569 Greenwald 2003, 113, referring, however, primarily to trade-remedy cases.

2570 For example Barfield 2001, 13.

2571 Kelly 2002, 372.

2572 Bown and Trachtman 2009, 130.

2573 Oesch 2003, 644.

2574 See the references in chapter, 2 section 4.2, but also Zeitler 2005, 755; statement by Lacarte-Muró in Taniguchi et al. 2008, 393.

quite different impression of the standard of review applied in WTO dispute settlement after *EC – Biotech Products* and *Hormones II* respectively. Some observers have actually identified changes in the WTO's judicial style over time, such as a movement away from formalism.[2575] It is perhaps even more important for the overall assessment of the WTO judicial style that what is considered acceptable varies – over time, across legal cultures, between individuals. In the WTO setting, this cacophony is probably even more marked, because the organization as such is controversial. As noted above, charges of judicial activism, overreaching etc. are often a mere *chiffre* for disliking a decision. In sum, characterizations of the WTO judicial style need to be taken with a measure of caution.

My own perspective, already briefly mentioned in the first chapter of this work, is that sticking the label "judicial activism" on a court's behaviour is of limited value. If we presume that law is indeterminate, to a degree at least, this means that more than one legal interpretation can often be justified as being in conformity with the law. Hence, there is often simply no established baseline from which a court could be said to depart or which it could be said to cross when adopting a specific interpretation.[2576] This does not mean that a court's behaviour cannot be described in objective terms as e.g. more deferential or less deferential regarding the measure under review. Indeed, this type of assessment is what this work has delivered. However, if a statement that a court is too "activist" or "creative", "making law" etc. is to be a meaningful signifier for identifiable court's behaviour, a definition would define the position of the lines are between an "activist/non-activist" behaviour or a "creative/non-creative" attitude, and also the difference between interpreting existing law and making new law. Exact definitions on these issues are difficult and are more likely to reflect the preferences of the individual producing the definition than they are to offer a meaningful description of judicial decision-making.

Against this background, the present work does not offer (debatable) statements on whether the Appellate Body is (too) activist or creative or engages in inappropriate judicial law-making. Instead, I have described the judicial style used by the WTO dispute settlement bodies using a set of indicators to determine how formalist/non-formalist they are. In addition, I have analysed how certain aspects of the WTO's judicial style contributes to legitimizing the decisions taken.

2575 See above n. 265 and 1859.
2576 Zarbiyev 2012, 5 seems to make a similar point.

6.2. Making sense of the judicial style of the WTO dispute settlement bodies

The previous section described the judicial style of the WTO dispute settlement. In this section, I will relate these insights on the WTO's judicial style to the literature discussed in chapter 1 that seeks to explain the judicial style of different courts.

As discussed in chapter 1, one widely held assumption in the literature is that one of the most important factors influencing the judicial style of a court is that judges try to win acceptance for their judgements and the judicial institution of which they are a part. The above analysis of individual aspects of the WTO's judicial style supports the assumption that this also applies to the WTO adjudicators. Moreover, the adjudicators indicate – in more or less explicit ways – that they are aware of the minefield they operate in[2577] and try to avoid what could be considered inappropriately activist steps, or as violating the boundaries of their mandate. This is evident from some of the quotes reproduced above (e.g. the Appellate Body's statement in *Hormones I* that it would not be prudent to make a general statement on the status of the precautionary principle in international law), but also from the extra-judicial statements of former Members of the Appellate Body.

However, as also discussed in the first chapter exactly which style a court adopts in a given legal and political setting is influenced by a number of factors. On this basis, I have developed the following hypothesis of what judicial style is to be expected in the WTO legal setting:

> "Consequently, it is to be expected that the WTO dispute settlement decisions – while predominantly formalist in style – will not look like those of the French *Court de Cassation* and will be considerably longer and supported by more arguments. It can also be expected that the Appellate Body will be very careful to present any of its findings as being rooted in WTO law and being justified by the use of established method of interpretation. It is also likely that the Appellate Body will seek to be or at least appear to be consistent in its decision-making by attributing its own case law some kind of precedential value. It is also

2577 See chapter 1, section 4.3.1 for a discussion why the WTO dispute settlement bodies are in a difficult situation, and probably more so than other newly established courts.

like that the adjudicators will avoid any appearance of being guided by their own political or economic preferences."[2578]

The characterization of the WTO's judicial style in the preceding section matches this – rather general – expectation: The WTO's style is predominantly formalist in orientation. Important elements of the WTO's judicial style are very long and detailed decisions, transparency about methods of interpretation, reliance on textual and other formal legal arguments rather than policy arguments, limited use of balancing, avoidance of bold and far-reaching use of potentially controversial principles, strong apparent reliance on precedents (which are, however, not always used correctly), use of certain techniques to avoid potentially controversial decisions, and an often appeasing rhetoric.

At the same time and taking features such as the length of the reports, the notable attempts at convincing the audience, or the transparency about methods of interpretations into account, it is safe to say that the WTO dispute settlement system draws on a discursive rather than an institutional model of authority. Thus, the WTO model appears to be a combination of a predominantly, but not exclusively, formalist style of justificatory reasoning and a predominantly discursive model of authority.

This combination is different from the one that Lasser found for the French *Cour de Cassation* and the US Supreme Court respectively. In the French setting, there is a combination of a formalist style of justificatory[2579] reasoning with an institutional model of authority, while in the US there is a combination of a non-formalist style of reasoning with discursive justification as the source of authority. These combinations have an inherent logic: A court that has a strong institutional legitimacy can simply derive judgements from that same source of authority, as if it did not have a choice in the matter. A court that does not have this type of institutional authority needs to explain itself more and better in order to convince its audience.

The combination of a predominantly formalist style with a discursive model of authority – which appears to exist for the WTO – seems perhaps less intuitive. Yet, considering some of the factors identified in the first

2578 See chapter 1, 4.6.

2579 Summers and Taruffo 1991, 504 briefly discuss, whether the French opinions can actually be described as "justificatory" at all, given how short they are, and whether "conclusory" might be a better description. They argue, however, that the French judicial decisions are also justificatory to a certain degree.

chapter[2580] as influencing judicial styles, it still makes sense[2581]. The WTO dispute settlement bodies could not draw on a reserve of institutional legitimacy right after their establishment. WTO law itself was contested – perhaps not such much among those that concluded the agreements, but among a wider public. The adjudicators thus needed to explain their decisions and do so in a way that ideally various audiences would understand. And they needed to avoid antagonising WTO Members. The judicial style of the WTO, formalism – but a formalism well explained – appears to be a plausible manner of dealing with this challenge. This holds true especially when combined, as in the WTO dispute settlement decisions, with other features such as reliance on other less contested legal rules outside of the WTO legal universe (international law more broadly) or simply avoiding to decide controversial issues to the extent feasible.

2580 See chapter 1, 3.2. and 3.3.

2581 It should be noted that I have not investigated empirically, which factors exactly have influenced the WTO's judicial style. It is therefore not possible to offer any definite conclusions on whether the theoretical insights summarized in chapter 1 on which factors influence judicial styles apply to the WTO context as well. None of the findings in this work appears to contradict these earlier insights, however. What is more, the hypothesis developed in the first chapter on the likely judicial style of the WTO dispute settlement bodies on the basis of applying these factors in the WTO context appears to be corroborated by the empirical analysis of the WTO's judicial style; this in turn would make it quite plausible that these factors are relevant to the WTO as well.

Chapter 4: Conclusions and outlook

> *"One cannot criticise the lawyers for doing what they are programmed to do – that would be to shoot the messenger."*[2582]

> *"Ladies and gentlemen, your analyses and comments in fact delight us [...]. In our judgments you find depths of meanings which were unbeknown to us! And for all that, you do not shy away from attributing us your own thoughts, and perform psycho-analytical miracles which massage our egos and fill us with pride."*[2583]

The Appellate Body is described by most commentators as a success, even though it is not always clear by which yardstick success is measured.[2584] This does not mean that certain interpretations or decisions taken in specific cases have not been subject to criticism – they have. This also does not mean that there are no voices critical of the judicial style and approach of the Appellate Body more generally – there are certainly outspoken critics and there are also reform proposals in the academic literature.[2585] Nevertheless, it is fair to say that there is no wide-spread, systematic discontent with the WTO case law or the Appellate Body's approach in the legal literature – quite the contrary.

What is more important in the present context is, however, that there appears to be no fundamental discontent among the majority of WTO Members with the WTO's dispute settlement mechanism – at least not one serious enough to spur action. The US blockade of the re-appointment of

2582 Flett 2011, 19.
2583 Mohammed Bedjaoui (2003), Former President of the ICJ in front of a group of international legal scholars, as quoted by Zarbiyev 2012, 25.
2584 See below, section 2.
2585 See chapter 2, section 4.2 and chapter 3, section 6.1.3.

Appellate Body Members is an exception, albeit a very impactful one, to this general picture. WTO Members are in fact the most important constituency for the WTO dispute settlement system.[2586] If they do not fundamentally oppose what the dispute settlement bodies do, this means that the dispute settlement bodies, and the Appellate Body in particular, have been successful in deciding the cases brought before it in a way that is acceptable to WTO Members; it also means that the legitimacy of the WTO dispute settlement system as a judicial institution is no longer fundamentally questioned (if, in fact, it ever was). Thus, in this section "success" is used interchangeably with empirical legitimacy, i.e. the *de facto* acceptance of the Appellate Body's decisions by WTO Members and its authority in taking these decisions as justified.

In this last chapter of the work, I would like to use the accumulated insights of this work to formulate plausible assumptions on how the Appellate Body has managed to generate that kind of legitimacy. I offer plausible assumptions rather than definite conclusions, because the methodology employed in this work does not allow definite conclusions on the causality between an observed behaviour of the Appellate Body and the reaction of the receiving audience to be drawn: the methodology did not entail a systematic survey of how content WTO Members and other constituencies are with the Appellate Body.

It should be stated again that the empirical bases for the conclusions I offer here are primarily the "trade and ..." cases and the provisions specifically relevant for them, enriched by insights from the literature and occasional references to other cases. Conversely, the US dissatisfaction with the Appellate Body's case law appears to be at least partially motivated by concerns over the handling of certain procedural issues and cases on subsidies, anti-dumping, trade remedies and other matters adjudicated under WTO agreements that were not within the scope of this work.[2587] A further limitation is that I have not systematically studied the political context of individual cases, notably the political actors involved and their stakes in a dispute or the wider preferences and attitudes of WTO Members towards the WTO dispute settlement system. The conclusions offered are therefore subject to corresponding limitations.

The chapter is structured as follows. In section 1, I will present some evidence supporting my claim that the majority of WTO Members is by and

2586 Krüger 2013, 57.

2587 See the list of issues mentioned in US Trade Representative 2020 and section 1.3 below.

large satisfied with what the Panels and the Appellate Body have done. For this purpose, I will look at potential countermeasures that the WTO Members might have taken against the dispute settlement system if dissatisfied with it, and the extent to which they actually have resorted to those countermeasures. In section 2, I will summarize existing literature on those aspects of judicial decision-making through which the Appellate Body has created legitimacy. In section 3, I will present my own version of that success story that expands on, modifies, or fine-tunes existing findings on the matter. Section 4 concludes the chapter and the work overall with a broader outlook on some of the issues discussed in this work.

1. *The success of the WTO dispute settlement system – the evidence*

The first chapter of this work[2588] presented research on how judicial decisions by international tribunals are influenced by the preferences of states that have access to a court or are bound by its decisions (e.g. the EU Member States in the case of the ECJ or the WTO Members in the case of the WTO); in the terminology of political science, states are also referred to as "principals" in this context. To recap, this kind of research has shown that courts are strategic actors that use whatever decision-making space they have in a way that might keep them from provoking hostile reactions from their principals or at least some particularly important principals.

Conversely, the principals (in the present context WTO Members), may be expected to take certain counter-measures when dissatisfied with individual dispute settlement decisions or when having more fundamental doubts about the dispute settlement system. The potential countermeasures relevant to the WTO universe, which were identified in chapter 1[2589] were as follows: a political reversal of substantive rules of WTO law in an attempt to change interpretations adopted by the dispute settlement bodies; modifications to the DSU changing the competences of the dispute settlement bodies; non-compliance with dispute settlement decisions; non-use of the dispute settlement system (including exit from the WTO), and refusal to re-appoint Appellate Body Members, in particular, but not limited to those, not liked by Members. I will consider what evidence there is of any of these events materializing in the following section. While these proxies are not the only way to measure the success of the Appellate

2588 See chapter 1, section 2.1.
2589 See chapter 1, section 4.4.1.

Body,[2590] they are both consistent with the theoretical framework of this work, and, perhaps more importantly, have the advantage of being relatively easy to apply.[2591]

The section is structured as follows: In the first part, I will show that none of the following potential countermeasures available to WTO Members has materialized to any significant degree or been taken by a significant number of WTO Members: preventing the (re)-appointment of Members of the Appellate Body (1.1), legislative overturn of judicial decisions (1.2), attempts at changing the functioning of the WTO dispute settlement bodies through altering their mandate or the rules governing their decision-making (1.3), non-compliance with the dispute settlement decisions (1.4), and the non-use of the system (1.5).

The conclusion is that none of these actions, any one of which would signal dissatisfaction with the functioning of the WTO dispute settlement system, has so far been taken to any significant degree or by a significant number of WTO Members. While the US refusal to re-appoint Appellate Body Members has far-reaching effects, effectively preventing the Appellate Body from functioning, the US is the only country to have taken such far-reaching action. Consequently, I discuss in 1.6 whether this may be because the WTO dispute settlement system is simply not important enough to cause WTO Members to take that kind of adverse reaction. Finally, I present the conclusions from the preceding sections in 1.7.

1.1. (Re)-appointment of Members of the Appellate Body

Two types of measures that WTO Members dissatisfied with the decision-making of the Appellate Body could take are blocking the appointment of new Appellate Body Members in general, or the (re)-appointment of indi-

---

2590 For other ways of assessing the success of the Appellate Body see Mavroidis 2006; van den Bossche 2006; Pauwelyn 2016b, 1123; Zdouc 2008, 370. It should also be noted that not all of these authors use the term "success" or "legitimacy". For example Shaffer, Elsig, and Puig 2016 refer to the "authority" of the Appellate Body; they seem to mean something similar to what I mean by empirical legitimacy, though.

2591 This is not the case for some alternative ways of conceptualizing and measuring "success". Notably, a systematic review of the minutes of the DSB sessions where WTO Members often state their view on a dispute settlement report comes to mind, but is not feasible within the scope of this work.

vidual candidates whose views on matters of WTO law and judicial decision-making they dislike.

Blocking the appointment of new Appellate Body Members in general is a measure to which one WTO Member, the US, has in fact resorted. The US had raised concerns over the Appellate Body's decision-making for a number of years[2592] before actually blocking the re-appointment of an Appellate Body Member in 2016 for the first time. One factor behind the US blockage is likely the fact that it has been the country against which most WTO complaints have been filed[2593]; in about 90 % of these cases there has been a finding of non-compliance of an US measure with WTO law.[2594] Factors that could explain the high number of disputes in which the US was a defendant are the importance of the US as a trading partner for many countries, but also the fact that, at least according to some evidence, the US is less compliant with international trade law than other countries[2595].

The underlying motives for the US blockage of the Appellate Body appear to go beyond the track record of the US in WTO dispute settlement, however, and could be a consequence of the US stance towards a rule-based international trading system in general. The Obama administration's position on the international trading system has been described as "economic nationalism".[2596] Conversely, the Trump administration has been characterised as marked by a high level of "aggression against international law" and "rejectionism" of an "economic order based on the international rule of law".[2597] Reflecting this, the first decision to block the re-appointment of an Appellate Body Member was taken by the US trade administration under President Obama[2598], but the policy was continued and exacerbated under President Trump[2599]. It has also been pointed out that the ini-

2592 See the various US documents and statements cited in the appendices of US Trade Representative 2020.

2593 See Reich 2017, 5 for cases until 2017; US Trade Representative 2020, 3 for a more recent figure.

2594 US Trade Representative 2020, 3.

2595 Reich 2017, 17ff.

2596 Charnovitz 2018, 228.

2597 P. J. K. 2018, 227ff maintains that there are "indications that the US wants simply to be rid of the AB".

2598 See Charnovitz 2018, 231; Picker 2020, 60.

2599 See for example the position of the US as recorded in Dispute Settlement Body, Minutes of the Meeting, 22 November 2019, para. 5.8.

tial agreement of the US to the creation of the Appellate Body was due to an expectation that the appeal mechanism

> "would only be used in rare cases, would not greatly prolong the process, and would most likely confirm panel findings, allowing the Unites States to apply retaliatory measures approved by WTO institutions".[2600]

Moreover, there is some evidence that the US stance is not motivated exclusively by a desire to see changes in the Appellate Body's functioning, but also by the US view that the refusal to re-appoint Appellate Body Members constitutes an effective leverage for changes that it wishes to see to WTO rules above and beyond dispute settlement.[2601] At the same time, the US has also been described as being "best at leveraging the judicial process to define the meaning of the rules in a way that suits their interests" among the WTO Members[2602] and it is also the country to have brought most complaints[2603]. The US stance concerning the WTO dispute settlement system is thus not without contradictions.[2604]

In stark contrast to the US position, a large majority of Members want to secure the continued functioning of the Appellate Body and have repeatedly called for re-launching the process of selecting new Appellate Body Members.[2605] A number of Members have even agreed on the establishment of an interim appeal system in light of the Appellate Body impasse;[2606] this system is based on Art. 25 DSU and only Members that join it are allowed to bring a claim or can be made a defendant. Thus, while other WTO Members seem to share, to a degree at least, the view that some aspects of how the WTO Appellate Body functions are in need of reform (see below, section 1.3), the position of one country cannot be taken as indicative of a wide-spread fundamental discontent of WTO Members with the system.

2600 Shaffer, Elsig, and Puig 2016, 245f.

2601 Pauwelyn 2019, 301; Bahri 2019, 7f.

2602 Daku and Pelc 2017, 236.

2603 According to figures by Reich 2017, 5 covering the period until 2017.

2604 This is also noted by Bahri 2019, 6.

2605 WTO, Members reiterate joint call to launch selection process for Appellate Body members, 22 November 2019, https://www.wto.org/english/news_e/news19_e/dsb_22nov19_e.htm.

2606 See European Commission, EU and 16 WTO members agree to work together on an interim appeal arbitration arrangement, 24 January 2020, https://trade.ec.europa.eu/doclib/press/index.cfm?id=2106.

With regards the re-appointment of specific individuals, there seems to be only one systematic and thorough study of whether Members have actually made use of this possibility.[2607] The study indicates that the (re)-appointment procedures have become more politicised over time, reflecting growing concern among WTO Members about judicial law-making at the WTO.[2608] In particular, the US is said to have been very active in trying to influence (re)-appointments of specific Appellate Body Members[2609] and has even rejected the-reappointment of two specific candidates in response to the position they took in certain cases[2610]. Many other WTO Members are or have become very active in the selection of new Appellate Body Members,[2611] but with the exception of the US not to the extent of blocking appointments of specific candidates.

In conclusion, the US has chosen to block the re-appointment of Appellate Body Members, likely partially as a result of its dissatisfaction with Appellate Body judicial decision-making and partially for other reasons. While the US stance has far-reaching effects for the WTO, it is the only one of more than 160 WTO Members to have taken such measures. The actions of one individual WTO Member, powerful as it may be, cannot be taken to signal systemic and wide-spread discontent with the decision-making of the Appellate Body among the WTO membership.

1.2. Legislative overturn of judicial decisions

Generally, there has been very little activity from WTO Members aimed at overturning specific interpretations by the WTO dispute settlement bodies. For example, there has been no decision by WTO Members constituting an authoritative interpretation of WTO law under Art. IX.2 WTO and modifying any of the findings of the Appellate Body.[2612] No important de-

---

2607 Elsig and Pollack 2012.

2608 Ibid., 15ff.

2609 Krüger 2013, 77f.

2610 Dunoff and Pollack 2017, 53f; Lee 2020, 263; Elsig and Pollack 2012, 19; P. J. K. 2018, 2f.

2611 Lee 2020, 263f.

2612 The point is made by Bacchus 2005, 518. Scully-Hill and Mahncke 2009, 148f note, that the Doha Declaration on TRIPS and Public Health may have a somewhat similar affect as decisions under Art. IX.2; Krüger 2013, 74 points to requests by the EU for an authoritative interpretation on which there was no agreement, however.

cision by the dispute settlement bodies has been reversed through a treaty revision.[2613]

Admittedly, the quorum for adopting such an interpretation would be high.[2614] However, if there was very serious or widespread concern about certain findings of the WTO adjudicators, such a decision could still be politically achievable. Indeed, WTO Members have managed to agree on some "trade and …" issues over the course of the years. The Doha "Declaration on the TRIPS agreement and public health"[2615] is an important example. It was motivated by wide-spread concerns over intellectual property rights inhibiting access to essential medicines for the poor. From a legal point of view, its status is not entirely clear; there are good arguments in favour of considering it a "subsequent agreement regarding the interpretation" of the TRIPS Agreement in the sense of Art. 31.3 VCLT.[2616] Moreover, some cases have also been identified where WTO Members voiced strong discontent with what the Appellate Body or a Panel had decided and this supposedly led to a modification in the adjudicators' stance (even though not to an explicit change in their jurisprudence).[2617]

In conclusion, the fact that WTO Members have not so far overturned any interpretation of WTO law adopted by the Appellate Body through a political decision is probably to a certain extent owed to the fact that the quorum for such a decision is difficult to attain. Yet there are some examples from the short history of the WTO, where WTO Members have actually managed to come to an agreement on certain issues. Therefore, the absence of political action aimed at overturning interpretations adopted in WTO dispute settlement can to a limited degree be taken to signal satisfaction of WTO Members with the dispute settlement system.

2613 Sweet and Brunell 2013, 66.

2614 See chapter 1, section 4.4.1 for a description of WTO decision-making procedures.

2615 Online at http://www.wto.org/english/thewto_e/minist_e/min01_e/mindecl_trips_e.htm.

2616 For various options how to qualify the legal status of the Declaration, see Gathii 2002, 299ff; Bloche 2002, 841f.

2617 Krüger 2013, 71ff identifies two "mildly successful examples of political intervention with judicial decision-making in the WTO", a Panel decision in a subsidies case that was allegedly in contravention of the "*ne ultra petita*" principle and the *amicus curiae* affair.

1.3. Attempts at changing the functioning of the dispute settlement bodies

WTO Members dissatisfied with the performance of the dispute settlement bodies could also try to change the mandate of these bodies or change the rules of the game in other ways, in an attempt to clip the wings of the judicial decision-makers. Indeed, debates concerning a reform of the DSU in the WTO have been ongoing for a while.[2618]

In a 2002 decision, the DSB introduced a requirement according to which amendments of the Appellate Body's working procedures require consultations with the entire WTO membership.[2619] According to Broude, this amendment has had little effect in terms of restricting the Appellate Body in practice.[2620]

More recently and more importantly, a mandate for negotiating a DSU reform was contained in the Doha Ministerial Declaration.[2621] According to that mandate, the negotiations should have been concluded in 2003, but consensus remains elusive. A progress report on the DSU reform negotiations conducted under the Doha mandate and dating from June 2019 notes "low expectations" in this regard.[2622] The same report lists the following 12 issues that WTO Members are discussing in the context of WTO DSU reform:

> "1) Mutually agreed solutions, (2) Third-party rights, (3) Strictly confidential information, (4) Sequencing, (5) Post-retaliation, (6) Transparency and amicus curiae briefs, (7) Timeframes, (8) Remand, (9) Panel composition, (10) Effective compliance, (11) Developing country interests, and (12) Flexibility and Member control".[2623]

2618 For academic contributions, see for example Sacerdoti, Yanovich, and Bohanes 2006, pt. IV.

2619 WTO Dispute Settlement Body, "Additional Procedures for Consultations Between the Chairperson of the DSB and WTO Members in Relation to Amendments for the Working Procedures for Appellate Review", adopted 19 December 2002, WT/DSB/31.

2620 Broude 2004, 149.

2621 Ministerial Declaration, Adopted on 14 November 2001, para. 30, http://www.wto.org/english/thewto_e/minist_e/min01_e/mindecl_e.htm#dispute.

2622 Special session of the Dispute Settlement Body, Report by the Chairman, Ambassador Coly Seck, TN/DS/3, 17 June 2019, para. 1.9.

2623 Ibid., para. 1.4.

The progress report also contains drafts for modified DSU clauses on the above topics. It also notes, however, that some of these issues are no longer very relevant to all of the WTO Members.[2624]

Of the above topics, "flexibility and Member control" seems to be the one that is most directly related to WTO Members seeking to impose certain restraints on WTO judicial decision-making. Under this heading, various individual proposals were discussed, including providing the DSB with the option to only partially adopt a dispute settlement report or to delete certain parts of a report before adopting it, adding an interim stage to appellate proceedings, as well as the issuance of guidance for the dispute settlement bodies on the use of public international law, the interpretative approach to be followed in WTO dispute settlement, and the measure under review in WTO dispute settlement.[2625] These proposals express a desire by WTO Members to enhance their control over the WTO judicial decision-making processes to a certain degree and thus – perhaps – the idea that the WTO dispute settlement bodies have strayed too far from what WTO Members want.

However, neither this or any other of the proposals for reforming the WTO dispute settlement system appears to have garnered wide-spread support among WTO Members. Consequently, an informal process to find solutions to the impasse that threatened to incapacitate the Appellate Body, was conducted at the WTO. It culminated in a draft decision on the functioning of the Appellate Body, submitted for adoption to the WTO General Council in December 2019.[2626] While the facilitator of the informal process stated that the draft decision reflected areas of convergence among the WTO Members[2627], the latter did not adopt it[2628].

The text of the draft decision expresses the Members' view that "the Appellate Body has, in some respects, not been functioning as intended" under the DSU. If adopted, the decision would have clarified two procedural issues, concerning the appointment of new Appellate Body Members and

2624 Ibid., para. 1.13.

2625 Ibid., section 2.12.1.

2626 Draft Decision on the Functioning of the Appellate Body, WT/GC/W/791, 28 November 2019.

2627 Informal process on matters related to the functioning of the Appellate Body – Report by the Facilitator, H. E. Dr. David Walker (New Zealand) and Draft Decision on the Functioning of The Appellate Body (WT/GC/W/791), 9 December 2019, JOB/GC/225, para. 1.7f.

2628 See WTO General Council 9 and 10 December 2019, Minutes of the Meeting, WT/GC/M/181, section 5.

those approaching the end of their term as well the timeframe for the issuance of Appellate Body reports. Even if WTO Members had agreed on adopting these clarifications, this would not have implied a fundamental discontent with the substance of the Appellate Body's decision-making or changed fundamental aspects of its decision-making.

However, the draft decision also covers several other issues that appear to be more closely related to Members' concern over perceived judicial activism in the WTO dispute settlement system or to result from a desire of WTO Members to exert stronger control over the Appellate Body. Notably, the draft decision emphasizes that according to Art. 17.6 DSU appeals are limited to issues of law covered in the Panel report and legal interpretations developed by a Panel and elaborates on the relevance of this clause both for the Appellate Body and the parties to a dispute. While most of the statements are mere repetitions of the legal text, the fact that at least some WTO Members appear to see a need for explicitly and formally expressing them is an indicator of a certain dissatisfaction with how the judicial decision-makers have interpreted WTO law and what role they have assumed in doing so.

Nonetheless, none of the proposals that appear to be supported widely among WTO Members would fundamentally change the mandate of the WTO dispute settlement bodies or reduce their case-load. They do not question the existence of an adjudicative mechanism at the WTO. Indeed, the above quoted progress report on the DSU negotiations notes that one of the reasons for the lack of progress in the negotiations was a lack of political will and engagement, "which undoubtedly reflects the fact that for much of its history the DSU has been widely seen as operating effectively and efficiently"[2629]. In fact, a significant number of WTO Members have stressed the importance of the continued functioning of the Appellate Body and expressed their dissatisfaction with the current impasse.[2630] The US position on WTO dispute settlement is an outlier and appears to be motivated partially by other factors than the actual functioning of the WTO dispute settlement system. These proposals can hence not be read as an expression of fundamental discontent with the functioning of the dispute settlement system to date among a majority of Members.

2629 Special session of the Dispute Settlement Body, Report by the Chairman, Ambassador Coly Seck, TN/DS/3, 17 June 2019, para. 1.10.

2630 See WTO General Council, 9 and 10 December 2019, Minutes of the Meeting, WT/GC/M/181, section 5.

In sum, while there are attempts by some WTO Members to better control the Appellate Body, these appear to be limited in ambition and/or lacking clear agreement amongst WTO Members. Thus, any existing dissatisfaction with the Appellate Body's functioning is at least not strong enough to effectively bring about a political backlash or more far-reaching counter-measures supported by a majority of WTO Members.

1.4. (Non)compliance with dispute settlement decisions

Non-compliance is another option for WTO Members that do not like a decision in cases where they were involved as defendants. In the WTO system, this could then lead to the winning party seeking authorization for retaliation measures which might be economically costly for the losing WTO Members, as well as having potential costs in political terms. These facts notwithstanding, non-compliance is still an option open to WTO Members.

In practice, there is no indication of a wide-spread lack of compliance with WTO dispute settlement decisions; to the contrary, compliance levels with WTO dispute settlement decisions have been very high. Obviously, there are certain major cases where a party did not comply, at least initially, mostly due to internal pressure (e.g. the *EC – Biotech Products* and *Hormones I* cases); generally, the EU's track record on compliance is worse than that of other Members, due to its internal decision-making processes.[2631] Yet in the broader picture, cases of non-compliance have remained the exception.[2632] It is estimated that the losing parties in a WTO dispute comply with the decision in 95 % of the cases; this rate is considerably higher than for the ICJ (62 %) and the Inter-American Court of Human Rights (5 %).[2633] There has been only a single instance where one party in a GATS case sought to withdraw a concession according to Art. XXI GATS for the type of service concerned as a result of a ruling against it.[2634]

2631 Krüger 2013, 84ff.

2632 Shaffer, Elsig, and Puig 2016, 256 citing a former director of the WTO Legal Secretariat in support.

2633 Figures compiled by Magnuson 2010, 134 from different publications. However, he does not indicate the time periods for which these rates apply.

2634 The US in *US – Gambling*. For a detailed description of the case history and Art. XXI, see Korotana 2009.

Besides statistical analysis, another indicator[2635] for the rate of compliance with dispute settlement decisions, albeit a vague one, is the number of times that a lack of compliance has been found under Art. 21.5 DSU and the number of times that an authorization for retaliation (e.g. according to Art. 22.6 DSU) has been granted by the dispute settlement bodies. In the latter proceedings, the dispute settlement bodies authorize the winning party in a WTO dispute to suspend concessions if the WTO Member held to be violating WTO law has not complied with the dispute settlement decision. The WTO website records six cases in which it was found that a Member had failed to bring itself in conformity with a prior dispute settlement finding. Additionally, there are eight ongoing compliance disputes. Authorization for retaliation, also pre-supposing non-compliance with a prior dispute settlement finding, was granted in eight cases and requests for authorization have been made in another twelve cases.[2636] In practice, the actual suspension of concessions is the exception rather than the norm.[2637] All in all, cases where non-compliance with a prior dispute settlement decision was officially confirmed through a second round of dispute settlement represent a tiny fraction of all cases decided.

Wide-spread non-compliance with the WTO dispute settlement decisions could be taken as an indication of an equally wide-spread discontent with the system amongst Members. The high compliance rate, whatever the precise reasons for it may be[2638], thus suggests a lack of such discontent.

2635 The frequency of this type of proceedings is only a vague indicator of how frequent lack of compliance is, because the parties to the dispute must, according to Art. 22.2 DSU, first try and agree among themselves on compensation for the party affected. Only if they cannot come to an agreement, the party affected by the WTO inconsistent measures can resort to the dispute settlement bodies under Art. 22.6 DSU.

2636 See WTO, Dispute Settlement – Current Status of Disputes, http://www.wto.org/english/tratop_e/dispu_e/dispu_current_status_e.htm, last visited 1 August 2020.

2637 Colares 2009, 389.

2638 For a discussion of compliance theories and their application to a WTO dispute settlement case, see Whitlock 2002, 755ff.

1.5. Non-use of the dispute settlement system

Another strategy that WTO Members could adopt if they were dissatisfied with the decisions produced by the WTO dispute settlement system would be to avoid using it.[2639] Whether or not disputes are initiated is completely in the hands of the WTO Members, as is any decision as to whether a particular Panel report is appealed.

Yet WTO Members do not appear to be using the WTO dispute settlement system significantly less over time. For example, Hughes noted in a 2009 contribution that dispute settlement had not abated over time and the WTO dispute settlement system continued to be the busiest international adjudicative system in existence.[2640] According to a more recent statistical analysis, the number of complaints per year that have resulted in Panel reports has remained largely stable over the years and the same is true for Appellate Body reports, with a somewhat higher number for the first decade of the WTO's existence than the later period.[2641] Another statistical analysis, covering the period 1995 - 2016, also indicates that while the number of Panel and Appellate Body reports issued annually varies over five-year periods, there is no general downward trend.[2642] It has also been noted that "more dispute settlement complaints […] were filed in 2018 than in any year since 1998" and this

> "suggests that despite the threat posed by the Appellate Body crisis, the WTO membership continues to view the dispute settlement system as an effective tool for resolving trade disputes".[2643]

In sum, there is no evidence of a trend of WTO Members resorting to the Appellate Body or the dispute settlement system *in toto* much less over time. However, Busch and Reinhardt argue that the number of complaints brought does not necessarily indicate "growing confidence" in the dispute settlement system; instead, it may be a result of the expansion of the scope of WTO law as well as growing world trade. They also point out that some cases – where one dispute keeps coming back to the system such as the

2639 See also Zdouc 2008, 369.

2640 Hughes 2009, 272.

2641 Krüger 2013, 63; Pauwelyn 2016b emphasizes the fact that more disputes were filed in the first decade of the WTO than in the 2nd and also points out that the overall number of disputes litigated at the WTO is still small compared to the overall number of (likely) violations of WTO law.

2642 See Leitner and Lester 2017, 177.

2643 Clifford Chance 2019, 2.

Hormones case – indicate a failure of the system to permanently settle a dispute, rather than its success.[2644] Yet none of these explanations is ultimately convincing. While the first of the three explanations may be of relevance when comparing the track records for the use of the dispute settlement procedures in the GATT and WTO eras respectively, it has less traction when looking at WTO dispute settlement over time. The WTO agreements have not fundamentally changed since the establishment of the WTO, even though there are now more WTO Members and additional Accession Protocols. The second alternative explanation would also need further substantiation to be convincing: While world trade continues to increase[2645], it is at least questionable whether there is a direct link between overall global trade volumes and the number of disputes arising: disputes are over trade barriers. If there is more trade globally, this could also be indicative of a decrease in trade barriers and thus imply the existence of fewer causes for trade disputes. With regard to the third of the alternative explanations, the number of cases that "bounce back" to the system is, after all, relatively small – most cases brought are indeed about disputes not yet decided by the WTO dispute settlement system. Altogether, the constant use of the system can be taken to indicate that the prevailing attitude amongst WTO members towards it is one of acceptance.

The assumption that WTO members largely support the system is further corroborated by the fact that they continue to resort to the WTO dispute settlement system even though dispute settlement mechanisms under regional or bilateral free trade agreements (FTAs) are often times available. A country may typically choose under which of the FTAs of which itself and the opponent country are parties to bring a dispute.[2646] In practice, the inter-state dispute settlement mechanisms of bilateral or regional FTAs are used much less than the WTO mechanism, however;[2647] one commentator has described them as being virtually idle[2648].

Factors that have been identified as leading states to choose the WTO dispute settlement mechanism rather than one under an FTA include – besides the extent to which the respective set of legal norms is favourable for

2644 Busch and Reinhardt 2002, 465.
2645 For example, according to WTO statistics, the global world merchandise trade volume grew by 26 % between 2008 and 2018, see WTO, World Trade Statistical Review 2019, p. 10, https://www.wto.org/english/res_e/statis_e/wts2019_e/wts2019chapter02_e.pdf.
2646 Busch 2007, 739; Hillman 2009, 195f; Melillo 2019, 96.
2647 Yoo-Sun Jung 2013, 2.
2648 Vidigal 2017, 928.

a complainant – the WTO's institutional support in dispute settlement proceedings[2649], the option of appellate review, the fact that the WTO dispute settlement procedures are more predictable for states than those of FTAs (e.g. because the mechanisms under FTAs allow the defending state to block dispute settlement proceedings, because the WTO dispute settlement system has deadlines and because there is already a body of case law)[2650], the fact that WTO Members not involved in a specific dispute may put pressure on a non-compliant Member[2651], the preference of WTO Members to create a multilateral *de facto* precedent at the WTO (as compared to a bilateral one under FTAs)[2652], the availability of compliance obligations and remedies, and the fact that FTA Panels often include representatives of the parties and WTO Panels do not[2653]. The general conclusion from this is that states would not prefer the WTO a forum for dispute settlement, if the WTO did not judicially deliver what they seek.

This is further corroborated by the fact that the number of cases decided in the WTO dispute settlement system is extraordinarily high when compared to decisions by other international courts: the Appellate Body issued 110 reports between its establishment and 2013, but corresponding numbers are considerably lower for the ICJ and ITLOS.[2654]

While obviously the decision by a WTO Member to initiate WTO dispute settlement proceedings in a given case is motivated by a number of factors,[2655] it is fair to say that the WTO dispute settlement system continues to be popular enough among WTO Members for them to actually use it.

1.6. An alternative explanation: do WTO Members not care (enough)?

Of course, the limited use of the above counter-measures by Members could also have another explanation: even Members that are very critical about the functioning of the WTO dispute settlement system may still not care *enough* to actually try to change it. There are a variety of possible ex-

2649 Trommer 2017, 505, 514ff.
2650 Porges 2011, 478; Vidigal 2017, 932ff.
2651 Porges 2011, 478; Vidigal 2017, 940.
2652 Busch 2007, 757f.
2653 Porges 2011, 478.
2654 See for the figures Bossche 2014.
2655 See chapter 1, section 4.4.1.

planations for why a Member might not care, and I will consider these in this section.

One reason is that a country that has never been involved as a party in any WTO dispute will be unlikely to be worried about the WTO dispute settlement system or to invest resources to change anything about it. There are quite a number of countries that this situation applies to.

Nevertheless, this is obviously not true for all WTO Members – a few of them have been involved quite regularly in WTO dispute settlement cases, notably the US and EU.[2656] Even when countries are frequently involved in disputes, there may be reasons why they make no attempt to change the WTO dispute settlement system, even if they are dissatisfied with it. By far not every case of a WTO-inconsistent regulation is taken to the WTO,[2657] which means that WTO Members do not have to be overly concerned about complaints being brought against them. For example, Weiler suggests a possible explanation for the absence of an "outcry" from Members concerning the Appellate Body's balancing ambitions:

> "Although in the small pond of WTO dispute settlement, one is impressed by the growing number of cases, the numbers are infinitesimally small in relation to the vast regulatory matrix of the modern state. In all but the most exceptional, public high-visibility cases […] a ruling against a measure, even if based on flawed methodology, is but a fleabite […]. […] the real-life specific gravity of these decisions is slight. The Members will continue, unperturbed, to set their level of acceptable risk in their regulatory regimes – and from time to time face a challenge."[2658]

Another explanation can be garnered from the wider literature on judicial decision-making and its relation with the preferences of states: states are no monolithic blocs, but there are different branches or actors within them. Their interests concerning WTO dispute settlement are not necessarily

2656 See Krüger 2013, 25.

2657 For example, many WTO Members have schemes supporting renewable energy generation that contain some kind of local content requirement. Whether such local content requirements are compatible with WTO law is a quite open question. However, among the many WTO Members that have such local content requirements, only a very limited number are faced with a WTO complaint until now, see Gerstetter et al. 2014.

2658 Weiler 2009, 143.

identical.[2659] In particular, the legislative branch has been identified as more critical of decisions by international organizations than the executive branch, given that contributing to such decisions and negotiating international agreements in the first place is mainly an executive domain.[2660] For example, it has been observed that the US usually complies quickly with WTO dispute settlement decisions when compliance requires only administrative action, but not when Congress has to take a decision for a ruling to be implemented.[2661] Yet if the reason for a lack of action against the WTO dispute settlement system is that there are diverging positions within a state, this means that the system has managed to assemble the support of at least some relevant actors within WTO member countries.

In conclusion, while the idea that WTO Members simply do not care enough about the WTO dispute settlement system to do anything about it may be a valid explanation for *some* countries, it is unlikely to be a convincing explanation for *all* countries, in particular those that frequently participate in WTO disputes.

1.7. Conclusions

Even when taking into account that some WTO Members may not overly care about WTO dispute settlement, the reluctance of WTO Members to try to effect fundamental changes in the way the WTO dispute settlement mechanism currently functions can reasonably be taken to mean that the Appellate Body has managed to gain acceptance as a legitimate judicial entity. Indeed, some long-time observers of the WTO world have concluded that WTO Members are quite satisfied with WTO jurisprudence[2662] or have accepted the authority of the Appellate Body[2663]. There is anecdotal evidence that WTO Members have generally expressed satisfaction with the course that the Appellate Body has steered. For example, Flett notes that WTO Members appear to have reacted rather positively to the Appellate Body's jurisprudence so far; he also indicates that while a Member that has lost a judicial case usually complains about the results in the relevant

2659 In this context, see also the discussion on the relevance of internal domestic constraints on WTO dispute settlement behavior for the outcome of WTO dispute settlement proceedings in chapter 2, section 4.2.

2660 Benvenisti and Downs 2012, 121.

2661 See the statement by Jackson in Taniguchi et al. 2008, 389.

2662 For example Jackson in ibid.

2663 Shaffer, Elsig, and Puig 2016, 238.

DSB session, these comments relate to specific cases rather than systemic issues.[2664] Knox also reports broad support by WTO Members for major "trade and …" decisions, even from the parties losing the respective case.[2665]

On the other hand, Members have also expressed concern repeatedly over alleged "judicial activism" on the part of the Appellate Body.[2666] There is indeed a degree of uneasiness among WTO Members about what is perceived as law-making by the Appellate Body[2667]and criticism of certain individual decisions.[2668] The reaction of the WTO membership to the Appellate Body's decision to accept *amicus curiae* briefs is a well-known example.[2669] Concerns about the direction of WTO dispute settlement seem to be more pronounced in some countries, such as the US[2670], than in others. Moreover, the lack of progress in multilateral negotiations could be taken as an indication that WTO Members are unwilling to produce more WTO law; and certainly NGOs continue to take a critical view of developments at the WTO.[2671] Thus, the picture is not uniform.

My claim is not that the WTO or its WTO dispute settlement system are above and beyond criticism from an empirical, let alone normative point of view, but instead that the criticism they do receive does not seem to be directed primarily and specifically against what the WTO dispute settlement system does and that the criticism is not as widespread and fundamental that it has led to backlash by a significant number of WTO Members. In these terms, the WTO dispute settlement system has been quite successful.

2664 Flett 2011, 6, 37.

2665 Knox 2004, 70ff.

2666 See for references Goldstein and Steinberg 2007, 25f.

2667 Steinberg 2004, 256 observes that concerns over judicial law-making are very regularly voiced by a high number of WTO Member States in various bodies of the WTO, both in public documents and confidential deliberations; for relevant statements from the US, see also Du 2011, 642; Krüger 2013, 71ff.

2668 For example, the EC in *European Communities – Conditions for the Granting of Tariff Preferences to Developing Countries, WT/DS246/AB/R* 2004 explicitly challenges the legitimacy of a certain decision by the Panel, see para. 14.

2669 See Krüger 2013, 71 for a description of WTO Members' reaction.

2670 See section 1.1 in this chapter.

2671 For example Howse and Levy 2013, 344 relate criticism by NGOs of the decision of the Appellate Body in *US – Clove Cigarettes* as incompatible with health protection.

2. *The literature: How has the WTO dispute settlement system successfully generated legitimacy?*

In section 1 of this chapter, I have shown that WTO Members have not taken counter-measures against the WTO dispute settlement system to any significant degree, which can be indicated as an expression of most WTO Members considering it to be legitimate.

Another approach to ascertaining the empirical legitimacy of the WTO dispute settlement system is considering the views of experts on the matter. Whether or not the Appellate Body has been successful and by which standards is only discussed explicitly in a handful of contributions.[2672] Yet there are more contributions discussing the functioning of the WTO dispute settlement system and its decisions in broader terms. The general conclusion here seems to be that the Appellate Body has – with some limited exceptions – been functioning well and/or has achieved considerable legitimacy.[2673] While the dominant positive view of WTO judicial decision-making can be seen as further corroborating the conclusion in section 1, such an assessment also needs to be viewed in the context of who expresses it: international lawyers are likely to have an inherent bias favouring international judicial institutions.

In this section, I would like to summarize the research on what features of the WTO's judicial decision-making have led to this success in terms of empirical legitimacy (aka acceptance) of the WTO dispute settlement system and the Appellate Body more specifically. I will also compare these finding to my own results. Previous studies have looked both at external, contextual factors[2674] behind the success of the WTO dispute settlement system as well as internal factors, i.e. those resulting from actions of the dispute settlement bodies themselves. In the following, I will limit myself

2672 Among these are Behboodi 1999; Howse 2016b; Lockhart 2006; Mavroidis 2008; Taniguchi et al. 2008.

2673 Instead of many, see Bacchus 2005, 502; Dunoff and Pollack 2017, 44; Hughes 2009, 271; Picker 2020, 56ff; Ruiz Fabri 2006, 130; Venzke 2012, 193; Zdouc 2008, 369; Trommer 2017, 517, who conducted more than 100 interviews with members of the trade policy communities in governments, the private sector, civil society and academia also concludes that the interviewees "were on the whole optimistic about the WTO's [...] adjudication functions". Conversely Pauwelyn 2016b, 1120 warns not to overestimate the extent legitimacy the Appellate Body has achieved. For more critical perspectives see chapter 2, section 4.2 and chapter 3, section 6.1.3.

2674 See generally Alter, Helfer, and Madsen 2016; for the WTO specifically Shaffer, Elsig, and Puig 2016.

to discussing internal factors controlled by the Panel and the Appellate Body, since the overall focus of this work is on judicial decision-making and thus on internal factors. This should not be read as a statement that other factors (e.g. the composition of the Appellate Body, with its members being international lawyers without a narrow focus on international trade law[2675]) are unimportant; it is just a limitation of my analysis.

There are a limited number of studies that identify certain individual features of the Appellate Body's decision-making explicitly as factors contributing to its empirical legitimacy.[2676] Yet there is a wider body of literature that discusses the success of the Appellate Body and the internal factors behind it more broadly, including how the Appellate Body has acted strategically to gradually build its authority and legitimacy[2677].

The main factors identified in both types of literature on why the Appellate Body has been successful (at generating legitimacy of itself) are the following[2678]:

- Reliance on the VCLT methods of interpretation and willingness to conceive of WTO law as part of international law[2679]
- The strong textual orientation of the Appellate Body[2680], but also its resorting to teleological interpretation in certain instances[2681]
- Quality and clarity of the Appellate Body's reasoning, as compared to that of the Panels[2682], and the "exhaustive and rigorous interpretation

2675 Krüger 2013, 97; van den Bossche 2006, 301ff; Venzke 2012, 193; see also comment by Zdouc, in Taniguchi et al. 2008, 402; with a slightly different focus Hughes 2008, 475.

2676 Shlomo-Agon 2015.

2677 See in particular Howse 2016b; Shlomo-Agon 2015; also Lang 2016.

2678 It should be noted that some of the authors cited in the following are very close to the WTO dispute settlement system or even employed by the WTO. This is likely to lead to some bias in assessing the functioning of the WTO dispute settlement system: Someone who works for the dispute settlement system is more likely to value its functioning positively than the opposite; if the system was assessed to not function well, such might to self-critically acknowledge that their efforts relating to WTO dispute settlement have failed, see on this point also Ruiz Fabri 2006, 1076.

2679 Ehlermann 2003a, 699; Howse 2001, 54; Lennard 2002, 61f; van den Bossche 2006, 306ff; van Damme 2010, 606; Zdouc 2008, 371, 374ff.

2680 Howse and Essermann 2006, 74; Shaffer, Elsig, and Puig 2016, 252; van Damme 2010, 641; Venzke 2012, 193.

2681 Shlomo-Agon 2015, 569.

2682 Van den Bossche 2006, 317.

and application of the law according to consistently applied interpretative rules"[2683]

- Building a coherent and consistent body of case law[2684] that results from the Appellate Body's way of making decisions, an agreed judicial policy that all Members of the Appellate Body abide by[2685]
- Adherence to precedents[2686]
- Showing institutional sensitivity to other international organizations (e.g. the WHO)[2687] and the reference to multilateral benchmarks in the judicial decisions[2688]
- Limiting findings to what is necessary to decide on claims[2689] and generally using various forms of judicial restraint[2690], thus maintaining flexibility for futures cases[2691]
- Demonstrated awareness among the adjudicators of the limits of their competence, as marked by Art. 3.2 and 19.2 DSU[2692]
- Striking of an appropriate balance in the decisions between trade objectives and other public policy goals in the case law[2693], among others things by not interpreting Art. XX GATT and other exceptions provisions too narrowly[2694] and by generally respecting the regulatory objectives of WTO Members as important[2695]
- Being responsive to the political implications of judicial findings and the political sensitivities and preferences in WTO countries[2696] and seeking solutions likely to be approved by the WTO Members[2697]

2683 Flett 2011, 6.
2684 Shany and Shlomo-Agon 2014, 208; Venzke 2012, 193.
2685 Ruiz Fabri 2006, 131.
2686 Howse 2016b, 31; Shany and Shlomo-Agon 2014, 208; Zdouc 2008, 372f.
2687 Shlomo-Agon 2015, 577ff.
2688 Howse and Essermann 2006, 74.
2689 Ibid.
2690 Krüger 2013, 93ff; Shany and Shlomo-Agon 2014, 207; Pauwelyn 2016b, 1125; van den Bossche 2006, 319.
2691 Lang 2016, 1101f.
2692 Petersmann 2006, 92f.
2693 Howse 2016b, 44f; Shaffer, Elsig, and Puig 2016, 255; van den Bossche 2006, 320ff; Venzke 2012, 193; Zdouc 2008, 377.
2694 Shlomo-Agon 2015, 555ff.
2695 Howse 2016b, 61ff.
2696 Krüger 2013, 121 and passim; Pauwelyn 2016b, 1120; Shlomo-Agon 2015, 260f.
2697 Knox 2004, 3.

- Emphasis on fair procedures being observed by WTO Members in adopting measures[2698], rather than on adjudicating substantive standards
- Findings that it is administrative decisions by WTO Members rather than their legislation that violates WTO law[2699]
- "Impartiality and integrity" of the Appellate Body[2700]
- The way that the Appellate Body has crafted the Working Procedures for Appellate Review, stressing the judicial character of the proceedings[2701] and collegiality[2702]
- The Appellate Body's striving for consensus and the infrequency of individual opinions[2703]
- The adjudicators' approach of accepting *amicus curiae* briefs, allowing external lawyers to represent WTO Members and opening hearings to the public[2704]
- Rejecting the idea that the judicial decision-makers would have to give deference to political/diplomatic processes in the WTO[2705]
- The Appellate Body's intense scrutiny of Panel reports, including the decision to complete the analysis on some occasions[2706]

Different authors have offered different views on the comparative importance of these factors[2707] and not all of them are undisputed. Yet it should be noted that in the wider literature both the outcome of cases and certain features of the WTO's judicial style are mentioned as success factors. This corroborates the assumption underling this work that both the outcome of case and the judicial style influence the legitimacy of judicial decisions.

2698 Howse and Essermann 2006, 74.
2699 Shaffer, Elsig, and Puig 2016, 254; Howse 2016b, 52.
2700 Hughes 2008, 474.
2701 Krüger 2013, 91f; van den Bossche 2006, 303ff.
2702 Howse 2016b, 31; Ruiz Fabri 2016, 1078; Shany and Shlomo-Agon 2014, 208; Zdouc 2008, 371.
2703 Ruiz Fabri 2016, 1079; Shaffer, Elsig, and Puig 2016, 253.
2704 Howse 2016b, 31; Shany and Shlomo-Agon 2014, 207; Shaffer, Elsig, and Puig 2016, 255f; Shlomo-Agon 2015, 554f.
2705 Howse 2016b, 31.
2706 Ibid.
2707 See for example Howse 2016a; and the various responses to his article: Pauwelyn 2016b; Ruiz Fabri 2016.

While I have not considered all of the aspects presented above,[2708] my research confirms the presence of the following characteristics in the findings of the Appellate Body:

- Reliance on the VCLT methods of interpretation and willingness to conceive of WTO law as part of international law
- Strong textual orientation, with some use of other teleological interpretation
- A policy of de-facto adherence to earlier case law, i.e. precedents, albeit with some instances where the substantive interpretations in earlier cases do not appear to be used entirely correctly
- eference to multilateral benchmarks
- Limiting of findings to what is necessary to decide claims by invoking judicial economy or insisting on the case-by-case character of a certain decision
- Striking a balance between trade and other objectives that does not always or consistently favour trade interests
  - Showing a certain level of awareness of political implications of findings and the political sensitivities and preferences in WTO countries, even though this may be sometimes more rhetoric than reality
- The Appellate Body's striving for consensus and the infrequency of individual opinions
- Accepting *amicus curiae* briefs

Whether any of these features have actually led to the success of the Appellate Body in the sense of acceptance from relevant constituencies is not only methodologically difficult to establish with any degree of reliability, but has generally not been investigated in the studies quoted above. Yet many of the above statements come from observers intimately familiar with the WTO dispute settlement universe on account of their having been involved in dispute settlement proceedings or the practice of WTO law in one capacity or the other.[2709] This suggests that these commentators are

2708 I have not looked in depth, for example, at the composition of the Appellate Body, fair procedures, or the frequency of appeals.

2709 For example, according to the biographical indications in the publications cited and biographies publicly available, Hughes was the former Director of the WTO Appellate Body Secretariat, Zdouc is the current one, Flett is an EU Commission official representing the EU in WTO disputes, Van den Bossche is a current Member of the Appellate Body and Petersmann is a former Legal Counsellor in the Division of Legal Affairs in the GATT and former Panelist.

likely to have a good sense of the views prevailing among WTO Members on the performance and acceptance of the WTO dispute settlement system. It is therefore more reasonable to assume that the factors that these commentators have identified and that are listed above have contributed to the acceptance of the WTO dispute settlement system by WTO Members, than to assume that there is no causal connection.

3. *My own version: (How) have the adjudicators managed to create legitimacy?*

Having looked at other authors' views, I will in this section summarize my own account on the approach that the Appellate Body has used for generating acceptance for its decisions and established a reputation for legitimate judicial decision-making.

As argued throughout this work, a court can influence the extent to which its decisions are perceived as legitimate in two important dimensions: the substantive outcome and the justification offered for it. My argument is that to understand how courts generate legitimacy it is not sufficient to look at either outcomes or style, but to consider both dimensions.[2710] Consequently, the WTO judicial decision-makers' model of creating legitimacy is also a combination of certain substantive outcomes coupled with a certain judicial style.

Before explaining this in greater detail, I would like to deal with potential objections to my presenting a "model" of legitimacy generation. First, the term implies a certain degree of stability and coherence over time and second, it implies intent.

Concerning the first point, the idea of stability over time may appear questionable given that WTO judicial decisions are made by different individuals – the Appellate Body Members serve for a maximum of eight years before they are replaced. It is reasonable to assume that there is also a certain degree of fluctuation among the other actors shaping the WTO's model of legitimacy generation, including the WTO Secretariat and the lawyers representing the parties in WTO disputes. Nonetheless, I would argue that a certain stability of the patterns described above can be expected. Certain features of the institutional set-up, the mandate and procedural rules of the WTO dispute settlement bodies and the characteristics of WTO law contribute to stabilizing the WTO's model of judicial legitimacy generation – and these features are unlikely to change any time soon. Moreover, main-

2710 For a similar approach see Shlomo-Agon 2015.

taining coherence and consistency of decisions over time is fundamental to the making of good and legitimate legal judgements. As the former Member of the Appellate Body Ehlermann notes with regard to the methods of interpretation used in WTO dispute settlement:

> "The choice of a certain interpretive method entails certain constraints. The interpreter has to follow the chosen method coherently and consistently. If he does not do so, his credibility – and therefore his authority and legitimacy – will suffer. In other words: the choice of a given interpretative method has its price."[2711]

This statement applies *mutatis mutandis* to other elements of the WTO's judicial model. For example, it is highly unlikely that the Appellate Body would suddenly change its approach to precedents. Empirically, the judicial style of tribunals tends to be stable over time.[2712] Nonetheless, what I describe in this work is a record of the past, not a prediction of the future. Changes in the WTO's judicial legitimacy model over time cannot be categorically ruled out; yet if they occur, imperatives of consistency and coherence of judicial reasoning suggest that they are more likely to take the form of gradual shifts than radical ruptures.

I will now turn to the second point, the connotations of intent implicit in the statement that the WTO adjudicators embrace a certain model of generating legitimacy. Such an intent may seem unlikely, given the number and diversity of the actors involved in producing the WTO's judicial discourse. In response, as I stated already in chapter 1,[2713] I do not purport to offer conclusive and definite statements on what individuals drafting a dispute settlement report may have thought, felt, intended, or which unconscious motivations may have guided their dispute settlement reports. Neither do I suggest that there is a master plan, set out after the creation of the WTO, that guides the WTO adjudicators' reasoning. There is no basis on which I could make such statements. Rather, my claims here are more modest, namely that there are certain identifiable characteristics of the WTO case law that can be ascertained and described. Furthermore, there are plausible accounts that conceive of courts as strategic actors that have an interest in both their decisions and their institution being perceived as legitimate. These accounts are corroborated for the WTO context by some statements of the Appellate Body in the reports as well as extra-curial state-

2711 Ehlermann 2003a, 701.
2712 See chapter 1, section 3.2.
2713 See chapter 1, section 5.1.

ments by (former) Members of the Appellate Body or staff working in the Appellate Body's secretariat,[2714] sometimes even on individual aspects of the Appellate Body's decisions-making[2715], as well as in the academic literature[2716]. Like other courts, the WTO adjudicators make political, moral, economic, and personal choices. Consequently it is reasonable to speak of a deliberate act of aiming at and creating judicial legitimacy, even though the individuals writing the reports may not at each and every stage of the proceedings be concerned with how their decisions may be received by others.[2717]

In addition, it should be noted that when I refer to a "model" of judicial legitimacy creation this does not automatically imply a judgement as to the success of any such model. Describing such a model means describing what a court does – not how other actors assess the functioning of the court. As demonstrated in the first two sections of this chapter, there is evidence that the WTO's model has in practice been quite successful at both being accepted as legitimate by WTO Members. While it is reasonable to assume that the *de facto* acceptance of a judicial body and its decisions by relevant actors is a result of that court's model of generating legitimacy, it is also theoretically conceivable that a court may strive to gain acceptance without success.

The present analysis is based on a limited number of fully adjudicated cases dealing with the norms at issue in this work and decided between the establishment of the WTO in 1995 and 2014.[2718] There are many WTO cases that fell outside the scope of this work – notably cases relating to the SCM, the Anti-dumping, Safeguards and TRIMS Agreements, i.e. the ones where primarily different economic interests are pitted against each other. The case selection is unlikely to affect the conclusions on the WTO judicial style, as judicial styles tend to be stable for a given court irrespective of the

2714 See chapter 1, section 4.2.

2715 See Shlomo-Agon 2015, 555ff for statements by WTO officials stating that the Appellate Body's decisions to admit *amicus curiae* briefs and to seek to strike a balance between trade and non-trade happened in response to concerns from the environmental community and other constituencies worried about a one-sided trade agenda of the WTO.

2716 See for example the seminal contribution by Howse 2016b, who identifies several "judicial policies" of the Appellate Body.

2717 On the degree to which the Appellate Body Members explicitly take account of the likely acceptance of their decisions and legitimacy issues, see the quote by a former staff member of the Appellate Body Secretariat in Shlomo-Agon 2015, 588.

2718 For a similar caveat Charnovitz 2007, 695.

matter decided. The result on the substantive outcome could, however, be different for "trade and ..." as compared to other cases; as described in the conclusion of chapter 2, charges of judicial activism and law-making seem, indeed, to be most pronounced concerning trade remedy cases.

Having clarified these issues, what comprises the specific WTO model of judicial legitimacy generation? The answer requires combining the insights on the substantive outcome of cases from chapter 2 with those on judicial style from chapter 3. This leads to the following characterization of the WTO's model of legitimacy creation.

On the substantive side, it consists of a relatively mixed outcome of cases, in terms of the interpretations chosen. The Appellate Body has neither adopted a line of interpretation that consistently favours trade interests nor one that systematically enhances the regulatory space of WTO Members. There is some evidence that this outcome corresponds to WTO Members' preferences. In terms of style and justification, the WTO's model can be described as relying on a discursive (rather than institutional) source of authority while at the same time being predominantly formalist in orientation. In greater detail, I consider the following among the many aspects of WTO case law discussed in in chapters 2 and 3 central to the WTO's model of judicial decision-making and legitimacy creation:

Balanced outcome in interpreting WTO law: The outcome of the "trade and ..." cases is relatively balanced in that the interpretations adopted do not consistently favour either trade interests or the regulatory freedom of WTO Members to adopt non-trade measures. Examples can be given for instances where the Appellate Body has chosen an interpretation that is more permissive of Members' regulatory measures than the one of earlier GATT Panels and WTO Panels, but there are also instances where the Appellate Body is stricter with WTO Members' measures than is suggested it ought to be by a significant number of WTO legal commentators.

Outcome in line with anticipated preferences of WTO Members: This balanced outcome also supports insights from existing research that the adjudicators at least sometimes act in line with the expected preferences of WTO Members. The numerous signals of appeasement that the adjudicators send in their written decisions can also be read as an attempt at reassuring WTO Members that their potential or actual concerns have been taken into account. The fact that the WTO dispute settlement bodies seem to be bolder on procedural matters also supports this point. The WTO dispute settlement bodies appear willing to resort to various sources of international law when considering procedural issues, including principles, and to fill gaps, and are maybe slightly less conscientious about the text than with regard to substantive matters. A more active and less textual stance is likely to meet with less criticism in relation to resolving procedural matters than if it was adopted in relation to substantive issues – procedural rules are the domain of the court.

The use of avoidance techniques also supports this point, as these techniques serve to avoid rulings that might be controversial among WTO Members or wider audiences. Similarly, the fact that there are a number of legal interpretations that have been embraced by the WTO adjudicators but that are subsequently not fully applied can be explained by the wish of the adjudicators to avoid antagonising WTO Members. A notable example is the Appellate Body's balancing formula for interpreting the term necessary in Art. XX GATT and XIV GATS. The importance of the regulatory goal at stake is one of the factors to be balanced according to the case law, but no regulatory objective has ever been described as "not important" or "less important" than others. Another example is the controversial decision to allow the admissibility of *amicus curia* briefs, following which the adjudicators have in most cases stated that they see no need to draw on such briefs in their decisions. In both cases, the legal interpretation offered by the adjudicators has generated criticism; subsequently, the adjudicators have not made full use of the legal options they have created through their interpretation.

Predominantly formalist style: The style of the adjudicators can be classified as predominantly, but not exclusively, formalist. The characteristics of the judicial reasoning of the WTO adjudicators that warrant this characterization are the following: the possibility of different interpretations is not too openly admitted; the implicit model of rationality is logico-deductive; the evaluative and creative role of the adjudicators is not openly acknowledged. A higher proportion of formal arguments are used in WTO dispute settlement as compared to substantive arguments: decisions are supported mostly by formal legal arguments such as the existence of precedent or a textual argument rather than in terms of policies, interests, or values.

Mainly discursive, not institutional sources of authority: WTO judicial decision-making is based on discursive, not institutional sources of authority. The dispute settlement bodies do not – and cannot – rely on any pre-accepted notion of institutional legitimacy and therefore hand down their judgements in a curt, magisterial fashion as does, for example, the French judiciary and to a lesser extent the ECJ. The absence of figures such as an Advocate General also means that there is no option to "outsource" part of the discourse that explains and legitimizes WTO judicial decisions. Therefore, adjudicators must seek to make the decisions acceptable to their audience by explaining them – in a formalist manner, but at the same in detail and at great length. At the same time, institutional sources of authority are not entirely absent from WTO dispute settlement. The frequent references to the common intention of WTO Members as well as to recognized rules of international law (e.g. the rules on treaty interpretation) can be understood as an attempt to support the dispute settlement findings by "borrowing" legitimacy from non-controversial institutional sources.

Maintaining and expanding space for future judicial decisions: Despite their lip-service to the letter of the law and strong acknowledgement of the supremacy of WTO Members as the makers of the WTO treaties, the Appellate Body has provided itself and the Panels with considerable adjudicative authority and discretion through some of its findings. The balancing formula used to interpret Art. XX GATT and XIV GATS is one example; the Appellate Body has here developed a substantively open-ended test that provides the adjudicators with considerable leeway to exercise discretion on how important the different elements of the balancing test are and what will be the result of applying the test in a given case. Other central norms of the WTO law have been interpreted as requiring a case-by-case approach, e.g. the "based on" standard in Art. 5.1 SPS. The standard of review is another example. Panels have a significant amount of discretion on how to deal with the facts, given that the Appellate Body sees only a wilful distortion of or egregious mistakes in dealing with the evidence as a violation of the requirement to conduct an objective assessment in the sense of Art. 11 DSU.

Divergence between rhetoric and reality: There are certain instances of a divergence between the rhetoric used in a WTO judgement and the reality of what that judgement actually means. A prominent example is the great emphasis that the adjudicators put on the right of Members to choose their appropriate level of protection – while in reality it is highly questionable whether the extent to which this right is counterbalanced by WTO Members' obligations leaves WTO Members as much freedom as the rhetoric suggests. Another example is the rhetoric on the chapeau. The Appellate Body stresses that the chapeau embodies a balance of rights and obligations of WTO Members and it is the task of the adjudicators to ascertain where precisely the "line of equilibrium" is in a given case. Yet striking a balance between the rights and obligations of WTO Members when applying the chapeau inevitably means striking a balance between trade and non-trade interests, too. This latter aspect is rarely acknowledged openly in the WTO dispute settlement reports. Yet another example of an at least potential divergence between rhetoric and reality is the Appellate Body's tendency to rely on precedents that do not entirely support what the Appellate Body states in a later case.

These elements are used flexibly in WTO dispute settlement – not all of them are necessarily present in each case, and they also partially overlap. So this is rather a toolbox from which certain tools can be and are used in a given case. The above elements are also quite dissimilar in character. For example, elements of a formalist style of judicial reasoning are present in each of the cases I have investigated (e.g. in the form of a strong tendency towards textual interpretation); yet, they may be more pronounced in one case, less in another. Other aspects, e.g. the use of judicial economy, cannot be observed in all cases. Moreover, the above mentioned aspects of WTO judicial decision-making are most likely not the only ones that have led to WTO judicial decisions being perceived (and complied with) as legitimate.

4. Outlook

This study contains an empirical description of how adjudicators at the WTO decide cases; it has also presented insights on potential reasons behind the observed outcomes and the judicial style identified. Throughout the study, I have only expressed my own more normative-political views on what the WTO dispute settlement bodies should do on a limited number of the legal questions discussed in this work. Yet a choice of a certain research question is often itself an expression of the respective scholar's more fundamental beliefs of what is worth researching and writing about. Therefore, it is worth stating my broader view of the WTO's judicial style and also the observed pattern of outcome of WTO cases more explicitly in this concluding section.

I share the assumption that law is indeterminate; indeed, rather more so than less so. By implication, I also share the view that while there are certain interpretations of the law that *cannot* be justified, there are often several interpretations than can be justified. If that is so, doctrinal legal work is rather to be viewed with a certain measure of distrust. Rather than yielding "objective" answers it can itself be regarded as dissimulating, often unconsciously, the political, moral, and strategic choices and motivations of the respective commentator when suggesting a certain interpretation.

Turning to the judicial style, my conclusion that the WTO adjudicatory bodies have, like other courts, adopted a certain judicial style and by implication a certain model of generating legitimacy does not entail any judgement on whether the observed behaviour is normatively desirable. In this respect, I would contend that adopting a certain judicial style is inevitable for any judicial body; doing so does not present a problem from a more normative political point of view. I see both strong and weak points to the concrete manner in which the Appellate Body has shaped its judicial style. For example, I disagree with the way that the Appellate Body uses some of its precedents. I find it legally or intellectually more appealing to spell out differences between earlier and later cases and explain if and why an earlier finding is actually upheld and why, than leaving it to the audience to figure it out from a given judicial decisions. I do not find it convincing to provide a dubious precedent as almost the only reason for adopting a specific interpreting of a term as central to WTO law as "necessary". Moreover, and in line with my position that WTO law often fails to predetermine the outcomes of cases, I would prefer WTO judgements to more openly acknowledge the policy issues behind the cases and deal with them openly. Pretending that a certain interpretation inevitably results from the often rather indeterminate text of the law does not make these policy issues go away. It just makes it more difficult to critically contest the reasons behind a certain WTO decision, especially for non-lawyers. Also, the adjudicators should be clearer regarding the basis on which they use or do not use non-WTO international law in their decisions. Finally, more deference when reviewing scientific evidence offered by WTO Members would certainly be warranted; as the examples of other courts show, it is quite possible for adjudicators to adopt such a more deferential stance.

Among the laudable aspects of the WTO's judicial style is, from my perspective, that the Appellate often (with the exception of the use of international law) carefully explains the methods of interpretation it uses. Similarly, I tend to think that comprehensiveness is generally better in judicial decisions than brevity – readers of a judgement should be in a position to understand why a decision has been taken. I would also support the relatively frequent use of judicial economy manifest in WTO dispute settlement decisions so far.

With regard to substance, while I have summarized some of the shortcomings of the case law as discussed in existing legal research as well as proposals on interpretation of WTO law alternative to that adopted by the Appellate Body, I have not as a general rule subscribed myself to any of these suggestions or conclusions. I would like to mention at least a few thoughts on this matter before concluding this study. I disclosed at the very beginning of the work that I belong in the "camp" of those sceptical of the benefits of trade liberalization and consider that it is likely to have, more often than not, negative impacts on other important policy objectives, such as protecting the environment, enhancing equality in societies, or combating poverty. From this viewpoint and in a more over-arching perspective, what the WTO adjudicators have done so far is no worst-case scenario – the outcome in terms of *interpretation* in "trade and ..." cases is rather balanced. At the same time, the overall record of the outcomes of WTO disputes is not a best-case scenario, either; complainants mostly win in WTO dispute settlement and non-trade regulatory measures (or at least aspects of them) tend to be struck down. Moreover, some of the interpretations chosen and practices followed in WTO dispute settlement (e.g. the conception of science) seriously constrain WTO Members' regulatory freedom, even though the text of the law appears to allow less-restrictive approaches.

This leads to the more general question of to what extent the WTO adjudicators can be blamed for outcomes that could be described as politically or economically inadequate in substance. Tentatively, I would rather locate the problem predominantly, but not exclusively with WTO law itself rather than the judicial decision-making of the Appellate Body. The Appellate Body often needs to make decisions on the basis of very thin and indeterminate legal rules,[2719] in a setting in which there are strongly divergent policy preferences not only among WTO Members, but also among the general public. Indeed, some of the Appellate Body Members have stated explicitly that they would welcome a clarification of certain aspects of WTO law[2720] – something that the WTO Members have not managed to do until today. Shlomo-Agnon also quotes a WTO official describing the situation of the Appellate Body in one of the "trade and ..." cases in the following terms:

> "[T]the poor old judge is put before a political question, and most judges, who are good judges, don't like that. ... And yet, the legislator,

2719 This observation is made for the standard of review and burden of proof issues, for example, by Spamann 2004, 529; Guzman 2008, 53.

2720 For example Matsushita 2005b, 629, suggests that WTO Members should clarify the WTO/MEA relationship, as provided for in the Doha agenda.

> the horrible legislator, has sent them that problem, because … the problem is in the treaty … And the horrible legislator has sent to the legislator what is a political problem … and nobody elected the judge and the judge is sitting there thinking, 'Well what am I going to do with this?'"[2721]

This also indicates that the WTO judicial decision-makers are not necessarily always happy about having to decide questions that WTO Members are unable to find a consensus on.

Altogether, more is wrong with the overall set-up of WTO law than with the functioning of the dispute settlement mechanism specifically; for example, non-trade objectives are conceived of as exceptions in the GATT and the GATS and the science-related disciplines of the SPS Agreement that have turned out to be a significant obstacle to WTO Members' regulatory measures cannot just be ignored by the adjudicators. The WTO dispute settlement system cannot fully remedy the shortcomings of WTO law, nor should it do so.[2722] Kulovesi, while being concerned with issues of environmental sustainability, concludes the following:

> "[…] I do not believe that the [sic] many of the problems identified […] could be solved with the WTO dispute settlement system by simply 'importing' substantive legitimacy and injecting a dose of international environmental law or ecological sensitivity into the domain of trade rules where appropriate. My argument is that when tackling its substantive legitimacy challenges, the WTO dispute settlement system must pay careful attention to the institutional and procedural factors underpinning the notion of formal legitimacy."[2723]

While I do not fully share Kulovesi's position on the formal constraints that the DSU imposes on the adjudicators,[2724] I do concur that the WTO judicial decision-makers should not seek to expand the reach of the WTO dispute settlement system or to exploit the boundaries of its formal mandate to the very limit. For example, instead of engaging in a more intensive balancing of the different interests at stake, the adjudicators should, to whatever extent is feasible, show deference to regulatory decisions at the national level. At the same time they should be transparent and clear about

---

2721 Shlomo-Agon 2015, 565.

2722 For a similar position, see Shany and Shlomo-Agon 2014, 213 with further references.

2723 Kulovesi 2011, 180.

2724 For her position, see ibid., 181ff.

the reasons motivating their decisions, including those relating to policy and values. Beyond that, whatever is wrong with the WTO and its dispute settlement mechanism needs to be remedied through more balanced and concise trade rules, through reforms of the (political) decision-making procedures at the WTO[2725] and/or judicial mechanisms in other areas of international law that are comparable in strength and sanctioning power to the WTO dispute settlement system.

2725 This has been proposed by a number of commentators, see for example Matsushita 2020, 49.

References

Abbott, Kenneth O. W., Robert Keohane, Andrew Moravcsik, Anne-Marie Slaughter, and Duncan Snidal. 2000. The Concept of Legalization. *International Organization* 54 (3): 401–419.

Abi-Saab, Georges. 2006. The Appellate Body and treaty interpretation. In *The WTO at ten: the contribution of the dispute settlement system*, edited by Alan Yanovich, Jan Bohanes, and Sacerdoti, Giorgio, 453–464. Cambridge/New York: Cambridge University Press.

Abi-Saab, Georges. 2008. WTO case law in an international law context – panel discussion. In *The WTO: governance, dispute settlement & developing countries*, edited by Merit E. Janow, Victoria Donaldson, and Alan Yanovich, 709–730. Huntington: Juris Publishing.

Afilalo, Ari, and Sheila Foster. 2003. The World Trade Organization's anti-discrimination jurisprudence: free trade, national sovereignty, and environmental health in balance. *Georgetown International Environmental Law Review*: 634–676.

Aleinikoff, Alexander. 1987. Constitutional law in the age of balancing. *Yale Law Journal* 96: 943–1005.

Alemanno, Alberto. 2013. Public perception of food safety risks under WTO law: a normative perspective. In *Research Handbook on Environment, Health and the WTO*, edited by Geert van Calster and Marie Denise Prévost, 270–303. Cheltenham/Northhampton: Edward Elgar.

Alexy, Robert. 1995. *Recht, Vernunft, Diskurs*. Frankfurt a.M.: Suhrkamp.

Allee, Todd, Manfred Elsig, and Andrew Lugg. 2017. The Ties between the World Trade Organization and Preferential Trade Agreements: A Textual Analysis. *Journal of International Economic Law* 20 (2): 333–363.

Alter, Karen, Laurence Helfer, and Mikael Madsen. 2016. How Context Shapes the Authority of International Courts. *Law and Contemporary Problems* 79 (1): 1–36.

Alter, Karen J. 1998. Who are the "masters of the treaty"? European governments and the European Court of Justice. *International Organization* 52 (1): 121–176.

Alter, Karen J. 2003. Resolving or exacerbating disputes? The WTO's new dispute resolution system. *International Affairs* 79 (4): 783–800.

Alvarez, José. 2008. The Factors Driving and Constraining the Incorporation of International Law in WTO Adjudication. In *The WTO: governance, dispute settlement & developing countries*, edited by Merit E. Janow, Victoria Donaldson, and Alan Yanovich, 611–633. Huntington: Juris Publishing.

Alvarez-Jiménez, Alberto. 2008. New approaches to the state of necessity in customary international law: insights from WTO law and foreign investment law. *American Review of International Arbitration* 19 (3–4): 463–488.

Alvarez-Jiménez, Alberto. 2009a. The WTO Appellate Body's decision-making process: a perfect model for international adjudication? *Journal of International Economic Law* 12 (2): 289–331.

Alvarez-Jiménez, Alberto. 2009b. The WTO Appellate Body's Exercise of Judicial Economy. *Journal of International Economic Law* 12 (2): 393–415.

Andenas, Mads, and Stefan Zleptnig. 2007. Proportionality and balancing in WTO law: a comparative perspective. *Texas International Law Journal* 42 (3): 371–423.

Appleton, Arthur E. 1999. Shrimp/turtle: untangling the nets. *Journal of International Economic Law* 2 (3): 447–496.

Arcuri, Alessandra. 2013. Law and economics of the SPS Agreement: a critical perspective. In *Research Handbook on Environment, Health and the WTO*, edited by Geert van Calster and Marie Denise Prévost, 164–206. Cheltenham/Northhampton: Edward Elgar.

Arup, Christopher J. 2003. The State of Play of Dispute Settlement "Law" at the WTO. *Journal of World Trade* 37 (5): 897–920.

Atik, Jeffery. 2013. On the efficiency of health measures and the "appropriate level of protection". In *Research Handbook on Environment, Health and the WTO*, edited by Geert van Calster and Marie Denise Prévost, 116–138. Cheltenham/Northhampton: Edward Elgar.

Babu, R. Rajesh. 2020. WTO Appellate Body Overreach and the Crisis in the Making: A View from the South. In *The Appellate Body of the WTO and Its Reform*, edited by Chang-fa Lo, Junji Nakagawa, and Tsai-fang Chen, 91–107. Singapore: Springer.

Bacchus, James. 2001. The role of lawyers in the WTO. *Vanderbilt Journal of Transnational Law* 34 (4): 953–961.

Bacchus, James. 2002. Table talk: around the table of the Appellate Body of the World Trade Organization. *Vanderbilt Journal of Transnational Law* 35 (4): 1021–1039.

Bacchus, James. 2003. The bicycle club – affirming the American interest in the future of the WTO. *Journal of World Trade* 37 (3): 429–441.

Bacchus, James. 2004a. A few thoughts on legitimacy, democracy, and the WTO. *Journal of International Economic Law* 7: 667–673.

Bacchus, James. 2004b. The strange death of Sir Francis Bacon: the dos and don'ts of appellate advocacy in the WTO. *Legal Issues of Economic Integration* 31 (1): 13–24.

Bacchus, James. 2005. Appellators: The Quest for the Meaning of and/or. *World Trade Review* 4 (3): 499–523.

Bahri, Amrita. 2019. *Appellate Body Held Hostage: Is Judicial Activism at Fair Trial?* Working Papers. Institute of European Law.

Barak, Aharon. 2005. *Purposive interpretation in law*. Princeton: Princeton University Press.

Barfield, Claude E. 2001. *Free trade, sovereignty, democracy – The future of the World Trade Organization*. Washington, D.C.: American Enterprise Institute Press.

Barfield, Claude E. 2002. *The constitutional flaws of the WTO and what to do about them*. Geneva.

Bartels, Lorand. 2001. Applicable law in WTO dispute settlement proceedings. *Journal of World Trade* 35 (3): 499–519.

Bartels, Lorand. 2002. Article XX of GATT and the problem of extraterritorial jurisdiction – the case of trade measures for the protection of human rights. *Journal of World Trade* 36 (2): 353–403.

Bartels, Lorand. 2004. The separation of powers in the WTO: how to avoid judicial activism. *International and Comparative Law Quarterly* 53: 861–895.

Bartels, Lorand. 2015. The Chapeau of the General Exceptions in the WTO GATT and GATS Agreements: A Reconstruction. *American Journal of International Law* 109 (1): 95–125.

Baum, Lawrence. 2006. *Judges and their audiences: a perspective on judicial behavior*. Princeton: Princeton University Press.

Beach, Derek. 2001. Between law and politics: taking the law seriously in rationalist models of judicial autonomy in the EU. Madison. Available at <http://aei.pitt.edu/2049/1/002092_1.PDF>.

Bechtler, Thomas W. 1978. American legal realism revaluated I. In *Law in a social context – Liber amicorum honouring Prof. Lon. L. Fuller*, edited by Thomas W. Bechtler, 5–47. Beventer: Kluwer.

Beck, Gunnar. 2012. *The legal reasoning of the European Court of Justice*. Oxford: Hart.

Behboodi, Rambod. 1999. Legal reasoning and the international law of trade: the first steps of the Appellate Body of the WTO. In *International trade law on the 50th anniversary of the multilateral trade system*, edited by Paolo Mengozzi, 303–367. Milano: A. Guiffrè.

Bentley, Philip. 2000. A re-assessment of Article XX, paragraphs (b) and (g) of GATT 1994 in the light of growing consumer and environmental concern about biotechnology. *Fordham International Law Journal* 24 (1): 107–131.

Benvenisti, Eyal, and George W. Downs. 2012. Prospects for the increased independence of international tribunals. In *International Judicial Lawmaking: On Public Authority and Democratic Legitimation in Global Governance*, edited by Armin von Bogdandy and Ingo Venzke, 99–129. Heidelberg/New York/Dordrecht/London: Springer.

Berger, Helge, and Michael Neugart. 2012. How German Labor Courts Decide: An Econometric Case Study. *German Economic Review* 13 (1): 56–70.

Beviglia Zampetti, Americo. 2003. Democratic legitimacy in the World Trade Organization: the justice dimension. *Journal of World Trade* 37 (1): 105–126.

Bhala, Raj. 1999a. The myth about stare decisis and international trade law (part one of a trilogy). *American University International Law Review* 14 (4): 845–956.

Bhala, Raj. 1999b. The precedent setters: de facto stare decisis in WTO adjudication (part two of a trilogy). *Journal of Transnational Law and Policy* 9 (Fall 1999): 1–151.

Blackmore, Dana T. 2004. Eradicating the long standing existence of a no-precedent rule in international trade law – looking toward stare decisis in WTO dispute settlement. *North Carolina Journal of International Law and Commercial Regulation* 29 (3): 487–518.

Bleckmann, Albert. 1981. Gedanken zur Repressalie – Ein Versuch der Anwendung der Interessenjurisprudenz auf das Völkergewohnheitsrecht. In *Staatsrecht, Völkerrecht, Europarecht - Festschrift für Hans-Jürgen Schlochauer zum 75. Geburtstag*, edited by Ingo von Münch, 193–213. Berlin, New York.

Bloche, M. Gregg. 2002. WTO deference to national health policy: Toward an interpretive principle. *Journal of International Economic Law* 5 (4): 825–848.

Böckenförde, Markus. 2003. Zwischen Sein und Wollen – Über den Einfluss umweltvölkerrechtlicher Verträge im Rahmen eines WTO-Streitbeilegungsverfahrens. *Zeitschrift für ausländisches öffentliches Recht und Völkerrecht* 63: 971–1005.

Bodansky, Daniel. 1999. The legitimacy of international governance: A coming challenge for international environmental law? *American Journal of International Law* 93 (3): 596–624.

Bogdandy, Armin von. 2001. Law and politics in the WTO: strategies to cope with a deficient relationship. *Max Planck Yearbook of United Nations Law* 5: 609–674.

Bogdandy, Armin von. 2003. Legitimacy of international economic governance: interpretative approaches to WTO law and the prospects of its proceduralization. In *International economic governance and non-economic concerns: New challenges for the international legal order*, edited by Stefan Griller, 104–148. Wien/New York: Springer.

Bogdandy, Armin von, and Ingo Venzke. 2012. Beyond dispute: international judicial institutions as lawmakers. In *International Judicial Lawmaking: On Public Authority and Democratic Legitimation in Global Governance*, edited by Armin von Bogdandy and Ingo Venzke, 3–33. Heidelberg/New York/Dordrecht/London: Springer.

Bogdandy, Armin von, and Ingo Venzke. 2013. On the Functions of International Courts: An Appraisal in Light of Their Burgeoning Public Authority. *Leiden Journal of International Law* 26 (1): 49–72.

Bohanes, Jan. 2002. Risk regulation in WTO law: A procedure-based approach to the precautionary principle. *Columbia Journal of Transnational Law* 40 (2): 323–389.

Bohanes, Jan, and Andreas Sennekamp. 2006. Reflections on the concept of "judicial economy" in WTO dispute settlement. In *The WTO at ten: the contribution of the dispute settlement system*, edited by Alan Yanovich, Jan Bohanes, and Sacerdoti, Giorgio, 424–449. Cambridge/New York: Cambridge University Press.

Bossis, Gaelle. 2001. La notion de sécurité alimentaire selon l'OMC: entre minoration et tolerance timide. *Revue générale de droit international public* 105 (2): 313–354.

Bourdieu, Pierre. 1987. The Force of Law: Toward a Sociology of the Juridical Field. *Hastings Law Journal* 38 (5): 805–853.

Bowen, Brandon L. 2000. The World Trade Organization and its interpretation of the Article XX: exceptions to the General Agreement on Tariffs and Trade, in the light of recent developments. *Georgia Journal of International and Comparative Law* 29 (1): 181–202.

Bown, Chad P. 2005. Participation in WTO dispute settlement: complainants, interested parties, and free riders. *The World Bank Economic Review* 19 (2): 287–310.

Bown, Chad P., and Joel P. Trachtman. 2009. Brazil – Measures Affecting Imports of Retreaded Tyres: A Balancing Act. *World Trade Review* 8 (1): 85–135.

Brewer, Scott. 1998. Scientific expert testimony and intellectual due process. *Yale Law Journal* 107 (6): 1535–1681.

Briggs, Lewis. 2001. Conserving "Exhaustible Natural Resources": The role of precedent in the GATT Article XX(g) exception. In *Reconciling environment and trade*, edited by Edith Brown Weiss and John H Jackson, 261–292. Ardsley: Transnational Publishers.

Brink, Tegan. 2010. Which WTO Rules Can a PTA Lawfully Breach? Completing the Analysis in Brazil – Tyres. *Journal of World Trade* 44 (4): 813–846.

Bronckers, Marco, and Keith E. Maskus. 2014. China – Raw Materials: a controversial step towards evenhanded exploitation of natural resources. *World Trade Review* 13 (2): 393–408.

Broude, Tomer. 2004. *International governance in the WTO: judicial boundaries and political capitulation*. London: Cameron May.

Broude, Tomer. 2006. *Genetically Modified Rules: The Awkward Rule-Exception-Right Distinction in EC-Biotech*. Research Paper. Jerusalem: Faculty of Law and Department of International Relations, Hebrew University of Jerusalem. Available at <http://205.251.117.79/articles/broudebiotech.pdf>.

Buchmüller, Christian. 2013. *Strom aus erneuerbaren Energien im WTO-Recht: zur Vereinbarkeit von Einspeisevergütungssystemen und Quotenmodellen mit Zertifikatehandel mit dem WTO-Recht*. Baden-Baden: Nomos.

Búrca, Gráinne de, and Joanne Scott. 2001. The impact of the WTO on EU decision-making. In *The EU and the WTO: Legal and constitutional aspects*, edited by Gráinne de Búrca and Joanne Scott, 1–30. Oxford: Hart.

Burley, Anne-Marie, and Walter Mattli. 1993. Europe before the Court: a Political Theory of Legal Integration. *International Organization* 47 (1): 41–76.

Busch, Marc L. 2007. Overlapping Institutions, Forum Shopping, and Dispute Settlement in International Trade. *International Organization* 61 (4): 735–761.

Busch, Marc L., and Krzysztof J. Pelc. 2010. The Politics of Judicial Economy at the World Trade Organization. *International Organization* 264 (2): 257–279.

Busch, Marc L, and Krzysztof J Pelc. 2019. Words Matter: How WTO Rulings Handle Controversy. *International Studies Quarterly* 63 (3): 464–476.

Busch, Marc L., and Eric Reinhardt. 2002. Testing international trade law: Empirical studies of GATT/WTO dispute settlement. In *The political economy of international trade law: Essays in Honor of Robert E. Hudec*, edited by Daniel L. M. Kennedy and James D. Southwick, 457–481. Cambridge/New York: Cambridge University Press.

Cameron, James, and Kevin G Gray. 2001. Principles of international law in the WTO dispute settlement body. *International and Comparative Law Quarterly* 50 (2): 248–298.

Canal-Forgues, Eric. 2001. Sur l'interprétation dans le droit de l'OMC. *Revue générale de droit international public* 105 (1): 5–24.

Carlone, Jonathan. 2014. An Added Exception to the TBT Agreement After Clove,Tuna II, and Cool. *Boston College International and Comparative Law Review* 37 (1): 103.

Cartland, Michel, Gérard Depayre, and Jan Woznowski. 2012. Is Something Going Wrong in the WTO Dispute Settlement? *Journal of World Trade* 46 (5): 979–1015.

Carvalho, Nuno Pires de. 2002. *The TRIPS Regime of Patent rights*. New York: Kluwer Law International.

Cass, Deborah Z. 2001. The "constitutionalization" of international trade law: judicial norm-generation as engine of constitutional development in international trade. *European Journal of International Law* 12 (1): 39–76.

Cass, Deborah Z. 2005. *The Constitutionalization of the World Trade Organization: Legitimacy, Democracy, and Community in the International Trading System*. Oxford/New York: Oxford University Press.

Ceva, Emanuela, and Andrea Fracasso. 2010. Seeking mutual understanding: a discourse-theoretical analysis of the WTO Dispute Settlement System. *World Trade Review* 9 (3): 457–485.

Chan, Alexsia T., and Beverly K. Crawford. 2017. The puzzle of public opposition to TTIP in Germany. *Business and Politics* 19 (4): 683–708.

Charlotin, Damien. 2017. The Place of Investment Awards and WTO Decisions in International Law: A Citation Analysis. *Journal of International Economic Law* 20 (2): 279–299.

Charnovitz, Steve. 1991. Exploring the environmental exceptions in GATT Article XX. *Journal of World Trade* 25 (5): 37–55.

Charnovitz, Steve. 2007. The WTO's environmental progress. *Journal of International Economic Law* 10 (3): 685–706.

Charnovitz, Steve. 2018. How American Rejectionism Undermines International Economic Law. *Trade, Law and Development* 10 (2): 226–269.

Charvat, Nicola. 2016. Amicus Curiae Briefs in WTO Disputes: An Opportunity for Participation. Available at <https://www.tradelab.org/single-post/2018/03/02/Amicus-Curiae-Briefs-in-WTO-Disputes-An-Opportunity-for-Participation>.

Cheyne, Ilona. 2006. The Precautionary Principle in EC and WTO Law: Searching for a Common Understanding. *Environmental Law Review* 8 (4): 257–277.

Cheyne, Ilona. 2007. Gateways to the precautionary principle in WTO law. *Journal of Environmental Law* 19 (2): 155–172.

Chi, Manjiao. 2014. 'Exhaustible Natural Resources' in WTO Law: GATT Article XX (g) Disputes and Their Implications. *Journal of World Trade* 48 (5): 939–966.

Cho, Sungjoon. 1998. Gasoline: United States – Standards for Reformulated and Conventional Gasoline. *European Journal of International Law* 9 (1). Available at <http://papers.ssrn.com/sol3/papers.cfm?abstract_id=1734488>.

Cho, Sungjoon. 2009a. Of the World Trade Court's Burden. *European Journal of International Law* 20 (3): 675–727.

Cho, Sungjoon. 2009b. United States – Continued Suspension of Obligations in the EC – Hormones Dispute. WT/DS320/AB/R. *American Journal of International Law* 103: 299–305.

Choi, Won-Mog. 2003. *"Like products" in international trade law: towards a consistent GATT/WTO jurisprudence*. Oxford/New York: Oxford University Press.

Christoforou, Theofanis. 2000. Settlement of science-based trade disputes in the WTO: a critical review of the developing case law in the face of scientific uncertainty. *New York University Environmental Law Journal* 8 (3): 622–648.

Chua, Adrian T. L. 1998. Precedent and principles of WTO Panel jurisprudence. *Berkeley Journal of International Law* 16 (1): 171–196.

Clifford Chance. 2019. The WTO Appellate Body crisis – a way forward? Available at <https://www.cliffordchance.com/briefings/2019/11/the-wto-appellate-body-crisis---a-way-forward-.html>.

Colares, Juscelino F. 2009. A Theory of WTO Adjudication: From Empirical Analysis to Biased Rule Development. *Vanderbilt Journal of Transnational Law* 42 (3): 383–439.

Colares, Juscelino F. 2011. The limits of WTO Adjudication: Is Compliance the Problem? *Journal of International Economic Law* 14 (2): 403–436.

Conconi, Paola, and Tania Voon. 2016. EC – Seal Products: The Tension between Public Morals and International Trade Agreements. *World Trade Review* 15 (2): 211–234.

Condon, Bradly J. 2004. GATT Article XX and proximity of interest: determining the subject matter of paragraphs b and g. *UCLA Journal of International Law and Public Affairs* 9 (2): 137–162.

Condon, Bradly J. 2010. Lost in Translation: Plurilingual Interpretation of WTO Law. *Journal of International Dispute Settlement* 1 (1): 191–216.

Condon, Bradly J. 2018. Captain America and the Tarnishing of the Crown: The Feud Between the WTO Appellate Body and the USA. *Journal of World Trade* 52 (4): 535–556.

Conrad, Christiane. 2007. The EC – Biotech Dispute and Applicability of the SPS Agreement: Are the Panel's Findings Built on Shaky Ground? *World Trade Review* 6 (2): 233–248.

Conrad, Christiane. 2011. *Processes and production methods (PPMs) in WTO law: interfacing trade and social goals*. Cambridge/New York: Cambridge University Press.

Conti, Joseph A. 2011. *Between law and diplomacy: the social contexts of disputing at the World Trade Organization*. Stanford: Stanford University Press.

Cooter, Robert D., and Thomas B. Ginsburg. 1996. Comparative Judicial Discretion: An Empirical Test of Economic Models. *International Review of Law and Economics* 16: 295–313.

Coroado, Susana, Nuno Garoupa, and Pedro C. Magalhães. 2017. *Judicial Behavior under Austerity: An Empirical Analysis of Behavioral Changes in the Portuguese Constitutional Court, 2002-2016*. Legal Studies Research Paper Series. Texas: Texas A. & M. University School of Law.

Costa, Jose Augusto Fontoura. 2011. Comparing WTO Panelists and ICSID Arbitrators: The Creation of International Legal Fields. *Oñati Socio-Legal Series* 1 (4).

Cottier, Thomas. 1998. Dispute Settlement in the World Trade Organization: Characteristics and Structural Implications for the European Union. *Common Market Law Review* 35 (2): 325–378.

Cottier, Thomas, Roberto Echandi, Rachel Liechti-McKee, Tetyana Payosova, and Charlotte Sieber. 2017. The Principle of Proportionality in International Law: Foundations and Variations. *The Journal of World Investment & Trade* 18 (4): 628–672.

Cottier, Thomas, and Matthias Oesch. 2003. The paradox of judicial review in international trade regulation: towards a comprehensive framework. In *The role of the judge in international trade regulation: experience and lessons for the WTO*, edited by Thomas Cottier and Petros C. Mavroidis, 287–306. Ann Arbor: University of Michigan Press.

Cottier, Thomas, and Krista Nadakavukaren Schefer. 2000. Good faith and the protection of legitimate expectations in the WTO. In *New directions in international economic law*, 47–68. London/The Hague/Boston: Kluwer Law International.

Craig, Paul, and Gráinne de Búrca. 2011. *EU Law: Text, Cases, and Materials*. Oxford/New York: Oxford University Press.

Crowley, Meredith A., and Robert Howse. 2014. Tuna – Dolphin II: a legal and economic analysis of the Appellate Body Report. *World Trade Review* 13 (2): 321–355.

Cunningham, Richard O., and Troy H. Cribb. 2003. Dispute Settlement Through the Lens of "Free Flow of Trade": A Review of WTO Dispute Settlement of US Anti-Dumping and Countervailing Duty Measures. *Journal of International Economic Law* 6 (1): 155–170.

Daku, Mark, and Krzysztof J. Pelc. 2017. Who Holds Influence over WTO Jurisprudence? *Journal of International Economic Law* 20 (2): 233–255.

Danziger, Shai, Jonathan Levav, and Liora Avnaim-Pesso. 2011. Extraneous Factors in Judicial Decisions. *Proceedings of the National Academy of Sciences* 108 (17): 6889–6892.

D'Aspremont, Jean, and Makane Moïse Mbengue. 2014. Strategies of Engagement with Scientific Fact-finding in International Adjudication. *Journal of International Dispute Settlement* 5 (2): 240–272.

Davey, William J. 2000. WTO dispute settlement: segregating the useful political aspects and avoiding "over-legalization". In *New directions in international economic law*, edited by Marco Bronckers and Reinhard Quick, 290–307. London/The Hague/Boston: Kluwer Law International.

Davey, William J. 2003. Has the WTO dispute settlement system exceeded its authority? A consideration of deference shown by the system to member government decisions and its use of issue-avoidance techniques. In *The role of the judge in international trade regulation: experience and lessons for the WTO*, edited by Thomas Cottier and Petros C. Mavroidis, 79–110. Ann Arbor: University of Michigan Press.

Davey, William J. 2005. The WTO dispute settlement system: the first ten years. *Journal of International Economic Law* 8 (1): 17–50.

Davey, William J., and André Sapir. 2009. The Soft Drinks Case: The WTO and Regional Agreements. *World Trade Review* 8 (1): 5–23.

Davies, Arwel. 2009. Interpreting the chapeau of GATT Art. XX in light of the "new" approach in Brazil tyres. *Journal of World Trade* 43 (3): 507–539.

Delbrück, Jost. 1997. Proportionality. In *Encyclopedia of public international law, Vol. 3*, edited by Rudolf Bernhardt, 1140–144. Amsterdam: North Holland.

Delimatsis, Panagiotis. 2011. Protecting Public Morals in a Digital Age: Revisiting the WTO Rulings on US – Gambling and China – Publications and Audiovisual Products. *Journal of International Economic Law* 14 (2): 257–293.

Desmedt, Axel. 2001. Proportionality in WTO law. *Journal of International Economic Law* 4 (3): 441–480.

De Waart, Paul de. 1998. Quality of life at the mercy of WTO panels: GATT's Article XX an empty shell? In *International economic law with a human face*, edited by Friedl Weiss, Erik Denters, and Paul de Waart, 109–131. London/The Hague/Boston: Kluwer Law International.

De Visser, Maartje. 2013. A cautionary tale: some insights regarding judicial activism from the national experience. In *Judicial activism at the European Court of Justice*, edited by Mark Dawson, Bruno Witte, and Elise Muir, 188–210. Cheltenham/Northhampton: Elgar.

Dickson, Brice. 2007. Comparing supreme courts. In *Judicial activism in common law supreme courts*, 1–17. Oxford/New York: Oxford University Press.

Diebold, Nicolas F. 2008. The Morals and Order Exceptions in WTO Law: Balancing the Toothless Tiger and the Undermining Mole. *Journal of International Economic Law* 11 (1): 43–74.

Dörr, Oliver, and Kirsten Schmalenbach, eds. 2012. *Vienna Convention on the Law of Treaties: a commentary*. Berlin/Heidelberg: Springer.

Doyle, Christopher. 2011. Gimme Shelter: The Necessary Element of GATT Article XX in the Context of the China – Audiovisual Products Case. *Boston University International Law Journal* 29 (1): 143–167.

Du, Michael M. 2010a. Autonomy in Setting Appropriate Level of Protection under the WTO Law: Rhetoric or Reality? *Journal of International Economic Law* 13 (4): 1077–1102.

Du, Michael M. 2010b. Standard of review under the SPS Agreement after EC – Hormones II. *International and Comparative Law Quarterly* 59 (April 2010): 441–459.

Du, Michael M. 2011. The Rise of National Regulatory Autonomy in the GATT/WTO Regime. *Journal of International Economic Law* 14 (3): 639–675.

Dunoff, Jeffrey L., and Mark A. Pollack. 2017. *The Judicial Trilemma*. Research Paper. Temple University Legal Studies. Temple University. Available at <https://papers.ssrn.com/abstract=2955172>. Accessed 7 March 2021.

Dutfield, Graham. 2003. *Trading in Knowledge: Development Perspectives on TRIPS, Trade and Sustainability*. Edited by Christophe Bellmann and Ricardo Melendez-Ortiz. London: Routledge.

Dworkin, Ronald. 1981. *Taking Rights Seriously*. London: Duckworth.

Eckert, Dieter. 1995. Die neue Welthandelsordnung und ihre Bedeutung für den internationalen Verkehr mit Lebensmitteln. *Zeitschrift für das gesamte Lebensmittelrecht* 22 (4): 363–395.

Eeckhout, Piet. 2010. The Scales of Trade – Reflections on the Growth and Functions of the WTO Adjudicative Branch. *Journal of International Economic Law* 13 (1): 3–26.

Eggers, Barbara. 2001. *The Precautionary Principle in WTO Law*. Available at <http://www.sub.uni-hamburg.de/opus/volltexte/2001/451/>.

Ehlermann, Claus-Dieter. 2002. Six years on the bench of the "world trade court": some personal experiences as member of the Appellate Body of the World Trade Organization. *Journal of World Trade* 36 (4): 605–639.

Ehlermann, Claus-Dieter. 2003a. Reflections on the Appellate Body of the WTO. *Journal of International Economic Law* 6 (3): 695–708.

Ehlermann, Claus-Dieter. 2003b. WTO dispute settlement and competition law: views from the perspective of the Appellate Body's experience. *Fordham International Law Journal* 26 (6): 1505–1558.

Ehlermann, Claus-Dieter, and Lothar Ehring. 2005. Decision-making in the World Trade Organization. *Journal of International Economic Law* 8 (1): 51–75.

Ehlermann, Claus-Dieter, and Nicolas Lockhart. 2004. Standard of review in WTO law. *Journal of International Economic Law* 7 (3): 491–521.

Eliason, Antonia. 2009. Science versus law in WTO jurisprudence: the (mis)interpretation of the scientific process and the (in) sufficiency of scientific evidence in EC – Biotech. *New York University Journal of International Law & Politics* 41 (2): 341–406.

El-Said, Hamed, and Mohammed El-Said. 2005. TRIPS, Bilateralism, Multilateralism & Implications for Developing Countries: Jordan's Drug Sector. *Manchester Journal of International Economic Law* 2 (1): 59–79.

Elsig, Manfred, and Mark A. Pollack. 2012. Agents, trustees, and international courts: The politics of judicial appointment at the World Trade Organization. *European Journal of International Relations* Online first version: 1–15.

Emmerich-Fritsche, Angelika. 2000. *Der Grundsatz der Verhältnismäßigkeit als Direktive und Schranke der EG-Rechtssetzung*. Berlin: Duncker & Humblot.

Enderlein, Wolfgang. 1992. *Abwägung in Recht und Moral*. Freiburg/München: Alber.

Epiney, Astrid. 2000. Welthandel und Umwelt: Ein Beitrag zur Dogmatik der Art. III, XI, XX GATT. *Deutsches Verwaltungsblatt* 115 (2): 77–86.

Epps, Tracey. 2008. *International trade and health protection: a critical assessment of the WTO's SPS Agreement*. Cheltenham/Northhampton: Edward Elgar.

Espa, Ilaria. 2012. The Appellate Body approach to the applicability of Article XX GATT in the light of China – Raw materials: a missed opportunity? *Journal of World Trade* 46 (6): 1399–1423.

Esty, Daniel C. 2002. The World Trade Organization's legitimacy crisis. *World Trade Review* 1 (1): 7–22.

Fastenrath, Ulrich. 1991. *Lücken im Völkerrecht – Zu Rechtscharakter, Quellen, Systemzusammenhang, Methodenlehre und Funktionen des Völkerrechts*. Berlin: Duncker & Humblot.

Feddersen, Christoph T. 2002. *Der ordre public in der WTO: Auslegung und Bedeutung des Art. XX lit. a) GATT im Rahmen der WTO Streitbeilegung*. Berlin: Duncker & Humblot.

Feteris, Eveline T. 1999. *Fundamentals of legal argumentation: a survey of theories on the justification of judicial decisions*. Dordrecht: Springer.

Fitzgerald, Peter L. 2011. "Morality" May Not Be Enough to Justify the EU Seal Products Ban: Animal Welfare Meets International Trade Law. *Journal of International Wildlife Law & Policy* 14 (3): 85–136.

Flett, James. 2010. Collective Intelligence and the Possibility of Dissent: Anonymous Individual Opinions in WTO Jurisprudence. *Journal of International Economic Law* 13 (2): 287–320.

Flett, James. 2011. *From the Green Room to the Court Room (and Back): Judicial Clarification of Ambiguity in WTO Law and the Effects on Subsequent Negotiations*. Oñati Socio Legal Series. Oñati: Oñati International Institute for the Sociology of Law.

Foltea, Marina. 2012. *International organizations in WTO dispute settlement: how much institutional sensitivity?* Cambridge/New York: Cambridge University Press.

Fontanelli, Filippo. 2012. Necessity killed the GATT – Art. XX GATT and the misleading rhetoric about "weighing and balancing". *European Journal of Legal Studies* 5 (2): 35–56.

Footer, Mary E. and Saman Zia-Zarifi. 2002. Case Note: European Communities – Measures Affecting Asbestos and Asbestos-Containing Products. *Melbourne Journal of International Law* 3 (1): 121–142.

Foster, Caroline E. 2008. Public Opinion and the Interpretation of the World Trade Organisation's Agreement on Sanitary and Phytosanitary Measures. *Journal of International Economic Law* 11 (2): 427–458.

Foster, Caroline E. 2009. Precaution, Scientific Development and Scientific Uncertainty under the WTO Agreement on Sanitary and Phytosanitary Measures. *Review of European Community & International Environmental Law* 18 (1): 50–58.

Francioni, Francesco. 2006. WTO law in context: the integration of international human rights and environmental law in the dispute settlement process. In *The WTO at ten: the contribution of the dispute settlement system*, edited by Alan Yanovich, Jan Bohanes, and Sacerdoti, Giorgio, 143–154. Cambridge: Cambridge University Press.

Franken, Lorenz, and Jan-Erik Burchardi. 2007. Beyond Biosafety – An Analysis of the EC – Biotech Panel Report. *Aussenwirtschaft* 62 (1): 77–106.

Fukunaga, Yuka. 2012. Standard of Review and "Scientific Truths" in the WTO Dispute Settlement System and Investment Arbitration. *Journal of International Dispute Settlement* 3 (3): 559–576.

Gaines, Stanford. 2001. The WTO's reading of the GATT Article XX chapeau: a disguised restriction on environmental measures. *University of Pennsylvania Journal of International Economic Law* 22 (4): 739–861.

Gallagher, Kevin P. 2009. *Handbook on Trade and the Environment*. Cheltenham/ Northhampton: Edward Elgar.

Garrett, Geoffrey, R. Daniel Kelemen, and Heiner Schulz. 1998. The European Court of Justice, national governments and legal integration in the European Union. *International Organization* 52 (1): 149–176.

Garrett, Geoffrey, and James McCall Smith. 2002. *The politics of WTO dispute settlement*. Los Angeles: UCLA International Institute. Available at <http://escholarship.org/uc/item/4t4952d7#page-1>.

Gathii, James Thuo. 2002. The legal status of the Doha Declaration on TRIPS and public health under the Vienna Convention on the Law of Treaties. *Harvard Journal of Law and Technology* 15 (2): 291–317.

Gazal-Ayal, Oren, and Raanan Sulitzeanu-Kenan. 2010. Let My People Go: Ethnic In-Group Bias in Judicial Decisions – Evidence from a Randomized Natural Experiment. *Journal of Empirical Legal Studies* 7 (3): 403–428.

Gehring, Markus W., and Marie-Claire Cordonier Segger. 2003. Precaution in World Trade Law: The Precautionary Principle and its Implications for the World Trade Organisation. *Journal of Environmental Law* 15 (3): 289–321.

Gelbert, Julia. 2001. *Die Risikobewältigung im Lebensmittelrecht auf internationaler, europäischer und nationaler Ebene: unter besonderer Berücksichtigung des Hormonfalls, der BSE-Krise und gentechnischer Verfahren bei der Lebensmittelherstellung und unter Beachtung des Vorsorgeprinzips*. Bayreuth: PCO.

Gerstetter, Christiane, and Matthias Leonhard Maier. 2005. *Risk regulation, trade and international law: Debating the precautionary principle in and around the WTO*. TranState Working Paper. Bremen: University of Bremen. Available at <http://www.sfb597.uni-bremen.de/pages/pubApBeschreibung.php?ID=20&SPRACHE=en>.

Gerstetter, Christiane, Nils Meyer-Ohlendorf, Christian Tietje, Tobias Zuber, and Martin Kohoutek. 2014. *Welthandelsrechtliche Grenzen des Ausbaus erneuerbarer Energien – Projekt im Auftrag des Bundesministeriums für Wirtschaft und Energie (BMWi)*. Ecologic Institute/Institut für Wirtschaftsrecht, Martin-Luther-Universität Halle-Wittenberg. Available at <http://www.erneuerbare-energien.de/EE/Redaktion/DE/Downloads/Berichte/welthandelsrechtliche_grenzen_des_ausbaus_ee.html>.

Ginsburg, Tom. 2006. *International Judicial Lawmaking*. Illinois Law and Economics Working Papers Series Working Paper. Illinois: University of Illinois, College of Law.

Glennon, Colin, and Logan Strother. 2019. The Maintenance of Institutional Legitimacy in Supreme Court Justices' Public Rhetoric. *Journal of Law and Courts* 7 (2). The University of Chicago Press: 241–261.

Godt, Christine. 1998. Der Bericht des Appellate Body der WTO zum EG-Einfuhrverbot von Hormonfleisch. Risikoregulierung im Weltmarkt. *Europäisches Wirtschafts- und Steuerrecht* 9 (6): 202–209.

Goh, Gavin, and David L. H. Morgan. 2007. Political Considerations and Pragmatic Outcomes in WTO Dispute Ruling. *University of New South Wales Law Journal* 30 (2): 477–503.

Goldstein, Judith, and Richard H. Steinberg. 2007. *Regulatory Shift: The Rise of Judicial Liberalization at the WTO*. 07-15. Law & Economics Research Paper Series. Los Angeles: UCLA.

Gourgourinis, Anastasios. 2011. The Distinction between Interpretation and Application of Norms in International Adjudication. *Journal of International Dispute Settlement* 2 (1): 31–57.

Gourgourinis, Anastasios. 2016. *Equity and equitable principles in the World Trade Organization: addressing conflicts and overlaps between the WTO and other regimes*. New York: Routledge.

Green, Andrew, and Tracey Epps. 2007. The WTO, science, and the environment: moving towards consistency. *Journal of International Economic Law* 10 (2): 285–316.

Greenwald, John. 2003. WTO Dispute Settlement: an Exercise in Trade Law Legislation? *Journal of International Economic Law* 6 (1): 113–124.

Gross, Oren, and Fionnuala Ní Aoláin. 2001. From discretion to scrutiny: revisiting the application of the margin of appreciation doctrine in the context of Article of the European Convention on Human Rights. *Human Rights Quarterly* 23 (3): 625–649.

Gruni, Giovanni. 2020. The unsustainable lightness of enforcement procedures: environmental standards in the EU-Mercosur FTA. Available at <https://blogdroiteuropeen.com/2020/05/13/the-unsustainable-lightness-of-enforcement-procedures-environmental-standards-in-the-eu-mercosur-fta-by-giovanni-gruni/>.

Gruszczynski, Lukasz. 2006. *The Role of Science in Risk Regulation under the SPS Agreement*. EUI Law Working Paper. Florence: European University Institute. Available at <http://papers.ssrn.com/abstract=891114>.

Gruszczynski, Lukasz. 2008. SPS measures adopted in case of insufficiency of scientific evidence – where do we stand after the EC – Biotech Products case? In *WTO judicial system: contributions and challenges*, edited by Julien Chaisse and Tiziano Balmelli, 91–140. Geneva: Ed. Interuniversitaires Suisses, Edis.

Gruszczynski, Lukasz. 2013. Standard of review of health and environmental regulations by WTO panels. In *Research Handbook on Environment, Health and the WTO*, edited by Geert van Calster and Marie Denise Prévost, 731–758. Cheltenham/Northhampton: Edward Elgar.

Gu, Bin. 2012. Applicability of GATT Article XX in China – Raw Materials: A Clash within the WTO Agreement. *Journal of International Economic Law* 15 (4): 1007–1031.

Guan, Wenwei. 2014. How general should the GATT general exceptions be?: a critique of the "common intention" approach of treaty interpretation. *Journal of World Trade* 48 (2): 219–258.

Guillaume, Gilbert. 2006. Methods and practice of treaty interpretation by the International Court of Justice. In *The WTO at ten: the contribution of the dispute settlement system*, edited by Alan Yanovich, Jan Bohanes, and Sacerdoti, Giorgio, 465–473. Cambridge/New York: Cambridge University Press.

Guthrie, Chris, Jeffrey J. Rachlinski, and Andrew J. Wistrich. 2007. Blinking on the bench: how judges decide cases. *Cornell Law Review* 93 (1): 1–43.

Guzman, Andrew, and Beth A. Simmons. 2002. To settle or empanel? An empirical analysis of litigation and settlement at the World Trade Organization. *Journal of Legal Studies* 31 (1): 205–236.

Guzman, Andrew T. 2008. Determining the Appropriate Standard of Review in WTO Disputes. *Cornell International Law Journal* 42 (1): 42–76.

Guzman, Andrew T., and Beth A. Simmons. 2005. Power Plays and Capacity Constraints: The Selection of Defendants in World Trade Organization Disputes. *Journal of Legal Studies* 34: 557–598.

Habermas, Jürgen. 1992. *Faktizität und Geltung: Beiträge zur Diskurstheorie des Rechts*. Frankfurt a.M.: Suhrkamp.

Harris, Allison P., and Maya Sen. 2019. Bias and Judging. *Annual Review of Political Science* 22: 241–259.

Hart, Herbert L. A. 1994. *The Concept of Law*. 2nd ed. Oxford: Clarendon.

Hathaway, Oona A., Sabria McElroy, and Sara Aronchick Solow. 2011. International law at home: enforcing treaties in U.S. courts. *Yale Journal of International Law* 37 (1): 51–106.

Haugen, Hans Morten. 2007. *The right to food and the TRIPS agreement*. The Raoul Wallenberg Institute human rights library: RAWA. Leiden: Martinus Nijhoff.

Hector, Pascal. 1992. *Das völkerrechtliche Abwägungsgebot – Abgrenzung der Souveränitätssphären durch Verfahren*. Berlin: Duncker & Humblot.

Henckels, Caroline. 2006. GMOs in the WTO: A Critique of the Panel's Legal Reasoning. *Melbourne Journal of International Law* 7 (2): 278–305.

Herwig, Alexia. 2008. Whither Science in WTO Dispute Settlement? *Leiden Journal of International Law* 21 (4): 823–846.

Herwig, Alexia, and Christian Joerges. 2013. The precautionary principle in conflicts of law perspectives. In *Research Handbook on Environment, Health and the WTO*, edited by Geert van Calster and Marie Denise Prévost, 3–40. Cheltenham/Northhampton: Edward Elgar.

Hestermeyer, Holger P., and Laura Nielsen. 2014. The Legality of Local Content Measures under WTO Law. *Journal of World Trade* 48 (3): 553–591.

Hey, Ellen. 2000. Considerations regarding the Hormones case, the precautionary principle and international dispute settlement procedures. *Leiden Journal of International Law* 13 (1): 239–248.

Higgins, Rosalyn. 1968. Policy Considerations and the International Judicial Process. *International & Comparative Law Quarterly* 17 (1): 58–84.

Hilf, Meinhard. 2001. Power, rules and principles – which orientation for WTO/GATT law? *Journal of International Economic Law* 4 (1): 111–130.

Hilf, Meinhard, and Goetz J. Goettsche. 2003. The relation of economic and non-economic principles in international law. In *International economic governance and non-economic concerns: New challenges for the international legal order*, edited by Stefan Griller, 5–46. Wien/New York: Springer.

Hilf, Meinhard, and Sebastian Puth. 2002. The principle of proportionality on its way into WTO/GATT law. In *European integration and international co-ordination*, edited by Armin von Bogdandy, Petros C. Mavroidis, Yves Mény, and Claus-Dieter Ehlermann, 199–238. The Hague/London/New York: Kluwer Law International.

Hillenkamp, Thomas. 2006. *32 Probleme aus dem Strafrecht, Allgemeiner Teil*. 12th ed. Neuwied: Luchterhand.

Hillman, Jennifer. 2009. Conflicts between Dispute Settlement Mechanisms in Regional Trade Agreements and the WTO – What Should WTO Do. *Cornell International Law Journal* 42 (2): 193–208.

Hippler Bello, Judith, and Maury D. Shenk. 1996. WTO Dispute Settlement Body – Article XX environmental exceptions to GATT – National Treatment – Consistency with GATT of U. S. rule regarding imports of reformulated gasoline. *American Journal of International Law* 90 (4): 669–674.

Hoekman, Bernard. 2016. The World Trade Order: Global Governance by Judiciary? *European Journal of International Law* 27 (4): 1083–1093.

Hoekman, Bernard and Trachtman, Joel. 2010. Continued Suspense: EC – Hormones and WTO Disciplines on Discrimination and Domestic Regulation Appellate Body Reports: Canada/United States – Continued Suspension of Obligations in the EC — Hormones Dispute, WT/DS320/AB/R,WT/DS321/AB/R, Adopted 14 November 2008. *World Trade Review* 9 (Special Issue 1): 151–180.

Hohmann, Harald. 2000. Der Konflikt zwischen freiem Handel und Umweltschutz in WTO und EG. *Recht der internationalen Wirtschaft* 2000 (2): 88–99.

Holmes, Peter. 1999. The WTO and the EU: Some Constitutional Comparisons. In *The EU and the WTO: Legal and Constitutional Issues*, edited by Gráinne de Búrca and Joanne Scott, 59–80. Oxford: Hart.

Howse, Robert. 2001. Adjudicative legitimacy and treaty interpretation in international trade law: the early years of WTO jurisprudence. In *The EU, the WTO and the NAFTA: towards a common law of international trade?*, edited by Joseph H. H. Weiler, 37–69. Oxford/New York: Oxford University Press.

Howse, Robert. 2002a. From politics to technocracy: and back again: The fate of the multilateral trading regime. *American Journal of International Law* 96 (1): 94–117.

Howse, Robert. 2002b. The Appellate Body rulings in the shrimp/turtle case: a new legal baseline for the trade and environment debate. *Columbia Journal of Environmental Law* 27 (2): 489–519.

Howse, Robert. 2002c. The Sardines Panel and AB rulings - some preliminary reactions. *Legal Issues of Economic Integration* 29 (3): 247–254.

Howse, Robert. 2003a. How to begin to think about the "democratic deficit" at the WTO. In *International economic governance and non-economic concerns: New challenges for the international legal order*, edited by Stefan Griller, 79–101. Wien/New York: Springer.

Howse, Robert. 2003b. India's WTO Challenge to Drug Enforcement Conditions in the European Community Generalized System of Preferences – A little known case with major repercussions for "political" conditionality in US trade policy. *Chicago Journal of International Law* 4 (2): 385–405.

Howse, Robert. 2003c. The most dangerous branch? WTO Appellate Body, jurisprudence on the nature and limits of the judicial power. In *The role of the judge in international trade regulation: experience and lessons for the WTO*, edited by edited by Thomas Cottier and Petros C. Mavroidis, 11–41. Ann Arbor: University of Michigan Press.

Howse, Robert. 2008. The use and abuse of international law in WTO trade/environment litigation. In *The WTO: governance, dispute settlement & developing countries*, edited by Merit E. Janow, Victoria Donaldson, and Alan Yanovich, 635–670. Huntington: Juris Publishing.

Howse, Robert. 2009. Moving the WTO forward – one case at a step. *Cornell International Law Journal* 42 (2): 223–231.

Howse, Robert. 2016a. The World Trade Organization 20 Years On: Global Governance by Judiciary. *European Journal of International Law* 27 (1): 9–77.

Howse, Robert. 2016b. The WTO 20 Years On: A Reply to the Responses. *European Journal of International Law* 27 (4): 1127–1129.

Howse, Robert, and Susan Essermann. 2006. The Appellate Body, the WTO dispute settlement system, and the politics of multilateralism. In *The WTO at ten: the contribution of the dispute settlement system*, edited by Alan Yanovich, Jan Bohanes, and Sacerdoti, Giorgo, 61–80. Cambridge/New York: Cambridge University Press.

Howse, Robert L., and Henrik Horn. 2009. European Communities – Measures Affecting the Approval and Marketing of Biotech Products. *World Trade Review* 8 (1): 49–83.

Howse, Robert, and Joanna Langille. 2011. Permitting pluralism: the seal products dispute and why the WTO should accept trade restrictions justified by noninstrumental moral values. *Yale Journal of International Law* 37 (Spring 2011): 367–432.

Howse, Robert, and Philip I. Levy. 2013. The TBT Panels: US – Cloves, US – Tuna, US – COOL. *World Trade Review* 12 (Special Issue 2): 327–375.

Howse, Robert, and Elisabeth Tuerk. 2001. The WTO impact on internal regulations – a case study of the Canada – EC asbestos dispute. In *The EU and the WTO: Legal and constitutional aspects*, edited by Gráinne de Búrca and Joanne Scott, 283–327. Oxford: Hart.

Hu, Jiaxiang. 2004. The role of international law in the development of WTO law. *Journal of International Economic Law* 7 (1): 143–167.

Hubmann, Heinrich. 1977. *Wertung und Abwägung im Recht*. Köln: Heymanns.

Hudec, Robert E. 2003. Science and "post-discriminatory" WTO law. *Boston College International and Comparative Law Review* 26 (2): 185–195.

Hughes, Valerie. 2008. Strengths, weaknesses, and future of the WTO appellate review. In *The WTO: governance, dispute settlement & developing countries*, edited by Merit E. Janow, Victoria Donaldson, and Alan Yanovich, 471–504. Huntington: Juris Publishing.

Hughes, Valerie. 2009. The institutional dimension. In *The Oxford Handbook Of International Trade Law*, edited by Daniel L. Bethlehem, Donald M. McRae, Rodney Neufeld, and Isabelle Van Damme, 269–297. Oxford/New York: Oxford University Press.

Huls, Nick, Maurice Adams, and Jacco Bomhoff, eds. 2009. *The Legitimacy of Highest Courts' Rulings: Judicial Deliberations and Beyond*. The Hague: Asser Press.

Iancu, Bogdan. 2009. Law/Politics Distinctions – The Elusive Reference Points. In *The law/politics distinction in contemporary public law adjudication*, edited by Bogdan Iancu, 1–17. Utrecht: Eleven.

Iida, Keisuke. 2003. Why Does the World Trade Organization Appear Neoliberal? The Puzzle of the High Incidence of Guilty Verdicts in WTO Adjudication. *Journal of Public Policy* 23 (1): 1–21.

Iida, Keisuke. 2004. Is WTO Dispute Settlement Effective? *Global Governance* 10 (2): 207–225.

International Institute for Sustainable Development (IISD), Canadian Environmental Law Association (CELA), and Ecojustice Canada. 2012. Amicus curiae submission before the Panel Canada – Certain Measures Affecting the Renewable Energy Generation Sector (DS412). Available at <https://www.iisd.org/pdf/2012/ecojustice_amicus_curiae_brief.pdf>.

Iynedjian, Marc. 2002. *L'accord de l'organsation mondiale du commerce sur l'application des mesures sanitaires et phytosanitaires: une analyse juridique*. Paris: Librairie Générale de Droit et de Jurisprudence.

Jacob, Marc. 2012. Precedents: lawmaking through international adjudication. In *International Judicial Lawmaking: On Public Authority and Democratic Legitimation in Global Governance*, edited by Armin von Bogdandy and Ingo Venzke, 35–68. Heidelberg/New York/Dordrecht/London: Springer.

Jacobs, Francis G. 1999. Recent developments in the principle of proportionality in European Community law. In *The principle of proportionality in the laws of Europe*, edited by Evelyn Ellis, 1–21. Oxford/Portland: Hart.

Jans, Jan H. 2000. Proportionality revisited. *Legal Issues of Economic Integration* 27 (3): 239–265.

Jetzlsperger, Christian. 2003. Legitimacy through jurisprudence? The impact of the European Court of Justice on the legitimacy of the European Union. Nashville, Tennessee. Available at <http://aei.pitt.edu/2880/1/119.pdf>.

Joerges, Christian. 1997. Scientific expertise in social regulation and the European Court of Justice: Legal frameworks for denationalized governance structures. In *Integrating scientific expertise into regulatory decision-making: national traditions and European innovations*, edited by Christian Joerges, Karl-Heinz Ladeur, and Ellen Vos, 295–324. Baden-Baden: Nomos.

Joerges, Christian. 2009. Judicialization and transnational governance: the example of WTO law and the GMO dispute. In *The law/politics distinction in contemporary public law adjudication*, edited by Bogdan Iancu, 67–84. Utrecht: Eleven.

Joerges, Christian, and Christine Godt. 2005. Free Trade: The Erosion of National and Birth of Transnational Governance. *European Review* 13 (Supplement No 1): 93–117.

Johannesson, Louise, and Petros C. Mavroidis. 2015. *Black Cat, White Cat: The Identity of the WTO Judges*. Working Paper. Stockholm: IFN.

Kapterian, Gisele. 2010. A critique of the WTO jurisprudence on "necessity". *International and Comparative Law Quarterly* 59 (January 2010): 89–127.

Kaufmann, Christine, and Rolf H. Weber. 2011. Carbon-related border tax adjustment: mitigating climate change or restricting international trade? *World Trade Review* 10 (4): 497–525.

Kaupa, Clemens. 2013. Maybe not activist enough? On the Court's alleged neoliberal bias in its recent labor cases. In *Judicial activism at the European Court of Justice*, edited by Mark Dawson, Bruno Witte, and Elise Muir, 56–75. Cheltenham/ Northhampton: Elgar.

Kelemen, R. Daniel. 2001. The Limits of Judicial Power: Trade-Environment Disputes in the GATT/WTO and the EU. *Comparative Political Studies* 34 (6): 622–650.

Kelly, Claire R. 2006. Power, Linkage and Accommodation: The WTO as an international actor and its influence on other actors and regimes. *Berkeley Journal of International Law* 24 (1): 79–128.

Kelly, J. Patrick. 2002. Judicial activism at the World Trade Organization: Developing principles of self-restraint. *Northwestern Journal of International Law and Business* 22 (3): 353–388.

Kennedy, Duncan. 1997. *A critique of adjudication {fin de siècle}*. Cambridge/London: Harvard University Press.

Kepplinger, Hans Mathias, and Thomas Zerback. 2009. Der Einfluss der Medien auf Richter und Staatsanwälte. *Publizistik* 54 (2): 216–239.

Klabbers, Jan. 1992. Jurisprudence in international trade law: Article XX of GATT. *Journal of World Trade* 26 (2): 63–94.

Kleinlein, Thomas. 2012. Judicial law-making by judicial restraint: The potential of balancing in international economic law. In *International Judicial Lawmaking: On Public Authority and Democratic Legitimation in Global Governance*, edited by Armin von Bogdandy and Ingo Venzke, 251–292. Heidelberg/New York/Dordrecht/London: Springer.

Kmiec, Keenan. 2004. The Origin and Current Meanings of Judicial Activism. *California Law Review* 92 (5): 1441–1477.

Kneubuehler, Lorenz. 2001. *Integration durch Rechtsprechung in der EG und der WTO*. Bern: Stämpfli.

Knox, John H. 2004. The judicial resolution of conflicts between trade and the environment. *Harvard Environmental Law Review* 28 (1): 1–78.

Koch, Hans-Joachim. 1996. Die normtheoretische Basis der Abwägung. In *Abwägung im Recht - Symposium und Verabschiedung Werner Hoppe am 30. Juni 1995 aus Anlaß seiner Emeritierung*, edited by Wilfried Erbguth, Janbernd Oebbecke, Hans-Werner Rengeling, and Martin Schulte, 9–24. Köln/Berlin/Bonn: Heymanns.

Kogan, Lawrence A. 2004. The Precautionary Principle and WTO Law: Divergent Views Toward the Role of Science in Assessing and Managing Risk. *Seton Hall Journal of Diplomacy and International Relations* V (1): 77–123.

Kolsky Lewis, Meredith. 2006. The lack of dissent in WTO dispute settlement. *Journal of International Economic Law* 9 (4): 895–931.

Korotana, M. Shabir. 2009. US – Gambling: Test of Limits of the WTO Dispute Settlement Process. *Journal of World Investment & Trade* 10 (1): 121–129.

Krajewski, Markus. 2001. Democratic legitimacy and constitutional perspectives of WTO Law. *Journal of World Trade* 35 (1): 167–186.

Krüger, Tilman. 2013. Strategic Litigation in the World Trade Organization. Doctoral thesis, microfiche version, Bremen: University of Bremen.

Krugmann, Michael. 2004. *Der Grundsatz der Verhältnismäßigkeit im Völkerrecht*. Berlin: Duncker & Humblot.

Kulick, Andreas. 2012. *Global public interest in international investment law*. Cambridge: Cambridge University Press.

Kulovesi, Kati. 2011. *The WTO Dispute Settlement System. Challenges of the Environment, Legitimacy and Fragmentation*. Aalphen an den Rijn: Wolters Kluwer.

Lacarte Muró, Julio. 2007. Os primeiros anos do Órgão de Apelação e do sistema de solução de controvérsias na OMC: uma perspectiva histórica. In *10 anos de OMC: uma análise do sistema de soluçã o de controvérsias e perspectivas*, edited by Baptista, Luiz O, Celli Junior Umberto, and Alan Yanovich. São Paulo: Aduaneiras.

Ladeur, Karl-Heinz. 2004. *Kritik der Abwägung in der Grundrechtsdogmatik*. Tübingen: Mohr Siebeck.

Lagomarsino, Jeffrey. 2011. WTO Dispute Settlement and Sustainable Development: Legitimacy Through Holistic Treaty Interpretation. *Pace Environmental Law Review* 28 (2): 545–567.

Landwehr, Oliver. 2000. *Globalisierung, Freihandel und Gesundheitsschutz (Trade and Health): Die Zulässigkeit gesundheitspolizeilicher und pflanzenschutzrechtlicher Maßnahmen im Lichte der Entscheidungen des EuGH und der GATT/WTO - Panels*. Frankfurt am Main: Peter Lang.

Lang, Andrew. 2016. The Judicial Sensibility of the WTO Appellate Body. *European Journal of International Law* 27 (4): 1095–1105.

Lanye, Zhu. 2003. The effects of the WTO dispute settlement panel and Appellate Body reports: is the dispute settlement body resolving specific disputes only or making precedent at the same time? *Temple International and Comparative Law Journal* 17 (1): 221–236.

Laowonsiri, Akawat. 2010. Application of the Precautionary Principle in the SPS Agreement. *Max Planck Yearbook of United Nations Law* 14: 565–623.

Lasser, Mitchel. 2001. Do Judges Deploy Policy. *Cardozo Law Review* 22 (3): 863–899.

Lasser, Mitchel. 2003. *Anticipating three models of judicial control, debate and legitimacy: the European Court of Justice, the Cour de cassation and the United States Supreme Court*. Jean Monnet Working Paper. Available at <https://www.jeanmonnetprogram.org/archive/papers/03/030101.pdf>.

Lasser, Mitchel. 2004. *Judicial Deliberations – A comparative Analysis of Judicial Transparency and Legitimacy*. Oxford/New York: Oxford University Press.

Lavranos, Nikolaos, and Nicolas Viellard. 2008. The Brazilian Tyres Case: Competing Trade and Non-Trade Interests and Competing Jurisdictions between MERCOSUR and WTO. *European Energy & Environmental Law Review* 17 (5): 306–318.

Lee, Po-Ching. 2020. Appointment and Reappointment of the Appellate Body Members: Judiciary or Politics. In *The Appellate Body of the WTO and Its Reform*, edited by Chang-fa Lo, Junji Nakagawa, and Tsai-fang Chen, 255–271. Singapore: Springer.

Leisner, Walter. 1997. *Der Abwägungsstaat: Verhältnismäßigkeit als Gerechtigkeit?* Berlin: Duncker & Humblot.

Leitner, Kara, and Simon Lester. 2017. WTO Dispute Settlement 1995–2016 – A Statistical Analysis. *Journal of International Economic Law* 20 (1). Oxford Academic: 171–182.

Lennard, Michael. 2002. Navigating by the Stars: Interpreting the WTO Agreements. *Journal of International Economic Law* 5 (1): 17–89.

Leyton, Patricio E. 2001. Evolution of the "Necessary Test" of Article XX (b): From Thai cigarettes to the present. In *Reconciling environment and trade*, edited by Edith Brown Weiss and John H. Jackson, 75–100. Ardsley: Transnational Publishers.

Lieberman, Sarah, and Tim Gray. 2008. The World Trade Organization's Report on the EU's Moratorium on Biotech Products: The Wisdom of the US Challenge to the EU in the WTO. *Global Environmental Politics* 8 (1): 33–52.

Lim, Chin Leng. 2017. Trade Law and the Vienna Treaty Convention's Systemic Integration Clause. In *International Economic Law and Governance: Essays in Honour of Mitsuo Matsushita*, edited by Julien Chaisse and Tsai-yu Lin, 94–112. Oxford: Oxford University Press.

Lim, Chin Leng, and J. H. Senduk. 2014. The wages of belonging: rare earths from China, and the return of GATT à la carte. *Global Trade and Customs Journal* 9 (9): 380–396.

Lindquist, Stefanie, and Frank Cross. 2009. *Measuring Judicial Activism*. Oxford/New York: Oxford University Press.

Lindroos, Anja, and Michael Mehling. 2006. Dispelling the Chimera of "Self-Contained Regimes" – International Law and the WTO. *European Journal of International Law* 16 (5): 857–877.

Livermore, Michael A. 2006. Authority and Legitimacy in Global Governance: Deliberation, Institutional Differentiation, and the Codex Alimentarius. *New York University Law Review* 81 (2): 766–801.

Lo, Chang-Fa. 2010. Good Faith Use of Dictionary in the Search of Ordinary Meaning under the WTO Dispute Settlement Understanding. *Journal of International Dispute Settlement* 1 (2): 431–445.

Lo, Chang-Fa. 2013. The Proper Interpretation of "Disguised Restriction on International Trade" under the WTO: The Need to Look at the Protective Effect. *Journal of International Dispute Settlement* 4 (1): 111–137.

Lockhart, John. 2006. Assessing the "success" of the Appellate Body over the first ten years. In *The WTO at ten: the contribution of the dispute settlement system*, edited by Alan Yanovich, Jan Bohanes, and Sacerdoti, Giorgoi, 285–288. Cambridge/New York: Cambridge University Press.

Loth, Marc A. 2009. Courts in quest for legitimacy: a comparative approach. In *The Legitimacy of Highest Courts' Rulings*, edited by Nick Huls and Jacco Bomhoff, 267–288. The Hague: T.M.C Asser Press.

Lovric, Daniel. 2010. *Deference to the Legislature in WTO Challenges to Legislation*. Alphen aan den Rijn: Kluwer Law International.

Lowe, Eric R. 2014. Technical Regulations to Prevent Deceptive Practices: Can WTO Members Protect Consumers from (un)Fair-Trade Coffee and (Less-Than) Free-Range Chicken? *Journald of World Trade* 48 (3): 593–627.

Lucy, William. 1999. *Understanding and explaining adjudication*. Oxford/New York: Oxford University Press.

Lydgate, Emily. 2017. Is it Rational and Consistent? The WTO's Surprising Role in Shaping Domestic Public Policy. *Journal of International Economic Law* 20 (3): 561–582.

Lydgate, Emily Barrett. 2012. Sustainable development in the WTO: from mutual supportiveness to balancing. *World Trade Review* 11 (4): 621–639.

MacCormick, D. Neil, and Robert S. Summers. 1991. Interpretation and justification. In *Interpreting statutes – a comparative study*, edited by D. Neil MacCormick and Robert S. Summers, 511–544. Aldershot: Darthmouth.

Magnuson, William. 2010. WTO Jurisprudence & Its Critiques: The Appellate Body's Anti-Constitutional Resistance. *Harvard International Law Journal Online* 51 (30 June 2010): 121–154.

Maier, Matthias Leonhard. 2017. *Lebensmittelstandards und Handelsrecht im Verbund internationaler Regime: Interaktion und Wandel von Codex-Alimentarius - Kommission und GATT/WTO, 1963 bis 2013*. Wiesbaden: Springer.

Manzini, Pietro. 1999. Environmental exceptions of Art. XX GATT 1994 revisited in the light of the rules of interpretations of general international law. In *International trade law on the 50th anniversary of the multilateral trade system*, edited by Paolo Mengozzi, 811–848. Milano: A. Guiffrè.

Marceau, Gabrielle. 1999. A call for coherence in international law – praises for the prohibition against "clinical isolation" in WTO dispute settlement. *Journal of World Trade* 33 (5): 87–152.

Marceau, Gabrielle. 2001. Conflicts of norms and conflicts of jurisdictions – the relationship between the WTO agreements and MEAs and other treaties. *Journal of World Trade* 35 (6): 1081–1131.

Marceau, Gabrielle. 2006. Balance and coherence by the WTO Appellate Body: who could do better? In *The WTO at ten: the contribution of the dispute settlement system*, edited by Alan Yanovich, Jan Bohanes, and Sacerdoti, Giorgio, 326–347. Cambridge/New York: Cambridge University Press.

Marceau, Gabrielle. 2018. Evolutive Interpretation by the WTO Adjudicator. *Journal of International Economic Law* 21 (4). Oxford Academic: 791–813.

Marceau, Gabrielle, Arnau Izaguerri, and Vladyslav Lanovoy. 2013. The WTO's influence on other dispute settlement mechanisms: a lighthouse in the storm of fragmentation. *Journal of World Trade* 47 (3): 481–574.

Marceau, Gabrielle, and Joel P. Trachtman. 2002. The Technical Barriers to Trade Agreement, the Sanitary and Phytosanitary Measures Agreement, and the General Agreement on Tariffs and trade: a map of the World Trade Organization law of domestic regulations of goods. *Journal of World Trade* 36 (5): 811–881.

Marceau, Gabrielle, and Joel P. Trachtman. 2014. The Technical Barriers to Trade Agreement, the Sanitary and Phytosanitary Measures Agreement, and the General Agreement on Tariffs and trade: a map of the World Trade Organization law of domestic regulations of goods. *Journal of World Trade* 48 (2): 351–432.

Marín Durán, Gracia. 2016. Measures with Multiple Competing Purposes after EC – Seal Products : Avoiding a Conflict between GATT Article XX-Chapeau and Article 2.1 TBT Agreement. *Journal of International Economic Law* 19 (2): 467–495.

Martineau, Anne-Charlotte. 2007. La technique du balancement par l'Organe d'appel de l'OMC (études de la justification dans les discours juridiques). *Revue du droit public et de la science politique en France et a l'étranger* 2007 (4): 991–1030.

Marwell, Jeremy C. 2006. Trade and Morality: The WTO Public Morals Exception after Gambling. *New York University Law Review* 81 (2): 802–842.

Maton, John, and Carolyn Maton. 2007. Independence under fire: Extra-legal pressures and coalition building in WTO dispute settlement. *Journal of International Economic Law* 10 (2): 317–334.

Matsushita, Mitsuo. 2003. Some Issues of the SPS Agreement. In *The role of the judge in international trade regulation : experience and lessons for the WTO*, edited by Thomas Cottier and Petros C. Mavroidis, 193–212. Ann Arbor: University of Michigan Press.

Matsushita, Mitsuo. 2004. Governance of international trade under World Trade Organization agreements – relationships between World Trade Organization agreements and other trade agreements. *Journal of World Trade* 38 (2): 185–210.

Matsushita, Mitsuo. 2005a. Some Thoughts on the Appellate Body. In *The World Trade Organization: Legal, Economic and Political Analysis*, edited by Patrick F. J. Macrory, Arthur E. Appleton, and Michael G. Plummer, 1389–1403. Boston: Springer US.

Matsushita, Mitsuo. 2005b. The Sutherland Report and its Discussion of Dispute Settlement Reforms. *Journal of International Economic Law* 8 (3): 623–629.

Matsushita, Mitsuo. 2020. Reforming the Appellate Body. In *The Appellate Body of the WTO and Its Reform*, edited by Chang-fa Lo, Junji Nakagawa, and Tsai-fang Chen, 43–52. Singapore: Springer.

Mattoo, Aaditya, and Petros C. Mavroidis. 1997. Trade, environment and the WTO: dispute settlement practice relating to Article XX of GATT. In *International trade law and the GATT/WTO dispute settlement system*, edited by Ernst-Ulrich Petersmann, 327–343. London/The Hague/Boston: Kluwer Law.

Mavroidis, Petros C. 2000. Trade and environment after the shrimps-turtles litigation. *Journal of World Trade* 41 (1): 73–88.

Mavroidis, Petros C. 2006. Looking for Mr and Mrs Right. In *The WTO at ten: the contribution of the dispute settlement system*, edited by Alan Yanovich, Jan Bohanes, and Giorgio Sacerdoti, 348–359. Cambridge/New York: Cambridge University Press.

Mavroidis, Petros C. 2008. Legal eagles? The WTO Appellate Body's first ten years. In *The WTO: governance, dispute settlement & developing countries*, edited by Merit E. Janow, Victoria Donaldson, and Alan Yanovich, 345–367. Huntington: Juris Publishing.

Mavroidis, Petros C. 2013. Driftin' too far from shore – Why the test for compliance with the TBT Agreement developed by the WTO Appellate Body is wrong, and what should the AB have done instead. *World Trade Review* 12 (3): 509–531.

Mavroidis, Petros C. 2016. The Gang That Couldn't Shoot Straight: The Not So Magnificent Seven of the WTO Appellate Body. *European Journal of International Law* 27 (4): 1107–1118.

McBride, Scott. 2001. Dispute settlement in the WTO: Backbone of the global trading system or delegation of awesome power? *Law and Policy in International Business* 32 (3): 643–675.

McCall Smith, James. 2003. WTO dispute settlement: the politics of procedure in Appellate Body rulings. *World Trade Review* 2 (1): 65–100.

McGinnis, John O. 2003. The appropriate hierarchy of global multilateralism and customary international law: the example of the WTO. *Virginia Journal of International Law* 44 (1): 229–284.

McGrady, Benn. 2008. Fragmentation of international law or "systemic integration" of treaty regimes: EC – Biotech Products and the proper interpretation of Article 31(3)(c) of the Vienna Convention on the Law of Treaties. *Journal of World Trade* 42 (4): 589–618.

McGrady, Benn. 2009. Necessity Exceptions in WTO Law: Retreaded Tyres, Regulatory Purpose and Cumulative Regulatory Measures. *Journal of International Economic Law* 12 (1): 153–173.

McNelis, Natalie. 2001. The role of the judge in the EU and WTO: Lessons from the BSE and hormones cases. *Journal of International Economic Law* 4 (1): 189–208.

McRae, Donald M. 2000. GATT Article XX and the WTO Appellate Body. In *New directions in international economic law*, edited by Marco Bronckers and Reinhard Quick, 219–236. London/The Hague/Boston: Kluwer Law International.

McRae, Donald M. 2006. Treaty interpretation and the development of international trade law by the Appellate Body. In *The WTO at ten: the contribution of the dispute settlement system*, edited by Alan Yanovich, Jan Bohanes, and Giorgio Sacerdoti, 360–371. Cambridge/New York: Cambridge University Press.

McWhinney, Edward. 2006. The International Court of Justice and International Law-Making: The Judicial Activism/Self-Restraint Antinomy. *Chinese Journal of International Law* 5 (1): 3–13.

Meagher, Niall. 2020. The Judicial Style of the Appellate Body. In *The Appellate Body of the WTO and Its Reform*, edited by Chang-fa Lo, Junji Nakagawa, and Tsai-fang Chen, 141–165. Singapore: Springer.

Melillo, Margherita. 2019. Informal Dispute Resolution in Preferential Trade Agreements. *Journal of World Trade* 53 (1). Kluwer Law International: 95–127.

Mestral, Armand C. M. de. 2013. Dispute Settlement under the WTO and RTAs: An Uneasy Relationship. *Journal of International Economic Law* 16 (4): 777–825.

Miller, Nathan. 2002. An international jurisprudence? The operation of "precedent" across international tribunals. *Leiden Journal of International Law* 15 (3): 483–526.

Mitchell, Andrew D. 2007. The Legal Basis for Using Principles in WTO Disputes. *Journal of International Economic Law* 10 (4): 795–835.

Montini, Massimiliano. 2001. The necessity principle as an instrument to balance trade and the protection of the environment. In *Environment, human rights and international trade*, edited by Franceso Francioni, 135–155. Portland: Hart.

Morosini, Fabio. 2010. The MERCOSUR trade and environment linkage debate: the disputes over trade in re-treaded tyres. *Journal of World Trade* 44 (5): 1127–1144.

Morrison, Peter, and Laura Nielsen. 2013. Trade, environment and animal welfare: conditioning trade in goods and services on conduct in another country. In *Research Handbook on Environment, Health and the WTO*, edited by Geert van Calster and Marie Denise Prévost, 207–230. Cheltenham/Northhampton: Edward Elgar.

Morrison Piehl, Anne, and Shawn D. Bushway. 2001. Judging Judicial Discretion: Legal Factors and Racial Discrimination in Sentencing. *Law & Society Review* 35 (4): 733–764.

Muir, Elise, Mark Dawson, and Bruno Witte. 2013. Introduction: the European Court of Justice as a political actor. In *Judicial activism at the European Court of Justice*, edited by Mark Dawson, Bruno Witte, and Elise Muir, 1–10. Cheltenham/Northhampton: Elgar.

Münch, Ingo, and Philip Kunig, eds. 2012. *Grundgesetz: Kommentar*. 6th ed. München: Beck.

Neugebauer, Regine. 2000. Fine-tuning WTO jurisprudence and the SPS Agreement: lessons from the beef hormone case. *Law and Policy in International Business* 31 (4): 1225–1283.

Neumann, Jan. 2002. *Die Koordination des WTO-Rechts mit anderen völkerrechtlichen Ordnungen*. Berlin: Duncker & Humblot.

Neumann, Jan, and Elisabeth Tuerk. 2003. Necessity revisited: Proportionality in World Trade Organization law after Korea – Beef, EC – Asbestos and EC – Sardines. *Journal of World Trade* 37 (1): 199–233.

Neumayer, Eric. 2001. Greening the WTO Agreements: can the treaty establishing the European Community be of guidance? *Journal of World Trade* 35 (1): 145–166.

Neyer, Jürgen. 2010. Justice or Democracy? Power and Justification in the EU and Other International Organizations. In *Conflict of Laws and Laws of Conflict in Europe and Beyond Patterns of Supranational and Transnational Juridification*, edited by Rainer Nickel, 33–47. Antwerp et al.: Intersentia.

Nickel, Rainer. 2010. Conflict of laws and laws of conflict – an introduction to the research agenda. In *Conflict of laws and laws of conflict in Europe and beyond: patterns of supranational and transnational juridification*, edited by Rainer Nickel, 1–9. Antwerpen: Intersentia.

Norpoth, Johannes. 2013. Mysteries of the TBT Agreement resolved? Lessons to learn for climate policies and developing countries exporters from recent TBT disputes. *Journal of World Tade* 47 (3): 575–600.

Notaro, Nicola. 2003. *Judicial approaches to trade and environment: the EC and the WTO*. London: Cameron May International Law Publishers.

Oesch, Matthias. 2003. Standards of review in WTO dispute settlement. *Journal of International Economic Law* 6 (3): 635–659.

Ortino, Federico. 2004. *Basic legal instruments for the liberalisation of trade: a comparative analysis of EC and WTO law*. Oxford/Portland: Hart.

Ortino, Federico. 2006. Treaty Interpretation and the WTO Appellate Body Report in US-Gambling – A Critique. *Journal of International Economic Law* 9 (1): 117–148.

Osiro, Deborah Akoth. 2002. GATT/WTO necessity analysis: evolutionary interpretation and its impact on the autonomy of domestic regulation. *Legal Issues of Economic Integration* 29 (2): 123–141.

Ossenbühl, Fritz, and W. Erbguth, eds. 1996. Abwägung im Verfassungsrecht. In *Abwägung im Recht - Symposium und Verabschiedung Werner Hoppe am 30. Juni 1995 aus Anlaß seiner Emeritierung*, 25–41. Köln; Berlin; Bonn: Heymanns.

P. J. K. 2018. From the Board: The US Attack on the WTO Appellate Body. *Legal Issues of Economic Integration* 45 (1). Kluwer Law International: 1–11.

Pair, Lara M. 2001. Judicial Activism in the ICJ Charter Interpretation. *ILSA Journal of International & Comparative Law* 8: 181–221.

Palmeter, David N, and Petros C Mavroidis. 1998. The WTO legal system: sources of law. *American Journal of International Law* 92: 398–413.

Pardo Quintillán, Sara. 1999. Free trade, public health protection and consumer information in the European and WTO context: Hormone-treated beef and genetically modified organisms. *Journal of World Trade* 33 (6): 147–197.

Parish, Matthew. 2010. On Necessity. *Journal of World Investment & Trade* 11 (2): 169–195.

Pauwelyn, Joost. 1999. The WTO Agreement on Sanitary and Phytosanitary (SPS) Measures as applied in the first three disputes – EC – Hormones, Australia – Salmon, Japan – Varietals. *Journal of International Economic Law* 2 (4): 641–664.

Pauwelyn, Joost. 2001a. Applying SPS in WTO disputes. In *Globalization and the environment: risk assessment and the WTO*, edited by David Robertson and Aynsley Kellow, 63–78. Cheltenham/Northhampton: Edward Elgar.

Pauwelyn, Joost. 2001b. The role of public international law in the WTO: how far can we go? *American Journal of International Law* 95 (3): 535–578.

Pauwelyn, Joost. 2002. Cross-agreement complaints before the Appellate Body: A case study of the EC-Asbestos dispute. *World Trade Review* 1 (1): 63–87.

Pauwelyn, Joost. 2003a. *Conflict of Norms in Public International Law: How WTO Law Relates to Other Rules of International Law*. Cambridge /York: Cambridge University Press.

Pauwelyn, Joost. 2003b. Does the WTO stand for "deference to" or "interference with" national health authorities when applying the agreement on Sanitary and Phytosanitary Measures (SPS Agreement?). In *The role of the judge in international trade regulation: experience and lessons for the WTO*, edited by Thomas Cottier and Petros C. Mavroidis, 175–192. Ann Arbor: University of Michigan Press.

Pauwelyn, Joost. 2003c. How to win a World Trade Organization dispute based on non-world trade organization law? Questions of jurisdiction and merits. *Journal of World Trade* 37 (6): 997–1030.

Pauwelyn, Joost. 2003d. The limits of litigation: "Americanization" and negotiation in the settlement of WTO disputes. *Ohio State Journal on Dispute Resolution* 19 (1): 121–140.

Pauwelyn, Joost. 2016a. Minority rules: precedent and participation before the WTO Appellate Body. In *Establishing Judicial Authority in International Economic Law*, 141–172. Cambridge: Cambridge University Press.

Pauwelyn, Joost. 2016b. The WTO 20 Years On: "Global Governance by Judiciary" or, Rather, Member-driven Settlement of (Some) Trade Disputes between (Some) WTO Members? *European Journal of International Law* 27 (4): 1119–1126.

Pauwelyn, Joost. 2019. WTO Dispute Settlement Post 2019: What to Expect? *Journal of International Economic Law* 22 (3). Oxford Academic: 297–321.

Pauwelyn, Joost, and Manfred Elsig. 2012. The Politics of Treaty Interpretation. In *Interdisciplinary Perspectives on International Law and International Relations: The State of the Art*, edited by Jeffrey L. Dunoff and Mark A. Pollack, 445–474. Cambridge: Cambridge University Press.

Pavot, David. 2013. The Use of Dictionary by the WTO Appellate Body: Beyond the Search of Ordinary Meaning. *Journal of International Dispute Settlement* 4 (1): 29–46.

Peel, Jacqueline. 2004. *Risk Regulation Under the WTO SPS Agreement: Science as an International Normative Yardstick?* Jean Monnet Working Paper. New York: New York School of Law. Available at <http://www.jeanmonnetprogram.org/archive/papers/04/040201.pdf>.

Peel, Jacqueline. 2012. Of apples and oranges (and hormones in beef): science and the standard of review in WTO disputes under the SPS Agreement. *International and Comparative Law Quarterly* 61 (2): 427–458.

Peel, Jacqueline. 2013. Scope of application of the SPS Agreement: a post-Biotech analysis. In *Research Handbook on Environment, Health and the WTO*, edited by Geert van Calster and Marie Denise Prévost, 332–362. Cheltenham/Northhampton: Edward Elgar.

Peresie, Jennifer L. 2005. Female Judges Matter: Gender and Collegial Decision-making in the Federal Appellate Courts. *Yale Law Journal* 114 (7): 1759–1790.

Perez, Oren. 1998. Reconstructing science: the Hormone conflict between the EU and the United States. *European Foreign Affairs Review* 3 (4): 563–582.

Perez, Oren. 2007. Anomalies at the Precautionary Kingdom: Reflection on the GMO Panel's Decision. *World Trade Review* 6 (2): 265–280.

Petersmann, Ernst-Ulrich. 2006. From "member-driven governance" to constitutionally limited "multi-level trade governance" in the WTO. In *The WTO at ten: the contribution of the dispute settlement system*, edited by Alan Yanovich, Jan Bohanes, and Sacerdoti, Giorgio, 86–110. Cambridge/New York: Cambridge University Press.

Picciotto, Sol. 2005. *The WTO's Appellate Body: Legal formalism as a legitimation of global governance*. Working Paper. London: School of Public Policy, University College London. Available at <https://eprints.lancs.ac.uk/id/eprint/29/>.

Picker, Colin B. 2020. The AB Crisis as Symptomatic of the WTO's Foundational Defects or: How I Learned to Stop Worrying and Love the AB. In *The Appellate Body of the WTO and Its Reform*, edited by Chang-fa Lo, Junji Nakagawa, and Tsai-fang Chen, 53–65. Singapore: Springer.

Pitschas, Christian, and Hannes Schloemann. 2012. *WTO compatibility of the EU seal regime: why public morality is enough (but may not be necessary)*. Beiträge zum Transnationalen Wirtschaftsrecht. Halle-Wittenberg: Transnational Economic Law Research Center, Martin-Luther-University. Available at <http://telc.jura.uni-halle.de/sites/default/files/BeitraegeTWR/Heft118.pdf>.

Poiares Maduro, Miguel. 1998. *We, The Court*. Oxford/Portland: Hart.

Pollicino, Oreste. 2004. Legal reasoning of the Court of Justice in the context of the principle of equality between judicial activism and self-restraint. *German Law Journal* 5 (3): 283–327.

Porges, Amelia. 2011. Dispute Settlement. In *Preferential Trade Agreement Policies for Development*, edited by Jean-Pierre Chauffour and Jean-Christophe Maur, 467–501. Washington DC: The World Bank.

Posner, Eric A., and Miguel F. P. de Figueiredo. 2005. Is the International Court of Justice Biased. *Journal of Legal Studies* 34 (2): 599–630.

Posner, Richard. 1995. Judges' Writing Styles (And Do They Matter?). *University of Chicago Law Review* 62: 1420–1449.

Prott, Lyndel V. 1970. The style of judgment in the international court of justice. *Australian Year Book of International Law* 75: 75–90.

Quick, Reinhard. 2013. Do We Need Trade and Environment Negotiations or Has the Appellate Body Done the Job? *Journal of World Trade* 47 (5): 957–983.

Quick, Reinhard, and Andreas Blüthner. 1999. Has the Appellate Body erred? An appraisal and criticism of the ruling in the WTO hormones case. *Journal of International Economic Law* 2 (4): 603–639.

Rafi, Anusheh. 2004. *Kriterien für ein gutes Urteil*. Berlin: Duncker & Humblot.

Rasmussen, Hjalte. 1986. *On Law and Policy in the European Court of Justice: A Comparative Study in Judicial Policymaking*. Dordrecht: Martinus Nijhoff Publishers.

Raz, Joseph. 1983. Legal Principles and the limits of the law. In *Ronald Dworkin and Contemporary Jurisprudence*, edited by Marshall Cohen, 75–87. Totowa: Rowman & Allanheld.

Regan, Donald H. 2003. The Dormant Commerce Clause and the Hormones Problem. In *The role of the judge in international trade regulation: experience and lessons for the WTO*, edited by Thomas Cottier and Petros C. Mavroidis, 91–117. Ann Arbor: University of Michigan Press.

Regan, Donald H. 2007. The meaning of "necessary" in GATT Article XX and GATS Article XIV: the myth of cost - benefit balancing. *World Trade Review* 6 (3): 347–369.

Reich, Arie. 2017. *The effectiveness of the WTO dispute settlement system: A statistical analysis*. EUI Working Papers Law. Florence: European University Institute. Available at <https://cadmus.eui.eu/bitstream/handle/1814/47045/LAW_2017_11.pdf?sequence=1>.

Reid, Emily. 2010. Regulatory Autonomy in the EU and WTO: Defining and Defending Its Limits. *Journal of World Trade* 44 (4): 877–901.

Reusch, Ralf. 2007. *Legitimation des WTO-Streitbeilegungsverfahrens*. Berlin: Duncker & Humblot.

Richieri Hanania, Lilian. 2009. Le principe de précaution et son application dans l'OMC. In *La circulation des concepts juridiques: le droit international de l'environnement entre mondialisation et fragmentation*, edited by Hélène Ruiz Fabri and Lorenzo Gradoni, 555–573. Paris: Société de législation comparée.

Rigod, Boris. 2015. *Optimal regulation and the law of international trade: the interface between the right to regulate and WTO law*. Cambridge/New York: Cambridge University Press.

Roessler, Frieder. 2000. The institutional balance between the judicial and the political organs of the WTO. In *New directions in international economic law*, edited by Marco Bronckers and Reinhard Quick, 325–345. London/The Hague/Boston: Kluwer Law International.

Ruffert, Matthias. 2001. Der Entscheidungsmaßstab im WTO - Streitbeilegungsverfahren – Prozessuale Relativierung materieller Verpflichtungen? *Zeitschrift für vergleichende Rechtswissenschaft* 100 (3): 304–321.

Ruiz Fabri, Hélène. 2006. Drawing a line of equilibrium in a complex world. In *The WTO at ten: the contribution of the dispute settlement system*, edited by Alan Yanovich, Jan Bohanes, and Sacerdoti, Giorgio, 125–142. Cambridge/New York: Cambridge University Press.

Ruiz Fabri, Hélène. 2016. The WTO Appellate Body or Judicial Power Unleashed: Sketches from the Procedural Side of the Story. *European Journal of International Law* 27 (4): 1075–1081.

Ruozzi, Elisa. 2009. L'application du principe de proportionalité en droit de l'organisation mondiale du commerce. In *La circulation des concepts juridiques: le droit international de l'environnement entre mondialisation et fragmentation*, edited by Hélène Ruiz Fabri and Lorenzo Gradoni, 475–492. Paris: Société de législation comparée.

Sacerdoti, Giorgio. 2006. The dispute settlement system of the WTO in action: a perspective on the first ten years. In *The WTO at ten: the contribution of the dispute settlement system*, edited by Alan Yanovich, Jan Bohanes, and Sacerdoti, Giorgio, 35–57. Cambridge/New York: Cambridge University Press.

Sacerdoti, Giorgio. 2008. WTO law and the "fragmentation" of international law: specificity, integration, conflicts. In *The WTO: governance, dispute settlement & developing countries*, edited by Merit E. Janow, Victoria Donaldson, and Alan Yanovich, 595–609. Huntington: Juris Publishing.

Sacerdoti, Giorgio, Alan Yanovich, and Jan Bohanes. 2006. *The WTO at Ten – The Contribution of the Dispute Settlement System*. Cambridge/New York: Cambridge University Press.

Schauer, Frederick. 1988. Formalism. *Yale Law Journal* 97 (4): 509–548.

Schauer, Frederick. 2009. *Balancing, Subsumption and the Constraining Role of Legal Text*. Public Law and Legal Theory Working Paper Series. University of Virginia Law School. Available at
<http://law.bepress.com/cgi/viewcontent.cgi?article=1197&context=uvalwps>.

Schebesta, Hanna, and Dominique Sinopoli. 2018. The Potency of the SPS Agreement's Excessivity Test: The Impact of Article 5.6 on Trade Liberalization and the Regulatory Power of WTO Members to take Sanitary and Phytosanitary Measures. *Journal of International Economic Law* 21 (1). Oxford Academic: 123–149.

Schmid, Christoph U. 2001. *A theoretical reconstruction of WTO constitutionalism and its implications for the relationship with the EU*. EUI Working Paper LAW. European University Institute. Available at <http://cadmus.eui.eu/bitstream/handle/1814/169/law01-05.pdf?sequence=1>.

Schmid, Christoph U. 2010. From effet utile to effet neoliberal – a critique of the new methodological expansionism of the European Court of Justice. In *Conflict of laws and laws of conflict in Europe and beyond: patterns of supranational and transnational juridification*, edited by Rainer Nickel, 295–314. Antwerpen: Intersentia.

Schropp, Simon A. 2012. Commentary on the Appellate Body Report in Australia – Apples (DS367): judicial review in the face of uncertainty. *World Trade Review* 11 (Special Issue 2): 171–221.

Schwarze, Jürgen, Ulrich Becker, Armin Hatje, and Johann Schoo, eds. 2012. *EU-Kommentar*. 3rd ed. Baden-Baden: Nomos.

Scott, Joanne. 2004a. *European Regulation of GMOs: Thinking about "Judicial Review" in the WTO*. Jean Monnet Working Paper. New York: NYU School of Law, Jean Monnet Program. Available at <http://www.jeanmonnetprogram.org/archive/papers/04/040401.pdf>.

Scott, Joanne. 2004b. International trade and environmental governance: relating rules (and standards) in the EU and the WTO. *European Journal of International Law* 15 (2): 307–354.

Scott, Joanne, and Ellen Vos. 2002. The juridification of uncertainty: observations on the ambivalence of the precautionary principle within the EU and the WTO. In *Good governance and administration in Europe's integrated market*, edited by Christian Joerges and Renaud Dehousse, 252–286. Oxford: Oxford University Press.

Scully-Hill, Anne, and Hans Mahncke. 2009. The Emergence of the Doctrine of Stare Decisis in the World Trade Organization Dispute Settlement System. *Legal Issues of Economic Integration* 36 (2): 133–156.

Shaffer, Gregory. 2009. A Structural Theory of WTO Dispute Settlement: Why Institutional Choice Lies at the Heart of the GMO dispute. *International Law and Politics* 41 (1): 1–102.

Shaffer, Gregory. 2012. *The WTO Tuna-Dolphin II Case: United States — Measures Concerning the Importation, Marketing and Sale of Tuna and Tuna Products*. Minnesota Legal Studies Research Paper. Minnesota: University of Minnesota – Twin Cities – School of Law. Available at <http://papers.ssrn.com/abstract=2176863>.

Shaffer, Gregory C. 2001. The World Trade Organization under challenge: democracy and the law and politics of the WTO's treatment of trade and environment matters. *Harvard Environmental Law Review* 25 (1): 1–93.

Shaffer, Gregory, Manfred Elsig, and Sergio Puig. 2016. The Extensive (But Fragile) Authority of the WTO Appellate Body. *Law and Contemporary Problems* 79 (1): 237–273.

Shahabuddeen, Mohamed. 1996. *Precedent in the world court*. Cambridge/New York: Cambridge University Press.

Shany, Yuval. 2005. Toward a General Margin of Appreciation Doctrine in International Law? *European Journal of International Law* 16 (5): 907–940.

Shany, Yuval, and Sivan Shlomo-Agon. 2014. The WTO Dispute Settlement System. In *Assessing the effectiveness of international courts*, edited by Yuval Shany, 189–222. International courts and tribunals series. Oxford/New York: Oxford University Press.

Shapiro, Martin. 1994. Judges As Liars. *Harvard Journal of Law & Public Policy* 17 (1): 155–156.

Shaw, Malcolm. 1991. *International Law*. Cambridge: Grotius.

Shell, G. Richard. 1995. Trade legalism and international relations theory: an analysis of the World Trade Organization. *Duke Law Journal* 44 (5): 829–927.

Shlomo-Agon, Sivan. 2015. Clearing the Smoke: The Legitimation of Judicial Power at the WTO. *Journal of World Trade* 49 (4). Kluwer Law International: 539589.

Silbergeld, Ellen K. 1991. Risk assessment and risk management: an uneasy divorce. In *Acceptable evidence: science and value in risk management*, edited by Deborah G. Mayo and Rachelle D. Hollander, 99–114. New York Oxford: Oxford University Press.

Slaughter, Anne-Marie, and Laurence R. Helfer. 1997. Toward a theory of effective supranational adjudication. *Yale Law Journal* 107 (2): 273–391.

Slotboom, Marco M. 1999. The Hormones case: an increased risk of illegality of sanitary and phytosanitary measures. *Common Market Law Review* 36 (2): 471–491.

Slotboom, Marco M. 2003. Do Public Health Measures Receive Similar Treatment in European Community and World Trade Organization Law? *Journal of World Trade* 37 (3): 553–596.

Smith, Adam M. 2004. "Judicial Nationalism" in International Law: National Identity and Judicial Autonomy at the ICJ. *Texas International Law Journal* 40 (2): 197–231.

Snoderly, Anna Beth. 1996. Clearing the Air: Environmental Regulation, Dispute Resolution, and Domestic Sovereignty under the World Trade Organization. *North Carolina Journal of International Law and Commercial Regulation* 22 (1): 241–306.

Soper, E. Philip. 1983. Legal theory and the obligation of a judge: the Hart/Dworkin dispute. In *Ronald Dworkin and Contemporary Jurisprudence*, edited by Marshall Cohen, 5–27. Totowa: Rowman & Allanheld.

Spamann, Holger. 2004. Standard of review for World Trade Organization Panels in trade remedy cases: a critical analysis. *Journal of World Trade* 38 (3): 509–555.

Stein, Eric. 2001. International integration and democracy: No love at first sight. *American Journal of International Law* 95 (3): 489–534.

Steinberg, Richard H. 2004. Judicial Lawmaking at the WTO: Discursive, Constitutional, and Political Constraints. *American Journal of International Law* 98: 247–275.

Stone Sweet, Alec. 2004. *The Judicial Construction of Europe*. Oxford/New York: Oxford University Press.

Study Group of the International Law Commission. 2006. *Report: Fragmentation of international law: difficulties arising from the diversification and expansion of international law (finalised by Martti Koskenniemi)*. New York: United Nations General Assembly.

Summers, Robert S. 1991. Statutory interpretation in the United States. In *Interpreting statutes – a comparative study*, edited by D. Neil MacCormick and Robert S. Summers, 407–459. Aldershot: Darthmouth.

Summers, Robert S., and Michele Taruffo. 1991. Interpretation and comparative analysis. In *Interpreting statutes – a comparative study*, edited by D. Neil MacCormick and Robert S. Summers, 461–510. Aldershot: Darthmouth.

Sun, Haochen. 2003. Reshaping the TRIPs agreement concerning public health: two critical issues. *Journal of World Trade* 37 (1): 163–197.

Sweet, Alec Stone, and Thomas L. Brunell. 2013. Trustee Courts and the Judicialization of International Regimes: The Politics of Majoritarian Activism in the European Convention on Human Rights, the European Union, and the World Trade Organization. *Journal of Law and Courts* 1 (1): 61–88.

Sykes, Alan O. 2002. Domestic regulation, sovereignty, and scientific evidence requirements: a pessimistic view. *Chicago Journal of International Law* 3 (2): 353–368.

Sykes, Katie. 2014. Sealing animal welfare into the GATT exceptions: the international dimension of animal welfare in WTO disputes. *World Trade Review* 13 (3): 471–498.

Tamanaha, Brian Z. 2009. *Beyond the Formalist - Realist Divide: The Role of Politics in Judging*. Princeton and Oxford: Princeton University Press.

Taniguchi, Yasuhei, John H. Jackson, Julio Lacarte Muró, George Bermann, Frieder Roessler, and Werner Zdouc. 2008. Panel discussion: Examining the dispute settlement system: how has it performed? In *The WTO: governance, dispute settlement & developing countries*, edited by Merit E. Janow, Victoria Donaldson, and Alan Yanovich, 387–405. Huntington: Juris Publishing.

Terris, Daniel, Cesare P. R. Romano, and Leigh Swigart. 2007. *The International Judge: An Introduction to the Men and Women Who Decide the World's Cases*. Waltham/Massachusetts: Brandeis University Press.

Thiedemann, Anke. 2005. *WTO und Umwelt – Die Auslegung des Art. XX GATT in der Praxis der WTO Streitbeilegungsorgane*. Münster: LIT.

Thomas, Sébastien. 2009. Trade and environment under WTO rules after the Appellate Body report in Brazil-retreated tyres. *Journal of International Commercial Law and Technology* 4 (1): 42–49.

Thomison, Andrew. 2007. New and Controversial Mandate for the SPS Agreement – The WTO Panel's Interim Report in the E.C.-Biotech Dispute. *Columbia Journal of Environmental Law* 32 (2): 287–307.

Tomkiewicz, Vincent. 2009. L'interprétation téléologique au sein de l'OMC et la question de la protection environnementale. In *La circulation des concepts juridiques: le droit international de l'environnement entre mondialisation et fragmentation*, edited by Hélène Ruiz Fabri and Lorenzo Gradoni, 243–266. Paris: Société de législation comparée.

Trachtman, Joel P. 1999. The domain of WTO dispute resolution. *Harvard International Law Journal* 40 (Spring 1999): 333–377.

Trachtman, Joel P. 2003. The agency model of judging in economic integration: balancing responsibilities. In *The role of the judge in international trade regulation : experience and lessons for the WTO*, edited by Thomas Cottier and Petros C. Mavroidis , 135–150. Ann Arbor: University of Michigan Press.

Trebilcock, Michael, and Julie A Soloway. 2002. International trade policy and domestic food safety regulation: The case for substantial deference by the WTO Dispute Settlement Body under the SPS Agreement. In *The political economy of international trade law: Essays in Honor of Robert E. Hudec*, edited by Daniel L. M Kennedy and James C Southwick, 537–574. Cambridge/New York: Cambridge University Press.

Trommer, Silke. 2017. The WTO in an Era of Preferential Trade Agreements: Thick and Thin Institutions in Global Trade Governance. *World Trade Review* 16 (3): 501–526.

Troper, Michel, Christophe Grzegorczyk, and Jean-Louis Gardies. 1991. Statutory interpretation in France. In *Interpreting statutes – a comparative study*, edited by D. Neil MacCormick and Robert S. Summers, 171–212. Aldershot: Darthmouth.

Tumonis, Vitalis. 2013. Adjudication Fallacies: The Role of International Courts in Interstate Dispute Settlement. *Wisconsin International Law Journal* 33 (1): 35–64.

Turk, Matthew C. 2011. Why Does the Complainant Always Win at the WTO?: A Reputation-Based Theory of Litigation at the World Trade Organization. *Northwestern Journal of International Law & Business* 31 (Spring 2011): 385–437.

Urakami, Kenichiro. 2001. Unsolved problems and implications for the chapeau of GATT Article XX. In *Reconciling environment and trade*, edited by Edith Brown Weiss and John H. Jackson, 167–184. Ardsley: Transnational Publishers.

US Trade Representative. 2020. *Report on the Appellate Body of the World Trade Organization*. Available at <https://ustr.gov/sites/default/files/Report_on_the_Appellate_Body_of_the_World_Trade_Organization.pdf>.

Van Calster, Geert. 2008. Faites Vos Jeux – Regulatory Autonomy and the World Trade Organisation after Brazil Tyres. *Journal of Environmental Law* 20 (1): 121–136.

Van Damme, Isabelle. 2009. *Treaty interpretation by the WTO Appellate Body*. Oxford/New York: Oxford University Press.

Van Damme, Isabelle. 2010. Treaty interpretation by the WTO Appellate Body. *European Journal of International Law* 21 (3): 605–648.

Van den Bossche, Peter. 2006. From afterthought to centrepiece: the WTO Appellate Body and its rise to prominence in the world trading system. In *The WTO at ten: the contribution of the dispute settlement system*, edited by Alan Yanovich, Jan Bohanes, and Sacerdoti, Giorgio, 289–325. Cambridge/New York: Cambridge University Press.Van den Bossche, Peter. 2008. Looking for Proportionality in WTO Law. *Legal Issues of Economic Integration* 35 (3): 283–294.

Van den Bossche, Peter L. H. van den. 2014. Reform of the WTO Dispute Settlement System – Fixing What Ain't Broke?, Melbourne Law School. Available at <http://www.law.unimelb.edu.au/files/dmfile/ReformoftheWTODisputeSettlementSystem-FixingWhatAintBrokeMelbourneLawSchool10Feb2014final.pdf>.

Venzke, Ingo. 2012. Making General Exceptions: The Spell of Precedents in Developing Article XX GATT into Standards for Domestic Regulatory Policy. In *International Judicial Lawmaking: On Public Authority and Democratic Legitimation in Global Governance*, edited by Armin von Bogdandy and Ingo Venzke, 179–249. Heidelberg/New York/Dordrecht/London: Springer.

Venzke, Ingo. 2016. Judicial authority and styles of reasoning: self-presentation between legalism and deliberation. In *Establishing Judicial Authority in International Economic Law*, edited by Henrik Palmer Olsen, Joanna Jemielniak, and Laura Nielsen, 240–262. Cambridge International Trade and Economic Law. Cambridge: Cambridge University Press.

Vidigal, Geraldo. 2017. Why Is There So Little Litigation under Free Trade Agreements? Retaliation and Adjudication in International Dispute Settlement. *Journal of International Economic Law* 20 (4). Oxford Academic: 927–950.

Voon, Tania S. 2009. China – Publications and Audiovisual Products. *American Journal of International Law* 103 (4): 710–716.

Vranes, Erich. 2009. *Trade and the environment: fundamental issues in international law, WTO law, and legal theory*. Oxford/New York: Oxford University Press.

Walker, Vern R. 1998. Keeping the WTO from becoming the "World Trans-science Organization": scientific uncertainty, science policy, and factfinding in the growth hormones dispute. *Cornell Journal of International Law* 31 (2): 251–319.

Walker, Vern R. 2003. The myth of science as a "neutral arbiter" for triggering precautions. *Boston College International and Comparative Law Review* 26 (2): 197–228.

Watkins-Bienz, Renée M. 2004. *Die Hart-Dworkin Debatte – Ein Beitrag zu den internationalen Kontroversen der Gegenwart*. Berlin: Duncker & Humblot.

Watson, James K. R. 2013. *The WTO and the environment: development of competence beyond trade*. Abingdon/New York: Routledge.

Weiler, Joseph H. H. 1991. The Transformation of Europe. *Yale Law Journal* 100 (8): 2403–2483.

Weiler, Joseph H. H., ed. 2000. *The EU, the WTO and the NAFTA: towards a common law of international trade?* Oxford/New York: Oxford University Press.

Weiler, Joseph H. H. 2001. The rule of lawyers and the ethos of diplomats: reflections on the internal and external legitimacy of WTO dispute settlement. *Journal of World Trade* 35 (2): 191–207.

Weiler, Joseph H. H. 2009. Brazil – Measures Affecting Imports of Retreaded Tyres (DS322). *World Trade Review* 8 (1): 137–144.

Weiler, Joseph H. H, and Iulia Motoc. 2003. Taking democracy seriously: the normative challenges to the international system. In *International economic governance and non-economic concerns: New challenges for the international legal order*, edited by Stefan Griller, 48–77. Wien/New York: Springer.

Weimer, Maria. 2014. *Risk Regulation, GMO's, and the Challenges to Deliberation in EU Governance - Politicization and Scientification as Co-Producing Trends*. Amsterdam Centre for European Law and Governance Research Paper. Amsterdam: University of Amsterdam. Available at <http://papers.ssrn.com/abstract=2400553>.

Weiss, Wolfgang. 2003. Security and predictability under WTO law. *World Trade Review* 2 (2): 183–219.

Wessel, Jared. 2006. Judicial Policy-Making at the International Criminal Court: An Institutional Guide to Analyzing International Adjudication. *Columbia Journal of Transnational Law* 44 (2): 377–452.

Whitlock, Joseph P. 2002. Japan – Measures affecting agricultural products: lessons for future SPS and agricultural trade disputes. *Law and Policy in International Business (now Georgetown Journal of International Law)* 33 (4): 741–776.

Whittington, Keith E. 2003. Legislative sanctions and the strategic environment of judicial review. *International Journal of Constitutional Law* 1 (3): 446–474.

Wiers, Jochem, and James Mathis. 2001. The report of the Appellate Body in the Asbestos Dispute: WTO Appellate Body Report 12 March 2001, WT/DS135/AB/R, European Communities – Measures affecting asbestos and asbestos-containing products. *Legal Issues of Economic Integration* 28 (2): 211–255.

Winham, Gilbert R. 2003. International regime conflict in trade and environment: the Biosafety Protocol and the WTO. *World Trade Review* 2 (2): 131–155.

Winickoff, David, Sheila Jasanoff, Lawrence Busch, Robin Grove-White, and Brian Wynne. 2005. Adjudicating the GM Food Wars: Science, Risk, and Democracy in World Trade Law. *Yale Journal of International Law* 30: 81–123.

Winter, Gerd. 2003. The GATT and environmental protection: problems of construction. *Journal of Environmental Law* 15 (2): 113–140.

Wirth, David A. 2006. The Transatlantic Dispute Against the European Communities: Some Preliminary Thoughts. In *EU and WTO Law: How Tight is the Legal Straitjacket for Environmental Product Regulation*, edited by Marc Pallmaerts, 175–208. Brussels: VUBPRESS Brussels University Press. Available at <http://lawdigitalcommons.bc.edu/cgi/viewcontent.cgi?article=1145&context=lsfp>.

Wofford, Carrie. 2000. A greener future at the WTO: The refinement of WTO jurisprudence on environmental exceptions to GATT. *Harvard Environmental Law Review* 24 (2): 563–592.

Wu, Mark. 2008. Free trade and the protection of public morals: an analysis of the newly emerging public morals clause doctrine. *Yale Journal of International Law* 33 (1): 215–251.

Xu Yi-chong, and Patrick Weller. 2004. *The governance of world trade – international civil servants and the GATT/WTO*. Cheltenham/Northampton: Edward Elgar.

Yavitz, Laura. 2001. The WTO and the environment: the shrimp case that created a new world order. *Journal of Natural Resources and Environmental Law* 16 (2): 203–255.

Yavitz, Laura. 2002. The World Trade Organization Appellate Body report, European Communities – measures affecting asbestos and asbestos containing products, Mar. 12, 2001, WT/DS135/AB/R. *Minnesota Journal of Global Trade (now Minnesota Journal of International Law)* 11 (1): 43–67.

Yoo-Sun Jung. 2013. Dispute Settlement Mechanisms and Power Asymmetry in Regional Trade Agreements. Available at <https://ncgg.princeton.edu/IPES/2013/papers/S930_rm2.pdf>.

Yung, Corey Rayburn. 2011. Flexing Judicial Muscle: An Empirical Study of Judicial Activism in the Federal Courts. *Northwestern University Law Review* 105 (1): 1–60.

Zangl, Bernhard, Achim Helmedach, Aletta Mondré, Alexander Kocks, Gerald Neubauer, and Kerstin Blome. 2012. Between law and politics: Explaining international dispute settlement behavior. *European Journal of International Relations* 18 (2): 369–401.

Zarbiyev, Fuad. 2012. Judicial Activism in International Law - A Conceptual Framework for Analysis. *Journal of International Dispute Settlement* 3 (2): 1–32.

Zdouc, Werner. 2008. Features of the Appellate Body that have defined its performance. In *The WTO: governance, dispute settlement & developing countries*, edited by Merit E. Janow, Victoria Donaldson, and Alan Yanovich, 369–385. Huntington: Juris Publishing.

Zeitler, Helge Elisabeth. 2005. "Good Faith" in the WTO Jurisprudence – Necessary Balancing Element or an Open Door to Judicial Activism? *Journal of International Economic Law* 8 (3): 721–758.

Zleptnig, Stefan. 2002. The standard of review in WTO law: an analysis of law, legitimacy and the distribution of legal and political authority. *European Business Law Review* 13 (5): 427–457.

Zleptnig, Stefan. 2010. *Non-economic objectives in WTO law: justification provisions of GATT, GATS, SPS and TBT agreements*. Leiden/Boston: Nijhoff.